THE FOOD LOVER'S GUIDE TO

PARIS

COMPLETELY REVISED FIFTH EDITION

THE FOOD LOVER'S GUIDE TO

PARIS

—❧ COMPLETELY REVISED FIFTH EDITION ☙—

THE BEST RESTAURANTS, BISTROS, CAFÉS, MARKETS, BAKERIES, AND MORE

PATRICIA WELLS

WITH EMILY BUCHANAN

ASSISTED BY SUSAN HERRMANN LOOMIS

PHOTOGRAPHS BY GIANLUCA TAMORRI

WORKMAN PUBLISHING • NEW YORK

Library of Congress Cataloging-in-Publication
Data is available.
ISBN 978-0-7611-7338-0

Design by Lisa Hollander
Cover and interior photographs by
Gianluca Tamorri

Workman books are available at special discounts
when purchased in bulk for premiums and
sales promotions as well as for fund-raising or
educational use. Special editions or book
excerpts also can be created to specification.
For details, contact the Special Sales Director
at the address below, or send an email to
specialmarkets@workman.com.

Workman Publishing Co., Inc.
225 Varick Street
New York, NY 10014-4381
workman.com

WORKMAN is a registered trademark of
Workman Publishing Co., Inc.

Printed in the United States of America
Fifth edition: First printing February 2014

10 9 8 7 6 5 4 3 2 1

To Walter, with gratitude
for his unwavering love, trust,
and support

ACKNOWLEDGMENTS

T hanks to the generosity, enthusiasm, and encouragement of many fine people over the years, much of the work on this book has been transformed into sheer pleasure. I am deeply grateful to everyone, past and present, who has been part of the *Food Lover's* team. For this edition in particular, I can never,

ever thank and praise enough my talented and diligent assistant, Emily Buchanan. I give thanks as well to my longtime associate and friend Susan Herrmann Loomis, and to our wonderful photographer Gianluca Tamorri, who so aptly captured Paris's nostalgic beauty as well as its modernity. I am constantly touched by the generosity of the Parisian chefs, bakers, restaurateurs, and shopkeepers who have given so freely of their time and expertise. None of this would have been possible without the remarkable confidence of the late Peter Workman and the expert attention of my editor Suzanne Rafer, who was there from the very beginning in 1983 and still supports the *Food Lover's* effort. Thanks also to Suzanne's assistant, Erin Klabunde; Mary Wilkinson for copyediting; Lisa Hollander, who designed the book; and Amanda Hong, production editor.

CONTENTS

INTRODUCTION

When I moved to Paris in January of 1980, I arrived with the dream and intention of researching and writing THE FOOD LOVER'S GUIDE TO PARIS. I quickly began reviewing restaurants for the *International Herald Tribune* but also wanted to share with readers all the pleasures of Paris that didn't include sitting in a restaurant: visiting the city's irresistible chocolate shops and bustling markets, savoring the finest *baguettes,* reveling over a perfect lemon tart.

When the first *Food Lover's Guide to Paris* was published in 1984, it became an instant travel bible and was acclaimed as "the book that cracks the code," suggesting that even newcomers to the city could feel perfectly at home in the food maze of restaurants, shops, and markets.

This book—my 15th, on the 30th anniversary of the first guide—is a totally revisited, revised, rewritten, rephotographed version of the first 1984 guide, but it remains completely in the spirit of the original. So much has changed in the Paris food scene since the fourth edition was published in 1999. Many chefs have come and gone. Others have matured into excellence. And, most exciting, I have had the pleasure of covering the new group of energetic young cooks who are expanding the culinary "musts" into up-and-coming Paris neighborhoods. There's also a new generation of bakers, pastry chefs, and chocolate makers, bringing us all new looks, flavors, excitements, temptations. The markets of Paris have remained strong and vibrant, as local and regional growers—as well as a strong contingent of organic farmers—help the city's fresh-food possibilities evolve.

As with the rest of the world, Paris has become a much more casual place. So in my latest guide I have continued with a chapter on Restaurants, Bistros, and Brasseries, but have included a totally expanded chapter on Cafés and Casual Bites. This reflects the flourishing of simple and generally inexpensive spots for quick meals: cafés offering expanded menus, a growing crop of *crêperies* and bakeries that offer more than just a sit-down spot for bread and pastries, some great pizzerias, additional spots for terrific coffee and food, more ethnic eateries, and an acknowledgment of the hamburger's explosion of popularity in the capital.

And while today Paris and its food offerings may in many ways resemble other world food capitals, the city has in no way lost its soul. Just walk through any neighborhood noted in this guide, and you'll discover a special, textured universe that will always be Paris, and France.

As in any international capital, Parisian establishments are always growing, changing, in flux. All the information included here is as accurate and up to date as possible at the time of publication. For updates and the most current information on new establishments, any change in prices, opening hours, and management, consult this book's companion, *The Food Lover's Guide to Paris* app for the iPhone and iPad, available from foodloversparis.com or directly from the iTunes store.

I hope that this new edition will inspire you to explore, discover, enjoy, and embrace the splendors of Paris.

PATRICIA WELLS
Paris, 2014

HOW TO USE THIS BOOK

ALPHABETIZING

Within each chapter, establishments are grouped by the *arrondissement* in which they are located, then listed in alphabetical order. Following French style, any articles such as *au, la,* or *le* and words such as *bistro, brasserie, café,* or *chez* that appear before the proper name of the establishment are ignored in the alphabetizing. For example, Bistrot Paul Bert and Le Petit Lutetia are all listed under the letter *P*. Restaurants and shops carrying the name of the chef or proprietor are listed under the first letter of the first name. For example, Guy Savoy is listed under *G*, not *S*.

WHAT'S AN *ARRONDISSEMENT?*

Many major cities are divided into districts for easy identification and organization. Paris is divided into 20 *arrondissements,* and within each may be several *quartiers,* or neighborhoods. The *arrondissements* are arranged numerically in a spiral, beginning in the center of the city on the Right Bank (with the 1st *arrondissement,* at the Louvre and Les Halles) and moving clockwise, making two complete spirals until reaching the central eastern edge of the city (with the 20th *arrondissement,* at Père Lachaise cemetery). In organizing the book we have listed establishments broadly by *arrondissement,* rather than specific neighborhoods or *quartiers.*

LISTINGS

Each listing in *The Food Lover's Guide to Paris* includes the following information: the name of the establishment; the type of establishment or cuisine served; the address and phone number; the closest *métro* stop; when it is open and closed; and, where they have them, website address and email. (In the case of restaurants, when an establishment keeps regular dining hours of noon to 3PM and 8 to 10PM, opening times are not listed.)

If applicable, any or all of the following information is also included for restaurants: the restaurant's atmosphere as relating to ambiance and whether a reservation is suggested or not; house specialties; and what you can expect to spend. Listings of establishments that have outdoor, private, and late dining; Michelin stars; vegetarian-friendly menus; and other particulars can be found in the Ready Reference section on page 427.

ABBREVIATIONS

The following abbreviations are used in the recipes to indicate weights and measurements:

CM: centimeter

ML: milliliter

L: liter

G: gram

KG: kilogram

CL: centiliter

The following abbreviations are used in some street addresses:

BIS: equivalent to *B* in a road numbering system; e.g., 3bis is equivalent to 3B

TER: equivalent to *C* in a road numbering system; e.g., 3ter is equivalent to 3C

THE FOOD LOVER'S GUIDE TO

PARIS

COMPLETELY REVISED FIFTH EDITION

RESTAURANTS, BISTROS, AND BRASSERIES

RESTAURANTS, BISTROTS, ET BRASSERIES

I am constantly being asked to name my favorite Paris restaurant. For me that is akin to trying to name my best friend, or favorite piece of music, film, or classic novel. The answer depends on the hour, the season, my mood, the company. This is a personal guide representing a cross section of Paris restaurants, bistros, and brasseries. I hope they will serve simply as a starting point, enabling you to begin exploring and sorting out until you discover the kinds of restaurants you like. You should not have a bad meal at most of the restaurants listed here. But this doesn't mean you can't.

I dine out in Paris four or five times each week. I always make a reservation and always arrive hungry, for that's one of the best compliments one can pay a chef. I try to dine anonymously and so am known at few of these restaurants. What do I look for? My final judgment rests on the quality of the ingredients, the chef's creativity and honesty, and overall service. In menus, I look for a healthy balance of dishes, seasonal use of ingredients, and good value. In wine lists, value and variety are essential. A good restaurant is like good theater: One leaves in a good frame of mind, with a feeling that the time and money have been well spent. You know it's a good restaurant when you are already planning and looking forward to a return visit before you pay the check. With that in mind, some restaurants included in earlier editions of the guide, such as Le Grand Vefour, have been eliminated, for they simply did not hold up.

In considering the elements of what

makes a great dining experience, your restaurants and meals should be chosen according to your own mood and appetite, the time of year, and of course the time of day.

When I first arrived in Paris in January of 1980, the *Michelin Guide* and the *Gault et Millau Guide* ruled where anyone dined in Paris. There were no blogs, minute-to-minute, or even daily, updates on where to dine in Paris. The city was still a very elegant, dressed-up place, where men wore suits and ties; women heels, short skirts, and mink coats. There were no blue jeans or sneakers to be seen on the streets. Fast food was just arriving, but not yet really making an impact.

Today, via Twitter, numerous blogs, and Facebook, restaurant openings become public knowledge the second the doors are unlocked and, sometimes unfairly, judgments are made before they are really established. Sometimes the restaurants go on to become favorites, other times they fade into oblivion. Yet diners have never had a greater choice than today, from top tables to simple eateries.

WHERE AM I, ANYWAY?

An American traveler once related this story: She was stopped on a street in Paris by another American visitor, who asked, in a state of sheer frustration, "What I don't understand is with all these restaurants, how do you tell which ones are French? You know, the ones that serve soufflés." Slightly less complicated, but equally frustrating for visitors, are the distinctions among bistro, brasserie, and restaurant. Although the lines between bistro and restaurant are often blurred, here are a few definitions that should clear up the matter:

BISTROS AND NEO-BISTROS

A traditional bistro is a rather small restaurant, traditionally a mom-and-pop establishment, with Mom at the cash register and Pop at the stove. Bistro menus are usually handwritten or mimeographed, and offerings are limited to a small selection of traditional home-style dishes. Wine is generally offered by the carafe, while wines available by the bottle are listed on the single-page menu. Bistro decor is usually simple, not fancy (though Paris's Belle Époque bistros have some of the city's most beautiful interiors), often with a long zinc bar, tiled floors, and sturdy, serviceable tableware. At some of the most modest establishments, diners may share long tables.

Today the definition of *bistro* has been widely expanded, due to an increasing appetite for restaurants that are casual and less expensive, offering contemporary decor and modernized traditional fare. So within this new crop of bistros, also called neo-bistros, one will find small, often out-of-the-way establishments, with ingredients carefully sourced and fare that's highly creative. Little attention is paid to the decor, and it may be bare-bones, but prices are generally reasonable.

BRASSERIES

Brasserie is French for "brewery," and almost all of Paris's large and lively brasseries have an Alsatian connection. That means lots of beer, Alsatian white wines such as Riesling and Gewürztraminer, and usually *choucroute*, that hearty blend of sauerkraut and assorted sausages. Brasseries tend to be brightly lit and full of the sounds of good times, fine places for going with a large group. Generally, snacks or full meals are available whenever the restaurant is open. Brasseries tend to keep late hours, and while a reservation is recommended, one can often get a table without one. Sadly, the quality of many Parisian brasseries has declined in recent years, and while the ambience remains uniquely Parisian, the quality of food at many establishments is dubious at best. I have of course listed the ones that I feel have been able to stay true to both their traditional charm and their menus.

RESTAURANTS

Beyond bistros and brasseries, Paris offers numerous sorts of full-fledged restaurants, establishments that usually have a more elaborate menu and wine list, and often more refined service and decor. Some serve elegant and classic cuisine; some specialize in creative, inventive modern cooking. Classifications for all the restaurants, bistros, and brasseries in the guide appear in the Ready Reference on page 427.

RESERVATIONS

Almost without exception, reservations are necessary and always helpful at all restaurants, bistros, and brasseries. For the grand restaurants, such as Taillevent, Pierre Gagnaire, Alain Ducasse au Plaza Athénée, and Astrance, reserve weeks to months in advance. For others, reservations should be made several days ahead for dinners at extremely popular restaurants, bistros, and brasseries, though for a weekday lunch, reserving the same day is often sufficient. Even so, to avoid disappointment call at least a week in advance for reservations. Some casual bistros have become so popular (particularly those open only for dinner) that it may be necessary to book weeks in advance. If you are unable to keep a reservation, call to cancel. Many restaurants now require that advance reservations be confirmed by telephone the day you plan to dine there. Another good reason for reserving: Restaurants freely, and without warning, change opening and closing times and vacation plans, particularly during summer months and holiday periods. So it is always safest to call to make sure the restaurant will be open when you plan to visit.

DINING HOURS

Set aside plenty of time for a Paris restaurant meal. In general, expect to spend anywhere from one and a half to three hours at the

table for a substantial lunch or dinner. If you want to be in and out within 30 minutes to an hour, visit a café, tea salon, wine bar, or brasserie, but don't attempt to rush through a meal at a serious restaurant. Currently, most Parisians begin lunch at 12:30 or 1PM (although one can begin at noon), and most start dinner at 8:30 or 9PM (although some restaurants will accept reservations as early as 7PM). Despite the later hours, most kitchens close early, so a 2PM lunch or 10PM dinner reservation would be stretching it. On the other hand, the majority of cafés and brasseries serve at almost any hour. A few restaurants, bistros, and brasseries continue taking orders after 10PM, and a list of those can be found in the Ready Reference beginning on page 427.

PRICES

The price range of restaurants listed here goes from low to high. I have made no attempt to include restaurants serving mediocre fare simply because they are inexpensive. Today, one finds more bargains than ever, especially with the new generation of young chefs offering good-value menus. But there are always ways to cut costs, even in the most expensive restaurants. Forgo the before-dinner drink, the after-dinner cognac, and share dishes, if you like. You are not obliged to order either cheese or dessert, and if they do not suit your budget or appetite, forget them. You can often cut costs by ordering from a fixed-price menu (though it is not always cheaper than ordering à la carte), or by opting for a glass of wine or an inexpensive house wine. Most restaurants offer wine by the glass, which is generally cheaper than a bottle or half bottle.

A few restaurants, such as Chez Georges and Le Cinq Mars, allow you to order a bottle and pay for only what you drink, a practice called *à la ficelle*. In all cases, the prices noted with each restaurant listing represent an average meal for one person, including a first

course, main course, and cheese or dessert, as well as the service charge, but not beverages. Generally, a good inexpensive meal for one person can be had for under 30€, a good moderately priced meal for 50€, while a luxury meal, in a higher class of restaurant with more expensive wines, will range from 200 to 300€. Diners looking to save money should always choose lunch over dinner for their big meal of the day. Even most of the top-rated restaurants offer well-priced lunch menus. Note that many good-value lunch menus are available on weekdays only, so plan to order à la carte on weekends.

ADVICE ON PAYING THE BILL AND TIPPING

No subject is more confusing to visitors than French restaurant bills. You need to remember only one fact: You are never required to pay more than the final "net" total on the bill. Service, which ranges from 12 to 15 percent, depending on the class of the restaurant, is already included in the price of the individual dishes, and is therefore already calculated in the price of the final bill. Etiquette does not require you to pay more than the total. If you have particularly enjoyed the meal, if you feel the *maître d'hôtel* or *sommelier* has offered exceptional service, if you are in a particularly generous mood, then you might wish to leave anywhere from a few euros to 5 percent of the total bill as an additional tip, preferably in cash.

CREDIT CARDS

Almost without exception, Paris restaurants accept credit cards. If you are sharing your bill with another person or couple and you both wish to pay by credit card, most restaurants will oblige by dividing the bill between two or more credit cards. Out of kindness to the waiters and *sommelier*, any tips (beyond the obligatory 12 to 15 percent service charge) should be left in cash.

WHAT TO EXPECT
AT THE TABLE

SUGGESTIONS ON ORDERING

There are several simple things to keep in mind when ordering in a Paris restaurant. First, think about what foods are likely to be fresh and in season. Thank goodness the French are still fanatical about freshness, and about eating what is naturally in season. Now more than ever, restaurants offer a *menu du marché*, a market menu dictated daily by the best seasonal ingredients. When dining out in Paris, I often go on seasonal "binges," eating asparagus, melon, scallops, oysters, or game day after day when they are at their peak. If you see melon on the menu in January, or scallops during July, beware. And do take the time to learn about the restaurant's specialties. Every restaurant has at least one or two dishes of which it is particularly proud, and the majority of restaurants either offer a *plat du jour* or underline or boldface their specialties. These dishes, assuming they are to your liking, will usually be a good buy, and generally fresh. Note that fish is freshest on Fridays (when the demand is greatest) and least fresh on Mondays, when the wholesale market is closed. But do stick to your guns and order the kind of food you really like to eat. This is a caveat to those diners who will blindly accept a critic's or a waiter's suggestion, then all too late realize that they hate tripe, or duck, or whatever it was that was recommended.

Finally, today many restaurants offer a tasting menu, or *menu dégustation,* which allows diners to sample portions from four to eight different dishes. I am generally opposed to such menus, for in the end they are rarely good buys and inevitably provide more food than it is humanly (and healthily) possible to eat. Because a tasting menu offers so many different dishes, it is difficult, if not impossible, to take with you a memorable impression of the meal or restaurant. While the *menu dégustation* is often easier on the kitchen, you may get the feeling that the dishes you are eating came off an assembly line.

Today many restaurants, such as Chateaubriand, Roseval, and Septime, have opted to offer a fixed-price, no-choice menu. These fixed (no à la carte) menus generally offer good value, and allow the chefs to change the menu regularly, remain seasonal, and keep costs down.

BUTTER

Most, but not all, restaurants offer butter at the table. If you don't see butter, just ask for it. Since the French do not always butter their bread, restaurants do not systematically offer it, unless you order a dish that generally calls for buttered bread—*charcuterie,* oysters served with rye bread, sardines, radishes, or the cheese course. Today many restaurants offer a choice of salted or unsalted butter, and some even offer a selection of butters flavored with herbs or spices.

COFFEE

The French have very specific coffee-drinking habits. Many Frenchmen begin their day with a *café au lait*—usually lots of hot milk with a little bit of coffee. During the rest of the day they drink either black coffee or *café crème* (coffee with steamed milk). In France, coffee is always taken at the very end of a meal (never with the meal), almost served as a course of its own. In finer restaurants, chocolates or petits fours might also be served.

FISH, MEAT, AND POULTRY

Almost all fish, meat, and poultry taste better

when cooked on the bone. If you have problems boning fish, ask if the dish you ordered is boned (*sans arêtes*), and if not, ask the waiter to debone it before serving (*enlevez les arêtes*). The French prefer their meat (beef, veal, and lamb) and some poultry (particularly duck) cooked quite rare, or rosé. If rare meat or poultry really bothers you, be insistent, and ask for it *bien cuit* (well done), but be prepared for the waiter to wince. For very rare meat, order it *bleu*; for rare meat, order it *rosé* (for lamb, veal, duck, or liver) or *saignant* (for beef); and for medium, *à point*.

SALT AND PEPPER

Some chefs are insulted if diners alter their creations with additional seasoning, and so they do not offer salt and pepper at the table. If you don't see them, just ask. But do be sure to taste the food before reaching for the mill or shaker.

WATER

I am always shocked when people ask, "Is it safe to drink the tap water in Paris?" Of course it is. Perhaps visitors assume that because the French are passionate about bottled water—a table of eight diners might order four preferred brands of mineral water—the tap water is unsafe. Either tap water (ask for *une carafe d'eau*) or mineral water (*plat* is flat bottled mineral water, *gazeuze* or *petillante* is bubbly) may be ordered with all meals. If ordering Perrier brand mineral water, don't be surprised if only small bottles are available. The French consider Perrier too gaseous to drink with meals, so most restaurants stock only small bottles, as an *apéritif* or to mix in drinks.

WINES AND LIQUORS

This is one area where I firmly advise you to follow the rule "When in Paris, do as the Parisians do." Most French people do not drink hard liquor before meals and few restaurants are equipped with a full bar. If you are accustomed to drinking hard liquor

before meals, try to change your habits during a Paris visit. The liquor will numb your palate for the pleasures to follow, and requests for a martini or whiskey before a meal will not put you in good stead with the waiter or the management. Almost all restaurants offer a house cocktail—most often a *kir*, a blend of either white wine or champagne with *crème de cassis* (black currant liqueur). I personally dislike most of these concoctions (which can be expensive and run up the bill) and always ask for the wine list when requesting the menu. Then I usually order as an *apéritif* a white wine that will be drunk with the meal, or at least the first course.

SELECTING AND ORDERING WINES

I have learned almost all I know about wines by tasting, tasting, tasting in restaurants. I study wine lists, keep track of average prices and favorite food-and-wine combinations, and am always eager to sample a wine that's new or unfamiliar to me. If you don't know a lot about wine, ask the *sommelier*'s advice. Give him a rough idea of your tastes and the price you'd like to pay. This assumes, of course, that you share a common language. If you do not, simply ask whether there is a *vin de la maison* (house wine). If you are knowledgeable about wine, you will want to study the wine list. Don't allow yourself to be pressured into making a quick decision (this isn't always easy), and if pressed, simply explain that you are fascinated by the restaurant's wonderful selection and would like a few minutes to examine and fully appreciate the list of offerings.

Prices for the same wines vary drastically from restaurant to restaurant. Some have large, long-standing wine cellars, others are just getting started. I love wine, consider it an essential part of any good meal, and probably tend to spend slightly more than the average diner on a good bottle. When dining in a bistro or brasserie, I often order the house wine, either by carafe or by the bottle.

VEGETARIAN OFFERINGS

Today many Paris restaurants offer a vegetarian main course with each menu. Another option is to order two vegetable-based first courses from the menu. Refer to the Ready Reference (page 427) for vegetarian-friendly dining. ❧

1ST ARRONDISSEMENT

LE CARRÉ DES FEUILLANTS

HAUTE CUISINE / MODERN FRENCH SOUTHWESTERN
14, rue de Castiglione
Paris 1
TEL: +33 1 42 86 82 82
alaindutournier.com/wp/carredesfeuillants
carredesfeuillants@orange.fr
MÉTRO: Tuileries, Pyramides, or Concorde
OPEN: Monday through Friday, and Saturday dinner

CLOSED: Saturday lunch, Sunday, and August
PRICES: 60€ lunch menu, 80 and 95€ lunch menus with wine. 145 and 205€ *dégustation* (tasting) menus. À la carte 120–160€.
SPECIALTY: Cheese tray
RESERVATIONS: Recommended
ATMOSPHERE: Formal. Suit jacket, but not tie, required for men.

Alain Dutournier, the outgoing and personable ambassador for France's Southwest cuisine, remains in fine form. Although Michelin awards him two stars, everything at his flagship Carré des Feuillants makes me vote for the ultimate three stars. The sleek, modern decor, attentive and professional service, top-rate ingredients, and Dutournier's magic touch make this one of the city's truly fine dining destinations. On the plate, you can see and taste his passion and enthusiasm for his craft. The scent alone of his bouillon of chestnuts and white truffles is enough to send you soaring toward heaven, and the sublime taste is a masterful mix of soft and smooth textures, soothing and exciting at the same time. The accompanying *tartine* of raw fresh chestnuts sliced paper-thin, and the warm toast slathered with white truffle butter, delivered a wave of surprise and pleasure at our table. All too often haute cuisine is littered with the trite litany of expensive ingredients—lobster and truffles, caviar and turbot, *foie gras* and *langoustines*—that seem to be there just to earn a label. But put those ingredients in Dutournier's hands and you feel as though he has truly thought through each one, treating them with dignity and respect. An alabaster morsel of turbot is topped with distinctive caviar from France's Aquitaine region and set on a bed of al dente black rice, a sophisticated play of black and white, soft and crunchy. But perhaps the star of the show at our dinner was his trio of wild *cèpe* mushrooms, some simply marinated, others turned into a warming vegetable pâté, a third sliced ever so thinly and carefully fried—a chip like none you've ever tasted. This sublime mushroom dish is the result of a brilliant chef treating a noble ingredient with intelligence and creativity, showing us its virtues and versatility. *Fougerous*—the bloomy-rind cow's-milk cheese from the Champagne region—is sliced in half like a layer cake, filled with a blend of mascarpone and minced white truffles, then reconstructed. If there is a truffle heaven, let me in! The wine list is impressive. My choices included the crisp, full-bodied white Clos Uroulat Cuvée Marie and the fine, concentrated Madiran Chapelle Lenclos. The 60€ lunch menu is one of the city's great bargains.

LA DAME DE PIC

HAUTE CUISINE / MODERN FRENCH
20, rue du Louvre
Paris 1
TEL: +33 1 42 60 40 40
ladamedepic.fr
contact@ladamedepic.fr
MÉTRO: Louvre-Rivoli

OPEN: Tuesday through Saturday
CLOSED: Sunday and Monday
PRICES: 49€ lunch menu. 79, 100, and 120€ lunch and dinner menus.
RESERVATIONS: Essential
ATMOSPHERE: Formal

Anne-Sophie Pic's La Dame de Pic, near the Louvre, is a pure and calming all-white space with crisp white linen table runners, sturdy modern wooden tables, and knives from Forge de Laguiole in the Auvergne region, all punctuated by a series of vases holding single, long-stemmed pink roses.

The restaurant—whose name is a play on words for "queen of spades"—is not a place for compromise. Nor is the herb-, spice-, and aroma-filled menu. Like the dining room itself, it offers a balance of elegance and comfort, haute cuisine and everyday fare, all bearing Anne-Sophie's unique, ultramodern imprint. She sports her feminine role, but does not flaunt it or play it cute. Ingredients are impeccable, preparations are complicated but not overdone, and the taste and texture theme throughout is one of softness and smoothness with a required touch of crunch. I would never think of pairing warm oysters with cauliflower, but Anne-Sophie offers a regal, cloudlike presentation of warm Gillardeau oysters bathed in a frank and fragrant cream of cauliflower and jasmine—surprising, as well as satisfying. Sardines are paired with some of the best-tasting leeks I have enjoyed, punctuated by *thé matcha*, making for an exotic turn on the everyday fresh Mediterranean sardine. Bresse chicken breast arrives meltingly tender, paired with a blend of cooked and raw spinach and a touch of finely sliced *couteaux* (razor clams) adding a bit of texture to the soft greens. But for me, the triumph of the meal was the vibrant pea soup (*le petit pois de montagne*), flavored with a touch of *réglisse* (licorice) and galanga (a gingerlike rhizome), and tasting as though the peas had been picked in the palace gardens only seconds before. The flavored butters are not to be missed—one green anise, another *thé matcha*—carefully if not sparingly spread on whole wheat or rye-miso bread. The cheese course consists of three perfectly aged Picodon goat's-milk cheeses from Anne-Sophie's home *département* of the Drôme—one young, one slightly aged, one firm and well-aged—served with a delicate rosemary gelatin and another gelatin of beer and honey. Although I am not a huge fan of *baba au rhum* (usually too boozy), hers is a delicate delight: tiny mouthfuls of light baba, paired with a burst-in-your-mouth passion fruit creation. The staff is casually but impeccably dressed in crisp blue jeans and blue shirts, and they all actually seem to be having a wonderful time serving the guests at La Dame de Pic. A tiny powerhouse of a woman with endless energy, Anne-Sophie will of course continue running her Michelin three-star restaurant in Valence, south of Lyon. She says she'll probably be in Paris a day or so a week. Before La Dame de Pic opened, most of the youthful Parisian chefs—cooking on a beautiful *plancha* (flat griddle) and induction range in an open kitchen overlooking the street—spent the summer working in Valence learning the tricks of the trade. They seem to be playing their cards right, as well.

CHEZ DENISE / LA TOUR DE MONTLHÉRY

CLASSIC BISTRO
5, rue des Prouvaires
Paris 1
TEL: +33 1 42 36 21 82
MÉTRO: Les Halles or Louvre-Rivoli
OPEN: Monday through Friday noon to 3PM
and 7:30PM to 5:30AM

CLOSED: Saturday, Sunday, and mid-July to
mid-August
PRICES: À la carte 35 to 50€ at lunch and
dinner
RESERVATIONS: Essential
ATMOSPHERE: Casual
SPECIALTIES: *Steak frites*, game, veal kidneys,
cassoulet, steak tartare, lamb's brains

Thank goodness for old-time bistros like Chez Denise. Those red-checkered tablecloths, efficient waiters, liter bottles of Brouilly, and nearly every bistro classic in the book: well-seared, rare, and juicy hanger steak (*onglet*), decent fries, *steak tartare,* lamb's brains (*cervelle d'agneau*), stuffed cabbage (*chou farcie*), veal kidneys (*rognons*) in mustard sauce, and *cassoulet* (white beans and varied meats). This is a good-time place for feasting, sitting elbow to elbow with your neighbors, living in carnivore utopia. I love the copious *frisée aux croutons,* wintry curly endive topped with croutons freshly made with the famed *pain Poilâne,* as well as the *haricot de mouton,* not mutton at all but a casserole of creamy white beans and the tenderest of lamb. Chez Denise is open until 5AM, so if you can't sleep and have a hunger for grilled pigs' feet (*pied de porc*), you know where to go.

IZAKAYA ISSÉ

JAPANESE
45, rue de Richelieu
Paris 1
TEL: +33 1 42 96 26 60
MÉTRO: Pyramides or Palais Royal–Musée du
Louvre
OPEN: Monday through Saturday

CLOSED: Sunday and holidays
PRICES: 12 to 19€ lunch menu. À la carte
35 to 40€ at dinner.
RESERVATIONS: Recommended
ATMOSPHERE: Casual
SPECIALTIES: *Domburi*, sake

With Japanese food always on my mind, I walked into Izakaya Issé on rue de Richelieu, hoping for a quick, flavorful, inexpensive, and light lunch. And that's just what I got, in the name of *domburi,* the Japanese bowl of rice covered with a diverse assortment of fish, shellfish, meat, or poultry.

I chose the salmon and avocado *domburi*—strips of bright-flavored salmon, chunks of avocado with a personality, and delicious, well-cooked rice flavored with just a touch of soy. The sprinkling of crunchy nori strips was as welcome as the frosting on a cake. Equally worthy was the *domburi* topped with carefully grilled eel and fine strips of omelet. At lunch, the tiny 20-seat diner offers four different *domburi*, priced at just 12 to 15€, with a small selection of desserts. The dinner menu features an assortment of brochettes, salads, vegetables, and sashimi. Wash it all down with sips of sake, choosing from a selection of more than 50 offerings.

▶ *Sake bar Izakaya Issé.*

RACINES 2

MODERN BISTRO
39, rue de l'Arbre Sec
Paris 1
TEL: +33 1 42 60 77 34
MÉTRO: Louvre-Rivoli or Pont Neuf
OPEN: Monday through Friday

CLOSED: Saturday, Sunday, 3 weeks in August, and between Christmas and New Year's
PRICES: À la carte 40 to 50€
RESERVATIONS: Recommended
ATMOSPHERE: Smart-casual

I love this peppy, loftlike, ground-floor modern bistro not far from the Louvre, with its spotless, open stainless-steel kitchen, a variety of dining spots (bistro tables, the bar, high stools, a cushy sofa), and a solid menu based on fresh, wholesome fare. A wintry lunch of creamy cauliflower soup; a pristine crab salad (quickly brought to life with a dusting of salt and pepper); firm, fresh scallops (*coquilles Saint-Jacques*) served with risotto (alas, overcooked); and a super-meaty capon paired with a rainbow of winter vegetables made my day. The wine list is extensive (treats from Château Rayas and Chave in the Côtes du Rhône), the service attentive but not intrusive, and I'd go back in a heartbeat for the creamy lemon tart (*tarte citronée*).

DOMBURI AU SAUMON ET AVOCAT D'IZAKAYA ISSÉ

Izakaya Issé's Salmon and Avocado Domburi

Domburi is Japan's original "fast food," created about 100 years ago when Japan began to modernize and there was more need for "on-the-go" food. A *domburi* is actually a deep bowl, usually made of porcelain, but the word is also commonly used to describe the dish that comes in it: hot boiled rice served with a topping of meat, fish, egg, or vegetables and various garnishes and condiments, often including a *dashi* sauce, traditionally a broth of dried kelp and bonito. *Domburi* is now popular outside Japan, and is the perfect quick snack to refuel during an afternoon exploring Paris's 1st *arrondissement*. Here's my take on Izakaya Issé's specialty.

EQUIPMENT:

4 porcelain *domburi* bowls or deep soup bowls

INGREDIENTS:

2 cups (450 g) short-grain Japanese rice (see Note)

½ cup (125 ml) *dashi*, or best-quality chicken stock or vegetable stock

2 tablespoons soy sauce, plus extra for serving

1 teaspoon sugar

1 large ripe avocado, preferably Hass

1 pound (500 g) ultra-fresh sushi-grade raw salmon, cut into bite-size portions, chilled

1 sheet dried seaweed or nori, sliced into thin matchsticks (or several tablespoons nori sprinkle)

1. In a medium-size saucepan with a lid, cover the rice with 2½ cups (590 ml) cold water and bring to a boil over a medium heat. As soon as the water begins to boil, cover and reduce heat to low. Cook until the rice is soft, about 15 minutes more. Remove from the heat and set aside for 10 minutes. (Alternatively, cook the rice in a rice cooker.)

2. In a small saucepan, combine the *dashi* or other stock, 2 tablespoons of the soy sauce, and the sugar. Bring to a boil over a high heat, then remove the pan from the heat.

3. Halve, pit, and peel the avocado. Cut the avocado halves lengthwise into thin slices, then cut each slice into thirds.

4. With a wooden spoon or paddle, fluff the rice.

5. Spoon the rice into the bowls. Pour several tablespoons of the *dashi*-soy mixture over the rice. Top each with slices of avocado and the salmon. Garnish with nori. Serve.

4 SERVINGS

NOTE: Thoroughly wash the rice by placing it in a sieve over a bowl. Fill the bowl with cold water so that the rice is immersed. Stir with your hand until the water becomes milky. Drain and repeat until the water runs clear, about 5 minutes. Do this 30 minutes to 1 hour before cooking the rice, then leave to drain in the open air.

SPRING

MODERN FRENCH
6, rue Bailleul
Paris 1
TEL: +33 1 45 96 05 72
springparis.fr
contact@springparis.fr
MÉTRO: Louvre-Rivoli or Pont Neuf
OPEN: For dinner only Tuesday through
Saturday 6:30 to 10:30PM. See website for
exceptions.

CLOSED: For lunch and all day Sunday and
Monday
PRICES: 76€ fixed menu; no à la carte
RESERVATIONS: Essential (via website, email,
phone, or in person from 10AM to 6PM Tuesday
through Friday, and from 3 to 6PM Saturday)
ATMOSPHERE: Smart-casual

Over the past few years, much ink has been spilled in the name of American Daniel Rose and his restaurant, Spring. Need I add more? Yes. His simple, market-driven cuisine sparked a Paris movement that won't stop. And although I could live without the media frenzy over anything identified as *new*, and the blogger blindness (or is it amnesia?), I'd like more of Rose's simple, straightforward style. A recent lunch at Spring left me feeling enormously satisfied, as though I had just witnessed a meal that was divine, pure, and memorable. No, the earth did not shake. But Rose delivered exquisite duck (meaty, cooked to rare perfection, with oh-so-crunchy, crusty skin); ultrafresh seared scallops paired with a single raw oyster (and tasteless razor clams); a pitch-perfect Pavlova (meringue that is crunchy on the outside, soothingly soft inside); and a superlative goat's-milk cheese sorbet. But the winner of the day was a humble, homey baked apple (better than my mother or grandmother made, alas). Tart Fuji wedges were first poached, then roasted in a touch of butter, turning golden, soft, succulent, welcoming. With all the delights of Rose's cuisine, however, some details here are annoying, such as the door buzzer at the entrance (this isn't a night club with a bouncer), a tacky coatrack inside the door, a bare window that looks out onto green plastic garbage cans being filled by building residents as we dine, a down-market plastic heater plugged in near the front window, and knives too dull to properly slice that perfect duck.

Predinner wine tastings in the 16th-century cellar can be organized for up to ten people. Inquire upon reservation.

VERJUS RESTAURANT

MODERN INTERNATIONAL
52, rue de Richelieu
Paris 1
TEL: +33 1 42 97 54 40
verjusparis.com
verjusparis@gmail.com
MÉTRO: Pyramides, Palais Royal–Musée du
Louvre, or Quatre Septembre

OPEN: For dinner only, Monday through Friday
CLOSED: Saturday and Sunday
PRICES: 60€ *dégustation* (tasting) menu.
No à la carte.
RESERVATIONS: Essential (by phone between
5 and 11PM, or email)
ATMOSPHERE: Smart-casual

For more than 30 years I have looked up at this tiny little restaurant space off the Palais Royal arcades and wondered what it would be like to be inside. Finally, only the image in my mind drew me in, never one of the slew of ever-changing restaurants with different names and different owners. But now I know. The space has a special allure—a cozy 25-seat dining room overlooking the brightly lit Theatre du Palais Royal—where recently, Americans Braden Perkins and Laura Adrian of Hidden Kitchen fame (they used to hold intimate and ultrapopular dinners in their own Palais Royal apartment) have opened a new restaurant, Verjus, adding a winning wine bar on the ground floor. Chef Braden's food is quiet, streamlined, and sophisticated, with a thoughtful, creative edge. The sober dining room is a good match, with its spectacular view of old Paris. The 55€ menu, with a wine pairing option at 85€, is on the expensive side; but it's worth venturing forth to sample Braden's tasty smoked eggplant (I had doubts about greeting this summer star in January) with a whisper of *ponzu,* a *crème fraîche semi-freddo,* and the requisite touch of beet. Each dish is a minor construction, a main ingredient decorated with a touch of spice, a hint of citrus, a bite of potato, a curl of greens. A fat filet of the freshest trout is teamed up with radicchio, grapefruit, potatoes, and buttermilk—warming, soothing fare that's light and almost felicitous. But my favorite of the evening was Braden's grilled Basque pork, seared to perfection on the outside, supermoist and pink on the inside, paired with little semolina *gnocchetti.* We chose the wine pairing and loved each and every sip, from the Domaine de Montcy Cour-Cheverny Plénitude (an easygoing, crisp Loire Valley white) to the Anjou Rouge Clos des Treilles Pompois (another friendly, light red from the Loire).

YAM'TCHA

MODERN FRENCH /
MODERN INTERNATIONAL
4, rue Sauval
Paris 1
TEL: +33 1 40 26 08 07
yamtcha.com
MÉTRO: Louvre-Rivoli or Les Halles

OPEN: Tuesday dinner, Wednesday through Saturday for lunch and dinner
CLOSED: Sunday, Monday, and Tuesday lunch
PRICES: 60€ weekday lunch menu, 100€ *dégustation* (tasting) menu at lunch and dinner
RESERVATIONS: Essential
ATMOSPHERE: Smart-casual

I s it worth the wait? Three months or more for dinner, slightly less for lunch? That's for you to decide, but each meal I have had at the postage stamp of a restaurant, Yam'Tcha, was memorable not only for the food, but for the experience throughout. It was evenhanded, carefully paced, not the least bit precious, and just a perfectly wonderful place to be on a rainy day in Paris. Chef Adeline Grattard's pedigree includes time spent with chefs Yannick Alléno, formerly of the Michelin three-star restaurant in the Hotel Meurice, and Pascal Barbot, of the Michelin three-star Astrance. With her Chinese tea–*sommelier* husband, Chiwah Chan, they make a rare team, she working elegantly in her tiny box of an open kitchen at the entrance, he with great ceremony (but not ceremoniously) delivering tiny cup after cup of soothing and remarkably matched teas that pair lusciously with her carefully constructed French-Asian cuisine. Each meal includes myriad ingredients and flavors: Tender Brittany mussels merged with fermented beans and pumpkin noodles, and were anointed with just the right touch of brown rice vinegar; a duet of giant wontons

▲ *Diners enjoying a bistro lunch in the Passage des Panoramas.*

stuffed with plump and full-flavored shrimp were paired with ultra-crunchy water chestnuts; a pad of steamed *foie gras* nuzzled a delightful blend of wakame seaweed and julienne of turnips, with a foam of dried scallops that emerged much like a sprig of parsley—not essential to the dish, but a pleasant nod. On one visit, we were wowed by the silken *lieu jaune* (Atlantic cod) set on a bed of black rice laced with garlic shoots. Each dish impresses with its intensity and freshness. There's no menu choice at this small, 16-seat restaurant, but I'm not complaining. The food is remarkably light, not a bit show-offy, and just different enough from all of our everyday fare to make one sit up and take notice. I love the decor, simple and elegant with lovely little chopsticks and Italian porcelain in pale earthy tones. The brief wine list is remarkable. We enjoyed two delicious and well-paired Burgundies. The white Nuits-Saint-Georges Jacques-Frédéric Mugnier Clos de la Maréchale was chardonnay to perfection, almost as though the winemaker was thinking of Grattard's fare as he vinified. Equally well paired was the pinot noir Nuits-Saint-Georges Les Boudots from Michel Noellat, a wine with a gentle touch of spice and smoke, elegant and right at home in this little jewel box of a restaurant. The name, by the way, is Mandarin for "drink tea," and you will!

2ND ARRONDISSEMENT

FRENCHIE

MODERN BISTRO
5–6, rue du Nil
Paris 2
TEL: +33 1 40 39 96 19
frenchie-restaurant.com
MÉTRO: Sentier
OPEN: For dinner only, Monday through Friday

CLOSED: For lunch, as well as all day Saturday and Sunday
PRICES: 45€ dinner menu
RESERVATIONS: Essential (online, by phone between 3 and 7PM weekdays, or in person at the restaurant). Note: There are two seatings at 7 and 9:30PM.
ATMOSPHERE: Casual

Ever since chef Grégory Marchand captured the hearts, minds, and palates of every blogger and Anglophone around the globe, this small, dinner-only farm-to-table restaurant has been booked solid, often months in advance. The last time I snagged a table, we feasted on Marchand's delectable pork with peaches, crunchy strips of fresh zucchini topped with a bounty of fresh herbs, and meltingly tender and meaty pigeon set on a bed of fresh corn, all garnished with nasturtium leaves. It was worth the wait. His well-priced nightly menu offers two choices for starters, mains, and dessert. The wine selection is extensive. If it's still on the list, revel in fresh, light, fruity Domaine de Montille's Volnay Champans, a red that Robert Parker's reviewer describes as a wine that "flows across the palate with the grace of a ballerina." Say no more. Note that guests at his bare-bones wine bar across the street regularly spill out into the cobblestone street, making for a festive air in a neighborhood not known for its great food. During the day, try the fish and chips or Reuben sandwich at Frenchie to Go, down the street, or buy ultra-fresh fish, meat, or organic coffee beans at the shops that make this a Parisian market street not to be missed.

CHEZ GEORGES

CLASSIC BISTRO
1, rue du Mail
Paris 2
TEL: +33 1 42 60 07 11
MÉTRO: Bourse or Sentier
OPEN: Monday through Friday

CLOSED: Saturday and Sunday, August, and one week at Christmas
PRICES: À la carte 40 to 70€
RESERVATIONS: Recommended
ATMOSPHERE: Casual

It's always a pleasure to return to a restaurant you loved decades ago and find it virtually unchanged. And maybe even better than you remember. That's Chez Georges, the dream bistro just off the place des Victoires. I am not sure, but it may be the first true bistro I dined in back in the 1970s. What I do know is that the menu remains unchanged; the quality is there, and especially the hustle-bustle of the dining room. Well-coiffed waitresses seem to skate through the aisles of this long, narrow dining room, with its mirrored walls and Gothic columns, effortlessly delivering giant bowls of herring; searingly hot, garlic-scented snails; bowls overflowing with curly *frisé* greens; and rich chunks of bacon, each adorned with a perfect poached egg. Everywhere there's a feeling of abundance and generosity and the sound of good times. The crowd is young, French, chic, and the ocher-toned dining room easily takes you back in time. I loved the moist, parsley-rich *jambon persillé;* the generous portion of tiny wild *girolle* mushrooms; the perfectly grilled sole; and the moist and meaty *steak de canard*, paired with a mix of wild mushrooms. Desserts of profiteroles, *tarte Tatin*, and *millefeuille* were just right. My only regret is that they were out of their *tarte au citron* by the time I placed my order. For a bistro, the wine list is extensive. There are plenty of bargain wines (the fruity red Côte Roannaise is an ideal bistro wine), and this is one restaurant that still offers wine *à la ficelle*. You pay only for what you have consumed from the bottle. Some good-value wines here include Alain Graillot's Crozes Hermitage, Olivier Leflaive's white Montagny, and Dagueneau Pouilly-Fumé.

GOUST

MODERN FRENCH
110, rue Volney
Paris 2
TEL: +33 1 40 15 20 30
enricobernardo.com
goust@enricobernardo.com
MÉTRO: Opéra or Madeleine

OPEN: Tuesday through Saturday
CLOSED: Saturday lunch, Sunday and Monday
PRICES: À la carte 35 to 50€ at lunch. 75 and 130€ dinner menus, à la carte 50 to 100€ at dinner.
RESERVATIONS: Essential
ATMOSPHERE: Smart-casual

Restaurateur Enrico Bernardo (named *Meilleur Sommelier du Monde* in 2004) has created a lovely, welcoming restaurant for grown-ups who are looking for a touch of surprise. Wine and food pairing has long been Bernardo's passion, as seen at his first restaurant, Il Vino, at 13, boulevard de la Tour-Maubourg in the 7th. Here, in a restored Napoleon III townhouse, you feel just a little bit special, as the super-attentive and friendly staff spoils you with a quick glass of pink champagne, as you dine on crisp white Quagliotti Italian linens, and admire the sparkling Puiforcat silver. But at center stage is the drama of the wine and food pairing, which could be seen as a gimmick, a game, if not played just right. With each dish,

Bernardo offers a glass of carefully chosen wine. The diner doesn't know what the wine is until about halfway through the course. At first I found it off-putting, but then got into the match. My first glass—a well-chosen young Meursault from Burgundy—totally tricked me: With the first sniff, I had declared, "I know it's not French; maybe Italian." My husband, Walter, and I guessed wrong a second time, so certain that his luscious red Volnay from Burgundy was a Bordeaux. As each wine developed in the glass, it changed, as it did with each bite of the carefully prepared food. The lesson here—at least for me—was to pay closer attention to each wine, and be aware of how it changes from the moment it is poured until the final sip is savored. Spanish

chef José Miguel Manuel offers a fine mix of Mediterranean-inspired fare, including a perfectly cooked filet of *bar*, or sea bass, bathed in pale green sauce laced with *verveine*, or lemon verbena, and dotted with fresh, crunchy peas. A first course of *langoustines*, or Dublin Bay prawns, cooked by a pro, were moist and still tasting of the sea, yet oddly paired with seared baby potatoes (colors and textures just wrong) but relieved by an unusual, tangy, and creamy sauce prepared with Spanish *turron*, or nougat. At Goust, which takes its name from the old French word for "taste," the air is relaxed, and the well-informed staff—both men and women dressed in black suits, white shirts, and red ties—help us enjoy a few moments of simple elegance.

LIZA

LEBANESE
14, rue de la Banque
Paris 2
TEL: +33 1 55 35 00 66
restaurant-liza.com
info@restaurant-liza.com
MÉTRO: Bourse
OPEN: For lunch Sunday through Friday. Dinner Monday through Saturday. Brunch Sunday noon to 3PM.

CLOSED: Saturday lunch and Sunday dinner
PRICES: 16 to 34€ lunch menus. À la carte 30€ at lunch. 42 and 49€ evening tasting menus (for minimum of two). À la carte 40 to 45€ at dinner. Sunday brunch 29€ menu (17€ for children under 12).
RESERVATIONS: Recommended
ATMOSPHERE: Casual

This young, hip, family-friendly, modern Lebanese restaurant near the Bourse is a hit. It's casual, with a menu that goes on and on in a positive way, and one of the most vegetarian-friendly restaurants around. Almost everything here is delicious, and the falafel—chickpea fritters that are expertly seasoned and carefully fried—is among the best I've ever tasted. The hummus (chickpea and sesame paste dip) and baba ghanoush (smoky eggplant dip) show you why they are Middle Eastern classics, and the halloumi—firm, white pan-fried young cheese—had that wonderfully squeaky quality and lovely mouthfeel. I adored the vegetarian "meatball," *kebbe batata*, a nicely seasoned potato creation that is great for dipping into the clean white *labné*, garlic and mint–laced drained fresh cheese. Only the tabbouleh was disappointing, soggy and lacking personality. There's a Sunday brunch for 31€, and an adjacent bakery and café.

SOUPE AU BROCCOLI DE PASSAGE 53

Passage 53's Broccoli Forest Soup

On my very first visit to the tiny Parisian restaurant Passage 53, this gorgeous green soup appeared as an appealing appetizer. Arranged in a tiny white cup, the soup resembled a spring-green forest, a creamy bottom layer topped with a crunchy halo of raw, shaved broccoli florets. The contrast of textures is a surprise to the palate, the flavor 100 percent pure broccoli. Here's my version. To your health!

EQUIPMENT:

A steamer; a food processor or a blender; a box grater; 4 small cups

INGREDIENTS:

1 pound (500 g) broccoli

⅓ cup (80 ml) plain whole-milk yogurt

3 tablespoons light cream or half-and-half

½ teaspoon fine sea salt

3 tablespoons chopped fresh mint leaves, for garnish

1. Trim the broccoli. Reserve 4 small florets for garnish. Finely chop the remaining florets and stems.

2. Prepare a large bowl of ice water.

3. Bring 1 quart (1 l) water to a simmer in the bottom of a steamer. Place the broccoli on the steaming rack. Place the rack over simmering water, cover, and steam just until a knife inserted into the stem pieces enters easily, about 7 minutes.

4. Plunge the broccoli into the ice water and cool for several minutes. Drain and transfer to the food processor or blender. Add the yogurt, cream, and salt, and puree. Taste for seasoning. Divide the puree among the small cups.

5. Using the large holes of the box grater, grate the reserved broccoli florets directly over the soup in the cups. Garnish with mint leaves. Serve. (The soup can be refrigerated, covered with plastic wrap, for up to 4 hours.)

VARIATION: Prepare with cauliflower for a white-on-white soup.

4 SERVINGS

PASSAGE 53

MODERN FRENCH
53, passage des Panoramas
Paris 2
passage53.com
TEL: +33 1 42 33 04 35
MÉTRO: Richelieu-Drouot or Grands
Boulevards

OPEN: Tuesday through Saturday
CLOSED: Sunday, Monday, 2 to 3 weeks in
August, December 25, and January 1
PRICES: 60€ fixed lunch menu, 130€ fixed
dinner menu. No à la carte.
RESERVATIONS: Essential
ATMOSPHERE: Smart-casual

Guillaume Guedj and Shinichi Sato know how to woo us with their streamlined, almost-too-beautiful-to-eat multicourse menus in this tiny, understated, salonlike restaurant tucked into the historic passage des Panoramas. Their work here is a play of brilliant colors, textures, and flavors

that surprise and astonish. An all-white offering of an alabaster serving of tender squid topped with feathery shavings of cauliflower recalled a tiny sonnet. The broccoli soup—I dubbed it broccoli forest soup—is little more than a smooth broccoli emulsion topped with carefully shaved bits of broccoli florets, offering brilliant color for the eye and intense textural contrast on the palate (see recipe on the facing page). In their hands, sole has true soul, paired with just a few bites of green beans and a shock of paper-thin red slices of radish. Moist, tender, succulent duck is paired with a delicate serving of cabbage, while their take on *tarte Tatin* arrives as a perfect rectangle with nothing but rich, memorable apple *confit*. Fans of chef Pascal Barbot, of Astrance, where Chef Sato once worked, will see the links here, for he is a worthy acolyte.

◀ *Passage des Panoramas, home of Passage 53 and the Gyoza Bar, and the oldest covered passage in Paris, opened to the public in 1799.*

POMMES PONT-NEUF

At the end of the 19th century, merchants with deep-fat fryers on rolling carts lined the Pont-Neuf bridge. They cut potatoes into slender sticks, fried them, and bundled them into paper cones. The French food writer Curnonsky exclaimed: "Fried potatoes are one of the most spiritual creations of the Parisian genius." But potatoes were not always so well loved. In 1787 Antoine Parmentier introduced the potato to France, with great hopes that this curious tuber would become so popular they would call it a *parmentier*. To promote the potato, he offered a dinner for 100 diners at the Hôtel des Invalides. The menu included potato soup, potato salad, potato fritters, a brioche made with potato flour, and to end the meal, potato liqueur.

SATURNE

MODERN INTERNATIONAL BISTRO
17, rue Notre-Dame des Victoires
Paris 2
TEL: +33 1 42 60 31 90
saturne-paris.fr
saturnetablecave@gmail.com
MÉTRO: Bourse

OPEN: Monday through Friday
CLOSED: Saturday and Sunday
PRICES: 37€, 55€, and 69€ fixed menus at lunch. 60€ fixed menu at dinner. No à la carte.
RESERVATIONS: Essential
ATMOSPHERE: Smart-casual

After my last lunch at Saturne, at the hands of young chef Sven Chartier, I knew this was a place I would want to return to again and again. What we want today is fresh, inventive fare that is at once familiar and surprisingly new, and Saturne delivers. The blond wood decor and airy glass roof are cheerful, and service is attentive and correct (despite a bit of confusion over a reservation). Sven loves his mandolin, and everything, from the veritable cornucopia of root vegetables to golden Comté cheese, is sliced paper-thin. The vegetables arrive as though they were lean, shiny sheets of colorful pasta, crisply guarding their integrity and flavor. Main courses, such as a moist *cochon de lait* (suckling pig) and fat slices of codfish, were cooked perfectly. And there are some pleasing surprises, such as the tiny buckwheat blinis paired with an effusive oyster mousse. I didn't love the wine I chose, a "natural" beverage, Domaine Valette Viré Clessé 2005. It had an oxidized edge, no balance of fruit and acid, and added, alas, nothing positive to the experience. Desserts were a bit heavy, with a thick *brioche perdu* and well-saturated *baba au rhum*. But I'd go back again and again just to sample baker Christophe Vasseur's *pain des amis*, a vibrant, thick-crusted loaf with a bright and nutty flavor (sourced from Du Pain et des Idées; see page 233). At lunchtime, you can order snacks and wine at the bar near the entrance.

3ᴿᴰ ARRONDISSEMENT

L'AMBASSADE D'AUVERGNE

CLASSIC BISTRO
22, rue du Grenier Saint-Lazare
Paris 3
TEL: +33 1 42 72 31 22
ambassade-auvergne.com
MÉTRO: Rambuteau or Étienne Marcel
OPEN: Daily noon to 2PM and 7:30 to 10PM
CLOSED: Sunday and Monday in July and
August, December 25 and 31 (for dinner), and
January 1
PRICES: 22€ weekday lunch menu. 42, 60, and
68€ lunch menus (for groups). 32€ regional
lunch and dinner menu. 42 and 68€ dinner
menus (for groups). À la carte 45€.
RESERVATIONS: Recommended
ATMOSPHERE: Smart-casual

Returning to the folkloric, dependable L'Ambassade d'Auvergne is like going to visit a favorite aunt and uncle. You settle in to enjoy a few sips of meaty Cairanne Côtes du Rhône from Domaine Brusset while examining the menu that's familiar and rich in the fiercely staunch traditions of the storied Auvergne, the mountainous center of France. Meat is king here, as in the delicious *pot-au-feu d'agneau,* a warming winter classic of chunks of lamb simmered with an avalanche of cold-weather vegetables. There are thick, seared slices of rich and fragrant *foie gras;* fat and rare-cooked *magret de canard,* or duck breast; a surprisingly modern take on *boudin noir,* or an individual upside-down tart with chunks of hearty blood sausage. In abundance is the region's pièce de résistance, the thick and creamy *aligot,* a potato puree laced with the fresh local cow's-milk cheese. For the first course—to prepare for the hearty fare that's to come—try the *tartare* of sea bass, filled with giant chunks of *bar,* tons of mustard, and fat, crunchy slices of celery, a refreshing starter if ever there was one. Save room for the smooth and addictive chocolate mousse, served out of giant bowls, and you are force-fully urged to go for seconds, even thirds.

L'AMI LOUIS

CLASSIC BISTRO
32, rue du Vertbois
Paris 3
TEL: +33 1 48 87 77 48
MÉTRO: Temple or Arts et Métiers
OPEN: Wednesday through Sunday
12 to 2PM and 7 to 11PM
CLOSED: Monday, Tuesday, three weeks in
August, and four days at Christmas
PRICES: À la carte 70 to 160€ at lunch and
dinner
RESERVATIONS: Essential
ATMOSPHERE: Casual
SPECIALTIES: *Steak frites,* game, roast chicken,
oysters

Caricature or the real deal? Are they pulling our leg or offering us authentic bistro fare? I guess it depends on one's history, outlook, or even mood. For sure, the decor at this 1930s bistro—which has been a world-famous icon since the 1960s—rates among the most faux-dilapidated in Paris. The patina is dingy, dark, and prized. But, oh, that roast chicken! Part of the secret, of course, is the kitchen's oak wood-fired oven, offering a sweet, soft, yet intense heat, making for a succulent bird that is up there with the best—if not *the* best—in Paris. Really. Maître d' Louis (that's his real name, though he's not the original chef) says the kitchen is on its fourth wood-burning oven since his arrival in 1978. In my earliest visits in the late 1970s, I remember the famed chef Antoine Magnin (whose photo hangs ceremonially in the dining room) cooking in an ancient blackened wood oven, his chef's whites punctuated by a red kerchief given to him by the actress Romy Schneider. "Nothing's changed," announces Louis, proudly, and he is quite right. Today's voluminous slabs of chilled *foie gras* are better than I remembered, carefully seasoned, with that nice touch of acidity. Most starters, like the *foie gras* and the generous serving of scallops, seared with plenty of butter, whole cloves of garlic, and a showering of parsley, can easily be shared. I have had better leg of lamb, this version tasting not as young as I'd like, though it was advertised as milk-fed. But it

was cooked to perfection in that wood oven. Towers of shoestring potatoes warm the heart of any potato lover, but my favorite "new" dish on the menu was the giant potato cake—they call it *pommes Béarnaise*—brilliantly executed, with tiny potatoes cooked in their skins, then baked in a round mold so the skins turn blistery and deep golden. The "cake" comes embellished with parsley and chopped raw garlic, though I wish they'd hold the garlic, especially in winter months when it's bitter no matter how "fresh" it may be. The wine list has improved a thousand-fold (both in selections and in value), and on my last visit I delighted in both the flinty white Sauvignon Blanc Henri Bourgeois Sancerre Jadis and the heady, deep purple, expressive Gigondas from Domaine la Bouïssière, at bargain prices by former L' Ami Louis standards. Not that the meal is a bargain: The chicken for two is 80€; the leg of lamb for two, 140€. If you are in a frugal mood, two people could get out of this iconic bistro for 136€, without wine, and that's not outrageous in this day and age. This is a place that every Paris food lover should experience at least once.

GRAZIE

ITALIAN / PIZZERIA
91, boulevard Beaumarchais
Paris 3
TEL: +33 1 42 78 11 96
graziegrazie.fr
MÉTRO: Chemin Vert or Saint-Sébastien–Froissart

OPEN: Daily. Continuous service on weekends.
CLOSED: One week in August, Christmas, and New Year's
PRICE: À la carte 30 to 40€
ATMOSPHERE: Casual
SPECIALTIES: Pizza

This loud and trendy Cohen-family outpost in the Northern Marais is just down the street from the family concept store Merci (see Cafés and Casual Bites, page 137), and is as much a cocktail lounge and bar as it is a pizzeria. The look could be called funky distressed industrial chic, with high ceilings, dark walls, and overstuffed armchairs. But the proof is on the plate, with exquisite thin-crusted pizzas direct from the wood-fired brick oven in the restaurant. Try the pizza Bianca (olive oil, *fleur de sel*, and rosemary) and the classic pizza Aurora (tomatoes, mozzarella, basil), as well as any variations topped with spicy pork sausages. The wine list offers some treasures: A favorite is the festive, well-structured Montepulciano d'Abruzzo from Emidio Pepe. Many complain that the restaurant is over the top, even in Paris's latest bobo (bohemian-bourgeois) land. You choose.

▶ *A Grazie chef throwing a pizza.*

CHEZ JENNY

BRASSERIE
39, boulevard du Temple
Paris 3
TEL: +33 1 44 54 39 00
chez-jenny.com
reservationchezjenny@blanc.net
MÉTRO: République or Temple
OPEN: Daily noon to midnight

PRICES: Lunch and dinner menus from 19.80€. Children's menu 11€. À la carte 35 to 50€.
RESERVATIONS: Recommended
ATMOSPHERE: Smart-casual
SPECIALTIES: Fish and shellfish, *choucroute* (sauerkraut and sausages), onion soup, children's menu

▼ *Setting up the dining room of the classic brasserie Chez Jenny.*

You'll feel as though you've taken a trip to Alsace as you enter this cute brasserie, all dolled up with folkloric wooden carvings and paintings from one of France's most welcoming regions. This is the place for some of the best *choucroute* in Paris, a well-seasoned sauerkraut (not the sort that tastes as though it's been reheated multiple times) served with hearty portions of sausages and pork. The sauerkraut is simmered gently with a touch of duck fat, grains of coriander, cumin, mustard seed, and juniper berries. I'd go back for the quartet of sausages alone—a carefully seasoned smoked pork sausage, another flavored with cumin, a white veal sausage, and a hot dog–like Strasbourg sausage. The dish also included a giant simmered pork knuckle, as well as smoked pork breast. Quality all around. A single 25€ serving was copious for two diners. The onion soup is *correct*, as the French say, meaning nothing special. So I'll pass next time. And the *flammekueche*—regional onion, bacon, and cream tart—could have been crispier. Do sample one of their well-priced, crisp, and dry white Rieslings.

CAFÉ DES MUSÉES

CLASSIC BISTRO
49, rue de Turenne
Paris 3
TEL: +33 1 42 72 96 17
cafedesmusees.fr
cafe.des.musees@orange.fr
MÉTRO: Chemin Vert or Saint-Paul
OPEN: Daily (kitchen open until 11PM)

CLOSED: First week of January and the first three weeks in August
PRICES: 15€ weekday lunch menu. 25€ dinner menu. À la carte 35€.
RESERVATIONS: Recommended
ATMOSPHERE: Casual
SPECIALTIES: Oysters, *steak frites*

This fun and funky corner café in the center of the Marais is a perennial favorite. I'd go just for platters of their delicate, silken, house-smoked salmon, served up with a tangle of greens and tangy dressing for dipping. Chef-owner Pierre Lecoutre is a master at the stove and diners can watch him perform in his tiny, open kitchen, shifting copper pots, stirring and searing, offering up gorgeous, giant *entrecôte* (beef rib steak), frying up deliciously crisp and golden French fries, roasting Basque pork topped with the famed smoked garlic from Arleux in the north of France. On my last visit I adored the *Parmentier de pintade fermière*, a winning *hachis parmentier*—traditionally a pie of minced beef topped with soothing mashed potatoes—served here with a twist: minced farm-raised guinea fowl. Café des Musées also offers briny Brittany oysters from Paimpol in season. The wine list and *medicaments du jour* (daily medicines) measure up to the cuisine, with a crisp and tart Champagne Drappier Zéro Dosage (meaning no sweet wine is added before bottling), and a spicy, mineral-rich Chardonnay Domaine de la Bongran Viré Clessé Quintaine. A good place to know anytime, but especially when visiting the Picasso and Carnavalet museums nearby.

4ᵀᴴ ARRONDISSEMENT

L'AMBROISIE

HAUTE CUISINE / MODERN FRENCH
9, place des Vosges
Paris 4
TEL: +33 1 42 78 51 45
ambroisie-paris.com
MÉTRO: Saint-Paul or Bastille
OPEN: Tuesday through Saturday

CLOSED: Sunday, Monday, two weeks in February (during school vacation), and August
PRICES: À la carte 300€ at lunch and dinner
RESERVATIONS: Essential
ATMOSPHERE: Formal. Suit jacket, but not tie, required for men.

I have followed and loved L'Ambroisie since the early 1980s when it was born as a contemporary nine-table restaurant on the Quai de la Tournelle. For 20 years now it has been beautifully installed on the elegant place des Vosges. Run by Bernard Pacaud and his wife, Danielle, the sumptuously decorated dining rooms make you feel as though you are eating in someone's home. The tapestries, sprays of flowers, and quiet tones can also make you feel as if you are in a private club. The staff is attentive, but not overly so. The clientele has to have deep pockets, for this may be the most expensive restaurant in Paris, with no fixed-price menu at either lunch or dinner. There is no way to trim the basic *addition* here: Most dishes are priced at 100 to 150€. Which raises the question, why include a restaurant that is so far beyond most of our means?

Well, if you do have the means there are great reasons to visit L'Ambroisie. Pacaud is a perfectionist and that commitment to perfection shows in the presentation of each dish. If the standard-bearers of French haute cuisine all turn in their aprons (and many have), where does that leave us? As a cook, I can see how Pacaud gently tweaks a dish each time it is made, refining and improving. That does not mean the "wow" factor always makes it to the plate. But subtlety can move us as much as a dish that hammers us on the head. Take the case of his *feuillantine de langoustines aux grains de sesame, sauce curry:* Gigantic *langoustines* are cooked gently and lightly, the curry sauce is divine, and the crunch of the thin sesame pastry is the perfect foil for the featherlight giant prawns. The prettiest dish of my last visit, and one I would go back for, is his *escalopines de bar, émincé d'artichauts, nages reduit au caviar.* Haute cuisine doesn't get much more altitudinous. The delicate sea bass is cooked tenderly, arranged in a mound like petals on a flower, the sauce is dotted with caviar, the artichokes arranged on a bed beneath the fish, all topped with a touch of nori, or dried seaweed. If I were queen of the world, I could imagine sampling this dish, say, once a week. Pacaud's insistence upon perfection continues to the dessert course, with one of the most densely flavored yet airy chocolate tarts one could imagine: an ultrathin crunchy crust, featherlight but rich chocolate filling, and a fine layer of cocoa on top. A delight with each bite.

BENOIT

CLASSIC BISTRO
20, rue Saint-Martin
Paris 4
TEL: +33 1 42 72 25 /6
benoit-paris.com
restaurant.benoit@alain.ducasse.com
MÉTRO: Châtelet or Hôtel de Ville
OPEN: Daily

CLOSED: August, December 24, 25, 31, and January 1
PRICES: 38€ lunch menu. À la carte 60 to 90€ at lunch and dinner.
RESERVATIONS: Recommended
ATMOSPHERE: Smart-casual
SPECIALTIES: *Cassoulet*, game, soufflés

Sometimes fond memories are what keep us cheerful, but memories can also be deceiving. A good friend once wrote to chef-owner Michel Petit (whose grandfather founded this iconic Parisian bistro in 1912), "Please reserve us a table next month, for we have the fondest Paris memories of our last anniversary meal at Benoit and plan to repeat it." Monsieur Petit responded in his always-direct, unemotional manner, "But, Madame, your memories may deceive you." As the French would say, you "risk" being disappointed. After Alain Ducasse became the owner of Benoit, and what has to be the most beautiful and authentic bistro decor in Paris, thus in the world, I had stomach pangs. Not because of Ducasse, indisputably a master, but because I feared that change might erase decades of memories of those voluptuous plates of *foie gras;* that salmon, cured like herring; the high-spirited banter of the waiters; and, most of all, Monsieur Petit's little smile as he peered over his glasses. After he left, I stayed away for a while, but on my last visit I made my peace. The evening was lovely, truly lovely—a little table for three up the winding stairway, a rainy night, a welcoming waiter, some well-priced white Burgundy, platters of silken smoked salmon with a salad of warm potatoes, the famed *cassoulet*, and the classic airy *millefeuille* and favored *tarte Tatin*. We were all happy, our memories intact. It remains a classic and an icon if ever there was one. Yes, it's the luxe version of a Paris bistro with etched glass, brass, and marble. And if you are looking for some relief on those prices—memorably elevated—reserve a table at lunchtime.

LET THEM EAT PEAS

"Eat peas with the rich and cherries with the poor" is an old French saying. The rich were able to afford the best crops of peas, the very earliest. The finest cherries of the season however, are the last: they are usually the ripest and most flavorful, also the cheapest and most plentiful.

During the 17th century, the French became impassioned over the fashionable pea. At court, women would dine with the king, feasting on peas, then return home to eat more before going to bed, even if it meant indigestion. "It is a fashion, a furor," wrote one court chronicler.

PETITS POIS ET CHAMPIGNONS, CRÈME D'ESTRAGON DE MON VIEIL AMI

Mon Vieil Ami's Peas and Mushrooms in Tarragon Cream

One of the many things to love about Mon Vieil Ami on the Île Saint-Louis is their generous offering of main-course vegetable dishes. If one is ever looking for inspiration for out-of-the-ordinary vegetable dishes to make at home, here is the place to go shopping. My version of this room-temperature dish has been on our home menu for years.

INGREDIENTS:

1 cup (250 ml)
    light cream or
    half-and-half

½ cup (125 ml) finely
    minced fresh
    tarragon, plus extra
    for garnish

Fine sea salt

1 tablespoon extra-virgin
    olive oil

4 ounces (125 g) fresh
    domestic mushrooms,
    trimmed, cleaned,
    and sliced lengthwise

1 cup (125 g) fresh or
    frozen peas, blanched
    and refreshed under
    cold running water

1. Combine the cream and the tarragon in a small saucepan, and simmer over low heat gently for 3 minutes. Let cool.

2. In a small skillet, heat the oil over medium heat until hot but not smoking. Add the mushrooms and sear until softened and cooked through, 3 to 4 minutes. Drain and set aside to cool.

3. Combine the peas, mushrooms, and tarragon cream. Toss to blend. Season with the salt to taste. Garnish with the minced tarragon and serve.

4 SERVINGS

CLAUDE COLLIOT

MODERN FRENCH
40, rue des Blancs-Manteaux
Paris 4
TEL: +33 1 42 71 55 45
claudecolliot.com
MÉTRO: Rambuteau or Hôtel de Ville
OPEN: Tuesday through Saturday

CLOSED: Sunday, Monday, and August
PRICES: 21, 24, and 29€ weekday lunch
menus. 59€ dinner menu. À la carte
50 to 65€ at lunch and dinner.
RESERVATIONS: Recommended
ATMOSPHERE: Smart-casual

Claude Colliot is on a roll. His inventive, modern fare is based on the classics and his food is always filled with authentic, intense flavors. Few chefs cook meat and poultry as well as he, and each visit to Colliot's modern Marais dining room offers new discoveries, new pleasures. I've been friends with Claude and his wife, Chantal, since their days at Bamboche on rue de Babylone in the 7th *arrondissement*. I count his signature oyster ice cream as one of the greatest dishes I've tasted in decades. He knows how to draw the purest of flavor from the meatiest cuts of lamb or a simple meringue. His *couleur maraichère* is a composition of the season's freshest vegetables. One early spring day, it was an all-white offering, the thinnest slices of cultivated mushrooms, celery root, capers, pistachios, and hazelnuts bathed in a perfect vinaigrette. His well-seasoned raw veal carpaccio is dusted with fresh minced coriander and a hint of licorice, while he cooks the most delectable squab, well seared, meaty, dense, and rosy rare. His *tout blanc* dessert—a memorable all-white trio of cardamom-flavored *fromage blanc*, fresh lychee sorbet, topped with rosewater-scented Italian meringue showered with *fleur de sel*—is already a modern classic.

ISAMI

JAPANESE
4, quai d'Orléans
Paris 4
TEL: +33 1 40 46 06 97
MÉTRO: Pont Marie
OPEN: Tuesday through Saturday

CLOSED: Sunday and Monday
PRICES: 40 to 60€ à la carte at lunch and
dinner
RESERVATIONS: Recommended
ATMOSPHERE: Casual
SPECIALTIES: Sushi and sashimi

If you are in the mood for super-fresh fish—no fireworks here but no surprises either—reserve a table at this discreet sushi restaurant situated on the Île Saint-Louis. The fabulous Seine-side location gives one the feeling of dining in a small seaside restaurant. The sushi menu offers a nice selection of sparkling fish, including extraordinary bonito and squid. A favorite here is the fresh mackerel marinated in rice wine vinegar. Chef-owner Katsuo Nakamura told me he simply marinates slices of the fish for five minutes in the rice wine vinegar. I've made it at home and it's delish!

MON VIEIL AMI

MODERN BISTRO
69, rue Saint-Louis en l'Île
Paris 4
TEL: +33 1 40 46 01 35
mon-vieil-ami.com
MÉTRO: Pont Marie
OPEN: Daily

CLOSED: January 1
PRICES: Lunch 15€ daily specials, 38€
vegetable menu, 46€ menu, 15€ children's
menu at lunch and dinner. À la carte 50 to
60€ at lunch and dinner.
RESERVATIONS: Essential
ATMOSPHERE: Casual

I confess that when I sit down to examine a restaurant menu and find a cornucopia of seasonal vegetables on the list, I want to get up and kiss the chef! Such was the case at my last lunch at Mon Vieil Ami, where the menu was loaded with fresh, seasonal produce: meaty *girolle* mushrooms, new carrots and heirloom tomatoes, new potatoes and last-of-season asparagus. Avocados, first-of-season ratatouille, fresh white beans (*cocos blancs*), zucchini, and fennel all starred. I relished a stunning and satisfying all-vegetarian meal, beginning with a giant platter of fresh heirloom tomatoes tossed in a fine vinaigrette, dollops of fragrant pesto, and just the right amount of *burrata*, the cream-filled mozzarella from Italy. Equally appealing was the mountain of fat golden *girolle* mushrooms—chanterelles—paired with an equal-size mountain of fresh peas cooked to al dente perfection, topped with a perfect soft-cooked egg slathered with a pungent tarragon cream. The well-priced Crochet white Sancerre was right at home with this fare. Other dishes were less exciting, with a bland *barigoule* of artichokes and fennel, and a ho-hum pea soup topped with a dollop of goat's-milk cheese. I loved the idea of the lemony chickpea puree paired with a well-cooked lamb shoulder, but think garlic would have been at home here, and the dish merited a better presentation. The charming, single-room restaurant holds just 40 diners, with space for 14 at a homey *table d'hôte*. We quickly made friends with our neighbors, even passing plates and sharing business cards. Two big pluses: Not surprisingly, there is a vegetarian menu, and the restaurant is open daily.

5TH ARRONDISSEMENT

L'A.O.C.

CLASSIC BISTRO
14, rue des Fossés Saint-Bernard
Paris 5
TEL: +33 1 43 54 22 52
restoaoc.com
aocrestaurant@wanadoo.fr
MÉTRO: Cardinal Lemoine

OPEN: Tuesday through Saturday
CLOSED: Sunday and Monday
PRICES: 21€ lunch menu. 29€ dinner menu.
À la carte 35 to 55€.
RESERVATIONS: Recommended
ATMOSPHERE: Casual

When I'm in the mood for classic bistro fare, A.O.C. is a place that always comes to mind: How can you miss, with an honest rotisserie chicken, meticulously sourced ingredients, and a generously priced and well-chosen wine list, topped off with the wheaty, crusty bread from Jean-Luc Poujauran?

Oh, and friendly, neighborly service, as well. I could do without the bright 1950s bistro lighting, and desserts can let you down (a *tarte Tatin* that tasted days old, a forgettable chocolate dessert), but that doesn't keep me from coming back for their bountiful *salade frisée* (curly endive salad teamed up with clean, salty cubes of bacon and crisp cubes of bread, all tossed in a vinegary dressing), moist rotisserie chicken, and portions of *cassoulet* that could feed an army. Their well-priced lunch and dinner menus might include an assortment of *charcuterie* from the Auvergne in central France, roasted suckling pig, varied cuts of well-seared beef, pork loin from the Basque village of Ospital, and freshly cut beef *tartare*. Wines I love here include Domaine Cauhapé's well-balanced Jurançon sec, Vincent Giardin's red Burgundy, the Santenay Vieilles Vignes, and Michel Richaud's meaty red Côtes-du-Rhône Terre de Galets. A.O.C., by the way, stands for *Appellation d'Origine Contrôlée*, a badge certifying the authenticity and quality of an agricultural product. The A.O.C. certifies excellence for wines, cheeses, butters, honey, poultry, and other products.

ATELIER MAÎTRE ALBERT

MODERN BISTRO
1, rue Maître Albert
Paris 5
TEL: +33 1 56 81 30 01
ateliermaitrealbert.com
ateliermaitrealbert@guysavoy.com
MÉTRO: Maubert-Mutualité or Saint-Michel
OPEN: Lunch Monday through Friday; dinner Sunday through Wednesday 6:30 to 11:30PM, and Thursday through Saturday 6:30PM to 1AM.

CLOSED: Saturday and Sunday lunch, and for two weeks in August
PRICES: 26 and 31€ lunch menus. 36€ dinner menu. À la carte 40 to 64€.
RESERVATIONS: Recommended
ATMOSPHERE: Smart-casual
SPECIALTIES: Roast chicken, rotisserie veal

Is there a better example of basic gastronomy than a simple, sublime, classic roast chicken? Golden, fragrant, its skin crisp and crackling, the humble *poulet rôti* is one of the world's greatest dishes, one that can stand on its own or serve as a soothing escort to all manner of potatoes, crying out to be paired with a red wine of some stature. In comes chef Guy Savoy, once again, to show us the way. His is a remake of one of the city's grand old Left Bank restaurants—Atelier Maître Albert—a warming spot with a giant fireplace at one end and a modern rotisserie at the other. Along with chef Emmanuel Monsallier and manager Laurent Jacquet, Savoy has figured out what we want today, and how to deliver. Walking in late one weeknight, it felt as though the place had been open for decades, as tables for two, four, and ten diners filled the room with sounds of fun and good times. A bistro classic and a favorite starter here is the seasonal green salad topped with seared chicken livers, wholesome and satisfying. Don't miss that golden rotisserie chicken, teamed with a warming potato puree. Daily specials might include a perfect roast duck and a potato gratin (with potatoes too thinly sliced for my taste) or a crispy-skinned veal shank and a fine "gratin" of spinach and mushrooms (see recipe on page 35).

▲ *Chef Emmanuel Monsallier, of Atelier Maître Albert.*

BRASSERIE BALZAR

BRASSERIE
49, rue des Écoles
Paris 5
TEL: +33 1 43 54 13 67
brasseriebalzar.com
MÉTRO: Cluny-La Sorbonne or Odéon
OPEN: Daily 8:30AM to 11PM Monday through Saturday. 8:30AM to 10:30PM Sunday.
CLOSED: Last week in July and first two weeks in August

PRICES: À la carte 35 to 65€. After 10PM menu 24.50€ (except during Christmas holidays). Children's menu 12.90€.
RESERVATIONS: Recommended
ATMOSPHERE: Casual
SPECIALTIES: *Steak frites*, roast chicken, oysters, *blanquette de veau, tête de veau, cassoulet, brandade de morue*

▲ *Contemplating the menu at Brasserie Balzar.*

n the mood for half a dozen oysters around 3PM? Or a steaming bowl of onion soup around 11PM? Your date wants a simple salad of goat's-milk cheese and greens; you want a well-seasoned, hearty hand-cut *steak tartare* with a salad and fries. Then reserve a table at the bustling Brasserie Balzar, one of the last good-food brasseries left in Paris. The lights are bright, the action is non-stop, tables are elbow to elbow, and everyone seems to be having a good time. On my last visit, we loved the moist and tender roast chicken, a well-thought-out dish of roasted leg of farm-raised lamb served with hearty white Tarbais shell beans and well-cooked slim green *haricots verts,* and the classic *gratinée à l'oignon,* or well-seasoned onion soup. The brief wine list offers a well-priced Châteauneuf-du-Pape, the Clos de l'Oratoire des Papes. This is one of the few restaurants left in Paris that offers consistent *plats du jour,* or daily specials, Monday through Saturday.

Monday: *Blanquette de Veau*
Tuesday: *Cuisse de Canard Confite*
Wednesday: *Tête de Veau, Sauce Ravigote*
Thursday: *Cassoulet*
Friday: *Brandade de Morue*
Saturday: *Onglet de Boeuf aux Echalotes Confites*

DANS LES LANDES

FRENCH SOUTHWESTERN
119, bis rue Monge
Paris 5
TEL: +33 1 45 87 06 00
MÉTRO: Censier Daubenton
OPEN: Daily Monday through Sunday noon to 11PM

CLOSED: December 22 to January 6 and three weeks in August
PRICES: À la carte 25 to 35€ lunch and dinner
RESERVATIONS: Essential on weekends, recommended during the week
ATMOSPHERE: Casual
SPECIALTY: Small plates and tapas

henever I am thinking of where to go to find an inexpensive, hearty lunch or dinner, I head over to the 5th *arrondissement* and pop into Dans les Landes, the second restaurant from the owners of a 15th-*arrondissement* favorite, Afaria. A rambling café just steps from the Rue Mouffetard market and the charming square Saint-Médard, this smart little spot is full of varied tapas-style tastes from France's Southwest, including meaty grilled quail breasts; tender fried *chipirons* (baby squid) sprinkled with a touch of sweet pepper; good spare ribs (*travers de porc*); and an adorable *salade landaise,* a take on Asian spring rolls—*foie gras,* salad, and duck breast wrapped in rice paper and cut into bite-size pieces. Surely don't miss the spicy Basque *xistora* (*merguez* sausage) tossed with tangy green *guindilla* peppers. Sip a glass of white Irouléguy, and enjoy!

GRATIN D'ÉPINARDS ET CHAMPIGNONS D'ATELIER MAÎTRE ALBERT

Atelier Maître Albert's Spinach and Mushroom Gratin

This appealing bistro dish is a specialty at a favorite Guy Savoy restaurant, Atelier Maître Albert (see page 31), where rotisserie chicken is always on the menu and, in the winter months, a warming fire awaits in the giant fireplace at the end of the room. Here is a vegetable gratin that is regularly on the menu and has long been a family favorite.

EQUIPMENT:

A 9-inch (23 cm) square baking dish

INGREDIENTS:

1 pound (500 g) baby spinach leaves, blanched and refreshed

¼ cup (60 ml) light cream or half-and-half

Freshly grated nutmeg

Fine sea salt

2 tablespoons extra-virgin olive oil

1 pound (500 g) fresh domestic mushrooms, trimmed, cleaned, and sliced lengthwise

1. Arrange an oven rack about 3 inches (7.5 cm) from the broiler. Preheat the broiler.

2. Toss the blanched and refreshed spinach with 2 tablespoons of the cream. Season with nutmeg and salt. Transfer to the baking dish.

3. In a skillet, heat the oil over medium heat until hot but not smoking. Add the mushrooms and saute until soft and cooked through, 2 to 3 minutes. Add the remaining 2 tablespoons of cream and cook 1 minute more. Taste for seasoning. Spoon the mushrooms on top of the spinach. Place under the broiler and broil until bubbling, about 3 minutes. Serve.

4 SERVINGS

CHEZ RENÉ

CLASSIC BISTRO
14, boulevard Saint-Germain
Paris 5
TEL: +33 1 43 54 30 23
MÉTRO: Jussieu or Cardinal Lemoine
OPEN: Tuesday through Saturday
CLOSED: Sunday, Monday, 10 days at

Christmas and New Year's, and all of August
PRICES: À la carte 40 to 55€ at lunch and
dinner. Plat du jour 15€ lunch and dinner.
RESERVATIONS: Recommended
ATMOSPHERE: Smart-casual
SPECIALTIES: *Steak frites*, black truffles

Anyone in the mood for classic Parisian bistro fare should reserve a table at the ultratraditional and purely authentic Chez René, set on a sunny corner along boulevard Saint-Germain. This has been a favorite haunt for decades, with copious portions of excellent preserved duck leg (*confit de canard*), whole veal kidneys (*rognons de veau*), and classic Burgundian beef stew (*boeuf Bourguignon*). The fries are hot and crispy and taste of real potatoes. The cheese comes from Madame Quatrehomme, so you know that the warm goat's-milk cheese salad (*chèvre chaud*) will be first-rate, with the greens a superb blend of lamb's lettuce (*mâche*) and arugula (*roquette*). In winter months there is a terrific starter, a gratin of *blettes* (Swiss chard), a recipe that uses the wilted leaves as well as the chopped stems, tossed with a flavorful béchamel and topped with plenty of beautifully gratinéed Gruyère cheese. On my last visit, the famed *saucisson de Lyon chaud pistaché* left me a bit disappointed: The potatoes were rather tasteless and not very warm, while the slices of pork sausage were a bit dry and ordinary. But I'll keep returning, for the service is thoroughly professional and the decor right out of central casting. The walls are filled with classic art show posters dating from the 1940s. Woody Allen would be right at home here!

▲ *Service is always attentive at Chez René.*

TERROIR PARISIEN

MODERN BISTRO
20, rue Saint-Victor
Paris 5
TEL: +33 1 44 31 54 54
yannick-alleno.com
reservation-mutualite@terroirparisien.fr
MÉTRO: Cardinal Lemoine or Maubert-
Mutualité

OPEN: Daily
PRICES: 15€ weekday plat du jour, à la carte 35
to 50€ at lunch and dinner
RESERVATIONS: Recommended
ATMOSPHERE: Casual
SPECIALTIES: *Croque monsieur,* onion soup,
steak frites

Thank you, Yannick Alléno, for bringing us yet another chic, casual, well-priced, good-food bistro that's open seven days a week. I am loving this trend. Alléno is the former Michelin three-star chef at the outstanding Hôtel Meurice, who, several years ago, began presenting a lunch menu built around products of the Paris region. He now presides over many restaurants around the world, in France, Morocco, Dubai, China, and Taiwan. Here in Paris the regionally sourced ingredients include carrots and onions, poultry and mushrooms, lettuces, and even beef and lamb. Terroir Parisien is a bright, light, airy space in the Maubert-Mutualité area of the 5th *arrondissement*. The location abounds in good food—it's home to the twice-weekly produce market, to Éric Kayser's abundant line of breads and pastries, and the top-flight cheese shop of Laurent Dubois. Most of the dishes here have a local history, relating to the days when the Parisian diet came mostly from the fields surrounding the city. There's a classic—and perfect—*salade de frisée, cresson à l'oeuf mollet et croûtons au lards,* tender curly endive and watercress topped with a flawless soft-cooked egg, crunchy croutons, and crisp rectangles of fragrant bacon. A few grindings of the pepper mill and I was good to go. I'd be proud to bring to the table their *navarin printanier d'agneau,* a moist, delicate spring lamb stew teamed up with baby carrots, potatoes, green beans, peas, and herbs. I have not seen the old-fashioned *merlan Colbert* (whole whiting breaded and deep fried) since the 1980s, when Joël Robuchon brought it back to the table at Jamin. Here the dish was as golden, tender, and crisp as can be, served with a delicate herb butter. There is also the classic French onion soup, stuffed cabbage, and platters of excellent *charcuterie* from Gilles Vérot's boutiques.

LE ZYRIAB BY NOURA

LEBANESE
Institut du Monde Arabe
1, rue des Fossés Saint-Bernard
Paris 5
TEL: +33 1 55 42 55 42
noura.com
MÉTRO: Jussieu or Cardinal Lemoine

OPEN: Tuesday through Sunday lunch
CLOSED: Sunday evening and Monday
PRICES: 48 and 56€ lunch menus. À la carte
25 to 30€. 72 and 84€ dinner menus. À la
carte 60 to 70€.
RESERVATIONS: Recommended
ATMOSPHERE: Smart-casual

As beautiful as Paris can be, it is not the place for restaurants with grand views or open terraces. Le Zyriab, perched high in the sky on the 9th floor of the *Institut du Monde Arabe* on the Left Bank, fills that bill.

The view is spectacular: Notre-Dame, the towers of Montmartre, and the Bastille are all there for your eyes to explore. The cuisine here is authentically Lebanese, and comes from the omnipresent house of Noura, with several restaurants, cafés, catering shops, and *patisseries* around the city. (See noura.com for details.) The dining room, which seats 90 guests indoors, is bright, spacious, and comfortable, and each table offers diners a stunning view. Service is efficient and warm, and the food clean, clear, well seasoned, and memorable. All the favorites are there, from the refreshing parsley-rich tabbouleh to a particularly spicy version of the chickpea puree, hummos Beyrouti. The thick, white drained *laban* cheese comes well adorned with crisp cucumbers, and the falafel (deep-fried balls of seasoned chickpeas) arrives crisp, crusty, moist, and satisfying. Do try the mixed grill, kebabs of moist, seasoned chicken breasts and lamb, as well as a particularly assertive version prepared with ground lamb. I could easily make a meal of the yeasted flatbreads—including *manakiche*, a pizzalike pleaser topped with *za'tar*, or a local blend of thyme leaves, sesame seeds, and sumac; and the lamb-stuffed *arayes*, a dish that with a touch of *laban* could become a major snack of its own. There's a good list of Lebanese wines, and we loved the white Château Kefraya from Lebanon Bekaa Valley, a complex blend of Viognier, Sauvignon Blanc, Ugni Blanc, and Chardonnay. This is a great place to go with a group, so one can share in a multitude of flavors.

6TH ARRONDISSEMENT

LE 21

MODERN FRENCH
21, rue Mazarine
Paris 6
TEL: +33 1 46 33 76 90
MÉTRO: Mabillon or Saint-Germain-des-Prés
OPEN: Tuesday through Saturday

CLOSED: Sunday, Monday, holidays, all of August, two weeks at Christmas, one week at Easter
PRICES: À la carte 70€ lunch and dinner
RESERVATIONS: Essential
ATMOSPHERE: Smart-casual
SPECIALTIES: Oysters, fish, and shellfish

Chef-owner Paul Minchelli is a fish and shellfish wizard who blends together dishes of ultimate simplicity (scallops barely steamed in the shell with a touch of seaweed, then topped with a gentle dollop of salty seaweed butter) or goes hog-wild with brilliant flavors in his colorful *mouriette à la sobrasada*, a lively dish of moist and tender cubes of young codfish married with spicy Spanish pork sausage, potatoes, and black olives. This earthy dish defines Minchelli's commitment to creativity and originality. I always love his *tartares*—the most recent a trio of scallops, salmon, and sea bass—punctuated with a fine Japanese accent of bits of seaweed and the crunch of sesame seeds. Equally lovely and delicious is his *supions à l'encre*, the tiniest and most tender of squid rings cooked in a jet-black sauce of squid ink and black rice. Yum! This discreet, dressed-up black-and-white bistro is the kind of place I could easily visit on a weekly basis. Didier Granier is a kindly, informed host who will lead you to some delicious wines, such as the very fish-friendly, lush, and flamboyant Condrieu from the fragrant Viognier grape, Georges Vernay's Les Chaillées de l'Enfer.

AZABU

JAPANESE
3, rue André-Mazet
Paris 6
TEL: +33 1 46 33 72 05
azabu.fr
MÉTRO: Odéon or Mabillon
OPEN: Tuesday through Sunday

CLOSED: Monday, Sunday lunch, two weeks in August and Christmas
PRICES: Lunch menus from 19 to 55€. Dinner menus from 43 to 62€. À la carte 40 to 80€.
RESERVATIONS: Recommended
ATMOSPHERE: Casual

Now that sushi has invaded all of Paris (albeit mostly bad sushi), a forgotten or ignored game in town is *teppanyaki,* a cooking method so simple as not to need a name at all. Quite simply, it's meats, vegetables, or fish cooked directly on a flat metal grill, similar to the also-ubiquitous Spanish *plancha,* with just a touch of oil and a bit of seasoning. (In Japanese, a *teppan* is an iron sheet, and *yaki* is stir-fried food.) The latest show in town is Azabu, a sushi-bar-size little spot near the Odéon, and one I can see myself returning to on a very regular basis. What is it about food cooked in front of you that makes it all the more pleasing? You want it all, even if it's not for you. You salivate, your nostrils flare, you are just so hungry. When you go, sit at the bar so you can watch the dexterous chef. He works like an artist preparing his palette, quietly concentrating on each detail, lining up all the ingredients and *bing! bang! zoom!*—they are flipped on the huge flat grill— scallops, chicken, squid, *foie gras,* beef, pork, you name it. Everything is cooked quickly and effortlessly, some covered with a metal hood to soften the heat and slow down the cooking. The raw items are good here, too, with a marvelous beef carpaccio, as well as a platter of fresh oysters served with a seriously delicious *ponzu* sauce, a fabulous blend of soy sauce, rice vinegar, lemon juice, and a touch of *kombu,* or kelp. (But these were rather difficult to eat with chopsticks, since there was nothing to cut the muscle.) Equally lovely was a starter carpaccio of salmon, served with fresh sheets of nori seaweed to wrap your own salmon packages. The main-course *teppanyaki* chicken was moist, copious, and delicious. On my last visit I adored the well-seasoned *salade aux algues* (seaweed salad) and extraordinary grilled eggplant brushed with fermented soybean paste, or miso. To wash it all down, the chilled house sake, or rice wine, is the perfect match.

LES BOUQUINISTES

MODERN BISTRO
53, quai des Grands-Augustins
Paris 6
TEL: +33 1 43 25 45 94
lesbouquinistes.com
bouquinistes@guysavoy.com
reserve@guysavoy.com (reservations)
MÉTRO: Saint-Michel or Odéon

OPEN: Monday through Saturday noon to 2PM and 7 to 10:30PM. Sunday 6:30 to 10PM.
CLOSED: Sunday lunch
PRICES: 31 and 35€ lunch menus, with a glass of wine. 89€ *dégustation* (tasting) menu. À la carte 60 to 80€ at lunch and dinner.
RESERVATIONS: Essential
ATMOSPHERE: Smart-casual

I always consider it a very positive sign when I am barely halfway through a dish I'm loving, and I'm already plotting how I'll prepare it at home. And how soon. That's what happened to me at a summer dinner at the longtime favorite modern bistro Les Bouquinistes, a star in chef Guy Savoy's already-brilliant galaxy. The starter in question included oh-so-gently-smoked trout cut into paper-thin slices and draped around a crunchy mix of cornichons, tomatoes, and radishes, bathed ever so lightly in a mildly acidulated cream dressing. Pretty, tasty, modern, light, satisfying—who could ask for more? I could easily have made a meal of it. Throughout the evening, I was struck by how every flavor on the plate was frank and forward. You knew that when you were eating an eggplant, it was eggplant, and when biting into a mushroom, there was no doubt what it was. No fussy disguises—it was clearly a mushroom. A winning starter was the tiniest of tuna squares topped with a smoked eggplant puree, hardly visible but highly present on the palate, paired with a pungent rice vinegar sauce I would die to copy. All was really fresh and welcoming. Another dish, a little round of brioche, was filled with a generous mound of wild mushrooms topped with a soft-cooked egg (cut at the table to run, golden and divine, as a sauce for the mushrooms). It could also have served as a meal on its own. The chocolate dessert is not to be missed: basically two brownie-like rich chocolate squares paired with a pool of warm chocolate sauce and cool chocolate sorbet, a mix that melts into one giant, soothing pool of pleasure. This classy bistro has worn well, and I love to find a window seat at lunch or at dinner in the summer, when you can look out on the Seine, or across to Notre-Dame and Pont Neuf, and know that you could not be anywhere else in the world but Paris.

LA CLOSERIE DES LILAS

CLASSIC FRENCH
171, boulevard du Montparnasse
Paris 6
TEL: +33 1 40 51 34 50
closeriedeslilas.fr
closeriedeslilas@orange.fr
MÉTRO: Raspail or Port-Royal (RER B)

OPEN: Daily
PRICES: Bistro 40 to 60€ à la carte at lunch
and dinner. Restaurant 50€ lunch menu,
80 to 100€ à la carte at lunch and dinner.
RESERVATIONS: Recommended for restaurant.
No reservations for bistro.
ATMOSPHERE: Casual

Is there a restaurant as mythically, historically Paris as La Closerie des Lilas? It would be a shame to not at least sip a coffee or glass of bubbly here at least once in one's life, enveloping oneself in an establishment situated at the end of boulevard du Montparnasse since 1847. You can go for the decor alone, admiring the elegant Art Deco details in the more casual brasserie's glass dividers and cabinetry. You can go for the history alone, for the list over the decades is long: Hemingway, Fitzgerald, Bacall, and for people-watching today, perhaps Mick Jagger or Johnny Depp. You can go for the terrace, just steps from the edge of the Luxembourg Gardens and shaded from the summer sun.

And you can go for the food: extraordinary oysters from the Gillardeau family in Brittany, all plump, fleshy, and iodine-rich. Regular customers swear by the bistro's pistachio-rich sausages and *steak tartare* and *frites*, while the more formal restaurant selections might include a welcoming lobster salad flanked with a mix of fresh, dressed seaweed from Brittany. Service is professional and generally comes with a smile.

LE COMPTOIR DU RELAIS

MODERN BISTRO
9, carrefour de l'Odéon
Paris 6
TEL: +33 1 44 27 07 97
hotel-paris-relais-saint-germain.com
hotelrsg@wanadoo.fr
MÉTRO: Odéon
OPEN: Monday through Friday noon to 6PM
(brasserie menu), one evening seating at
8:30PM (bistro menu only). Saturday and
Sunday noon to 11PM (brasserie menu only).

CLOSED: No summer closure, although hours
may change during the year according to school
holidays. Best to call ahead to confirm.
PRICES: À la carte 35 to 45€ at lunch. 60€
fixed dinner menu, no à la carte.
RESERVATIONS: Essential (only for dinner
Monday to Friday)
ATMOSPHERE: Casual

Yves Camdeborde hits the jackpot with his vest-pocket bistro that overflows with diners. The no-reservation lunches (get there early!) are fantastic, with an array of salads, cheese platters, and great wines by the glass. Some favorites include his protein-rich salad of lobster and green beans bathed in a light and delicate sauce of yogurt, and a warming winter starter of baked eggs topped with fresh black truffles. His bistro repertoire is classically based but totally personal, with plenty of meaty terrines, *cochonailles* (various hams, sausages, and pâtés), pigs' feet, veal, and beef cheeks. The menu is heavy on meats and *abats* (organ meats), but one can also find platters of seasonal vegetables and fish selections, and there's always a fine cheese assortment.

FOGÓN

SPANISH
45, quai des Grands-Augustins
Paris 6
TEL: +33 1 43 54 31 33
fogon.fr
fogon@fogon.fr
MÉTRO: Odéon or Saint-Michel
OPEN: Tuesday through Friday dinner only (7PM
to midnight). Saturday and Sunday lunch and
dinner (noon to 2:30PM and 7PM to midnight).

CLOSED: Monday
PRICES: 48€ paella menu (for two). 55€ tapas
menu (for the entire table). 35€ menu after
10:30PM. À la carte 10 to 50€.
RESERVATIONS: Recommended
ATMOSPHERE: Casual
SPECIALTIES: Paella, Spanish wines

Welcome to a *real* Spanish meal, not a caricature of a giant paella steaming at an outdoor market. Alberto Herráiz and his wife, Vanina, are true ambassadors for a great cuisine, offering a personal, vital Spanish table. Herráiz is a fourth-generation cook and if the proof is in the tasting, he has truly inherited the right DNA. Flavors here are bold, and often very salty, so come forewarned. Paella is king, in many guises: al dente, richly flavored rice—each grain a separate tiny, delicious morsel—escorting lobster or snails, tuna or vegetables, or the famed Ibérico ham. The paella is first cooked stovetop to help create a dense crust, then baked so that flavors marry and ingredients soften. Starter tapas are totally original, ranging from a brilliant, vibrant yellow pepper soup to toast topped with black olive tapenade and a section of fresh grapefruit, a lovely contrast of salty and acidic. The tapas tasting menu is in a league all its own. I have never tasted such original flavors anywhere, and served with elegance and flair. Some are just little bites (a giant green grape stuffed with fish eggs, a sweet-salty explosion on the palate), while others are truly substantial dishes, such as the most tender marinated octopus I have ever tasted, topped with a shower of tangy arugula. Herráiz offers us a giant platter of colorful, roasted fall root vegetables, all glossy and glazed and topped with tiny bits of his tangy *botarga,* or dried mullet roe; sea bream comes with a trio of sauces; while moist, tender quail arrives bathed in a deep red wine sauce. Service in this small, long, and narrow dining room is attentive as well as instructive. Two wines to suggest here include the pale white Marfil, a wine that will carry you through the entire meal, or the more intense house red, a blend of Tempranillo and Grenache. If it's on the menu that day, do not miss the outstanding pear sorbet—intense, fruity, satisfying. Or the Manchego sheep's-milk cheese, teamed with a flavorful quince paste. A great place to go on a Sunday night, when most other restaurants are closed.

HUÎTRERIE RÉGIS

OYSTER BAR
3, rue de Montfaucon
Paris 6
TEL: +33 1 44 41 10 07
huitrerieregis.com
contact@huitrerieregis.com
MÉTRO: Mabillon or Saint-Germain-des-Prés
OPEN: Tuesday through Sunday

CLOSED: Monday. Annual closing from mid-July to third week of September (depending upon the availability of oysters at the start of the season).
PRICES: 27, 31, and 36€ menus at lunch and dinner. Oysters 18.50 to 62€ per dozen.
RESERVATIONS: Not taken
ATMOSPHERE: Casual

From the moment you approach this spotless, all-white postage-stamp-size oyster bar, you know you are in for a treat. Clean, briny, top-of-the-line oysters are what you will find here, especially the Marennes-Oléron from the Poitou-Charentes in Southwest France, aged in ocean beds for up to two months once they come of age. At Régis there is room for only 14 diners indoors and 8 at tiny tables outside. Régis is simple and efficient: You must have at least a dozen oysters per person here and you can watch as the briny bivalves are opened. You should have no trouble polishing off their tiny *fines de claires*, delights that taste of the ocean; or, my other favorite, the meatier *spéciales de Claire* No. 3 (the smaller of the two choices), with a true hint of hazelnuts. These are oysters that leave your palate with a welcome cleansing aftertaste for hours to come. There is wine by the glass, carafe, or bottle. A favorite here is Alphonse Mellot's Sancerre Desmoiselles, a truly stunning Sauvignon Blanc with chalky, mineral-rich overtones. The oysters and wine seem to lock elbows at the table! Depending on the season, Régis may also have a few cooked shrimp, some sea urchins (*oursins*), or raw clams (*palourdes*). There is carryout as well as a delivery service for opened oysters.

LE PETIT LUTETIA

BRASSERIE / CLASSIC BISTRO
107, rue de Sèvres
Paris 6
TEL: +33 1 45 48 33 53
MÉTRO: Vaneau
OPEN: Daily

CLOSED: December 23 and 24
PRICES: 28 and 37€ lunch and dinner menus.
À la carte 45 to 50€.
RESERVATIONS: Not necessary
ATMOSPHERE: Smart-casual
SPECIALTIES: Game

Some restaurants just hit the spot from the moment you walk through the door and this 1920s dolled-up bistro-brasserie does just that, with its jocular waiters, bentwood chairs, brass shelves, stamped tin ceiling, and shiny copper pots hanging on the walls. The food is fine classic bistro fare, with a huge array of fresh oysters, a delicious offering of smoked herring and potatoes, and fresh goat-cheese salad prepared with cheese from *fromagerie* Quatrehomme down the street. I loved their sauté of *sanglier* (wild boar), tender and flavorful. The *tranche de gigot* (sliced leg of lamb) was grilled to perfection, though I've had better-quality lamb. A good place to know about while shopping at the Bon Marché department store nearby, as well as on days when other restaurants are closed.

OYSTERS

"I don't think one could ever tire of oysters."

—Leon Daudet, French author (1867–1942)

And the French don't tire of them. Indeed, oyster consumption in France hovers around 92,000 tons a year. That's a lot of oysters!

Up until the 1850s, oysters were so plentiful in Paris that they were considered poor man's food, even though the journey from the coasts where they were harvested to Paris was never simple. Oysters traveled in wooden carts laden with ice. As the ice melted, it was regularly replenished at icehouses set along the route.

During the 18th century, oyster criers filled the streets of Paris, carrying wicker hampers on their backs filled with their inexpensive and weighty fare. Although the colorful hawkers are gone today, France remains Europe's premier oyster producer—cultivating some 2,000 tons of precious, flat-shelled *Belon*-style *plates* oysters and more than 100,000 tons of deep, elongated, crinkle-shelled *creuses* oysters.

From Cherbourg in the north to Toulon along the Mediterranean, more than 18,000 French oystermen in high rubber boots and thick jerseys carry out their battle with nature. They nurse the fragile baby oyster from infancy to maturity, a labor that takes three to four years.

Near-microscopic oyster larvae begin life floating in the sea with plankton. The larvae search for something to grip on to. Their survival rate is low; out of millions of spawn, just three or four grow to the adult stage.

Four to ten months later the larvae have grown to seed oysters and are now about the size of a fingernail. At this stage they are harvested and put into *parcs* (oyster beds), where they remain for up to two and a half years.

Then, the flat-shelled *plates* are often dispatched to river estuaries, where the warmish blend of salt and fresh water helps them develop their captivating, slightly metallic flavor.

The more common *creuses*—which grow twice as fast as the *plates*—might be transferred several times before they swing into their final stage of development. The most vaunted spend the last months of their lives in swampy, shallow, slightly alkaline fattening beds known as *claires*, where they pick up their unusual green tinge by feasting on certain microscopic blue algae. The longer the oysters spend in the fattening beds, the greener and more richly flavored, and more valuable, they become.

Just before oysters are ready for the market, they spend a few days being purified in reservoirs. There, they are dipped in and out of water so they learn to keep their shells shut. As long as the oyster remains chilled and the shell stays closed during transport, the oyster can survive on its own store of saline solution. Once out of the water, it will easily stay alive for eight days in winter, two days in warmer summer months.

Oysters are generally available in a number of sizes. The larger are more expensive, though not necessarily better. No matter the size, oysters are best eaten raw on the half shell, from a bed of crushed ice, with no dressing—neither lemon juice nor vinegar. They need no further embellishment than a glass of Muscadet or Sancerre white wine and a slice of buttered rye bread.

PLATES. The two most popular types of flat French oysters (*plates*) are the prized *Belon*—a small, elegant oyster that is slightly salty, faintly oily, with a hint of hazelnut—and the fringy, green-tinged *Marennes*. *Plates* are calibrated according to their weight: The smallest and least expensive, No. 6, offers about

.75 ounce (20 g) of meat; while the largest, No. 000 (sometimes called *pied de cheval*, or horse's hoof), offers up to 4 ounces (125 g) of meat.

CREUSES. France's most common oyster—deep, elongated, and crinkle-shelled, the *creuse* is sometimes called the *Portugaise*, even though this variety was essentially replaced by the *Japonaise* after the *Portugaise* was struck by disease in 1967.

The *creuse* oyster has several subcategories related to the method of final aging and size. Two subcategories relate to size: *Fines* are the smaller and *spéciales* are larger. *Huîtres fines de claire* have been "aged" at least one month in special fattening beds where there are 20 oysters for each square meter; *huîtres spéciales de claire* have been "aged" for two months at 10 oysters per square meter; *huîtres spéciales pousse en claire* have been "aged" at least four months at 5 to 10 oysters a square meter.

Creuses are calibrated according to weight, from the smallest and least expensive, No. 5, weighing about 1 ounce (30 g), to the largest, No. 0, weighing more than 5 ounces (150 g).

"As I ate the oysters with their strong taste of the sea and their faint metallic taste that the cold white wine washed away, leaving only the sea taste and the succulent texture, and as I drank their cold liquid from each shell and washed it down with the crisp taste of the wine, I lost the empty feeling and began to be happy and to make plans."

—Ernest Hemingway, *A Moveable Feast*

▼ *L'Écailler du Bistrot (see page 98).*

LES SHIITAKES DE SEMILLA

Semilla's Seared Shiitake Mushrooms

Chef Eric Trochon and owners Juan Sanchez and Drew Harré have a winner on their hands with this casually serious restaurant, Semilla, in the heart of Saint-Germain in the 6th *arrondissement*. This unforgettable, simple mushroom dish has been on the menu since the restaurant's early days in 2012. The meaty mushrooms make a perfect starter or vegetable side dish. I love to serve them with a simple roast leg of lamb. Note that while these mushrooms can be cooked on a grill, I find they tend to lose their precious juices to the coals. If shiitake mushrooms are not available, other large, cultivated mushroom caps are a worthy substitute.

EQUIPMENT:

A flat griddle or a *plancha*

INGREDIENTS:

1 tablespoon best-quality toasted sesame oil, such as Leblanc brand

1 tablespoon Japanese soy sauce, preferably organic

16 fresh shiitake mushrooms or other fresh, cultivated mushrooms

1 tablespoon finely minced fresh chives

1. Heat the griddle or *plancha* over high heat.

2. In a small bowl, combine the sesame oil and soy sauce and whisk to blend.

3. Trim the mushroom stems and reserve for making stock. Brush the mushroom caps and undersides with the oil–soy sauce mixture. (This can be done 10 minutes in advance, allowing the mushrooms to absorb the sesame and soy flavors.) Place the mushrooms, cap side down, on the griddle or *plancha*. Press down slightly on the mushrooms to flatten them, and cook for 3 to 4 minutes. Turn the mushrooms over and press down slightly on them to flatten the caps even more. Cook for 1 minute more. Brush once more with the oil–soy sauce mixture. Shower with chives and serve.

**2 SERVINGS AS A FIRST COURSE,
4 SERVINGS AS AN APPETIZER OR SIDE DISH**

◀ *Drew Harré, partner in the popular restaurant Semilla.*

AU PIED DE FOUET (Saint-Germain)

CLASSIC BISTRO
3, rue Saint-Benoit
Paris 6
TEL: +33 1 42 96 59 10
aupieddefouet.com
MÉTRO: Saint-Germain-des-Prés

OPEN: Monday through Saturday
CLOSED: Sunday
PRICE: À la carte 24€
RESERVATIONS: Not taken
ATMOSPHERE: Casual

Established more than 150 years ago in Paris, Au Pied de Fouet now has three locations around the city (see the 7th and 11th *arrondissements*), where the young and old sit elbow to elbow in search of the kind of old-fashioned bistro fare now often hard to find:

gesiers confit (confit of duck gizzards), *foie de volaille* (chicken livers), *foie de veau* (calf's liver), *hachis parmentier* (ground beef and potato casserole), and *tarte Tatin*. Your satisfaction at this simple, always-bustling bistro depends on how you order. On my last visit, the *chou farci* (stuffed cabbage) was fluffy, light, full-flavored, delicious. The calf's liver was cut too thin and cooked too long. I did keep eyeing the *confit de canard* (preserved duck confit) being devoured on my left and on my right, and plan to sample it on my next visit. We loved the starter of herring and warm potatoes and the well-priced Perrin brothers Vieille Ferme red Côtes du Ventoux. The *tarte Tatin* is pretty good, too, as is the cheery, efficient service.

PIZZA CHIC

ITALIAN / PIZZERIA
13, rue de Mézières
Paris 6
TEL: +33 1 45 48 30 38
pizzachic.fr
pizzachic@sjcohen.fr

MÉTRO: Saint-Sulpice or Rennes
OPEN: Daily
CLOSED: One week in August
PRICES: Lunch and dinner à la carte 15 to 30€
RESERVATIONS: Essential
ATMOSPHERE: Casual

Despite the dreadful name—Pizza Chic—I vote this restaurant's Pizza Aurora the best in town. Simple is best: thick, fresh tomato sauce, soft pillows of rich mozzarella, a touch of basil set on a full-flavored crust and baked to perfection in a wood-fired oven. When it's on the menu,

the *burrata* pizza is spectacular: delicate, cream-filled mozzarella is added just after the pizza comes from the oven and melts softly into the tomato topping. Service ranges from decent to nonchalant. Critics are all over this place complaining of the prices, which are outlandish for pizza. But I don't mind paying a price for a delicious and satisfying dinner in the center of Paris.

SEMILLA

**MODERN FRENCH /
MODERN INTERNATIONAL**
54, rue de Seine
Paris 6
TEL: +33 1 43 54 34 50
MÉTRO: Saint-Germain-des-Prés or Mabillon

OPEN: Daily 12:30 to 2:30PM lunch. Dinner 7 to
11PM. Sunday brunch noon to 3PM, with continued
limited service until 11PM.
PRICES: 23€ lunch menu. À la carte 35 to 55€.
RESERVATIONS: Recommended
ATMOSPHERE: Casual

American Juan Sanchez and New Zealander Drew Harré have become fixtures in the Saint-Germain neighborhood (with restaurants Fish and Cosi, and the wine shop La Dernière Goutte). My good friends have hit yet another grand slam with their newest endeavor, Semilla, a tapas (small plate–style) restaurant. They produced one winning dish after the other, with chef Eric Trochon (who holds the coveted title of *Meilleur Ouvrier de France*) at the helm. The menu features a mix of totally new and amazingly to-the-point inventions, as well as soothing classics updated with a modern edge.

Juan, Drew, and their crew spent more than a year gutting and then fine-tuning this lovely spot, updating the beams-and-brick decor into a clean, white yet bistro-like space, with an all-stainless open kitchen. On the menu: paper-thin slices of delectable *charcuterie* from Corsica; an amazing starter of grapefruit, coconut cream, and Asian herbs; a creamy *velouté* of mushrooms; a must-have plate of shiitake mushrooms grill-seared with just a touch of sesame oil, soy sauce, and chives (see recipe, page 46); fabulous skate wing topped with a peppy *sauce vierge;* a state-of-the-art *blanquette de veau;* a rosy-rare *côte de boeuf;* a dessert of winning citrus-based *soupe d'agrumes.* The wine list offers an abundance of dependable and affordable selections from Juan the Magnificent.

LA SOCIÉTÉ

MODERN FRENCH
4, place Saint-Germain des Prés
Paris 6
TEL: +33 1 53 63 60 60
restaurantlasociete.com
MÉTRO: Saint-Germain-des-Prés

OPEN: Daily 8AM to 2AM
PRICES: À la carte 60 to 80€ at lunch and
dinner
RESERVATIONS: Recommended
ATMOSPHERE: Smart-casual

No matter how often I visit this chic, trendy spot hidden off the place Saint-Germain (there is no sign; just look for the staid gray building diagonally across from La Bonaparte café), I always leave uplifted. I love the summer outdoor dining space, nicely sheltered from the wind, rain, and sun, and well heated for chilly days when you simply must dine outdoors. Indoors or out, the place is always a scene, with a lean, alluring waitstaff who look as though they just walked off the fashion runway. The menu here is eclectic, international, modern, with something for everyone, ranging from giant club sandwiches, a rich lobster salad, convincing Vietnamese *nems* (spring rolls) with plenty of mint and a spicy sauce for dipping, salads of carefully stacked baby lettuce leaves topped with green beans and a vinegary dressing, creamy macaroni with morel mushrooms, and salads of king crab and avocado. Only the sole here has been unconvincing, rubbery, and tasteless. Chic is not cheap, but you'll still find me sitting in the shadow of the Église Saint-Germain on many sunny summer days.

LE TIMBRE

MODERN BISTRO
3, rue Sainte-Beuve
Paris 6
TEL: +33 1 45 49 10 40
restaurantletimbre.com
MÉTRO: Notre-Dame des Champs or Vavin

OPEN: Tuesday through Saturday
CLOSED: Sunday and Monday
PRICES: 22 and 26€ lunch menus. Starters 8€, mains 17€, desserts 7€ at lunch and dinner.
RESERVATIONS: Essential
ATMOSPHERE: Casual

It's the size of a postage stamp, so why not name the restaurant Timbre! Restaurants don't get much smaller than this, a single simple room with space for no more than 20 diners. Le Timbre is always jam-packed and has a kind of cheap and cheerful "let's play" restaurant air. But there is nothing amateurish about the fine and honest bistro fare, with just the proper modern touch. Owner Christopher Wright keeps himself super-busy in the dining room, and one may have to wait a bit for service, so be forewarned. I can attest to the freshness of his ingredients, for I often pass this restaurant early in the morning after a run in the Luxembourg Gardens. Crates of produce are piled high right outside the door and Wright is already in the kitchen, working on the day's creations. He loves root vegetables and pairs *panais*, or parsnip, with seared sea scallops, or transforms them into a hearty soup. Cured anchovies are piled atop a soothing onion compote, while a hearty *daube de boeuf* arrives with a mountain of penne, tossed with cheddar for that British touch, and a well-made *confit* of duck is served on a wintry bed of lentils. His brief wine list offers some treasures, including Domaine du Vissoux's granite-tinged Fleurie and Moulin à Vent, and Jean-Baptiste Senat's complex, pungent Minervois la Nine.

TOYO

JAPANESE
17, rue Jules Chaplin
Paris 6
TEL: +33 1 43 54 28 03
MÉTRO: Vavin
OPEN: Monday dinner through Saturday
CLOSED: Sunday, Monday lunch, 3 weeks in August, and December 24 to 30.

PRICES: 39 and 49€ lunch menus. 89€ dinner menu. 120€ *dégustation* (tasting) menu. 79€ Japanese menu on Monday evenings only.
RESERVATIONS: Recommended
ATMOSPHERE: Smart-casual
SPECIALTIES: Fish and shellfish

Some years ago, fashion designer Kenzo discovered Toyomitsu Nakayama cooking in one of the many Japanese eateries along rue Sainte Anne in Paris's 1st *arrondissement.* He quickly lured Toyo away as his private chef. Toyo had a fine time with that but, after nearly a decade of cooking for Kenzo, decided to go it alone. I figured that what's good enough for Kenzo's palate might be good enough for me, and I was not disappointed. Toyo's sleek, quiet little restaurant on a hard-to-find street in the Montparnasse neighborhood in the 6th *arrondissement* is a gem. I arrived for lunch famished, and in a bit of a tizzy from a stressful morning. Within a few moments I felt calm, relaxed, unhurried. Everyone in this spotless restaurant works with a sense of elegance and precision. Toyo is there in the open kitchen, cooking on his griddle and induction cooktop, creating a cuisine that's not Japanese and not French, but completely his own. The streamlined lunch menus offer just enough choices, and

the series of small plates make for a fun way to witness Toyo's talents. He offers tiny rectangles of perfectly cooked *merlan* (whiting) showered with flakes of salty *bottarga* (dried, salted mullet or tuna), set upon a bed of giant *cèpe* mushrooms. The dish was not only beautiful but rich, complex, and comforting. A star of the meal was the single seared shrimp leaning against a delicious rectangle of white radish with the surprising texture of polenta. That was achieved through a delicate blend of grated radish, mushroom broth, and soy. For dessert, a stunning green tea ice cream topped with a warm red bean broth set me on my way to face the afternoon, floating in a sea of calm.

YEN

JAPANESE
22, rue Saint-Benoit
Paris 6
TEL: + 33 1 45 44 11 18
restau.yen@wanadoo.fr
MÉTRO: Saint-Germain-des-Prés or Mabillon
OPEN: Monday through Saturday

CLOSED: Sunday and two weeks in August
PRICES: 38.50€ lunch menu. 68€ dinner menu. À la carte 20 to 80€.
RESERVATIONS: Recommended
ATMOSPHERE: Casual
SPECIALTIES: Fish and shellfish, soba noodles

Where to lunch on a cold, gray January day in Paris? Soba noodle heaven, of course. Yen, a Zenlike, two-story affair just steps behind Café Flore in the 6th *arrondissement,* is a Japanese treasure, offering silken tofu that's as smooth as pudding, featherlight tempura, and deliciously satisfying al dente

soba noodles bathed in a fragrant mahogany-toned broth that both fills and satisfies. With every bite, every sip, you feel as though you are offering yourself a "good health" treatment. I sampled soba noodles and broth paired with the shrimp and vegetable tempura, as well as a version offering plump and pleasingly moist poached oysters touched with a flourish of brilliant green spinach. The

tofu starter, served in gorgeous white bowls and topped with pungent fresh ginger, thin rounds of spring onion, sesame seeds, and soy sauce, was subtle but simply ethereal. For dessert, try the unusual black sesame ice cream, smoky, with a touch of crunch, and the intense green tea ice cream. As I walked out the door, my soul was full of sunshine and I hardly noticed the leaden skies above.

ZE KITCHEN GALERIE VELOUTÉ DE POTIRON AU LAIT DE COCO ET AUX CÈPES

Ze Kitchen Galerie Pumpkin and Coconut Milk Soup with Wild Mushrooms

Leave it to the talented, ever-curious chef-restaurateur William Ledeuil to come up with a marriage of Asian-French flavors using pumpkin and coconut milk, lemongrass and wild *cèpe* (boletus) mushrooms, Thai basil as well as cilantro. This lovely, lively soup is a winter's dream. When I am in a hurry, I make just the soup and omit the mushrooms, but include the final herb garnish.

EQUIPMENT:

A food processor or a blender; 4 warmed, shallow soup bowls

INGREDIENTS:

4 tablespoons extra-virgin olive oil

1 pound (500 g) raw pumpkin, cubed

2 cups (500 ml) homemade chicken or vegetable stock

2 cups (500 ml) coconut milk, stirred to blend

3 stalks lemongrass, bottom third only, trimmed, outer leaves removed, and minced

Celery salt to taste

FOR THE MUSHROOMS:

4 large wild *cèpe* (boletus) mushrooms, or substitute cultivated mushrooms, cleaned, stems trimmed

2 tablespoons extra-virgin olive oil

2 shallots, peeled and minced

18 fresh Thai basil leaves or traditional fresh basil leaves

Small handful of fresh cilantro leaves

2 stalks fresh Chinese chives or 4 leaves traditional fresh chives, minced

Toasted peanut oil or fruity olive oil, for garnish (optional)

1. In a large saucepan, heat 2 tablespoons of the extra-virgin olive oil until hot but not smoking. Add the pumpkin cubes and cook for 2 to 3 minutes. Add the stock and coconut milk, and cook until the pumpkin is tender, about 10 minutes.

2. In a small skillet, heat the remaining 2 tablespoons of oil over medium heat until hot but not smoking. Add the lemongrass. Cook until fragrant, about 2 to 3 minutes. Add to the pumpkin mixture, along with the celery salt. Taste for seasoning. Puree the soup in the food processor or blender.

3. Prepare the mushrooms: Slice the mushrooms lengthwise on the diagonal. In a nonstick skillet, heat the extra-virgin olive oil until hot but not smoking. Add the mushrooms and cook for 2 to 3 minutes. If juices have collected in the pan, pour them into the soup and cook the mushrooms for 2 to 3 minutes more. This will give them a more intense flavor. Add the shallots and cook to soften, 1 minute more. Add the basil and cilantro leaves and the chives off the heat so that they retain their lively flavors and do not cook.

4. Divide the mushroom-shallot mixture among the warm, shallow soup bowls, and pour the hot soup over the vegetables. If desired, add a few drops of toasted peanut oil or very fruity olive oil.

4 SERVINGS

ZE KITCHEN GALERIE

**MODERN FRENCH /
MODERN INTERNATIONAL**
4, rue des Grands Augustins
Paris 6
TEL: +33 1 44 32 00 32
zekitchengalerie.fr
MÉTRO: Saint-Michel or Pont Neuf
OPEN: Monday through Saturday

CLOSED: Saturday lunch and Sunday
PRICES: 39.60, 46, and 70€ *dégustation*
(tasting) menus at lunch. 82€ evening
dégustation (tasting) menu. À la carte 80€
at dinner.
RESERVATIONS: Recommended
ATMOSPHERE: Smart-casual

It is impossible to count the number of great meals I have had at the hands of the talented, ambitious, outgoing chef William Ledeuil. Early on, at his first "big" job at Guy Savoy's first Bistrot de l'Étoile on Rue Troyon; later at Les Bouqinistes; and now at his own home, Ze Kitchen Galerie. I could cherish a meal here once a week without a problem. Ledeuil has a way with ingredients, and when he combines his classic French training with his passion for all things Asian, fireworks fly. Try his wasabi and *tarama* combo with smoked tuna and *poutargue*, the unforgettably strong and salty cured codfish eggs. It sounds so complex in the reading and yet is so simple, enjoyable, and surprising on the palate. Always craving pasta, I leapt at his offering of *cappelletti*, mussels, and razor clams (*couteaux*), all soothing in a seafood broth laced with lemongrass. (I wanted to race home and get it ready for the next day's lunch.) What is amazing about Ledeuil's food is that he does it with nary a touch of fat. He coaxes satisfaction from vegetables, fruits, herbs, and spices, the Asian way. Meat eaters will not go away unhappy: Try the Ibérique pork, cooked to melting tenderness, a true *confit*, then grilled and served with a condiment of ginger and gooseberry. Or go for the meaty, tender veal shank (*jarret*) with a teriyaki juice and white peach condiment. On my last visit, I loved the simple Domaine de la Janasse red Côtes du Rhône, as well as, yes, a little *coupe de Champagne*.

▼ *William Ledeuil (far right) with his kitchen staff.*

7ᵀᴴ ARRONDISSEMENT

35° OUEST

MODERN FRENCH
35, rue de Verneuil
Paris 7
TEL: +33 1 42 86 98 88
35degresouest@orange.fr
MÉTRO: Rue du Bac
OPEN: Tuesday through Saturday

CLOSED: Sunday, Monday, August, and two weeks at Christmas
PRICES: 35€ lunch menu. À la carte 60 to 100€ at lunch and dinner.
RESERVATIONS: Recommended
ATMOSPHERE: Smart-casual
SPECIALITIES: Fish and shellfish

When you reserve a table at 35° Ouest, here's what you can expect: pristine fish and shellfish, simply prepared in a place that is intimate, understated, and accessible. Run by the outgoing Pascal Yar, this compact, contemporary dining room is almost Zenlike in its clean lines and soothing tones of gray green, and there are no more than a dozen tables. This is the place I go when I have had it with wow-factor meals, über-trendiness, or elbow-to-elbow dining. I go for what's on the plate, including a classic, well-seasoned Granny Smith apple and crab rémoulade; a satisfying *coquilles Saint-Jacques* (scallops) *tartare* with a welcoming hint of Japanese *yuzu* zest (from October to May; see recipe, page 55); a fine *sole meunière;* and giant *langoustines* roasted in the oven and topped with a touch of tarragon butter. There are many fish- and shellfish-friendly wines on the list.

AIDA

JAPANESE
1, rue Pierre Leroux
Paris 7
TEL: +33 1 43 06 14 18
aida-paris.com
MÉTRO: Vaneau or Saint-François-Xavier

OPEN: Dinner only, Tuesday through Sunday
CLOSED: Monday
PRICES: 160€ *omakassé* (tasting) menu. 210€ truffle menu (in season).
RESERVATIONS: Essential (call after 2PM)
ATMOSPHERE: Smart-casual

Chef Koji Aida's evening procession of pure Japanese tastes is a mix of subtle and explosive maneuvers that arise from his steady hand and a magical teppanyaki grill. This austere restaurant set on a quiet 7th-*arrondissement* street near the Bon Marché department store may not be for everyone. Some will find flavors too subtle, or will consider the ceremony more of a sideshow, even what some call the "Benihana experience." But to my mind, lovers of pure Japanese food and artistry should do themselves a favor and reserve for an evening's pleasure. The restaurant is small, with room for just nine at the counter, four in a private room, and two spots for table-side dining. A single set menu offers a steady procession of creative, ultra-fresh offerings. In a single dinner, Aida manages to cover extensive ground, with fish, shellfish, meat, eggs, and plenty of herbs, spices, and vegetables woven into the combination. On a recent visit we had treasured seats at the bar, right in front of the spotless

mackerel rolled around a mound of sushi rice, then wrapped in rectangles of nori. The chef deftly toasts the seaweed, then takes a blowtorch to the prepared rice and mackerel bundles, an explosive taste that is luxurious in the mouth. The meal has a clear rhythm, a "wow" taste followed by one more subtle. After the mackerel came a tiny taste of glistening, line-caught sea bass (*bar de ligne*) escorted by a dab of freshly grated wasabi. Alongside, a bit of crunch and freshness came in the form of a finely shredded cucumber and radish salad. Who would have thought to deep-fry a naked scallop, but here a duet of fried *coquilles Saint-Jacques* is sliced in half to display the scallop's amazing progression of textures and colors. A simple mound of *fleur de sel* on the side served as a singular seasoning. Beef tenderloin—from none other than Paris's star butcher Hugo Desnoyer—is seared on the hot griddle, then cut into bite-size cubes and sauced ever so lightly. What should have been the star of the meal came out just a bit too dry for my palate: Aida worked like an orchestra conductor constructing his showpiece, a studied mix of grilled lobster, lobster roe, sushi rice, eggs, and gentle seasoning, all gathered into a perfect mound on the griddle and delivered to diners in the restaurant's signature hand-crafted pottery. Nothing is left to chance here, and for some that may lack drama. I love the place, and after the finale, clementine sorbet with a touch of clementine puree, I walked out into the night feeling fresh and oh, so light.

stainless steel griddle. I will never forget—and will forever try to imitate—Aida's plump, soft-cooked egg yolk set in a clear glass vessel, topped with a seaweed and bonito broth laced with bits of black winter truffle. A beautiful work of art on its own, the dish offered lovely textures, mouth pleasures, color, aromas (see recipe, page 57). Other favorite memories of the 11-course meal include a palate-opening *tartare* of veal and oysters bathed in tangy golden bits of gelatin, and a stunning dish of

L'AFFABLE

MODERN BISTRO

10, rue de Saint-Simon
Paris 7
laffable.fr
TEL: +33 1 42 22 01 60
MÉTRO: Rue du Bac or Solférino

OPEN: Monday through Friday
CLOSED: Saturday and Sunday
PRICES: 28€ lunch menu. À la carte 50 to 70€.
RESERVATIONS: Recommended
ATMOSPHERE: Smart-casual

CARPACCIO DE COQUILLES SAINT JACQUES 35° OUEST

35° Ouest's Scallop Carpaccio

From October to May one can find the freshest and finest scallops in Paris markets and restaurants. Pascal Yar, owner of the tiny Left Bank fish restaurant 35° Ouest, does wonders with them, here marinating the alabaster delights in a variety of citrus juices, zest, and peel, adding a tiny touch of sesame seeds for that essential crunch. Here's my version of this elegant dish.

EQUIPMENT:

A small jar with a lid;
4 chilled salad plates

INGREDIENTS:

2 tablespoons *yuzu* juice, or freshly squeezed lime or lemon juice

6 tablespoons extra-virgin olive oil

½ teaspoon fine sea salt

8 ultra-fresh, sushi-quality scallops

Zest of 1 lime or lemon, preferably organic

2 tablespoons candied citrus peel (*yuzu*, lemon, or orange), very finely minced

1 tablespoon toasted sesame seeds

Fleur de sel

Toasted sourdough bread, for serving

1. In the jar, combine the citrus juice, olive oil, and fine sea salt. Cover and shake to blend. Pour about half of this dressing mixture onto a platter.

2. Slice the scallops crosswise into 6 to 8 very thin slices. Arrange the slices, side by side, on the platter. Turn each slice over to coat the second side of the scallop with the citrus mixture.

3. Divide the scallop slices among the 4 chilled salad plates. Drizzle with the remaining dressing. Garnish with the citrus zest, candied peel, and sesame seeds. Season very lightly with the *fleur de sel*. Serve with the toasted sourdough bread.

4 SERVINGS

▶ *A Parisian fishmonger with shellfish at the ready.*

With two airy red, white, and black dining rooms looking onto the quiet rue de Saint-Simon off boulevard Saint-Germain in the 7th, L'Affable hits the spot, a contemporary bistro with an instant feel of familiarity and easy comfort. Chef Jean-François Pantaleon (formerly of Apicius and Grand Cascade) hits some high notes with his modern, personality-driven bistro fare. Noteworthy were a winning, perfectly seared Argentine *filet de boeuf* (moist, chewy, full-flavored) set upon an unusual but delicious bed of crunchy Frenched fresh green beans tossed with fresh bean sprouts; and a *bar de ligne*—line-caught sea bass—as tender as a pillow, served with a soothing portion of wintry fennel bulb. Service here comes with a smile, and the simple but elegant room is filled with the sounds of camaraderie and good times. I was less enthusiastic about the *ravioles de queue de boeuf*, served lukewarm in a Thai broth, with flavorless oxtail and timid seasoning. And his *sucettes de volailles*—boned chicken legs—lacked personality, although the accompanying ginger-flecked butternut squash soup packed a wallop of flavor. Our neighbors ordered a giant, appetizing veal chop for two, and that dish will definitely be on my list for the next visit to the affable L'Affable. Jean-Luc Poujauran's country loaf, a touch of salty butter, and sips of fruity Brouilly all make the visit a hit.

L'AMI JEAN

MODERN BISTRO / BASQUE
27, rue Malar
Paris 7
TEL: +33 1 47 05 86 89
amijean.eu
MÉTRO: Invalides or La Tour-Maubourg
OPEN: Tuesday through Saturday

CLOSED: Sunday and Monday, last week in July to end of August and December 25 to January 1
PRICES: 35 and 42€ lunch menus. À la carte 40€ at lunch. 75€ dinner menu. À la carte 70€ at dinner.
RESERVATIONS: Essential
ATMOSPHERE: Casual
SPECIALTIES: Game

We arrived one sunny evening in May, on time but before our table was ready, so we were offered a seat at a table on the sidewalk and our quartet settled into a glass of bubbles, conversation, and laughter. By the time we were seated at the long common table inside, we were ready for more fun. Giant platters of fat, multitoned asparagus, purple, green, and white, topped with a modern-style *mimosa* garnish (chopped eggs, crunchy bits of croutons, all manner of herbs); huge portions of *bonite*, or albacore tuna, from the port of Saint Jean de Luz, teamed up with cucumbers and a composition of citrus; sweetbreads, roasted then braised, served with crisp, fresh spring peas and bits of ham. And there are always the giant boards of varied sausages to keep us all occupied and happy. Everything here comes from the hands of star chef Stéphane Jégo, who holds court at this longtime Basque stronghold. This is the sort of bistro that guests either love or hate. Service can be brisk, even rude: A reservation at 8PM might not get you a seat before 8:30, and then you'll be squeezed next to loud neighbors. As long as you understand this, I think it's worth a try to sample Jégo's ever-changing, seasonal, updated, and totally original modern French fare. In the fall and winter months, L'Ami Jean offers an extensive selection of game.

OEUF MAGIQUE D'AIDA
Aida's Magical Egg

Restaurant Aida is like an inner sanctum Japanese restaurant. Little chatter, surely no cell phones, simply reverence for what chef Koji Aida is dreaming up that evening. On one visit we did not opt for the pricey black truffle menu but were allowed to watch all the drama. I could not figure out what Aida was doing with all those eggs in the shell. Only much later, after having sampled his "magic egg yolk," did I figure out what he had done. The eggs were poached in their shells, then each yolk was poured into an elegant wineglass and topped, of course, with a touch of stock and truffles. Pure, pure elegance with the mouthful of a soothing, warm poached egg yolk bursting with color, aroma, flavor. Top with a touch of chicken stock and, if you have one, a few slices of fresh truffle. Or top with stock and some lovely cooked mushrooms. Here's my version of this elegant dish.

EQUIPMENT:

A 6-quart (6 l) saucepan; a slotted spoon; 6 ramekins; 6 small, clear-footed wineglasses; 6 demitasse spoons

INGREDIENTS:

1 teaspoon fine sea salt

2 tablespoons distilled white vinegar

6 large eggs, preferably free-range and organic, at room temperature

About 1 cup (250 ml) warmed chicken stock

About 12 thin slices or julienne slices fresh truffle or several tablespoons minced truffle shavings, or several cooked mushrooms of any variety, minced

1. Prepare a large bowl of ice water.

2. Add 2 quarts (2 l) of water to the saucepan. Add the salt and vinegar and bring to a bare simmer over medium heat. With a slotted spoon, carefully lower the whole eggs in their shells into the water and maintain the water at a bare simmer. Small bubbles should surround the eggs. Cook for 5½ minutes.

3. With a slotted spoon, remove the eggs and transfer them to the ice water to cool completely, at least 1 minute.

4. Crack the chilled egg in half into a ramekin. The yolk should hold its form and most of the white remain attached to the shell. (The egg white is not used for this preparation.) Carefully transfer the whole yolk to the wineglass. Gently spoon the warmed chicken stock over the yolk. Arrange truffles or mushrooms on top of the stock. Repeat for the remaining servings. Serve immediately.

NOTE: The eggs can be cooked up to 2 days in advance, and refrigerated in the shell. To reheat the eggs, bring to room temperature. Place them in a bowl and cover with the hottest-possible tap water for 1 minute. Eggs that have been reheated will generally be much easier to peel.

6 SERVINGS

ARPÈGE

HAUTE CUISINE / MODERN FRENCH
84, rue de Varenne
Paris 7
TEL: +33 1 47 05 09 06
alain-passard.com
MÉTRO: Varenne
OPEN: Monday through Friday

CLOSED: Saturday and Sunday
PRICES: 135€ lunch menu. 395€ *dégustation* (tasting) menu at lunch and dinner. À la carte 350€.
RESERVATIONS: Essential
ATMOSPHERE: Formal. Suit jacket, but not tie, required for men.

Chef Alain Passard has evolved dramatically since creating his vegetable-friendly menu in 2001. Now he shows what experience in the kitchen, as well as a full-fledged garden outside Paris, can do for his diners. His vegetable-centered 10-course lunch menu (which also includes a course of either fish or meat) offers an expansive palate of colors, flavors, and sensations. It shows off what can be accomplished with vegetables, herbs, exotic oils, and cooking techniques such as smoking as well as roasting on a bed of salt. For my palate, the winners of the day included a colorful plate of varied tomatoes, sliced almost paper thin, including *blanche arpège,* orange banana, black iceberg, green zebra and black prince, seasoned with salt and anointed with a touch of *huile de sureau* (elderflower oil); and his delicate "gratin" of red baron onions, sliced paper thin, barely cooked, and showered with Parmesan cheese and minced, bright-green sorrel leaves. Each dish leaves the palate filled with powerful, herbal, vegetal flavors, an uncommon collection of sensations for almost every diner. His creative mind reels, and includes his classic, first-course tomato gazpacho paired with a celery and mustard ice cream (always a winner), as well as a surprising and welcoming "risotto" of cubed celery root tossed with Parmesan and set in a bed of frothy parsley sauce. I loved, as well, his wild salad, a custom-made mesclun mix of Asian miuzuna, mibuna, choho, and wild mustard, seasoned with a touch of smoked almond praline. Less convincing was the multicolored vegetable-filled ravioli in a vegetal consommé, a dish that felt unfinished, with some dramatic element largely lacking. Service can be professional and attentive, with a very knowledgeable wine staff that will find just the right wine for the moment, for the menu.

L'ATELIER DE JOËL ROBUCHON SAINT-GERMAIN

HAUTE CUISINE / MODERN FRENCH
5, rue Montalembert
Paris 7
TEL: +33 1 42 22 56 56
joel-robuchon.net
latelierdejoelrobuchon@wanadoo.fr
MÉTRO: Rue du Bac
OPEN: Daily 11:30AM to 3:30PM and 6:30PM to midnight
CLOSED: December 24

PRICES: Small plates 15 to 50€. À la carte 70 to 120€ at lunch and dinner. 199€ *dégustation* (tasting) menu.
RESERVATIONS: Essential. Lunch seatings at 11:30AM, 12:30, 2:00, and 3:30PM. Dinner reservations 6:30PM only. Remaining seating is first come, first served.
ATMOSPHERE: Smart-casual
SPECIALTIES: Game, lamb, fish carpaccio, Spanish ham, potato puree

For more than 30 years I've been writing about chef Joël Robuchon, and together we've written two books. So blind objectivity is not what

VÉLOUTÉ DE CHATAIGNE AU FOIE GRAS DE L'ATELIER DE JOËL ROBUCHON SAINT-GERMAIN

L'Atelier de Joël Robuchon Saint-Germain's Chestnut and Foie Gras *Soup*

I can't count how many times I sampled this soothing, elegant soup from Robuchon's talented chefs. I make it often at home, and depending on time, prepare it both with and without the *foie gras*, bacon, and celery root garnish. When fresh black truffles are in season, a garnish of thin slices of the black diamond are a welcome addition.

EQUIPMENT:

A food processor or blender; a fine-mesh sieve; 4 warmed, shallow soup bowls

INGREDIENTS:

6 tablespoons (¾ stick; 90 g) unsalted butter

14 ounces (400 g) vacuum-packed cooked chestnuts

2 cardamom pods

Fine sea salt

Coarse, freshly ground black pepper

1 large egg yolk, preferably free-range and organic

6 tablespoons heavy (whipping) cream

2 teaspoons coarse sea salt

4 ounces (125 g) celery root, trimmed and cut into ½-inch (1-cm) cubes (about 24)

4 ounces (125 g) trimmed smoked bacon, cut into 1-inch (2 cm) cubes (about 24)

4 ounces (125 g) *foie gras*, cut into 1-inch (2-cm) cubes (about 24)

1. In a large saucepan, melt 2 tablespoons (1 ounce; 30 g) of the butter over low heat. Add the chestnuts and cook without coloring for 2 to 3 minutes. Add 1 quart (1 l) of water, the cardamom pods, and season with salt and pepper to taste. Bring to a boil over high heat. Reduce the heat and simmer for 10 minutes.

2. In the food processor or blender, process the chestnut mixture until smooth and velvety, about 2 minutes. Add the egg yolk, heavy cream, and remaining 4 tablespoons (60 g) of butter and blend again. Taste for seasoning. Pass through the fine-mesh sieve back into the saucepan and cover to keep warm. (The soup can be made up to 1 day ahead, stored in an airtight container in the refrigerator.) Reheat at serving time.

3. Bring 1 quart (1 l) of water to a boil in a large saucepan. Add the coarse sea salt and the celery root cubes. Blanch the celery root for 2 minutes. Transfer the celery root to the fine-mesh sieve and refresh under cold running water. Drain.

4. In a small, dry skillet, brown the bacon over medium heat until crisp and golden, about 5 minutes. Add the celery root and cook 1 minute more, to warm the celery root. With a slotted spoon, transfer the bacon and celery root to several layers of paper towel to absorb the fat. Blot the top of the bacon and celery root with several layers of paper towel to absorb any additional fat. Transfer to a plate and season with salt and pepper.

5. In the warmed bowls, evenly scatter the celery root, bacon, and *foie gras*. Ladle the hot chestnut soup over the trio. Serve immediately.

4 SERVINGS

I bring to any encounter with his food. He's the best chef cooking today, in my often-tested opinion, and the Atelier on rue de Montalembert is simply one of my favorite restaurants in Paris. It's the place I go to celebrate a half or a full marathon, ready to dine on whatever chef Axel Manes suggests I sample that evening. If anyone was going to reinvent the restaurant as we know it—more casual, more open—Robuchon was the one to do it. Since he opened here in 2002, his small-plate menu has charmed the world. Diners gather on plush upholstered stools and watch the kitchen action. From giant *langoustines* seasoned with coarse salt, *steak tartare* and fries, a thimble of gazpacho paired with paper-thin slices of perfectly aged ham from Spain, to an outstanding *vitello tonnato* (cold sliced veal topped with a creamy tuna sauce),

everything wears the sign of perfection here. A perennial favorite is the sea bream carpaccio, feathery petals of fish marinated in citrus juice, plenty of lime zest, olive oil, and salt—a painting on the plate, a pleasure on the palate (see recipe, page 61). As you enjoy it, don't miss the chance to sip Comte Lafon's stunning Macon. In season, sample the most substantive of wild *cèpe* mushrooms, almost tasting more like meat than meat, moist and full-flavored, with scents of the forest and of herbs, accented with a touch of arugula. Lamb chops are so tiny you can finish them off in a few bites, but what pleasure! Accompanied by a puddle of his famous buttery mashed potatoes topped with a bouquet of fresh thyme, they're gift-wrapped like a precious present. For dessert, a puckery lemon sorbet, an arresting espresso. Need I say more?

LES BOTANISTES

MODERN BISTRO
11, bis rue Chomel
Paris 7
TEL: +33 1 45 49 04 54
lesbotanistes.com
restaurant.lesbotanistes@orange.fr
MÉTRO: Sèvres-Babylone

OPEN: Monday through Saturday
CLOSED: Sunday and August
PRICES: 26€ lunch menu. À la carte
40 to 50€ at lunch and dinner.
RESERVATIONS: Recommended
ATMOSPHERE: Casual

I t is always a pleasure to be reunited with old acquaintances, and I had a wonderful surprise one night when my husband and I walked into Les Botanistes on rue Chomel in the 7th *arrondissement,* close to the chic Bon Marché department store. Restaurateur Jean-Baptiste Gay met us warmly at

the door to his art deco bistro and the good times began! It had been ten years to the day since I wrote about his former bistro, Jean-Baptiste, then in the 17th *arrondissement.* We loved that spot and once again we are in love with Les Botanistes, an address that under previous ownership was known as La Gorille Blanche and before that as La Cigale. I believe that restaurant locations have good karma or they don't. This one has it in spades, with its classic red-and-white-checkered

tile floors; bare, varnished oak tables; and a decorative old wall clock that forgot to tell the time long ago. Jean-Baptiste and his wife, Virginie, are gracious and professional hosts, who turn out such satisfying bistro fare as plump white asparagus with a peppy vinaigrette; roasted guinea fowl cleverly paired with cubes of *topinambours* (sunchokes) as home fries; plump Spanish piquillo red peppers stuffed with goat's-milk cheese. We also had the pleasure of enjoying

CARPACCIO DE POISSON BLANC DE L'ATELIER DE JOËL ROBUCHON SAINT-GERMAIN

*L'Atelier de Joël Robuchon Saint-Germain's
White Fish Carpaccio*

When this beautiful and carefully seasoned carpaccio is on the menu at Robuchon's Saint-Germain Atelier, it's my first taste, my first course, on every visit. I regularly prepare the carpaccio at home as well, for the sea-fresh flavors marry so beautifully with the touch of spice, zest of lime, gentle crunch of the chives. The best choice of fish here is Alaskan wild-caught Pacific halibut or Atlantic pole-and-line mahi-mahi.

EQUIPMENT:

A pastry brush; 4 chilled dinner plates; a very sharp knife

INGREDIENTS:

2 tablespoons freshly squeezed lemon juice

Fleur de sel

½ teaspoon coarse, freshly ground black pepper

3 tablespoons extra-virgin olive oil

1 pound (500 g) ultra-fresh, sushi-grade white fish filets, well chilled

Zest of 1 lime, preferably organic

¼ teaspoon ground *piment d'Espelette* or other mild chile pepper

Several tablespoons minced fresh chives

1. In a bowl, combine the lemon juice, about ¼ teaspoon of the *fleur de sel,* the black pepper, and olive oil and mix well. With the pastry brush, brush the chilled plates with this dressing.

2. With the knife, cut the filets into paper-thin slices, beginning with the thickest part of the filet. Arrange the slices in an even, single layer on top of the dressed plates. Cover each with plastic wrap and refrigerate for 20 minutes.

3. At serving time, season each with the lime zest, chile pepper, chives, and more *fleur de sel.* Serve immediately.

4 SERVINGS

▶ *Young and talented: the chef at L'Atelier de Joël Robuchon Saint-Germain, Axel Manes.*

a classic Lyonnais bistro dish we have not seen in decades: *clapotins*, or sheep's trotters, braised in vinegar and mustard, then dressed with a creamy egg and mustard dressing.

When you go, sample Philippe Gilbert's citruslike Menetou-Salon from the Loire Valley or Rémi Jobard's classic Bourgogne Blanc from Burgundy.

LE CINQ MARS

MODERN BISTRO
51, rue de Verneuil
Paris 7
TEL: +33 1 45 44 69 13
cinq-mars-restaurant.com
cinq-marsrestaurant@wanadoo.fr
MÉTRO: Musée d'Orsay, Rue du Bac, or Solférino

OPEN: Monday through Saturday
CLOSED: Sunday
PRICES: 17 and 21.50€ menus. À la carte 25 to 40€.
RESERVATIONS: Recommended
ATMOSPHERE: Casual

Le Cinq Mars is the easygoing, cozy sort of bistro we are all searching for. Don't expect the earth to move here, and the sun will still shine if you miss a visit, but this is a great place to know when browsing the antiques shop–filled streets of the 7th or before or after a visit to the

Musée d'Orsay. They got the decor just right, hip enough but not a touch of grunge, welcoming and open, with huge windows looking out onto the quiet rue de Verneuil, sturdy polished oak tables, and a funnily formal chandelier lighting the back of the bistro. This is the place to come for a quick omelet (cooked *baveuse*, or soft and runny), a favorite salad of goat's-milk cheese and cucumbers, a warming *pot-au-feu* (a huge chunk of well-cooked beef with broth and vegetables), or their absolutely unforgettable *mousse au chocolat*. It's got real chocolate flavor and my luncheon partner and I ate the whole thing! There's a well-priced selection of wines, many available *à la ficelle*, meaning you pay only for what you drink from the bottle set before you.

◀ *Bistro conviviality at the modern eatery Le Cinq Mars.*

LES COCOTTES DE CHRISTIAN CONSTANT

MODERN BISTRO
135, rue Saint-Dominique
Paris 7
No telephone
maisonconstant.com/les-cocottes/

MÉTRO: École Militaire
OPEN: Daily
PRICES: 24€ menu. À la carte 30 to 50€.
RESERVATIONS: Not taken
ATMOSPHERE: Casual

O n a cold, rainy day, there is nothing more comforting than sitting in this casual, friendly dining spot nurturing oneself with a warming *cocotte,* or casserole. My choice on the miserable day of my visit was veal stew, a magical bistro dish here paired with an avalanche of vegetables, including artichokes, fennel, potatoes, and carrots, and showered with colorful parsley. Specialties change day to day and may include tender lamb shoulder stew, a soup of carrots and coriander, and their famed tarts, both lemon and chocolate. This is a place for all ages, the very young to the rather old, alone or in groups. There are seats at the bar and classic table seating, as well as high tables for sampling the simple, sturdy fare while seated on stools.

RESTAURANT ES

MODERN FRENCH
91, rue de Grenelle
Paris 7
TEL: +33 1 45 51 25 74
MÉTRO: Solférino
OPEN: Tuesday through Saturday
CLOSED: Sunday and Monday

PRICES: 55€ fixed weekday menu at lunch, 75€ at lunch on Saturday. 75 and 105€ fixed weekday menus at dinner. 105€ fixed menu at Saturday dinner. No à la carte.
RESERVATIONS: Recommended
ATMOSPHERE: Smart-casual

Y ears ago, chef Joël Robuchon told me that his trips to Japan greatly influenced his own personal style of cuisine. He felt that the French and the Japanese shared a great sensibility and respect for food, showing special consideration for flavors, colors, textures, and presentation. Today in Paris, diners can see how intensely Japanese-born chefs are responding to that shared awareness. Many—like Akihiro Horihoshi at La Table d'Aki and Shinichi Sato at Passage 53—have worked in some of the finest kitchens in Europe. Chef Takayuki Honjo—with a CV that includes Astrance, Noma, and Le Mugartiz—joins the club with his tiny, quiet, all-white, angelic, monastic dining room, ES, on rue de Grenelle on the Left Bank. Taka's food is beautiful in every sense of the word. I feel as though he has been immensely influenced by Pascal Barbot's food at Astrance, just across the Seine. But he's not a copycat. And his flavors are direct and forthright— not a slammer, but a gentle tap. One of the best dishes sampled at his table was a roasted guinea fowl (*pintade*), teamed up with a delicate and colorful green pool of spinach cream, a shower of perfectly cooked autumn *girolles* (chanterelles), and the tiniest, most flavorful sautéed baby new potatoes—each the size of an olive. But the crowning glory came in the way of a soothing hazelnut cream, applied like a palette knife to the plate, a nutty luxury that unified the entire dish. A creation triumphant in its simplicity and clarity of flavors. I would be proud to make and serve his caramelized codfish, and loved the idea of his cream of corn soup, flavored with a jasmine essence. Dessert almost hit the ball out of the park: a delicate, tiny meringue shell filled with a sweet, fruity poached peach, topped with a peach sorbet (too forcefully flavored with almond extract), and set in a pool of soothing, bright-pink peach jelly. Crusty country bread from baker Jean-Luc Poujauran and wines from a favored winemaker, Simon Bize in Burgundy, all add to the pleasure. The restaurant name is a translation of the Freudian "id," meaning the component of personality at birth that is the source of our wants, desires, impulses, and drives. So use your id and go to ES.

LES FABLES DE LA FONTAINE

FRENCH SOUTHWESTERN
131, rue Saint-Dominique
Paris 7
TEL: +33 1 44 18 37 55
lesfablesdelafontaine.net
MÉTRO: École Militaire or La Tour-Maubourg
OPEN: Daily

PRICES: 30 and 35€ lunch menus. 120€ evening *dégustation* (tasting) menu. À la carte 85 to 110€ at lunch and dinner.
RESERVATIONS: Recommended
ATMOSPHERE: Smart-casual
SPECIALTIES: Fish and shellfish, oysters

S ébastien Gravé (also chef and co-owner of Pottoka—see page 67) and David Bottreau are quite a duo. With Les Fables de la Fontaine, they've created a one-of-a-kind fish restaurant with a true personality. And you'll feel as though you've hit the jackpot if you arrive on a warm, sunny day and dine on the compact terrace facing the fountain on rue Saint-Dominique. (Though it would be nice if they could hide the garbage cans.) Thanks to Gravé's Basque heritage, the menu favors specialties of France's Southwest, including a *ttoro*, or Basque fish soup. Here it arrives in its classic form—several varieties of fish and shellfish in a wine-based sauce, garnished with a spicy mayonnaise—as well as a modern *gelée* version. All manner of fish and shellfish are featured, from oysters and *langoustines* to smoked eel, cod, turbot, sole, and *maigre*, a sea-bass-like variety from the Atlantic. A starter of red tuna tartare was my kind of fare, with the wasabi-seasoned fish set on a soothing bed of avocado puree and topped with a delicate, bright-flavored mousse of kaffir lime. Modern, refreshing, satisfying. The *maigre* was perfectly seared *à la plancha* and teamed up with seasonal white beans from Paimpol to the north, tossed with a touch of pesto from the south, and a Basque touch in the name of tender baby squid, or *chipirons*. My neighbor's turbot—simply seared—looked fabulous, and I'll be sure to seek that out on my next visit. Weekday lunches are well priced, with a 30€ special that includes a glass of wine. With my terrace lunch I enjoyed Leon Beyer's always-dependable, bone-dry Riesling Les Ecaillers. Its overtones of peach and lime made it a perfect choice.

LA FONTAINE DE MARS

CLASSIC BISTRO / FRENCH SOUTHWESTERN
129, rue Saint-Dominique
Paris 7
TEL: +33 1 47 05 46 44
fontainedemars.com
lafontainedemars@orange.fr

MÉTRO: École Militaire or La Tour-Maubourg
OPEN: Daily
CLOSED: Christmas and New Year's
PRICES: 21€ plat du jour, 35 to 80€ à la carte at lunch and dinner
RESERVATIONS: Recommended
ATMOSPHERE: Smart-casual

If La Fontaine de Mars did not exist, we'd have to make it up. Red-checkered tablecloths, wicker chairs, a charming terrace overlooking a newly restored fountain, and all the bistro classics, from a meaty pâté served with a *confit* of onions to the famed *boudin* (blood sausage) from Christian Parra. On a recent visit I loved the compressed oxtail (*queue de boeuf*) terrine topped with *foie gras* and served with a tangle of greens, the moist roast chicken with a so-so potato puree, and a thick veal chop paired with a fine potato gratin. The *pot* (little carafe) of house Brouilly is a worthy choice, as is the stunning Vacqueyras from Domaine Le Sang des Cailloux. The classic bistro dates from 1908 and was revived in 1991 by Christiane and Jacques Boudon, model hostess and host.

▶ *La Fontaine de Mars, a classic favorite.*

RESTAURANT JEAN-FRANÇOIS PIÈGE

HAUTE CUISINE / MODERN FRENCH
79, rue Saint-Dominique
Paris 7
TEL: +33 1 47 05 79 79
thoumieux.fr
MÉTRO: La Tour-Maubourg or Invalides
OPEN: Monday through Friday

CLOSED: Saturday, Sunday, three weeks in August, and December 22 to 25.
PRICES: 99€ lunch menu. 119, 149, and 239€ (with wine) lunch and dinner menus. No à la carte.
RESERVATIONS: Essential
ATMOSPHERE: Formal. Suit jacket, but not tie, required for men.

Put on your highest heels, your tightest and shortest black dress, your biggest diamond studs, and reserve a table at the newest offering from Jean-François Piège, ex-Crillon, ex-Les Ambassadeurs, ex-Louix XV, ex-Plaza Athenée. But don't rush to dress before you call for a reservation, because you may have to wait for one, and then wait in line for a table at this tiny, 20-seat dining room. But the wait is worth it. Well, pretty much. Piège, like so many major French chefs before him, starting with Joël Robuchon in the 1990s, decided to ditch the potentially suffocating Michelin three-star drama and create his own route to gastronomic stardom. He shed some pounds, created his own space, and re-created his very own version of a restaurant. Bravo! I am all for it, though we diners do pay a price for his experiment. Nothing is perfect. But I have to say that Piège's food is among the prettiest and most ethereal I have tasted in a long time, and I can't wait to go back for more of his repertoire. The menu is called Règle du Je(u), which recalls *les règles du jeu,* or the rules of the game, but is a *jeu de mot* (pun) that easily translates as "rules of my game." It's unique. The place, a Hollywood-style setting on the second level with an unsigned, speakeasy-like entrance on the rue Saint-Dominique, may not be for everyone. You're seated at plush banquettes, the waitstaff is as slim and tall (and as accommodating) as they come, and there is no menu—just a list of ingredients of the day. Each represents one course, if not more than one. You choose as many as you wish, by price. That day's list included caviar, *coquilles Saint-Jacques* (scallops), *langoustines* (Dublin Bay prawns), *bar de ligne* (line-caught sea bass), and *ris de veau* (sweetbreads). The menus are not cheap but each includes a generous and beautiful selection of starters (all surprises, not on the menu), and, of course, dessert. The wine list is as extensive as any palate, expertise, or budget could imagine. So what did we eat and what did we love? Best taste of the day was Piège's huge serving of *langoustines* with a pungent and delicious kaffir-lime-based sauce, paired with a rectangle of perfectly seared *foie gras.* Fabulous and gorgeous. Equally flavorful and beautiful was the carpaccio of beef with a crisscross of Parmesan cream. A delight! I was much less enthusiastic about the beautiful but bland sea bass paired with wild mushrooms and the seared beef from Chile that, I am sorry to say, was nicely cooked but tough and inedible. But I applaud Piège's ability to create a new idea of what a restaurant can be. He seems relaxed and at home, working the room with smiles, in blue-jean casual, with a clientele that seems happy. To be continued!

LE JULES VERNE

HAUTE CUISINE / MODERN FRENCH
Tour Eiffel
avenue Gustave Eiffel
Paris 7
TEL: +33 1 45 55 61 44
lejulesverne-paris.com
MÉTRO: Bir-Hakeim
OPEN: Daily

PRICES: 90€ weekday lunch menu, 125€ with wine. 165 and 210€ *dégustation* (tasting) menu. 210€ dinner menu, 301€ with wine. À la carte 150 to 200€.
RESERVATIONS: Essential
ATMOSPHERE: Formal. Suit jacket, but not tie, required for men.

The one true thing I can say about dining at Le Jules Verne in the Eiffel Tower is *go!* If only once in your life, and at a weekday lunch when prices are the best you'll find, and the view is the only one of its kind. Chef Alain Ducasse should be applauded for what he has done with this historic, mythical spot, for the food here is not only accessible to all diners but beautiful, delicious, well-conceived, and, in many ways, unforgettable. A recent lunch here was a symphony of colors and flavors, including a burnished golden *velouté de moules* (mussel soup) garnished with all manner of julienned vegetables; a down-home bistro-style medley of farm chicken paired with mushrooms and carrots in a delicate cream sauce; and an astonishingly perfect savarin (ring-shaped cake soaked in syrup) topped with whipped cream and a dash of well-aged Armagnac. Service is impeccable, under the direction of Jean-Jacques Michel. My only regret is that most diners here have no respect. On my last visit, seats were filled with diners in workout clothes and torn jeans. Alas!

AU PIED DE FOUET (Babylone)

CLASSIC BISTRO
45, rue de Babylone
Paris 7
TEL: +33 1 47 05 12 27
aupieddefouet.com
MÉTRO: Saint-François-Xavier or Vaneau

OPEN: Monday through Saturday
CLOSED: Sunday
PRICES: À la carte 24€
RESERVATIONS: Not taken
ATMOSPHERE: Casual

A bustling bistro that offers all the French classics. See page 47 for full commentary.

POTTOKA

MODERN BISTRO / BASQUE
4, rue de l'Exposition
Paris 7
TEL: +33 1 45 51 88 38
pottoka.fr
contact@pottaka.fr
MÉTRO: École Militaire

OPEN: Daily
PRICES: 20 and 25€ weekday lunch menus.
60€ evening *dégustation* (tasting) menu.
À la carte 35€.
RESERVATIONS: Recommended
ATMOSPHERE: Casual

This totally Basque modern bistro (there's even *piment d'Espelette* on each table in place of salt and pepper) is a dream. Clean, direct, earthy fare from France's Basque country in the Southwest, lots of delicious organic Irouléguy wines, and service with a smile. The long, narrow dining room is uncluttered, with warm wooden tables, serious wineglasses, crisp linen napkins, comfortable chairs. And the varied, seasonal fare is not only beautiful but prepared with professional care and attention. Tender beef cheeks, cooked slow and long, arrive in a steaming white terrine flanked by artichoke hearts, an avalanche of meaty *trompettes* mushrooms, strips of bright red pepper, and baby potatoes. Nothing could be more beautiful or welcoming than a starter of fresh crabmeat set on a bed of crushed and seasoned avocado, topped with a paper-thin, glistening slice of beet, as well as a dollop of cream. Chef Sébastien Gravé (also chef and co-owner of Les Fables de la Fontaine—see page 64—he has trained with some of France's top chefs, including Joël Robuchon, Philippe Braune, and Christian Constant) knows his way around the kitchen, and we're the better for it. Ingredients come direct from the source, with *charcuterie* from Ospital and cheese from the Ferme Béthanoun.

LA TABLE D'AKI

MODERN FRENCH
49, rue Vaneau
Paris 7
TEL: +33 1 45 44 43 48
MÉTRO: Vaneau or Saint-François-Xavier
OPEN: Tuesday through Saturday

CLOSED: Sunday and Monday
PRICES: À la carte 38 to 50€ at lunch and dinner
RESERVATIONS: Essential
ATMOSPHERE: Smart-casual
SPECIALTIES: Fish and shellfish

Akihiro Horikoshi brings new meaning to the phrase "one-man show." His 16-seat restaurant has a staff of two: himself and a single server. He shops, he creates the menu, he cooks, he cleans up. And this is the way the Tokyo native wants it. He has been on his own at La Table d'Aki since January 2010, having worked under the tutelage of Bernard Pacaud at the Michelin three-star L'Ambroisie since 1991. The spotless, tiny restaurant is bathed in light and white from head to toe, with a few flashes of red from the lamp cables that bring the room together in a quiet, festive way. His food, too—pure, simple, and sensational in an understated way—is white. A giant alabaster ravioli filled with sweet, fresh *langoustines* dotted with herbs arrives with a thin but potent meat sauce that makes the dish resemble dessert. A delicate, moist *fricassée* of chicken with carefully turned potatoes and baby onions tastes as though it was dropped from on high by the angels. The delicate *lieu-jaune* (cod) is offset with the punch of a *brunoise* of celery root, all precision-cut cubes with a nice hit of capers. Dessert, all white again, arrives as silken *crème caramel*, paired with an apple baked with a touch of cake inside, a pleasant surprise on the palate. At night, Aki cooks only fish. On the menu for a winter visit, the freshest scallops from Brittany. The food has the Aki signature, as well as the echo of Pacaud's sublime perfection. La Table d'Aki is a welcome little star in Paris's ever-glistening sky.

LE TOURETTE BY IBÉRIQUE GOURMET

SPANISH
70, rue de Grenelle
Paris 7
Tel: +33 1 45 44 16 05
MÉTRO: Rue du Bac or Sèvres-Babylone
OPEN: Lunch Monday through Friday. Dinner Friday and Saturday.

CLOSED: Dinner Monday through Thursday, Saturday lunch, and Sunday
PRICES: Starters, 7 to 12€; main courses, 12 to 21€; wines by the glass, 3 to 5€
RESERVATIONS: Recommended
ATMOSPHERE: Casual
SPECIALTY: Tapas

Take a trip to this tiny, 22-seat bistro-canteen that looks, feels, smells, and tastes like Spain. It's called Le Tourette, a cheery, newly revived gathering spot dating from the 1920s, a classic bistro that survived well into the 1980s. Owner Olivier Mourin (also proprietor of the Ibérique Gourmet, a Spanish specialty shop nearby at 3, rue Paul-Louis Courier) has garnered a band of Spanish specialists to offer diners an authentic Spanish treat. The silken, fragrant, delicate Ibérian ham is expertly hand-cut paper-thin before your eyes, served with excellent *pan con tomate*, or crisp slices of baguette rubbed with both garlic and fresh red tomatoes. *Bouqerones* (classic Spanish vinegar-marinated anchovies) arrive glistening, layered on slices of grilled country bread, surrounded by gigantic cured caper berries and thin slices of yellow heirloom tomatoes. I loved the *riz noir aux calamars,* a huge portion of wholesome rice cooked in squid ink and flanked by moist, delicate baby squid. The *poulpe à la galicienne* arrives as a colorful, paprika-dusted portion of steamed baby potatoes in their skins and bite-size pieces of the most tender octopus. There are just 10 stools and a *table d'hôte* that seats 12. Everything here is generous, personal, and friendly.

YUZU

JAPANESE
33, rue de Bellechasse
Paris 7
TEL: +33 1 47 05 28 84
MÉTRO: Solférino
OPEN: Tuesday through Sunday
CLOSED: Sunday lunch and Monday

PRICES: 20 to 30€ lunch menus. À la carte 30€ at lunch. 50€ dinner menu and 70€ *dégustation* (tasting) menu. À la carte 45 to 60€ at dinner.
RESERVATIONS: Recommended
ATMOSPHERE: Casual
SPECIALTIES: Sushi

This tidy little Japanese restaurant just off the boulevard Saint-Germain serves some of the most interesting Asian fare in town. I'd walk miles just to sample their black-and-gold sesame-studded shrimp tempura; it's pure perfection, with giant, moist, and tender shrimp dipped in the lightest of batters and carefully fried by the young woman chef Megumi Yanase, better known as Megu. If you take a seat at the counter, you'll get to watch sushi master Nao Takemoto (known as Take) and Megu work their magic. The generous bento box lunch is a luxurious blend of sashimi, maki, tempura, and deliciously fresh poached salmon. A sure bet.

8ᵀᴴ ARRONDISSEMENT

RESTAURANT ALAIN DUCASSE AU PLAZA ATHÉNÉE

HAUTE CUISINE / MODERN FRENCH
25, avenue Montaigne
Paris 8
TEL: +33 1 53 67 65 00
plaza-athenee-paris.com
adpa@plaza-athenee-paris.com
MÉTRO: Alma-Marceau
OPEN: Lunch Thursday and Friday only. Dinner Monday through Friday.

CLOSED: Saturday, Sunday, and all of August
PRICES: 360€ lunch and dinner menu. À la carte 195 to 335€.
RESERVATIONS: Essential
ATMOSPHERE: Formal. Suit jacket, but not tie, required for men.
SPECIALTIES: Black truffles, cheese cart

If you are of the opinion that French haute cuisine is boring and passé, think again. For Christophe Saintagne, chef at the illustrious Alain Ducasse au Plaza Athénée, has taken his cooking completely out of the box and certainly proves that today, "fine dining" can be anything the chef says it is. There's not a touch of preciousness in his food; in fact, "earthy" is the word I'd apply to many of his dishes. One look at the streamlined, abbreviated menu and you begin to get the message. One dish reads only *langoustines rafraichies, caviar.* Another simply *turbot, coquillages, blette.* You know this is going to be all about the ingredients.

When did you last have an *amuse-bouche* like this? The tall, lean, handsome waiter arrives and places a hot-off-the-stove sauté pan in the center of the table. Two long-handled seafood forks rest on a mound of spicy, hot, brilliant pink baby shrimp, the bodies sautéed and the cleaned heads deep-fried to a perfect crisp. We ate the entire portion. That could have been lunch.

A first course of giant *langoustines* cooked ever so slightly, then chilled, arrived as a lineup of perfectly dainty bite-size portions, topped with a dollop of glistening caviar. Dip them into a delicate *langoustines* broth, then follow up with a sip of lemongrass and ginger–laced broth. Magnificent. The golden crayfish bisque came topped with a giant shellfish-flavored *oeuf à la neige,* which is then bathed in a rich, pumpkin-flavored shellfish sauce, making for a stunning dish with myriad textures, flavors, taste sensations. Forceful and brilliant. Next came the turbot-lover's dream. (That's me, the turbot lover.) A giant rectangular portion of alabaster turbot arrives on a mattress of fresh seaweed, gorgeous and fragrant, served with a delicate fish broth and all manner of baby shellfish and strips of Swiss chard. A sea festival, completely satisfying. It's hard to decide which was the best dish of the day, though the beauty-pageant winner was surely the gratin of fresh *cèpe* mushrooms served in a clean white bowl and garnished with parsley flowers. I took one look at the dish—painstakingly layered slices of sautéed mushroom—and asked myself why I hadn't thought of that. The chef had carefully cubed and sautéed mushrooms, then topped that base with the thinly sliced portions. It made me realize that whole, cooked *cèpes* are like meat. Sliced mushrooms are pure vegetable. The only ho-hum dish of the meal was the accompanying soup, cubed *cèpes* floating in a bronze-colored broth, with flavors that were simply nondescript.

And just when I thought I had had enough fresh purple figs for the year, the chef insisted I try his autumnal creation. I am glad I did. He layered a small *cocotte* with fresh fig leaves and buried them with fresh whole purple figs. Once they were cooked, he added sliced raw figs, then topped it all with a sharp *granité* of sweet Italian wine. Thank you, October.

Service led by *maître d'* Denis Courtiade is totally down to earth and friendly, while *sommelier* Laurent Roucayro breaks the mold of the snooty wine waiter. His choice of wines—Pascal Jolivet's clean and expressive Pouilly-Fumé and Pierre Usseglio's crisp, full-bodied white Châteauneuf-du-Pape—brought harmony and happiness to a lovely meal.

CHEZ ANDRÉ

CLASSIC BISTRO

12, rue Marbeuf
Paris 8
TEL: +33 1 47 20 59 57
gerard-joulie.com
MÉTRO: Alma-Marceau or George V
OPEN: Daily noon to 1AM

PRICES: 35€ menu. À la carte 35 to 55€ lunch and dinner.
RESERVATIONS: Recommended
ATMOSPHERE: Smart-casual
SPECIALTIES: *Steak frites*, roast chicken, onion soup, oysters

The laughter begins as the phone rings off the hook in this bustling 1930s bistro off the Champs-Élysées. We are awaiting our table, standing right in front of the ringing beast as a pert, tiny waitress in black and white turns to my husband and with a joking reprimand shouts,

"Why don't you answer it!" With a good laugh we take a seat on the banquettes that have stood the test of time, and order up! Sizzling bowls of onion soup with delicious hearty broth and plenty of melting cheese; platters of briny oysters from grower Gillardeau that make us smile with pleasure; a giant, succulent roasted *daurade* (porgy or sea bream) large enough for two. A friend orders a huge portion of *foie de veau* (calf's liver), something he has not seen on a New York menu in ages. A classic *sole meunière* (or grilled

simply *à la plancha* if you prefer) arrives hot from the kitchen as the all-female staff continues to joke and cajole, all part of the best bistro banter. Seek out their wine treasures, such as the mineral-rich Sauvignon Blanc Monts Damnés, and the seldom-seen second wine from Château de la Nerthe in Châteauneuf-du-Pape, Clos de la Granière, a sturdy red. Service here is nonstop from noon until 1AM, meaning that bowl of *gratinée oignon* will be waiting for you at just about any hour.

ÉPAULE D'AGNEAU FONDANTE AUX ÉPICES DU CINQ

Le Cinq's 11-Hour Braised Lamb Shoulder

I like to joke that I never got up at 6AM to start dinner before attempting this recipe, but now I don't mind. The results are totally amazing, with tender, moist lamb that is literally falling off the bone, spiced with cumin, coriander, black peppercorns, and a fresh, homemade curry powder. The recipe comes from Eric Briffard, chef at the Hotel George V's Le Cinq. Currently, many Parisian chefs enjoy the results of cooking meats at low temperatures for many hours.

INGREDIENTS:

1 bone-in lamb shoulder
  (2 to 3 pounds; 1.1 to 1.2 kg)

Fine sea salt and freshly ground
  black pepper

3 tablespoons extra-virgin olive oil

AROMATIC GARNISH:

3 large onions, minced

2 large carrots, minced

1 celery rib, left whole with leaves

1 small bunch fresh flat-leaf
  parsley

1 small bunch fresh thyme

1 fresh or dried bay leaf

½ head garlic, unpeeled

1 sprig fresh rosemary

SPICE MIX:

1 tablespoon whole coriander seeds

1 tablespoon whole cumin seeds

1 tablespoon Homemade Curry
  Powder (recipe follows)

1 tablespoon fine sea salt

1 teaspoon whole black
  peppercorns

8 sprigs fresh thyme

2 sprigs fresh rosemary

2 plump, moist garlic cloves,
  crushed

Harissa or other favorite hot
  sauce, for serving

1. Preheat the oven to 160°F (70°C).

2. Season the lamb all over with salt and pepper. In a large cast-iron casserole with a cover, heat the oil over low heat. Very slowly brown the lamb on both sides, about 10 minutes. Add the aromatic garnish and brown 10 minutes more. Add the spice mix and ⅓ cup (80 ml) water.

3. Cover the casserole and place in the oven for 11 hours. The lamb needs no attention during this time.

4. At serving time, preheat the broiler. Transfer the lamb and all the ingredients in the casserole to a roasting pan. Place the grill pan under the broiler until the meat is crusty and golden, about 15 minutes.

5. Carve the lamb and serve with harissa or other hot sauce.

4 TO 6 SERVINGS

Homemade Curry Powder

Homemade curry powder has long been an essential part of my pantry. The recipe may change from season to season, whim to whim, but I am always sure to have a small jar of the freshly ground mixture in my refrigerator at all times. (Yes, refrigerator: I keep essential spices that might lose their power in a cool spot, in a tiny jar, very tightly sealed, to give it the honor and care that it deserves.)

EQUIPMENT:

An electric spice mill

INGREDIENTS:

2 whole, small dried red chiles

2 tablespoons whole coriander seeds

1 tablespoon whole cumin seeds

1 teaspoon black mustard seeds

1 teaspoon whole black peppercorns

1 teaspoon ground ginger

1 teaspoon ground turmeric

1. In a small, dry skillet combine the chiles, coriander seeds, cumin seeds, mustard seeds, and peppercorns and toast over medium heat, shaking the pan often to prevent burning, 2 to 3 minutes.

2. Combine the toasted spices, ginger, and turmeric in the spice mill, and grind to a fine powder. (Store in an airtight container in a cool place for up to 1 month.)

MAKES ⅓ CUP

SORBET PISTACHE DU CINQ

Le Cinq's Pistachio Sorbet

I have followed Le Cinq's chef Eric Briffard's career path since working closely with him in the 1980s while he was a lead man in the kitchens of Joël Robuchon. This sorbet is simple and sublime. I serve it two ways, either topped with toasted, salted pistachios for a sweet and savory contrast, or as I once sampled it at the neighbhood bistro Les Botanistes, where chef Jean-Baptiste Gray served a pistachio sorbet with fresh raspberries, a beautiful as well as delicious combination.

EQUIPMENT:

An ice-cream maker;
8 ice-cream bowls,
chilled in the freezer

INGREDIENTS:

1½ cups (375 ml)
whole milk

¾ cup (185 ml) heavy
(whipping) cream

2 teaspoons invert
sugar syrup (recipe
follows), or light corn
syrup

¾ cup (150 g) unrefined
cane sugar, preferably
organic

3 tablespoons dried
whole milk powder

6 tablespoons (100 g)
pistachio paste

Toasted, salted pistachio
nuts, for garnish
(optional; recipe
follows)

4 ounces (125 g)
fresh raspberries,
for garnish (optional)

In a large bowl, combine the milk, cream, and invert sugar syrup. Whisk to blend. Whisk in the sugar and milk powder. Whisk in the pistachio paste. Chill thoroughly. Transfer to an ice-cream maker and freeze according to the manufacturer's instructions. For best results, serve the sorbet as soon as it is frozen. Do not refreeze. At serving time, divide the sorbet among the chilled ice-cream bowls. Garnish each serving with toasted, salted pistachio nuts or with fresh raspberries.

8 SERVINGS

TRÉMOLINE

Invert Sugar Syrup

Invert sugar is basically a very thick, clear sugar syrup, with the consistency of liquid honey or light corn syrup. The French call it *trémoline*. The syrup makes for a smoother mouthfeel in sorbets and ice creams and also controls crystallization. It is simple to make, and stores for up to 6 months in the refrigerator.

EQUIPMENT:

A 2-quart (2-l) stainless steel saucepan; a heatproof jar with a lid

INGREDIENTS:

2¼ cups (450 g) refined white cane sugar (do not use dark, unrefined sugars)

1 cup (250 ml) water

2 teaspoons freshly squeezed lemon juice

Combine the sugar, water, and lemon juice in a 2-quart saucepan and bring to a boil over high heat. Do not stir. Reduce the heat to low and simmer until the mixture is slightly thick and viscous, like corn syrup or a liquid honey, 8 to 10 minutes. The mixture should not darken or caramelize. Be aware that the liquid will thicken as it cools. I find it better to err on the runny side rather than risk a syrup that is too thick and nearly impossible to pour. Transfer to a heatproof jar and let cool. Cover and refrigerate for up to 6 months.

MAKES ABOUT 1¾ CUPS (435 ML)

PISTACHES GRILLÉ

Toasted, Salted Pistachio Nuts

These toasted pistachio nuts make a great snack, but are equally delicious on top of Le Cinq's Pistachio Sorbet (facing page), a fantastic sweet-savory combo.

INGREDIENTS:

4 ounces (125 g) shelled pistachio nuts

1 teaspoon best-quality pistachio oil (such as Leblanc brand), or extra-virgin olive oil

¼ teaspoon fine sea salt

In a small skillet set over medium heat, combine the pistachios, oil, and salt, and toss to blend. Toast, shaking the pan regularly, until the nuts are fragrant, evenly toasted, and begin to crackle and sizzle, 3 to 4 minutes. Watch carefully! They can burn quickly. Transfer the nuts to a large plate to cool. Store in an airtight container at room temperature for up to 1 week.

MAKES 4 OUNCES (125 G)

L'ATELIER DE JOËL ROBUCHON ÉTOILE

HAUTE CUISINE / MODERN FRENCH
133, avenue des Champs-Élysées
(Publicis Drugstore)
Paris 8
TEL: +33 1 47 23 75 75
joel-robuchon.net
MÉTRO: Charles de Gaulle-Étoile
OPEN: Daily 11:30AM to 3:30PM and 6:30PM
to midnight

PRICES: Small plates from 15 to 50€. 37, 57,
and 77€ lunch menus. 165€ *dégustation*
(tasting) menu.
RESERVATIONS: Essential. Lunch seatings at
11:30AM, 12:30, 2:00, and 3:30PM. Dinner
reservations 6:30PM only. Remaining seating is
first come, first served.
ATMOSPHERE: Smart-casual
SPECIALTIES: Small plates, fish and shellfish,
game, black truffles, cheese tray

Intense, explosive flavors and imaginative fare await diners at Joël Robuchon's newest addition to the Paris restaurant scene, L'Atelier de Joël Robuchon Étoile. Situated in the lower level of the Publicis Drugstore at the Étoile, the bright red-and-black space is full of glittery Las Vegas–style drama. But the

real scene is what's on the plate and what happens to your palate with each pleasurable bite. As we were finishing our multicourse tasting lunch, one of my dining companions said in disbelief, "This must be what it feels like to take LSD! The reds are more alive, everything is more focused, more extreme." I second that. The menu offers some welcoming Robuchon classics, many dating back to the 1980s and the early days of his first iconic Paris restaurant, Jamin. But with Japanese chef Yosuke Suga in charge, an entirely new line of Asian-inspired aromas and flavors shares the limelight. Suga previously served as head chef at the Atelier branches in New York and Taipei, and is a member of the very tightly knit group of Robuchon chefs who travel the world to make sure each of the many Ateliers stays on top of its game. That lunch served as a case study as to how old dishes can become new again. Once a dish is perfected—as only Robuchon can—it can live on forever. His classic creation of caviar in lobster jelly, topped with cauliflower cream, offers an explosion with every bite, with the magical grains of caviar almost suspended in the rich jelly, and the cream there to intensify and smooth out the flavors at the same time. The presentation alone—the unctuous

mélange is served in tiny glass bowls with clear glass lids—would be sufficient drama, but you also get the inestimable pleasure of eating it. Another specialty not to be ignored is the penetrating bite of smooth and pungent *foie gras* set in a dense port jelly, topped with a soothing Parmesan cream. Mouth-filling, intense, unforgettable. Joël's classic potato-and-truffle salad has been turned inside out and appears here as a beautiful architectural offering, with smooth curls of *foie gras,* paper-thin shards of toast, slim disks of truffles, thick slices of potatoes, shavings of Parmesan, and just a few whispers of arugula. The textures and flavors saunter arm in arm. (Still, I would have loved the dish more if the potatoes had been warm.) Chef Suga's addition of *Les Shishitots*—the bright green, tiny, thin-skinned Japanese peppers that are slightly sweet and barely spicy—gets a big winter welcome when any touch of greenery on the plate demands applause. It's hard to pick a best taste of the day here, but the little peppers pierced with wooden skewers and placed between meaty mushrooms were cooked to perfection on their flat-plate *plancha.* A tiny dollop of brilliant green, extra-mild wasabi mousse topped it all off. I could have easily gone for a second portion. But then what about the salsify? Who knew salsify could taste so great! The theme of many of the newer dishes here seems to be a lot of rectangles and squares, and in the case of the much-maligned and ignored salsify, the rectangles of the winter root vegetable are lined up side by side and topped with golden, crispy salsify chips.

LE CINQ (FOUR SEASONS)

HAUTE CUISINE / MODERN FRENCH
31, avenue George V
Paris 8
TEL: +33 1 49 52 70 00
fourseasons.com/paris/dining/restaurants/le_cinq
MÉTRO: George V or Alma-Marceau

OPEN: Daily for breakfast, lunch, and dinner
PRICES: 44 to 57€ breakfast menus, à la carte 20 to 90€ for individual dishes. Lunch and dinner 180 to 265€ à la carte.
RESERVATIONS: Recommended
ATMOSPHERE: Formal (jacket required, tie recommended)

While this grand, illustrious dining room may suggest to diners that they will be served some classic (read: old-fashioned, trite) fare, think again. Chef Eric Briffard, whom I first met in Joël Robuchon's kitchen at Jamin in the 1980s, is part of Paris's well-trained band of kitchen wizards, chefs who have been *so* classically trained but are well-grounded in the modern era. Briffard, like Robuchon before him, is all about sourcing the best and freshest. (Robuchon always said, "I don't care what you charge me, but if it isn't the best, I'll send it back.") So on his ever-changing menu in this glorious dining room, you will find everything from *langoustines* to kumquats, morels to the freshest of fish, capers and nuts, fig leaves and pistachios (see recipes, pages 74–75), lamb (see recipe, page 72), and fresh black truffles, all treated with the honor they deserve. A meal you will not regret.

RESTAURANT DOMINIQUE BOUCHET

MODERN FRENCH
11, rue Treilhard
Paris 8
TEL: +33 1 45 61 09 46
dominique-bouchet.com
message@dominique-bouchet.com
MÉTRO: Miromesnil

OPEN: Monday through Friday
CLOSED: Saturday, Sunday, public holidays, and three weeks in August
PRICES: 55€ lunch menu, 105€ dinner menu. À la carte 60 to 92€.
RESERVATIONS: Recommended
ATMOSPHERE: Smart-casual

Entering this luxurious enclave will make you feel as though you're taking a secret little vacation. Dominique Bouchet, who made his name at the Tour d'Argent when it had three Michelin stars, opened this elegant little restaurant in 2006. Usually in the open kitchen supervising the details, he is a master of the humble. Because he spends part of his time in Japan, Bouchet tends to drizzle soy here, use tempura there, and wasabi has been known to sneak in on occasion. But mostly, his food is traditional and seasonal, with an ultralight touch. In his hands, *tête de veau* (calf's head) comes to the table as a crisp, toothsome *galette* garnished with tender root vegetables, tiny beet greens, and a velvety sauce *gribiche*, here a mayonnaise with capers and cornichons. Roasted sea bass (*bar*) reaches a tender-crisp height as it comes seasoned with vanilla oil, capers, and lemon, and sits on a bed of small crushed potatoes. Fat scallops (*coquilles Saint-Jacques*) arrive golden on both sides, tender in the center, and perched like little towers on beds of endives laced with orange-scented veal stock. His signature chestnut soup is beguiling with its base of coconut milk, and *foie gras* seasoned with sake is an ideal cultural and gastronomic marriage. Desserts, too, are lovely, particularly the *crème brûlée* baked in half a pear, set on a tender butter cookie and served with caramel ice cream; and the sliver of bitter chocolate tart with sorbet. Save room, too, for the after-meal truffles. They alone are worth the trip to this very classy little spot.

EPICURE AU BRISTOL

HAUTE CUISINE / MODERN FRENCH
Hotel Bristol
112, rue du Faubourg Saint-Honoré
Paris 8
TEL: +33 1 53 43 43 40
lebristolparis.com
MÉTRO: Miromesnil
OPEN: Daily for breakfast, lunch, and dinner

PRICES: 130€ lunch menu and 290€ *dégustation* (tasting) menu at lunch and dinner. À la carte 350€.
RESERVATIONS: Essential
ATMOSPHERE: Formal. Suit jacket, but not tie, required for men.
SPECIALTIES: Cheese cart

C hef Eric Frechon is a modern-day master, taking all the classic rhythms and making them look and taste ultramodern, while remaining profoundly true to his roots. Throughout a meal here in the new, modern dining room overlooking the well-tended private garden, Frechon and his team work their magic, offering clean, crisp, intense flavors that don't skip a beat. Here, mushrooms taste purely of mushrooms, basil has that extra intensity, and tomatoes taste as though they were harvested just moments before. And he knows how our palate loves crunch, so there's always a little crisp and crackle along with the smooth. He manages to bundle satisfaction better than any chef I know. Two little bites of his featherlight pizza appetizer make you feel as though you've enjoyed an entire pizza (see recipe on facing page). Nothing here is an afterthought; each bite has purpose. Frechon's first course of *langoustines*, caviar, and touches of *yuzu* (a fragrant and flavorful Japanese citrus), elegant mouthfuls packed with a citrus wallop, make you feel like royalty. A favorite here is his *tourteau mayo en gelée de tomate verte parfumé à l'estragon et fleur de ciboulette:* Gigantic pieces of crab claws are stacked like boulders along the seashore, bound together with the tangy green tomato *gelée*. He stuffs sole with the tiniest of wild *girolle* (chanterelle) mushrooms; tender filets of *merlan* (whiting) are contrasted with thin almond wafers; duck breast is served spicy, teamed up with a carpaccio of fresh figs; while a dessert finale—a frozen meringue of green apple, basil, and lime—sent me out onto the street in a happy haze. You will be in good hands with the charming *sommelier* Marco Pelletier, who knows his cellar by heart. We loved, as always, the well-priced Mâcon-Villages from the Domaine des Héritiers du Comte Lafon.

CROUSTILLANT SAVEUR PIZZA D'EPICURE AU BRISTOL

Epicure au Bristol's Crispy Pizza Bites

E ric Frechon of the Bristol Hotel's restaurant Epicure is surely one of France's most creative and talented chefs. One sunny day in July we savored these tiny bites as part of a glorious procession of appetizers, one more stunning than the next. The delicate, elegant pizza morsels are a sure crowd pleaser.

EQUIPMENT:

2 baking sheets, each lined with baking parchment; a food processor or blender

INGREDIENTS:

2 sheets phyllo dough

Extra-virgin olive oil spray

4 tablespoons (30 g) freshly grated Parmigiano-Reggiano cheese

½ teaspoon fresh thyme leaves

¼ teaspoon ground *piment d'Espelette* or other dried chile pepper

⅛ teaspoon *fleur de sel*

TOPPING:

1 tablespoon extra-virgin olive oil

1 small onion, minced

¼ teaspoon fine sea salt

1 small tomato, cored, peeled, seeded, and chopped

1 small, fresh hot chile pepper, such as jalapeño, minced

¼ teaspoon best-quality sherry wine vinegar

1. Center a rack in the oven. Preheat the oven to 350°F (175°C).

2. Place a sheet of phyllo dough on the baking parchment. Spray with oil. Shower with the cheese, thyme, chile pepper, and salt. Cover with the second sheet of phyllo dough. Cut the dough into 1- by 3-inch (2.5- by 7.5-cm) rectangles. Spray once more with oil. Cover with the second sheet of parchment. Cover the parchment with the second baking sheet.

3. Place the covered phyllo in the oven and bake for 7 minutes. Remove to a rack to cool.

4. While the phyllo is cooling, prepare the topping: In a saucepan, combine the oil, onion, and salt, and cook, covered, over low heat until soft, about 3 minutes. Add the tomato and chile pepper and cook over low heat for 15 minutes. Stir in the vinegar. Transfer the mixture to the food processor or blender and puree. Taste for seasoning.

5. At serving time, spread the onion mixture on top of half the phyllo rectangles. Top each with a second rectangle and serve.

MAKES 26 BITES

LAURENT

HAUTE CUISINE / MODERN FRENCH
41, avenue Gabriel
Paris 8
TEL: +33 1 42 25 00 39
le-laurent.com
info@le-laurent.com
MÉTRO: Champs-Élysées–Clemenceau
OPEN: Monday through Saturday

CLOSED: Saturday lunch, Sunday, and holidays
PRICES: 95€ lunch menu. 180€ *dégustation*
(tasting) menu at lunch and dinner. À la carte
200€ at lunch and dinner.
RESERVATIONS: Essential
ATMOSPHERE: Formal. Suit jacket, but not tie,
required for men.
SPECIALTIES: Game, black truffles

Restaurant Laurent is one of a kind, both classic and timeless. This historic, pastel-pink, 19th-century former hunting lodge set in the gardens of the Champs-Élysées is the sort of rare restaurant that makes Paris, Paris. Its tidy terrace shaded beneath giant chestnut trees sets the stage for romance.

And under the guidance of the ultra-professional director, Philippe Bourgignon, and talented chef Alain Pégouret, Laurent is a sure win. Pricey, yes, though the 88€ lunch menu is hard to beat in terms of value and pure pleasure. If you love wine, the restaurant should be added to your to-try list, for Bourgignon and trusted *sommelier* Patrick Laer appear to intimately know, love, and respect every offering in its 30,000-bottle cellar. Lunch highlighted the chef's ability to combine upgraded classic French dishes with items rarely found on luxury menus. Fresh meaty morels in a foam of sauce *poulette,* the tenderest cod cheeks paired with artichokes and mushrooms, beautifully braised veal flank teamed with juicy Swiss chard ribs, and the restaurant's classic spider crab bound in lobster jelly and topped with fennel cream are all dishes made in heaven. A few sips of the fragrant white Puligny-Montrachet Clos de la Mouchère from winemaker Henri Boillot,

and the pleasure trip is assured. Add the perfectly executed crispy "waffle" filled with almond milk cream and wild strawberries and that trip is complete!

LAZARE

BRASSERIE
Gare Saint-Lazare (front side, street level)
rue Intérieure
Paris 8
TEL: +33 1 44 90 80 80
lazare-paris.fr
resa@lazare-paris.fr

MÉTRO: Saint-Lazare
OPEN: Daily 7:30AM to midnight
PRICES: 9€ breakfast menu. 25 to 80€
à la carte at lunch and dinner.
RESERVATIONS: Essential
ATMOSPHERE: Smart-casual

The super-talented chef Eric Frechon (of Paris's Hotel Bristol and the Mini Palais) brings us a modern, up-to-date brasserie called Lazare, serving, as he likes to say, "real, authentic food and a return to what's essential at the table: history, memory, laughs, tears, family meals, and a simple dinner tête à tête." Set at the ground-floor entrance of the Gare Saint-Lazare—the train station near the Madeleine that sends travelers to Normandy and points west—the bright and contemporary brasserie offers good food, fine service, a cheerful setting, and hours that are hard to beat: 7:30AM to midnight, nonstop. You don't have to be traveling to love the place, and I can imagine popping in for a quick breakfast or a snack while shopping at the department stores Printemps or Galeries Lafayette nearby. Frechon hopes to bring back the authentic Parisian brasserie, a loud and happy-sounding spot with such classics as mussels in cream, *steak tartare*, seven-hour leg of lamb, and a green bean salad. The decor is modern—shelves filled with stacks of white plates and rows of shiny copper pots; a recipe for their Paris-Deauville dessert, handwritten on a huge blackboard; and an industrially exposed ceiling, painted all white. I'd go back again and again for the moist, perfectly cooked lamb, falling off the bone, set on a bed of well-seasoned bulgur, the meat itself flavored with black olives, tomato, thin slices of lemon, and whole pieces of star anise. Yum! Just right for pairing with a glass of Marcel Lapierre's Morgon. I love as well his rendition of the classic green bean salad, paired with freshly cooked artichokes, whole hazelnuts, and a hazelnut oil dressing. On one visit we feasted on a giant portion of the tiniest *girolles* (chanterelles), enough for a vegetarian main course! I was less convinced of the roast codfish (*cabillaud*) served in pleasant green sauce (*sauce vierge*) and topped with lightly cooked baby spinach. His rhubarb tart is delicious, perfectly tangy with a crisp, not-too-sweet crust. And cheese comes from young cheesemonger Claire Griffon (see Cheese Shops, page 257). Do try the perfectly aged young goat cheese—*chèvre*—marinated in fresh thyme and olive oil.

PAVILLON LEDOYEN

HAUTE CUISINE / MODERN FRENCH
1, avenue Dutuit (Cárre Champs-Élysées)
Paris 8
TEL: +33 1 53 05 10 01
ledoyen.com
MÉTRO: Champs-Élysées–Clemenceau
OPEN: Monday through Friday, and Saturday dinner
CLOSED: Saturday lunch, Sunday, and three weeks in August
PRICES: 128€ lunch menu. 250€ *dégustation* (tasting) menu (350€ with wine) at lunch and dinner. À la carte 250 to 300€.
RESERVATIONS: Recommended
ATMOSPHERE: Formal. Suit jacket, but not tie, required for men.

This *pavillon*, first built as a hunting lodge set in the gardens of what is now the Champs-Élysécs, is, for sure, out of another era. The bright pink stucco, the grand entry, the imposing staircase, may surely intimidate. But don't let all this stop you from sampling chef Christian Le Squer's superlative contemporary interpretation of classic French cuisine, with moist, meaty, eye-opening roasted sweetbreads (*ris de veau*) that will set you begging for more, or his gigantic *langoustines,* one of France's greatest gifts to gastronomy. Each dish is presented as though it had been blessed by a jeweler, but never too precious to touch, devour, savor. Go at lunch, when the prices are more comfortable, and take pleasure in the balanced mix of Old and New World France.

MINI PALAIS

MODERN FRENCH

Grand Palais Museum
Avenue Winston Churchill
Paris 8
TEL: +33 1 42 56 42 42
minipalais.com
resa@minipalais.com
MÉTRO: Champs-Élysées–Clemenceau

OPEN: Daily 10AM to midnight
PRICES: 28€ lunch menu. À la carte 35 to 50€ at lunch and dinner.
RESERVATIONS: Recommended
ATMOSPHERE: Smart-casual
SPECIALTIES: Steak tartare and fries, duck burger with foie gras

Consider this: a Paris restaurant with a welcoming outdoor terrace, open nonstop seven days a week from 10AM to midnight, service that's polite (if a bit slow), and food that is utterly modern, fresh, and seasonal. I'd call it Le Grand Slam, but the restaurant's true name is Mini Palais, located in the historic Grand Palais Museum. While the alluring, vast black-and-gray dining room is designed to evoke an artist's atelier, the terrace colonnade is one of the city's most inviting outdoor dining spaces. Outfitted with sturdy wicker-style chairs and banquettes, colorful mosaics on the floor and walls, giant stone columns, potted palms, pale linens, and pure-white Bernardaud china, this has become one of my favorite spots for enjoying the city's constant elegance and infrequent sunshine. Consultant Eric Frechon (Michelin three-star chef at the Hotel Bristol) has done a fine job of creating a menu that's up-to-date, original, and appealing (though I did want to run into the kitchen and take the salt mill from his hands). I adored his tomato trio: a colorful green tomato tartare topped with a red tomato sorbet and set in a pool of yellow tomato broth. This dish was seasoned perfectly, and embellished with a paper-thin slice of toast topped with slivers of fresh garlic and pungent fresh thyme. I can't wait to copy it in my own kitchen. Another fine starter that I'll make again and again was composed of thin strips of creamy burrata cheese topped with thin slices of ham, then showered with fresh basil, toasted pine nuts, and sun-dried tomatoes. Line-caught merlan, or whiting, was brilliantly prepared under a thick coating of toasted, ground almonds, while a piece of Saint-Pierre, or John Dory, rested atop a bed of delicious eggplant puree. The meal began with puffy, golden trencherman-size gougères made with aged Comté cheese—a fine companion to sips of Olivier Merlin's magical Chardonnay, a wine that's intense and mineral-rich. The most popular dish here seemed to be the gorgeous steak tartare, paired with golden fries peeking out of a crisp white cup. And I'll be sure to sample that on my next visit.

NEVA CUISINE

MODERN FRENCH
2, rue de Berne
Paris 8
TEL: +33 1 45 22 18 91
MÉTRO: Europe or Liège
OPEN: Monday through Friday

CLOSED: Saturday, Sunday, three weeks in
August, and between Christmas and New Year's
PRICES: 32 and 39€ lunch and dinner menus.
RESERVATIONS: Recommended
ATMOSPHERE: Casual

Neva Cuisine's owners Yannick Tranchant and Beatriz Gonzalez know what they are doing, and they do it well. Everything in this clean, white 1900s bistro is honest, unforced, natural, and without pretense. Chef Gonzalez offers a resolutely modern and appealing style of cooking and

makes this the sort of restaurant you go to for Just Good Food. The same can be said for Yannick Tranchant's Just Good Service. Many of Gonzalez's dishes have a familiar air, such as the classic and delicious chilled gazpacho, kicked up a notch by the addition of airy, whipped fresh mozzarella cheese, making this a dish I could have for lunch many a day. Her seared Saint-Pierre fish (John Dory) was ultra-fresh and cooked to perfection, teamed up with a brilliant "cannelloni"

of zucchini—long, thin strips of zucchini wrapped around crunchy quinoa, and bathed in a frothy, light, and creamy sauce. I loved her molten chocolate dessert, reminiscent of the chocolate "pearl" from La Table d'Eugène in the 18th *arrondissement*, a thin, delicate sphere of chocolate melted at the table with a drizzle of hot chocolate. The wine list is appealing, with my ever-favorite Sancerre from Henri Bourgeois.

OKUDA

TRADITIONAL JAPANESE
7, rue de la Trémoille
Paris 8
TEL: +33 1 40 70 19 19
MÉTRO: Alma-Marceau
OPEN: Tuesday through Sunday
CLOSED: All day Monday and Tuesday lunch

PRICE: 180€ fixed menu at lunch,
250€ fixed menu at dinner, no à la carte
RESERVATIONS: Essential
ATMOSPHERE: Smart-casual
SPECIALTY: *Kaiseki* (a multi-course, seasonal,
haute cuisine Japanese meal)

Once you watch Japanese master Toru Okuda wield a knife, you'll never want to touch one again. Precision. Care. Attention. Discipline. Perfection. Okuda—whose stable of Tokyo restaurants include both a Michelin three-star and Michelin two-star—has come to Paris. And we diners are the

better for it. His serene, pale-wood, pottery-filled trio of dining rooms (a main-floor counter for seven; a downstairs dining room for ten; and a private room for four) transport you directly to Japan, with all the accompanying courtesy and gentleness one expects. There is only a single, multi-course *kaiseki*

menu, and diners are presented with a simple printed list of the offerings as they begin their pleasant journey. I was lucky enough to be seated at the bar, with Chef Okuda in front of me, demonstrating his amazing proficiency with a knife. It is hard to choose a favorite of the eight courses, but I guess I would have to say soothing, delicate crab flan, rich with fresh crab meat, and a perfect foil of warm autumn mushrooms (*flan salé au tourteau, sauce épaisse aux champignons*). It was course number two, and if I had to stop there, I would have been a happy woman. Brilliantly fresh tuna, paper-thin slices of squid from the L'Île de'Yeu, and delicate white flounder (*carrelet*) arrive as a sashimi selection, seasoned with the most delicious sea greens, including an unforgettably bright-flavored freshwater nori. Not that the dish needed embellishment, we were instructed to season one bite of the squid with the dollop of caviar set on the plate, and take a second bite paired with fresh wasabi that had been grated only seconds earlier. Mouth in heaven, mouth on fire! It will be a while before I forget the grilled *bar*—oh-so-perfectly cooked over a charcoal fire—just lightly smoky, falling easily into chopstick-worthy bites, seasoned with salt and sesame. And who would think to actually fry an avocado, transforming both the texture and flavor, making me think of a freshly harvested butternut squash, cooked to create an autumn-worthy puree. Morsels of charcoal-grilled French Limousin beef filet from butcher Hugo Desnoyer arrive so tender you can eat them with a chopstick, while just about every dish leaves your palate with a clean, citrusy aftertaste. But the one dish that I will be making at home is Okuda's spectacular dessert: It consisted of a peach compote, using no less than three varieties (a white peach, a *pêche plate* and the rare *pêche de vigne*) set in a glistening crystal bowl, surrounded by a fragrant and fruity-sweet sparkling peach jelly, and of course a perfect peach sorbet, garnished with pungent leaves of fresh mint.

PIERRE GAGNAIRE

HAUTE CUISINE / MODERN FRENCH
6, rue Balzac
Paris 8
TEL: +33 1 58 36 12 50
pierregagnaire.com
MÉTRO: George V
OPEN: Monday through Friday

CLOSED: Saturday, Sunday, August, November 11, Christmas, and first week of January
PRICES: 110€ lunch menu. 280€ dinner menu. À la carte 285 to 380€.
RESERVATIONS: Essential
ATMOSPHERE: Formal. Suit jacket, but not tie, required for men.
SPECIALTIES: Game, black truffles

For my palate, and the pleasure of your own, one Parisian restaurant not to miss is the home of Pierre Gagnaire, the hyperactive, super-creative, sometimes off-the-wall-crazy chef who manages to woo us with amazing combinations, remarkable presentations, and, most of all, flavorful surprises that please even the most jaded of palates. I first met Gagnaire in the mid-1980s, when he was a brash young chef working out of a playful skylit restaurant in the town of Saint-Étienne in deepest central France. I remember my first meal as though it were yesterday, especially the astonishingly rich chocolate soufflé, so creamy he called it a soup. He was like a jumping bean, so full of ideas and challenges that just being within earshot you felt the energy, excitement, and enthusiasm. Some decades later, Gagnaire is still working his magic. As with most of us, maturity has brought a bit of sobriety (but not *too* much) and clearer focus on what he is after. Many adjectives come to mind after a meal in his tranquil, enveloping gray-and-white Right Bank dining room. Exciting. Intelligent.

Generous. Challenging. Audacious. A while back I told Gagnaire that I thought he was the most intellectual of chefs, because it is hard to tear into a dish of his without thinking of all the elements there. Why and how did he come up with the combination of fresh morels in curry powder, paired with frog's legs with tarragon, and *écrevisses* (crayfish) with vegetables in a chervil pesto? Just looking at the food makes your head spin with questions. His response was "But we have all these incredible ingredients at hand, so why not use them all?" Of course, you can look at his food both ways: Take it at face value (it tastes great—I'll have another bite), or plunge into thought, trying to get into the mind of the slightly mad scientist. A main dish of turbot paired with leeks and codfish and a juice of highbush cranberries, set off by tiny mackerel in anchovy sauce, in the end is really all about that firm, white-fleshed star of the sea from Brittany. And who but Gagnaire would tempt you, lure you, make you fall in love with a simple giant raspberry rolled in sugar? Or a single wild strawberry, or *fraise des bois,* presented on a wooden spoon? Gagnaire makes us sit up and take notice, become reverent in front of two of nature's most perfect, most beautiful, full-flavored fruits. Pop the single morsels in your mouth and you wonder why we cook at all! His starter of a hot, seared ball of *foie gras* served with a tiny square of Japanese dried seaweed is another special moment: a miniature mouthful that offers big-time pleasure. He almost lost me on the caramelized popcorn at one lunch, but why not have fun while we're at it? But Gagnaire is dead serious with his tiny clams fried with polenta and set on a bed of mushroom puree; he wows us with a Mediterranean fish flan served with a slice of monkfish cooked in tandoori spices; and he makes us all take notice with his tiny serving of grated coconut paired with bits of cauliflower, all linked with a puree of celery root. Gagnaire has done away with the cheese cart and now serves a single amazing plate of many different tastes. On one visit, the offering included a thin slice of rich cow's-milk *Beaufort* set on a dab of almond cream, and a slice of cow's-milk blue *Fourme d'Ambert* set on a slice of raw pear. Another time, the cheese plate included a dollop of fresh goat's-milk cheese topped with a red beet sauce; a slice of *Beaufort* on a slice of crispy buckwheat bread; and a welcome trio of pears, including a slice of fresh pear, a paper-thin slice of dried pear, and a dollop of pear puree. But go, see, and taste for yourself. It will be a memorable meal.

TAILLEVENT

HAUTE CUISINE / CLASSIC FRENCH

15, rue Lamennais
Paris 8
TEL: +33 1 44 95 15 01
taillevent.com
resa@taillevent.com
MÉTRO: George V
OPEN: Monday through Friday

CLOSED: Saturday, Sunday, and August
PRICES: 86€ (102€ with wine) lunch menu.
218€ *dégustation* (tasting) menu, 320€
seasonal menu. À la carte 200€.
RESERVATIONS: Essential
ATMOSPHERE: Formal (jacket required,
tie recommended)
SPECIALTIES: Game, black truffles

An American friend spends part of each year in Paris and when he is there, his rule is to lunch at Taillevent each and every Friday. A worthy goal, I say! This was one of the first Michelin three-star restaurants I ever visited, back in the 1970s. Over the years, the elegant, understated dining room has been our family's choice to celebrate birthdays, anniversaries, awards. Today, the clublike restaurant is as alive, alert, and up-to-date as any I know. As it always did, it provides the very definition of modern French haute cuisine. Chef Alain Solivérès and his pastry chef Matthieu Bijou make this one of the finest dining spots in the country. They both know how to update classics to modern-day tastes and expectations, working always with the finest of ingredients. Fish, shellfish, game, poultry, and meat are all treated with the utmost respect. I have re-created the chef's gorgeous crab rémoulade, sweet and delicately seasoned crab topped with a crown of colorful and crunchy radish rounds, though I know that I could never duplicate his lobster *boudin*, an Asian-inspired lobster sausage bathed in a delicate cream with a touch of caviar. On one visit, he wowed me with flowerlike *tartare* of fresh sea scallops topped with a nice hit of Asian herbs, followed by ultra-tender venison filets served with a melting, warm touch of *foie gras*. In winter months, black truffles reign here, with a creamy risotto of Provençal *épeautre* (spelt) topped with a crown of truffles; a magical *lièvre à la royale* fashioned into a rich, fragrant, perfectly seasoned wild hare terrine studded with truffles and served with a well-matched saffron-sauced pasta; and an outrageous portion of smooth and buttery potato *mousseline* showered with minced truffles and a golden egg yolk. Save room for Bijou's desserts. I dream of his super-perfect chocolate tart (the thinnest of crusts, the most ethereal chocolate), while his vanilla *millefeuille* has to be one of the lightest and flakiest in Paris. One cannot dine here without regretting the absence of perhaps the city's greatest restaurateur of modern times, Jean-Claude Vrinat. We will always miss him. Jean-Marie Ancher, long Vrinat's right-hand man, carries on with absolute attention and care, while the extensive wine list remains one of the glories of the establishment.

9TH ARRONDISSEMENT

KIKU

JAPANESE
56, rue Richer
Paris 9
TEL: +33 1 44 83 02 30
odo-fuyuanfeng.com
MÉTRO: Cadet or Notre-Dame de Lorette
OPEN: Monday through Saturday

CLOSED: Saturday lunch, Sunday, Christmas holidays, and part of August
PRICES: 27€ fixed lunch menu. 35€ fixed dinner menu. 55€ *dégustation* (tasting) menu. No à la carte.
RESERVATIONS: Recommended
ATMOSPHERE: Casual

Chef Kyoichi Kai from the southern Japanese island of Kyushu brings a fresh approach to Japanese cooking in Paris. His journey here via Tokyo, Sydney, and London is evident in his food—rustic yet elegant, creative and surprising, yet firmly rooted in Japanese culinary tradition. The simple wooden and stone interior of this small basic restaurant in the 9th *arrondissement* belie the sophistication to be found on the plate. The three-course fixed-price menu offers two *amuse-bouches*, a starter, and a main course, accompanied by miso soup and earthy rice, anointed with an assortment of grains. Chef Kyoichi's inventiveness is perhaps most apparent in his pre-starters, so pay attention from the beginning! The menu changes frequently, but on a recent visit I encountered two perfectly executed *amuse-bouches* beautifully presented in mismatched but exquisite Japanese ceramic bowls: a cold king crab *brandade* with warm buttery okra and perfectly seasoned with red Japanese pepper; and a harmonious combination of a single creamy scallop enrobed in thinly sliced pork, pan-fried and served with a paper-thin onion salad and a *yuzu* dressing that gave a zesty citrus punch. Fish and shellfish dominate the starter menu—soft shell crab, a light and airy tempura, fish *tartare* and sashimi—so for non-fish-eaters, this is not the restaurant for you. Opening the lid to the *cocotte* of the main course of *bar* (sea bass) released a fragrant aroma of lime zest and lemongrass from the rich poaching broth. The fish was tender and creamy, accompanied by bamboo shoots and lotus root, and a side dipping dish of citrusy *ponzu* sauce. In addition to the 35€ menu, you can order from a large range of sakes; green, jasmine, or oolong tea; Japanese beer; or perhaps you'll be adventurous enough to try the *yuzu* wine.

L'ORIENT D'OR

CHINESE
22, rue de Trévise
Paris 9
TEL: +33 1 48 00 07 73
MÉTRO: Cadet or Grands Boulevards
OPEN: Tuesday through Sunday

CLOSED: Monday
PRICES: 8.80€ lunch menu. 11.50, 14, and 17€ dinner menus. À la carte 18 to 30€.
RESERVATIONS: Recommended
ATMOSPHERE: Casual
SPECIALTIES: Hunanese cuisine

I f you are craving hot and spicy Chinese food with loads of flavor, then you won't be disappointed by L'Orient d'Or. The cuisine here is Hunanese, from the province in southeast China, and is known for its complex spices and generous use of chiles. The Chinese dumplings were unremarkable, as were the pumpkin beignets that are often cited as a must-try. But things start to pick up with the *galettes croustillantes au canard* (crispy duck pancakes): small rectangles of duck meat and skin encrusted with sesame seeds, served in the style of Peking duck with pancakes, Chinese chives, and hoisin sauce. A hit all around at the table. Next up, spicy cumin lamb, where the Hunanese reputation for spice really comes into its own. This dish, ordered spicy (a nonspicy version is available, but not nearly as adventurous), is not for the fainthearted. Despite the force of the chiles, the cumin spice comes through beautifully and makes for an extraordinarily flavorsome dish. The smoked pork belly was delicately savory, and the eggplant and pork, and spicy sautéed cabbage, were welcome additions to the table. For the dedicated, and organized, call ahead to order the two house specialties (they must be ordered 24 hours in advance): the Zuo Zong-tang chicken (*poulet de Zuo Zong-tang*), marinated, then deep fried—crispy and delicious, served with a mound of chiles yet surprisingly subtle in spiciness; and the highly recommended Chairman Mao braised pork (*porc en sauce rouge style Mao*). Succulent and full of flavor, this dish is worth the extra effort. The classic Chinese restaurant atmosphere is complete with plenty of large round tables with lazy Susan spinning trays in the center, and plastic chile peppers hanging from the ceiling. Prices are easy on the wallet, especially when ordering in large groups (which the staff handles with ease); you can feast here for under 30€ per person.

LE PANTRUCHE

MODERN BISTRO
3, rue Victor Massé
Paris 9
TEL: +33 1 48 78 55 60
lepantruche.com
MÉTRO: Saint-Georges or Pigalle

OPEN: Monday through Friday
CLOSED: Saturday and Sunday
PRICES: 18€ lunch menu, 14€ plat du jour,
34€ dinner menu
RESERVATIONS: Recommended
ATMOSPHERE: Casual

L e Pantruche, with its 1930s patina—large oak bar, mirrors that make a small place grand, warming chestnut-toned banquettes, and simple oak chairs—is the sort of place everyone wants to have within walking distance of home. Chef Franck Baranger and associates Nicolas Chatellain and

Edouard Bobin run their contemporary bistro with enthusiasm and personality, and the Pigalle spot is always filled with the sounds of guests having a fine time. Baranger (who spent time with the chef Christian Constant at Violon d'Ingres and Les Cocottes) takes the classic bistro repertoire, wraps it around in his mind, and comes out with some appealing, personal, modern fare. I'll begin with a few "bones to pick" with Baranger. I begged him to toss his truffle oil (produced in the chemistry lab and nothing more than perfume, and no more an ingredient for the table than Shalimar or hand purifier). And I wish he would turn up the heat in his kitchen, for too many ingredients come out lukewarm, their potential lost. That said, I'll be back to try once again his signature oyster tartare set in a brilliant green cream of lettuce soup (*huître en tartare, crème de laitue*). The raw, well-seasoned scoop of minced oysters bathes in the creamy soup, topped with a palate-opening dollop of nutmeg-scented cream, a soothing opener if ever there was one. A wintry serving of jet-black braised wild hare sits atop a warming and pungent puree of celery root (*céleri-rave*), while a daily special of braised beef cheeks left me kicking up my heels. A few sips of Foillard's Morgon

added to the pleasure. Now, if the staff could only speed up the service, we'd all leave with a bigger grin on our faces. The best news is that the bill does not break the bank.

10ᵀᴴ ARRONDISSEMENT

ABRI

MODERN FRENCH
92, rue du Faubourg-Poissonnière
Paris 10
TEL: +33 1 83 97 00 00
MÉTRO: Poissonnière
OPEN: Monday and Saturday lunch
(sandwiches only), Tuesday through Friday for
4-course lunch. Tuesday through Saturday for
6-course dinner.

CLOSED: Sunday and Monday dinner
PRICES: 13€ *tonkatsu* sandwich (Monday and
Saturday lunch only), 25€ fixed lunch menu.
40€ fixed dinner menu. No à la carte.
RESERVATIONS: Essential
ATMOSPHERE: Casual

Inexpensive, vest-pocket restaurants keep turning up in the most amazing places in Paris, and that's great for all budget-conscious diners. Worth the detour is Katsuaki Okiyama's latest venture, a tiny "hole in the wall" steps from the Poissonnière *métro* in the 10th *arrondissement*. Carefully decorated on a budget—simple but pleasant hanging lamps, exposed stone walls, an efficient open kitchen—Abri, as its French name suggests, is indeed a refuge from some of the expensive, mundane fare one might find elsewhere. The Japanese chef—who trained with Joël Robuchon and at Taillevent—offers simple, carefully prepared food, no surprises but no real disappointments, either. Fresh, seasonal fare prepared right in front of you: What more could one ask? The 22€ lunch menu offers a daily choice of either fish or poultry/meat as the main course, with a no-choice starter and dessert. A first-course carpaccio of *daurade* (sea bream) was a feathery light, protein-rich starter, showered with paper-thin slices of fennel and radish, alas a bit too salty for even my salt-loving palate. Main courses might include carefully seared and roasted duck breast, meaty and full-flavored, adorned with a light port reduction, garnished with *ratte* (bite-size) potatoes, or delicate *lieu jaune* (pollack, in the cod family) in a yellow tomato sauce. The sure star of the meal was the chocolate tart, a delicate layer of pastry topped with a thick and soothing ganache, paired with a light chocolate sorbet. When a simple café or wine-bar meal can easily cost way more than 22€, Abri is definitely worth the *métro* ride.

LE GALOPIN

MODERN BISTRO
34, rue Sainte-Marthe
Paris 10
TEL: +33 1 42 06 05 03
le-galopin.com
MÉTRO: Belleville or Colonel Fabien
OPEN: Dinner only Tuesday through Saturday

CLOSED: Lunchtime daily and all day Sunday
and Monday. Closed April 23 to May 14 and
Christmas.
PRICES: 46€ fixed menu, no à la carte.
RESERVATIONS: Essential
ATMOSPHERE: Casual

Top Chef star Romain Tischenko rose to bistro stardom right off the bat with his bare-bones, 20-seat bistro overlooking the quiet place Saint-Marthe in the bobo (bohemian-bourgeois) land's 10th *arrondissement.* It may not be worth a trip across town, but modern bistro-hoppers can't get enough of this ultra-lean chef's contemporary fare. A visit to taste the evening-only *dégustation* (tasting) menu will find a very democratic group of diners, young and old, with fork and knife and satisfied postures, watching Tischenko cooking his heart out in the small, open kitchen. The chef is a fish lover, so on any given day—the menu changes daily—you may find the likes of wild *daurade* (porgy) with the pungent Japanese citrus *yuzu,* or organic codfish (*kbio*) soothingly paired with wild *lactaire* mushrooms, garlic, and a touch of citrus. I loved the warming, giant ravioli stuffed with tender white *merlu* (whiting), with a touch of shellfish broth. The giant duck breast was cooked to a rare perfection, teamed with wintry beets and Brussels sprouts. Desserts are divine, with a lovely al dente *riz au lait* (rice pudding) and a finely poached pear served with walnuts and touch of goat-cheese sorbet. Marcel Richaud's always dependable Côtes-du-Rhône is on the wine list, so go for it. (By the way, this Galopin has no relationship to the brasserie of the same name in the 2nd *arrondissement.*)

CHEZ MICHEL

CLASSIC BISTRO / BRETON

10, rue de Belzunce
Paris 10
TEL: +33 1 44 53 06 20
MÉTRO: Gare du Nord or Poissonnière
OPEN: Monday dinner through Friday

CLOSED: Monday lunch, Saturday and Sunday, July 20 to August 20, and December 20 to 30
PRICES: 28€ lunch menu and 34€ dinner menu
RESERVATIONS: Essential
ATMOSPHERE: Casual
SPECIALTIES: Game, cheese tray

Chez Michel, long a popular bistro just steps from the Gare du Nord, is an ideal spot for a meal just as you are leaving Paris, or for a celebratory return to the city. There is much to love about this small, classic bistro. Chef-owner Thierry Breton clearly knows who he is and what he wants, and offers impeccable ingredients—a recent spring starter of white and green asparagus, *morilles* (morels) in a mushroom broth, and a poached egg was truly satisfying—some of the best baked-on-the-premises bread in town (perhaps the best country rye bread to be found for kilometers), and a changing blackboard menu that's so varied, every diner should find something to his or her liking. In winter months you'll find every sort of game (from wild boar, duck, and rabbit prepared in a variety of ways) and always fresh fish and shellfish from Breton's native Brittany (from briny oysters and plump fresh scallops to wild *Barreau*—similar to sea bass). Desserts are classic and generous, and the sticky, caramelized *tarte Tatin* is one of the best you'll find on any bistro menu. Breton's recently revised menu prices make this rustic bistro a great value, but beware of the supplement prices on many of the menu's dishes, which can really hike up the bill.

PHILOU

MODERN BISTRO
12, avenue Richerand
Paris 10
TEL: +33 1 42 38 00 13
MÉTRO: Goncourt or Jacques Bonsergent
OPEN: Tuesday through Saturday

CLOSED: Sunday and Monday
PRICES: 19€ lunch menu, 27 and 34€ dinner menus, no à la carte
RESERVATIONS: Recommended
ATMOSPHERE: Casual

M odern Parisian bistros know no bounds these days. There is no way that diners ate better in the "good old days." Today food is fresher, unmasked, and more wholesome. The bright and lively Philou, home of Philippe Damas (last seen at Square Trousseau) is a case in point. Damas offers old-time ingredients—like pigs' cheeks and calf's liver—and serves them up with a simplicity and freshness that is thoroughly appealing. He pairs slow-cooked, moist, and meaty pigs' cheeks with a tangy celery root *boulangère* (baked in a gratin dish with nothing but chicken stock until all the stock is absorbed) and cooks calf's liver like a giant piece of meat, with a deeply seared outer crust and moist, rosy interior (see recipe, page 92). I also loved the beautifully marinated fresh sardines, paired with a julienne of apples and set on a bed of warm, baked potatoes. The choice of wines is excellent. Try the superb Domaine de la Vieille Julienne Côtes du Rhône, which could easily pass as a Châteauneuf-du-Pape. This tiny place off the Canal Saint-Martin is super-loud and super-fun.

▼ *At Philou, diners settle in for a modern bistro meal.*

FOIE DE VEAU DE PHILOU

Philou's Seared and Roasted Calf's Liver

I still remember a dish of calf's liver that I sampled for lunch in a Paris bistro sometime in the early 1980s. It was served whole and roasted with a thick, impressive coating of coarsely ground black pepper. The presentation was dramatic and such a change of pace from the thin, shoe leather–like version one finds in more traditional preparations. More recently, a similar preparation turned up at the popular Paris bistro Philou. Here the chef treats the liver like meat, searing, seasoning, then roasting to a rare perfection.

INGREDIENTS:

1 tablespoon (½ ounce; 15 g) unsalted butter

1 tablespoon best-quality vegetable oil

1 pound (500 g) fresh calf's liver in a single piece

Fine sea salt

Coarse, freshly ground black pepper

1. Center a rack in the oven. Preheat the oven to 425°F (220°C).

2. In a skillet just large enough to hold the liver, melt the butter in the oil over medium heat. Increase heat to high and add the liver. Sear it well on all sides, about 1 minute per side. Season generously with salt and pepper.

3. Transfer the liver to a roasting pan just large enough to hold it. Roast until firm and cooked to desired doneness, about 20 minutes for medium-rare, longer for medium or well-cooked. Season once again with pepper. Cut the liver into thick slices and serve on warmed dinner plates.

4 SERVINGS

▶ *Philippe Damas, owner of Philou.*

11ᵀᴴ ARRONDISSEMENT

LE 6 PAUL BERT

MODERN BISTRO
6, rue Paul Bert
Paris 11
TEL: +33 1 43 79 14 32
MÉTRO: Faidherbe-Chaligny, Rue des Boulets, or Charonne
OPEN: Lunch Tuesday through Friday, dinner Monday through Friday

CLOSED: Saturday, Sunday, Monday lunch and August
PRICES: 18 and 19€ lunch menus, 38 and 44€ dinner menus, no à la carte
RESERVATIONS: Essential
ATMOSPHERE: Smart-casual

Just down the street from the now legendary Bistro Paul Bert, this combination wine bar and *épicerie* is a welcome addition to the city's growing number of casual, well-priced eateries. Owner Bertrand Auboyneau hits another home run here, offering such tasty treats as asparagus with black truffles, crispy skinned *porcelet* (suckling pig), and tender, grilled squid in a vibrant herb oil. Natural wines are featured here, including the always reliable offerings from Domaine Gramenon.

ASTIER

CLASSIC BISTRO
44, rue Jean-Pierre Timbaud
Paris 11
TEL: +33 1 43 57 16 35
restaurant-astier.com
MÉTRO: Parmentier or Oberkampf
OPEN: Daily

CLOSED: December 25, January 1
PRICES: 23.50, 29.50, and 39€ lunch menus. 35 and 45€ dinner menus. À la carte 25 to 35€ at lunch and dinner.
RESERVATIONS: Recommended
ATMOSPHERE: Casual
SPECIALTIES: Cheese tray

This lovely old-time bistro in Paris is a longtime favorite, just off the place de la République. My best memories of a recent dinner include the classic favorite *lapin à la moutarde* (slow-cooked rabbit with mustard sauce) and the more than generous cheese tray, a tradition that, alas, is slowly dying.

We were greeted at the door by a handsome 40-something gentleman with jet-black hair and a winning smile. My friend and I smiled as the daily specials appeared on a blackboard set before us. The choices were SEASONAL, in caps! The season was autumn and all sorts of wild game were on offer—partridge, wild hare, venison—along with cured herring fresh from the market, autumnal quince, and, of course, fresh scallops from Brittany. We were overwhelmed. But after conferring, we opted to try the smoked young herring and agreed it was truly the best ever. All too often herring is too salty, too smoky, too rich. This had a silken quality, and was anointed with just the faintest hint of smoke. Served, of course, in a classic rectangular white porcelain terrine, with tiny potatoes that I found just a bit on the bland side. I chose another starter of rabbit *rillettes*, moist, flavorful, not too fatty, and served with giant pink pickled shallots, a recipe I need to perfect ASAP! The roasted codfish wrapped in ham and served with fresh white shell beans and a touch of tomato offered a lovely, light touch, and the dessert of poached quince hit the spot. You will find all the bistro classics: asparagus with poached egg; Lyonnais sausage with warm sliced potatoes; grilled *entrecôte* with anchovy butter; pork breast braised in hay; and *tête de veau,* or calf's head, with a brilliant sauce *ravigote.* There are good wines, too, including Jean Foillard Morgon Côte du Py, Ghislaine Barthod Burgundy, and Maxime Graillot Domaine des Lises Crozes-Hermitage. Run, don't walk, to Astier, and be sure to look in at their lovely *épicerie*/restaurant/carryout, Jeanne A (see Cafés and Casual Bites, page 162) with a rotisserie right next door.

BONES

MODERN BISTRO / MODERN INTERNATIONAL
43, rue Godefroy Cavaignac
Paris 11
TEL: +33 9 80 75 32 08
bonesparis.com
contact@bonesparis.com
MÉTRO: Voltaire

OPEN: Dinner only, Tuesday through Saturday
CLOSED: Sunday and Monday
PRICES: 47€ fixed menu; no à la carte in the restaurant. 3 to 12€ small plates at the bar.
RESERVATIONS: Essential (from two weeks in advance)
ATMOSPHERE: Casual

Young Australian chef James Henry first made waves in the Paris restaurant scene with his inventive small-plate dishes at Au Passage. After a two-week temporary position that turned into a year running the kitchen, and put Au Passage on the culinary map of Paris, Henry has now branched out with his own restaurant, Bones, in one of Paris's most "culinary" neighborhoods. Henry stripped back an Irish pub to its bare bones (hence the name of the restaurant) and the result is a raw and relaxed neo-bistro space segmented in two with the dining room and open kitchen in the rear, and a well-laid-out bar space at the front, where you can order oysters, *charcuterie*, and wine by the glass or bottle. In the main dining room Henry offers an *à la carte* menu showcasing his talent for inventive seasonal fare, in which the produce is the star of the plate: green asparagus, anchovies, and Pecorino (sheep's-milk) cheese; barbecued smoked oysters; or for the more adventurous, veal heart, marrow, and shiitake mushrooms. Time spent in the kitchen of Andrew MacDonald at Cumulus Inc. in Melbourne, and cooking in remote Tasmania, has informed his honest locavore approach. Henry is serious about cooking seasonally and locally when possible, sourcing the best ingredients France has to offer from the likes of Terroir d'Avenir (see Specialty Food Shops, page 339) and Joël Thiebault (see Marché Président Wilson, page 202). He even makes his own *charcuterie*, butter, and bread. Wines are low in sulphite and are sourced from small producers, handpicked by *sommelier* Pierre Derrien. I loved Pierre's recommendation of the Burgundy from Fanny Sarbre. Expect loud music from the bar, super-friendly and unpretentious service, and a reservations waiting list of at least a week.

GLACE AU LAIT RIBOT DU DAUPHIN

Le Dauphin's Buttermilk Sorbet
with Fresh Thyme and Olive Oil

Basque chef Inaki Aizpitarte is one of the most sought-after chefs in Paris, and his two restaurants, Le Dauphin and Chateaubriand, are highly desired tables. I love both places and after one visit to Le Dauphin, I returned home to re-create the flavors of his memorable buttermilk sorbet, sprinkled with fresh thyme leaves and a touch of fruity olive oil. A surprise as well as a pleasure.

EQUIPMENT:

A food processor or a blender; an ice-cream maker; 8 ice-cream bowls, chilled in the freezer

INGREDIENTS:

⅓ cup (80 ml) freshly squeezed lemon juice

Grated zest of 1 lemon, preferably organic

¾ cup (185 ml) honey

2 cups (500 ml) buttermilk, shaken to blend

2 teaspoons fresh thyme leaves, stemmed

About 2 tablespoons extra-virgin olive oil

In the food processor or blender, combine the lemon juice, zest, and honey. Pulse to blend. Add the buttermilk and pulse again. Chill thoroughly. Transfer to the ice-cream maker and freeze according to manufacturer's instructions. At serving time, divide the sorbet among the chilled bowls and garnish each portion with thyme leaves and olive oil.

8 SERVINGS

SBRISOLONA DE CAFFÉ DEI CIOPPI

Caffé dei Cioppi's Almond Cookie-Cake

Not a cookie, not a cake, but as pastry goes, this crunchy, rich almond delight is one of the world's most delicious and appealing sweets. The owners of the tiny Italian Caffé dei Cioppi—Fabrizio Ferrara and Federica Manicioppi—offer up fat meatballs and great pastas, as well as this delicacy, a specialty of Verona in Italy.

EQUIPMENT:

A food processor;
a baking sheet lined
with baking parchment

INGREDIENTS:

10 ounces (300 g)
unblanched whole
almonds

2½ cups (360 g)
unbleached all-
purpose flour

⅞ cup (225 g) quick-
cooking polenta

2½ sticks (20
tablespoons; 300 g)
unsalted butter,
melted

1½ cups (300 g) organic
unrefined cane sugar

1 large egg and 1 egg yolk,
preferably free-range
and organic, lightly
beaten

Grated zest of 1 lemon,
preferably organic

½ teaspoon pure vanilla
extract

¾ teaspoon fine sea salt

40 SERVINGS

1. Center a rack in the oven. Preheat the oven to 350°F (180°C).

2. In the bowl of the food processor, coarsely chop the almonds.

3. In a large bowl, combine the almonds, flour, and polenta. Toss to blend.

4. In another large bowl, combine the butter, sugar, egg, egg yolk, lemon zest, vanilla extract, and salt, and stir to blend. Add the dry ingredients to the liquid ingredients and stir to combine until the mixture is well blended. The texture should be like that of a thick cookie dough.

5. Rub the dough between your hands and let it drop onto the baking sheet, so that it covers the entire rectangular sheet.

6. Place the baking sheet in the oven and bake the cake until it is deep golden and crisp, 20 to 30 minutes. Remove to a baking rack to cool. Let cool at least 20 minutes before serving. This crumbly almond cake is not cut with a knife but simply broken into pieces with your fingers. The cake keeps well, and can be stored in an air-tight container for several weeks.

LE CHATEAUBRIAND

MODERN BISTRO
129, avenue Parmentier
Paris 11
TEL: +33 1 43 57 45 95
lechateaubriand.net
anomalia@voila.fr
MÉTRO: Goncourt
OPEN: Dinner only, Tuesday through Saturday

CLOSED: Sunday, Monday, and Christmas week
PRICE: 60€ fixed menu, no à la carte
RESERVATIONS: Essential for 7:30 to 8:30PM seating (from two weeks in advance); no reservations for 9:30PM seating (groups of 4 people maximum). Call between 3 and 7:30PM.
ATMOSPHERE: Casual

Thank goodness for chefs like Inaki Aizpitarte, the Basque-born chef of this lively neo-bistro in the 11th. With flair and strong, forward flavors, he redefines modern bistro cooking, challenging diners to open their minds and their palates. What's that coffee bean doing in my golden pumpkin broth? Why are there poppy seeds on my *gougères* (cheese puffs)? Who let him turn a *ceviche* into a citrus-filled "shooter"? Why not marry a cucumber *granité* with just a murmur of soothing crabmeat? There are bright flavors and brilliant combinations all around. And he's a magician with a mandolin, slicing everything—a turnip, an onion, a wedge of Basque sheep's-milk cheese—into ethereal thinness to eke out maximum flavor from each ingredient. And dessert does not have to be sweet: Take some soft, fresh buttermilk—*lait ribot*—and top it with a garnish of mint and coriander. Inspired it is! And just a bit crazy. On one of my visits, a couple walked out because they didn't want a no-choice menu. I'd put Aizpitarte in charge of my palate any day. Service is ultra-friendly, the wine list a mystery, loaded with so-called natural wines that I have yet to embrace. Though you'll find some sure bets, such as Gramenon's dependable Viognier (Vie On Y Est) and Foillard's all-purpose Morgon.

CAFFÉ DEI CIOPPI

ITALIAN
159 rue du Faubourg Saint-Antoine
(passage Saint-Bernard)
Paris 11
TEL: +33 1 43 46 10 14
METRO: Faidherbe-Chaligny or Ledru-Rollin

OPEN: Tuesday through Friday
CLOSED: Saturday, Sunday, three weeks in August, and two weeks over Christmas
PRICES: À la carte 30 to 40€ lunch and dinner
RESERVATIONS: Essential
ATMOSPHERE: Casual

Once you watch owners Fabrizio Ferrara and Federica Mancioppi juggle casseroles in their tiny kitchen, you will never again have the right to self-pity about your cramped cooking quarters. With tables for just 14 diners, plus a quartet of mismatched stools at a makeshift bar, this is more of an elbow-to-elbow diner than restaurant. But eager diners flock to this disheveled 11th *arrondissement passage* for the steaming bowls of fat macaroni and meatballs, platters of smoked mozzarella served with a *confit* trio of winter vegetables, and the rarely seen dessert popular in the Verona region of Italy, *sbrisolona*, a rich almond and butter cookie-cake that should be enshrined in a special food museum as one of the world's great simple desserts (see recipe, facing page).

L'ÉCAILLER DU BISTROT

FISH AND SHELLFISH
22, rue Paul Bert
Paris 11
TEL: +33 1 43 72 76 77
MÉTRO: Faidherbe-Chaligny or Rue des
Boulets
OPEN: Tuesday through Saturday

CLOSED: Sunday, Monday, and August
PRICES: 19€ weekday lunch menu. 55€ lobster
menu. À la carte 40 to 60€.
RESERVATIONS: Essential for dinner
ATMOSPHERE: Casual
SPECIALTIES: *Plateau de fruits de mer*
(seafood platter), oysters

Anyone searching for the freshest of fish and shellfish simply but expertly prepared should reserve a table at the charming and always jovial L'Écailler du Bistrot, run by the outgoing Gwen Cadoret. She's the wife of bistrotier Bertrand Auboyneau, with his great and classic Bistrot Paul Bert (see facing page) right next door. Come here for the briny oysters and other treasures from Gwen's home port of Guilvinec in Brittany. Treats I have loved include an impeccable *tartare* of *bar* (sea bass), and the state-of-the-art *sole meunière*. The wine list offers many fish-friendly choices, and the adorable blue-and-white tilefish bistro decor is sure to please. The generous *plateau de fruits de mer* (platter of raw and cooked shellfish) is one of the best in town. If available, try the rare *Spéciales #3*, tiny oysters with a faint hint of hazelnuts, or the Utah Beach #3, plump and iodine-rich. From October to May, don't miss the giant scallops (*coquilles Saint-Jacques*) prepared in many ways. A favorite is lightly roasted in the shell—they're trembling, tender, and a treat.

LE MANSOURIA

MOROCCAN
11, rue Faidherbe
Paris 11
TEL: +33 1 43 71 00 16
mansouria.fr
contact@mansouria.fr
MÉTRO: Faidherbe-Chaligny
OPEN: For lunch Wednesday through Saturday

and dinner Monday through Saturday
CLOSED: Sunday, Monday lunch, Tuesday
lunch, May 1, and for lunch in August
PRICES: 28 and 36€ lunch and dinner menus.
À la carte 40€.
RESERVATIONS: Recommended
ATMOSPHERE: Smart-casual
SPECIALTIES: Couscous, *tagine*

Take a little trip to Morocco with this cheery, vibrant restaurant first opened by chef Fatéma Hal in 1985. The decor takes you away from the bright lights of Paris and into a series of intimate rooms colored in vivid yellow, red, and orange. The menu here offers something for everyone and allows you to sample a variety of Moroccan specialties. The 28€ menu *Diaffa* will lead you to the flaky *briwatte au fromage*, triangular pastries laced with fresh goat's-milk cheese and mint; the fragrant vegetable couscous laden with colorful vegetables; or the generous chicken *tagines*, flavored with plump olives and pungent lemon *confit*. A favorite is the *tagine mourouzia*, a stunning, well-seasoned, lamb-based *tagine*, based on a 17th-century recipe. The meat is flavored with the authentic *ras el hanout*, composed of some 27 different spices and cooked in a thick and fragrant honey sauce, accompanied by raisins and almonds. Service is friendly and efficient, and you'll be sure to want to return to sample more of Fatéma's litany of specialties.

▲ *A rainy, romantic night in Paris.*

BISTROT PAUL BERT

CLASSIC BISTRO
18, rue Paul Bert
Paris 11
TEL: +33 1 43 72 24 01
bistrotpaulbert@gmail.com
MÉTRO: Faidherbe-Chaligny or
Rue des Boulets
OPEN: Tuesday through Saturday

CLOSED: Sunday, Monday, August, and
December 24 and 25
PRICES: 19€ lunch menus. 38€ lunch and
dinner menu. À la carte 35 to 50€.
RESERVATIONS: Essential
(only taken 15 days in advance)
ATMOSPHERE: Casual
SPECIALTIES: *Steak frites*, game, *soufflés*,
Paris-Brest, macarons

I n another life, should I come back as a restaurant, I'd like to be the Bistrot Paul Bert, my idea of the quintessential Paris bistro. There's the larger-than-life owner Bertrand Auboyneau holding court, cajoling customers, behind the bar. This classic, old-fashioned eatery with an intelligent modern touch is exceptional for a lot of reasons, but what really stands out are the impeccable ingredients prepared with flair and care. While meat and game reign here, fish lovers will also find a good selection, such as *sole meunière* or scallops roasted whole in their shell. Here, each seasonal ingredient is treated with reverence and respect: slim asparagus in spring, all manner of wild mushrooms and game in autumn, the wonderful winter black truffle come December. Bistrot Paul Bert's classic version of *steak frites* is among the best in town. I have returned again and again for the roasted baby pork (*cochon de lait*) and creative salads—a favorite is their crunchy, colorful vegetable salad that includes ethereally thin slices of heirloom yellow and orange carrots, multihued red-and-white beets, a thin julienne of raw asparagus, and a toned-down dressing that allows the vegetables to shine. Also on the menu: fresh morel mushrooms surrounding a duet of perfectly fried eggs, their famed sweet *Paris-Brest,* and a newer entry, gigantic macarons. The food, the authentic old-bistro decor, and the sounds of good times all make this well worth the journey. The wine list is extensive and includes some favorites, including the meaty Rhône reds from Domaine Gramenon, and Lucien Crochet's citrusy Sancerre.

AU PIED DE FOUET (Oberkampf)

CLASSIC BISTRO
96, rue Oberkampf
Paris 11
TEL: +33 1 48 06 46 98
aupieddefouet.com
MÉTRO: Rue Saint-Maur

OPEN: Monday through Friday, and Saturday dinner
CLOSED: Saturday lunch and Sunday
PRICE: À la carte 24€
RESERVATIONS: Not taken
ATMOSPHERE: Casual

A bustling little restaurant where you will find all kinds of classic bistro fare. See page 47 for full commentary.

SASSOTONDO

ITALIAN
40, rue Jean-Pierre Timbaud
Paris 11
TEL: +33 1 43 55 57 00
sassotondo.com
reservations@sassotondo.com
MÉTRO: Parmentier or Oberkampf

OPEN: Thursday through Monday
CLOSED: Tuesday, Wednesday, and August
PRICES: 16 and 34€ lunch menus.
34€ dinner menu. À la carte 30 to 40€.
RESERVATIONS: Recommended
ATMOSPHERE: Smart-casual

Restaurateur Fréderic Hubig (of the fine classic Bistro Astier; the modern bistro Café Moderne; and Jeanne A, the *épicerie*/rotisserie/restaurant where you can dine in or take your food away) has another hit on his hands with Sassotondo, a comfortable, casual, lively spot they call a *taverne Toscane.* There's everything to love about this place: the easygoing setting; the partially open kitchen that lets you sort of keep an eye on the action; the friendly Tuscan chef, Michele Dalla Valle; and the outgoing, well-informed, and friendly *sommelier,* Sicilian Gianluca de Simone. You can go for just a platter of the excellent Viani-brand *charcuterie* from San Gimignano, or try the *dégustation* menu upon request for the table. The brief menu changes regularly, but if it's on the menu that night go for the *gnocchi del casentino,* bite-size ricotta and spinach gnocchi bathing happily in a fine, delicate stock. I could have had two portions and called it dinner! But then I might have missed the *sella e carre di agnello da latte con carote,* moist, tender, delicate milk-fed lamb chops and saddle served with full-flavored carrots grown in sandy soil, giving them a character other carrots simply can't achieve. The all-Italian wine list offers some real treasures. Do try the Lazio Cori Rosso Capolemole, a red from central Italy, made from old vines and old varieties rarely seen. Rich, vibrant, well balanced. Don't think twice about Sassotondo. Go!

SEPTIME

MODERN BISTRO
80, rue de Charonne
Paris 11
TEL: +33 1 43 67 38 29
septime-charonne.fr
MÉTRO: Charonne or Ledru-Rollin
OPEN: Monday dinner through Friday

CLOSED: Monday lunch, Saturday, Sunday, the last week of July, and the first three weeks of August
PRICES: 28€ lunch menu. 55€ lunch and dinner menus. No à la carte.
RESERVATIONS: Essential. Reservations taken by phone 10AM to noon and 5:30 to 7PM only.
ATMOSPHERE: Casual

On the Paris food scene since May 2011, this industrial-chic bistro in the 11th *arrondissement* has become the home of young chef Bertrand Grébaut, who cut his teeth in some substantial kitchens, like those of Joël Robuchon and Alain Passard. Freshness of produce and simplicity on the plate mark his calling card, and both were much in evidence on a chilly January afternoon. A *tartare* of veal was given a salty hit by an unusual but successful pairing with oysters, topped with a smooth potato puree—an excellent mix of clean, bright flavors with the comfort of creamy potatoes. A mound of crisp, thinly shaved *héliantis* (a root vegetable much like a Jerusalem artichoke) sat atop a creamy *héliantis* puree, balanced by a finely seasoned cider vinaigrette and finished off with a generous helping of shaved *foie gras*. The *pluma* (a cut of pork from near the animal's neck) was tender and buttery, served with seasonal root vegetables and a sweet squash puree. *Merlan* (whiting) was cooked to a delicate perfection, elevated by a rich mussel and tandoori emulsion. The dessert—one to re-create at home—arrived as a refreshing combination of orange segments, mandarin and orange sorbet, lemon curd topped with a crunchy, nutty crumble, and a teaspoon of buttermilk ice cream (*glace lait ribot*) to round it off. When we asked for an end-of-meal herbal tea, we were presented with a glass flask filled with fresh-cut thyme, rosemary, orange, lemon rind, and lemon leaves that made for the perfect end to a very satisfying meal. Service was a bit slow, but understandable considering the packed dining room, and was made up for by the warm attention we were given when we were served.

LE SOT-L'Y-LAISSE

MODERN BISTRO
70, rue Alexandre Dumas
Paris 11
TEL: +33 1 40 09 79 20
MÉTRO: Alexandre Dumas or Rue des Boulets
OPEN: Monday through Saturday

CLOSED: Monday and Saturday lunch, Sunday, between Christmas and New Year, and two weeks in August
PRICES: 18 and 24€ lunch menu. À la carte 50€.
RESERVATIONS: Recommended
ATMOSPHERE: Casual

Japanese-born chef Eiji Doihara has been at the helm of this tiny, 20-seat classic Parisian bistro since October 2011, and has quickly found a loyal following. No wonder. His food is honest, authoritative, distinctive, and, in truth, a welcome change from the sameness of many of the new, overblown, wunderkind, blog-buster spots. I love the restaurant's name, Le Sot-l'y-Laisse, which translates as "a fool leaves it," referring to the moist, tender nuggets of meat tucked into the hollow of the bone on the back side of poultry, also known as "oysters." Of course they are served here as a delicious first course mixed with mushrooms and a creamy broth. I love his rendition of oysters, the real kind, poached in a clear bouillon and teamed with a duet of parsley bouquets wrapped in ham, a brilliant idea and one that succeeds on the plate and the palate. Lovers of classic bistro fare will adore his succulent *pieds de porc* (pigs' feet) wrapped in caul fat and set in a pool of carefully seasoned lentils, a fine cold-weather dish if ever there was one. The chef is a master of searing and grilling and intelligently treats vegetables like meat or fish, grilling thin crosswise slices of leeks so they take on a smoky richness. He sears tender *rascasse* (scorpion fish) on just one side, adding intense color and flavor at the same time. The *rascasse* was set in a cream of celery root, surrounded by a welcome chorus of roasted spring onions, halved and grilled Brussels sprouts, and leaves of Swiss chard that had been "burnt" on the grill to a pleasant crisp. The wholesome sourdough bread comes from baker Rodolphe Landemaine and tea and coffee from the dependable house of Verlet. The decor here is simple, 1950s bistro with large mirrors on the walls, bare wooden tables, and bottles of wine to serve as the wine list. Reserve in advance, and enjoy!

UNICO

ARGENTINE STEAKHOUSE
15, rue Paul Bert
Paris 11
TEL: +33 1 43 67 68 08
resto-unico.com
unico@resto-unico.com
MÉTRO: Faidherbe-Chaligny or Rue des Boulets

OPEN: Tuesday lunch through Saturday. Monday dinner through Saturday 8 to 10:30PM.
CLOSED: Sunday and Monday lunch
PRICES: 17€ lunch menu. À la carte 25 to 45€.
RESERVATIONS: Recommended
ATMOSPHERE: Casual

L ooking for the perfect steak? You needn't look any further than Unico, the Argentine steakhouse on rue Paul Bert. Transformed from a 1970s *boucherie* and complete with original brown wall tiles and cabinetry, this is the perfect setting for one of the best steakhouses in Paris, where the steaks are buttery, tender, and full of flavor. The starters menu offers several Argentine specialties: empanadas (breaded chicken, meat, and corn), *ceviche* (marinated fish), Argentine sausage, and charcoal-grilled bone marrow. Steak, mostly Argentine Angus beef, except for a few cuts of choice French beef, is all that is on the main menu here. The beef comes from young animals, 24 to 36 months of age, which accounts for its tenderness. Steaks are ordered by the cut, cooked Argentine-style on a wood charcoal grill, and served with *chimichurri* sauce and aioli, and a choice of potato wedges, grilled vegetables, or salad. They recommend ordering steaks *à point*, or medium rare, as served in Argentina. For those who like their meat well cooked, order the filet, which is slightly fattier, stands up best to longer cooking, and so remains extremely tender. And for those rare vegetarians who are willing to accompany their meat-eating pals to such a place, large vegetarian salads are also on the menu.

LE VILLARET

CLASSIC BISTRO
13, rue Ternaux
Paris 11
TEL: +33 1 43 57 89 76
MÉTRO: Parmentier or Oberkampf
OPEN: Monday through Friday, and Saturday dinner
CLOSED: Saturday lunch, Sunday, holidays, Christmas week and New Year's, and three weeks in August

PRICES: 20 and 25€ lunch menus. 32€ dinner menu. 55€ *dégustation* (tasting) menu. À la carte 50 to 60€ at lunch and dinner. 95€ truffle menu in season (late November to March).
RESERVATIONS: Recommended
ATMOSPHERE: Casual
SPECIALTIES: Game, roast chicken, black truffles

You'll enter this crisp, lively bistro set on a dreary side street in the 11th *arrondissement* and announce, if only to yourself, "This is the bistro I have been dreaming of for years." From the elegant, high-back 1930s chairs, to the friendly, unpretentious attitude, the place is a gem. Chef Olivier Gaslain serves an ideal mix of classic and modern bistro fare, with an ever-changing assortment of classics such as *sole meunière*, a chicken *pot-au-feu*, an always-reliable and delicious salmon *tartare*, and leg of lamb, though each is treated with a contemporary freshness. A favorite is a powerfully satisfying medley of root vegetables—turnips and salsify, standard artichokes and Jerusalem artichokes—bathed in a deep, dense poultry stock, showered with chives and draped with a paper-thin slice of *foie gras*. Delicious! It's a dream dish, served in a simple white bowl with the restaurant's spectacular dense, crusty country bread. Other winners include a duo of artichokes and asparagus, cooked in that same intense stock and topped with a perfect poached egg; a trio of salmon preparations (a well-seasoned *tartare*, a pair of *brochettes*, a delicately cured filet), and an Asian-inspired dish of oyster ravioli with fresh coriander. I couldn't get enough of the roasted country chicken, set on a bed of curly green cabbage and covered in a creamy sauce made with the sherry-like Arbois wine from the Jura. The chicken was moist, firm, and well flavored, and the potato *galette* served with it made for pure crunchy pleasure. The lamb shoulder arrives in a polished copper pot, with meat that's perfectly roasted and set on a bed of potatoes, turnips, and broad beans. Leg of lamb is served with giant white beans (on one visit marred by an excess of salt), and the hearty veal breast comes with chanterelles and smooth broad beans. During truffle season, from late November to March, they also offer a truffle menu that includes a truffle-studded *croque monsieur*. The wine list gives goose bumps to wine lovers and is worth a *métro* ticket all on its own, with a broad and well-priced selection of Burgundies. In short, this is a caring, spotless place to put on your to-try list. Or your let's-go-again list.

12TH ARRONDISSEMENT

À LA BICHE AU BOIS

CLASSIC BISTRO
45, avenue Ledru-Rollin
Paris 12
TEL: +33 1 43 43 34 38
MÉTRO: Gare de Lyon or Quai de la Rapée
OPEN: Monday dinner through Friday

CLOSED: All day Saturday, Sunday, and Monday lunch
PRICE: 19 and 24.50€ lunch menus, 29.80€ fixed menu. À la carte 35€ at lunch and dinner.
RESERVATIONS: Recommended
ATMOSPHERE: Casual
SPECIALTIES: *Steak frites*, game, cheese tray

À la Biche au Bois is one restaurant where you definitely get what you came for: hearty food, good wine, a super-generous cheese platter, and classic desserts. Whether you're in the mood for *biche* (young female deer) or *canard sauvage* (wild duck), this classic welcoming bistro is sure to please.

The soothing potato puree (made with the firm, golden Agatha variety of potatoes and 10 percent butter, or so the waiter assured me) is worth the detour all on its own. So is the sumptuous cheese tray, with treasures stacked one on top of the other, with favorites Brie, raw-milk Camembert, and *bleu de Causses* all in perfect ripeness. There's a parade of terrines—rabbit, duck, or a mix of meats—all classic and rich, all outdoing one another. I don't remember the last time I saw *coq au vin* on a menu, but you'll find it here, meaty and bathed in a vibrant red wine sauce. Oh, and yes, the chocolate mousse is the reason you come to Paris to dine. If the always-reliable Clos du Caillou Côtes du Rhône is still on the wine list, go for it. The meaty red is a worthy stand-in for a Châteauneuf-du-Pape. This is a bistro where you'll find a mixed crowd, from the well-fed national railroad conductor to youthful locals to happy tourists, all feasting on treasures of the day.

AU TROU GASCON

CLASSIC FRENCH SOUTHWESTERN
40, rue Taine
Paris 12
TEL: +33 1 43 44 34 26
autrougascon.fr
MÉTRO: Daumesnil
OPEN: Monday through Friday

CLOSED: Saturday, Sunday, August, and Christmas week
PRICES: 40 to 58€ lunch menus. 62€ dinner menu. À la carte 60 to 80€.
RESERVATIONS: Recommended
ATMOSPHERE: Smart-casual
SPECIALTIES: *Cassoulet*, game, *foie gras*, wild mushrooms

There are days when your spouse wants a hearty *cassoulet* (that famous concoction of fat white beans, rich duck *confit*, lamb chops, and pork sausage) but you're in the mood for something light and seasonal, such as a delicate last-minute *tartare* of rich sea scallops, bathed in an emulsion of artichokes and Swiss chard. That's when to reserve a table at Nicole and Alain Dutournier's compact dining room off place Daumesnil in the 12th *arrondissement*. I adored the scallop *tartare,* cut into cubes just big enough to enjoy their texture, a refreshing dish that perfectly suited my mood. Next came a generous dish of the tiniest, brightest-orange, most flavorful *girolles* (chanterelles) I have ever tasted—perfectly seared (not soggy, mushy, or laden in oil as they often are served), topped with a fine poached egg, all runny and tender as a gift package when I broke it over the mushrooms. Equally successful is the *crevettes qwehli à la plaque,* giant bright-pink organic farm-raised shrimp from Madagascar, seared and bathed in a rich shellfish broth I would be proud to make. *Foie gras* lovers will adore the version here, seared and served with a tangy quince *confit.* Also notable is the unique Southwestern *tourtière,* the warm, flaky-crusted dessert filled with apples and served with a winning salted-caramel ice cream. The only disappointment of the meal was the famous duck *confit*—just a bit too dry and stringy, and served with a small potato gratin that was a bit too fatty. As ever, we adored the Jurançon Sec Cuvée Marie from Clos Uroulat, a crisp, nicely acidic, full-bodied white, a star of the Southwest made with the Gros Manseng grape.

14TH ARRONDISSEMENT

LE DÔME

BRASSERIE
108, boulevard du Montparnasse
Paris 14
TEL: +33 1 43 35 25 81
MÉTRO: Vavin
OPEN: Daily
CLOSED: Sunday and Monday from mid-July to end of August

PRICES: À la carte 80 to 100€ at lunch and dinner
RESERVATIONS: Recommended
ATMOSPHERE: Smart-casual
SPECIALTIES: Oysters, fish and shellfish, *sole meunière*

love the beginning of a season and *hate* it when it ends. That's the story with oysters, best of course in months with an "R." So on Sundays in season—from September to April—I feast on plump *huitres Tsarskaya* from the oyster beds off Cancale. Huge, meaty, slightly briny, with a hint of hazelnuts. For more than 30 years, my husband and I have made Le Dôme our Sunday lunch restaurant, always loving the ambience of the well-lit terrace, the friendly *maître d's* Jacques and Stéphane. Following the oysters, there is always a perfect *sole meunière*, noble turbot, or glistening Saint-Pierre filleted tableside. All you need is a touch of fragrant extra-virgin olive oil and a squeeze of lemon to send you off to gustatory heaven.

LE DUC

FISH AND SHELLFISH
243, boulevard Raspail
Paris 14
TEL: +33 1 43 20 96 30
MÉTRO: Raspail
OPEN: Tuesday through Saturday

CLOSED: Saturday lunch, Sunday, Monday, 2 weeks in August, and two weeks over Christmas
PRICES: 55€ lunch menu. À la carte 90 to 110€ at lunch and dinner.
RESERVATIONS: Essential
ATMOSPHERE: Smart-casual

Diners with a bent toward nostalgia will love this clubby, wood-paneled dining room designed to resemble a luxury yacht, where since 1967 fish and shellfish oh-so-simply prepared are the order of the day. When your *tartare* of *Saint-Jacques* (sea scallops) arrives, you'll look down and swear the plate is empty, the alabaster shellfish is sliced so meticulously thin you can see straight through the clear glass plate. My dish was delicate, almost ethereal. Equally sublime was the bowl full of tender *palourdes* (clams) bathed in cream. The sweet-fleshed *rougets* (prized Mediterranean rockfish) arrive whole, all the better to enjoy their meaty richness. On some dishes, I would have welcomed a touch of acid, a little hit of citrus. As a wine accompaniment, try the herbal, saline Ostertag Riesling Muenchenberg, a perfect match for this simple cuisine. And don't miss the Berthillon mango sorbet—delish!

LE SEVERO

CLASSIC BISTRO
8, rue des Plantes
Paris 14
TEL: +33 1 45 40 40 91
MÉTRO: Alésia or Mouton-Duvernet
OPEN: Monday through Friday

CLOSED: Saturday, Sunday, one week at Christmas, Easter, last week in July, and three weeks in August
PRICES: À la carte 40€
RESERVATIONS: Essential
ATMOSPHERE: Casual
SPECIALTIES: *Steak frites*

Owner-chef William Bernet—who began his career as a Paris butcher— runs a bistro to build a dream on. Fantastic Limousin beef, astonishing fries, and a wine blackboard that fills an entire wall of the tiny room,

offering some fine sips indeed. Need I say more? Meals I've loved here include Bernet's spring asparagus, delicious salads prepared with the freshest of greens, the best *steak tartare* and seared steaks in the city, well-seasoned *boudin noir* (blood sausage), giant thick veal chops, and excellent cheese. The place is always elbow-to-elbow crowded; no frills, just honest ingredients, honest fare. Vegetarians, however, will be hard-pressed to find much on the menu.

◀ *Le Severo's blackboard with its meaty menu.*

SPICE AND WINE

THAI
142, avenue du Maine
Paris 14
TEL: +33 1 43 20 61 27
spiceandwine.fr
spiceandwine@gmail.com
MÉTRO: Pernety or Mouton-Duvernet

OPEN: Monday through Friday, Saturday dinner
CLOSED: Saturday lunch, Sunday, and three weeks in August
PRICES: À la carte 25 to 35€
RESERVATIONS: Recommended
ATMOSPHERE: Casual

The ex-chef of the famed Blue Elephant restaurant in Paris, Nopporn Siripark, is now at the helm of this small Thai restaurant tucked away just south of the Luxembourg Gardens. Flavors are pungent, fresh, and authentically well balanced. Two favorites on the menu are the massaman lamb curry and the whole sea bass poached with Thai spices and lemongrass and served with a spicy lime dressing. As the restaurant's name suggests, wine is celebrated here, and the *sommelier* is more than happy to recommend a label that will match well with Thai flavors.

15ᵀᴴ ARRONDISSEMENT

AFARIA

**MODERN BISTRO / FRENCH
SOUTHWESTERN**
15, rue Desnouettes
Paris 15
TEL: +33 1 48 42 95 90
restaurant-afaria.fr
MÉTRO: Convention
OPEN: Tuesday through Saturday noon to 2PM
and 7 to 11PM

CLOSED: Sunday, Monday, three weeks in
August, and Christmas week
PRICES: 22 and 26€ lunch menus. 45€
dégustation (tasting) menu at lunch and dinner.
À la carte 38€ at lunch and dinner.
RESERVATIONS: Recommended
ATMOSPHERE: Casual

B asque-born chef Julien Duboué offers a totally personal look at the hearty, heritage-rich cuisine of France's Southwest, with his filet of turbot topped with tiny tender baby Basque *chipirons* (squid); a favorite blood sausage (*boudin*) served with potatoes and a healthy dose of mustard; and *magret de canard* (fatted duck breast) that is rarely seen grilled on the bone and over vine clippings (the woody shoots trimmed from the vine's previous year's growth, often used as kindling). And that in Paris's 15th *arrondissement*! I love this place, as well as its smartly priced wine list.

L'ÉPICURISTE

CLASSIC BISTRO
41, boulevard Pasteur
Paris 15
TEL: +33 1 47 34 15 50
MÉTRO: Pasteur
OPEN: Tuesday through Saturday

CLOSED: Sunday, Monday, three weeks in
August, public holidays, and Christmas week
PRICES: 25 and 29€ lunch menus. 32 or 37€
dinner menu. No à la carte.
RESERVATIONS: Recommended
ATMOSPHERE: Casual
SPECIALTIES: Wild game, scallops

H ow's this for a lineup of cold-weather bistro fare? *Coq faisan roti, fine choucroute de navet* (roasted pheasant with turnip sauerkraut); *pot-au-feu de joues de boeuf* (beef cheeks with winter vegetables); *quasi de veau roti, potiron gratiné* (roast rump of veal with pumpkin gratin); *lièvre à la royale* (slow cooked wild hare in red wine and blood sauce); and the triple-threat *oreilles, pied, et poitrine de porc et petit salé* (pigs' ears, feet, and breast with pork belly and lentils). There's all that and more at L'Épicuriste, the 15th-*arrondissement* home of Stéphane Marcuzzi and chef Aymeric Kräml. Diners last saw them at the small and charming L'Épigramme in the 6th, where the pair outgrew the minuscule kitchen and set out in search of a bit of breathing room. The space is spare, but the welcome, the service, and the cuisine easily make up for that. One recent night the restaurant was filled with sounds of good times, as diners tucked into the same soothing, earthy fare I loved at L'Épigramme.

The *coquilles Saint-Jacques roties au beurre demi-sel persillé* (fresh scallops roasted with salted butter topped with parsleyed garlic puree) was just as I remembered. The triple-threat pork specialty was not only beautifully presented but unctuous, *confit*-like, velvety, rich, and earthy, and not the least bit heavy. The same can be said of the succulent wild hare stew, all mahogany and glistening, a masterful example of what can be accomplished with long, slow cooking. The wine list is brief and well priced, and the well-balanced red Grand Tinel Côtes du Rhône was a perfect match for this hearty fare. I'll be back for sure—I'm already looking forward to the beef cheeks and pheasant! From September through November, L'Épicuriste offers game on a regular basis.

LE GRAND PAN

MODERN BISTRO
20, rue Rosenwald
Paris 15
TEL: +33 1 42 50 02 50
legrandpan.fr
contact@legrandpan.fr
MÉTRO: Plaisance or Convention
OPEN: Monday through Friday

CLOSED: Saturday, Sunday, three weeks in August, between Christmas and New Year's, and one week April–May
PRICES: 29€ à la carte at lunch. 40€ à la carte at dinner.
RESERVATIONS: Recommended (only by phone)
ATMOSPHERE: Smart-casual
SPECIALTIES: *Steak frites*, game, black truffles

This elbow-to-elbow meat lover's paradise, tucked away in the southern edge of the 15th *arrondissement,* is a classic of its genre, a bistro where friends gather with two thoughts in mind: copious food and lots of laughter, both facilitators of good times. Waiters seem to skate through the crowded duet of dining rooms, arms held high to deliver gigantic seared steaks cooked rare and juicy, rosy double-thick veal chops, thick pork chops, and giant bowls of oversize French fries. There's a good Morgon on the list from winemaker Georges Descombes, a smooth wine with a pleasing flavor of lightly smoked meat. The service is familiar and friendly in the best sort of way, while in the winter months the menu might announce a lovely baked egg topped with slices of authentic, fresh black truffles. If so, don't think twice!

16TH ARRONDISSEMENT

AKRAME

MODERN BISTRO / MODERN INTERNATIONAL
19, rue Lauriston
Paris 16
TEL: +33 1 40 67 11 16
akrame.com
contact@akrame.com
MÉTRO: Charles de Gaulle-Étoile or Kléber

OPEN: Monday through Friday
CLOSED: Saturday, Sunday, August, and at Christmas
PRICES: 40€ lunch menu. 70 and 90€ (110 and 140€ with wine) lunch and dinner menus.
RESERVATIONS: Recommended
ATMOSPHERE: Casual

Akrame Benallal is a chef to watch. When I dine out, I want to be surprised, but not too much. I want the familiar, but not too familiar. I want to be tested: What *is* that spice I can't quite put my finger on? But most of all, I want to leave satisfied and with my wallet still intact. Benallal—having

trained with Pierre Gagnaire and Ferran Adrià—understands and fulfills all of these desires. I don't know many Paris restaurants where you can enjoy a two-course lunch like his for 25€, or 35€ if you add dessert. His modern, all-gray dining room seats just 20 or so diners, with an open kitchen and a stool-height *table d'hôte*. His food is spontaneous, light, and both playful and serious at the same time. Benallal is a fan of *sous-vide* (cooking ingredients vacuum-sealed in a low-temperature water bath). And he loves to get to the essence of an ingredient, turning it into dried powders that work a special magic. I loved his complex and satisfying first course of a *sous-vide* egg set atop a pungent avocado

puree, topped with strips of haddock, a smoky white foam, and a crunchy corn powder reminiscent of corn chips. Sound weird? It wasn't. Just great flavors, full of surprises. A main course of steamed codfish appeared a bit more mainstream, though the alabaster fish was topped with a bright green sprinkling of spinach powder and accompanied by a cup of flavorful carrot essence that I would have taken for a more forward-flavored butternut squash. Dessert was ethereally light, a blending of essence of vanilla and essence of raspberry, a mysteriously cloudlike creation that was neither a cream nor a mousse but just substantially satisfying.

ASTRANCE

HAUTE CUISINE / MODERN FRENCH
4, rue Beethoven
Paris 16
TEL: +33 1 40 50 84 40
MÉTRO: Passy
OPEN: Tuesday through Friday
CLOSED: Saturday, Sunday, and Monday

PRICES: 70, 150, and 230€ menus at lunch (120, 230, and 350€ with wine). 230€ menu at dinner (350€ with wine).
RESERVATIONS: Essential (reservations open on the first Tuesday of each month for the following month)
ATMOSPHERE: Smart-casual

Pascal Barbot is in top form, offering food that is light, laced with herbs, spices, and an avalanche of varied citrus flavors. I left his 12-course lunch with pep in my step and a palate coated with extraordinary taste memories. How to decide the best bite of the meal? The demitasse-

size condiment of spinach and *piquillo* peppers? The baby ravioli filled with a tangy bite of *cédrat* or citron? The chile pepper sorbet brilliantly paired with lemongrass and ginger? Or the almost-too-pretty-to-eat lemon meringue *sablé* cookies? Then there is the warm and golden brioche spread with fragrant, salty butter of rosemary and

lemon. And of course, the chestnut honey madeleines. For fine dining, the 70€ (120€ including wines) lunch menu is one of the city's best buys. Pascal Barbot and partner Christophe Rohat have always done it their way, discreetly, professionally, with a smile. And we are the lucky beneficiaries of their talents.

SOUPE DE PAIN GRILLÉ D'ASTRANCE

Astrance's Smoky Grilled Bread Soup

When chef Pascal Barbot and partner Christophe Rohat first opened the Parisian Right Bank restaurant Astrance in 2005, this intriguing soup was on the menu. To this day, they often serve the magical liquid as a first course, offering no hint of its ingredients. They don't present it as a test, really, or even a game, but it's fun to sit at the table and try to figure out what the contents might be. Over time, we've guessed mushrooms, truffles, maybe divined a bit of smoky bacon, but never thought of burnt bread.

EQUIPMENT:

A fine-mesh sieve; a food processor or a blender; an immersion blender; 6 demitasse cups

INGREDIENTS:

1 thick slice trimmed, smoked bacon (about 2 ounces; 60 g), cubed

2 cups (500 ml) vegetable or chicken stock, or more if needed

3 thick slices sourdough bread

2 cups (500 ml) whole milk

1 teaspoon French mustard

Fleur de sel

Coarse, freshly ground black pepper

1. In a skillet with no added fat, brown the bacon over medium heat until crisp and golden, about 5 minutes. Drain on paper towels.

2. In a saucepan, bring the stock to a simmer. Add the bacon to the stock. Cover and simmer for 20 minutes, allowing the bacon to infuse its flavors and aromas into the stock. Strain the stock through the fine-mesh sieve set over a bowl. Discard the bacon. Return the stock to the saucepan.

3. Grill or toast the bread until very dark, almost burnt. Break the bread into small, bite-size pieces. Add the bread to the stock in the saucepan. Add the milk and mustard. Bring the liquid to a simmer, covered, and simmer for 20 minutes more. Pour the mixture into the food processor or blender and process until smooth. Taste for seasoning. (The soup can be made up to this point, 3 days in advance. Store in an airtight container in the refrigerator.)

4. At serving time, pour the soup into a saucepan and bring to a simmer. Taste for seasoning. If the soup is too thick, add additional stock to thin it out. With an immersion blender whisk the soup to create a thick foam. Pour into demitasse cups and serve warm as an appetizer.

MAKES 1½ CUPS (750 ML) OR 6 DEMITASSE SERVINGS

VARIATIONS: Add a few spoonfuls of truffle juice or, better yet, the juice as well as a few thin slices of fresh black truffles.

THE SECRET: Infuse, infuse, infuse. While it may seem strange and even wasteful to cook bacon, infuse vegetable stock with its smoky flavor, and then discard the bacon, the end result is a lovely, mysterious soup base.

LE PRÉ CATELAN

HAUTE CUISINE / MODERN FRENCH
Route de Suresnes
Bois de Boulogne
Paris 16
TEL: +33 1 44 14 41 14
restaurant-precatelan.com
MÉTRO: Ranelagh (Note that the nearest *métro* stations are a distance from the restaurant, so a taxi is recommended.)
OPEN: Tuesday through Saturday

CLOSED: Sunday, Monday, the first week of November, two weeks in February, three weeks in August
PRICES: 105€ lunch menu (140€ with wine). 200 and 260€ *dégustation* (tasting) menus at lunch and dinner. À la carte 250€.
RESERVATIONS: Essential
ATMOSPHERE: Formal. Suit jacket, but not tie, required for men.
SPECIALTIES: Black truffles

I first met chef Frédéric Anton when he was working at Joël Robuchon's Jamin in the late 1980s. He was in charge of every item of food ordered and accepted (or just as often rejected) as it came through the doors in the morning; long before the term "market driven" became the overused credo of the day, Anton was *the* ingredient man. He was the first I knew to list his menu by ingredients—tomato, crab, egg, *foie gras*, chocolate—and treat each with respect, rigor, precision. At the helm of the august Le Pré Catelan since 1997, he brought the chalet-like restaurant back to glory, capturing three Michelin stars in a very short time. Less than a palace and more like a home, the cozy, elegant dining rooms nestled beneath the trees in the Bois de Boulogne are among the most romantic in the city, and one of my favorites for special occasions and celebrations. *Maître d'* Jean-Jacques Chauveau should run a training school, so masterful is he at his métier. Each *sommelier* clearly knows and loves each bottle in the cellar, and along with each waiter, this place operates as a team whose players love to be where they are. A rare Paris spot with a working fireplace, this is the place to come on a cold winter's night. And on that occasional day of great summer weather, the outdoor terrace has no parallel. In a short time Anton has created some true classics, such as the delicate crab meat starter paired with an intense hit of fennel. And one can almost always be sure to find his rendition of deep-fried *langoustines* (Dublin Bay prawns, a Robuchon classic), here presented on a crisp, folded napkin, offset by a festive, deep-fried Romaine lettuce leaf, and served with a bowl of Romaine lettuce gazpacho, as well as paprika-flavored whipped cream, for dipping the rich, crunchy, ethereal wonders. Anton manages to create surprising combinations, as in his pan-fried fresh morels set in a puree of celery root and cinnamon, all topped with a tempura of tiny fried garlic flowers. Equally energizing is his rectangle of fresh turbot, set in a bed of watercress pesto, topped with pine nuts and shavings of Parmigiano-Reggiano. On one visit he surprised us with the most tender, most perfect trio of lamb chops, set on a black stone and served with a gorgeous herb bouquet of fresh rosemary, thyme, sage, and parsley, elegantly entwined on a trio of bamboo skewers. Who ever said food is not fashion?

SHANG PALACE (SHANGRI-LA HOTEL)

CHINESE / HAUTE CUISINE
10, avenue d'léna
Paris 16
TEL: +33 1 53 67 19 92
shangri-la.com/en/paris/shangrila/dining
shangpalace.slpr@shangrila.com
MÉTRO: léna
OPEN: Thursday through Monday
CLOSED: Tuesday, Wednesday, and mid-July to

late August
PRICES: 52€ dim sum lunch menu
(not available on Sunday). 98€ lunch and
dinner menus. 128€ dinner menu. À la carte
50 to 100€ at lunch and dinner.
RESERVATIONS: Essential
ATMOSPHERE: Formal. Suit jacket, but not tie,
required for men.
SPECIALTIES: Peking duck

Early into the first visit to any restaurant, the best thing one can say is, "I can't wait to come back." Those were my exact words about Shang Palace, open since September 2011, and Paris's first Chinese fine-dining restaurant. I could not applaud it more. The classic Chinese haute-cuisine decor

transports you right to the finest hotel dining rooms in Hong Kong. Service is informed and attentive, and the food on a par with the best Cantonese fare in Asia. Located in the luxury Shangri-La Hotel, the restaurant is luxurious but its prices are fair. When you go, try for a group of four or more to have more to sample. The dim sum is hands down among the most elegant and original versions I have sampled, including those in Hong Kong, Shanghai, and Beijing. Elegant and ethereal, arriving in a kaleidoscope of colors, each little mouthful delivers surprise as well as pleasure. The classic *ha kao* shrimp dumpling will ruin you for the rest of your life, as you will find disappointment in impostors. At the Shang Palace, they arrive as alabaster jewels, moist rice *crêpes* wrapped around ultra-fresh shrimp laced with a miraculous crunch. But the star of the show was the shrimp-filled red rice flour rolls, a Technicolor blend of red rice *crêpes* enveloping the most elegant shrimp filling, anointed by a single thin bright green slice of raw asparagus. The scallop dumplings, wrapped in a pale green spinach *crêpe*, also top the list, and vie for honors with the featherlight barbecued pork buns. The crispy Peking duck offers equal pleasure

◀ *Expertly carving the Shang Palace specialty, Peking duck.*

(it's worth a visit just to witness the skilled and ceremonious carving of the duck), with gorgeous, glistening crispy duck skin ready for wrapping in some of the thinnest, airiest rice flour *crêpes* imaginable. The classic second course—wok-fried minced duck meat wrapped in a lettuce leaf—is full-flavored and light. And don't miss the mahogany-toned fried egg noodles, paired with shredded chicken and bean sprouts. At lunchtime, one can order a simple, well-orchestrated dim sum lunch for 58€ or splurge a bit more on the 70€ Jade menu, which offers an authentic, tasty variety of dim sum, an astonishing soup of shredded bean curd that would certainly cure any ills, a generous portion of steamed cod with black mushrooms, chicken steamed with black mushrooms, and fried rice with diced scallops. There's also a curious but delicious dessert of pancake rolls with whipped cream and chilled fresh fruit. Tastes are fresh, delicate, heaven-bound. I savored every bite, and when the portions overwhelmed, the kindly waiter suggested we "do as in China, and take a doggie bag home." I'll return, again and again, in hopes of sampling the crispy suckling pig; the stir-fried crab meat with crab coral and scrambled eggs; the steamed sole filet with ham and black mushrooms; beggar's chicken (chicken in a lotus leaf cooked in a clay pot; requires 24-hour advance notice); and deep-fried eggplant with crispy garlic and chili. The wine list is extensive, with a well-priced Chenin Blanc, a Loire Valley Savennières Château de Chamboureau.

▼ *The plush and elegant dining room at Shang Palace.*

17ᵀᴴ ARRONDISSEMENT

L'ENTREDGEU

CLASSIC BISTRO
83, rue Laugier
Paris 17
TEL: +33 1 40 54 97 24
MÉTRO: Porte de Champerret
OPEN: Tuesday through Saturday

CLOSED: Sunday, Monday, first three weeks in August, and between Christmas and New Year's
PRICES: 25 and 35€ lunch menus. 35€ dinner menu. No à la carte.
RESERVATIONS: Recommended for Thursday through Saturday evenings.
ATMOSPHERE: Smart-casual

P énélope and Philippe Tredgeu run one of Paris's most appealing little bistros, with a blackboard menu full of bargain-priced treasures, ranging from breaded and expertly fried Utah Beach oysters set on a bed of sauce *ravigote* (here a tangy mayonnaise with capers, onions, and herbs) to a starter of the freshest scallops (*coquilles Saint-Jacques*), properly seared and served on a bed of parsnips (*panais*). The two small daffodil-colored old-time bistro dining rooms fill with the sounds of good times, Fabien Coche-Bouillot's Burgundy runs freely, while Chef Philippe turns out truly professional, well-studied bistro fare. His *lapin* with *porchetta* is a wonder—ultra-moist rabbit entirely boned, then filled with a vegetable stuffing, rolled, and gently cooked on top of the stove. A *quasi de veau* (rump of veal) arrives moist and tender, perfectly rare, paired with an irresistible portion of cheese-covered macaroni gratin. Desserts—an unconvincing chocolate cake and a winter fruit soup—were not on a par with the rest of the meal. But don't let that stop you: Pénélope and her staff are there to please, and Philippe's precision cooking is worth a detour.

FRÉDÉRIC SIMONIN

HAUTE CUISINE / MODERN FRENCH
25, rue Bayen
Paris 17
TEL: +33 1 45 74 74 74
fredericsimonin.com
MÉTRO: Ternes or Charles de Gaulle-Étoile
OPEN: Tuesday through Saturday
CLOSED: Sunday, Monday, August, and Christmas

PRICES: 39 and 55€ lunch menus. 85€ dinner menu, 145€ evening *dégustation* (tasting) menu. À la carte 80 to 100€ at lunch and dinner.
RESERVATIONS: Recommended
ATMOSPHERE: Formal. Suit jacket, but not tie, required for men.

D iners last saw the talented Frédéric Simonin at Joël Robuchon's former Table du Joël Robuchon in the 16th *arrondissement*. His current cuisine echoes some favorite dishes there—including the memorable starter of Parmesan, *foie gras,* and port reduction as well as the appetizer crab and avocado salad—though flying on his own he continues to shine. Simonin has already created some modern classics with his well-seared, tender *côte de veau*, pairing a brilliant mix of Swiss chard leaves and stems bathed in a faintly creamy sauce; as well as a featherlight *yuzu* soufflé, flavored with the fragrant, intense Japanese citrus. On one visit, we fell in love with his simply titled starter *les légumes* (vegetables), both a salad and a vegetable dish, a colorful, flavorful combination of thin shavings of seasonal vegetables wrapped around tender greens, paired with varied anchovy, *tapenade*, and spicy pepper sauce. In the late fall and winter months, you'll find all manner of game on the menu—wild hare, venison, wild duck. The elegant black-and-white dining room suggests you are in for some serious food, and you are. Simonin's 39€ lunch menu is a veritable bargain, but if you go for dinner, hope someone else is picking up the tab. An all-time favorite wine here is the mineral-scented white Mâcon Milly-Lamartine from Domaine Les Héritiers du Comte Lafon.

GUY SAVOY

HAUTE CUISINE / MODERN FRENCH

18, rue Troyon
Paris 17
TEL: +33 1 43 80 40 61
guysavoy.com/en
reserv@guysavoy.com
MÉTRO: Charles de Gaulle-Étoile
OPEN: Tuesday through Saturday
CLOSED: Saturday lunch, Sunday, Monday, and Christmas week

PRICES: 110€ three-course lunch menu, for one table by online reservation only. 330 and 360€ dinner menus. À la carte 170 to 300€ at lunch and dinner.
RESERVATIONS: Essential
ATMOSPHERE: Formal. Suit jacket, but not tie, required for men.
SPECIALTIES: Black truffles, game, cheese cart

Hands down, Guy Savoy is one of the most creative and beloved chefs on the planet. I have followed his brilliant career, from his one-man-band kitchen in the 16th *arrondissement* in the early 1980s to his present illustrious Michelin three-star dining rooms near the Étoile. Always, his food has been full of style, following but not hobbled by tradition, loaded with ideas I've never seen elsewhere. One minute he is presenting you with the ultimately moist *jarret de veau* (veal knuckle), falling off the bone and roasted to a melting tenderness. The next he shocks you as the waiter arrives with rectangles of shiny fresh salmon and proceeds to "cook" them on a bed of dry ice. He has created many classics over the years: the always welcome artichoke soup with truffles; the buttery truffled brioche that comes with it; his tangy, refreshing, and beautiful grapefruit terrine. Years ago, Savoy was one of the first chefs to champion vegetables, to work directly with his growers and do honor to the small farms across the land. The wine list is exceptional and his wine experts are there to hold you by the hand. His dinner menus may be pricey, but his 110€ lunch is a definite must for those eager to experience French dining at its best, but whose budget would not allow for a more expensive meal. Savoy has grand plans to move his restaurant to the stunning quai-side location of the Musée de la Monnaie de Paris in the 6th in mid-2014. He will also be opening a more casual eatery, Métal Café, in the same location. Check *The Food Lover's Guide to Paris* iPhone app later in 2014 for details and a review.

18ᵀᴴ ARRONDISSEMENT

LE COQ RICO

MODERN BISTRO
98, rue Lepic
Paris 18
TEL: +33 1 42 59 82 89
lecoqrico.com
reservation@lecoqrico.com
MÉTRO: Lamarck-Caulaincourt

OPEN: Daily
PRICES: 15€ lunch plat du jour at lunch,
à la carte
40 to 70€ at lunch and dinner
RESERVATIONS: Recommended
ATMOSPHERE: Smart-casual
SPECIALTIES: Roast chicken

I don't like restaurants that make me feel guilty. But I'm not blaming Antoine Westermann, owner of Le Coq Rico in Montmartre. First of all, reserve right away—the place is fantastic and open seven days a week, so there's no excuse. You'll be rewarded by Westermann's novel concept.

How much of a genius do you have to be to come up with a single-theme restaurant? The theme is poultry, meaning chicken and guinea fowl, duck and pigeon. And the potential that those birds bring to the table. The reason that Le Coq Rico makes me feel guilty is how cleverly it uses every bit of those tender birds, turning kidneys, hearts, livers, and wings into miraculous morsels. You see, I don't use them. I stuff my freezer full of chicken livers

TARTARE DE POISSON BLANC DE LA TABLE D'EUGÈNE

La Table d'Eugène's White Fish Tartare

With each visit to this tiny, out-of-the-way bistro run by the talented Geoffroy Maillard, I have more respect and admiration for his talent. He marches to the beat of his own drum but always manages to please diners with some of the more classic combinations (sausages and lentils) while stunning us with his chocolate "pearl," a dish that melts on your plate as your eyes watch with pleasure. This *tartare* is often on the menu, in many guises and variations. Be sure to use ultra-fresh sushi-grade fish or shellfish. Good choices include Pacific Alaskan halibut, farmed or wild-caught striped bass, or farmed bay scallops.

EQUIPMENT:

A small jar with a lid; 4 chilled salad plates; a 3-inch (8-cm) square or round ring mold or form

INGREDIENTS:

2 tablespoons grated fresh ginger

4 tablespoons chervil leaves (optional)

2 tablespoons freshly squeezed *yuzu* juice or Meyer lemon juice

1 tablespoon Japanese soy sauce, preferably organic

6 tablespoons extra-virgin olive oil

1 tablespoon grated fresh wasabi or wasabi paste

1 pound (500 g) ultra-fresh sushi-grade fish filets or scallops

Small handful of alfalfa, radish, or lentil sprouts, or other microgreens

Small handful of fresh cilantro leaves

1. In the jar, combine the ginger, chervil (if using), citrus juice, soy sauce, and oil. Tighten the lid. Shake to blend. Taste for seasoning, adding wasabi to taste.

2. Cut the fish into small cubes and place them in a bowl. Add the dressing, tossing very gently to blend. Taste for seasoning.

3. Place the mold or form in the center of a salad plate. Gently spoon the *tartare* into the mold. Gently tap down to even out the *tartare*. Remove the mold or form. Scatter the top of the *tartare* with sprouts and cilantro leaves. Repeat for the remaining servings.

4 SERVINGS

for the terrine I never make. I stuff the birds with hearts and gizzards as I roast them, when I should be treating those less-than-noble parts with greater honor. Chef Thierry Lébé and his ultra-professional staff cook with precision and quiet perfection, roasting farm-raised poultry whole, from all parts of France (each comes with a pedigree and the name of the farmer), on a rotisserie set in their small but efficient kitchen. Diners can choose to sit at the bar and watch the action, or at a table in one of the two small dining rooms. The place is bright, modern, understated. The menu offers something for everyone: from a golden-brown, intense poultry and celery-root broth ladled over tender ravioli filled with *foie gras*, to their signature *planchette de béatilles*—poultry hearts seared, gizzards cooked tenderly in fat, wings lacquered, and little curried balls of herbs deep-fried. I love pigeon but am never 100 percent satisfied with my preparation of the bird. Lébé's is a classic model—roasted perfectly rare and rosy, teamed up with mushrooms and bacon, with the tender liver crushed atop a rectangle of toast. A single serving of Challans farm-raised chicken is a wonder of nature—moist, tender, as it should be but not always is. And, well, the fries are about the best ever, deep golden brown, crispy, can't-stop-eating-them delicious. Even the little green salad here is fresh and attentively dressed. After all that, I couldn't imagine having room for dessert, though somehow I did: The *île flottante* is gorgeous, rich, and flawless; the seasonal salad of pineapple and pineapple sorbet, with a touch of ginger and lime zest, adds a tonic that takes you bravely into the cold winter air.

GUILO GUILO

JAPANESE
8, rue Garreau
Paris 18
TEL: +33 1 42 54 23 92
guiloguilo.com
MÉTRO: Abbesses
OPEN: For dinner only Tuesday through Saturday (for even months) and Tuesday through Sunday (for odd months)

CLOSED: Sunday (for even months) and Monday
PRICE: 45€ fixed menu. No à la carte.
RESERVATIONS: Essential
ATMOSPHERE: Smart-casual

One can wait weeks to be one of the chosen few who gather around the 20-seat rectangular bar that makes up the small Montmartre Japanese restaurant known as Guilo Guilo. We joined the believers for the 7PM (first) seating and, like everyone, had a ringside seat for the show.

Slight and elegant chef Eiichi Edakuni holds court (he even calls himself *Le Président*), directing the multicourse meal like an orchestra leader. The rest of the cheery, agile staff scurry about in very tight quarters, clearly organized and motivated. There is no written menu and no choice—just a set 45€ menu each evening. Ours included some real highs, some lows, and a few ho-hums. Tops on my list was the elegant, memorable, cold-smoked mackerel, strips of that fabulous fatty fish garnished with a nori sprinkle and piled on a bed of a fine julienne of shiso and black radish, with a garnish of pungent ginger puree. (It was so good that our neighbor asked for a second serving at the close of the meal.) I also loved the originality of the crunchy corn and shrimp tempura, arriving hot and crisp. Another dish with happy, bright, intense flavors came in the form of what they called

Japanese *boeuf Bourguignon*, a tiny bowl of rice topped with a rich beef stew showered with spring onions and nori. There is something wonderful about a roomful of strangers all eating the same food, as at a banquet, a festival, a communion of souls. Several of the offerings lacked punch and character, including a rather bland tofu and crab soup, essentially a deep-fried bundle floating in a delicate broth; and an underwhelming turbot rolled in a sesame coating. If you go, don't bother with the famed *foie gras* sushi, which most diners order for an 11€ supplement. The restaurant goes into Benihana mode as the chef tosses cubes of *foie gras* in flour, sautés and sauces them with flair, and sets the bite-size morsels on a mound of rice. The result is rather mushy, tasteless, fatty, effects I could have done without. Guilo Guilo offers an extensive sake menu, including an intriguing bubbly version.

LA TABLE D'EUGÈNE

MODERN FRENCH
18, rue Eugène Sue
Paris 18
TEL: +33 1 42 55 61 64
latableeugene@orange.fr
MÉTRO: Marcadet-Poissoniers or Jules Joffrin
OPEN: Tuesday through Saturday

CLOSED: Sunday, Monday, the last week of February, first three weeks in August, and one week at Christmas
PRICES: 29 and 35€ weekday lunch menus. 52, 68, and 88€ evening tasting menus. À la carte 65€.
ATMOSPHERE: Casual

There seems to be no end to "outer borough" bargain-priced dining spots, and La Table d'Eugène in the 18th *arrondissement* is surely one to add to the list. Chef-owner Geoffroy Maillard has his finger on it all: a lovely varied menu that makes you want to try everything; service that is as efficient as it can be, even when the tiny dining room is packed (as it always is); a knack for beautiful food prepared with top-rate ingredients. Lunch choices might include a stunning *millefeuille*-like *dorade tartare* stacked between thin slices of daikon and topped with an herb-garden salad; an ultra-fresh portion of cod topped with thin slices of *pata negra* ham and a vinaigrette of *piquillo* peppers and chives, teamed with a brilliantly devised (though sadly overcooked) watercress risotto; and a soothing seven-hour *gigot* paired with the freshest of brilliant carrots. There's a nice selection of wines by the glass, including the always-reliable Clos Uroulat Jurançon Sec Cuvée Marie from

THAT PARISIAN PALLOR

"City dwellers of long standing and newly arrived rustics were widely different in appearance and manners. The former were large and plump, pink, and white, their complexion unspoilt by work in the fields, and their physical ideal was the round-bellied bulk of the self-made bourgeois, accustomed to good food and unwearied by manual labour. The *patronnes* of inns and brothels were always fresh and pale, real Parisians who neither knew nor liked the sun, which scarcely penetrated the narrow streets of the old *quartiers*."

—DANIEL ROCHE, "The People of Paris: An Essay in Popular Culture in the 18th Century" the Southwest. Desserts are spectacular, including a chocolate "pearl" melted at the table with a drizzle of hot chocolate seasoned judiciously with Tasmanian peppercorns; and a pineapple "carpaccio" set on a crunchy chocolate and lemon "biscuit," accompanied by a super-rich yogurt ice cream. If the restaurant is booked out (which will certainly be the case if you don't reserve at least a week in advance), try Maillard's second address, La Rallonge, a modern small plates and tapas wine bar just two doors down the street (see Wine Bars, page 184, for full commentary).

19ᵀᴴ ARRONDISSEMENT

QUEDUBON

CLASSIC BISTRO
22, rue du Plateau
Paris 19
TEL: +33 1 42 38 18 65
MÉTRO: Buttes Chaumont or Pyrénées
OPEN: Tuesday through Saturday

CLOSED: Saturday lunch, Sunday, and one week at Christmas
PRICES: 15 and 17.50€ lunch menus.
À la carte 30 to 50€.
RESERVATIONS: Recommended
ATMOSPHERE: Casual
SPECIALTIES: Cheese tray

It was another short, gray, chilly day in Paris, so the only solace was to seek out some warming bistro fare. When I heard that *bistrotier* Gilles Bénard had left one of my favorite bistros, Chez Ramulaud in the 11th, for a small and no-frills spot in the 19th *arrondissement* near the Parc de Buttes Chaumont,

I headed over there. And was I rewarded! Another simple but great bistro to add to the list. How to decide between the braised oxtail with orange and an avalanche of fragrant and delicious carrots and baby turnips, moist roast pork with mounds of soft and succulent cabbage, farm chicken with braised endive? As the oxtail and pork arrived, warming aromas wafted from the table; it was time to salivate and dig in. A few glasses of Jean Foillard's raspberry-rich Morgon Côtes du Py helped take off the January chill, and we smiled in self-satisfied contentment at our choices. The food was not just *bon*, but the carrots tasted like the best carrots I've ever had (and I am not a carrot fan). The oxtail was properly falling off the bone, seared to perfection then braised. Likewise, the pork had backbone, personality, and perfect texture. At Ramulaud, I always looked forward to the generous cheese course and remember envying their little wooden cheese house on wheels. At Quedubon, Bénard offers a small choice of three cheeses, but what quality! It had been years since I tasted *Morbier,* the semisoft cow's-milk cheese from the Jura, with its thin strip of ash in the center. All too often it resembles Velveeta and has about as much taste. But this one was aromatic, lactic, beautifully made, and perfectly aged. Likewise for the aged Comté, a fruity and memorable choice. The giant blackboard lists up to 150 different wines, including Richard and Couturier from the Southern Rhône, Chave from Hermitage, and Leccia from Corsica. *Que-du-bon,* by the way, roughly translates as "everything is good."

20ᵀᴴ ARRONDISSEMENT

CHATOMAT

MODERN FRENCH
6, rue Victor Letalle
Paris 20
TEL: +33 1 47 97 25 77
MÉTRO: Ménilmontant
OPEN: Tuesday through Saturday and first
Sunday of the month for dinner only

CLOSED: Sunday, Monday, and last two weeks
of August
PRICES: À la carte 35 to 40€
RESERVATIONS: Essential
ATMOSPHERE: Casual

This small 18-seat neighborhood bistro on a hidden-away cobblestone street in the 20th *arrondissement* is characteristic of what is so exciting about casual dining in Paris today. Two ambitious young chefs, who have cut their teeth with big-name chefs in London and Paris, have ventured out on their own to create original and exciting fare at a very reasonable price. Alice di Cagno and Victor Gaillard, a couple both in and out of the kitchen, shot to bistro fame when they opened Chatomat in 2011, quickly gaining the Le Fooding Best Table 2012 award, which has ensured them a steady stream of loyal customers both local and international. Produce is fresh and of excellent quality, and the intelligently thought-out menu (*à la carte* only) changes on a monthly basis. A late-spring meal began with a refreshing *amuse-bouche*

of ultra-fresh *tartare de truite* (finely diced sashimi trout) paired with avocado cream, a mango coulis, and punctuated with a surprising touch of powdered coffee. The chefs had my attention! I adored my entrée of white asparagus with grapefruit and crab, which was brought alive by a zesty hazelnut and preserved lemon butter. The *poitrine et ris d'agneau* (lamb breast and sweetbreads) were in perfect balance with the *crème de* *maïs* (creamed corn), *petits pois* (peas), *coriandre* (cilantro), and *poireau* (leeks). It was hard to choose between the poached rhubarb with white chocolate ganache and the ricotta mousse with honey and lemon sorbet, mint, and tarragon, so we ordered both and we weren't disappointed. This place has my vote for an excellent modern bistro in a part of Paris that still remains somewhat of a culinary wasteland.

ROSEVAL

MODERN BISTRO
1, rue d'Eupatoria
Paris 20
TEL: +33 9 53 56 24 14
roseval.fr
MÉTRO: Ménilmontant
OPEN: Monday through Friday, dinner only

CLOSED: Saturday and Sunday
PRICES: 35€ fixed menu (42€ with cheese course, 62 and 67€ with wine pairings). No à la carte.
RESERVATIONS: Essential
ATMOSPHERE: Smart-casual

Expectations run high for two chefs hailing from the kitchens of Inaki Aizpitarte (Le Chateaubriand) and Giovanni Passerini (Rino) when they strike out on their own. But chefs Simone Tondo and Michael Greenwold are indeed rising to the occasion with their modern bistro Roseval, set on a charming square at the foot of the imposing church Eglise Notre Dame de la Croix in the 20th *arrondissement*. Though a distance from central Paris, food pilgrims willingly make the evening journey. (Note that Roseval is just a short walk from the Ménilmontant *métro*.) In summer one can relish the few outdoor tables, watching the stars and the show of starlings flying back and forth between the trees. No matter what the season, you will also find a spectacle on the plate, with Tondo and Greenwold's unusual flavor accents and pairings. The menu changes daily, but you might find the likes of gambas and *tete de couchon* (pig's head) with a delicate hit of preserved lemon and fennel flowers; a cloudlike Mediterranean invention of cod filet on a bed of *pan con tomat*, veiled in an olive emulsion; or wild mallard duck, aubergine, green beans, and mussels. Service can be totally neutral and lackluster, though the wine choice is vast and exciting, with many natural Italian wines to discover.

◀ *Classic Parisian bars like this one are popular hangouts in outer-borough neighborhoods like the 20th.*

PARIS ENVIRONS

MA COCOTTE

MODERN FRENCH
106, rue des Rosiers
93400 Saint-Ouen
TEL: +33 1 49 51 70 00
macocotte-lespuces.com
infos@macocotte-lespuces.com
MÉTRO: Porte de Clignancourt

OPEN: Monday through Friday noon to 3PM
and 7 to 11PM, Saturday and Sunday 9AM to 11PM
PRICES: À la carte 25 to 40€ at lunch and
dinner
RESERVATIONS: Recommended
(no reservations taken for lunch on weekends)
ATMOSPHERE: Casual

D esigner Philippe Starck has finally given us flea market lovers a smart, trendy, easy place to lunch before or after wandering the stalls. I've been a regular visitor to the Clignancourt market since 1980, and have furnished many a room with treasures gleaned from long and leisurely Sunday strolls.

Starck's Ma Cocotte, right at the parking entrance of the Paul Bert market, is conveniently located, and since its opening in October 2012 has been a surefire hit, especially at lunch on weekends, when no reservations are taken. So go early, and walk off the lunch as you stroll the aisles. The food here is nothing more than "correct," but if you go with that in mind, you're not likely to be disappointed. The huge open kitchen sports a giant rotisserie, with roasted chicken and beef often on the menu. Simple salads of beets, lamb's lettuce, and soft-cooked egg arrive fresh and perky, while the first course of smoked salmon is divine. The bread is outrageously delicious, and the wine list—which includes some well-priced Burgundies from Olivier LeFlaive—make the experience all that much more digestible. The restaurant is comfortable and not an in-your-face Starck experience. There is plenty of space for outdoor dining, the all-white bathrooms are a must-visit, and service is, as the French would say, without a fault.

▶ *An evening stroll through a quiet Parisian street.*

AT A GLANCE

1ST ARRONDISSEMENT

Le Carré des Feuillants
La Dame de Pic
Chez Denise
Izakaya Issé
Racines 2
Spring
Verjus
Yam'Tcha

2ND ARRONDISSEMENT

Frenchie
Chez Georges
Goust
Liza
Passage 53
Saturne

3RD ARRONDISSEMENT

L'Ambassade D'Auvergne
L'Ami Louis
Grazie
Chez Jenny
Café des Musées

4TH ARRONDISSEMENT

L'Ambroisie
Benoit
Claude Colliot
Isami
Mon Vieil Ami

5TH ARRONDISSEMENT

L'A.O.C.
Atelier Maître Albert
Brasserie Balzar
Dans les Landes
Chez René
Terroir Parisien
Le Zyriab by Noura

6TH ARRONDISSEMENT

Le 21
Azabu
Les Bouquinistes
La Closerie des Lilas
Le Comptoir du Relais
Fogón
Huîtrerie Régis
Le Petit Lutetia
Au Pied de Fouet
Pizza Chic
Semilla
La Société
Le Timbre
Toyo
Yen
Ze Kitchen Galerie

7TH ARRONDISSEMENT

35° Ouest
Aida
L'Affable
L'Ami Jean
Arpège
L'Atelier de Joël Robuchon
   (Saint-Germain)
Les Botanistes
Le Cinq Mars
Les Cocottes de Christian
   Constant
Restaurant ES
Les Fables de la Fontaine
La Fontaine de Mars
Restaurant Jean-François Piège
Le Jules Verne
Pottoka
Au Pied de Fouet
   (Saint-Germain)
La Table d'Aki
Le Tourette by Ibérique
   Gourmet
Yuzu

8TH ARRONDISSEMENT

Restaurant Alain Ducasse au
   Plaza Athénée
Chez André
L'Atelier de Joël Robuchon
   Étoile
Le Cinq (Four Seasons)
Restaurant Dominique Bouchet
Epicure au Bristol
Laurent
Lazare
Pavillon Ledoyen
Mini Palais
Neva Cuisine
Okuda
Pierre Gagnaire
Taillevent

9TH ARRONDISSEMENT

Kiku
L'Orient d'Or
Le Pantruche

10TH ARRONDISSEMENT

Abri
Le Galopin
Chez Michel
Philou

11TH ARRONDISSEMENT

Le 6 Paul Bert
Astier

Bones
Le Chateaubriand
Caffé dei Cioppi
L'Écailler du Bistrot
Le Mansouria
Bistrot Paul Bert
Au Pied de Fouet (Oberkampf)
Sassotondo
Septime
Le Sot-l'y-Laisse
Unico
Le Villaret

12TH ARRONDISSEMENT

À la Biche au Bois
Au Trou Gascon

14TH ARRONDISSEMENT

Le Dôme
Le Duc
Le Severo
Spice and Wine

15TH ARRONDISSEMENT

Afaria
L'Épicuriste
Le Grand Pan

16TH ARRONDISSEMENT

Akrame
Astrance
Le Pré Catalan
Shang Palace (Shangri-la Hotel)

17TH ARRONDISSEMENT

L'Entredgeu
Frédéric Simonin
Guy Savoy

18TH ARRONDISSEMENT

Le Coq Rico
Guilo Guilo
La Table d'Eugène

19TH ARRONDISSEMENT

Quedubon

20TH ARRONDISSEMENT

Chatomat
Roseval

PARIS ENVIRONS

Ma Cocotte

CHAPTER 2

CAFÉS AND CASUAL BITES

CAFÉS ET TABLES DÉCONTRACTÉS

I t is impossible to imagine Paris without its cafés. Parisians are sun worshippers, and the attraction of an outdoor sidewalk stopping place perfectly suits their inclination. Until recently, the city's outdoor terrace life began in February, sunshine or not, as café doors would open wide,

wicker chairs tumble out, and the season began. Today, with the advent of convenient gas and electric heaters, most terraces stay open year-round, with colorful awnings often sheltering customers from the vagaries of the weather. The city has some 7,000 cafés (historians suggest there were as many as 45,000 in the 1800s!) varying in size, grandeur, and significance. As diverse as Parisians themselves, the café serves as an extension of the French living room, a place to start and end the day, gossip and debate, read the daily news, chat with a friend—a place for seeing and being truly alone. Many offer free Internet access, so it's common to see customers on laptops and cell phones. The outdoor café is also one spot that allows smoking in a public place.

Today's diverse casual dining life in Paris—with regional French *crêperies* and tapas bars; Japanese noodle and dumpling spots for quick snacks or meals; top-rated pizza parlors; Indian, Chinese, British, and Spanish specialty eateries—are all an extension of the long history of café life and culture in Paris.

No book on Paris literary, artistic, or social life is complete without details of café life, who sat where, when, and with whom—and what they drank. One wonders how writers and artists accomplished as much as they did if they really whiled away all those hours at sidewalk tables sipping *café au lait*, Vichy water, and *ballons* of Beaujolais.

When did it start? The café billed as the oldest in Paris is Le Procope, opened in 1686 by a Sicilian, Francesco Procopio dei Coltelli, the man credited with turning France into a coffee-drinking society. He was one of the first men granted the privilege of distilling and selling wines, *liqueurs,* and *eaux-de-vie,* as well as selling coffee, tea, and chocolate, with a status equal to a baker or butcher. Le Procope attracted Paris's political and literary elite, and its past is filled with history. It has been reported that it was there that Voltaire drank forty cups of his favorite brew each day, a blend of coffee and chocolate, which some credit with inspiring his spontaneous wit. When Benjamin Franklin died in 1790 and the French assembly went into mourning for three days, Le Procope was entirely draped in black in honor of France's favorite American. Even the young Napoleon Bonaparte spent time at Le Procope: When still an artillery officer, he was forced to leave his hat as security while he went out in search of money to pay for his coffee. Le Procope still exists at the original address, 13, rue de l'Ancienne Comédie in the 6th *arrondissement,* but as a restaurant, not a café.

By the end of the 18th century, all Paris was intoxicated with coffee. Some haunts were like all-male clubs, with many serving as centers of political life and discussion. It is not a surprise to find that one of the speeches that precipitated the fall of the Bastille took place outside the Café Foy at the Palais-Royal. By the 1840s, the men who congregated and set the tenor of the times included journalists, playwrights, and writers who became known as *boulevardiers,* because they spent so much time at the cafés situated along the city's wide boulevards. Certain cafés did have special rooms reserved for women, but in 1916 a law was passed that prohibited serving women sitting alone on the terraces of those along the boulevards.

At the same time, the sidewalk cafés along boulevard du Montparnasse—Le Dôme, La Rotonde, and later La Coupole—became the stronghold of artists; those along boulevard Saint-Germain—Les Deux Magots, Flore, and Lipp—were the watering holes and meeting halls for the literary. When the "lost generation" of expatriates arrived in Paris after World War I, they established themselves along both boulevards, drinking, talking, arguing, writing.

Cafés still serve as picture windows for observing contemporary life. The people you see today at Les Deux Magots, Café de Flore, and Lipp may not be the great artists of the day, but faces worth watching just the same.

If you know how to nurse a beer or coffee for hours, café sitting can be one of the city's best buys. No matter how crowded a café may be, waiters will respect your graceful loafing and won't insist that you order another round just to hold the table. Coffee is generally less expensive if you are willing to stand at the bar. At mealtime, if you see a table covered with a cloth or even a little paper place mat, that's a sign the table is reserved for dining. If the table is bare, you are welcome to sit and have just a drink. Note that the service charge is automatically added to all café bills, so you are required to pay only the final total and need not leave an additional tip, although most customers leave some loose change.

As modern Paris expands, the city offers a wealth of spots beyond cafés, and whether these are bakeries, *crêperies*, or ethnic eateries, you'll find it has never been easier to get a quick, simple bite around the capital. ❧

1ˢᵀ ARRONDISSEMENT

ANGELINA (Rivoli)

CLASSIC FRENCH / TEA SALON
226, rue de Rivoli
Paris 1
TEL: +33 1 42 60 82 00
angelina-paris.fr
angelina@groupe-bertrand.com
MÉTRO: Tuileries
OPEN: Monday through Friday 7:30AM to 7PM.
Saturday and Sunday 8:30AM to 7PM.

PRICES: Breakfast menu 20 to 29€. À la carte 15 to 20€ at lunch.
RESERVATIONS: Recommended between midday and 2PM. Reservations not taken after 2PM.
SPECIALTIES: Hot chocolate, Mont Blanc, red berry tart, thin apple tart, *croque monsieur*

A ngelina is mythical. Just the name evokes dreams of its rich, extra-thick hot chocolate. No one has ever been let in on the secret recipe, which is just as well since it is quite impossible to imagine sipping it without the elegant, baroque-style surroundings of this century-old tea salon. Sitting in the Angelina tearoom is like experiencing yesteryear, as the stern, black-and-white-clad staff bustles to serve the small, crowded tables and the *maître d'hôtel* surveys the humming rooms, making sure nothing is amiss. Angelina's signature pastry is the Mont Blanc, a mound of squiggled chestnut purée hiding crisp meringue and vanilla-scented whipped cream. Tender and achingly sweet, it's another century-held house secret. Other delicacies include a thin, crisp caramelized apple tart scented with cinnamon, a vanilla éclair topped with white chocolate, and a sweet-crusted tart piled with berries. Full meals and savory snacks are also served throughout the day; however, the quality is not of the same standard as the pastries and hot chocolate menu.

ANGELINA (Musée du Louvre)

CLASSIC FRENCH / TEA SALON
Musée du Louvre
Richelieu Wing
Café Richelieu
Paris 1
TEL: +33 1 49 27 93 31

MÉTRO: Palais Royal–Musée du Louvre
OPEN: Wednesday and Friday 10AM to 9PM.
Thursday and Saturday through Monday 10AM to 5PM.
CLOSED: Tuesday
RESERVATIONS: Not necessary

Although not as grand as the Angelina Rivoli tea salon, there is always a quality of living in yesteryear when sipping tea or hot chocolate in one of these baroque cafés, not at all inappropriate for a location in the Louvre. See above for full commentary.

CLAUS

GERMAN / MODERN INTERNATIONAL
14, rue Jean-Jacques Rousseau
Paris 1
TEL: +33 1 42 33 55 10
clausparis.com
contact@clausparis.com

MÉTRO: Louvre-Rivoli
OPEN: Monday through Friday 8AM to 5PM;
Saturday and Sunday 9:30AM to 5PM
PRICES: 14 to 26€ breakfast menus, 15 to 20€
lunch menu, à la carte items from 3€
RESERVATIONS: Recommended

This charming, modern German café is a big hit with connoisseurs of the *petit-déjeuner* and brunch. The bright and cheery downstairs *épicerie* showcases an array of beautiful tarts, cakes, and pastries, and offers a whole selection of artisanal breakfast products. The upstairs *salon* is outfitted with retro-chic yellow banquettes, geometric cushions, and vintage wooden tables. The menu comprises a variety of healthy and super-fresh *formule* options for any size appetite, and includes homemade Bircher muesli prepared the day before; granola; *viennoiseries* (breakfast pastries) from Masion Landemaine and bread baskets served with artisanal jams; *oeuf à la coque* (soft-cooked eggs), scrambled or fried; smoked salmon; and *charcuterie.*

LE CAFÉ MARLY

MODERN INTERNATIONAL CAFÉ
93, rue de Rivoli
Paris 1
TEL: +33 1 49 26 06 60
beaumarly.com
contact@beaumarly.com
MÉTRO: Palais Royal–Musée du Louvre

OPEN: Daily 8AM to 2AM
PRICES: À la carte 15 to 52€ at lunch and
dinner
RESERVATIONS: Not necessary
SPECIALTIES: *Croque monsieur*, club sandwich,
omelet (until 8PM only), dim sum from Yoom,
green beans with mushrooms

What could be better than sitting on a protected terrace at the Louvre, overlooking the glass Pyramid and, if you're in the right seat, having a view of the Eiffel Tower, too? This classy, classic, trendy all-day spot offers rather a traditional international menu (overseen by Michelin-starred chef Jean-François Piège), ranging from a good club sandwich and excellent omelets to smoked salmon and lobster salad. But there are also very good Vietnamese *nems* (spring rolls) and spicy penne with tomatoes. Like all of the Costes brothers' establishments, the

▶ *Lunch in style on one of Paris's most spectacular terraces at Le Café Marly.*

waitstaff is attentive and competent, but its members are also well chosen for their good looks and sex appeal. That's just all part of the Parisian scene. A good place to know about for breakfast, lunch, or dinner—or when you want a ringside seat in the center of Paris.

KOTTERI RAMEN NARITAKE

JAPANESE
31, rue des Petit-Champs
Paris 1
TEL: +33 1 42 86 03 83
MÉTRO: Pyramides, Quatre Septembre or Palais Royal–Musée du Louvre

OPEN: Wednesday through Monday
CLOSED: Tuesday
PRICES: À la carte at lunch and dinner 12 to 20€
RESERVATIONS: Not taken
SPECIALTY: Ramen (buckwheat noodles)

While there is an abundance of Japanese restaurants around rue Sainte-Anne, it is often surprising how difficult it can be to find satisfying, authentic Japanese fare in this neighborhood. Naritake Kotteri Ramen, however, is like a direct import, serving genuine ramen—buckwheat noodles in a thick *kotteri* pork-based broth. Noodles and side dishes of rice and gyoza (Chinese-style dumplings filled with pork and chives, lightly fried on one side, which are a popular accompaniment to ramen in Japan) are all you will find on the menu here, but believe me, you will leave feeling satisfied! You can choose between a lighter *shoyu* (soy) flavored broth or a thick gravy-like miso (soy paste) broth to accompany the firm, springy noodles that are made in-house every morning. And just as in Japan, you choose your toppings à la carte. The house special is a generous portion of succulent roast pork served with a showering of spring onions. Once inside the restaurant, watch your step—the floor is scattered with salt to soak up the inevitable splashes of broth from the tables of enthusiastic diners. The downside? Naritake seats only about 20 people, and with the instant popularity of the restaurant, queuing is almost inevitable, but if ramen is your thing it's worth the wait.

LE PAIN QUOTIDIEN
(Palais Royal)

BAKERY / CAFÉ
5, rue des Petits-Champs
Paris 1
MÉTRO: Palais Royal–Musée du Louvre
SPECIALTIES: Soups, salads, sandwiches, and pastries

LE PAIN QUOTIDIEN
(Saint-Honoré)

BAKERY / CAFÉ
18, place du Marché Saint-Honoré
Paris 1
MÉTRO: Pyramides or Tuileries
SPECIALTIES: Soups, salads, sandwiches, and pastries

This popular all-day Belgian café/bakery chain has healthy, organic menus for any time of day. These two cafés are conveniently located near two of Paris's most beautiful parks, so why not get your *tartine* (open-faced sandwich) to go, and dine in the luxury of the Palais Royal Gardens, near the rue des Petits-Champs café, or the Jardin des Tuileries (just a short walk from the café on the place du Marché Saint-Honoré). See Bakeries, page 222, for full commentary.

VERJUS BAR À VINS

MODERN INTERNATIONAL
47, rue de Montpensier
Paris 1

MÉTRO: Palais Royal–Musée du Louvre or Pyramides
SPECIALTIES: Sandwiches

This great little wine bar is also open at lunch, adding an American-inspired gourmet sandwich menu (weekday lunchtime only) to their repertoire of delicious dining in Paris. This is the place to go for a gourmand carryout picnic lunch to enjoy in the adjacent Palais Royal gardens. See Wine Bars, page 173, for full commentary.

2ND ARRONDISSEMENT

FRENCHIE TO GO

MODERN INTERNATIONAL
9, rue du Nil
Paris 2
No telephone
frenchietogo.com
MÉTRO: Sentier

OPEN: Tuesday through Saturday, 8:30AM to 4:30PM
CLOSED: Sunday and Monday
PRICES: À la carte menu items 10 to 22€
RESERVATIONS: Not taken

Hot on the heels of the success of Frenchie Bar à Vins, Grégory Marchand has opened his third eatery on the rue du Nil and it's another winner. Inspired by New York delis, Marchand focuses his attention for super-fresh ingredients on casual dining, with a menu of pastrami sandwiches, lobster rolls, hamburgers, and fish and chips. This is no ordinary carryout diner: Australian chef Sebbie Kenyon elevates the humble fast food to new and delicious heights. The fish and chips are the best you will find anywhere, using line-caught hake sourced from the reputable Terroir d'Avenir fishmongers (see page 339)—conveniently located opposite— and wrapped in a light and crusty batter. The *frites* too are fried to a golden perfection and served with a punchy *sauce tartare*. They don't take reservations, and the small 15-seat space fills up fast, so plan on arriving early for lunch or later in the afternoon if you want to eat in. In fine weather, a place at the streetside bar terrace, with a grilled Reuben sandwich—complete with 12-day brined pastrami, Keen's British Cheddar, pickled red cabbage, and mustard on *Pain des Amis* bread from Du Pain et des Idées (see Bakeries, page 233)— and an iced tea just might make Frenchie To Go the best casual-bite spot in the city.

GRILLÉ

TURKISH / MIDDLE EASTERN
15, rue Saint-Augustin
Paris 2
TEL: +33 01 42 96 10 64
MÉTRO: Quatre-Septembre

OPEN: Monday through Friday, noon to 3PM
CLOSED: Saturday and Sunday
PRICES: 8.5€ kebabs, 3€ homemade fries
RESERVATIONS: Not taken
SPECIALTY: Kebabs, homemade fries

If this is the future of street food in Paris, then we have a lot to look forward to. Conceived by Frédéric Peneau (cofounder of Le Chateaubriand and Le Dauphin), Hugo Desnoyer (celebrity butcher), and Marie Carcassonne (Founder of Dynamo, a luxury project management company), Grillé is

the simplicity of easy street food, using thoroughbred ingredients: Turkish flatbread handmade onsite from white flour and organic spelt flour; milk-fed veal from Desnoyer himself, grilled to perfection on a vertical kebab rotisserie, seasoned with olives and herbs from Annie Bertin (an impeccable source of aromatic herbs); and served with a choice of *sauce blanche* (a yogurt-like white sauce seasoned with horseradish) or *sauce vert* (a green tomato coulis with green chiles and sweet onions). Be prepared for long queues (but they move swiftly and it's worth the wait). There is minimal seating, so in fine weather, find a spot by the fountain in the nearby Square Louvois (rue de Louvois, just off rue Saint-Anne).

GYOZA BAR

JAPANESE
56, passage des Panoramas
Paris 2
TEL: +33 1 44 82 00 62
gyozabar.com
MÉTRO: Richelieu-Drouot or Grands
Boulevards

OPEN: Monday through Saturday, noon to 2:30PM and 6:30 to 11PM
CLOSED: Sunday
PRICES: 6 to 8€ for 8 to 12 dumplings
RESERVATIONS: Not taken
SPECIALTY: Gyoza (Japanese dumplings)

Fans of those spicy, addictive Japanese dumplings known as gyoza should make a beeline for this modern, streamlined bar set in the historic Passage des Panoramas. Find a stool and settle into a mini-feast. Chefs Guillaume Guedi and Shinichi Sato of the nearby Michelin two-star

restaurant Passage 53 had an instant hit on their hands when they opened in 2011, offering simplicity at its best with their wheat-flour dumplings filled with succulent ground pork loin from star butcher Hugo Desnoyer and spiced with *yuzu* zest (from that fragrant Japanese citrus) and ground chile pepper. The dumplings are seared right in front of you in a touch of oil in customized cast-iron pans, sprinkled with a touch of water, then steamed, so one side is golden and crunchy, the other soft and soothing. Dip the crescent-shaped goodies into a citrus-rich *ponzu* sauce touched with grapefruit and orange, and your palate breaks into a smile. The contrast of textures, a touch of spice, and a hit of citrus make for one happy diner. The only other offerings here include a tiny bowl of bean sprouts laced with nutty sesame oil, and a simple serving of white rice. There's both Yebisu and Kirin beer to wash it all down. The bar is efficiency personified, with excellent service from a trio of young Japanese women. The decor is pure, understated Japanese—all wood, gray stone, and glass, a perfect contrast to the *passage*, with its charming patina of age.

▲ *Télescope co-owner Nicolas Clerc.*

TÉLESCOPE

COFFEE BAR
5, rue Villedo
Paris 2
TEL: +33 1 42 61 33 14
telescopecafe.com
info@telescopecafe.com
MÉTRO: Pyramides or Palais Royal–Musée du
Louvre

OPEN: Monday through Friday 8:30AM to
6:30PM. Saturday 9:30AM to 6:30PM.
CLOSED: Sunday
RESERVATIONS: Not taken
SPECIALTIES: Coffee, breakfast, and light
snacks

Another excellent addition to the recent flourish of high-quality coffee bars in Paris. American David Flynn, who has been at the heart of the new coffee movement here, has joined up with Frenchman Nicolas Clerc to bring unbeatably good coffee to the 2nd *arrondissement.*

The pair rent a roaster for a few hours a week to roast their beans to their own specifications. Coffee is king here, but there is a light breakfast menu of granola and *tartines,* and a selection of Anglo-style pastries throughout the day.

LE PAIN QUOTIDIEN (Montorgueil)

BAKERY / CAFÉ
2, rue des Petits Carreaux
Paris 2

MÉTRO: Sentier
SPECIALTIES: Soups, salads, sandwiches, and
pastries

You can't go wrong with the simple, rustic menu of Le Pain Quotidien for breakfast, lunch, or even a light evening meal. See Bakeries, page 222, for full commentary.

3ᴿᴰ ARRONDISSEMENT

AL TAGLIO (Marais)

ITALIAN / PIZZERIA
22, rue de Saintonge
Paris 3
TEL: +33 9 50 48 84 06
altaglio.fr
MÉTRO: Filles du Calvaire or
Saint-Sébastien–Froissart

OPEN: Daily noon to 11PM. Until midnight
Friday and Saturday.
CLOSED: First two weeks in August
PRICES: 26.30 to 38.80€ per kilo
RESERVATIONS: Not taken
SPECIALTY: Pizza by the slice

A long with the wood-oven treasures from Pizza Chic (see page 47), I declare Al Taglio (literally, "by the slice") pizzas among the best in Paris. Walk into this small, casual eatery at noon and the chef will already have three or four giant rectangles of steaming pizza set out before you. On one visit we sat at the long communal tables and found mouthwatering Margherita; mozzarella and Parma ham; a version topped with truffle cream and thin disks of potato; and porcini and Parmesan. The crust is thick and airy, the kind of chewy, long-rise dough my Italian mother used to make, and all ingredients are fresh. You indicate the size of slice you want, they weigh it, and you pay by the weight. I'll be going back to sample the spicy sausage and artichoke variation. Note: They make deliveries of whole pizzas, serving 8 to 10, if ordered 24 hours in advance.

BREIZH CAFÉ

BRETON / CRÊPERIE
109, rue Vieille du Temple
Paris 3
TEL: +33 1 42 72 13 77
breizhcafe.com
contact@breizhcafe.fr
MÉTRO. Saint-Sébastien–Froissart or Filles du
Calvaire

OPEN: Wednesday through Sunday 11:30AM
to 11PM
CLOSED: Monday, Tuesday, and three weeks
in August
PRICES: *Galettes* and *crêpes* 4.50 to 14.50€
RESERVATIONS: Essential on weekends,
recommended during the week
SPECIALTIES: *Galettes, crêpes*, oysters, cider

T his noisy, bustling Breton *crêperie* in the Marais serves some of the finest thin buckwheat flour *galettes* I have ever tasted: deep golden brown with a fine crisp edge and embellished with a nonstop list of fillings. I am partial to the *Nordique*, garnished with first-class smoked Scottish salmon (*label rouge*), *crème fraîche* from the farm, and a touch of chives. Other excellent choices include the *Complète Chorizo*, inspired by Basque flavors and filled with an *oeuf miroir* (lightly fried egg), sliced chorizo sausage, and cheese. A restorative winter selection might be the *Cancalaise*, filled with potatoes, herring, the tangy, rich Bordier *crème fraîche* from Brittany, and salty herring eggs. One could easily come here once a week to sample a new flavor since Breizh Café also has a blackboard noting four or five daily

specials. On one visit, we loved the *galette* filled with the fine blue *fourme d'Ambert* cheese and topped with a tossed salad that included pine nuts and raisins. As a starter, don't miss the *Amuse-Galettes,* served in bite-size "rolls" and filled with your choice of butter (Bordier's smoked or seaweed-flavored), cheese and ham, chorizo, blue cheese with honey and walnuts; or smoked salmon with chive cream. The list of dessert wheat and buckwheat flour *crêpes* is enough to keep you busy for months. I highly recommend the *Carrément Sarrasin,* a warm and warming buckwheat flour *crêpe* drizzled with buckwheat honey and a scoop of buckwheat ice cream. Do order their top-of-the-line cider, Sydre Argelette, a delicate, easy-drinking beverage with a touch of elegance and charm. Breizh Café also has sister *crêperies* in Cancale in Brittany, and in Tokyo.

CUISINE DE BAR (Marais)

SANDWICH BAR
38, rue Debelleyme
Paris 3
TEL: +33 1 44 61 83 40
cuisinedebar.fr
MÉTRO: Saint-Sébastien–Froissart or
Filles du Calvaire

OPEN: Tuesday through Sunday 8:30AM to 8:30PM
CLOSED: Monday and the month of August
PRICES: 13.50€ all-day menu. À la carte breakfast 7.90 to 12.10€. Lunch *tartines* 9.50 to 11.90€. Teatime 7.20€.
RESERVATIONS: Not taken
SPECIALTY: *Tartines* (open-faced sandwiches)

Much like its Saint-Germain counterpart, this Northern Marais outpost of Poilâne bakery's eat-in breakfast and sandwich bar serves up some of the best *tartines,* or open-faced sandwiches, in Paris—all on perfectly grilled Poilâne sourdough bread. Even in the dead of winter, I've loved the tomato and mozzarella *tartine*. It's filling, fresh, and hearty, recreating the pleasure of a pizza on toasted Poilâne. The chicken *tartine* is moist and flavorful, studded with thin slices of roast chicken and garnished with capers and anchovies. Choices are vast, with toppings of smoked salmon, sardines, tapenade, goat's-milk cheese, ham, tuna, chicken, vegetables, and smoked duck breast with cheeses. The salads are less interesting (I could do without the corn and raisins on several of them) and the wine list needs improvement.

LOUSTIC

COFFEE BAR
40, rue Chapon
Paris 3
TEL: +33 9 80 31 07 06
MÉTRO: Arts et Métiers or Rambuteau

OPEN: Monday through Friday 8AM to 6PM, Saturday 10AM to 7PM, Sunday 11AM to 6PM
PRICES: 10 to 12€ at breakfast and lunch
SPECIALTIES: Soups, salads, and cakes

Just one sip of the expertly filtered coffee served at Loustic will change the way you feel about coffee forever. Owner Channa Galhenage sources his roasted beans from Caffènation in Antwerp, Belgium, simply because they are the very best that he can find. Galhenage is a seasoned barista and serious about the quality of the coffee he serves. Equally important is the café atmosphere, and alongside interior designer Dorothée Meilichzon, he has created a gorgeous retro-chic ambiance, where you can elegantly while away the hours. Snacks are available all day long, from breakfast to closing, including a homemade cardamom and apple granola, sweet pastries, sandwiches, and quiches.

MERCI

CONCEPT STORE WITH CAFÉS
111, boulevard Beaumarchais
Paris 3
TEL: +33 42 77 00 33
merci-merci.com
MÉTRO: Saint-Sébastien–Froissart
OPEN: Monday through Saturday 10AM to 7PM
CLOSED: Sunday
SPECIALTIES: Soups, salads, and cakes

Choose from one of three cafés—Used Book Café, Cinéma Café, and La Cantine de Merci —in the superchic concept store Merci, for a modern and inexpensive menu of salads, soups, coffee, and cake, at almost any time of the day. See Kitchen and Tableware Shops, page 375, for full commentary.

▶ *Waiting for cake at Merci's Cinéma Café.*

NANASHI (Charlot)

JAPANESE
57, rue Charlot
Paris 3
TEL: +33 9 60 00 25 59
nanashi.fr
MÉTRO: Filles du Calvaire

OPEN: Monday through Saturday noon to midnight. Sunday noon to 6PM.
PRICES: Bentos 13 to 15€. À la carte 12 to 25€.
RESERVATIONS: Recommended
SPECIALTY: Bento (a traditional Japanese meal in a box-shaped container, usually rice, fish, or meat, with cooked vegetables)

This casual Japanese-inspired trio of healthy, well-priced canteens (the other two are in the 6th and 10th *arrondissements*, respectively) offer a breath of fresh air in a world surrounded by *steak frites* and ever-present hamburger variations. The specialty here is a liberally translated bento box, featuring a protein and a grain on one side, and vegetables and salad on the other. (The vegetarian version might include wedges of tofu with a soy sauce glaze and sesame seeds.) We loved the moist, seared mackerel atop a delicious rice and grain mixture, while the accompanying salad was a healthy mix of potatoes, cauliflower, white beans, and broccoli with a toss of tender greens. The *chirashi* arrived as a warm bowl of rice topped with raw, seasoned salmon. This no-guilt concept comes packaged in an airy room of natural light with bright white walls, cheerful, primary-colored chairs, and a green chalkboard full of good-for-you treats. The rue de Touron branch, in the Bonpoint baby clothing and accessory boutique, offers a menu for babies, colorful high chairs, and a courtyard terrace for fine-weather dining.

ROSE BAKERY (Marais)

BRITISH CAFÉ / MODERN INTERNATIONAL
30, rue Debelleyme
Paris 3
TEL: +33 1 49 96 54 01
MÉTRO: Filles du Calvaire or Saint-Sébastien–Froissart

OPEN: Tuesday through Sunday 9AM to 6PM
CLOSED: Monday
PRICES: À la carte 10 to 30€
RESERVATIONS: Not taken
SPECIALTY: Carrot cake

Why seek out a British café and tea shop in the middle of Paris? Well, it's reason enough that no one does carrot cake quite like the British, and particularly Rose, of the Rose Bakery. It was this sweet little round cake that first caught the attention of Parisians, and now there are several incarnations of the Rose Bakery. You will find the two main cafés, here and on rue des Martyrs, packed at lunchtime and on weekends for brunch. There are inspired organic vegetarian salads each day with deliciously well-seasoned dressings, and the square vegetable quiches with light, flaky golden pastry are some of the best you'll find anywhere. In some shops food is served on beautiful Made in Cley glazed stoneware (from the town of Cley-next-the-Sea, near Norfolk in the East of England) that completes the homey, earthy atmosphere.

GÂTEAU AUX CAROTTES DE ROSE BAKERY
Rose Bakery's Carrot Cake

The carrot cake at the Rose Bakery shops is among the best in the world. And Anglophones craving a touch of home can't get enough if it!

EQUIPMENT:

A 10-inch (25-cm) nonstick springform pan; a heavy-duty mixer fitted with a whisk and paddle attachment

INGREDIENTS:

Unsalted butter, for buttering the pan

4 large eggs, preferably free-range and organic

1 cup (225 g) vanilla sugar

1¼ cups (300 ml) sunflower oil

5 medium carrots (about 10 ounces, 300 g total), trimmed, peeled, and finely grated

2 cups (280 g) unbleached, all-purpose flour, sifted

1 teaspoon ground cinnamon

1 teaspoon baking powder

½ teaspoon baking soda

½ teaspoon salt

1½ cups (150 g) finely chopped walnuts

THE FROSTING:

8 tablespoons (1 stick; 125 g) unsalted butter, softened

1 cup (250 g) cream cheese

½ teaspoon natural vanilla extract

½ cup (50 g) confectioners' sugar

1. Center a rack in the oven. Preheat the oven to 350°F (175°C).

2. Generously butter the pan.

3. In the bowl of the mixer, whisk the eggs and sugar at maximum speed until thick and lemon colored, about 2 minutes. Add the oil and whisk until all the ingredients are thoroughly incorporated.

4. Fold the carrots into the mixture, followed by the flour with the cinnamon, baking powder, baking soda, and salt. Finally, fold in the walnuts.

5. Pour the mixture into the buttered pan and bake until a knife inserted comes out clean, about 45 minutes. Remove to a rack to cool. After 10 minutes, run a knife along the sides of the pan. Release and remove the side of the springform pan, leaving the cake on the pan base.

6. While the cake is cooling, prepare the frosting. In the bowl of the mixer fitted with a paddle, beat the butter and cream cheese until smooth. Add the vanilla extract and confectioners' sugar.

7. When the cake has cooled, spread the frosting on the top and sides of the cake.

8 SERVINGS

▶ *One of Rose's talented pastry chefs.*

4TH ARRONDISSEMENT

L'AS DU FALLAFEL

MIDDLE EASTERN
34, rue des Rosiers
Paris 4
TEL: +33 01 48 87 63 60
MÉTRO: Saint-Paul
OPEN: Sunday and Tuesday through Thursday
11:30AM to midnight. Friday 11AM to 4:30AM.

CLOSED: Saturday, Monday, and some holidays
PRICES: 5 to 10€ at lunch and dinner
RESERVATIONS: Not necessary
SPECIALTY: Falafel (deep-fried patties or balls
made from spiced, ground chickpeas, often
served with pita bread)

You won't have any trouble finding L'As du Fallafel on the rue des Rosiers. Just look for the telltale queue stretching down the street from the takeout window, where they are selling the virtually undisputed best falafel in Paris. Don't worry—the line will move fast and the wait will be worth it for

the crispy, freshly fried falafel between generous layers of cucumber and red cabbage, slathered with a rich garlic sauce (the spicy sauce is optional), encased in a thick, pillowy pita sleeve. The sit-down canteen is somewhat grim. It's better to pay your 5€ and (weather permitting) enjoy your prize in the sunshine around the corner on the rue Payenne, where there are two public parks.

COMME À LISBONNE

PORTUGUESE
37, rue du Roi de Sicile
Paris 4
TEL: +33 1 7 61 23 42 30
MÉTRO: Saint-Paul or Pont-Marie
RESERVATIONS: Not taken (no seating area)
SPECIALTY: *Pateis de nata* (baked custard tarts)

For some of the best *pateis de nata* outside of Portugal, and beautifully packaged Mediterranean-inspired aperitifs, make a pit stop at this bright and fun hole-in-the-wall café.

LE PAIN QUOTIDIEN (Marais)

BAKERY / CAFE
18–20, rue des Archives
Paris 4

MÉTRO: Hôtel de Ville
SPECIALTIES: Soups, salads, sandwiches, and
pastries

See Bakeries, page 222, for full commentary.

5TH ARRONDISSEMENT

LA MOSQUÉE SALON DE THÉ

MOROCCAN / TEA ROOM
39, rue Geoffroy Saint-Hilaire
Paris 5
TEL: +33 1 43 31 38 20
la-mosquee.com
contact@la-mosquee.com

MÉTRO: Place Monge or Censier-Daubenton
OPEN: Daily 9AM to 11:30PM
PRICES: 2€ mint tea, pastries from 2€
RESERVATIONS: Not necessary
SPECIALTIES: Sweet mint tea and Moroccan pastries

Sipping mint tea in the outdoor *salon de thé* of La Mosquée de Paris (The Paris Mosque) under the pleasant shade of cedar and fig trees and listening to the friendly chatter of sparrows is like transporting yourself to the garden of an idyllic *riad* (house with a courtyard) in Morocco. Be sure to order a sampling of their delicious pastries: A particular favorite is the almond cake infused with orange blossom water, a pastry that is moist and not too sweet, and luckily so, as the mint tea itself is very sugary. This courtyard is a tranquil refuge early in the morning, before the crowds arrive; fun when it is packed; and perfect to know about after a visit to the Institut du Monde Arabe, the next-door Jardins des Plantes, or of course, after a relaxing *hammam* at La Mosquée itself.

LE CAMION QUI FUME

AMERICAN / FOOD TRUCK
Four roving locations (Place de la
Madeleine, Canal Saint-Martin,
Porte Maillot, and Bibliothèque
François Mitterand)
TEL: +33 01 84 16 33 75
@LeCamionQuiFume
lecamionquifume.com

contact@lecamionquifume.com
OPEN: Tuesday through Sunday.
See website, Twitter, or Facebook for
when and where to find the truck.
CLOSED: Monday
PRICES: Burger and fries 10€
SPECIALTY: Hamburgers

American chef Kristen Frederick is a game changer. Her hugely successful food truck Le Camion Qui Fume (that translates as The Smoking Truck), which serves up authentic and quite frankly delicious burgers, has reinvented Parisian street food. Although Frederick was certainly not the first to popularize burgers in Paris—they have been growing increasingly ubiquitous on Parisian café menus for several years now—she is responsible for bringing the first food truck of this type to Paris, and with its success has helped to create an explosion of street food culture in the capital. Her daily growing fan club (over 30,000 Facebook fans and over 17,000 Twitter followers) in Paris check in via their preferred social media to find out where and when they can get their burger fix. The truck pumps out more than 150 burgers at every service, and queues have been known to be up to two hours (so go early!). You cannot go wrong with *le Classique*, a perfectly executed classic beef burger. *Le Végétarian*, packed full of meaty mushrooms, is equally as satisfying—a must for vegetarians and burger lovers alike. While I could do without the mediocrity of the café burger frenzy, I applaud Frederick for inspiring street food entrepreneurialism in Paris, and would happily sit down on the steps of the Madeleine or the side of the Canal Saint Martin any day to enjoy one of her burger creations.

Frederick's burgers can also be enjoyed at the super-hip diner Le Depanneur (27, rue Pierre Fontaine, Paris 9), for those who prefer a seated experience. Aside from the inventive and well-executed cocktails, the burger is by far the best item on the menu there.

6TH ARRONDISSEMENT

L'AVANT COMPTOIR

CLASSIC FRENCH
3, carrefour de l'Odéon
Paris 6
No telephone
MÉTRO: Odéon

OPEN: Daily noon to 11PM
PRICES: Small plates 3 to 22€
RESERVATIONS: Not taken
(no tables, standing room only)
SPECIALTY: Small plates and tapas

Yves Camdeborde gives new meaning to the expression "small plates." His always-jammed, hit-the-jackpot, standing-room-only eatery is a smash, with a constantly changing array of tiny, perfect bites. His *croquette jambon* tastes like a grown-up version of the satisfying mac and cheese without the pasta. The *saucisses herbes* are no more than a few memorable bites of well-seasoned grilled pork sausage bathed in a surprising horseradish foam. The *piments poêlés* are the famed tiny *padron* peppers just seared ever so quickly on the grill in the tiny open kitchen, and packing a good deal of fire, while the wintry hare stew topped with mashed potatoes *(parmentier de lièvre)* made me want to order seconds, maybe thirds.

L'Avant Comptoir also offers generous platters of ham, sausage, *boudin noir* (blood sausage), and chorizo, as well as a plate of Basque sheep's-milk cheese. When you go, be sure to look up, for the menu is on the ceiling . . . really. There is also window service for made-on-the-spot *galettes* (savory buckwheat *crêpes*) and sweet dessert *crêpes*. And a fine selection of wines is offered by the glass or bottle.

LE BONAPARTE

CLASSIC FRENCH CAFÉ
42, rue Bonaparte
Paris 6
TEL: +33 1 43 26 42 81
MÉTRO: Saint-Germain-des-Prés

OPEN: Daily 8AM to 2PM
PRICES: À la carte 7 to 25€ at lunch and dinner
RESERVATIONS: Not necessary
SPECIALTIES: *Steak tartare*, onion soup

In fine weather the sun streams into this popular Saint-Germain café, a haunt that's set back away from the crossroads bustle of the more touristy Les Deux Magots (see page 145). This is a dressed-up spot, with a warming interior decor, spiffed-up waiters, and lots of specialties, including meats

▲ *Le Bonaparte, a favorite Saint-Germain café.*

from the Auvergne (seared steaks and carpaccio), as well as a warming onion soup (gratinée d'oignons) that merits a visit, with its rich homemade broth, thin layer of bread, and excellent cheese. The popular hamburger can be a bit dry and lifeless. (I once watched a Frenchman pouring ketchup on top of his bun, a sight to see! He ate it with a knife and fork, of course.) At this café, you will always find something that appeals, with their large selection of salads and omelets.

COSI

SANDWICH BAR
54, rue de Seine
Paris 6
TEL: +33 1 46 33 35 36
MÉTRO: Mabillon, Odéon, or Saint-Germain-des-Prés

OPEN: Daily noon to 11PM (midnight Friday and Saturday)
PRICES: Sandwiches from 5.50€ to 9.50€
RESERVATIONS: Not taken

For a completely satisfying sandwich experience in Saint-Germain, don't think twice about heading to Cosi. It's the original one (no longer affiliated with the U.S. franchise) created and still owned by New Zealander Drew Harré (who is virtually taking over the street with his co-owned restaurant Fish and latest venture Semilla). This sandwich bar has become a cult pit stop in the area for hungry locals and tourists alike. All sandwiches are made with the freshest focaccia bread, cooked on the premises in a brick oven. There is a huge selection of creative filling combinations. Try the sandwich of roast beef, roast tomatoes, onions, and green salad; the fresh roasted salmon with ricotta, walnuts, and lemon juice; or one of the many vegetarian options. Don't fancy a sandwich? A smaller menu of soups, salads, and desserts is also on offer, with an unbeatable menu *formule* of sandwich, dessert, and beverage from 9.50€. On sunny days this is the perfect portable picnic to take over to the Seine or the nearby park in the place Saint-Germain. If you prefer a table, there are plenty of seats in the upstairs canteen-style floor of the restaurant.

BAR DE LA CROIX ROUGE

CLASSIC FRENCH CAFÉ
2, carrefour de la Croix Rouge
Paris 6
TEL: +33 1 45 48 06 45
MÉTRO: Sèvres–Babylone

OPEN: Monday through Saturday 7AM to 10PM
CLOSED: Sunday
PRICES: À la carte 10 to 30€
RESERVATIONS: Not taken

No matter where we travel in the world, Walter, my husband, and I always look forward to certain rituals once we land in Paris. The breakneck taxi ride home, my own espresso, the familiar shower, and the unceremonious lunch at a café just a few blocks from our apartment, Bar de la Croix Rouge. For the two of us, it is a reassuring sign that we are grounded and home. On the menu for us, always, is the *Assiette Saint-Germain,* an open-faced sandwich—or *tartine*—of perfectly toasted Poilâne bread lightly spread with butter, then topped with ultra-thin slices of the most delicious rare-roasted beef. The garnish is pretty much an afterthought: a few forgettable slices of tomato, a touch of greens dressed with a classic creamy mustard vinaigrette, and some welcome, puckery cornichons. There is always a jar of pungent mustard on the table, as well as a small glass (or two) of chilled Brouilly. Welcome home, indeed!

CUISINE DE BAR (Saint-Germain)

SANDWICH BAR
8, rue du Cherche-Midi
Paris 6
TEL: +33 1 45 48 45 69
cuisinedebar.fr
MÉTRO: Sèvres-Babylone or Saint-Sulpice
OPEN: Tuesday through Saturday
8:30AM to 7PM

CLOSED: Sunday, Monday, and three weeks from the end of July to mid-August
PRICES: 13.50€ all-day menu. Breakfast 7.90 to 12.10€. Lunch *tartines* 9.50 to 11.90€. Teatime 7.20€.
RESERVATIONS: Not necessary
SPECIALTY: *Tartines* (open-faced sandwiches)

This animated, always-busy little shop next to the landmark Poilâne bakery (and operated by it) serves up some of the best *tartines*, or open-faced sandwiches, in Paris. See page 136 for full commentary.

LES DEUX MAGOTS

CLASSIC FRENCH CAFÉ
6, place Saint-Germain-des-Prés
Paris 6
TEL: +33 1 45 48 55 25
lesdeuxmagots.fr
contact@lesdeuxmagots.fr
MÉTRO: Saint-Germain-des-Prés

OPEN: Daily 7:30AM to 1AM. Dinner menu 7 to 11PM.
PRICES: À la carte café menu items from 7.50 to 28€ at lunch, à la carte restaurant menu items 10.50 to 35€
RESERVATIONS: Not necessary

This landmark café at the crossroads of boulevard Saint-Germain and rue Bonaparte—with its bright white-and-green awnings, wicker chairs, and glistening café tables—is perhaps the ultimate Paris café. Many prefer Café de Flore a few doors away, but I love them both, for different reasons.

The food, coffee, and sunshine are better at Les Deux Magots, and people-watching is superior at Flore. I love sitting in the shadow of the Église Saint-Germain with its towering spires, sipping a glass of Chablis with my *croquet Provençal,* a substantial creation of *pain de mie,* cooked ham, fresh tomatoes, herbs, and cheese, grilled to perfection. Equally fine are their slices of Poilâne toast with excellent smoked salmon. The coffee here is delicious and they offer pastries from two excellent pastry chefs, Pierre Hermé and Philippe Gosselin. If they have it that day, dive into Hermé's *2,000 Feuilles,* a gorgeous *millefeuille* with a crispy golden puff pastry and layers of chocolate cream and almond cream. Almost a meal in itself. In season, try Gosselin's *tarte aux figues,* a lovely creation with a cookie-like crust, a thin wisp of pastry cream, and delicious fresh figs. A good place to stop any time of day or night, the café has been pleasing patrons since 1884.

CAFÉ DE FLORE

CLASSIC FRENCH CAFÉ
172, boulevard Saint-Germain
Paris 6
TEL: +33 1 45 48 55 26
cafedeflore.fr
info@cafedeflore.fr

MÉTRO: Saint-Germain-des-Prés
OPEN: Daily 7AM to 2AM
PRICES: À la carte menu items 7.50 to 35€ at lunch and dinner
RESERVATIONS: Not taken

Few spots say "Paris" like the Café de Flore: landmark, historic, almost mythical. Sitting on the sun-dappled terrace at any hour of the day, you always feel as though you are at the right place at the right time. Call in for a quick coffee with the morning papers, linger with friends over a lunch of smoked salmon and a glass of Chablis, pop in for a late-night glass of bubbly. The food here inspires not at all (bland onion soup, dry *croque monsieur*) but it's the scene you want, and that's not dry or bland, and there's more than enough to go around. The warming, rich hot chocolate is worth the detour on a cold wintry day.

LADURÉE (Saint-Germain)

CLASSIC FRENCH TEA SALON
21, rue Bonaparte

Paris 6
MÉTRO: Saint-Germain-des-Prés

Transport yourself to a more elegant and gracious era that is the world of Ladurée. Here there is a pastry counter for carry-out purchases, a tea salon, and a shop full of sweet-scented Ladurée items, perfect for gifts. See Pastry Shops, page 298, for full commentary.

"I was often alone, but seldom lonely: I enjoyed the newspaper and books that were my usual companions at the table, the exchanges with waiters, barmen, booksellers, street vendors . . . the sound of the conversations of others around me, and finally, the talk of the girls I ended some evenings by picking up."

—A. J. LIEBLING

▶ *Whiling away the hours at a café with a coffee and a notebook. A timeless Paris tradition.*

BRASSERIE LIPP

BRASSERIE
115, boulevard Saint-Germain
Paris 6
TEL: + 33 1 45 48 53 91
groupe-bertrand.com/lipp.php
MÉTRO: Saint-Germain-des-Prés

OPEN: Daily 9AM to 1AM (last order at 12:45AM)
PRICES: À la carte 50€ at lunch and dinner
RESERVATIONS: Not necessary
ATMOSPHERE: Casual
SPECIALTIES: Oysters, from September through April

When I am in the mood for oysters—from September through April— I sit myself down on the popular covered sidewalk terrace of the landmark Brasserie Lipp, order up half a dozen of their well-chilled, delicious, briny *spéciales*, as well as a carafe of their very drinkable house

Riesling, and watch the Left Bank world go by. I'll follow that with a classic *salade de mâche et betterave,* a wholesome mix of lamb's lettuce, hard-cooked eggs, and giant cubes of beets, all topped with a tangy mustard dressing. I *never* dine inside, where the atmosphere is haughty and hurried.

▶*An unlikely reunion: Monsieur Luc Pignon was photographed holding a tray of freshly opened oysters in the first two editions of* The Food Lover's Guide to Paris, *for which he also appeared on the back cover, in 1984 and 1988. Here, he holds the third edition, where he is featured on page 78.*

LITTLE BREIZH

BRETON / *CRÊPERIE*
11, rue Grégoire de Tours
Paris 6
TEL: +33 1 43 54 60 74
creperielittlebreizh@gmail.com
MÉTRO: Mabillon, Odéon, or Saint-Germain-des-Prés
OPEN: Tuesday through Saturday

CLOSED: Sunday, Monday, three weeks in August, and between Christmas and New Year's
PRICES: 9 to 13.50€ weekday lunch menu, cider included. À la carte 10 to 19€.
RESERVATIONS: Not taken
SPECIALTIES: Organic buckwheat *crêpes* and *galettes*

This postage-stamp-size *crêperie,* hidden away on a tiny street near the Odéon, is a real find for an early lunch. The buckwheat *galettes* are prepared with a very dense and earthy black-flecked organic flour (*blé noir*) coarsely milled especially for the owners—brother and sister team Pierre and

Claire Goasdoué—who put their hearts and souls into this little enterprise. Stone walls, giant wooden beams, and bistro chairs give it a true neighborhood air. I could lunch here every day, sampling the elegant, filling ham-and-cheese *galette,* a creation that is like a love poem to Brittany. The *galette* is paper-thin, crisp and crunchy, with a deep, rich, freshly milled texture. Wash it down with a cup of chilled cider and you have a meal for under 10€. The salmon *galette* is equally appealing, and service comes with smiling cheerfulness—and excellent spoken English. This is a good place to know about for a late morning meal (*galettes* for breakfast, anyone?) since it opens at 11AM. It's also child- and vegetarian-friendly. (And in case you were wondering, *Breizh* means "Brittany" in the Breton language.)

▶ *Claire and Pierre Goasdoué, proud owners of the adorable Little Breizh.*

NANASHI (Bonpoint)

JAPANESE
6, rue de Tournon
Paris 6
TEL: +33 1 43 26 14 06
nanashi.fr
MÉTRO: Odéon or Mabillon
OPEN: Tuesday through Saturday 10AM to 7PM

CLOSED: Sunday and Monday
PRICES: Bentos 13 to 15€.
À la carte 12 to 25€.
RESERVATIONS: Not necessary
SPECIALTY: Bento (a traditional Japanese meal in a box-shaped container, usually rice, fish or meat, with cooked vegetables); baby menu

Healthy salads and Japanese-inspired bentos are Nanashi's specialty. Here in the downstairs café space of the chic Bonpoint baby clothing store, they supply high chairs and a baby puree menu, most certainly the only one in Paris! See page 138 for full commentary.

LE PAVILLON DE LA FONTAINE

CAFÉ
Luxembourg Gardens
Paris 6
TEL: +33 1 56 24 38 40
MÉTRO: Odéon or Luxembourg (RER B)

OPEN: Daily until park closing (changes seasonally)
PRICES: À la carte 7 to 21€ at lunch and dinner
RESERVATIONS: Not taken

When I want to feel just a little bit as though I am on vacation, I sit myself down at one of the pale-green tables of Le Pavillon de la Fontaine, a café set beneath the soaring aged chestnut trees near the eastern edge of the Luxembourg Gardens. Parisians and tourists alike savor the clean air along with the welcome, gurgling sounds of the romantic Medici Fountain nearby. I'll order a chilled glass of Sancerre, one of the several *tartines* (open-faced sandwiches) prepared with the sturdy Poilâne sourdough bread, and savor the moment. My favorite here is the Luxembourg, a combination of grilled ham, cheese, and sliced tomatoes.

DA ROSA

CAFÉ / *ÉPICERIE* / SPANISH / ITALIAN
62, rue de Seine
Paris 6
TEL: +33 1 40 51 00 09
MÉTRO: Mabillon or Saint-Germain-des-Prés

OPEN: Daily 11AM to 11PM
PRICES: À la carte 30€ at lunch and dinner
RESERVATIONS: Not necessary
SPECIALTIES: Spanish ham and *charcuterie*, *foie gras*, caviar, spices

This Spanish *épicerie*/wine bar/restaurant is a great place to know when looking for a good, quick authentic bite in the Saint-Germain neighborhood. Fast food doesn't have to mean bad food! Take their legendary soup with a vegetable bouillon base and an addition of carrots, celery leaves, potatoes, and zucchini. Diners get three more ingredients to complete the dish: choose from flecks of Spanish ham, chickpeas, split peas, white beans, or spelt, and you have a complete meal to enjoy on the sidewalk terrace, indoors, upstairs or down, or to take away. I highly recommend their *tartines*, open-faced sandwiches on ultra-thick slices of country bread, mostly slathered with tomato pulp and olive oil and "extras." The Catalane is embellished with Serrano ham and Manchego cheese; the *Pan con Tomate* is layered with pungent, vinegary *boquerones* (anchovies marinated in white vinegar) and a shower of Basque *Espelette* peppers. There are Italian touches here as well, with warming bowls of *penne à l'arrabbiata* (spicy tomato sauce and basil) and *pasta della mamma* (carrots, zucchini, celery, red onions, basil, asparagus, and olive oil). The gleaming plates of raw-milk *burrata* (mozzarella with a center of cream) and

fresh, raw-milk buffalo mozzarella continue the added Italian accent. Da Rosa offers the extraordinary *boudin noir* (blood sausage) from Frenchman Christian Parra, a spicy, earthy dish that I love to eat at least once each year, for no reason other than that it is unique and delicious. In short, this is a place not to miss when you are looking for big flavors, a lively atmosphere, and a quality meal that will not break the bank. It's difficult not to leave without a pink-and-white Da Rosa shopping bag full of goodies to take home. There are seven varieties of prized Spanish hams, five types of Italian *salumerie*, famed Portuguese ham, a huge selection of Spanish, Portuguese, and Italian wines, as well as *foie gras*, smoked fish, caviar, and *tarama* (a dip or spread made from fish roe, olive oil, and bread). The sheep's-milk Spanish Manchego cheese is excellent and I am a big fan of their paper-thin sliced chorizo. For those too tired to cross the street to the Italian ice-cream shop Grom (see Pastry Shops, page 298), you can stay put and have your Grom ice cream right where you are. And tarts and pastries come from only the best, Philippe Conticini's La Pâtisserie des Rêves (see Pastry Shops, page 303).

TSUKIZI

JAPANESE SUSHI BAR
2 bis rue des Ciseaux
Paris 6
TEL: +33 1 43 54 65 19
MÉTRO: Saint-Germain-des-Prés or Mabillon
OPEN: Tuesday through Saturday and Sunday dinner

CLOSED: Sunday lunch, all day Monday, two weeks at Christmas, and August
PRICES: 17€ lunch menu. À la carte 35 to 55€.
RESERVATIONS: Recommended
SPECIALTIES: Sushi, sashimi, fish and shellfish, sake

Since the early 1980s, this small, serious, no-frills Japanese restaurant has been pleasing diners with its authentic, ultra-fresh sushi and sashimi. I love to come and sit at the bar to watch the action as everything is prepared on the spot. I look forward to feasting on a lunch of ginger-packed, cubed mackerel, red tuna, salmon, and a freshly made cucumber-filled maki. There is always a bowl of hot soup, and appetizers such as cucumbers for dipping in rich miso or tender monkfish livers. Add a few sips of cold sake and I'm restored and ready for an afternoon of intense writing.

YOOM (Saint-Germain)

CHINESE
5, rue Grégoire de Tours
Paris 6
TEL: +33 1 43 54 94 56
MÉTRO: Mabillon or Odéon
OPEN: Tuesday through Saturday
CLOSED: Sunday and Monday

PRICES: 15€ lunch menu, 20€ vegetarian menu, 25€ *decouverte* menu, and à la carte 25 to 30€ at lunch and dinner. Dim sum from 5.50€.
RESERVATIONS: Recommended; essential on weekends
SPECIALTY: Dim sum (small, bite-size steamed dumplings and other delicacies)

When two Parisian friends came back after several years in Hong Kong, what they missed was dim sum, those endearing little steamed dumplings stuffed with meat, seafood, vegetables, and all manner of herbs. So the pair set out to learn the intricacies of dim sum with the help of

Chinese chefs. Today, they have not one but two dim sum restaurants: their spot on the fabulous market street rue des Martyrs in the 9th, and another on rue Grégoire de Tours in the 6th. Their places are hip and modern-looking, and while you don't have the grand-ballroom steamy setting of old Hong Kong (or the refined elegance of Paris's own Shang Palace), Yoom is a fine spot for a quick, light lunch when you need an Asian hit. I love that their combinations are a little out-side the box, with vibrant-tasting dump-lings filled with beef, ginger, soy, and basil;

others stuffed with mushrooms, carrots, satay sauce, chicken, peanuts, and corian-der. The small menu moves all around Asia, with some delightful Thai shrimp meatballs (*boulettes thai pimentées aux crevettes*), and soothing Vietnamese rice paper *crêpes* filled with chunks of smoked sausage, fish sauce, and chili sauce. Yoom is a bit pricey (5 or 6€ for just two to three dumplings), and too many dishes arrive lukewarm, reducing the pleasure by half. So ask for everything to be served steaming hot. And don't come too hungry or too poor.

7TH ARRONDISSEMENT

COUTUME

CAFÉ / COFFEE BAR
47, rue de Babylone
Paris 7
TEL: +33 1 45 51 50 47
coutumecafe.com
info@coutumecafe.com

MÉTRO: Saint-François-Xavier or Vaneau
OPEN: Monday through Friday 8AM to 7PM.
Saturday and Sunday 10AM to 7PM.
RESERVATIONS: Not taken
SPECIALTY: Coffee

Paris is famous for café culture, not so much coffee culture, and a smooth, well-roasted coffee is hard to come by if you don't make it yourself. But Coutume Café is a standout in a handful of serious coffeehouses whose mission is to change that. Tucked away on the rue Babylone, not far from

Le Bon Marché, the airy industrial-style space is part café, part laboratory. Beans are roasted on-site and there are numerous extraction methods available to fulfill every caffeine-related whim: espresso, siphon, cone filter, or 24-hour cold-drip filter. Prepare to be educated! Tea lovers will be happy here, too, with a fine selection of organic teas, all to

be accompanied by fresh delicious cakes from the nearby Pâtisserie des Rêves (see page 303). The 7€ breakfast menu of mini pas-tries, freshly squeezed juice, and a hot drink is unbeatable. Soups and salads are available for a perfect light lunch. And, of course, all their coffee is sold for home use—ground or whole bean.

TARTINE POILÂNE DE CAFÉ LE RASPAIL

Café Le Raspail's Poilâne Tartine

The homey, charming Café Le Raspail (at 58, boulevard Raspail) is the perfect spot for enjoying a sip of wine and a hearty *tartine* (open-faced sandwich) while overlooking the lively Tuesday and Friday market set up along a tree-lined stretch that divides the boulevard Raspail. The café is just steps from the Poilâne bakery, at 8, rue du Cherche-Midi. This is my re-creation of one of Café Le Raspail's classic *tartines*.

EQUIPMENT:

An oven with a broiler; a toaster; a baking sheet

INGREDIENTS:

2 thick slices sourdough bread

2 teaspoons French mustard

8 ultra-thin slices cooked ham (3 ounces; 100 g)

4 ounces (125 g) freshly grated Swiss Gruyère cheese

1. Arrange a rack in the oven about 3 inches (7.5 cm) from the heat source. Preheat the broiler.

2. In the toaster, toast the bread. Arrange the slices of bread side by side on the baking sheet.

3. Spread the mustard over each slice of toast. Arrange the ham on top of the mustard. Sprinkle the cheese on top of the ham.

4. Place the baking sheet under the broiler and broil just until the cheese melts, 30 seconds to 1 minute. Serve immediately.

2 SERVINGS

PATRICK LIRON

huitres-normandie.fr

Oyster-loving Parisians know exactly where to find Normandy's finest iodine-rich crustaceans in the capital, and now you do, too: Patrick Liron's *écaillier* stands open every Friday, Saturday, and Sunday during oyster season from October to the end of March.
See Brasserie aux PTT (below) for descriptions of Liron's oyster varieties.

17, rue des Petits Carreaux	28, rue des Archives	54, rue Cler (outside Brasserie aux PTT)	68, avenue de la Motte Picquet
Paris 2	Paris 4	Paris 7	Paris 15
MÉTRO: Sentier	MÉTRO: Hôtel de Ville	MÉTRO: École Militaire	MÉTRO: La Motte-Piquet–Grenelle
OPEN: Friday through Sunday 10AM to 10PM	OPEN: Saturday only 9AM to 10PM	OPEN: Friday and Saturday 9AM to 9PM and Sunday 9AM to 2PM	OPEN: Friday 11AM to 9PM, Saturday 10AM to 9PM, and Sunday 9AM to 2PM
FOR ORDERS: Call Stéphane, +33 6 03 02 55 11	FOR ORDERS: Call +33 1 42 78 56 66	FOR ORDERS: Call Stéphane, +33 6 87 21 30 34	FOR ORDERS: Call Jean Etienne, +33 6 40 24 96 48

BRASSERIE AUX PTT

BRASSERIE
54, rue Cler
Paris 7
TEL: +33 1 45 51 94 96
ADVANCE OYSTER ORDERS:
+33 6 87 21 30 34
MÉTRO: École Militaire

OPEN: Café open Monday through Saturday 7AM to 10PM. Oysters at the café or carryout (in season, October–March) 9AM to 9PM Friday and Saturday, 9AM to 2PM Sunday (carryout only).
CLOSED: Sunday (café)
RESERVATIONS: Not taken
SPECIALTIES: Fish and shellfish, oysters

When I am in Paris, on most Saturdays of the "R" months, I can be found lunching on an incomparable oyster feast at the Brasserie aux PTT. (The café is next to the neighborhood post office, or PTT, which stands for Postes, Télégraphes et Téléphones, the original national designation for the French postal service, formed in 1921.) My longtime friend and fellow oyster lover Maggie Shapiro introduced us to the most delicious oysters, all from grower Patrick Liron in Normandy. I don't know when I've sampled oysters with such finesse. Even the largest and priciest—the meaty *Viroise Speciales* from Isigny, with an almost buttery aftertaste—offer an elegance that other oysters simply can't match. The choice is vast and includes the lean and rustic *Pleine Mer* from Blainville, a spot with the strongest tides in Europe; the *Speciales Saint-Vaast,* found as far north as oysters will grow in France, offering a hint of hazelnuts; the *Belle du Liron,* an oyster with a lovely equilibrium and a healthy touch of iodine; and the rich and meaty *Spéciales* from Utah Beach, with an extraordinarily long finish. Be sure to say hello to the charming master *écaillier* (oyster and shellfish shucker) Stéphane Labozec and sip a little Pouilly-Fumé for me. (Note that the fresh oysters are available only from October to the end of April, only on Friday and Saturday at the café and on Sunday for carryout. The café has of course a regular café menu of salads, cheese, meats, poultry, and fish during all open hours.)

LE PAIN QUOTIDIEN (Rue du Bac)

25, rue de Varenne
Paris 7
MÉTRO: Rue de Bac or Sèvres-Babylone

See Bakeries, page 222, for full commentary.

SPECIALTIES: Soups, salads, sandwiches, and pastries

ROSE BAKERY (Bon Marché)

BRITISH CAFÉ / MODERN INTERNATIONAL
2nd floor, Bon Marché Department Store
24, rue de Sèvres
Paris 7
TEL: +33 1 42 22 60 00

MÉTRO: Sèvres–Babylone
OPEN: Monday through Saturday 10AM to 7PM
CLOSED: Sunday and public holidays
PRICES: À la carte 10 to 30€
RESERVATIONS: Not taken
SPECIALTY: Carrot cake

The earthy British tearoom Rose Bakery has had a makeover for its Bon Marché incarnation. A sleek white interior with gold trim is an elegant backdrop for the pristine cakes and tarts that are on display. Here you will find a small menu with well-considered options for breakfast, lunch, or afternoon tea. See page 138 for full commentary.

CAFÉ VARENNE

CLASSIC FRENCH CAFÉ
36, rue de Varenne
Paris 7
TEL: +33 1 45 48 62 72
MÉTRO: Rue du Bac or Sèvres–Babylone
OPEN: Monday through Friday 7:30AM to 10:30PM. Saturday 9AM to 8PM.

CLOSED: Sunday, holidays, and two weeks in August
PRICES: À la carte 30€ at lunch and dinner
RESERVATIONS: Not necessary
SPECIALTIES: Steak frites, roast chicken, salads, steak tartare

A convenient location if you're shopping along the rue du Bac or heading to the Rodin Museum. The menu is varied, but roast chicken is a constant, as are copious fresh salads. The blackboard lists daily specials, like a hearty sausage or *saucisson* with potato puree, or a dependably fresh fish choice. That's also where to look for the wines of the moment. And of course this is a café, and a welcoming stop for a caffeine hit or late-afternoon beer. Since the arrival of new owners, Sylvain and Agnès Didier, the quality of the food took a giant leap forward. Full disclosure: My husband, Walter, is honored to have his name on the wall over one of the tables.

A BIT OF PARISIAN COFFEE HISTORY

When Louis XIV first tasted coffee in 1664, he was not impressed. But Parisian high society fell in love with the intoxicating brew, enjoying it at lavish and exotic parties arranged by the Turkish ambassador, who arrived in 1669.

By 1670, the general public got a taste of the rich caffeinated drink when an Armenian named Pascal hawked it at the Saint-Germain fair in the spring. He hired formally dressed waiters to go out among the crowds and through the streets, crying as they went, "Café. Café." Later Pascal opened a little coffee boutique like those he had seen in Constantinople. It was not a smashing success, but he survived with the help of his wandering waiters, who even went door to door with jugs of the thick black brew. Then, as now, doctors discussed the merits and drawbacks of coffee. Those who favored the drink argued that it cured scurvy, relieved smallpox and gout, and was even recommended for gargling to improve the voice. *Café au lait* was lauded for its medicinal qualities, and in 1688, Madame de Sévigné, whose letters record the life of the period, noted it as a remedy for colds and chest illnesses.

By the time the city's first café, Le Procope, opened in 1686, coffee was well on its way to winning the Parisian palate.

LES BERGES

Along the Seine riverbank
lesberges.paris.fr

Until recently, a picnic on the edge of the Île Saint Louis, a padlock offering to the Pont des Arts, or a visit to Paris Plage were your best options to appreciate La Seine. However, Paris Mayor Bertrand Delonoë's bold move to close off the Left Bank *quai* in central Paris and give it over to pedestrians, cyclists, runners, and gourmands has been one of the city's most exciting public developments in many years. For 1.5 miles (2.3 km) between the Pont d'Alma and Pont Royal, there are large oak benches to sit on and watch the world and the river go by, shipping containers repurposed into cozy cabanas (called "Zzz boxes") with their own landscaped gardens, a ton of fun activities for children, a fitness trail, free outdoor yoga classes, public concerts, and happily, some fantastic street food options.

Here are my picks for snacking along the Seine.

MOZZA & CO.

Port de Solférino between Pont de la
Concorde and Pont Royal bridge
mozzaandco.it
MÉTRO: Assemblée Nationale
OPEN: Daily 11AM to midnight

Situated in a repurposed shipping container, Mozza & Co. specializes in Italian salads and focaccia sandwiches, with mozzarella as the star of the show.

OMNIVORE RIVES

Port de Solférino between Pont de la
Concorde and Pont Royal bridge
MÉTRO: Assemblée Nationale
OPEN: Tuesday through Thursday 11AM to 7PM, Friday through Sunday 10AM to 11PM
CLOSED: Monday

The first actual food location to be conceived by the Omnivore Food Festival crew, selling sandwiches, salads, and the ubiquitous burger. They also cater picnic baskets for the Zzz boxes.

EN ATTENDANT ROSA

Port des Invalides between Pont Alexandre
III and Pont de la Concorde bridges
MÉTRO: Invalides
OPEN: Wednesday through Sunday, 8AM to midnight. Note opening hours change seasonally and are likely to be shorter in the colder months.

The huge terrace of picnic benches and swinging festoon lights might make you think you're in Mexico, until you take a look to your left at the golden angels of the Pont Alexandre III. A fun place to have a drink and casual tapas, and enjoy the not-so-casual view!

8TH ARRONDISSEMENT

LADURÉE (Champs-Élysées)

CLASSIC FRENCH TEA SALON
75, avenue des Champs-Élysées
Paris 8
MÉTRO: George V

What could be more glamorous than dining in baroque splendor on one of Paris's most iconic streets? This beautiful tea salon will transport you to another, more gracious era.

See Pastry Shops, page 298, for full commentary.

LADURÉE (Rue Royale)

CLASSIC FRENCH TEA SALON
16, rue Royale
Paris 8
MÉTRO: Madeleine

This original 1862 Ladurée, down the street from the Church of the Madeleine, is a favorite, with its ceiling decor of fat cherubs baking brioches in the heat of the sun.

9TH ARRONDISSEMENT

ANGELINA (Galeries Lafayette)

CLASSIC FRENCH TEA SALON
Galeries Lafayette
First floor women's fashion
40, boulevard Haussmann
Paris 9

MÉTRO: Havre-Caumartin or Chausée d'Antin-La Fayette
OPEN: Monday through Saturday 9:30AM to 6:30PM
RESERVATIONS: Not necessary

While this department store outpost of the famous Angelina *salon de thé* is not nearly as spectacular as dining in the main Rivoli tea room, this is a good spot to refuel with a hot chocolate or pastry while shopping up a storm at the Galeries Lafayette. See page 129 for full commentary.

LADURÉE (Printemps de la Mode)

CLASSIC FRENCH TEA SALON
Printemps de la Mode Haussmann
64, boulevard Haussmann

Paris 9
MÉTRO: Havre-Caumartin

Visiting Ladurée is how you begin one of the most romantically nostalgic of Parisian experiences. The small boutique and café on the second floor of Printemps de la Mode has all the charm of Ladurée's larger cafés, where you will find yourself in a different, more gracious era. Here you can pick up macarons, sweet tarts, and Ladurée merchandise. See Pastry Shops, page 298, for full commentary.

LES PÂTES VIVANTES

CHINESE
46, rue du Faubourg–Montmartre
Paris 9
TEL: +33 1 45 23 10 21
lespatesvivantes.net
MÉTRO: Le Peletier

OPEN: Monday through Saturday
CLOSED: Sunday
PRICES: À la carte 12 to 25€ at lunch and
dinner. 19€ dinner menu.
RESERVATIONS: Recommended
SPECIALTY: Hand-pulled noodles

I was hungry for Asian and something fiery, so I settled at a window table at the small, casual Les Pâtes Vivantes on rue du Faubourg-Montmartre. The satisfying and amazingly long, alabaster hand-pulled noodles are made right before your eyes, and you can even follow the action from the street, thanks to a screen that hangs in front of the shop and broadcasts live video. There are tons to choose from here, but we headed straight for the heat, the spicy *crevettes touchant la ciel*, a giant bowl of soothing wheat noodles teamed with squares of soft tofu, Chinese cabbage, shrimp in the shell, and plenty of Szechuan peppercorns. All that, shared—and even then, unfinished—for 12.50€. I was in seventh heaven! A great starter here is the mustard green salad, bathed in a sesame oil dressing, with plenty of garlic and whole almonds. And this is one of the few places in Paris where a "doggy bag" is not just allowed, but offered!

ROSE BAKERY (Martyrs)

**BRITISH CAFÉ / MODERN
INTERNATIONAL**
46, rue des Martyrs
Paris 9
TEL: +33 1 42 82 12 80
MÉTRO: Saint-Georges or Pigalle

OPEN: Tuesday through Sunday 9AM to 6PM
CLOSED: Monday
PRICES: À la carte 10 to 30€
RESERVATIONS: Not taken
SPECIALTIES: Carrot cake

For a touch of British, try the health-conscious Rose Bakery. See page 138 for full commentary.

YOOM (Martyrs)

CHINESE
20, rue des Martyrs
Paris 9
TEL: +33 1 56 92 19 10
MÉTRO: Saint-Georges or
Notre-Dame de Lorette
OPEN: Daily
PRICES: 15€ lunch menu, 20€ vegetarian

menu, 25€ *decouverte* menu, and à la carte
25 to 30€ at lunch and dinner. Dim sum from
5.50€.
RESERVATIONS: Recommended, essential on
weekends
SPECIALTY: Dim sum (small bite-size steamed
dumplings and other delicacies)

Dim sum in a modern setting. See page 150 for full commentary.

10TH ARRONDISSEMENT

KRISHNA BHAVAN

INDIAN CANTEEN
24, rue Cail
Paris 10
TEL: +33 1 42 05 78 43
MÉTRO: Louis Blanc, La Chapelle, or Gare du Nord

OPEN: Daily 11AM to 11PM
PRICES: À la carte 10 to 20€ at lunch and dinner
RESERVATIONS: Recommended on weekends

For the warm aromatic spices of Tamil cooking and a veritable vegetarian feast, Krishna Bhavan is a sure bet. Off the beaten Parisian track amid sari stores and Indian grocers, Krishna Bhavan is an unassuming basic canteen-style restaurant that serves up light and delicious Indian classics. The *thaali* is a fantastic value, offering an assortment of lentil *dhal* and vegetable stews and curries, served with rice. The light-as-air *dosa* (fried *crêpe* of rice and black lentils) is crispy and comes with your choice of filling, and is served with traditional dipping sauces and chutneys. Finish off your meal with a yogurt-based mango *lassi* or a pistachio *kulfi* (Indian-style ice cream).

NOTE: This restaurant is completely vegetarian and does not serve alcohol.

NANASHI (Paradis)

JAPANESE
31, rue de Paradis
Paris 10
TEL: +33 1 40 22 05 55
nanashi.fr
MÉTRO: Poissonière or Château d'Eau

OPEN: Monday through Saturday noon to midnight. Sunday noon to 6PM.
PRICES: Bentos 13 to 15€. À la carte 12 to 25€.
RESERVATIONS: Recommended
SPECIALTY: Bento (a traditional Japanese meal in a box-shaped container, usually rice, fish, or meat, with cooked vegetables)

A bright and breezy canteen serving Japanese-inspired bentos. See page 138 for full commentary.

THE SUNKEN CHIP

BRITISH
39, rue des Vinaigriers
Paris 10
TEL: +33 1 53 26 74 46
MÉTRO: Jacques Bonsergent

OPEN: Wednesday through Saturday noon to 2:30PM and 7PM to 10:30PM
CLOSED: Monday and Tuesday
PRICES: 14€ and 16€ menus. 10€ children's menu.
RESERVATIONS: Not taken
SPECIALTY: Fish and chips

This is the import of food culture at its best. If you are going to transfer something *so British!* (as the French so dearly love to say) to Paris, it had better be good. And Michael Greenwold (co-chef and owner of the excellent modern bistro Roseval; see Restaurants, page 123) and fellow Englishman and bar owner James Whelan have hit the mark with their minimalist white tiled diner that is the first dedicated fish-and-chip shop in the French capital. The ultra-fresh fish, caught sustainably in Brittany and delivered daily, is sublime, arriving in a cardboard boat and enveloped in a light, golden-crusted batter. The fries are authentically English: fat and, for my taste, a little on the dry side (but improved with the classic malt vinegar you find in every English chippy). Go for the hake (*Merlu*) or haddock if they have it as a daily special, rather than the pollack (*lieu jaune* or *lieu noir*), which I find to be an inferior fish that often lacks substance and flavor. Be sure to try the bright, mushy peas anointed with mint, and the tangy homemade tartar sauce. The menu is rounded off with such classics as fish nuggets, chip butty (a chip sandwich), as well as English beers and soda pops. Go early if you want to grab a seat at one of the long wooden communal tables, or take a picnic rug and find yourself a spot along the Canal Saint-Martin, just steps away. Either way, this is a sinking chip that you want to be on.

TEN BELLES

COFFEE BAR
10, rue de la Grange-aux-Belles
Paris 10
TEL: +33 1 42 40 90 78
info@tenbelles.com
MÉTRO: Goncourt, Jacques Bonsergent, or Colonel Fabien

OPEN: Monday through Friday 8AM to 6PM, Saturday and Sunday 9AM to 7PM
PRICES: Coffee 2 to 4€. Pastries 3.50€. Lunch 15€.
RESERVATIONS: Not taken
SPECIALTY: Coffee

You may think you're in Amsterdam, not Paris, when you take a seat in this breezy and friendly canal-side café. Expect perfectly crafted coffee by owner and famous Parisian barista Thomas Lehoux, and a light lunch menu and pastries prepared by the talented Brits from the kitchen of Le Bal Café. This ranks as one of the best coffee bars in Paris and, no surprise, as part of the new "coffee mafia," the roasted beans are supplied by Télescope Café (see page 134).

11TH ARRONDISSEMENT

CHEZ ALINE

SANDWICHES
85, rue de la Roquette
Paris 11
TEL: +33 1 43 71 90 75
MÉTRO: Voltaire

OPEN: Monday through Friday 11AM to 7PM
PRICES: Sandwiches 4.50 to 8.50€, *plat du jour* 9 to 10€
RESERVATIONS: Not taken

For gourmet *casse-croûte* (sandwiches and casual snacks) in the Bastille neighborhood, be sure to add Chez Aline to your list. Delphine Zampetti, hailing from well-known bistro addresses such as La Baratin and Le Verre Volé, has an almost cult following since she transformed this tiny former horse butcher shop into a lunchtime destination for delicious and unusual salads and excellently conceived sandwiches. The menu doesn't change often but Zampetti offers a variety of filling options, made to order on either baguette or a soft sesame seed bun, such as Prince of Paris cooked ham, pine nut pesto and goat cheese; or bonito, hard-cooked egg, mayonnaise, and guindilla chile peppers.

AL TAGLIO (Oberkampf)

ITALIAN / PIZZERIA
2, bis rue Neuve Popincourt
Paris 11
TEL: +33 1 43 38 12 00
MÉTRO: Parmentier
OPEN: Daily noon to 11PM
(until midnight Friday and Saturday)

CLOSED: First two weeks of August
PRICES: 26.30 to 38.30€ per kilo at lunch and dinner
RESERVATIONS: Not taken
SPECIALTY: Pizza by the slice

The best pizza by the slice in Paris. See page 135 for full commentary.

COME A CASA

ITALIAN
7, rue Pache
Paris 11
TEL: +33 1 77 15 08 19
comeacasa7.tumblr.com
MÉTRO: Voltaire

OPEN: Monday through Saturday noon to 2:30PM and 6 to 10:30PM
CLOSED: Sunday
PRICES: À la carte 40€
RESERVATIONS: Recommended

Flavia Federici is an architect, born in Rome and transplanted to Paris. Her passion for food, design, and all things Italian led her to open her tiny, welcoming trattoria just steps from the Voltaire *métro* in the 11th *arrondissement*. Walk into the casually but carefully appointed brocante-decorated eatery and you instantly feel as though you've been transported to Italy: the aromas, Flavia's earnest smile and accent, the assortment of aged Pecorino cheeses sitting like a still life in the window. Her enthusiasm and energy are evident everywhere, in the careful selection of the 1950s cast-off chairs and tables, the serving plates, as well as silverware. On the menu you'll find a carefully crafted assortment of Pecorino sheep's-milk cheese brought in regularly from a small producer in Umbria: some smoked, some aged in stone *grottes,* or natural caves, served with homemade *confiture.* Fat slices of rye bread from the Parisian bakery Blé Sucré (see page 310) arrive lightly toasted, rubbed gently with fresh garlic, topped with outrageously delicious *ricotta salata* (firm, aged, and salty, from the same Umbrian cheesemaker) and sprigs of fresh rosemary. One could make a meal of that! But don't stop there: My favorite here is the ethereally light lasagna with fillings that change from day to day, with such variations as artichokes, spinach, or pesto, all topped with slivers of fragrant Parmesan and a touch of arugula. The wine list is compact, including a spicy, elegant Mazzi Brunello di Montepulciano and the dry Tuscan Sangiovese red, Lodola Nuova Vino Nobile de Montepulciano.

DEUX FOIS PLUS DE PIMENT

CHINESE CANTEEN
33, rue Saint-Sébastien
Paris 11
TEL: +33 1 58 30 99 35
MÉTRO: Saint-Sébastien–Froissart or
Saint-Ambroise
OPEN: Daily noon to 2PM and 5:30 to 10PM

CLOSED: Wednesday for lunch
PRICES: Lunch menu 6, 8, and 9.80€ Monday,
Tuesday, Thursday, and Friday only. À la carte
15 to 20€ at dinner.
RESERVATIONS: Recommended
SPECIALTY: Szechuan cuisine

Szechuan restaurant Deux Fois Plus de Piment (which translates as Twice the Spice) is aptly named. This small canteen-style eatery makes no concessions to the untrained palate, so be prepared to accompany your meal with several glasses of water, or better still, cold beer or a sweetened soy-milk drink. This spot is best for group dining, when you can order several dishes to share among many. Don't miss the spicy dried beef (*boeuf seché sauté au piment*), doused liberally in Szechuan peppers, or the *nouilles froides*—but don't be fooled by the cold noodle description, for these, too, have heat to them, as does the eggplant (*aubergine*) in fish sauce. The beef soup is hot and oily with tender beef, a dish that packs a punch. Don't say you weren't warned!

JEANNE A

MODERN FRENCH
42, rue Jean-Pierre Timbaud
Paris 11
TEL: +33 1 43 55 09 49
jeanne.a.comestibles@gmail.com
MÉTRO: Parmentier or Oberkampf
OPEN: Daily 10AM to 10:30PM. Carryout from
noon to 10:30PM.

CLOSED: August
PRICES: 15 and 17€ weekday lunch menus.
23 and 27€ menus at lunch and dinner
Saturday and Sunday. À la carte 15 to 35€
at lunch and dinner.
RESERVATIONS: Recommended
ATMOSPHERE: Casual

Jeanne A is the little sister restaurant-cum-delicatessen-cum-*épicerie* to its neighbor, the classic bistro Astier. The counter at the front is brimming with freshly made delights—Breton artichokes, veal and *foie gras*-stuffed cabbage, marinated squid stuffed with Swiss chard, terrines, pigeon and *foie gras torte*—all to eat in or to carry out. The walls are lined with a variety of gourmet food products: oils, spices, salts, dried mushrooms, Rösle cooking utensils, as well as fresh vegetables. But what you should really go here for is the roast chicken. Their permanent lunch menu consists of a succulent golden-roasted chicken breast (from Challans, the area of the Vendée famous for its fowl), *dauphinoise* potatoes, and salad, sparkling or still water, and dessert, all for just 15€. If this doesn't appeal, you can order soups, vegetable pies, or specialties on the delicatessen menu. Their extraordinarily good weekday-only sandwich, *le pain pain*—roasted Challans chicken, avocado mayonnaise, chorizo sausage, black olives, semi-dried tomatoes, and dried lemon zest, in a lightly toasted Kayser baguette—is perfect for an impromptu canal-side picnic.

WEST COUNTRY GIRL

BRETON / CRÊPERIE
6, passage Saint-Ambroise
Paris 11
TEL: +33 1 47 00 72 54
westcountrygirl.com
westcountrygirls@gmail.com

MÉTRO: Rue Saint-Maur or Parmentier
OPEN: Tuesday through Saturday
CLOSED: Sunday, Monday, and August
PRICES: *Galettes* 9.50 to 12.80€, *crêpes* 5 to 8€
RESERVATIONS: Recommended
SPECIALTIES: *Galettes* and *crêpes*, oysters, cider

The West Country refers to the west of France, Brittany, where you will find some of the most delicious *galettes,* classic buckwheat crêpes filled with ham, cheese, and an egg. *Galettes* can be leaden or ethereal, and here in this small, 1950s-style diner, they are truly outstanding—parchment-paper-thin, crisp, and golden. The selection is huge, including Mimolette cheese and spinach; Camembert and bacon; goat's-milk cheese and spinach; bacon and mushrooms. Dessert offerings might include a memorable sweet *crêpe* topped with meltingly delicious salted caramel. Go for what's on the plate and for the charming service. The floors are bare concrete, walls distressed plaster, chairs colorful castoffs from the 50s. Lunch will set you back around 9 to 12€. Oysters are also on the menu later in the week.

12TH ARRONDISSEMENT

ROSE BAKERY (La Maison Rouge)

BRITISH CAFÉ / MODERN INTERNATIONAL
10, boulevard de la Bastille
Paris 12
TEL: +33 1 46 28 21 14

MÉTRO: Quai de la Rapée
OPEN: Wednesday through Sunday 11AM to 7PM
CLOSED: Monday and Tuesday
PRICES: À la carte 10 to 30€

Rose Bakery's artistic outpost in the gallery La Maison Rouge. See page 138 for full commentary.

13TH ARRONDISSEMENT

PHO 14

VIETNAMESE CANTEEN
129, avenue de Choisy
Paris 13
TEL: +33 1 45 83 61 15
MÉTRO: Tolbiac

OPEN: Daily 9AM to 11PM
PRICES: 10€ at lunch and dinner
RESERVATIONS: Not taken
SPECIALTY: Pho (Vietnamese soup of broth, rice noodles, herbs, and meat)

Pho, that bottomless bowl of beef soup from Vietnam, is one of the world's great bargain dishes. It's inexpensive to prepare, filling, healthy, and endlessly varied. The best is made with a rich beef broth (usually prepared with marrow bones and cuts of beef for boiling), enhanced with ginger, onion, shallots, Vietnamese fish sauce, star anise, and sometimes dried shrimp. To the strained aromatic broth one adds dried rice noodles (*banh pho*), spring onions, sawtooth coriander, Thai basil, and cilantro. Garnishes generally also include fresh bean sprouts, wedges of lime, and plenty of thin rounds of red chile peppers. As many times as I have had the soup all over the world, including in Vietnam, I have never been able to finish a bowl. Pho 14 is a good spot for sampling the soup, where 6.50€ will buy you a bowl of classic soup, with variations served with thin slices of raw beef, pieces of cooked chicken,

a meatless version, and another that blends both cooked and raw beef. Worthy starters here include delicious *banh cuon* (steamed Vietnamese ravioli, stuffed with pork, ham, and black mushrooms); and the *cha gio* (deep-fried spring rolls stuffed with ground pork or chicken). Wash it all down with some chilled Saigon beer. The place is always crowded with lines of diners ready to take a seat at the small indoor restaurant or simple outdoor terrace. All you need to feel as though you are in Hanoi are a million motorcycles roaring down the avenue de Choisy. Pho 14 opens at 9AM, so if you love pho for breakfast, this is the place to go!

16TH ARRONDISSEMENT

ANGELINA (Jardin d'Acclimatation children's park)

CLASSIC FRENCH TEA SALON
Bois de Boulogne
Paris 16
TEL: +33 7 86 05 25 20
MÉTRO: Les Sablons

OPEN: Daily 10AM to 7PM April through September. 10AM to 6PM October through March.
RESERVATIONS: Not necessary

Sip hot chocolate with the angels in this small Angelina café situated in the Jardin d'Acclimatation, the children's fun park and petting zoo in the Bois de Boulogne forest. See page 129 for full commentary.

17TH ARRONDISSEMENT

ANGELINA (Porte Maillot)

CLASSIC FRENCH TEA SALON
Palais du Congrès
2, place de la Porte Maillot
Paris 17
TEL: +33 1 40 68 22 50

MÉTRO: Porte Maillot
OPEN: Monday through Friday 9AM to 7PM, Saturday, Sunday, and public holidays 10AM to 7PM
RESERVATIONS: Not necessary

Settle in for a decadent hot chocolate or pastry in a baroque setting, before or after picking up some luxury food items at the Galeries Gourmandes supermarket (see Speciality Food Shops, page 358). See page 129 for full commentary on Angelina.

SURF WHILE YOU SIP: WI-FI CAFÉS

For those who like to be connected while they sip their coffee, here's a list of favorite Wi-Fi cafés in the capital:

COUTUME
47, rue de Babylone
Paris 7

See page 151 for full commentary.

KB CAFESHOP
53, avenue Trudaine
Paris 9
TEL: +33 1 56 92 12 41
MÉTRO: Pigalle
OPEN: Daily

The savory snacks and cakes are nothing spectacular, but as you could expect at an Australian café, the coffee is excellent.

CAFÉ CRAFT
24, rue des Vinaigriers
Paris 10
TEL: +33 1 40 35 90 77
MÉTRO: Jacques Bonsergeant
OPEN: Monday through Saturday 9AM to 7PM

A laptop-friendly café near the canal Saint-Martin with customized work spaces for freelancers and bloggers.

TEN BELLES
10, rue de la Grange-aux-Belles
Paris 10

See page 160 for full commentary.

LA BAUHINIA–SHANGRI-LA
10, avenue d'Iéna
Paris 16
TEL: +33 1 53 67 19 98
MÉTRO: Iéna
OPEN: Breakfast 6:30 to 11AM, lunch noon to 3PM, tea 3:30 to 5:30PM (weekdays) and 4:30 to 5:30PM (weekends)

Breakfast, lunch, or take tea in style while you email at this beautifully appointed café in the Shangri-la Hotel.

MARCEL
1, villa Léandre
Paris 18

See page 166 for full commentary.

LES NOVICES
123, rue Caulaincourt
Paris 18
TEL: +33 1 42 64 71 37
MÉTRO: Lamarck-Caulaincourt
OPEN: Daily 8AM to 2PM

A comfy neighborhood spot serving classic bistro fare, Les Novices offers reasonably priced lunch menus and plenty of tables on which to pull out your laptop and work while you dine, including two large wooden tables at the rear of the restaurant.

SOUL KITCHEN
33, rue Lamarck
Paris 18

See page 166 for full commentary.

18TH ARRONDISSEMENT

GONTRAN CHERRIER

BAKERY
22, rue Caulaincourt
Paris 18
TEL: +33 1 46 06 82 66

MÉTRO: Lamarck-Caulaincourt
RESERVATIONS: Not taken
SPECIALTIES: Sandwiches and pastries

This fresh and modern bakery has a window-facing bar so you can enjoy a flaky croissant with a *café crème*, a freshly made sandwich or savory tart, or one of Cherrier's seriously superior sweet pastries, while watching the world go by. See Bakeries, page 242, for full commentary.

JEANNE B

MODERN FRENCH
61, rue Lepic
Paris 18
TEL: +33 1 42 51 17 53
jeanne-b-comestibles.com

jeanne.b.comestibles@gmail.com
MÉTRO: Lamarck-Caulaincourt
OPEN: Daily 10AM to 10:30PM
PRICES: 15€ lunch menu, à la carte 15 to 35€
RESERVATIONS: Not necessary

The delights of Jeanne A replicated in a Montmartre location. See page 162 for full commentary.

MARCEL

CAFÉ / MODERN INTERNATIONAL
1, villa Léandre
Paris 18
TEL: +33 1 46 06 04 04
MÉTRO: Lamarck-Caulaincourt

OPEN: Monday through Friday 10AM to 11PM,
Saturday and Sunday 10AM to 7PM
PRICES: 25 to 35€ at lunch and dinner
RESERVATIONS: Essential on weekends,
recommended during peak lunch hour times

Marcel counts among the better Anglo-style cafés that are becoming more and more popular in Paris. Situated on a wide, leafy residential avenue, on the corner of one of the prettiest cul-de-sac streets in Montmartre, this breezy modern eatery is perfect any day of the week. Stop by after 10AM for a weekday breakfast where the choices include porridge with caramelized banana, granola, and bagels. The lunch menu (the same menu at dinner) is bursting with delicious starters and salads that are hearty, generous, and always fresh. The *burrata* with seasonal vegetables is a great choice, the creamy juices mopped up with slices of baguette from the local star baker, Gontran Cherrier. And on weekends you will find a vast brunch menu, à la carte (unlike so many overpriced, fixed-price brunch menus you find in Parisian cafés these days), with all manner of eggs, pancakes, waffles, salads, sandwiches, and desserts, including cheesecake that is not bad but may leave some New Yorkers wanting. And to make a good thing even better, there is a small sidewalk terrace for sitting outdoors when the weather is fine. Reservations are not always essential during the week, but definitely so on weekends for brunch. *Local tip:* Parisians arise late on weekends, so if you don't have a reservation, arrive before noon and you'll have a good chance of getting a table.

SOUL KITCHEN

CAFÉ / MODERN INTERNATIONAL
33, rue Lamarck
Paris 18
TEL: + 33 1 71 37 99 95
allo@soulkitchenparis.fr

MÉTRO: Lamarck-Caulaincourt
OPEN: Tuesday through Friday 8:30AM to 7PM,
Saturday and Sunday 10AM to 7PM
CLOSED: Monday
PRICES: 12.50 and 14.50€ lunch menus

This bright and airy coffee shop nestled into the hillside of Montmartre was inspired by the owner's sun-filled trips to California. Here you will find excellent Coutume roasted coffee, delicious breakfast granola, healthy vegetarian lunch menus, and super-friendly service. In hot weather, grab a seat on the sloping sidewalk terrace and order up a refreshing pitcher of their homemade *citronnade* (lemonade).

AT A GLANCE

1ST ARRONDISSEMENT

Angelina (Rivoli)
Angelina (Musée du Louvre)
Claus
Le Café Marly
Kotteri Ramen Naritake
Le Pain Quotidien
  (Palais Royal)
Le Pain Quotidien
  (Saint-Honoré)
Verjus Bar à Vins

2ND ARRONDISSEMENT

Frenchie To Go
Grillé
Gyoza Bar
Télescope
Le Pain Quotidien
  (Montorgueil)

3RD ARRONDISSEMENT

Al Taglio (Marais)
Breizh Café
Cuisine de Bar (Marais)
Loustic
Merci
Nanashi (Charlot)
Rose Bakery (Marais)

4TH ARRONDISSEMENT

L'As du Fallafel
Comme à Lisbonne
Le Pain Quotidien (Marais)

5TH ARRONDISSEMENT

La Mosquée Salon de Thé

6TH ARRONDISSEMENT

L'Avant Comptoir
Le Bonaparte
Cosi
Bar de la Croix Rouge
Cuisine de Bar
  (Saint-Germain)
Les Deux Magots
Café de Flore
Ladurée (Saint-Germain)
Brasserie Lipp
Little Breizh
Nanashi (Bonpoint)
Le Pavillon de la Fontaine
Da Rosa
Tsukizi
Yoom (Saint-Germain)

7TH ARRONDISSEMENT

Coutume
Brasserie aux PTT
Le Pain Quotidien (Rue du
  Bac)
Rose Bakery (Bon Marché)
Café Varenne
Mozza & Co.
Omnivore Rives
En Attendant Rosa

8TH ARRONDISSEMENT

Ladurée (Champs-Élysées)
Ladurée (Rue Royale)

9TH ARRONDISSEMENT

Angelina (Galeries Lafayette)
Ladurée (Printemps de la
  Mode)
Les Pâtes Vivantes (Faubourg-
  Montmartre)

Rose Bakery (Martyrs)
Yoom (Martyrs)

10TH ARRONDISSEMENT

Krishna Bhavan
Nanashi (Paradis)
The Sunken Chip
Ten Belles

11TH ARRONDISSEMENT

Chez Aline
Al Taglio (Oberkampf)
Come a Casa
Deux Fois Plus de Piment
Jeanne A
West Country Girl

12TH ARRONDISSEMENT

Rose Bakery (La Maison
  Rouge)

13TH ARRONDISSEMENT

Pho 14

16TH ARRONDISSEMENT

Angelina (Jardin
  d'Acclimatation)

17TH ARRONDISSEMENT

Angelina (Porte Maillot)

18TH ARRONDISSEMENT

Gontran Cherrier
Jeanne B
Marcel
Soul Kitchen

WINE BARS

BISTROTS ET BARS À VIN

Enter into the land of bread and Beaujolais, tapas and organic wines, cheese and *charcuterie*. From the exterior, many resemble ordinary cafés, yet once you've entered and sipped a glass of silky, scented Fleurie or fresh and flinty Sancerre, and sampled an open-faced sandwich of garlic and thyme-flecked *rillettes* (spreadable pork or goose pâté), on thick slices of sourdough bread, you understand the difference.

There is always food and conviviality, but more important, there is wine—by the glass, the carafe, the bottle. For many years, light and fruity Beaujolais was king, but today one finds a greater range, such as the delicate Bourgueil from the Touraine; young wines from Bordeaux, Chinon, and Côtes du Rhône; the Atlantic Coast's stony, mineral-rich white Muscadet (a natural partner for oysters); the Jura's honeysuckle-scented white Arbois; and Provence's heady, vigorous Gigondas. Obviously, not every wine bar stocks every wine, but most offer from a dozen to thirty wines by the glass, along with—at the very least—platters of cheese or *charcuterie* (sausages, terrines, pâtés). Some wine bars are casual affairs, with no printed menu, but wine selections and daily specials handwritten on blackboards set behind the bar. Others serve as full-fledged restaurants, with full menus and an extensive wine cellar.

Is there a reason to go to a wine bar rather than a café for a glass of wine? Categorically, yes. The wine sold at many cafés can be mass-produced and bland. The wine served in wine bars is generally carefully chosen by the *bistrotier* (owner), most often a dedicated man or woman who is passionate about wine, visiting vineyards regularly, and creating friendships with winemakers.

The food, simple and unpretentious as it may be, is chosen with the same care. Most offer platters of French cheese, several kinds of hams, sausages, pâtés, and bread often from some of the city's top bakers, such as Poilâne, Poujauran, or Éric Kayser. Some wine bars offer even heartier fare, such as wintry daubes (stews), platters of cooked sausages, and *confit d'oie* (preserved goose). Some of the more modern wine bars may serve tapas-style small plates as well as full meals. (As one *bistrotier* put it, "Wine is made to go with food. Tasting wine alone should be left to the experts.")

Best of all, wine bars serve as a tasting and testing ground for wines yet to be discovered, as well as for familiar favorites. Since many wine bars offer lesser-known, small-production wines by the glass, this is the time to acquaint oneself with wines you may have never heard of, or have heard of and have been eager to try. ❧

1ST ARRONDISSEMENT

LES FINES GUEULES

MODERN FRENCH
43, rue Croix des Petits-Champs
Paris 1
TEL: +33 1 42 61 35 41
lesfinesgueules.fr
lesfinesgueules@free.fr

MÉTRO: Palais Royal–Musée du Louvre
OPEN: Daily
PRICES: Lunch & dinner: à la carte 35 to 50€
RESERVATIONS: Recommended
ATMOSPHERE: Casual
SPECIALTY: Organic and biodynamic wines

This trendy, stylish, bustling wine bar on the ground floor of a gorgeous turreted building near the Place des Victoires is great to know about when everything else is closed, for it's open seven days a week. Its fresh menu and *charcuterie* and cheese platters available between services mean you should find something appealing, no matter what the hour. Meats come from star butcher Hugo Desnoyer (see Specialty Food Shops, page 365), so I'd swear by their beef *tartare* and veal *carpaccio*. The creamy *burrata* is served showered with toasted almonds, olive oil, and curls of olives, while in season their heirloom tomato platter is hard to beat. While I have experienced a few mishaps on visits there—a veal tenderloin coated in that most-hated truffle oil (fabricated in a lab and a distant approximation of a real truffle aroma), and a couple of oddly out-of-season dishes that didn't fit the profile of *cuisine du jour*—I still find this friendly wine bar an excellent choice for the neighborhood. With draws like the huge attention paid to the quality of the produce, the warm and jovial service, and the sidewalk terrace in warmer months, this is a place I will return to again and again. The wine list is extensive, with a smooth, light, textbook example of a young and well-priced Burgundy, the red Hautes-Côtes-de-Beaune from the Domaine des Rouges-Queues.

JUVENILES

CLASSIC BISTRO FARE
47, rue de Richelieu
Paris 1
TEL: +33 1 42 97 46 49
MÉTRO: Palais Royal–Musée du Louvre,
Bourse, or Pyramides

OPEN: Monday 6 to 11PM, Tuesday through
Saturday noon to 11PM
CLOSED: All day Sunday and Monday at lunch
PRICES: 16.50€ lunch menu. 22€ and 32€
dinner menus. À la carte 35 to 40€.
RESERVATIONS: Recommended
ATMOSPHERE: Casual

Anyone looking for a fine glass of wine, a grand platter of British cheeses, and a good time should step through the door of the no-frills wine bar/wine shop Juveniles, one of the city's favorite spots for great sips. On the menu you'll find platters of *saucisson,* chorizo, mixed *charcuterie* with toast and butter, and my favorites, the Coston Basset Stilton and Montgomery unpasteurized farmhouse Cheddar. Salads vary from toasted *chèvre* (goat's cheese) on toast, to a salad of endives, Stilton, and nuts. Daily specials might include *blanquette de veau* or grilled sausage with mashed potatoes. The wine selection is a candy store full of discoveries, including a glass of fruity white Condrieu from Domaine Pichon; the sweet Jurançon from Charles Hours; and owner Tim Johnston's own Purple, a red wine he vinifies with Côtes du-Rhône winemaker Marcel Richaud. Order a full bottle and you'll have even greater choice, with my favorite Jurançon Sec from Charles Hours; Domaine Clape's Saint Péray; and a new discovery for me, Domaine de la Biscarelle's red Châteauneuf-du-Pape, a 99 percent Grenache that's medium-bodied and easy drinking.

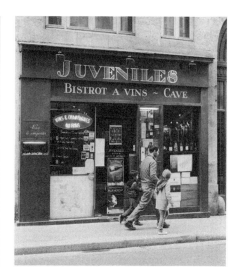

LE RUBIS

CLASSIC BISTRO FARE
10, rue du Marché Saint-Honoré
Paris 1
TEL: +33 1 42 61 03 34
MÉTRO: Tuileries or Pyramides
OPEN: Monday through Friday 7AM to 10PM.
Saturday 9AM to 4PM. Hot meal at lunch only.

CLOSED: Sunday, one week at Christmas, and three weeks in August
PRICE: À la carte 30€
RESERVATIONS: Not taken
ATMOSPHERE: Casual

I remember wandering the Marché Saint-Honoré for what seemed like hours some 30 years ago, trying to find the famed 1936 wine bar Le Rubis. I must have been circling the *place,* not the *rue,* but eventually I found it and fell instantly in love. Today the hangout remains virtually unchanged, just as boisterous, pushy, jam-packed, and old-fashioned as ever, the spot for a bargain 11€ platter of *confit de canard* (duck cooked in fat) and a thick potato gratin; meaty *petit salé aux lentilles* (braised salted pork with brown lentils); as well as a hearty and succulent *tête de veau* (braised calf's head), served with boiled potatoes and the biggest portion of tangy *sauce gribiche* (mayonnaise with capers, cornichons, hard-cooked eggs, and herbs) that I have ever seen. Though Le Rubis is known for its wine, I found the Chiroubles just a tad thin. This is the sort of place where you'll strike up a conversation with your neighbors (dining here is about as elbow-to-elbow as it gets), and my husband, Walter, and I spent an hour in the cramped upstairs dining room chatting with the French teacher from Andorra who sat to my left, and the Irish architect from Sydney to my right, talking of everything from our shared love of Paris to the sadness of the brain drain of the young French. We left sated and satisfied, and you should, too. In good weather you can lunch outdoors, standing at the wine barrels that serve as makeshift tables.

WILLI'S WINE BAR

MODERN INTERNATIONAL
13, rue des Petits-Champs
Paris 1
TEL: +33 1 42 61 05 09
williswinebar.com
info@williswinebar.com
MÉTRO: Bourse, Palais Royal–Musée du
Louvre, or Pyramides

OPEN: Monday through Saturday, noon to
2:30PM and 7 to 10:45PM
CLOSED: Sunday and August
PRICES: 23.80€ lunch menu, 36€ dinner
menu.
RESERVATIONS: Recommended
(online reservations taken)
ATMOSPHERE: Smart-casual
SPECIALTY: Chocolate terrine

A s eager diners, we focus all too often on the newest address or the chef with the latest hype as we race to keep up with the flavor of the week. Rather, we should stop every now and then and reflect on great places we've been taking for granted or pushing to the back of our minds. The solid, classic,

dependable old friends who will always be there once the hyped-up spots have been forgotten or have closed their doors. I confess it had been years since I visited Mark Williamson's landmark wine bar, established in 1980 and still going as strong as ever. But I finally returned and my last visit was a revelation and a delight: food with character and history, a chef with a classic education at the stove, a wine list that's hard to beat anywhere in the world, a staff that is well trained and seems to enjoy being there. I love the attention to detail, the menu designed to satisfy the

customer, a place that is what it is (fabulous!) and not trying to prove anything. The food on that visit was superb: a beautiful plate of Roseval potatoes, warm, bathed in a light and tangy sauce, showered with the freshest grilled walnuts and bits of salty bacon; a flavorful, wintry bed of mixed wild mushrooms topped with a round of fresh pasta. The chef, François Yon, there since 1993, understands searing like no one else. That evening, Walter and I feasted. I have since returned for the moist and perfectly cooked farm-raised breast of veal, with a thick, mahogany-toned

▲ *Lost in a book at Willi's Wine Bar.*

exterior and a delicately tender interior—a truly juicy morsel set upon a bed of carrots, leeks, potatoes, and turnips. The same can be said of his super-seared farm-raised guinea hen (*pintade*), set on the same soothing bed of vegetables. His chocolate terrine (see recipe, page 174) should go in the record books as one of the best ever, and, of course, Willi's wine list will bring any wine lover to his or her knees. The red Châteauneuf-du-Pape Domaine de Marcoux from sisters Sophie and Catherine Armenier is a dream, a balanced blend of opulence and refinement, as well as tons of pleasure.

VERJUS BAR À VINS

MODERN INTERNATIONAL
47, rue Montpensier
Paris 1
TEL: +33 9 53 94 36 76
verjusparis.com
verjusparis@gmail.com
MÉTRO: Palais Royal–Musée du Louvre or Pyramides

OPEN: Monday through Friday 6 to 11PM; Tuesday through Friday for sandwiches 12:30 to 2PM
CLOSED: Saturday and Sunday
PRICES: Sandwich menu 15€, small plates in the evening 4 to 14€.
RESERVATIONS: Not taken
ATMOSPHERE: Smart-casual
SPECIALTIES: Small plates and tapas

This cozy and fabulously located wine bar tucked away at the north end of rue Montpensier in the Palais Royal is run by the clever and always friendly American duo Laura Aiden and Braden Perkins. They came to fame with their underground supper club The Hidden Kitchen, operated out of their Paris apartment several years ago. Today, they are decidedly above ground, but no less sought after, with their restaurant Verjus, opened in 2012 (see Restaurants, page 14). As always it's tough to get a booking, but with the Verjus Bar à Vins located right downstairs from the restaurant, you can pull up a stool with no reservations required to sample some of Braden's culinary musings on the small plates/bar snack menu, and Laura's excellently chosen wine list. The menu changes frequently but you might find such interesting combinations as braised, grass-fed short ribs, salsify, sweet onion, *mizuna* (a peppery Asian salad green), soft polenta, pumpernickel, and saffron-pickled turnips (yes, that's just one small plate!), or celery root dumplings with *dan-dan* sauce (a spicy Szechuan sauce made with sesame paste and soy sauce), chives, and toasted peanuts. The buttermilk fried chicken is a permanent fixture on the menu, and for good reason—it's delicious. As is the current trend, you'll find your fair share of natural wines here. If the wine choices are unfamiliar, Laura is always happy to talk you through the list. The bar is open at lunchtime as well, offering a gourmet sandwich menu, not to be missed if you're looking to picnic in the nearby Palais Royal Gardens.

TERRINE AU CHOCOLAT DE WILLI'S WINE BAR

Willi's Wine Bar's Bittersweet Chocolate Terrine

This irresistible chocolate dessert is one of my Paris favorites. Mark Williamson, owner of the popular Willi's Wine Bar, generously shared this recipe, noting alongside, "Chef François has managed to achieve a good balance between solid, dense, unforgivably rich chocolate and an almost *foie gras*–like texture. On a good day." He also added, "Depending upon one's level of extreme *gourmandise*, this will make 15 to 18 portions." While the original recipe calls for unsalted butter, I like to make it with salted butter, for it gives the terrine a bright, surprising edge. I also like a touch of vanilla in my chocolate desserts and so added a tiny dose. Note that the eggs in this recipe are not cooked.

EQUIPMENT:

A double boiler; a heavy-duty mixer fitted with a whisk; a 1-quart (1-l) rectangular bread pan, lined with foil

INGREDIENTS:

10 ounces (300 g) bittersweet chocolate, such as Valrhona Guanaja 70%

12 tablespoons (1½ sticks; 180 g) salted butter, at room temperature

½ teaspoon pure vanilla extract

4 large egg yolks, preferably organic and free-range

6 large egg whites, preferably organic and free-range

1. Break the chocolate into medium-size pieces. Cube the butter.

2. In the top of the double boiler set over, but not touching, simmering water, melt the chocolate, stirring from time to time. The process should take about 3 minutes. Remove the top of the double boiler from the heat and whisk in the butter, cube by cube, until it melts. Whisk in the vanilla extract. The mixture should be smooth, glossy, and shiny, not dull and oily. Let cool for 5 minutes. Whisk in the egg yolks, one by one. Transfer the mixture to a large bowl.

3. In the bowl of the mixer, whisk the egg whites at highest speed until stiff but not dry, about 1 minute.

4. Add about one third of the beaten egg whites to the chocolate mixture, thoroughly whisking until no streaks of white remain. This will lighten the chocolate mixture and make it easier to blend with the remaining egg whites. Add the remaining whites to the chocolate mixture, and with a spatula, gently fold them in until no streaks of white remain.

5. Pour the mixture into the prepared pan. Cover securely with aluminum foil and refrigerate for a minimum of 6 hours and up to 3 days. To serve, carefully remove the terrine from the pan and cut into slices.

16 SERVINGS

2ND ARRONDISSEMENT

FRENCHIE BAR À VINS

MODERN FRENCH
5–6, rue du Nil
Paris 2
TEL: +33 1 40 39 96 19
frenchie-restaurant.com/menu_bar_fr
MÉTRO: Sentier
OPEN: Monday through Friday 7 to 11:30PM

CLOSED: Saturday and Sunday
PRICES: Small plates 10 to 25€
RESERVATIONS: Not taken. Arrive before 7PM
to put your name on the list for a table.
ATMOSPHERE: Casual
SPECIALTY: Small plates and tapas

Gregory Marchand's hugely popular wine bar (directly opposite his restaurant, Frenchie) is the kind of place I'd make my hangout if it were right around the corner. Pristine ingredients in both common and uncommon combinations make this a hit. You can walk in for a glass of wine at the bar and a plate of extraordinary Spanish *jamón ibérico de bellota*. This is a great place for sharing small bites with friends, such as the unlikely but delicious slaw of squid and carrots; and a refined and superb veal *tartare*, beautifully seasoned with a surprise in each bite: cornichons, a tangle of arugula, baby *girolles* mushrooms, summer truffles, hazelnuts. Although I am not a fan of the highly touted "natural wines" (most simply taste unfinished to me), I did enjoy the meaty Les Gamines from Domaine de la Marfée in the Languedoc, a blend of Grenache, Syrah, and Mourvèdre. Other worthy wines to note here: selections from the cooperative Les Vignerons d'Estézargues in the Gard; Alain Graillot's Crozes-Hermitage; Lalou Bize-Leroy's Bourgogne Rouge; and the Burgundian Givry from Domaine Joblot.

6TH ARRONDISSEMENT

AMBASSADE DE BOURGOGNE

CLASSIC FRENCH
6, rue de l'Odéon
Paris 6
TEL: +33 1 43 54 80 04
ambassadedebourgogne.com
contact@ambassadedebourgogne.com
MÉTRO: Odéon
OPEN: Monday 5PM to midnight. Tuesday

through Saturday 10AM to midnight. Sunday
noon to midnight.
PRICES: Small plates 4 to 12€ at lunch and
dinner
RESERVATIONS: Not taken
ATMOSPHERE: Casual
SPECIALTY: Small plates and tapas

Lovers of the lush and lovely wines of Burgundy will be happy to take a seat at this tiny, modern wine bar/wine shop that features just about every dream wine one could want from the region. Many of the great names are here—Grantet-Pansiot, Edouard Lamy, Ghislaine Barthod, Thévenet—

to sample by the bottle or by the glass. This place is all about wine, of course, but it's also a great spot to know when you just want a quick platter of cheese (they offer different selections to go with white and red wines), or an abundant plate of *charcuterie,* featuring some of the most delicious *jambon persillé* (jellied, parsleyed ham) I have ever tasted, prepared by Marc Colin in Chablis. The well-thought-out red-wine cheese tray includes all cow's-milk cheeses, including the nutty Saint Nectaire, the trufflelike Chaource or Brillat-Savarin, and the creamy cheese from the Abbaye de Cîteaux in Burgundy. My friend Andrew and I adored the Chambolle Musigny from winemaker Ghislaine Barthod. Be sure to check their website for information on regular wine tastings.

FISH LA BOISSONNERIE

MODERN BISTRO FARE
69, rue de Seine
Paris 6
TEL: +33 1 43 54 34 69
laboissonnerie@wanadoo.fr
MÉTRO: Mabillon or Odéon
OPEN: Daily, 12:30 to 2:30PM and 7PM to 12:30AM (kitchen closes at 10:45PM). Open on public holidays.

CLOSED: One week in August
PRICES: 26.50€ lunch menu. 31.50 and 35€ dinner menus.
RESERVATIONS: Recommended. Walk-ins without reservations taken at 7PM.
ATMOSPHERE: Casual
SPECIALTIES: Fish and shellfish

I confess that I could easily lunch or dine at the wine bar/restaurant Fish La Boissonnerie once a week, and would be totally happy just sipping some delicious wine (our own Clos Chanteduc Côtes du Rhône is often on the list now!) and eating the warm and golden brick-oven bread from Cosi, just across the street. The friendly Anglophone spot reminds me of the coffee shop from *Friends,* where you always run into someone you know and always feel at home. I love to go for Sunday lunch, with the charming Colombian Angela Jaramitto taking orders and delivering fresh bread every few minutes or so. I crave the simple arugula, date, and Parmesan salad, as well as the *daurade* on a welcoming bed of poached vegetables, including leeks, tomatoes, potatoes, and bits of citrus. The wine is always a delight, such as the Mâcon-Villages Quintaine, 100 percent Chardonnay from Pierette and Michel Guillemot, a white with a surprising amount of acidity and vigor.

OENOSTERIA

ITALIAN
40, rue Grégoire de Tours
Paris 6
TEL: +33 1 77 15 94 13
MÉTRO: Odéon

OPEN: Daily 10AM to 2AM. Final orders taken at midnight.
PRICES: Small plates 10 to 19€ at lunch and dinner
RESERVATIONS: Not taken
ATMOSPHERE: Casual

Take a little trip to a village *osteria* in the Tuscan hillsides as you sip some stellar Sangiovese reds, tuck into wooden boards laden with all manner of silken, top-quality *charcuterie,* and chat with the outgoing Fabiana, the

Siena-born Italian who treats her roomful of diners as though they were family. This casual, 1950s-style wine bar and carryout shop near the Odéon bustles with multilingual sounds—French, Italian, English—as guests feast on delicious *crostini* (I love the grilled bread topped with Pecorino sheep's-milk cheese and fennel-flecked salami; see recipe, page 178), pleasant frittatas (we had one filled with zucchini, potatoes, and herbs), or a giant salad of arugula, pine nuts, sheep's-milk cheese, and thinly sliced *bresaola,* or air-dried beef. Oenosteria is small and cheery, filled with tables topped with bright red Formica or bare wood, with walls of stone, marble, and glass. The wine bar fills up quickly at mealtimes, so go very early or very late to assure a seat, or sit at the bar to watch the kitchen action. The list of wines from throughout Tuscany is extensive, including a personal favorite, the Tenuta di Capezzana's Villa Capezzana, a stunning red blend of 80 percent Sangiovese and 20 percent Cabernet Sauvignon that's smoky and radiant with flavors of fat, dark, ripe red cherries. Try also the award-winning white Azienda Biologica Boriassi Mezzaluna, a 100 percent Vermentino from the hills of Colli di Luni,

> "They drank with unbuttoned bellies."
> —Rabelais

between Liguria and Tuscany. Oenosteria is a good place to know about during off-hours, since it's open from 10AM to 2AM (last orders accepted at midnight) every day of the week. And the coffee from a small supplier in Florence is outstanding.

10ᵀᴴ ARRONDISSEMENT

ALBION

MODERN BISTRO FARE
80, rue du Faubourg-Poissonnière
Paris 10
TEL: +33 1 42 46 02 44
restaurantalbion.com
MÉTRO: Poissonnière

OPEN: Monday through Friday
CLOSED: Saturday, Sunday, two to three weeks in August and one week at Christmas
PRICES: À la carte 30 to 50€ at lunch and dinner
RESERVATIONS: Recommended
ATMOSPHERE: Casual

A friendly, outgoing welcome from owner Hayden Clout (a New Zealander); bargain-priced, well-chosen wines by the glass; and no-frills, down-to-earth cooking from chef Matt Ong—what more need one ask? This duo, formerly seen at Fish la Boissonnerie in the 6th, has fittingly taken up residence on the rue du Faubourg-Poissonnière, keeping *poisson,* so to speak, in the family. All my favorite

CROSTINI DI PECORINO E FINOCCHIONA DA OENOSTERIA

Oenosteria's Sheep's-Milk Cheese and Fennel Sausage Crostini

Many weekdays I can be found grabbing a simple, satisfying lunch at my favorite neighborhood Italian *osteria*, Oenosteria. Here the always-smiling Fabiana serves up delicious, ever-changing *crostini*, open-faced sandwiches made with toasted slices of hearty bread from Éric Kayser's bakery nearby. This is my version of one of my favorites. Like much Italian cooking, it is very simple, but the success depends upon top-quality ingredients.

EQUIPMENT:

Baking sheet

INGREDIENTS:

2 thick slices sourdough bread

4 ounces (125 g) freshly grated best-quality sheep's-milk cheese, such as Pecorino-Romano

8 ultrathin slices fennel-scented cured pork sausages

1. Place a rack in the oven about 3 inches (7.5 cm) from the heat source. Preheat the broiler.

2. In a toaster, toast the bread. Arrange the slices of bread side by side on the baking sheet.

3. Sprinkle the cheese on top of the toasted bread. Arrange the slices of sausage on top of the cheese.

4. Place the baking sheet under the broiler and broil just until the cheese melts, 30 seconds to 1 minute. Serve immediately.

2 SERVINGS

wines are here either by the glass, the 46 cl pot, or the 75 cl bottle, including Legras & Haas Champagne, Domaine de Villargeau's easy-drinking white Côteaux du Giennois Sauvignon Blanc, Sainte Cosme's meaty red Côtes du Rhône, and Vissoux's welcoming Beaujolais Les Griottes. Simple dishes—many that Fish fans will remember—include

a lovely oyster vichyssoise, smoked eel paired with a delicate horseradish (*raifort*) cream, succulent braised beef cheeks, hearty portions of seared salmon, a classic chocolate tart, and a nice selection of cheeses, among them Reblochon, Comté, and Pélardon goat's-milk cheese.

VIVANT TABLE

MODERN FRENCH / ITALIAN
43, rue des Petites Écuries
Paris 10
TEL: +33 1 42 46 43 55
MÉTRO: Poissonnière, Château d'Eau, or Bonne Nouvelle
OPEN: Monday through Friday

CLOSED: Saturday and Sunday
PRICES: 40€ lunch menu. À la carte 35 to 45€ at lunch. 60€ evening *dégustation* menu (130€ with wine), no à la carte.
RESERVATIONS: Recommended
ATMOSPHERE: Casual
SPECIALTY: Natural wines

After hitting it big with his wine bar, Racines, then taking a year off, Pierre Jancou is back with another winner, the tiny Vivant, in a lively part of the 10th *arrondissement*. The long, narrow room began its life around 1900 as a shop that sold pet birds, as the lovely ceramic murals attest.

As at his former establishment, Jancou is all about ingredients. So we have the incomparable *boudin noir* from Christian Parra; the

moist, meaty duck from Challans in France's Southwest; lovely Italian *burrata* (that incomparable mozzarella filled with rich, tangy cream); and equally amazing smoked mozzarella. This is a wintry, meaty sort of place, but not necessarily heavy. An autumn meal here linked summer and fall, with an entire *burrata* bathed in a puddle of delicious olive oil, seasoned with coarse salt, pepper, herbs, and a tiny garden of late-season cherry tomatoes. We ushered in fall with another hit: crunchy polenta topped with wild *pleurote* (oyster) mushrooms and a meltingly rich round of smoked mozzarella that humorously resembled a giant mushroom cap. A main course of Challans duck—moist, tender, meaty—was set upon a golden bed of mashed potatoes, with the crunch of coarse salt and thin slices of red onion. An equally succulent *cochon de lait* was served with an ocher square of polenta, soft and moist inside, crunchy on the outside. All was escorted by a glass or two of the lively Côtes du Rhône Villages red, P-U-R, and golden crisp baguettes from Le Grenier à Pain nearby.

11TH ARRONDISSEMENT

LE DAUPHIN

MODERN FRENCH
131, avenue Parmentier
Paris 11
TEL: +33 1 55 28 78 88
restaurantledauphin.net
MÉTRO: Goncourt or Parmentier
OPEN: Tuesday through Saturday
CLOSED: Saturday lunch, Sunday, and Monday. Annual closing over Christmas.

PRICES: 23 and 27€ lunch menu. Small plates, cheese, and dessert from 5 to 35€.
RESERVATIONS: Essential for lunch and 7:30 to 9:30PM service. No reservations for 9:30 to 11PM service. Call 10AM to midday and 5 to 7:30PM.
ATMOSPHERE: Smart-casual
SPECIALTIES: Small plates and tapas, natural wines

S uperstar Basque chef Inaki Aizpitarte has done it again. He's hit a home run way out of the park with his ultramodern wine bar Le Dauphin, on the same block as his winning restaurant Le Chateaubriand. I could do without the cold and sterile decor of architect Rem Koolhaas (all white marble, glass, and mirrors) but will put up with it for the chance to sample Aizpitarte's inventive cuisine. He comes up with combinations most of us would never dream of, such as a soothing ceviche of *mulet* (large, mild ocean fish) bathed in a powerful, bright green cucumber water. But even standard combinations—perfectly fried crunchy baby shrimp (*crevettes grises*)—come off as surprising and satisfying. This is small-plate heaven, where diners share every order, though I would love to have had a little plate of my own, rather than pick from the common tapas-style servings. Everything has a personality here, from the rounds of *poulpe* (octopus) with their tandoori seasoning to a warming bowl of mushrooms on a bed of barley (*orge*), flecked with bits of nettles (*ortie*). Desserts are mostly of the fluffy sort in style today, with a single rectangle of lemon meringue pie (the pastry was dry and tough), but I left the restaurant with a smile, having fallen in love with the *glace lait ribot* (buttermilk ice cream) drizzled with olive oil and showered with pungent fresh thyme. Service is swift and gentle, and the wine list offers some real treats, including Michèle Aubrey's fresh yet powerful Domaine Gramenon Vinsobres Côtes du Rhône.

FARINATA DE VIVANT

Vivant's Baked Chickpea Crêpe

Run by French chef and media darling Pierre Jancou, Vivant is a restaurant/wine bar where lovely small plates and tastes inspired by Italy grace the tables. This is just one.

EQUIPMENT:

A 9-inch (23-cm) baking dish

INGREDIENTS:

2 cups (250 g) chickpea flour

1 teaspoon fine sea salt, plus more for seasoning

2 cups (250 ml) water

6 tablespoons extra-virgin olive oil

Coarse, freshly ground black pepper

½ teaspoon freshly squeezed lemon juice

2 thin slices San Daniele or Parma ham, each cut into 4 pieces, for garnish

Fresh sage or wild mint leaves, for garnish

1. In a bowl, whisk together the flour, salt, and water. The batter should be thin and *crêpe*-like. Let it rest for 3 hours.

2. Center a rack in the oven. Preheat the oven to 450°F (240°C).

3. Remove any froth that forms on top of the batter. Stir in 5 tablespoons of the olive oil. Then pour the batter into the baking dish. Place in the center of the oven and bake until golden, about 20 minutes. Remove from the oven and let cool. Cut into squares.

4. In a large, nonstick skillet, heat the remaining 1 tablespoon of oil and brown each square of the *farinata* on both sides until golden. Season with salt, pepper, and several drops of lemon juice. Top with the ultrathin slices of San Daniele or Parma ham and the herbs, such as sage or wild mint.

VARIATIONS: Serve with mozzarella, slices of scallion, and a drizzle of extra-virgin olive oil.

8 SERVINGS

AU PASSAGE

MODERN FRENCH
1, bis passage Saint-Sébastien
Paris 11
TEL: '33 1 43 55 07 52
baraupassage@gmail.com
MÉTRO: Saint-Sébastien–Froissart

OPEN: Monday through Saturday for dinner,
Thursday and Friday for lunch
CLOSED: Sunday
PRICES: 18€ lunch menu. À la carte 20 to 35€
at dinner.
RESERVATIONS: Recommended
ATMOSPHERE: Casual

Anyone looking for a simple, bargain-priced meal prepared with excellent ingredients should stop in at Au Passage, a no-frills wine bar off the boulevard Beaumarchais in the 11th *arrondissement*. The lunch offerings allow a small choice, but we loved our first course, a small plate of top-quality beef *tartare* embellished with thin slices of fresh artichokes, a few capers, the tiniest of baby radishes and turnips, and strips of Parmigiano-Reggiano. A delicious in-season main course of fresh *thon germon* (albacore tuna) from the Mediterranean was expertly seared and placed atop a bed of plump mussels, crunchy green *salicorne* (sea greens), a light cream sauce, and tasty flowers of fresh cilantro. A flinty white Sancerre from the Vignoble Dauny helped make a sunny day even sunnier. In the evenings, a menu of small plates is a sure bet, with carefully thought-out combinations using super-fresh ingredients, such as sashimi bonito with an anchovy vinaigrette, *saucisse au couteau* (hearty pork sausages from the Vosges, seasoned with cumin) served with thin shavings of cauliflower on a bed of cauliflower puree, or roasted pumpkin with salted ricotta.

SEPTIME LA CAVE

MODERN FRENCH
3, rue Basfroi
Paris 11
TEL: +33 1 43 67 14 87
MÉTRO: Ledru-Rollin or Voltaire
OPEN: Tuesday through Saturday 4 to 11PM

CLOSED: Sunday and Monday
PRICES: Small plates 4 to 14€
RESERVATIONS: Not taken
ATMOSPHERE: Casual
SPECIALTIES: Small plates and tapas, natural
wines

If you don't already have great expectations for this small wine bar of exceptional parentage—as the offspring of the neighborhood's superstar bistro Septime—then the invitation posted on the window might give you a clue about what awaits you: "We expect that wine should surprise us, disturb us, seduce us, and finally convince us. *Bon dégustation!*"

Here you will find some, if not all, of these qualities on their thorough list of natural wines, including favorites such as Fanny Sabre and Les Foulards Rouge, all at very affordable prices. This is perhaps more wine shop than eatery, but grab a seat if you can to try their simple snack menu that is delivered directly from the mother ship's kitchen, some 50 meters away. While not the superbly conceived dishes you might expect to find at the Septime bistro, there is beauty in the simplicity of their offerings (excellent *charcuterie*, anchovies with ricotta, *foie gras*, and smoked eel) and the produce is of the same high quality as you will find around the corner.

14ᵀᴴ ARRONDISSEMENT

LE JEU DE QUILLES

MODERN FRENCH
45, rue Boulard
Paris 14
TEL: +33 1 53 90 76 22
jdequilles.fr
MÉTRO: Mouton-Duvernet

OPEN: Tuesday evening through Saturday
CLOSED: Sunday, Monday, Tuesday lunch, three weeks in August, and two weeks at Christmas
PRICES: 20€ lunch menus. À la carte 50€.
RESERVATIONS: Recommended

If you want to sample the meat sold to the star chefs of France, but do not want to cook it yourself or pay sky-high prices at a restaurant, the best bet is to take a look at the remarkable display at Hugo Desnoyer's incredible butcher shop in Paris's 14th *arrondissement* (see Specialty Food Shops, page 365),

then move one step farther into the appealing wine bar next door, le Jeu de Quilles. This tiny, friendly, open spot offers Desnoyer's lamb from Aubrac and beef from the Auvergne and Normandy, as well as fresh Brittany *langoustines* and razor clams, heirloom tomato salad in season, and a carefully chosen list of wines—including well-priced Châteauneuf-du-Pape selections from some of the top young growers, among them Marcoux and Giraud; Côtes du Rhône from Gramenon; Morgon from Foillard; and Chiroubles from Descombes. The sturdy, moist country bread comes from baker Dominique Saibron. Owners Benoît Reix and Romulaud Le Comte act as though they are welcoming you into their homes, with a friendly *table d'hôte*, as well as tables for two, three, or four. The place is spotless and the meat all gorgeous, but I am certain that flavors would be improved with more careful seasoning, a bit more searing, and a

▲ *Le Jeu de Quilles owner, Benoît Reix.*

little resting time to allow each ingredient to reach its full potential. I loved the idea of an apricot *tatin* but alas, the fruit was cooked too long and the taste had turned toward a bitter edge. But I'll go back. The place is too easy, friendly, and generous not to. (And do take note of the beautiful steak knives used in the wine bar, all made in the Atelier Perceval in Thiers in the Auvergne. They can be purchased next door at the butcher shop, as well as online at couteau.com.)

18TH ARRONDISSEMENT

LA RALLONGE

MODERN FRENCH / SPANISH / BASQUE
16, rue Eugène Sue
Paris 18
TEL: +33 1 42 59 43 24
larallonge.fr
contact@larallonge.fr
MÉTRO: Jules Joffrin or Marcadet-Poissonniers
OPEN: Tuesday through Saturday from 7PM

CLOSED: Monday, Sunday, one week at the end of February, three weeks in August, and December 21 through 30
PRICES: Lunch menu 18 to 24€. À la carte 25 to 35€.
RESERVATIONS: Recommended
ATMOSPHERE: Casual
SPECIALTY: Small plates and tapas

Montmartre can now add another top table to its growing list of great eateries with the opening of Geoffroy Maillard's second restaurant, La Rallonge (which translates as "The Extension"), just two doors down from his first triumph, La Table d'Eugène. This small plates–and–tapas wine bar was an immediate neighborhood hit, and for good reason. It's the perfect casual dining spot whether you are eating alone, *en deux,* or in a group. Maillard's menu combines Spanish tapas classics such as a fresh and zesty *pan con tomate* (toasted bread scrubbed with fresh tomatoes) and a Spanish Manchego and quince paste plate with more adventurous dishes like *nems de langoustines à la menthe avec salade thai* (prawn and mint spring rolls with Thai salad), and *ravioles de tendron de veau liées à la ricotta et pignons de pin, salade de pousses d'épinard au beurre noisette, espuma aux morilles* (veal rib ravioli with ricotta, pine nuts, baby spinach with hazelnut butter, and a morel emulsion). The *cochon fermier à la plancha* (farm-raised pork with truffle juice) is browned to perfection on a flat griddle, and pairs nicely with the *cèpe* (boletus mushroom) and truffle *"risotto" de coquillettes* (small pasta shells)— both tapas incarnations of dishes that have appeared on La Table d'Eugène's menu. The menu varies monthly but you're likely to find that some house favorites and classics are permanent fixtures. The wine list is as agreeable as the service: friendly, inviting, and likely to make you want to while away the hours there. La Rallonge has so many of my favorites on their list, I had a hard time choosing. Try the always reliable white Domaine de Villargeau Coteaux du Giennois white, a Sauvignon Blanc with overtones of lime and passion fruit; or the crispy, nicely acidic Clos Urolat Jurançon Sec Cuvée Marie, an unusual wine made of 100 percent Gros Manseng grape. Seating is on stools at the bar or at high tables.

20ᵀᴴ ARRONDISSEMENT

LE BARATIN

MODERN BISTRO FARE
3, rue Jouye-Rouve
Paris 20
TEL: +33 1 43 49 39 70
MÉTRO: Belleville or Pyrénées

OPEN: Monday through Saturday
CLOSED: Saturday lunch and Sunday
PRICES: 19€ lunch menu. À la carte 35 to 55€.
RESERVATIONS: Essential
ATMOSPHERE: Casual

Argentine-born chef Raquel Carena is one of few women behind the stove in Paris today. Her home-style cuisine draws a broad crowd of locals, as well as diners who will cross town to take a seat at this humble little bistro, with a bargain 18€ lunch that might include *pomme purée* and the freshest of *cabillaud* (mashed potatoes and codfish), a no-frills *fricassée* of chicken with rice, a dense chocolate cake (*fondant au chocolat amer*), or a slab of farm-fresh Saint-Nectaire cheese. The welcoming Saint-Veran white goes down really well, as does the ruby Morgon. Don't go without a reservation. Located just off the rue Belleville strip of popular Chinese restaurants, Le Baratin has a loyal following.

AT A GLANCE

1ST ARRONDISSEMENT

Les Fines Gueules
Juveniles
Le Rubis
Willi's Wine Bar
Verjus Bar à Vins

2ND ARRONDISSEMENT

Frenchie Bar à Vins

6TH ARRONDISSEMENT

Ambassade de Bourgogne
Fish La Boissonnerie
Oenosteria

10TH ARRONDISSEMENT

Albion
Vivant Table

11TH ARRONDISSEMENT

Le Dauphin
Au Passage
Septime La Cave

14TH ARRONDISSEMENT

Jeu de Quilles

18TH ARRONDISSEMENT

La Rallonge

20TH ARRONDISSEMENT

Le Baratin

MARKETS

MARCHÉS

Morning is my favorite time of day, and I often walk through the charming roving market on the center island of boulevard Raspail on my way to a run. After a sunny jog around the Luxembourg Gardens, I extract a string bag from my pocket and, on my way home, return to the market. There, on that tree-lined stretch of land each Tuesday, Friday, and Sunday, I search out the best that the fishmongers, vegetable and cheese merchants, as well as bakers have to offer.

A tour of Paris's markets offers a rare glimpse of an immensely important ritual, since it allows one to examine the authentic fabric and texture of contemporary French society. Parisians devote a good part of each day to marketing, and it's obvious that what many Frenchmen do between meals is make shopping lists, shop for food, and talk about meals past and future. Daily marketing is still the rule in Paris, where everything from Camembert to cantaloupe is sold to be eaten that day, preferably within a few hours. I still smile appreciatively when the cheese merchant asks if the Camembert will be savored that afternoon, or perhaps that evening, then shuffles through his larder, touching and pinching, to come up with a cheese that's perfectly ripe and properly creamy.

I love watching the extensive process of setting up the Raspail market for the day. The vegetable merchants admirably attack their *métier* like true artists. Fruits and vegetables are arranged in orderly rows, with careful attention paid to shapes, textures, and shading. The result is a colorful, vibrant mosaic: Fat stalks of celery rest next to snow-white cauliflower, the ruffled green leaves of Swiss chard beside them, followed by alabaster Belgian endives, bright green artichokes, then—zap!—rosy tomatoes or ruby red peppers. Across the aisle, green Granny Smith apples line up alongside the sweet Italian blood oranges called *sanguines* (favored for their juice, which runs the color of a brilliant sunset), while bananas from Martinique and walnuts from the Périgord in southwestern France complete the palette.

Mastering the intricacies and etiquette of French marketing is no simpler than learning French, and easily as frustrating. And it requires patience. A serious marketing trip—which will get you through only the next meal or two—can take an hour or more. Lines can be long, particularly at weekend markets, and waiting for your turn can require some patience, as those ahead of you chat away with the stall owner, discussing what is on the dinner menu for that evening, and how best to prepare what they have bought. This is all part of the market experience, though, and once it is your turn, your perseverance will

▲ *Discussing cooking techniques with the market poultry vendor.*

pay off as etiquette dictates that you can take as long as you need. So do not feel pressured, and make the most of the time you have with the stall owner to ask any questions you have about the produce, fish, meat, poultry, or dairy and how best to store or cook it—many

> "The air was laden with the various smells of the city and its markets: the strong smell of leeks mingled with the faint but persistent scent of lilacs, all carried along by the pungent breeze which is truly the air of Paris."
> —Jean Renoir

stall owners know their products very well and can be a mine of information.

Paris offers three basic sorts of markets: *marchés volants* (roving or "flying" markets); *rues commerçantes* (merchant streets); and *marchés couverts* (covered markets). Paris has 82 official markets in total: 69 *marchés volants*, including 3 organic markets, and 11 *marchés couverts*.

The *marchés volants* include more than 5,000 independent merchants moving from neighborhood to neighborhood on given days. (Workers from the city of Paris set standards and awnings in place the night before the market, so that merchants can set up shop in the early morning hours. As soon as the market is completed in early afternoon, the city workers tear down the structure, do a huge cleanup, and move on to another part of the city to set up markets for the following day.) As a shopper, if you move from various *marchés volants* from day to day, you may well see many of the same merchants.

The *rues commerçantes*, or merchant streets, are stationary indoor-outdoor street markets, not "official" markets in the strict sense, and are generally large, rambling, and open six days a week. A large *rue commerçante*, such as rue Poncelet, might include half a dozen *boulangeries* and *patisseries;* a butcher; a good dozen fruit and vegetable merchants; a coffee, tea, and spice shop; four shops for fish and shellfish; a *foie gras*, sausage, and poultry specialist; a horsemeat butcher; two *fromageries;* and a supermarket. And depending upon the length of the lines and the merchants' chatter, each individual purchase can take five to ten minutes.

The old-fashioned *marchés couverts*, or covered markets, have basically not been able to withstand modern-day competition from supermarkets and other open-air markets, and are most often less interesting and vibrant than the other markets.

Paris's markets, like its neighborhoods, reflect a variety of cultures and classes, and a tour of one or several will tell you much about the daily life of the city and the habits of those living in each neighborhood. ❧

ROVING MARKETS
MARCHÉS VOLANTS

Officially, the roving markets are open Tuesday through Friday from 7AM to 2:30PM, and from 7AM until 3PM on weekends. In reality, however, markets generally begin opening around 8AM and begin to close up by 1PM on weekdays and 2PM on weekends. They tend to be less expensive than greengrocers and specialty shops (such as butchers and fishmongers), and you will often find more local, more unusual produce here, but sometimes less variety. Unlike farmers markets, not all the produce at these markets comes directly from farmers. Many stall owners are simply resellers who buy the produce from the huge wholesale market Rungis, on the outskirts of Paris. Look for signs that say *Direct du Producteur*, meaning direct from the producer, as this often guarantees fresher, better produce. Stall owners must label the provenance of their produce, which is noted on the price flags.

Roving markets are usually set up along the center islands of major boulevards or on city squares, and generally offer a full range of products, including fruits, vegetables, meats, poultry, fish, cheese, and fresh flowers, as well as kitchen items, clothing, and sometimes antiques.

5TH ARRONDISSEMENT

MAUBERT

Place Maubert
Paris 5
MÉTRO: Maubert-Mutualité

OPEN: Tuesday, Thursday, and Saturday
8:30AM to 1PM

Place Maubert is a bustling, animated square resembling a tiny village, peppered with a full contingent of merchants offering produce, honey, packaged goods, jewelry, and clothing. The outdoor market is surrounded by food shops offering endless treasures, including the outstanding Fromagerie

Laurent Dubois, one of France's top cheesemongers (47, boulevard Saint-Germain); freshly roasted coffee beans at the Brûlerie Maubert (3, rue Monge); and outstanding

Paris baker Éric Kayser, who sells his remarkably varied assortment of breads (I am addicted to the cheese-filled *pain au fromage*) and pastries at numbers 8 and 14, rue Monge. La Pirée (47, boulevard Saint-Germain) is a family-run Greek deli offering fresh, high-quality salads, including excellent *tarama* (a spread made from carp roe) and roasted red pepper and garlic dip, as well as garlic-flecked olives. And a complete line of fresh Asian greens and packaged goods can be had for a song at the jam-packed See Sou Quan (35, place Maubert). A bit of Paris history: The square has been home to a produce market only since 1920, with some 125 merchants then, compared with about 45 today. In the 19th century it was known as the *Marché aux Mégôts*. Drifters would wander the city collecting *mégôts* (cigarette butts) and would gather in the square in the morning to resell the butts to industrialists, who would recycle the tobacco.

6TH ARRONDISSEMENT

RASPAIL

Boulevard Raspail, between rue du Cherche-Midi and rue de Rennes
Paris 6

MÉTRO: Rennes
OPEN: Tuesday and Friday 8:30AM to 1PM

This lively market has appeared on the tree-lined middle stretch of boulevard Raspail since 1920. Since moving to the Left Bank, I have walked through it three times a week on my way to and from the Luxembourg Gardens (see commentary on the Sunday organic market, page 192). On the first pass, I make a mental note of what looks good that day. As I jog through the park I plan the night's menu, then make my purchases on my way home. On Tuesdays and Fridays, merchants come from all over France, bringing an excellent selection of produce, nuts and dried fruits, pristine fish and shellfish (don't miss the Goldenfish stall), and the freshest of poultry.

▶ *Fantastically fresh meat from butcher Bruno at the Raspail market.*

ASPERGES AUX RICOTTA, JAMBON, ET PARMESAN

Braised Asparagus with
Whipped Ricotta, Ham, Parmesan, and Herbs

Asparagus first comes to market in Paris at the very end of February, shipped from asparagus growing beds in Provence. Braising asparagus—cooking it in a small amount of liquid, covered—seems to bring out the vegetal qualities of this sublime vegetable. Adding a touch of fresh rosemary and bay leaf only intensifies its bright, herbal flavors. Here a white cloud of whipped ricotta adds a contrast of textures and colors, while a touch of Parmesan, ham, and a shower of fresh herbs turns this salad into a meal.

EQUIPMENT:

A heavy-duty mixer fitted with a whisk; a large skillet with a lid; 4 warmed salad plates

INGREDIENTS:

2 cups (8 ounces; 25 g) best-quality sheep's-milk or cow's-milk ricotta

4 tablespoons whole milk

½ teaspoon fine sea salt

16 plump spears (about 2 pounds; 1 kg) fresh green asparagus, trimmed

1 tablespoon lemon oil or extra-virgin olive oil

1 teaspoon coarse sea salt

Several fresh or dried bay leaves

Several sprigs fresh rosemary

Zest and juice of 1 lemon, preferably organic

THE GARNISH:

About 40 shavings (about 2 ounces; 60 g) Parmigiano-Reggiano cheese

About 3 ounces (90 g) ham or sausage, cut into matchsticks

Fresh thyme leaves

Fresh parsley leaves

Minced fresh rosemary

Fleur de sel

1. Prepare the ricotta: In the bowl of the mixer, whisk together the ricotta and the milk until light and fluffy. Add the fine salt and whisk once more.

2. Prepare the asparagus: In a skillet large enough to hold the asparagus in a single layer, combine the asparagus, oil, coarse salt, bay leaves, and rosemary. Add enough water to cover the asparagus by about one third. Cover. Cook over high heat just until the oil-and-water mixture begins to sizzle.

3. Reduce heat to medium and braise the asparagus, turning from time to time, just until the vegetables begin to brown in spots and offer no resistance when pierced with the tip of a knife, 6 to 8 minutes. (The cooking time will depend on the thickness of the asparagus.) Remove and discard the bay leaves and rosemary. Shower the lemon zest and juice over the asparagus.

4. Arrange 4 asparagus on each salad plate. While still warm, shower with the cheese strips, the meat matchsticks, and herbs. Place a scoop of whipped ricotta alongside the asparagus. Season lightly with *fleur de sel*. Serve immediately.

4 SERVINGS

RASPAIL (Organic)

Boulevard Raspail, between rue du
Cherche-Midi and rue de Rennes
Paris 6

MÉTRO: Rennes
OPEN: Sunday 9AM to 1PM

O n Sundays, the regular Tuesday and Friday Marché Raspail transforms itself into one of the most chic markets in Paris. Set up in 1989, this was the city's first organic market. Shoppers swarm, eager to choose from the vast selection of fresh produce, poultry, cheese, and meat offered at around 50 organically certified stalls. Go early, for by noon you'll find yourself tripping over baby strollers and shopping carts. Don't miss the potato and onion *galette* stand at the rue du Cherche-Midi end of the market, or the Technicolor display of fruits and vegetables across the way. There's sparkling fish from the dependable fish merchant Diget and a spectacular range of dried fruits and nuts, and you will also find English muffins, fabulous yogurt and *fromage blanc*, a good selection of Italian products, freshly squeezed organic orange juice, and excellent vanilla beans and hot chocolate. Throughout the market prices are high, sometimes verging on the ridiculous, so remember to pack a bundle of euros as you leave home—it's a cash business.

7ᵀᴴ ARRONDISSEMENT

SAXE-BRETEUIL

Avenue de Saxe, between avenue de Ségur and
place de Breteuil
Paris 7

MÉTRO: Ségur
OPEN: Thursday and Saturday 8:30AM to 1PM

D ating from 1873, the Saxe-Breteuil market was one of the many open-air markets established as the city's covered markets lost favor. With some 76 stands, this is one of Paris's largest and best. Where else can you buy carrots and cabbage as you look up at the Eiffel Tower? Buy a pound of the rare and coveted potatoes from Noirmoutier and you'll be given a little sachet of *fleur de sel* to top off their seasoning. Get to La Boulange des Marchés stand early for their *pain pepitas*, made with 60 percent rye flour and studded with *grains de courges* (pumpkin seeds). But my favorite stand is Le Nouveau Verger, with 38 varieties of apples. Try the Chantecler, a

▶ Artichauts *(artichokes), in the markets from May to September, always find their way into my market basket.*

RAGOÛT D'ARTICHAUTS, TOMATES, CÂPRES, ET OLIVES NOIRES

Artichoke, Tomato, Caper, and Black Olive Ragout

From May to September Paris markets offer the fresh and tiny artichokes known as *artichauts violets*, grown mostly in Provence and Brittany. This Provençal preparation is a favorite, combining many of my favorite ingredients: tomatoes, black olives, and capers.

INGREDIENTS:

10 plump, moist garlic cloves, peeled, halved, and green germ removed

Fine sea salt

3 tablespoons extra-virgin olive oil

4 artichokes plus 1 lemon, prepared (see Note), or two 9-ounce (270-g) packages frozen artichoke hearts

1 can (28 ounces; 765 g) cubed tomatoes in juice

½ cup best-quality black olives

¼ cup capers in vinegar (drained, then measured)

1. In a large saucepan combine the garlic, 1 teaspoon of salt, and the oil, and sweat (cook, covered, over low heat until the garlic begins to soften), about 5 minutes.

2. Add the prepared artichokes, tomatoes, olives, and capers, and cook, covered, over low heat, until the artichokes are soft and cooked through, about 20 minutes. Taste for seasoning. Serve warm as a vegetable dish, or as a pizza or pasta sauce.

6 SERVINGS

NOTE: To trim fresh artichokes: Prepare a large bowl of cold water. Halve the lemon, squeeze the juice, and add the juice plus the lemon halves to the water. With your hands, break off the stem from the base of the artichoke. Bend back the tough outer green leaves, one at a time, and snap them off at the base. Continue snapping off leaves until only the central cone of yellow leaves with pale green tips remains. Lightly trim the top cone of leaves to just below the green tips. Trim any dark green areas from the base. Since you do not need perfect artichoke bottoms for this dish, the vegetable can be sliced lengthwise, making it easier to remove the choke. Halve the artichoke lengthwise. With a small spoon or a melon baller, scrape out and discard the hairy choke from each half. Cut each trimmed artichoke half lengthwise into 8 even slices. Return each slice to the lemony water. Repeat for the remaining 3 artichokes. Set aside. (If using frozen artichokes, thaw but do not precook them. Drain the artichokes well.)

BUYING LOCAL

There are now several online companies through which you can order fruit and vegetable boxes (*paniers*) in Paris. Order online, pay in advance, and collect your box of seasonal produce from a predesignated location, normally a local shop. Not all the companies source all their produce from local farmers, but there are a few whose produce comes direct from farmers on the outskirts of Paris and the surrounding *départements*:

JOËL THIEBAULT, vegetable grower to the star chefs of Paris, delivers weekly boxes to Paris from his farm in the Yvelines, to the west of Paris, through *Tous Primeurs*. He specializes in heirloom varieties of vegetables. (tousprimeurs.com)

THE RIGAULT FAMILY farm in Herblay, northwest of Paris, also specializes in "forgotten" varieties of fruit and vegetables and delivers to locations all over Paris on a weekly basis. (tousprimeurs.com)

BIO NIYA is one of the few companies that will deliver directly to your home or workplace from their farm in Nemours, south of Paris, and gives you the option to order à la carte although these extra services come at a price. (panierslegumes.fr)

LES PLAISIRS DU JARDIN delivers organic bags of fruit and vegetables, picked the day before or day of delivery. Bags can be preordered up to the day before, or can be bought impromptu directly at the pickup points, while stock is available. (panierbiocergy.com)

The organic seasonal produce from **LES PANIERS BIO DU VAL DE LOIRE** comes largely from 20 family-run farms in the Loire Valley. (lespaniersduvaldeloire.fr)

LE CAMPANIER delivers organic and biodynamic produce from farms a little farther afield, in Brittany, Vertou (Western France), and Graveson, south of Avignon. (lecampanier.com)

If you wish to buy directly from a farm, the website Cervia has a map detailing farms around Paris that sell directly to the public as well as farms that allow you to pick your own (*cueillette*) fruit and vegetables. (saveursparisidf.com)

LA RUCHE QUI DIT OUI! (The Hive That Says Yes!) is a fantastic new system in Paris that allows Parisians to buy directly from local farmers, *à la carte*. A "hive" is set up by someone in a local community; then members and food producers join the hive and collaborate online to form a simple and direct food-distribution system. Food producers set a minimum purchase amount, the items go on sale online via La Ruche Qui Dit Oui! website, members do their weekly shopping (or every two weeks, depending on each particular hive), and if the minimum purchase level is reached, the producer delivers to the pickup point on the organized day of delivery. If the minimum purchase level isn't reached, that item is simply deleted from your cart. There is no subscription fee or obligation to make an order regularly. By cutting out the middleman, the farmers are better paid for their produce, and the consumer gets local produce at a reasonable price, with the bonus of being able to meet and talk with the farmers who grow their food. (laruchequiditoui.fr)

◀ *A winter display of fresh vegetables.*

great variety with nice acidity and one that won't fall apart in your *tarte Tatin.* Other varieties to look for include Gala, Reinettes du Mans, Sainte Germaine, Canada Golden Doré, and Court Pendu Suntan, a tiny late-season apple that is tart and delicious. But the list goes on and on. At other stands, Evelyne Bernard brings geese from the Périgord; Patrick Buisson sells his potato specialties; Charcuterie Leconte offers a flavorful *terrine de cabillaud aux fines herbes* (cod terrine with *fines herbes*); Madame Verbel makes delicious homemade jams; father and daughter Stéphane and Dominique Frémont, especially known for their milk-fed veal from the Périgord, also sell lamb from the Charentes, ducks, *pintades* (guinea fowl), and sausages. Right opposite is the famous fishmonger Jacky Lorenzo. Also try the Lebanese "pizza" cooked on the spot. Before or after the market, visit one of the city's last artisanal wells at the tiny place de Breteuil. A touch of history: The Champ de Mars—originally marshland used by the clergy to grow vegetables—was cleared to make a training ground for soldiers when the École Militaire was built in 1760. Land nearby was subsequently chosen in 1889 as the site for the Eiffel Tower and was transformed into the landscaped garden that we enjoy today.

8ᵀᴴ ARRONDISSEMENT

BATIGNOLLES (Organic)

Along the center island of the boulevard des Batignolles, between numbers 27 and 48
Paris 8

MÉTRO: Rome or Place de Clichy
OPEN: Saturday 8AM to 1PM
SPECIALTY: Organic foods

Bordering the 8th and 17th *arrondissements,* along the leafy boulevard des Batignolles, is the sister market of the pricey Sunday organic market on boulevard Raspail. This is a small (just 34 stalls) but plentiful market, with a collection of merchants selling produce direct from the farm. Stands are piled high with earth-encrusted local seasonal produce: carrots, pumpkins, parsnips, and salad leaves fresh from the farms around Paris. You can also find an array of exotic imported organic fruits from stalls that purchase organic produce at the Rungis wholesale market. Stop by Laure & Mathieu Thiriet for fresh cuts of organic meat. For cheese, look out for *fromager* Philippe Grégoire. At the Moulin de la Vierge pastry stand, you'll want to grab a vanilla-rich *pain aux raisins* for breakfast, or take home a loaf of the organic rye bread.

▶ *Thick, sturdy carrots, plucked fresh from the farmer's garden.*

9TH ARRONDISSEMENT

ANVERS

Place d'Anvers, along the east and south sides
of Square d'Anvers
Paris 9

MÉTRO: Anvers
OPEN: Friday 3 to 8:30PM

I n the shadow of the Sacré-Coeur Basilica, alongside the square d'Anvers, is the small but charming *marché* d'Anvers. In this market made up of some 20-odd stalls, you will find your basket overflowing with excellent produce before you know it: organic fruit and vegetables (not direct from the farm, but the produce is ultra-fresh); French honeys, bread, and pastries; goat's-milk cheese from La Ferme de La Prairie, a family-run farm in Chabris in the center of France; and oysters and shellfish from Lecardonnel, in Normandy.

11TH ARRONDISSEMENT

BASTILLE

Boulevard Richard-Lenoir, between rue Amelot
and rue Saint-Sabin
Paris 11

MÉTRO: Bastille or Bréguet-Sabin
OPEN: Thursday 7AM to 2:30PM and Sunday
7AM to 3PM

O ne of the city's largest open-air food markets, with more than 100 merchants, the Bastille market is also one of the liveliest, particularly on a Sunday. Stretching for several blocks from the place de la Bastille toward the canal Saint-Martin, the market is filled with a huge variety of produce.

Here you will find excellent meat, poultry, and the freshest of fish and shellfish by one of the most famous fishmongers in Paris, Jacky Lorenzo. Fabulous *crèmeries* sell all manner of seasonal cheeses from all over France, as well as fresh cream, butter, and *fromage blanc*. Throughout the market you can find numerous stalls that sell *direct du producteur*, or direct from the producer (much of the produce at outdoor markets these days comes via the wholesale market at Rungis on the outskirts of Paris). Look for the merchant at the Bréguet-Sabin end of the market who has a huge variety of apples, pears, and apple cider direct from the farm. If all this makes you instantly hungry, there is a wide range of premade fare to be tasted as well: *paella*, Lebanese "pizzas" grilled on what resemble overturned woks, roasted chicken, and Middle Eastern dips and spreads alongside every imaginable type of olive. On Thursdays there's a smaller version of the bustling weekend market. On a Sunday, go before 10AM if you don't like crowds!

BELLEVILLE

Along the center island of boulevard de
Belleville, between *métros* Belleville and
Ménilmontant
Paris 11

marchedaligre.free.fr
METRO: Ménilmontant, Couronnes, or
Belleville
OPEN: Tuesday and Friday 8:30AM to 1PM

The lively *marché* Belleville is a true reflection of the diversity of the northeastern *arrondissements,* perhaps recalling North Africa more than Paris. Here you are more likely to hear Arabic spoken than French as you weave your way through the crowds, surrounded by mounds of fresh coriander and mint, *figues de barbarie* (prickly pears), melons, pomegranates, persimmons, and peppers in all colors. Grab some spicy lamb *merguez* sausages, spices, marinated olives, or preserved lemons for a couscous dish—all are on offer here. This is one of Paris's least expensive markets—promises of 1€ bargains are called out by every stall owner, reminiscent of London's vibrant Dalston market. If you can, try to pick out your own produce, or you could end up with less than the best quality. Start at Ménilmontant and make your way through the kilometer of stalls until you reach the Belleville *métro* station, where you will find yourself in Paris's second Chinatown. Head up to 35, rue de Belleville to the restaurant Le Pacifique for a quick lunchtime snack. Don't bother with the main menu—the dim sum is what they do best.

▲ *The Bastille Sunday morning market in full swing.*

POPINCOURT

Boulevard Richard Lenoir, between rue
Oberkampf and rue Jean-Pierre Timbaud
Paris 11

MÉTRO: Oberkampf
OPEN: Tuesday and Friday 7AM to 2:30PM

This charming neighborhood market is a smaller sibling to the Bastille market (see page 196). You will see many familiar faces here from stands in the Thursday and Sunday market farther down the boulevard Richard Lenoir.

12TH ARRONDISSEMENT

BEAUVAU-SAINT-ANTOINE (MARCHÉ D'ALIGRE)

Rue d'Aligre and place d'Aligre
Paris 12
marchedaligre.free.fr
MÉTRO: Ledru-Rollin or Gare de Lyon
OPEN: Open-air and antiques market Tuesday

through Sunday 7AM to 2PM (sales end at 1:30PM).
Covered market Tuesday through Friday 9AM to
1PM and 4 to 7:30PM. Saturday 9AM to 1PM and
3:30 to 7:30PM. Sunday 8:30AM to 7:30PM.
CLOSED: Monday

Bustling from 7AM to 7:30PM (except for 2 to 4PM), the Marché Beauvau-Saint-Antoine (better know as le Marché d'Aligre) is in fact three markets in one: an open-air fruit and vegetable market, a covered market, and an antiques market. It is the only market in Paris that combines all three,

and unlike other markets, is open every day of the week except Monday, when most food markets are closed. The outdoor section containing 58 vendors stretches from the rue du Faubourg Saint-Antoine up rue d'Aligre to the place d'Aligre and the Beauvau covered market, built in 1779. At the height of its popularity, this market was as famous as Les Halles, the central Paris food halls that were removed to Rungis in 1969. During the heyday of the Les Halles market, more than 1,000 stalls spread through the area's streets, attracting people from all levels of Parisian society. These days, the Marché d'Aligre is humbler in size, but it remains a vibrant hub for the rapidly gentrifying neighborhood of the 12th *arrondissement*. Half of the place

d'Aligre gives over to the flea market: You'll find tables of mismatched plates and vintage ceramic pots, secondhand clothes and hats, and all kinds of knickknacks. There are treasures to be found, but you do have to dig. After a stroll through the market, stop at the famous Baron Rouge wine bar for a glass with the locals, perhaps ordering a plate of cheese or *charcuterie*. You'll find crowds on weekends, most likely due to the Arcachon oysters and 2€ wine. While in the area, don't miss Blé Sucré (7, rue Antoine Vollon; see page 310), an adorable sparkly pastry shop on the square Trousseau, which excels at classic pastries such as lemon tart (*tarte au citron*) and *millefeuille* (made only on weekends).

TO MARKET, TO MARKET

Paris's first food market was established during the 5th century on what is now the Île de la Cité. As the city expanded, other small markets were created, first at the city gates and then, beginning in the 13th century, at the old ironworks between rue Saint-Denis, rue Saint-Honoré, and rue Croix-des-Petits-Champs, the site of the present Forum des Halles shopping mall.

At the time, the big *halles*, or market, was shared by merchants, craftsmen, and peddlers offering an international array of goods. To encourage trade here, other city merchants and craftsmen were ordered to close their shops two days each week.

It was not until the 16th century, when Paris had 300,000 inhabitants, that produce and other foodstuffs came to dominate the market.

By 1546 Paris boasted four major bread markets and one live-animal market. In the 17th century, the quai de la Mégisserie, along the Seine's Right Bank—now the site of the live-bird market, then known as the "valley of misery"—was the chicken, wild game, lamb, goat, and milk-fed-pig market; rue de la Poissonnière was established as the fish market; and the wine market was installed on the Left Bank's quai Saint-Bernard.

The French Revolution of 1789 put an end to the royal privilege of authorizing markets and transferred the power to the city. By 1860 Paris had 51 markets, 21 of them covered and the rest open-air affairs.

By the mid-19th century, the central Les Halles was badly in need of repair, so a new hall with iron girders and skylight roofs—reminiscent of the still-existing Gare de l'Est—was built by the architect Baltard between 1854 and 1866. The design, complete with vast underground storehouses and linked by roofed passages and alleys, became a model for markets throughout France and the rest of the world. As the city's population grew, the market space eventually became inadequate, and in 1969 the market was moved to Rungis, south of Paris, near Orly airport. Les Halles was torn down to make way for a major modern shopping complex, now a frenetic neighborhood of shops and restaurants with gardens at the center.

▼ *A truffle and* foie gras *extravaganza at the Raspail market.*

SORBET AUX FIGUES RÔTIES

Roasted Fig Sorbet

When figs fill the city's markets from late summer to early autumn, this is one of my favorite desserts. Figs, much like cherries and other delicately flavored fruits, sometimes need coaxing to bring out their true goodness: Roasting does the trick here!

EQUIPMENT:

A food processor or a blender; an ice-cream maker; 8 ice-cream bowls, chilled in the freezer

INGREDIENTS:

2 pounds (1 kg) fresh figs, stems trimmed and discarded, halved lengthwise

6 tablespoons unrefined cane sugar, preferably organic

Grated zest of 1 lemon, preferably organic

1 teaspoon fresh thyme leaves

2 tablespoons sweet red wine, such as port or a *vin doux naturel* from Rasteau

1 cup (250 ml) Greek-style plain whole-milk yogurt

2 tablespoons Invert Sugar Syrup (page 75) or light corn syrup

1. Center a rack in the oven. Preheat the oven to 400°F (200°C).

2. In a baking dish, combine the figs, cane sugar, lemon zest, thyme, and wine. Toss to blend. Place in the oven and roast, uncovered, until hot and bubbly, about 30 minutes. Remove from the oven. Transfer to a container and chill thoroughly.

3. In the food processor, combine the roasted figs, yogurt, and sugar syrup. Place the mixture in the ice-cream maker and freeze according to the manufacturer's instructions. For best results, serve the sorbet in well-chilled ice-cream bowls as soon as it is frozen. Do not refreeze.

8 SERVINGS

14ᵀᴴ ARRONDISSEMENT

EDGAR QUINET

Along boulevard Edgar Quinet, beginning at rue
du Départ
Paris 14

MÉTRO: Edgar Quinet
OPEN: Wednesday, Saturday, and Sunday
9ᴀᴍ to 1ᴘᴍ

This truly neighborhood market in Montparnasse serves as a classic example of a traditional Parisian *marché volant*: Shoppers and merchants all seem to know one another ("Will you be here Saturday? It's a holiday," asks a well-dressed matron), and quality is there for the asking. Favorite merchants here include Chenus Volailles, a stunning poultry merchant who makes delicious (and hard to find) turkey sausage (*saucisses de dinde*) and offers a beautiful selection of game in the fall and winter months, the seldom-seen duck from Challans (*canard de Challans*) prized by the city's finest chefs, as well as the plump, gorgeous Noir de Kervor, an ancient breed of black-eyed rabbits traditionally fed on flaxseed (*lin*), making the meat rich in omega-3. (The Chenus family can also be found at the Convention market on Thursday and Sunday.) In autumn, I love the festive array of wild mushrooms from J. L. Testard, including shiitakes, fairy mushrooms (*mousserons*), wild boletus (*cèpes*), and of course, year-round, the always-delicious *champignons de Paris* cultivated mushrooms. There are a number of market gardeners, or *maraichers,* including the Douilly family from Picardie, with multiple varieties of potatoes, more offerings of apples than you can imagine, and a huge choice of pears as well as quince (*coing*) in season. There's rotisserie chicken, hard-to-resist just-roasted spare ribs (*travers de porc*), and every kind of *charcuterie* you might desire, including the fall and winter specialty of *choucroute* (sauerkraut) and an avalanche of pork products.

15ᵀᴴ ARRONDISSEMENT

DUPLEIX-GRENELLE

Boulevard de Grenelle, between rue Lourmel
and rue de Commerce
Paris 15

MÉTRO: Dupleix or La Motte-Picquet–
Grenelle
OPEN: Wednesday and Sunday 9ᴀᴍ to 1ᴘᴍ

This bustling, always crowded market sheltered beneath the elevated *métro* lines in the 15th *arrondissement* is one of the finest examples of a roving neighborhood Paris market. With more than 140 merchants, this is one of the largest markets in the capital, with many stellar merchants. It is a market that truly specializes: One merchant sells nothing but honey from Burgundy; another only eggs from free-range chickens; there's a snail lady and a goat farmer/

cheesemaker offering clean and supple goat cheeses from their farm, la Ferme de la Prairie, in the Loire. Several *maraichers,* or market gardeners (also called *producteurs*), bring their homegrown produce direct from the farm to Paris markets and do a land-office business with lines flowing down the center aisle of this active *marché.* My favorite apple lady is there from Le Nouveau Verger, as well as the Deshaies family, who offer nothing but plump, fresh homegrown oysters from the Marennes-Oléron along the Atlantic coast north of Bordeaux. This is a good market to know about on a rainy day, for the elevated lines offer a nice bit of shelter from the elements. From October to May, oyster grower Patrick Liron sets up a stand outside the café Le Bouquet de Grenelle, 68, avenue de la Motte-Picquet. Note that Sunday is the liveliest day, since some merchants make the trip only on weekends.

16TH ARRONDISSEMENT

COURS DE LA REINE / PRÉSIDENT WILSON

Avenue Président Wilson, between rue Debrousse and place d'Iéna
Paris 16

MÉTRO: Alma-Marceau or Iéna
OPEN: Wednesday and Saturday 8:30AM to 1PM

This is the market Parisians will cross town for. With nearly 130 merchants, the upscale outdoor institution has been here since 1873, and today offers perhaps the best and most abundant selection of fresh fish and shellfish in the city, and at reasonable prices. On one visit, I found live, squiggling shrimp in several sizes, seldom-seen *sébaste* (ocean perch) from the Atlantic Ocean, and of course, pristine turbot, *bar* (sea bass), giant rose-colored *rougets* (red mullet), sparkling *raie* (skate), fresh *hareng* (herring), and 000-size *huîtres* (oysters as big as the palm of a hand). In season, this is a game lover's paradise, with wild hare (skinned right before your eyes), a whole haunch of baby wild boar (*marcassin*), pheasant, and partridge. Joël Thiebaut, the famed vegetable grower to the star chefs, has a stunning display of the freshest and most colorful heirloom vegetables all year, and several of the Asian vendors offer seldom-seen *combava*, or dried kaffir lime leaves, as well as a remarkable assortment of baby vegetables. A snail vendor offers ready-to-heat snails, clams, and mussels, all stuffed with a tangy parsley and garlic butter, and spice vendors sell vanilla beans and pods at reasonable prices. I've been known to turn a trip here into breakfast and lunch, snacking first on the salty *manaeesh* (Lebanese flatbread) sprinkled with *za'tar* (a savory spice blend of thyme, sumac, and sesame seeds) and cooked on the spot on a gas cooker that resembles an upside-down wok. That was followed by a sit-down snack of fresh-from-the-griddle buckwheat *galettes* stuffed with cheese, ham, and egg, all washed down with a glass of chilled cider. The flower vendors here always have colorful and unusual offerings, the Italian cheese selection is vast, and I counted 12 different varieties of potato at one vegetable stand. Come February, several stands offer the remarkable *merenda* tomatoes, grown in greenhouses in Sicily.

▲ *Pumpkin delivery on rue Cler.*

MARKET STREETS

RUES COMMERÇANTES

While every shop on these market streets keeps its own hours, generally shops are open Tuesday through Sunday, and are closed Monday. Many specialty shops such as butchers, grocers, and cheesemongers still close for lunch, and opening hours are likely to be 9AM to 1PM and 4 to 7PM Tuesday through Saturday and Sunday 9AM to 1PM. Pastry shops, chocolate shops, and cafés stay open through lunchtime; however, it is always best to check opening times for specific shops you plan to visit to avoid disappointment.

These merchant or market streets vary in style from neighborhood to neighborhood. Some are long, rambling streets with many choices of merchants from which to do your weekly shopping; others are smaller with less variety, but have a truly neighborhood feel to them. Here are my favorites in the capital.

7TH ARRONDISSEMENT

RUE CLER

From avenue de la Motte-Piquet to rue Saint-Dominque
Paris 7

MÉTRO: École Militaire
OPEN: Tuesday through Sunday
CLOSED: Monday

This lively market street is one of the prettiest in Paris, with a wide walking *allée* for strolling without traffic, flanked by shops and restaurants on either side. This is a strong family neighborhood, so you may compete for

space with strollers and children on scooters. There are many treasures here: If you start at the crossroads of rue Cler and avenue de la Motte-Piquet, don't miss, from October to March, the oysters opened by master *écailler* Stèphane Labozec at the Brasserie aux PTT (No. 54, see page 153); the stunning array of *charcuterie* (*foie gras*, of course; *jambon persillé*; all manner of sausages; carryout salads) at Jeusselin (No. 37); and across the street the mouthwatering Italian offerings from *charcuterie* Davoli (No. 34). Ice-cream and sorbet

lovers must make a stop at Martine Lambert (No. 39, see page 302) for her organic raw-milk specialties. While in the neighborhood, stop at one of the city's finer cheese shops, Marie-Anne Cantin at 12, rue du Champ de Mars (see page 258); Moulin de la Vierge wood-oven sourdough breads at 64, rue Saint-Dominique (see page 230); and Secco pastry and bread at 20, rue Jean-Nicot. If you have shopped well, you shouldn't have to cook lunch or dinner for days!

9TH ARRONDISSEMENT

RUE DES MARTYRS

Beginning at rue Notre-Dame de Lorette, up to boulevard Clichy
Paris 9

MÉTRO: Notre-Dame-de-Lorette or Pigalle
OPEN: Tuesday through Sunday
CLOSED: Monday

In 1787 this street boasted 25 *auberges* or restaurants for every 58 houses. While today there isn't quite the ratio of almost one eatery for every two houses, rue des Martyrs is one of Paris's most vibrant *rues commerçantes*

for food sellers. You can spend an entire morning browsing the many food specialty shops and come away with bags of delicious produce, so start at the bottom of the street and head uphill to work up an appetite for the spoils you are sure to acquire. The *Quincaillerie Droguerie* at 1, rue des Martyrs will set you up for any kitchen supplies you may be lacking. Look out for La Chambre aux Confitures (No. 9) for its fragrant and well-balanced jam and marmalade combinations (see page 362). Pop into Premier Pression Provence next door for a quick olive oil tasting from small olive producers in Provence. You won't want to miss the beautiful and spacious pastry shop Pâtisserie des Martyrs

(No. 22, see page 307), but leave room for a few small *choux à la crème* bites at Popelini (No. 44, see page 309), and Henri Le Roux's CBS (*caramel au beurre salé*) salted butter caramel chocolates at No. 24 (see page 279). Cleanse your palate with some organic salads at the Rose Bakery (No. 46, see page 158) and a coffee at KB Cafeshop at No. 62 (the "flat white" cappuccino-style coffee is their specialty). The list is indeed almost endless but other shops of note include Terra Corse at No. 42 for their Corsican specialties, particularly the *saucisson*; Pascal Beillevaire *fromager* (No. 48, see page 261); and La Fabrique for their addictive freshly baked cookies (No. 47).

17ᵀᴴ ARRONDISSEMENT

RUE PONCELET-BAYEN

Rue Poncelet and rue Bayen
Paris 17
MÉTRO: Ternes

OPEN: Tuesday through Sunday
CLOSED: Monday

For more than 20 years this high-quality street market was my neighborhood *marché*, and I still cross town for the sparkling fresh fish and shellfish at Daguerre Marée (4, rue Bayen), fruits and vegetables from Planète Fruits (5, rue Bayen), and state-of-the-art, attentively aged cheese from Alléosse (10, rue Poncelet). Be sure to walk around the corner to 16, avenue des Ternes to at least press your nose against the glass at Maison Pou for a look at the wondrous selection of classic French *charcuterie*.

18ᵀᴴ ARRONDISSEMENT

RUE DAMRÉMONT

From rue Marcadet to just past rue Lamarck
Paris 18
MÉTRO: Lamarck-Caulaincourt

OPEN: Tuesday through Sunday
CLOSED: Monday

Weekends in this *gourmand* section of rue Damrémont are animated and bustling, full of Montmartre locals doing their weekly shopping. You'll need time and patience, as queues can be long, but the atmosphere is jovial and within just a couple of blocks you have all the shops you will need to prepare almost any kind of feast you can imagine. The best choice for fruit and vegetables is Les Halles Damrémont (No. 72). While the quality is high, and the charming *vendeurs* will pick out the ripest produce for you, not everything here is French, so if you really want to shop local, pay attention to the provenance on the price flags. *Poissonnerie* Au Bon Port delivers fresh fish and shellfish daily at No. 61. There'll most likely be a wait at Maertens Boucherie Nouvelle (No. 72), but the quality of the meat and the service (mostly) is worth it and the butchers are happy to give you advice on meat preparation and cooking times. Across the road, more queues for the bright and perky dessert pastries at Delmontel (No. 57, see page 244). Make sure to try their dense and flavorful *tourte Auvergnate* rye loaf, sold as a quarter (*un quart*), a half (*un demi*), or a whole loaf. Next door, Arnaud Lahrer is a fierce rival with his macarons, chocolates, and pastry desserts. La Brûlerie coffee roaster adds a touch of neighborhood charm with live music playing every second weekend of the month. While in the neighborhood, you must visit *fromagerie* Chez Virginie (No. 54, see page 266) for some of the finest selections of cheeses in Paris, and excellent-quality milk and whipping cream from Normandy. And

for *la table*, Urtillo Fleurs (No. 70) has beautiful and long-lasting flowers.

RUE LEPIC

Beginning at place Blanche
Paris 18
MÉTRO: Blanche

OPEN: Tuesday through Sunday
CLOSED: Monday

The somewhat grubby street of rue Lepic, between place Blanche and rue des Abbesses, still retains an old-fashioned Montmartre charm, especially if you stop into the Lux Bar (No. 12), a neighborhood café with original tile murals and Art Nouveau woodwork from 1910. Have a quick coffee on the terrace of Café des Deux Moulins, made famous by Jean-Pierre Jeunet's film *Amélie,* as long as you don't mind being photographed by throngs of passing tourists. Les Petits Mitrons (No. 26) artisanal *pâtisserie* bakes some of the most beautiful fruit tarts to be found in Paris, with chewy, caramelized pastry bases. The roast chickens at Les Rotisseurs du Roy (No. 20) are excellent (don't forget to ask for *le jus*), as are the goat's-milk cheeses at Fromagerie Lepic next door. At the top of the hill there is the ultra-fresh Poissonnerie Pepone fishmonger (No. 65), across from the 18th *arrondissement* outpost of Le Pain Quotidien (see page 222). Take a right into rue des Abbesses, where you will find award-winning bakery (best baguette in Paris 2010) Le Grenier à Pain (No. 38). Le Sancerre (No. 35), a lively wine bar/café, is a fun spot for a *tartine* and a glass of wine on the *terrasse.* While in the neighborhood, it's certainly worth a detour to check out bakery Gontran Cherrier (22, rue Caulaincourt; see page 165), Chez Virginie cheesemonger (54, rue Damrémont; see page 266), and two favorite dining spots in Montmartre: Le Coq Rico (98, rue Lepic; see page 117) and Jeanne B (61, rue Lepic; see page 166).

▶ *The fresh fish at Poissonnerie Pepone on rue Lepic always draws a crowd.*

COVERED MARKETS

MARCHÉS COUVERTS

NOTE: DURING AUGUST, MANY OF THE STALL OWNERS TAKE THEIR VACATIONS.

3RD ARRONDISSEMENT

MARCHÉ DES ENFANTS ROUGES

39, rue de Bretagne
Paris 3
MÉTRO: Temple or Filles du Calvaire
OPEN: Tuesday through Thursday 8:30AM
to 1PM and 4 to 7:30PM. Friday and Saturday

8:30AM to 1PM and 4 to 8PM. Note: The cafés in
the market remain open during lunchtimes.
CLOSED: Sunday. Note: Some cafés remain
open on Sundays.

The Marché des Enfants Rouges is quite possibly the most charming covered market in Paris, and you won't find anything else like it. Hidden away off rue de Bretagne, it is the oldest recorded market in Paris,

dating back to the 16th century. Renovated at the end of the 1990s, this small hive of activity hosts several fresh fruit and vegetable vendors and a florist. The outer edge of the market is made up of cafés and deli-style food vendors—Moroccan, Italian, Lebanese. Favorites include Chez Taeko, with reasonably priced bentos and *domburi* (8 to 15€); and the stall run by the cheerful Alain le Boulanger, for an organic buckwheat *crêpe*, sandwich, or *socca*—a chickpea-flour *crêpe* that is a specialty of Nice.

◀ *Lunchtimes and weekends are always bustling at the open-air eateries in the Marché des Enfants Rouges.*

Name that *Passage*

At 16, rue Montmartre, there's a curiously named *passage*, the Queen of Hungary Passage (*passage Reine de Hongrie*). Sometime during the 18th-century reign of Marie-Antoinette, the queen was passing through the alley when she was handed a petition by a woman who ran a market stall. The queen commented on the merchant's likeness to the queen of Hungary, and soon the alley was renamed.

6TH ARRONDISSEMENT

SAINT-GERMAIN

4–6, rue Lobineau
MÉTRO: Mabillon
OPEN: Tuesday through Friday 8:30AM to 1PM

and 4PM to 8PM, Saturday 8:30AM to 1:30PM
and 3:30 to 8PM, Sunday 8AM to 1:30PM

The Saint-Germain covered market, not far from the always bustling Saint-Germain/rue de Rennes crossroads, almost gets lost in the shadows of the neighborhood's wealth of food shops, restaurants, cafés, and clothing stores. But it's worth a detour for the excellent selection of produce, both Greek and Italian grocers, a good florist, and a worthy cheese merchant.

10TH ARRONDISSMENT

SAINT-MARTIN

31–33, rue du Château d'Eau
MÉTRO: Château d'Eau
OPEN: Tuesday through Friday 9:30AM to 1PM

and 4 to 7:30PM, Saturday 9AM to 7:30PM,
Sunday 9AM to 1:30PM

This small covered market not far from the Strasbourg Saint-Denis gates does not have a vast selection of stalls, but the produce at the two fruit and vegetable stands, the fishmonger, butcher, cheesemonger, and a stand of organic products, are all fresh and of good quality. (The organic stand is a unique feature of this market, as one wouldn't typically find a whole organic stand in a covered market like this.) However, perhaps the most interesting find in this market is Au Comptoir de Brice, the small eatery at the edge of the market set up by the 2010 *Top Chef* finalist Brice Morvent. His daily changing menu offers a selection of original dishes using ultra-fresh ingredients. Open Tuesday through Saturday noon to 6PM, Sunday 11AM to 1:45PM. Closed Monday. Reservations not taken. Price: 30 to 35€ for three courses.

AT A GLANCE
ROVING MARKETS BY DAY

Roving markets are closed on Monday.

PARIS 2

Bourse
Place de la Bourse
Métro: Bourse
Open: 12:30 to 8:30PM

PARIS 5

Maubert
Place Maubert
Métro: Maubert-Mutualité
Open: 7AM to 2:30PM

Port Royal
Boulevard Port Royal, along
the length of the Hospital Val
du Grace
Métro: Port-Royal (RER B)
Open: 7AM to 2:30PM

PARIS 6

Raspail
Boulevard Raspail, between rue
du Cherche-Midi and rue de
Rennes
Métro: Rennes
Open: 7AM to 2:30PM

PARIS 8

Aguesseau
Place de la Madeleine, on the
left side of the church where
the *place* meets boulevard
Malesherbes
Métro: Madeleine
Open: 7AM to 2:30PM

PARIS 11

Belleville
Along the center island of
boulevard de Belleville,
between *métros* Belleville and
Ménilmontant
Métro: Belleville
Open: 7AM to 2:30PM

Père-Lachaise
Boulevard de Ménilmontant,
between rue des Panoyaux
and rue des Cendriers
Métro: Ménilmontant
Open: 7AM to 2:30PM

Popincourt
Boulevard Richard Lenoir,
between rue Oberkampf and
rue Jean-Pierre Timbaud
Métro: Oberkampf
Open: 7AM to 2:30PM

PARIS 12

**Beauveau Saint-Antoine
(Marché d'Aligre)**
Place d'Aligre and along rue
d'Aligre toward rue du
Faubourg Saint-Antoine
Métro: Ledru-Rollin
Open: 7AM to 1:30PM

Daumesnil
Boulevard de Reuilly, between
rue de Charenton and place
Félix Eboué
Métro: Daumesnil or
Dugommier
Open: 7AM to 2:30PM

PARIS 13

Auguste-Blanqui
Boulevard Blanqui,
between place d'Italie and
Barrault
Métro: Corvisart or Place d'Italie
Open: 7AM to 2:30PM

Bobillot
Along rue Bobillot, between
place Rungis and rue de la
Colonie
Métro: Tolbiac
Open: 7AM to 2:30PM

Salpêtrière
Boulevard de l'Hôpital, along
square Marie-Curie
Métro: Saint-Marcel
Open: 7AM to 2:30PM

PARIS 14

Mouton-Duvernet
Place Jacques Demy
Métro: Mouton-Duvernet
Open: 7AM to 2:30PM

PARIS 15

Convention
Rue Convention, between rue
Al. Chartier and rue l'Abbé
Groult
Métro: Convention
Open: 7AM to 2:30PM

Saint-Charles
Rue Saint-Charles, between
rue de Javel and the Saint-
Charles roundabout
Métro: Javel-André Citroën
Open: 7AM to 2:30PM

PARIS 16

Gros-La-Fontaine
Rue Gros and rue La Fontaine
Métro: Ranelagh
Open: 7AM to 2:30PM

Point du Jour
Avenue de Versailles, from rue
le Marois to rue Gudin
Métro: Porte de Saint-Cloud
Open: 7AM to 2:30PM

Porte Molitor
Place de la Porte Molitor *centre
sportif* (sports center)
Métro: Porte Molitor
Open: 7AM to 2:30PM

PARIS 17

Navier
Rue Navier, rue Lantiez, and
rue des Epinettes
Métro: Guy Moquet
Open: 7AM to 2:30PM

PARIS 18

Ornano
Boulevard Ornano, between
rue Mount-Cenis and rue
Ordener
Métro: Simplon
Open: 7AM to 2:30PM

PARIS 19

Jean-Jaurès
Avenue Jean-Jaurès, between rue
  Adolphe Mille and No. 195
Métro: Ourcq or Porte de Pantin
Open: 7AM to 2:30PM

Crimée-Curial
Even-numbered side of rue de
  Crimée, between Nos. 236
  and 246
Métro: Crimée
Open: 7AM to 2:30PM

Place des Fêtes
Place des Fêtes
Métro: Place des Fêtes
Open: 7AM to 2:30PM

PARIS 20

Davout
Boulevard Davout, between
  avenue de la Porte de
  Montreuil and rue
  Mendelssohn
Métro: Porte de Montreuil
Open: 7AM to 2:30PM

WEDNESDAY

PARIS 1

Saint-Honoré
Place du Marché Saint-
  Honoré
Métro: Pyramides
Open: 12:30 to 8:30PM

PARIS 4

Baudoyer
Place Baudoyer
Métro: Hôtel de Ville
Open: 12:30 to 8:30PM

PARIS 5

Monge
Place Monge
Métro: Place Monge
Open: 7AM to 2:30PM

PARIS 11

Charonne
Between 129, boulevard
  de Charonne and rue
  Alexandre Dumas
Métro: Alexandre Dumas
Open: 7AM to 2:30PM

PARIS 12

**Beauveau Saint-Antoine
(Marché d'Aligre)**
Place d'Aligre and along rue
  d'Aligre toward rue du
  Faubourg Saint-Antoine
Métro: Ledru-Rollin
Open: 7AM to 1:30PM

Bercy
Between 14, place
  Lachambeaudie and 11, rue
  Baron-le-Roy
Métro: Cour Saint-Émilion
Open: 3 to 8PM

Cours de Vincennes
On the cours de Vincennes,
  between boulevard Picpus and
  rue Arnold Netter
Métro: Nation or Porte de
  Vincennes
Open: 7AM to 2:30PM

PARIS 13

Alésia
Even-numbered side of rue de la
  Glacière and odd-numbered
  side of rue de la Santé from No.
  137 until the end
Métro: Glacière
Open: 7AM to 2:30PM

Vincent-Auriol
Boulevard Vincent Auriol,
  between No. 64 and rue
  Jeanne d'Arc

Métro: Chevaleret
Open: 7AM to 2:30PM

PARIS 14

Edgar-Quinet
Along the center island of
boulevard Edgar Quinet,
between rue du Départ and
36, boulevard Edgar Quinet
Métro: Edgar Quinet
Open: 7AM to 2:30PM

Villemain
Avenue Villemain and rue
d'Alesia
Métro: Plaisance
Open: 7AM to 2:30PM

PARIS 15

Cervantes
Between rue Bargue and rue de
la Procession
Métro: Volontaires
Open: 7AM to 2:30PM

Grenelle
Boulevard de Grenelle, between
rue Lourmel and rue du
Commerce
Métro: La Motte-Piquet–
Grenelle
Open: 7AM to 2:30PM

Lecourbe
Rue Lecourbe, between rue Vasco
de Gama and rue Leblanc
Métro: Balard or Lourmel
Open: 7AM to 2:30PM

Lefebvre
Boulevard Lefebvre, between rue
Olivier de Serres and rue de
Dantzig
Métro: Porte de Versailles
Open: 7AM to 2:30PM

PARIS 16

Auteuil
Place Jean Lorrain
Métro: Michel-Ange–Auteuil
Open: 7AM to 2:30PM

Cours De La Reine / Marché
Président Wilson
Avenue du Président Wilson,
between rue Debrousse and
place d'Iéna

Métro: Alma-Marceau or Iéna
Open: 7AM to 2:30PM

Amiral Bruix
Boulevard Bruix, between rue
Weber and rue Marbeau
Métro: Porte Maillot
Open: 7AM to 2:30PM

PARIS 17

Berthier
Boulevard de Reims, along the
square André-Ulmann
Métro: Porte de Champerret
Open: 7AM to 2:30PM

PARIS 18

Barbès
Boulevard de la Chapelle, across
from Lariboisière Hospital
Métro: Barbès–Rochechouart
Open: 7AM to 2:30PM

Ordener
Along rue Ordener, between
rue Montcalm and rue
Championnet
Métro: Guy Moquet or Jules
Joffrin
Open: 7AM to 2:30PM

PARIS 19

Villette
Boulevard de la Villette, between
Nos. 27 and 41
Métro: Belleville
Open: 7AM to 2:30PM

Porte Brunet
Avenue de la Porte-Brunet
Métro: Danube
Open: 7AM to 2:30PM

PARIS 20

Belgrand
Rue Belgrand, rue de la Chine,
and place Piaf
Métro: Gambetta
Open: 7AM to 2:30PM

Télégraphe
Rue du Télégraphe, between rue
de Belleville and Nos. 40 and
43 rue du Télégraphe
Métro: Télégraphe
Open: 7AM to 2:30PM

THURSDAY

PARIS 1

Saint-Eustache-Les Halles
Rue Montmartre, between
rue Rambuteau and rue
du Jour
Métro: Châtelet–Les Halles
Open: 12:30 to 8:30PM

PARIS 5

Marché Maubert
Place Maubert
Métro: Maubert-Mutualité
Open: 7AM to 2:30PM

Port Royal
Boulevard-Port-Royal, along
the length of the Hospital Val
du Grace
Métro: Port-Royal (RER B)
Open: 7AM to 2:30PM

PARIS 7

Saxe-Breteuil
Avenue de Saxe, between
avenue de Ségur and place
de Breteuil
Métro: Ségur
Open: 7AM to 2:30PM

PARIS 11

Bastille
Boulevard Richard Lenoir,
between rue Amelot and rue
Saint-Sabin
Métro: Bastille
Open: 7AM to 2:30PM

PARIS 12

Beauveau Saint-Antoine
(Marché d'Aligre)
Place d'Aligre and along
rue d'Aligre toward rue du
Faubourg Saint-Antoine
Métro: Ledru-Rollin
Open: 7AM to 1:30PM

Ledru-Rollin
Avenue Ledru-Rollin, between
rue de Lyon and rue de
Bercy
Métro: Gare de Lyon or Quai de
la Rapée
Open: 7AM to 2:30PM

Porte Dorée
Even-numbered side of avenue
Daumesnil, between boulevard
Poniatowski and avenue du
Général Michel-Bizot
Métro: Porte Dorée
Open: 7AM to 2:30PM

Saint Eloi
36–38, rue de Reuilly
Métro: Reuilly–Diderot
Open: 7AM to 2:30PM

PARIS 13
Maison-Blanche
Avenue d'Italie, between
Nos. 110 and 162
Métro: Maison Blanche
Open: 7AM to 2:30PM

Jeanne d'Arc
On two sides of place
Jeanne d'Arc
Métro: Nationale
Open: 7AM to 2:30PM

PARIS 14
Brune
Between l'impasse Vandal and
781 boulevard Brune
Métro: Porte de Vanves
Open: 7AM to 2:30PM

PARIS 15
Convention
Rue Convention, between
rue Al. Chartier and
rue l'Abbé Groult
Métro: Convention
Open: 7AM to 2:30PM

PARIS 16
Point du Jour
Avenue de Versailles,
from rue le Marois to
rue Gudin
Métro: Porte de Saint-Cloud
Open: 7AM to 2:30PM

PARIS 18
Ney
Boulevard Ney, between rue
Jean Varenne and rue Camille
Flammarion
Métro: Porte de Saint-Ouen or
Porte de Clignancourt
Open: 7AM to 2:30PM

PARIS 19
Jean-Jaurès
Between rue Adolphe Mille and
195 avenue Jean-Jaurès
Métro: Ourcq or Porte de Pantin
Open: 7AM to 2:30PM

Joinville
Place de Joinville and across
from No. 1 rue de Joinville
Métro: Crimée
Open: 7AM to 2:30PM

PARIS 20
Mortier
Even-numbered side of
boulevard Mortier, between
No. 90 and rue Maurice
Berteaux
Métro: Saint-Fargeau or
Pelleport
Open: 7AM to 2:30PM

Pyrénées
Rue des Pyrénées, between
rue de l'Ermitage and rue de
Ménilmontant
Métro: Jourdain
Open: 7AM to 2:30PM

Réunion
Place de la Réunion
Métro: Alexandre Dumas
Open: 7AM to 2:30PM

FRIDAY

PARIS 2
Bourse
Place de la Bourse
Métro: Bourse
Open: 12:30 to 8:30PM

PARIS 5
Monge
Place Monge
Métro: Place Monge
Open: 7AM to 2:30PM

PARIS 6
Raspail
Boulevard Raspail, between rue
du Cherche-Midi and rue de
Rennes
Métro: Rennes
Open: 7AM to 2:30PM

PARIS 8
Aguesseau
Place de la Madeleine, on left
side of church, where the *place*
meets boulevard Malesherbes
Métro: Madeleine
Open: 7AM to 2:30PM

PARIS 9
Anvers
Place d'Anvers opposite Nos. 2
to 10, and avenue Trudaine
opposite Nos. 15 to 17, along the
sides of place d'Anvers
Métro: Anvers
Open: 3 to 8:30PM

PARIS 11
Belleville
Along the center island of
boulevard de Belleville,
between *métros* Belleville and
Ménilmontant
Métro: Belleville
Open: 7AM to 2:30PM

Père-Lachaise
Boulevard de Ménilmontant,
between rue des Panoyaux and
rue des Cendriers
Métro: Ménilmontant
Open: 7AM to 2:30PM

Popincourt
Boulevard Richard Lenoir,
between rue Oberkampf and
rue Jean-Pierre Timbaud
Métro: Oberkampf
Open: 7AM to 2:30PM

PARIS 12
Beauveau Saint-Antoine (Marché d'Aligre)
Place d'Aligre and along rue
d'Aligre toward rue du
Faubourg Saint-Antoine
Métro: Ledru-Rollin
Open: 7AM to 1:30PM

▲ *Sausages at bargain prices.*

Daumesnil
Boulevard de Reuilly, between
rue de Charenton and place
Félix Eboué
Métro: Daumesnil or
Dugommier
Open: 7AM to 2:30PM

PARIS 13
Auguste-Blanqui
Boulevard Blanqui, between
place d'Italie and rue Barrault
Métro: Corvisart or Place d'Italie
Open: 7AM to 2:30PM. Sunday
7AM to 3PM.

Bobillot
Rue Bobillot, between place
Rungis and rue de la Colonie
Métro: Tolbiac
Open: 7AM to 2:30PM

Salpêtrière
Boulevard de l'Hôpital, along the
square Marie-Curie
Métro: Saint-Marcel
Open: 7AM to 2:30PM

Paris Rive Gauche
Rue Jean Anouilh, and on the
pavement of rue Neuve Tolbiac
opposite Nos. 18 and 20
Métro: Bibliotheque-François
Mitterrand
Open: noon to 8:45PM

PARIS 14
Mouton-Duvernet
Place Jacques Demy
Métro: Mouton-Duvernet
Open: 7AM to 2:30PM

PARIS 15
Brassens
Place Marette
Métro: Convention
Open: 3 to 8:30PM

Saint-Charles
Rue Saint-Charles, between rue
de Javel and the Saint-Charles
roundabout
Métro: Javel–André Citroën
Open: 7AM to 2:30PM

PARIS 16
Gros-La-Fontaine
Rue Gros and rue La Fontaine
Métro: Ranelagh
Open: 7AM to 2:30PM

Porte Molitor
Place de la Porte Molitor
Métro: Porte Molitor
Open: 7AM to 2:30PM

PARIS 17
Navier
Rue Navier, rue Lantiez, and rue
des Epinettes
Métro: Guy Moquet
Open: 7AM to 2:30PM

PARIS 18
Ornano
Boulevard Ornano, between rue
Mount-Cenis and rue Ordener
Métro: Simplon
Open: 7AM to 2:30PM

PARIS 19

Place des Fêtes
Place des Fêtes
Métro: Place des Fêtes
Open: 7AM to 2:30PM

Crimée-Curial
Even-numbered side of
    rue de Crimée, between
    Nos. 236 and 246
Métro: Crimée
Open: 7AM to 2:30PM

PARIS 20

Davout
Boulevard Davout, between
    avenue de la Porte de
    Montreuil and rue
    Mendelssohn
Métro: Porte de Montreuil
Open: 7AM to 2:30PM

SATURDAY

PARIS 1

Saint-Honoré
Place du Marché Saint-Honoré
Métro: Pyramides
Open: 7AM to 3PM

PARIS 4

Baudoyer
Place Baudoyer
Métro: Hôtel de Ville
Open: 7AM to 3PM

PARIS 5

Maubert
Place Maubert
Métro: Maubert-Mutualité
Open: 7AM to 3PM

Port Royal
Along the length of the Hospital
    Val du Grace, on boulevard de
    Port-Royal
Métro: Port-Royal (RER B)
Open: 7AM to 3PM

PARIS 7

Saxe-Breteuil
Avenue de Saxe, from avenue de
    Ségur to place Breteuil
Métro: Ségur
Open: 7AM to 3PM

PARIS 8

Batignolles (Organic)
27-48, boulevard des Batignolles
Métro: Rome or Place de Clichy
Open: 7AM to 3PM

PARIS 11

Charonne
Between 129 boulevard de
    Charonne and rue Alexandre
    Dumas
Métro: Alexandre Dumas
Open: 7AM to 3PM

PARIS 12

**Beauveau Saint-Antoine
(Marché d'Aligre)**
Place d'Aligre and along rue
    d'Aligre toward rue du
    Faubourg Saint-Antoine
Métro: Ledru-Rollin
Open: 7AM to 1:30PM

Cours de Vincennes
On the cours de Vincennes,
    between boulevard Picpus and
    rue Arnold Netter
Métro: Nation or Porte de
    Vincennes
Open: 7AM to 3PM

Ledru-Rollin
Avenue Ledru-Rollin, between
    rue de Lyon and rue de Bercy
Métro: Gare de Lyon or Quai de
    la Rapée
Open: 7AM to 3PM

PARIS 13

Alésia
Even-numbered side of rue de la
    Glacière and odd-numbered
    side of rue de la Santé from No.
    137 until the end
Métro: Glacière
Open: 7AM to 3PM

Vincent-Auriol
Boulevard Vincent Auriol,
    between No. 64 and rue
    Jeanne d'Arc
Métro: Chevaleret
Open: 7AM to 3PM

PARIS 14

Brancusi (Organic)
Place Constantin Brancusi
Métro: Gaité
Open: 9AM to 3PM

Edgar-Quinet
Along the center island of
    boulevard Edgar Quinet,
    between rue du Départ and No.
    36, boulevard Edgar Quinet
Métro: Edgar Quinet
Open: 7AM to 3PM

PARIS 15

Cervantes
Between rue Bargue and rue de
    la Procession
Métro: Volontaires
Open: 7AM to 3PM

Lecourbe
Rue Lecourbe, between rue
    Vasco de Gama and rue
    Leblanc
Métro: Balard or Lourmel
Open: 7AM to 3PM

Lefebvre
Boulevard Lefebvre, between rue
    Olivier de Serres and rue de
    Dantzig
Métro: Porte de Versailles
Open: 7AM to 3PM

PARIS 16

Amiral Bruix
Boulevard Bruix, between rue
    Weber and rue Marbeau
Métro: Porte Maillot
Open: 7AM to 3PM

Auteuil
Place Jean Lorrain
Métro: Michel-Ange–Auteuil
Open: 7AM to 3PM

**Cours De La Reine/
Président Wilson**
Avenue du Président Wilson,
    between rue Debrousse and
    place d'Iéna
Métro: Alma-Marceau or Iéna
Open: 7AM to 3PM

PARIS 17

Berthier
Boulevard de Reims, along
   André-Ulmann Square
Métro: Porte de Champerret
Open: 7AM to 3PM

PARIS 18

Barbès
Boulevard de la Chapelle, across
   from the Lariboisière Hospital
Métro: Barbès–Rochechouart
Open: 7AM to 3PM

Ordener
Along rue Ordener, between
   rue Montcalm and rue
   Championnet
Métro: Guy Moquet or Jules
   Joffrin
Open: 7AM to 3PM

PARIS 19

Porte Brunet
Avenue de la Porte Brunet
Métro: Danube
Open: 7AM to 3PM

Villette
Boulevard de la Villette, between
   Nos. 27 and 41
Métro: Belleville
Open: 7AM to 3PM

PARIS 20

Belgrand
Rue Belgrand, rue de la Chine,
   and place Piaf
Métro: Gambetta
Open: 7AM to 3PM

Télégraphe
Rue du Télégraphe, between
   rue de Belleville and Nos. 40
   and 43
Métro: Télégraphe
Open: 7AM to 3PM

SUNDAY

PARIS 1

Saint-Eustache-Les Halles
Rue Montmartre, between rue
   Rambuteau and rue du Jour
Métro: Châtelet–Les Halles
Open: 7AM to 3PM

PARIS 5

Monge
Place Monge
Métro: Place Monge
Open: 7AM to 3PM

PARIS 6

Raspail (Organic)
Boulevard Raspail, between rue
   du Cherche-Midi and rue de
   Rennes
Métro: Rennes
Open: Sunday 9AM to 3PM

Réunion
Place de la Réunion
Métro: Alexandre Dumas
Open: 7AM to 3PM

PARIS 10

Alibert
Rue Alibert, between avenue
   Parmentier and rue Bichat
Métro: Goncourt
Open: 7AM to 3PM

▼ *Seasoned olives, anchovies, and beans: the perfect appetizers.*

PARIS 11

Bastille
Boulevard Richard Lenoir,
between rue Amelot and rue
Saint-Sabin
Métro: Bastille
Open: 7AM to 3PM

PARIS 12

Beauveau Saint-Antoine (Marché d'Aligre)
Place d'Aligre and along rue
d'Aligre toward rue du
Faubourg Saint-Antoine
Métro: Ledru-Rollin
Open: 7AM to 1:30PM

Bercy
Between 14, place
Lachambeaudie and 11, rue
Baron-le-Roy
Métro: Cour Saint-Émilion
Open: 7AM to 3PM

Porte Dorée
Even-numbered side of avenue
Daumesnil, between boulevard
Poniatowski and avenue de
Général-Michel-Bizot
Métro: Porte Dorée
Open: 7AM to 3PM

Saint Eloi
36–38, rue de Reuilly
Métro: Reuilly-Diderot
Open: 7AM to 3PM

PARIS 13

Auguste-Blanqui
Boulevard Blanqui, between
place d'Italie and rue Barrault
Métro: Corvisart or Place d'Italie
Open: 7AM to 3PM

Jeanne d'Arc
On two sides of place Jeanne
d'Arc
Métro: Nationale
Open: 7AM to 3PM

Maison-Blanche
Avenue d'Italie, between Nos.
110 and 162
Métro: Maison Blanche
Open: 7AM to 3PM

PARIS 14

Brune
Between l'impasse Vandal and
71, boulevard Brune
Métro: Porte de Vanves
Open: 7AM to 3PM

Villemain
Avenue Villemain
Métro: Plaisance
Open: 7AM to 3PM

PARIS 15

Convention
Rue Convention, between rue Al.
Chartier and rue l'Abbé Groult
Métro: Convention
Open: 7AM to 3PM

Grenelle
Boulevard de Grenelle, between
rue Lourmel and rue du
Commerce
Métro: La Motte-Piquet–
Grenelle
Open: 7AM to 3PM

PARIS 16

Point du Jour
Avenue de Versailles, from rue le
Marois to rue Gudin
Métro: Porte de Saint-Cloud
Open: 7AM to 3PM

PARIS 18

Ney
Boulevard Ney, between rue
Jean Varenne and rue Camille
Flammarion
Métro: Porte de Saint-Ouen or
Porte de Clignancourt
Open: 7AM to 3PM

Ornano
Boulevard Ornano, between rue
Mount-Cenis and rue Ordener
Métro: Simplon
Open: 7AM to 3PM

PARIS 19

Jean-Jaurès
Avenue Jean-Jaurès, between
rue Adolphe Mille and No. 195
avenue Jean-Jaurès
Métro: Ourcq or Porte de Pantin
Open: 7AM to 3PM

Joinville
Place de Joinville, and across
from No. 1 rue de Joinville
Métro: Crimée
Open: 7AM to 3PM

Place des Fêtes
Place des Fêtes
Métro: Place des Fêtes
Open: 7AM to 3PM

PARIS 20

Mortier
On the even-numbered side of
boulevard Mortier, between
No. 90 and rue Maurice
Berteaux
Métro: Saint-Fargeau or
Pelleport
Open: 7AM to 3PM

Pyrénées
Rue des Pyrénées, between
rue de l'Ermitage and rue de
Ménilmontant
Métro: Jourdain
Open: 7AM to 3PM

COVERED MARKETS

PARIS 3

Marché des Enfants Rouges
39, rue de Bretagne
Métro: Filles du Calvaire
Open: Tuesday through
Thursday 8:30AM to 1PM
and 4 to 7:30PM. Friday and
Saturday 8:30AM to 1PM and
4 to 8PM.

PARIS 6

Saint-Germain
4–6, rue Lobineau
Métro: Mabillon
Open: Tuesday through Friday
8:30AM to 1PM and 4 to 8PM.
Saturday 8:30AM to 1:30PM
and 3:30 to 8PM. Sunday 8AM
to 1:30PM.

PARIS 8

Treilhard
1, rue Corvetto
Métro: Villiers
Open: Monday through
Saturday 8:30AM to 8:30PM

PARIS 10

Saint-Martin
31–33, rue du Château d'Eau
Métro: Château d'Eau
Open: Tuesday through Friday
9:30AM to 1PM and 4 to
7:30PM. Saturday 9AM to
7:30PM. Sunday 9AM to
1:30PM.

Saint-Quentin
85, bis boulevard Magenta
Métro: Gare de l'Est
Open: Tuesday through Friday
9AM to 1PM and 4 to 7:30PM.
Saturday 9AM to 1PM and 3:30
to 7:30PM.

PARIS 12

Beauvau
Place d'Aligre
Métro: Ledru-Rollin
Open: Tuesday through Friday
9AM to 1PM and 4 to 7:30PM.
Saturday 9AM to 1PM and 3:30
to 7:30PM. Sunday 8:30AM to
1:30PM.

PARIS 16

Passy
Place de Passy
Métro: Muette
Open: Tuesday through Friday
8AM to 1PM and 4 to 7PM.
Saturday 8:30AM to 1PM and
3:30 to 7PM. Sunday 8AM to
1PM.

Saint-Didier
Rue Mesnil and rue Saint-Didier
Métro: Victor Hugo
Open: Monday through Friday
8AM to 7:30PM. Saturday 8AM
to 1:30PM.

PARIS 17

Batignolles
96, bis rue Lemercier
Métro: Brochant
Open: Tuesday through Friday
8:30AM to 1PM and 3:30 to
8PM. Saturday 8:30AM to 8PM.
Sunday 8:30AM to 2PM.

Ternes
8, bis rue Lebon
Métro: Ternes
Open: Tuesday through Saturday
8AM to 1PM and 4 to 7:30PM.
Sunday 8AM to 1PM.

PARIS 18

La Chapelle
10, rue l'Olive
Métro: Marx Dormoy
Open: Tuesday through Friday
9AM to 1PM and 4 to 7:30PM.
Saturday 9AM to 1PM and 3:30
to 7:30PM. Sunday 8:30AM
to 1PM.

BAKERIES

BOULANGERIES

Of the hundreds of Parisians I've interviewed over the decades, I love the bakers best. Years ago they were roly-poly men in worn white T-shirts who came to Paris from little French towns and villages to make their way. They are family men,

who never seem to have enough time to sleep, and who are passionate—almost crazily, over-the-edge passionate—about bread. So am I. Today, however, I may spend time with Parisian baker-businessmen with perhaps 100 *boulangeries* around the world. But they retain the same passion.

One of my greatest gastronomic Parisian treats is to walk into a favorite or newly discovered *boulangerie* before noon, my stomach growling with hunger. I order a crusty baguette, *bien cuite* (well-cooked), and before I have plunked down my centimes I've bitten off the heel. Chewy, yeasty ecstasy. Bread *is* life. It's food that makes you feel good, feel healthy; food that goes with everything, and goes especially well with the foods we love most about France—fine cheese, great wine.

How does one tell the good loaf from the bad, and what makes the difference? The good French loaf is made with respect for the simple nature of the ingredients: wholesome, stone-milled wheat grown in France; a fresh sourdough starter (*levain*) or fresh yeast (*levure*); pure water; and a minimum of salt. This is true whether it is a thin, crisp, golden baguette or *ficelle;* a plump, round

country-style *pain de campagne;* or a made-to-eat-with-cheese loaf studded with hazelnuts, walnuts, or raisins. In the best bakeries, ovens are fired all day long, ensuring that customers can purchase loaves just minutes old throughout the day. (Most classic French breads contain no fat and thus quickly go stale.)

Almost all dough is kneaded mechanically, but the best is done slowly, so the flavor is not killed by over-kneading. Good dough is allowed to rise slowly, several times, with plenty of rest between kneadings. At the finest bakeries, every loaf is formed by hand. Good bread has a thick crust, a dense and golden interior, with lots of irregular air holes, and a fresh wheaty aroma and flavor.

In the 1970s French bakers organized a nationwide "good bread campaign," a loose attempt to bring back the kind of bread made before World War II brought modernization to the corner bakery. Today there is a clear renaissance of artisanal breads. Sourdough baguettes, and hearty and crusty country loaves, now vie for space with such novelty breads as *pain à l'emmental et noix* (Emmentaler cheese and walnut bread) and *pain aux plantes* (whole-grain bread baked with herbs), not to mention ten-grain loaves baked with everything from flaxseeds to pumpkin seeds.

This artisanal trend has also spawned a bevy of high quality brand-name breads. Bakeries buy the flour and the recipe that goes with it, and bake loaves with wholesome-sounding names like Mannedor, Rétrodor, Baguepi, and Pain Passion. And the modern Parisian rage for hamburgers has many bakers offering delicious buns, often custom-made for restaurants.

At the same time, the interest in all things natural and *biologique* (organic) is stronger than ever, but no longer new. What is great is that the growing demand has pushed passionate bakers to create (or re-create) innovative variations on the country theme—*pains campagnotte, triple alliance, vieille France, paillasse,* and *bûcheron,* to name a few. While I can't promise you will find great bread on every corner or even in every neighborhood, I've done my best to scour the city for the best breads that Paris has to offer. ❧

1ST ARRONDISSEMENT

ÉRIC KAYSER (Opéra)

33, rue Danielle Casanova
Paris 1
TEL: +33 1 42 97 59 29
maison-kayser.com
contact@maison-kayser.com

MÉTRO: Opéra or Pyramides
OPEN: Monday through Saturday
7AM to 8:30PM
CLOSED: Sunday

Y ou won't need to go far in Paris in search of Éric Kayser's crusty baguettes or super-tasty flavored loaves—his bread empire includes 17 shops across Paris. See box (facing page) for full commentary.

GOSSELIN (Saint-Honoré)

125, rue Saint-Honoré
Paris 1
TEL: +33 1 45 08 03 59
boulangerie-patisserie-artisanale-paris1.com

phgoss@wanadoo.fr
MÉTRO: Louvre-Rivoli
OPEN: Sunday through Friday 7AM to 8PM
CLOSED: Saturday

P hilippe Gosselin offers one of the most dependable baguettes in Paris. It has a great crunch, a tender *mie* (interior), and the smell of freshly milled wheat. The natural crust has a golden-brown glow with just the right amount of cracking, dusted ever so lightly with flour. His 7th-*arrondissement*

shop is in my neighborhood, so it has quickly become my go-to baguette. Try also the fine sourdough *pain au levain* and sturdy *pain de*

seigle. Winner of the Best Baguette in Paris 1996 and fifth place in 2010. A father-and-son operation since 1989.

ÉRIC KAYSER—BOULANGER

Éric Kayser has become the world's bread czar, with 17 boutiques in Paris and outposts in 13 foreign cities from Taipei to Dakar (Senegal), Moscow to Dubai, even New York City. He's also added a restaurant (le Restaurant du Boulanger Éric Kayser) to his stable of activities in the restored 19th-century wine-warehouse district in the 13th *arrondissement*. This youthful redheaded, fourth-generation baker remains modest, enthusiastic, and forcefully dedicated to good breads and pastry. He likes to say "good bread does not lie," and puts that to the test regularly, working to produce daily miracles. He has built his bread empire systematically, starting with his first boutique at 8, rue Monge in 1996. Today he offers 50 varieties of bread, 50 pastries, and 25 *viennoiseries* (croissants and *pain au chocolat*). I am a regular customer in his boutiques and swear by his whole-grain baguette, studded inside and out with flax, golden shiny sesame, and poppy seeds. I am fairly addicted to his *pain au fromage* and love to bite off any cheese dripping from the edges as I exit the boutique. (Once home, I toast it and eat it with cheese. Cheese on cheese—why not?) His fillings are always generous, and while his tomato quiche is not quite as satisfying as a pizza fresh from the oven, it is still serious, with good cheese, crispy—not soggy—puff pastry, and lots of tomato. I also look forward to his *ciabatta aux graines de courge*, a pumpkin-seed-studded bread that's great toasted; the *toursade aux olives*, stuffed with olives black and green; and cranberry-raisin bread that pairs perfectly with a well-chosen cheese tray. The simplest compliment one can pay is that his breads "taste like wheat." And the pastries? I am still working my way through them, but his pistachio *financier*—a buttery golden brick of heaven—is super-moist, with an authentic taste of pistachios.

▲ *A helpful shop assistant at Éric Kayser Saint-Germain.*

BOULANGERIE JEAN-NOËL JULIEN (Saint-Honoré)

75, rue Saint-Honoré
Paris 1
TEL: +33 1 42 36 24 83
boulangerie-patisserie-artisanale-paris.com
boulangerie.julien@wanadoo.fr

MÉTRO: Les Halles or Louvre-Rivoli
OPEN: Monday through Saturday 6:30AM to 8PM
CLOSED: Sunday

Jean-Noël Julien is one competitive baker and pastry chef, gathering awards all around for his crisp baguettes, winning *pains au chocolat,* and flaky croissants. I love all three: His *baguette aux céréales* is one I could happily sample on a daily basis; when you bite into his *pain au chocolat*, with its two giant rectangles of dark chocolate folded inside, you feel as though you've won the lottery; and his classic croissants are airy, buttery, irresistible. I am also a fan of his *pain Méditérranée*, a dark-colored yet light rye bread studded with sesame, flax, and oats. It's delicious toasted and spread with a wisp of butter. His *mendiants* (the traditional mix of figs, almonds, hazelnuts, and raisins) are gorgeous to look at, but on last tasting were disappointingly dry, old, and crumbly.

LE PAIN QUOTIDIEN (Palais Royal)

18, rue des Petits-Champs
Paris 1
TEL: +33 1 42 60 15 24
lepainquotidien.fr
MÉTRO: Pyramides, Bourse or Palais Royal–Musée du Louvre
OPEN: Daily 8AM to 8PM

LE PAIN QUOTIDIEN (Saint-Honoré)

18, place du Marché Saint-Honoré
Paris 1
TEL: +33 1 42 96 31 70
lepainquotidien.fr
MÉTRO: Pyramides or Tuileries
OPEN: Daily 8AM to 10PM

Organic breads and pastries from Belgium. In fine weather, order your sandwiches or croissants to go for a picnic in one of Paris's two most luxurious parks: the Palais Royal Gardens or the Jardin des Tuileries—a short walk from the marché Saint-Honoré.

See box (below) for full commentary.

LE PAIN QUOTIDIEN

Le Pain Quotidien—"Daily Bread"—is a Belgian import that now spans the world, yet each shop (there are seven in Paris) manages to maintain its own bright and airy personality. The bakeries serve as gathering spots for breakfast, lunch, snacks, and even a light dinner, and most are located near parks or monuments. Long, wooden communal tables and giant ivory bowls for coffee have become Quotidien signatures, and most shops sport terraces for outdoor dining on a sunny day. The philosophy here is organic, whenever possible. Their *baguette à l'ancienne* is state-of-the-art perfection, with a super-crispy crust and golden interior. Their giant round of dark rye bread is one of the best in town, and I have a soft spot for their *mendiant*, a giant cookie/cake studded with whole hazelnuts, walnuts, almonds, and pecans. There is a huge selection of *tartines*, or open-faced sandwiches (I love the versions topped with beef, basil, and Parmesan; or another with ricotta, radishes, and arugula), and copious salads, such as the grilled organic vegetable creation that combines grilled eggplant and zucchini with ricotta, Parmesan, and mozzarella.

▲ *A vast selection for your daily bread.*

PISSALADIÈRE

Onion, Anchovy, and Black Olive Tart

While this onion, anchovy, and black olive tart is a traditional Provençal specialty, you'll find it at most Paris bakeries and pastry shops, often offered in individual servings, perfect for snacking as you stroll the city's streets.

EQUIPMENT:

A large skillet with a lid; a baking sheet lined with baking parchment

INGREDIENTS:

3 tablespoons extra-virgin olive oil

1 pound (500 g) onions, peeled, halved lengthwise, cut into thin half moons

½ teaspoon fine sea salt

2 plump, moist garlic cloves, peeled, halved, green germ removed, and thinly sliced

2 large tomatoes, cored, peeled, seeded, and chopped

A 10-ounce (300-g) sheet of Quick Puff Pastry (page 308), or store-bought all-butter puff pastry, thawed if frozen (see Note)

12 flat oil-cured anchovy filets, drained

12 best-quality brine-cured black olives, pitted and halved lengthwise

Coarse, freshly ground black pepper

½ teaspoon fresh thyme leaves

1. Center a rack in the oven. Preheat the oven to 450°F (230°C).

2. In a large skillet with a lid, combine the oil, onions, salt, and garlic. Toss to coat the onions with the oil. Cover and cook over low heat until the onions are meltingly soft and pale golden, about 10 minutes. Add the tomatoes and stir to blend. Increase the heat to high and cook, uncovered, until most of the liquid has evaporated, about 5 minutes.

3. On a lightly floured work surface, roll out the pastry dough into a 13-inch (33-cm) round. Fold the dough in half and carefully transfer it to the prepared baking sheet lined with parchment. Unfold the dough. Spread the onion-tomato mixture evenly over the dough, going right out to the edges. Arrange the anchovies in a spokelike pattern on top of the mixture. Scatter the olives over the onion mixture. Season generously with coarse, freshly ground black pepper.

4. Place the baking sheet in the oven and bake the *pissaladiere* until the dough is crisp and golden, and the onions tinged with a touch of black, about 15 minutes. Remove from the oven and garnish with the thyme leaves. Transfer to a cutting board and cut into 8 wedges. Serve immediately.

ONE 13-INCH (33-CM) *PISSALADIÈRE*

NOTE: In our tests, we have preferred Dufour brand frozen puff pastry, available at most specialty supermarkets. Be sure to leave ample time for thawing frozen dough—at least 6 hours in the refrigerator.

2ND ARRONDISSEMENT

ÉRIC KAYSER (Bourse)

16, rue des Petits-Carreaux
Paris 2
TEL: +33 1 42 33 76 48
maison-kayser.com
contact@maison-kayser.com

MÉTRO: Sentier
OPEN: Monday through Saturday
7AM to 8:30PM
CLOSED: Sunday

Éric Kayser makes over 50 varieties of bread to sell in his shops, which are spread out all across Paris. Try his whole-meal baguette with sesame, flax, and poppy seeds or his *tourasde aux olives,* a loaf studded with olives and cranberries to accompany a cheese platter. See box (page 221) for full commentary.

LE PAIN QUOTIDIEN (Montorgueil)

2, rue des Petits-Carreaux
Paris 2
TEL: +33 1 42 21 14 50

lepainquotidien.fr
MÉTRO: Sentier
OPEN: Daily 8AM to 8PM

Reliably good organic loaves for your daily bread. See box (page 222) for full commentary.

3RD ARRONDISSEMENT

134 RDT

134, rue de Turenne
Paris 3
TEL: +33 1 42 78 04 72
barapain.com

MÉTRO: Filles du Calvaire or Oberkampf
OPEN: Monday through Friday 7:30AM to
8:30PM. Saturday 8:30AM to 1:30PM.
CLOSED: Sunday

Boulanger Benjamin Turquier understands bread and lures us bread lovers with his dense, German-style *Schwarzbrot,* the *baguette de tradition* (which placed second in the Paris competition in 2009), a chocolate bread studded with chunks of chocolate, and an all-rye *tourte de seigle.*

His list of specialty breads is totally seductive, with selections flavored with whole-grain *moutarde à l'ancienne;* spices and pastis; pistachios, apricots, and honey; as well as figs, apricots, hazelnuts, and walnuts. While I found his croissants flaky, golden, and satisfying, the *pain au chocolat* was less convincing. Turquier also offers tours of his kitchen and classes for his breads and pastries. Check out his website for details. You will find his treasures at various Paris restaurants, including the fabulous Willi's Wine Bar (see Wine Bars, page 172). Turquier also owns the nearby Bar à Pains (27, boulevard du

Temple, Paris 11, Tel +33 1 42 74 18 53), open for special groups, as well as Sunday brunch from 9AM to 3PM. After your time at the *boulangerie,* be sure to hop across the street to Jacques Genin's fantasy chocolate shop (see Chocolate Shops, page 272).

4TH ARRONDISSEMENT

BOULANGERIE JEAN-NOËL JULIEN (Hôtel de Ville)

24, rue Saint-Martin
Paris 4
TEL: +33 1 48 87 46 17
boulangerie-patisserie-artisanale-paris.com
boulangerie.julien@free.fr

MÉTRO: Hôtel de Ville or Châtelet
OPEN: Monday through Saturday
7:30AM to 8:30PM
CLOSED: Sunday

An award-winning baker who makes a crisp *baguette aux céréales* with sesame, flax, and oats. See page 221 for full commentary.

LE PAIN QUOTIDIEN (Marais)

18–20, rue des Archives
Paris 4
TEL: +33 1 44 54 03 07

lepainquotidien.fr
MÉTRO: Hôtel de Ville
OPEN: Daily 8AM to 10PM

Good to know about for a satisfying breakfast or a light lunch after shopping at the BHV Marais department store or a visit to the National Archives Museum. See page 222 for full commentary.

5TH ARRONDISSEMENT

ÉRIC KAYSER (Sorbonne)

8, rue Monge
Paris 5
TEL: +33 1 44 07 01 42
maison-kayser.com
contact@maison-kayser.com
MÉTRO: Maubert-Mutualité
OPEN: Monday and Wednesday through Friday
6:45AM to 8:30PM. Saturday and Sunday
6:30AM to 8:30PM.
CLOSED: Tuesday

ÉRIC KAYSER (Sorbonne II)

14, rue Monge
Paris 5
TEL: +33 1 44 07 17 81
maison-kayser.com
contact@maison-kayser.com
MÉTRO: Maubert-Mutualité
OPEN: Wednesday through Sunday
8AM to 8:15PM. Tuesday 7AM to 8:15PM.
CLOSED: Monday

You never have to travel too far in Paris to find an Éric Kayser bakery. Here in rue Monge he has two almost next door to each other! The boutique at No. 8, established in 1996, was the first of Kayser's now vast empire of *boulangeries/pâtisseries* both domestic and international. See page 221 for full commentary.

6TH ARRONDISSEMENT

ÉRIC KAYSER (Luxembourg)

87, rue d'Assas
Paris 6
TEL: +33 1 43 54 92 31
maison-kayser.com
contact@maison-kayser.com
MÉTRO: Vavin or Port Royal RER B
OPEN: Monday through Saturday 7AM to 8PM
CLOSED: Sunday

ÉRIC KAYSER (Odéon)

10, rue de l'Ancienne-Comédie
Paris 6
TEL: +33 1 43 25 71 60
maison-kayser.com
contact@maison-kayser.com
MÉTRO: Odéon or Mabillon
OPEN: Monday through Saturday
7AM to 8:30PM
CLOSED: Sunday

ÉRIC KAYSER (Montparnasse)

1, boulevard du Montparnasse
Paris 6
TEL: +33 1 47 83 75 39
maison-kayser.com
contact@maison-kayser.com
MÉTRO: Duroc
OPEN: Monday through Saturday
7AM to 8:30PM
CLOSED: Sunday

Éric Kayser is the bread czar of Paris, or indeed the world, with 17 shops in the capital and a baker's dozen of international locations. Whatever his formula is, it works, as the quality of his baked goods remains impeccable. See page 221 for full commentary.

BOULANGERIE JEAN-NOËL JULIEN (Luxembourg)

54, rue Notre-Dame des Champs
Paris 6
TEL: +33 1 43 54 99 54
boulangerie-patisserie-artisanale-paris.com

MÉTRO: Notre-Dame des Champs or Vavin
OPEN: Monday through Saturday
7:30AM to 8PM
CLOSED: Sunday

An award-winning baker who often appears in the top-ten rankings for the Best Baguette in Paris competition. See page 221 for full commentary.

POILÂNE (Cherche-Midi)

8, rue du Cherche-Midi
Paris 6
TEL: +33 1 45 48 42 59
poilane.fr
info@poilane.fr

MÉTRO: Sèvres-Babylone or Saint-Sulpice
OPEN: Monday through Saturday
7:15AM to 8:15PM
CLOSED: Sunday

Not to be missed—the most famous, and to my mind, the best bread in Paris. See box (facing page) for full commentary.

POILÂNE

In Paris, in France, in the world, the name Poilâne is synonymous with huge, healthy loaves of country sourdough bread baked in traditional wood-fired ovens. Each day, more than 3 percent of Paris's 10 million residents enjoy this bread, produced in wholesome 5-pound (2-kg) loaves scored with the famous *P*. Whether spread with salted butter or jam, paired with oysters, or served to accompany delicious raw-milk cheeses, the thick slices are a feast.

Lionel Poilâne and I were good friends and his death in 2002 was a big personal loss. He was so much more than a famous baker: a modern businessman, an inquisitive philosopher, a husband and father. After each of our encounters, which occurred over more than two decades, I left his presence enriched and inspired, as though I had been given a very special vitamin for the day. We shared a passion for music, for quirky jokes, for one-liners that always got a laugh.

Fortunately, his daughter Apollonia—a student at Harvard when her parents died in a helicopter accident—valiantly and brilliantly keeps this successful business true to its roots, even expanding specialties and shops. To my mind, and to my palate, Poilâne makes the best bread there is, for it is both as basic as bread can be and as complex. Its fragrance is ethereal and its texture so sturdy it could almost stand on its own as a meal. I think of it as a symbol of France and of the culture's ability to thrive, maintaining what is best from the past, while adapting confidently to the present. There's more than bread in the Poilâne collection: pastries include one of the best *tartelettes* in Paris—caramelized apples in a rich cloud of buttery puff pastry—and the equally famous buttery baby *sablé* (shortbread) cookies. Visitors to the colorful shop on rue du Cherche-Midi will occasionally be allowed to visit the wonderfully fragrant, flour-dusted cellar to watch the famous bread being mixed,

▲ *This Poîlane baker rose in the small hours of the morning to produce the fresh, delicious loaves that stock the shelves of the boutique on rue du Cherche-Midi.*

kneaded, shaped, and expertly placed in the ancient wood-burning oven lodged beneath the street. Personalized decorated *miches* (large round loaves), as well as miniature personalized rolls, can be ordered several days in advance. (All breads and pastries sold in the shop are baked there. Outside Paris, the artisanal Poilâne baking center called "Le Manufacture" operates around the clock, stoking 20 wood-burning ovens identical to the city ovens and manned in the same manner, to the same standards, producing handmade breads for shipment all over the world.) Poilâne will deliver bread to your door in Paris, so that you never will want for a wholesome loaf! Poilâne also has two cafés, both called Cuisine de Bar—one next door to the Cherche-Midi bakery, and one in the 3rd *arrondissement*—selling some of Paris's best *tartines* (open-faced sandwiches). See Cafés and Casual Bites, pages 136 and 145, for more details.

SECCO (Rennes)

101, rue de Rennes
Paris 6
TEL: +33 1 45 48 35 79

MÉTRO: Rennes or Saint-Placide
OPEN: Monday through Saturday 7AM to 8PM
CLOSED: Sunday

Stéphane Secco, who has moved from the Rue Jean-Nicot boutique of famed baker Jean-Luc Poujauran (who now bakes bread exclusively for Parisian restaurants), continues to turn out wonders. The classic sourdough *baguettes au levain* and country-style *boules de campagne* are to be recommended, as is the lemon tart and my favorite tomato tart, a simple but sublime puff pastry topped with slices of fresh tomatoes, a touch of cheese, and a shower of black olives.

▲ *The French idiom* long comme un jour sans pain, *meaning "long as a day without bread," is used to describe something that is interminably long.*

7TH ARRONDISSEMENT

ÉRIC KAYSER (Musée d'Orsay)

18, rue du Bac
Paris 7
TEL: +33 1 42 61 27 63
maison-kayser.com

contact@maison-kayser.com
MÉTRO: Rue du Bac or Solférino
OPEN: Tuesday through Sunday 7AM to 8PM
CLOSED: Monday

This bakery has a seating area, making it a perfect café stop before or after a visit to the nearby Musée d'Orsay. See page 221 for full commentary.

STREET NAME MENU

It should come as no surprise to find that in Paris, a city so devoted to food, dozens of street names have a food connection. Here are a few, with the *arrondissement* in which they are now located.

RUE DES BOULANGERS (5th *arrondissement*). When the street was named in 1844, it was lined with numerous bakeries. Today there's not a loaf of bread for sale on "Baker's Street."

PASSAGE DE LA BRIE (19th *arrondissement*). Named for the region east of Paris known for its wheat, pastures, butter, and of course, cheese.

RUE BRILLAT-SAVARIN (13th *arrondissement*). Named in honor of the gastronome and author of the famous *Physiology of Taste*.

RUE BRISE-MICHE (4th *arrondissement*). During the Middle Ages, it was on this street that clergymen distributed bread to the needy. Brise-miche, named in 1517, literally means "break bread."

RUE CURNONSKY (17th *arrondissement*). Named in memory of the gastronome Maurice-Edmond Sailland, who took on the Russian-sounding pseudonym around the turn of the 20th century, when everything Russian was fashionable in Paris. The author of the multi-volume *La France Gastronomique* died in 1956, and the street was later named in his honor.

RUE DES EAUX (16th *arrondissement*). In 1650, when this road was opened in the Passy district, workers had discovered the area's mineral waters. (Passy is now one of the more upper-class neighborhoods of Paris.) The source dried up during the 18th century, but the name "Street of the Waters" remained. Who knows—if the source still existed, we could all be drinking Passy water instead of Perrier.

RUE DE LA FAISANDERIE (16th *arrondissement*). A pheasant preserve, or *faisanderie*, once existed here.

RUE DES FERMIERS (17th *arrondissement*). There are no farmers, or *fermiers*, left here today, but in the 1800s there were still a few farms in this now-citified neighborhood not far from Parc Monceau. The street was named in 1840, when the area became part of Paris.

RUE DES JEÛNEURS (2nd *arrondissement*). The name perhaps comes from a sign that hung above one of the houses in 1715, during the reign of Louis XV. It read: *Aux Déjeuners*, or "Lunches Here."

RUE DES MARAÎCHERS (20th *arrondissement*). During the 18th century, vegetable garden markets, or *maraîchers*, bordered the region. The street was named in 1869.

IMPASSE MARCHÉ AUX CHEVAUX (5th *arrondissement*). There are many Paris streets named after past or still-existing markets, but this is one story I particularly enjoy. Beginning in 1687, this was a major market site. Early each Wednesday and Saturday, pigs were brought to market for sale, then later in the day mules, donkeys, and horses (*chevaux*) were sold, giving the street its name. On Sundays they sold wagons and dogs.

RUE DES MEUNIERS (12th *arrondissement*). The street of the millers takes its name from the flour mill that existed there in the 18th century. Today there's no sign of a mill.

RUE DES MORILLONS (15th *arrondissement*). Morillon is the name of a grapevine that flourished in the Parisian climate at a time when Parisians and those living on the outskirts still had room to grow grapes. The path that led from the vineyard was declared a road in 1730, and a street in 1906. Vineyards have once again been planted in the nearby Parc Georges-Brassens, but they're of the Pinot Noir variety, not Morillon.

GOSSELIN (Musée d'Orsay)

258, boulevard Saint-Germain
Paris 7
TEL: +33 1 45 51 53 11
boulangerie-patisserie-artisanale-paris7.com
boulangerie.gosselin@orange.fr

MÉTRO: Solférino
OPEN: Monday through Friday 7AM to 8PM.
Saturday 7:30AM to 7:30PM.
CLOSED: Sunday

This bright, spacious boutique at the exit of Solférino *métro*, just steps from the Musée d'Orsay, is my go-to bakery for a crunchy, golden baguette. See page 220 for full commentary.

LE MOULIN DE LA VIERGE (Invalides)

64, rue Saint-Dominique
Paris 7
TEL: +33 1 47 05 98 50
lavierge.com
saintdominique@lemoulindelavierge.com

MÉTRO: Invalides or La Tour-Maubourg
OPEN: Wednesday through Monday
7:30AM to 8:30PM
CLOSED: Tuesday

A passion for bread is the only explanation for Basile Kamir's extraordinary and creative variety. A bite into one of his sourdough loaves (baked in one of the city's rare wood-fired ovens) reminds you that this is what bread should taste like: moist and slightly tangy on the inside, surrounded by a thick,

earthy crust. Kamir's delicious, dense, golden country loaves, made from organically grown wheat, are among the best in town. Come here to find a perfect *fougasse,* crispy and golden on the outside with a rich olive and anchovy interior. (It also comes plain and with a variety of other fillings.) The moist sourdough rye dons a crater-like crust that seems to erupt with walnuts—and it, too, comes in a plain version and another one yummy with raisins. Do try the simple and unusual provincial pastry specialties, like the *carré dijonnaise,* a sandwich of brown butter *sablés* that resemble rich graham crackers filled with raspberry jam; the *galette charentaise* (an overgrown wheel of melt-in-your-mouth butter *galette* doused with almonds); or the *cannelés* (sweet miniature molded butter cakes, a specialty of Bordeaux). I am currently addicted to Kamir's *carré au miel,* sweet pastry topped with a colorful mix of

almonds, dried fruits, and honey. They're rich, but just a tiny bite satisfies.

▶ *Two happy customers at the Moulin de la Vierge bakery.*

LE PAIN QUOTIDIEN (Rue du Bac)

25, rue de Varenne
Paris 7
TEL: +33 1 45 44 02 10

lepainquotidien.fr
MÉTRO: Rue du Bac or Sèvres-Babylone
OPEN: Daily 8AM to 8PM

This shop is worth visiting after a morning of shopping at the nearby Bon Marché department store. See page 222 for full commentary.

SECCO (Varenne)

31, rue de Varenne
Paris 7
TEL: +33 1 45 48 46 50

MÉTRO: Rue du Bac
OPEN: Monday through Saturday 7AM to 8PM
CLOSED: Sunday

A favorite bakery in this neighborhood, Secco turns out excellent *baguettes au levain* and a sublime apple tart. See page 228 for full commentary.

8TH ARRONDISSEMENT

ÉRIC KAYSER (Monceau)

85, boulevard Malesherbes
Paris 8
TEL: +33 1 45 22 70 30
maison-kayser.com
contact@maison-kayser.com

MÉTRO: Villiers or Miromesnil
OPEN: Monday through Saturday
7AM to 8:15PM
CLOSED: Sunday

This shop is good to know about when gathering together a quick picnic lunch to enjoy in the nearby Parc Monceau. See page 221 for full commentary.

9TH ARRONDISSEMENT

ARNAUD DELMONTEL (Martyrs)

39, rue des Martyrs
Paris 9

TEL: +33 1 48 78 29 33
MÉTRO: Saint-Georges or Pigalle

Pâtisserie may be Delmontel's forte but don't leave this shop without a rustic *baguette à la fleur de sel* (he won 5th place in the Best Baguette in Paris competition in 2012 for his *baguette tradition*) or the rich and dense rye *tourte Auvergnate*. See Pastry Shops, page 305, for full commentary.

ÉRIC KAYSER (Galeries Lafayette)

Lafayette Gourmet
40, boulevard Haussmann
Paris 9
No telephone
maison-kayser.com
contact@maison-kayser.com

MÉTRO: Havre-Caumartin or Chaussée d'Antin–La Fayette
OPEN: Monday through Saturday 8:30AM to 9:30PM
CLOSED: Sunday

This is a small stand in the Galeries Lafayette gourmet supermarket, where you will find ever-dependable Kayser breads, sandwiches, savory tarts, and pastries. See page 221 for full commentary.

LE PETRIN MEDIEVAL

31, rue Henry Monnier
Paris 9
TEL: +33 1 44 53 05 02

MÉTRO: Pigalle or Saint-Georges
OPEN: Monday through Saturday 7AM to 8PM
CLOSED: Sunday

This tidy, appealing shop just a few blocks from the Saint-Georges *métro* in the 9th is a true find. The *boulangerie* itself is a stage set, with a warming black-and-gold storefront and an antique bicycle in the window. Once you're inside, the choice is vast and appealing. A variety of quiches come from the wood-fired oven at around 11AM, as do the classic *miches au levain*, giant *boules* of sourdough bread cooked with that smoky-oven tenderness. Also deadly delicious are their *pepitos*, tiny wands of puff pastry rolled with a ton of chocolate chips. What I loved most for a quick lunch was the *chèvre-épinard* (goat's milk cheese and spinach) in puff pastry.

10ᵀᴴ ARRONDISSEMENT

DU PAIN ET DES IDÉES

34, rue Yves Toudic
Paris 10
TEL: +33 1 42 40 44 52
dupainetdesidees.com

MÉTRO: Jacques Bonsergent
OPEN: Monday through Friday 6:45AM to 8PM
CLOSED: Saturday and Sunday

If I thought about relocating in Paris, I would definitely consider living around the corner from Christian Vasseur's boutique, where his *pain des amis* is pure perfection—moist, gigantic, crusty, golden, delicious. His giant loaves of bread can be found here, of course, but also at the tables of such illustrious restaurants as Alain Ducasse at the Plaza Athénée and Saturne. If that were all Vasseur offered the world, it would be enough. But his romantic, classic 1890s *boulangerie* (classified as a *monument historique*) seduces you from the sidewalk, drawing you in to sample his award-winning baguettes, sourdough *boule de céréales*, and his *mini-pavés* stuffed with feta. I have been less convinced by the pastries, which I find mundane and without a lot of charm.

12ᵀᴴ ARRONDISSEMENT

LA FOURNÉE D'AUGUSTINE (Nation)

24, place de la Nation
Paris 12
TEL: +33 1 43 43 77 36
MÉTRO: Nation

OPEN: Monday through Saturday
7:30AM to 8PM
CLOSED: Sunday

The bright blue-and-gold shop front of la Fournée d'Augustine draws you into this spotless little boutique. Rustic, sturdy breads and traditional sweet pastries are what baker Pierre Thilloux is known for. Among his huge collection of serious breads, try the version filled with prunes and pine nuts, the dense *raboliot* (studded with raisins and hazelnuts), or the *ficelle aux olives*. His specialty is the *baguette tradition*, for which he won the Best Baguette in Paris award in 2004. All are sturdy breads and worth sampling. The fruit tarts are gorgeous and I plan to return to sample the golden pine nut and cherry *tartelette*.

PAIN AU LEVAIN

• ———————— •

Sourdough Bread

I have been baking sourdough bread for more than 30 years. For the longest time, when the bread worked, I didn't know why it rose so beautifully and browned so well. When the bread turned out more like a dry pancake, I didn't understand why it didn't work, either. Then my husband, Walter, and I along with good friend Todd Murray spent a week at the San Francisco Institute of Baking with professor Didier Rosada. He is a master teacher, and I returned home to France, following all the rules we learned that week. Slowly, I broke one rule at a time and came up with this recipe, one that I and friends have used with great success for years.

Here are a few rules, not to be broken:

Be sure to keep your starter pure, nothing but water and flour. If the dough is not rising as you want, it is okay to add 1 teaspoon or less of dry yeast when adding water to the *levain* (starter), until your starter is lively and bubbly.

Before you begin, measure everything and have a dough scraper handy. Be sure to dust your bowl or your cotton- or linen-lined basket (*banneton*) with plenty of flour, measure out all the flours, have a clean container for your *levain*, and so on. Your hands will get sticky and the more you do in advance while your hands are clean, the better!

Your first several loaves may not rise very much. You can adjust rising time, from 6 hours to 24 hours, depending on your schedule and the vitality of the starter. If you bake every few days, the starter will get more and more active and the bread will rise more quickly and will be lighter.

EQUIPMENT:

A small bowl; an airtight container; a kitchen scale; a large bowl or basket (*banneton*); a cotton or linen towel; a shaker filled with flour for dusting; a heavy-duty mixer fitted with a paddle; a baking stone; a pizza peel lined with baking parchment; a razor blade; an instant-read thermometer

1. Prepare the starter: In a small bowl, combine ¼ cup (60 ml) of the water and ½ cup (70 g) of the flour and stir until the water absorbs all of the flour and forms a soft dough. Transfer to an airtight container, and set aside at room temperature for 24 hours. The mixture should rise slightly and take on a faintly acidic aroma. Repeat this for 3 more days, each day adding an additional ¼ cup (60 ml) of water and ½ cup (70 g) of flour to the dough. Each day the starter should rise slightly and should become more acidic in aroma. By day 5 you should have 1 pound (500 g) of lively starter. If you are in doubt, as you prepare the next loaf of bread, add 1 teaspoon of dry active yeast when combining the starter and water.

2. On baking day, line the bowl or basket with a cotton or linen towel and dust the cloth generously with flour.

3. In a large bowl, combine all the flours and mix to blend. In the bowl of the heavy-duty mixer fitted with a flat paddle (not the dough hook), combine the starter and the 3 cups (750 ml) of water, and mix at low speed to dissolve the starter. Add the flour mixture, cup by cup, mixing just until the dough

INGREDIENTS:

FOR THE STARTER (LEVAIN):

1 cup (250 ml) water, at room temperature

2 cups (280 g) white bread flour

FOR THE BREAD:

3 cups (420 g) white bread flour, plus some for dusting the basket

1 cup (140 g) light whole-wheat bread flour

1 cup (140 g) rye flour

1 cup (140g) spelt (épeautre) flour

1 pound (500 g) sourdough starter (levain)

3 cups (750 ml) water, at room temperature

2 tablespoons malt flakes or malt powder (see Note)

1 tablespoon coarse sea salt

1 cup (150 g) mixed seeds: equal parts sesame, flax, and sunflower seeds

NOTE: Malt powder, known as diastatic malt powder, can be found in my Amazon store, accessed via my home page, PatriciaWells.com. Malt powder adds color and flavor to the bread and also allows the bread to stay fresh longer.

is hydrated. This should take 1 to 2 minutes. Do not overmix; let the flour and water do all the work.

4. Remove 1 pound (500 g) of the dough and transfer it to an airtight container to reserve as a starter for the next baking. (Refrigerate the starter in the container for up to 3 days. It can also be frozen almost indefinitely. Thaw at room temperature for 24 hours before the next baking.)

5. Add the malt flakes, salt, and seeds to the remaining dough, mixing at low speed just until all the ingredients are well incorporated, 1 to 2 minutes. The dough will be loose and sticky. Transfer the dough to the flour-dusted bowl or basket. You do not need to shape the dough. It will take on a nice, round form as it rises. Cover and let rise for 6 hours, or until the dough has risen slightly. (To gauge how the dough is rising, leave the starter, in its see-through airtight container, on the counter. If the starter is rising nicely—with big air bubbles throughout—you can be assured that your bread dough is rising as well.)

6. About 30 minutes before baking the bread, place a baking stone in the oven and preheat the oven to 500°F (260°C).

7. Carefully invert the risen dough onto the pizza peel lined with baking parchment. With the razor blade, lightly score the loaf: I usually make 4 long slashes in a tic-tac-toe pattern. Transfer the dough and the baking parchment to the baking stone in the oven and bake for about 25 minutes, or until the loaf is evenly browned. Reduce heat to 425°F (220°C), and bake until the bread reaches an interior temperature of 200°F (95°C), another 20 minutes. Watch carefully, since ovens vary; if the bread seems to be browning too quickly, reduce the heat.

8. Transfer the bread to a wire rack to cool. The bread continues to bake as it cools, so resist the temptation to cut the bread before it is thoroughly cooled, at least 4 hours (though I do cheat from time to time.) Store the bread at room temperature in a cloth towel or cloth bag, slicing off only as much as you need at a time. The bread will stay fresh for 1 week. (When there are just two of us at home, I cut the bread into quarters, then cut each quarter into slices. I place about half a dozen slices in ziplock bags and store the bags in the freezer. Then when we want fresh bread, we just take a package from the freezer. And we never have a problem with bread going stale!)

ONE 3-POUND (1.5-KG) LOAF

BAGUETTES

The crackling-crisp, slender baguette—the name comes from the French word for "wand"—is not as old as some people think. And it wasn't born; it evolved essentially out of consumer demand. According to Raymond Calvel, one of France's more respected bread experts, the baguette came into being just before World War I when the classic French loaf had two shapes: the round *miche*, weighing about 5 pounds (2.5 kilos), and the *pain long*, an 8- by 30-inch (20.5- by 76-cm) loaf of the same weight. The *mie*, or interior, of the *pain long* was dense and heavy, the crust crisp and flavorful. Most consumers preferred the crust and bakers accommodated, making the bread thinner and thinner to obtain maximum crust, reducing the loaf's volume until they came up with the traditional 30-inch (76-cm) baguette, weighing 8 ounces (250 g).

Other historians suggest that the baguette evolved from the *viennois*, a long, thin Austrian-type loaf popular around the turn of the 19th century. The loaf has the same form as the baguette, but the dough is sweetened with sugar and softened with milk.

JACQUES BAZIN

85, bis rue de Charenton
Paris 12
TEL: +33 1 43 07 75 21
MÉTRO: Ledru-Rollin

OPEN: Monday, Tuesday, and Friday through Sunday 7AM to 8PM
CLOSED: Wednesday, Thursday, one week in February, and one month in summer (July or August)

Jacques Bazin's jam-packed historic bakery holds many wonders, including his five-grain baguette, so loaded with crunchy seeds you are sure you'll wake up extra-healthy the next morning. His mind-boggling assortment of enormous *pains fermier* is sold by the gram, with golden breads filled with almonds, hazelnuts, and Emmental cheese (a favorite toasted and served with still more cheese), as well as others with cranberries and apricots. They all rest like jewels, stacked on the old-fashioned, festive, wrought-iron baker's shelves. Bazin has even trademarked his own baguette, calling it the Bazinette.

VANDERMEERSCH

278, avenue Daumesnil
Paris 12
TEL: +33 1 43 47 21 66
boulangerie-patisserie-vandermeersch.com

c.vandermeersch@orange.fr
MÉTRO: Porte Dorée
OPEN: Wednesday through Sunday 7AM to 8PM
CLOSED: Monday and Tuesday

This tiny, orderly, old-fashioned *boulangerie* is definitely worth a detour for bread lovers. Just steps from the Porte Dorée *métro* stop, it's great for a visit on Thursday and Sunday mornings, when a produce market sets up just in front of the 1890s boutique. Stéphane and Céline Vandermeersch spoil us with an embarrassment of riches: how to decide between the irresistible 12-pound (6-kg)

Raboliot, a dense rye, walnut, hazelnut, and raisin bread (Thursday only) that they'll slice as thick as you desire or the *Rétro-Grains* (available daily), a crusty baguette loaded with sunflower seeds, millet, poppy seeds, and flax? Stéphane is also a fine pastry chef who has won awards for his *galette des rois* and *millefeuille*. Pastry fans also swear by his orange-flower-water-scented *kougelhof*. All the flour comes from the flour mill Minoterie Viron, a Parisian quality brand and point of reference.

13ᵀᴴ ARRONDISSEMENT

ÉRIC KAYSER (Bercy)

77, quai Panhard-et-Levassor
Paris 13
TEL: +33 1 56 61 11 06
maison-kayser.com
contact@maison-kayser.com

MÉTRO: Bibliothèque François Mitterrand
OPEN: Monday through Saturday
7AM to 8:15PM
CLOSED: Sunday

Éric Kayser has over 50 varieties of breads that he sells at his 17 boutiques in Paris, and in locations in 13 countries around the world. See page 221 for full commentary.

14ᵀᴴ ARRONDISSEMENT

DOMINIQUE SAIBRON

77, avenue du Général Leclerc
Paris 14
TEL: +33 1 43 35 01 07
dominique-saibron.com

contact@dominique-saibron.com
MÉTRO: Alésia
OPEN: Tuesday through Sunday 7AM to 8:30PM
CLOSED: Monday

D ominique Saibron has been sent from the heavens for us to devour his carefully crafted breads and pastries. I can never decide between his *baguette Alésiane* (hand-shaped, whole wheat, fabulous golden interior, crusty exterior—a state-of-the-art baguette made with his own yeast, honey, and spices) and the *boule bio* (made from stone-ground semi-whole-wheat flour, again with his own honey and spices, and with a specific, tangy flavor). I am less enthralled by his *pain aux olives*, made with less-than-perfect green olives. His pastries are a world of their own to explore: the croissant praliné is amazing, filled with chocolate and hazelnuts and a touch of salt. And the puff pastry is a wonder of perfection. He uses A.O.C. (*Appellation d'Origin Controlée*) butter from the Charentes and adds milk for a lighter puff. This is one shop with enough space for you to actually sit and enjoy breakfast, lunch, or a snack, so don't miss it, just steps from the Alésia *métro*.

LA FOURNÉE D'AUGUSTINE (Plaisance)

96, rue Raymond-Losserand
Paris 14
TEL: +33 1 45 43 42 45
MÉTRO: Plaisance or Pernety

OPEN: Monday through Saturday
7:30AM to 8PM
CLOSED: Sunday

The bright blue and gold shop front of La Fournée d'Augustine draws you into this spotless little boutique, which offers a huge collection of serious breads. See page 233 for full commentary.

LE MOULIN DE LA VIERGE (Plaisance)

105, rue Vercingétorix
Paris 14
TEL: +33 1 45 43 09 84

MÉTRO: Plaisance or Pernety
OPEN: Daily 7:30AM to 8PM

The bright red, old-fashioned, turn-of-the-century bakery sits as a historical monument in the middle of block after block of impersonal, modern high-rise buildings at the southern edge of town. Don't give up trying to find it, as it is worth the trek for Basile Kamir's delicious and dense country loaves. (Here's my route: From the Plaisance métro take the rue Décres exit, walk down rue d'Alésia, pass rue de l'Ouest, then make a right on Vercingétorix.) Note that all the organic *boules de campagne* are baked here in the wood-fired oven and transported to Kamir's other bakeries. Pastries and other breads are baked in traditional ovens. See page 230 for full commentary.

LE QUARTIER DU PAIN (Montparnasse)

93, rue Raymond Losserand
Paris 14
TEL: +33 1 45 42 23 98
lequartierdupain.com
contact@lequartierdupain.com

MÉTRO: Pernety or Plaisance
OPEN: Monday through Wednesday and
Friday 7AM to 8PM. Saturday and Sunday
7:30AM to 7:30PM.
CLOSED: Thursday

Baker Frédéric Lalos, with the hard-earned honor of *Meilleur Ouvrier de France* (Best Artisan in France), shares his passions with allure and conviction. His *boulangeries* scattered around Paris pull us in with the beauty of his artistry and the rich aroma of the wheat and rye he sources from some of the best flour mills in the Auvergne, in the center of France. Don't miss out on his *pain barbecue,* a golden triangle stuffed with green pepper and tomatoes; or his *pain sarrasin,* made with buckwheat flour and sporting a substantial crumb, an incredibly crunchy crust, and real sourdough flavor. His all-rye, state-of-the art *Tourte Auvergnate* is rustic, fragrant, dense, and satisfying. The sandwiches all look serious, as do the pastries. And if you need another vote of confidence, Guy Savoy serves Lalos's breads at his Michelin three-star restaurant.

15TH ARRONDISSEMENT

ÉRIC KAYSER (Émile Zola)

79, rue du Commerce
Paris 15
TEL: +33 1 44 19 88 54
maison-kayser.com
contact@maison-kayser.com

MÉTRO: Commerce
OPEN: Monday through Saturday 6:45AM to
8:15PM
CLOSED: Sunday

There's no stopping Éric Kayser with his 17 Paris boutiques and locations in 13 more cities around the world. See page 221 for full commentary.

MAX POILÂNE

87, rue Brancion
Paris 15
TEL: +33 1 48 28 45 90
max-poilane.fr

MÉTRO: Porte de Vanves
OPEN: Monday through Saturday 7:30AM to
8PM. Sunday and holidays 8AM to 7PM.
CLOSED: Christmas and New Year's

I love Max Poilâne's super-acidic hand-fashioned sourdough *miche,* a lightweight bread with a heavyweight attitude. He's also a master with rye bread, nut-filled *pain aux noix,* and raisin-studded rye *pain au raisins.* His charming little boutique bakery in a quiet residential neighborhood in the 15th is home to one of a handful of wood-fired ovens left in Paris. A good place to know when shopping at the Porte de Vanves flea market on the weekends.

LA BOULANGERIE PICHARD

88, rue Cambronne
Paris 15
TEL: +33 1 43 06 97 37
MÉTRO: Vaugirard

OPEN: Wednesday through Sunday
7AM to 1:30PM and 4 to 8PM
CLOSED: Monday and Tuesday

S'unday is the day for a visit to the Boulangerie Pichard, when the nearby active rue Lecourbe shopping street is in full swing. Baker Frédéric Pichard wins us over with his *boule de pain aux figues,* rye-based and generously filled with chunks of moist dried figs, delicious with fresh goat cheese! His baguette made with a touch of *fleur de sel* is not only a competition winner, but perfection on the palate: that golden touch, that essential crunch. His buttery croissant (also a competition winner) is pure success in the eating, buttery and flaky—though I wish he had left it in the oven a few more minutes to attain a deep, golden tone. And a fine Androuët cheese shop just across the street at No. 93 makes this a corner of gustatory heaven!

POILÂNE (Grenelle)

49, boulevard de Grenelle
Paris 15
TEL: +33 1 45 79 11 49
poilane.fr
info@poilane.fr

MÉTRO: Dupleix or Bir-Hakeim
OPEN: Tuesday through Sunday
7:15AM to 8:15PM
CLOSED: Monday

Poilâne also has two cafés, both called Cuisine de Bar, selling some of Paris's best *tartines* (see Cafés, pages 136 and 145). See page 227 for full commentary on Poilâne.

LE MOULIN DE LA VIERGE (Breteuil)

166, avenue de Suffren
Paris 15
TEL: +33 1 47 83 45 55
suffren@lemoulindelavierge.com

MÉTRO: Sèvres-Lecourbe or Ségur
OPEN: Friday through Wednesday
7:30AM to 8PM
CLOSED: Thursday

A bite into one of Basile Kamir's sourdough loaves will remind you of what a perfect one should taste like. See page 230 for full commentary.

LE QUARTIER DU PAIN (Émile Zola)

74, rue Saint-Charles
Paris 15
TEL: +33 1 45 78 87 23
MÉTRO: Charles Michels
OPEN: Monday through Friday 7AM to 8PM.
Saturday 7:30AM to 7:30PM.
CLOSED: Sunday

LE QUARTIER DU PAIN (Vaugirard)

270, rue de Vaugirard
Paris 15
TEL: +33 1 48 28 78 42
MÉTRO: Vaugirard
OPEN: Monday through Friday 7AM to 8PM.
Saturday 7:30AM to 7:30PM.
CLOSED: Sunday

As a *Meilleur Ouvrier de France,* baker Frédéric Lalos knows his trade, seeking all manner of interesting flours from the best mills in the Auvergne, in the center of France. See page 239 for full commentary.

SECCO (Eiffel Tower)

75, boulevard de Grenelle
Paris 15
TEL: +33 1 45 67 17 40
MÉTRO: Dupleix

OPEN: Tuesday through Saturday
8AM to 8:30PM
CLOSED: Sunday and Monday

I love Stéphane Secco's *baguette au levain* and *boule de compagne,* but my favorite here is his extraordinary fruit tart laden with plump, delicious apples. See page 228 for full commentary.

16TH ARRONDISSEMENT

ÉRIC KAYSER (Auteuil)

79, avenue Mozart
Paris 16
TEL: +33 1 42 88 03 29
maison-kayser.com

contact@maison-kayser.com
MÉTRO: Jasmin
OPEN: Monday through Saturday 7AM to 8PM
CLOSED: Sunday

As Éric Kayser says, "Good bread doesn't lie," and the quality of his breads and pastries is consistently excellent and dependable. See page 221 for full commentary.

LE PAIN QUOTIDIEN (Victor Hugo)

150, avenue Victor Hugo
Paris 16
TEL: +33 1 47 04 79 11

lepainquotidien.fr
MÉTRO: Victor Hugo or Rue de la Pompe
OPEN: Daily 8AM to 8PM

Excellent organic bread from Belgium, for breakfast, lunch, or a light evening meal. See page 222 for full commentary.

17TH ARRONDISSEMENT

ARNAUD DELMONTEL (Villiers)

25, rue de Lévis
Paris 17

TEL.: +33 1 42 27 15 45
MÉTRO: Villiers

Along with pastry desserts that are small works of art, you can also rely on Delmontel for a crisp *baguette à la fleur de sel* with a firm crumb, and a dense and flavorful *Tourte Auvergnate* rye bread. See Pastry Shops, page 305, for full commentary.

ÉRIC KAYSER (Ternes)

19, avenue des Ternes
Paris 17
TEL: +33 1 43 80 23 28
maison-kayser.com
contact@maison-kayser.com

MÉTRO: Ternes
OPEN: Monday through Saturday
7AM to 8:15PM
CLOSED: Sunday

The prolific Éric Kayser continues to impress me with his dependable quality and vast selection of over 50 bread varieties. See page 221 for full commentary.

LA FOURNÉE D'AUGUSTINE (Batignolles)

31, rue des Batignolles
Paris 17
TEL: +33 1 43 87 88 41

MÉTRO: Rome or La Fourche
OPEN: Monday through Saturday 7AM to 8PM
CLOSED: Sunday

The specialty here is the *baguette tradition,* for which baker Pierre Thilloux won the Best Baguette in Paris award in 2004. But there are a variety of delicious, sturdy breads that are all worth trying. See page 233 for full commentary.

GONTRAN CHERRIER (Wagram)

8, rue Juliette-Lamber
Paris 17
TEL: +33 1 40 54 72 60
gontrancherrierboulanger.com
contact@gontrancherrierboulanger.com

MÉTRO: Wagram
OPEN: Monday, Tuesday, and Thursday through Saturday 7:30AM to 8PM. Sunday 8AM to 8PM.
CLOSED: Wednesday

G ontran Cherrier (all by itself, his unusual name makes you sit up and take notice) is a wild man. His breads are like Halloween costumes: arugula green, paprika orange, squid-ink black. And he doesn't stop there, infusing breads with flavors of cumin and caraway, golden curry powder, even red miso and squid! I love him, his shop, his ambition, his sense of humor; and his bad-boy good looks make him a stand-in for Brad Pitt. I also adore his spiced Lebanese flatbread; sandwiches on squid-ink buns filled with smoked haddock, ham, and arugula; his flaxseed buns with salmon and *fromage blanc.* And I would kill to re-create his totally perfect lime tart with a good crunchy crust and tangy not-too-sweet filling. Next time, I hope to try his baguette filled with ham, *yuzu* butter, shiso leaves, and Japanese plum salt. Cherrier was the fourth-place winner for Best Baguette in Paris 2011.

THE DAILY LOAF

The following are just a few breads—of various sizes, flours, and shapes—found in the Parisian *boulangerie*.

BAGUETTE: The standard loaf of French bread, there are specific criteria to its shape and content. In Paris, the baguette weighs 8 ounces (250 g), and is about 30 inches (75 cm) long. It is made from flour, water, salt, and yeast, though it can contain a percentage of fava or soybean flour, malt, gluten, sourdough powder, or vitamin C. Traditionally made with white flour, today it is made with all sorts of flours and has everything from grains to olives added to it. Since the French Revolution, when the people cried out for affordable bread, the price of a baguette has been regulated. Today, the cost is 90 centimes (about $1.20). There are many "brand-name" baguettes made with different types of flours, which can be sold at a higher price. They include Retrodor, Parisse, Banette, Tradition, Campagrain, Bucheron. These breads are generally made according to traditional methods. Since 1993, all bread sold in *boulangeries* must be mixed, shaped, and baked on the premises.

BAGUETTE AU LEVAIN: sourdough baguette

BOULE: ball, or round loaf, either small or large

CHAPEAU: small, round loaf topped with a *chapeau*, or hat

COURONNE: ring-shaped loaf

LE FER À CHEVAL: horseshoe-shaped loaf

FICELLE: thin loaf that weighs exactly half that of a baguette

FOUGASSE: generally, a flat, rectangular, lacy bread made of baguette dough; can be filled with onions, herbs, spices, cheese, olives, bacon. It can also be made of puff pastry.

MICHE: large, round country-style loaf

PAIN BIO: made with organic flour

PAIN BIS: made with flour that is less refined than white flour

PAIN DE CAMPAGNE: made with white flour and a percentage (up to 50 percent) of rye

PAIN AUX CÉRÉALES: made with white flour and a variety of grains

PAIN COMPLET: made entirely with whole-wheat flour

PAIN DE FANTAISIE: any bread other than baguette

PAIN AU LEVAIN: any bread made with sourdough and a longer rising time

PAIN DE MIE: rectangular white sandwich loaf that is nearly all *mie* (or crumb) and very little crust. It is made for durability and is used for, among other things, sandwiches, croutons, and toast points.

PAIN AUX NOIX AND PAIN AUX NOISETTES: most often rye or wheat, filled with walnuts or hazelnuts

PAIN POLKA: bread that is slashed in a crisscross pattern; usually a large country loaf cut in this pattern

PAIN AUX RAISINS: most often rye or wheat bread studded with raisins

PAIN DE SEIGLE: made from two-thirds rye flour and one-third white flour

PAIN DE SON: a "health bread" recommended to help digestion, it contains a percentage of wheat germ

PAIN VIENNOIS: Shaped like a baguette, this tender white-flour loaf was the first bread in France to be made with yeast, in 1840. It usually contains flour, sugar, powdered milk, water, and yeast.

LE MOULIN DE LA VIERGE (Batignolles)

6, rue de Lévis
Paris 17
TEL: +33 1 43 87 42 42
levis@lemoulindelavierge.com

MÉTRO: Villiers
OPEN: Thursday through Tuesday
7:30AM to 8PM
CLOSED: Wednesday

Basile Kamir's delicious, dense, golden country loaves, made from organically grown wheat, are among the best in town. See page 230 for full commentary.

LE QUARTIER DU PAIN (Wagram)

116, rue de Tocqueville
Paris 17
TEL: +33 1 47 63 16 28
MÉTRO: Wagram

OPEN: Monday through Friday 7AM to 8PM.
Saturday 7:30AM to 7:30PM.
CLOSED: Sunday

Having the honor of *Meilleur Ouvrier de France* (Best Artisan in France), it is unsurprising that baker Frédéric Lalos seeks out flour from the best mills in Auvergne, in the center of France, for his breads. Favorites are the *pain sarrasin*, a buckwheat flour loaf with a substantial crumb, and a rustic and satisfying *Tourte Auvergnate* rye loaf. See page 239 for full commentary.

18TH ARRONDISSEMENT

ARNAUD DELMONTEL (Montmartre)

57, rue Damrémont
Paris 18

TEL: +33 1 42 64 59 63
MÉTRO: Lamarck-Caulaincourt

Pastries may be Arnaud Delmontel's strong suit, but when visiting this pretty-in-pink shop, don't leave without a rich and dense *Tourte Auvergnate*. See Pastry Shops, page 305, for full commentary.

GONTRAN CHERRIER (Montmartre)

22, rue Caulaincourt
Paris 18
TEL: +33 1 46 06 82 66
gontrancherrierboulanger.com
contact@gontrancherrierboulanger.com

MÉTRO: Blanche or Lamarck-Caulaincourt
OPEN: Monday, Tuesday, and Thursday through
Saturday 7:30AM to 8PM. Sunday 8AM to 8PM.
CLOSED: Wednesday

Gontran Cherrier is a talented and ambitious baker, with an eye for the bold and a palate for the unusual. I am happy that his tidy little shop on the charming rue Caulaincourt can be reached on my *métro* line, so it's easy to keep my kitchen stocked with his irresistible rye bread tinged with a salty touch of miso. His pastries, sandwiches, and savory tarts are excellent, too, so go for breakfast or lunch, sit at the window-side counters, and enjoy! See page 242 for full commentary.

LE PAIN QUOTIDIEN (Lepic)

31, rue Lepic
Paris 18
TEL: +33 1 46 06 79 98

lepainquotidien.fr
MÉTRO: Blanche or Abbesses
OPEN: Daily 8AM to 10PM

This shop is worth knowing after visiting the Sacré Coeur, Moulin Rouge, or the Cimetière de Montmartre. See page 222 for full commentary.

AU PAIN D'ANTAN

2, rue Eugène Sue
Paris 18
TEL: +33 1 42 64 71 78
aupaindantan.com
MÉTRO: Jules Joffrin or Marcadet-Poissonniers

OPEN: Monday through Friday 7AM to 8PM.
Saturday 7AM to 7PM.
CLOSED: Sunday and either the month of
July or August

This shop is a dreamworld of bread, with so many choices that it makes your head spin. Do try the 3-pound (2-kg) loaf of rectangular *seigle long,* sturdy rye bread that smells and tastes as it should, not a pale impostor. Normally they will slice off a piece and sell it by weight, but on one memorable visit I had to buy the entire loaf since the saleslady declared it too warm to slice. (Lucky me!) I am less enthralled by some of their specialty breads, which look great, though the *lardons-fromage* was too bready and the olives in the *fougasse aux olives* tasted rancid. They bake in a giant brick-lined oven that is more than 125 years old and was converted from wood to gas several years ago. Plan to visit before or after dining at one of my favorite Paris restaurants, La Table d'Eugène (see Restaurants, page 120).

19TH ARRONDISSEMENT

LA BOULANGERIE PAR VÉRONIQUE MAUCLERC

83, rue de Crimée
Paris 19
TEL: +33 1 42 40 65 55
MÉTRO: Laumière or Botsaris
OPEN: Wednesday through Friday 8AM to

1:30PM and 3:30 to 8PM. Saturday and Sunday
8AM to 8PM. Brunch beginning at 10:30AM
Thursday through Sunday.
CLOSED: Monday and Tuesday

Véronique Mauclerc is one rare lady: a female *boulangère* in a male-dominated baker's world, with a historic wood-fired oven for baking the varied treasures found in her charming boutique just steps from the fanciful *parc des Buttes Chaumont* at the northern edge of Paris.

The biggest problem here is deciding which breads and pastries I'll tuck into my shopping bags. Her spicy chickpea (*pois chiches*) and cumin bread is a favorite, perfect for toasting and spreading with a homemade chickpea spread (hummus). I could begin every day with her seriously delicious *pain au chocolat* embellished with a touch of raspberry. It's a revelation: Of course the combination of chocolate and raspberry is a marriage made in heaven, but add buttery puff pastry and how can you lose? She also offers a stunning *pain emmental et noisettes,* generously studded with cheese and hazelnuts, another brilliant bread for toasting and enjoying with fresh goat's-milk cheese. Fragile pastries are wisely displayed in a refrigerated glass case. I could become truly addicted to her picture-perfect *tarte au citron,* all lemony, buttery, with an ultra-thin, delicate crust. Everything here has that nice wood-oven glow—not burnt, just *bien cuit.* Shoppers can also settle into a quick bite Thursday through Sunday mornings from 10:30AM, seated at a homey table set up between the boutique and warming wood oven.

20TH ARRONDISSEMENT

BOULANGERIE AU 140

140, rue de Belleville
Paris 20
TEL: +33 1 46 36 92 47
au140.com

MÉTRO: Jourdain or Place des Fêtes
OPEN: Tuesday through Friday 7AM to 8PM. Saturday 7:30AM to 8PM. Sunday 7AM to 7PM.
CLOSED: Monday

Artisanal baker Pierre Demoncy should be proud. His *baguette 140* was named best in Paris in 2001 (which meant he got to supply bread to the president's table at the Elysée Palace for the year—cool!) and his flaky croissant—a marvel in the mouth—won second prize that same year.

He does not rest on his laurels, but rather continues to supply us with earthy *pain d'autrefois,* with a cracking crust and a sturdy base of rye flour; crusty *baguette de campagne;* and a large assortment of *pains bio,* prepared with organic flours. Visit on Friday or Sunday morning when the charming Place des Fêtes market is in full swing. And don't miss Pascal Beillevaire's inviting and impressive cheese shop at the same address.

AT A GLANCE

1ST ARRONDISSEMENT

Éric Kayser (Opéra)
Gosselin (Saint-Honoré)
Boulangerie Jean-Noël Julien
  (Saint-Honoré)
Le Pain Quotidien
  (Palais Royal)
Le Pain Quotidien
  (Saint-Honoré)

2ND ARRONDISSEMENT

Éric Kayser (Bourse)
Le Pain Quotidien
  (Montorgueil)

3RD ARRONDISSEMENT

134 RDT

4TH ARRONDISSEMENT

Boulangerie Jean-Noël Julien
  (Hôtel de Ville)
Le Pain Quotidien (Marais)

5TH ARRONDISSEMENT

Éric Kayser (Sorbonne)
Éric Kayser (Sorbonne II)

6TH ARRONDISSEMENT

Éric Kayser (Luxembourg)
Éric Kayser (Montparnasse)
Éric Kayser (Odéon)
Boulangerie Jean-Noël Julien
  (Luxembourg)
Poilâne (Cherche-Midi)
Secco (Rennes)

7TH ARRONDISSEMENT

Éric Kayser (Musée d'Orsay)
Gosselin (Musée d'Orsay)

Le Moulin de la Vierge
  (Invalides)
Le Pain Quotidien
  (Rue du Bac)
Secco (Varenne)

8TH ARRONDISSEMENT

Éric Kayser (Monceau)

9TH ARRONDISSEMENT

Arnaud Delmontel (Martyrs)
Éric Kayser
  (Galeries Lafayette)
Le Petrin Medieval

10TH ARRONDISSEMENT

Du Pain et des Idées

12TH ARRONDISSEMENT

La Fournée d'Augustine
  (Nation)
Jacques Bazin
Vandermeersch

13TH ARRONDISSEMENT

Éric Kayser (Bercy)

14TH ARRONDISSEMENT

Dominique Saibron
La Fournée d'Augustine
  (Plaisance)
Le Moulin de la Vierge
  (Plaisance)
Le Quartier du Pain
  (Montparnasse)

15TH ARRONDISSEMENT

Éric Kayser (Émile Zola)
Max Poilâne

La Boulangerie Pichard
Poilâne (Grenelle)
Le Moulin de la Vierge
  (Breteuil)
Le Quartier du Pain
  (Émile Zola)
Le Quartier du Pain
  (Vaugirard)
Secco (Eiffel Tower)

16TH ARRONDISSEMENT

Éric Kayser (Auteuil)
Le Pain Quotidien
  (Victor Hugo)

17TH ARRONDISSEMENT

Arnaud Delmontel (Villiers)
Éric Kayser (Ternes)
La Fournée d'Augustine
  (Batignolles)
Gontran Cherrier (Wagram)
Le Moulin de la Vierge
  (Batignolles)
Le Quartier du Pain (Wagram)

18TH ARRONDISSEMENT

Arnaud Delmontel
  (Montmartre)
Gontran Cherrier
  (Montmartre)
Le Pain Quotidien (Lepic)
Au Pain d'Antan

19TH ARRONDISSEMENT

La Boulangerie par Véronique
  Mauclerc

20TH ARRONDISSEMENT

Boulangerie au 140

CHAPTER 368

CHEESE SHOPS

FROMAGERIES

I f all France had to offer the world of gastronomy was bread, cheese, and wine, that would be enough for me. Each element in the trinity is made by the hands of men and women, and each is a fermented product. Think of the simplicity: Bread is just flour and water, cheese just milk and a fermenting

culture, wine nothing more than grapes fermented to often glorious heights. I cannot imagine a more understated, unified French meal than one perfectly crusty and fresh baguette, a single Camembert so ripe and velvety it won't last another hour, and a glass or two of young, fruity, well-balanced red wine. And I can't imagine a better place to discover French cheese than in Paris, where dozens of *fromageries* line the streets, each shop as distinctive and different as the personality of its owner, each offering selections that vary with the seasons.

The French have always produced many varieties of cheese, geographically reflecting the regional landscape and its many kinds of soil, climate, and vegetation. From the milk of cows, goats, and sheep nurtured on the flat green lands of Normandy, the steep mountains of the Alps, and the plains of Champagne east of Paris comes a veritable symphony of aromas, textures, colors, forms,

and flavors. Cheese fresh from little farms and dairies to large cooperatives, cheese to begin the day and to end it. The French consume a great deal of cheese—more than 26 kilos (almost 58 pounds) per capita per year compared to the Americans' average of just under 15 kilos (or less than 33 pounds).

How many varieties of French cheese are there really? The French are not a people given to simple agreement. When Charles de Gaulle said, "How can anyone govern a nation that has 246 different kinds of cheese," he was responding to a bit of cheese hype. The real figure, experts say, is more like 150 to 200 serious varieties, with perhaps an additional 100 cheeses that are minor variations.

There's an old *New Yorker* magazine cartoon that describes the confusion perfectly. An elderly woman is sitting on a sofa, poring over maps of France. She looks up at her husband and says, "Has it ever occurred to you, dear, that most of the villages and towns in France seem to have been named after a cheese?"

Don't let anyone convince you that the cheese you eat in France and the French cheese you eat in the United States are necessarily the same. A major reason they don't taste the same has to do with the United States Department of Agriculture regulations barring the importation of raw-milk (unpasteurized) cheeses that have been aged less than sixty days. Pasteurization may make cheese "safe," but in the process it kills microbes that give the cheese its character and flavor, that keep it a live, ever-changing organism. There is no question that pasteurized milk can produce uniformly bland cheese without much character. The regulation rules out the importation of France's finest fresh young cheese, including raw-milk Camembert and Brie and dozens of varieties of lively, delicate goat's-milk cheese, although on occasion a few may slip through.

Yet even in France, cheese made from pasteurized milk is increasingly common. For instance, less than 10 percent of the Camembert produced in France each year is made from raw milk. The advantage, of course, is that cheese made with pasteurized milk can be made available year-round, and will have more stable keeping qualities. And smart, entrepreneurial cheesemakers in France have made strides in recent years, creating a very acceptable Camembert made with pasteurized milk and thus easily exported. The best way to find them is by asking cheese merchants in gourmet grocery stores and sampling what is available.

When in France, take the time to get a true taste of fresh French cheese. Specify raw-milk cheeses by asking for *fromage au lait cru*. These cheeses are produced in limited quantities, the result of traditional production methods. Paris has dozens of *fromageries* that specialize in raw-milk cheese (it will say so on the label), some offering as many as 200 varieties. Note that cheese merchants do much more than simply buy and sell cheese. Their selection is rigorous and they often work directly with artisanal cheesemakers to help them create the form, color, texture, and even name of the cheese. Cheese shop owners often take the cheese from the farmer or dairy in its young, raw state, aging and refining the cheese in underground cellars that are carefully controlled for temperature and humidity. The process is called *affinage,* and it can last from days to months to years, depending upon the cheese. As each cheese matures, it takes on its own personality, influenced by the person responsible for its development. Maturing cheese needs daily attention. Some are washed with beer, some with a brine of salt and water, some with fruity *eau-de-vie.* Some are turned every day, moved from one cellar to another as the aging process continues. Each merchant has his or her own style of aging, and there are varying opinions on how cold and how humid the cellar should be; whether the cheese should be aged on clean straw or old straw, paper, wood, or even plastic mats; or whether the cheese should be turned daily or just every now and then. And each merchant has a different opinion on when cheese is ripe, and thus ready to be put on sale.

I adore watching the dedicated *fromagers,* whose love and enthusiasm for cheese is totally infectious. In their cellars they are in heaven, as they vigorously inhale the heady, pungent aromas that fill the air, and give the cheese little "love taps" the same way that bakers give their unbaked loaves a tender touch before putting them in the oven.

A few words on selecting cheese: Be sensitive to the seasons. For instance, don't expect to find a Jura mountain Vacherin in the middle of summer. Ask about the seasonal specialties in a given shop. (Some shops regularly create a platter of seasonal specialties, making it that much easier to learn about cheese.) When choosing cheese for a *dégustation* (either for sampling at home or in a restaurant), choose three or four different varieties, generally including a semisoft cow's-milk cheese, such as a Camembert; a goat's-milk cheese, such as a Crottin de Chavignol; and a blue, such as Roquefort. Eat the milder cheese first, then move on to the stronger flavors. ❧

1ST ARRONDISSEMENT

FROMAGERIE HISADA (Palais Royal)

47, rue de Richelieu
Paris 1
TEL: +33 1 42 60 78 48
hisada.fr
fromageriehisada@orange.fr

MÉTRO: Pyramides or Palais Royal
(Musée du Louvre)
OPEN: Tuesday through Saturday
11:30AM to 8PM
CLOSED: Sunday, Monday, and July 31
through August 15

A tiny, tidy gem nestled between sushi shops and Japanese bakeries, this is the place to find some unusual cheeses, including an intriguing fresh goat's-milk creation—*cabrion nature à la feuille*—wrapped in fragrant wild blackberry leaves that penetrate its alabaster dome. Equally interesting is the *Bouyguette du Segala*, a mild and lactic goat's-milk cheese made in a small dairy in France's Southwest, hand-formed and shaped like a little boat with an herbal fragrance of thyme and rosemary. The welcome here is warm and there is also a small selection of *charcuterie,* as well as the extraordinary Bordier butter. This is one of the few places in Paris with a small tasting salon, where you can sample the cheeses offered in the shop.

▶ *A spaceship-like cheese display at Fromagerie Hisada.*

3RD ARRONDISSEMENT

JOUANNAULT

39, rue de Bretagne
Paris 3
TEL: +33 1 42 78 52 61
MÉTRO: Filles du Calvaire or Temple

OPEN: Tuesday through Friday 8:30AM to 1PM and 3:30 to 7:30PM. Saturday 8:30AM to 7:45PM. Sunday 8:30AM to 1:30PM.
CLOSED: Sunday afternoon and Monday

William Jouannault runs a tidy, well-stocked cheese shop that welcomingly opens onto the rue de Bretagne market street in the Marais, just around the corner from the lively Marché des Enfants Rouges. For the uninitiated (as well as those with tons of cheese knowledge),

their blackboard lists the top three seasonal cheeses of the moment. The cheeses are all well aged and most can be purchased in smaller half sizes if you want to sample several. Some favorites here include the runny, creamy *Saint-Marcellin* cow's-milk cheese from the region south of Lyon; the fragrant *Vacherin Mont d'Or*, a cow's-milk cheese from the Jura, available from October to March; and a beautifully aged *Coulommiers* cow's-milk cheese from the Champagne region, which can rival most Brie. There is also a lovely selection of goat's-milk cheeses in season, as well as some beautifully aged *Comté* cow's-milk cheese from the Jura.

◄ *William Jouannault in his tidy street-side cheese shop.*

4TH ARRONDISSEMENT

PASCAL BEILLEVAIRE (Marais)

77, rue Saint-Antoine
Paris 4
TEL: +33 1 42 78 48 78
fromagerie-beillevaire.com

MÉTRO: Saint-Paul
OPEN: Tuesday through Saturday 8:30AM to
8PM. Sunday 9AM to 1PM.
CLOSED: Sunday afternoon and Monday

The large family enterprise of Pascal Beillevaire includes cheesemaking, cheese aging (*affinage*), and more than 80 points of sale all over France. The shops in Paris offer a mouthwatering selection of raw-milk cheeses (many of which are exclusive to Beillevaire), yogurts, desserts, and an irresistible *demi-sel croquant* unpasteurized butter. Exceptional cheeses to look out for include the rarely seen *Tomme Brulée* sheep's milk, with its bright orange crust, ivory interior, and rich, fruity flavor. I love the *Thym Tamarre*, a delicate goat's-milk cheese available from April to October. The tiny, 3-ounce (90-g) cheese is shaped like a little boat (*navette*), with a branch of thyme pressed into the cheese while it's still young and fresh. Made only from the rich, intense milk of the Rove breed of goats, it's a delicacy to savor, like a fine wine. The firmer, triangular goat's-milk cheese from the Poitou region of France, *Trois Cornes de Vendée*, is shaped to mimic a goat's horns, and aged for two to four weeks. It's a delight when spread on a crisp baguette. The Beillevaire website is a cheese lover's glossary, offering detailed commentary on each cheese, a bit of history, and advice on wine pairings. The shops in the Paris region promise to deliver cheese trays within three hours and will also prepare an entire cheese meal, delivered in a wicker basket. Most of the shops will also vacuum-seal (*sous-vide*) your purchases for travel.

5TH ARRONDISSEMENT

ANDROUËT (Mouffetard)

134, rue Mouffetard
Paris 5
TEL: +33 1 45 87 85 05
androuet.com
MÉTRO: Censier-Daubenton

OPEN: Tuesday through Friday 9:30AM to 1PM
and 4 to 7:30PM. Saturday 9:30AM to 7:30PM.
Sunday 9:30AM to 1:30PM.
CLOSED: Sunday afternoon and Monday

This shop, run by Pascal Euzet at one end of the folkloric Mouffetard market street, is worth a detour for its fine quality aged cheeses from all over France. See page 255 for full commentary.

ALLUMETTES AU CUMIN ET PARMESAN ANDROUËT

Androuët's Matchsticks with Parmesan and Cumin

Not only are Androuët's cheese shops marvels for cheese lovers, but their website—androuet.com—is a veritable cheese cookbook, featuring more than 1,500 recipes for cheese-related appetizers, main courses, and desserts. Here's one we make frequently.

EQUIPMENT:

A pizza cutter or a very sharp knife; a baking sheet lined with baking parchment

INGREDIENTS:

A 14-ounce (400-g) sheet of Quick Puff Pastry (page 308), well-chilled, or store-bought all-butter puff pastry, thawed if frozen (see Note)

½ cup (50 g) freshly grated Parmigiano-Reggiano cheese

2 tablespoons cumin seeds or caraway seeds

1. Center a rack in the oven. Preheat the oven to 425°F (220°C).

2. On a well-floured surface, roll the pastry into a 13-inch (33-cm) round. Sprinkle with the cheese and seeds. With the pizza cutter or knife, cut the pastry into strips about 1 inch (2.5 cm) wide and 4 inches (10 cm) long.

3. Transfer the matchsticks to the lined baking sheet. Place in the center of the oven and bake until golden, 12 to 15 minutes.

4. Remove from the oven and transfer to a serving plate. The matchsticks are best consumed the day they are baked.

ABOUT 40 SERVINGS

NOTE: In France my choice for purchased all-butter puff pastry is Marie's brand. In the United States, I favor Dufour brand frozen puff pastry, available at most specialty supermarkets. See dufourpastrykitchens.com. Be sure to leave ample time for thawing frozen dough, at least 6 hours in the refrigerator.

ANDROUËT

Since 1909, the name Androuët has been synonymous with quality aged cheese in France.

When I moved to Paris in 1980, the original Androuët shop in the 9th *arrondissement* was still in full swing. To learn about cheese, I would march to the shop every Saturday armed with Pierre Androuët's famed *Guide Marabout des Fromages de France et du Monde Entier* and select three or four seasonal choices. I made notes and comments on each cheese and soon began to understand the textures, aromas, flavors, and charms of many of the hundreds of French cheeses. Today, each Parisian Androuët boutique has its own personality, with each trained manager selecting his own specialties. Since it can be mind-boggling to enter a shop and know just what you want to choose from hundreds of offerings, it's best simply to ask the salesperson what's best and in season. Some of their boutiques have a blackboard noting *en ce moment* (at this time), the best cheese recommendations.

Here are some of my favorites to try when in season: *Brie Noir de Nanteuil*—the famed cow's-milk cheese from the Champagne region—is aged for 8 to 12 months in dry cellars, offering us the pleasure of a hint of hazelnuts and sometimes even black truffles; a firm, distinctive cheese with a lot of personality. The cheese named *1909 Centenaire* celebrates Androuët's 100th birthday: This sheep's-milk cheese, soft with a natural rind, is a fragrant offering filled with the perfume of the fields. Another worthy offering is the *Bleu de Chèvre*, a creamy blue-veined goat's-milk cheese from the Languedoc-Roussillon. I love this cheese with a slice of freshly toasted rye bread. Many shops also offer a rare selection of cheeses from Britain's leading cheesemonger, Paxton and Whitfield. Androuët's website, available in English, offers information on cheeses from all over the world. I love that if you choose a wine, the site will generate a list of well-matched cheeses.

◀ *Ask for a custom-made cheese platter to be assembled by one of Ardrouët's master cheesemongers.*

LAURENT DUBOIS (Maubert-Mutualité)

47, boulevard Saint-Germain
Paris 5
TEL: +33 1 43 54 50 93
fromageslaurentdubois.fr
contact@fromageslaurentdubois.fr

MÉTRO: Maubert-Mutualité
OPEN: Tuesday through Saturday
8:30AM to 7:30PM. Sunday 8:30AM to 1PM.
CLOSED: Sunday afternoon and Monday

aurent Dubois likes to say that when you enter one of his shops, you enter "a universe of cheese," and that's not the half of it. The biggest disappointment here is that you simply can't eat it all! This perfectionist won the coveted *Meilleur Ouvrier de France* (Best Artisan in France) award for the cheese profession in 2000, and his passion is on parade throughout his shops, where picture-perfect cheeses await your attention. Everything is here: cow, sheep, goat, fresh cheeses, rare cheeses, well-aged versions, from the mountains and from the rolling hills. Dubois loves to embellish young goat's-milk cheese with basil or chives or, my favorite, mildly spicy *piment d'Espelette* from the Basque region. He offers an exceptional assortment of Corsican and Italian cheeses, including an outstanding, clean, and fresh *Broccio Passu*, a ricotta-like Corsican sheep's-milk cheese that is soft, creamy, and finely textured with a strong lactic flavor, even a bit of spice. As with any well-stocked cheese shop, the Dubois boutiques can overwhelm, making selection difficult. When in doubt, simply ask for an assortment of the best cheeses for the season. For dinner parties, they will prepare cheese platters with handwritten labels, as well as vacuum-seal (*sous-vide*) cheeses for travel. The Saint-Germain shop is particularly lively on Tuesday, Thursday, and Saturday mornings, when the adjacent market on place Maubert adds a festive air.

7ᵀᴴ ARRONDISSEMENT

ANDROUËT (Musée d'Orsay)

36, rue de Verneuil
Paris 7
TEL: +33 1 42 61 97 55
androuet.com

MÉTRO: Rue du Bac
OPEN : Monday 4 to 7:30PM. Tuesday through Saturday 9:30AM to 1PM and 4 to 7:30PM.
CLOSED: Monday morning and Sunday

Established in 1909 to showcase cheeses from all the regions of France to Parisians, the name Androuët continues to be synonymous with quality aged cheese. This small, jam-packed boutique is run by the outgoing Emmanuel Monnoyer, a member of the Guilde des Fromagers, France's elite cheese brotherhood. On the charming rue de Verneuil (the street itself is like a small, quiet village), just steps from the Musée d'Orsay, this is a must. See page 255 for full commentary.

THE RIND

The million-dollar question: Should you eat the rind or shouldn't you? Even the experts don't agree. According to *Larousse des Fromages*, the French cheese bible, it is all a question of personal taste. Larousse advises, however, not to leave a messy plate full of little bits of crust. Pierre Androuët, the former dean of Paris cheese merchants, is more definite. Never eat the rind, he says, because it harbors all the cheese's developing molds and yeasts and can emit an alkaline odor. The truth? It's really up to you, though let logic rule. The rinds of soft-ripened cheeses such as Brie and Camembert are definitely edible, and when the cheese is perfectly ripe, the thin, bloomy *croute* adds both flavor and texture. However, with another soft cheese, *vacherin*, the rind is always removed, and the creamy cheese is scooped out with a spoon. The rinds of semi-soft cheeses, such as Reblochon, can have a nutty flavor. The crust is always discarded when eating hard mountain cheese, such as Emmenthal, Gruyère, and *tête-de-moine*.

BARTHÉLÉMY

51, rue de Grenelle
Paris 7
TEL: +33 1 45 48 56 75
MÉTRO: Rue du Bac

OPEN: Tuesday through Thursday 8:30AM to 1PM and 3:30 to 7:15PM. Friday and Saturday 8:30AM to 7PM.
CLOSED: Sunday and Monday

Whenever I enter Nicole Barthélémy's tiny, well-stocked shop, I wish there were a way to push out the walls, giving us cheese lovers room to stand back and explore all the treats inside. When you visit this Left Bank landmark, come with a shopping list or at least an idea of what you want to purchase, since service does not always come with a smile and patience is not the shop's strong suit. From November to March, no 7th-*arrondissement* dinner party would be complete without the rich and earthy rounds of mountain *Vacherin de Mont d'Or,* one of the shop's specialties. The choice of goat's cheese is vast, the *Époisses* is well aged, and the Camembert comes from the dependable Coopérative d'Isigny.

GRIFFON

23, bis avenue de la Motte Picquet
Paris 7
TEL: +33 1 45 50 14 85
fromagerie-griffon.com

MÉTRO: École Militaire or La Tour-Maubourg
OPEN: Tuesday through Saturday 9AM to 7:30PM
CLOSED: Sunday and Monday

In December of 2012, having worked for illustrious cheese merchants Marie-Anne Cantin and Laurent Dubois, the young Claire Griffon set off on her own, opening a jewel of a shop just steps from the rue Cler market in the 7th. Even the warm gray-and-white storefront exudes a sense of calmness, care, and honor for the gems inside. Each cheese is displayed with respect and attention, many sheltered beneath glass domes, carefully labeled, with larger cheeses cut into convenient serving sizes. If she has it in the boutique, try the perfumed *tomme de montagne aux fleurs sauvages.* It's a Swiss mountain cow's-milk cheese, the rind coated with dried mountain herbs and flowers, which infuse this very special cheese with fragrance and flavor. Equally fine is the goat's-milk *pavé de Pontlevoy,* a fresh, fine lactic cheese from the Loire. Claire and her staff will be happy to put together a cheese tray, either a seasonal selection or an assortment of more unusual cheeses, such as the *tomme de montagne* and a *fourme d'Ambert* seasoned with raisins and Sauternes.

MARIE-ANNE CANTIN

12, rue du Champ de Mars
Paris 7
TEL: +33 1 45 50 43 94
cantin.fr
MÉTRO: École Militaire

OPEN: Monday 2 to 7:30PM. Tuesday through Saturday 8:30AM to 7:30PM. Sunday 8:30AM to 1:30PM.
CLOSED: Sunday afternoon and Monday morning

Marie-Anne Cantin and husband Antoine Dias have managed this shop for several decades, offering sterling versions of firm and fragrant *Beaufort d'Alpage,* artisanal Roquefort, creamy Reblochon, and a wide choice of goat's-milk cheeses. Visit while the active market on the nearby rue Cler is in full swing, particularly on the weekends.

SCENTS OF PARIS

"It was the Camembert above all that they could smell. The Camembert with its gamey scent of venison had conquered the more muffled tones of Maroilles and Limbourg. . . . Into the middle of this vigorous phrase the Parmesan threw its thin note on a country flute, while the Brie added the dull gentleness of damp tambourines.

Then came the suffocating reprise of a Livarot. And the symphony was held for a moment on the high, sharp note of an aniseed Gérôme, prolonged like the note of an organ."

—Émile Zola, *Le Ventre de Paris*

QUATREHOMME (Sèvres)

62, rue de Sèvres
Paris 7
TEL: +33 1 47 34 33 45
quatrehomme.fr
MÉTRO: Vaneau or Duroc

OPEN: Tuesday through Thursday 8:45AM to 1PM and 4 to 7:45PM. Friday and Saturday 8:45AM to 7:45PM.
CLOSED: Sunday and Monday

Marie Quatrehomme is a model merchant, unfailingly gracious, outgoing, attentive, personable, and responsible. Along with her husband, Alain, she runs one of the finest cheese shops in the land. Marie was the first woman in the French food trade to be awarded the coveted *Meilleur Ouvrier de France*

(Best Artisan in France) title, and her dedication to quality shines in her well-tended shop. Whether you think you know everything there is to know about cheese or just want to learn, her shop is educational. Each week, she spotlights at least three seasonal cheeses on the table in the center of the boutique. There's generally one French, one foreign, and another that most of us have never seen. I learn something each time I enter the shop. Some favorites here include her house-smoked *Crottin de Chavignol* goat's-milk cheese, summer mountain cow's-milk Beaufort aged for more than 18 months, and a spectacular, seasonal *Vacherin du Mont d'Or,* the cow's-milk cheese found from mid-September to the middle of May. The

cow's-milk blue *Fourme d'Ambert* is the most distinctive and creamy version of that cheese I have ever tasted, the Napoleon sheep's-milk cheese from the Basque region is not to be missed, and the choice of both Italian and Spanish cheeses is vast. The entire staff here is extremely knowledgeable and amiable, and will be sure to help shoppers put together an excellent seasonal cheese tray. The best time to shop is on Saturdays, when the Quatrehomme team brings out a selection of well-aged cow's-milk Comté from the Jura, and often an aged Manchego sheep's-milk cheese from Spain. After shopping at the rue de Sèvres boutique, be sure to stop in at the Orangerie de Vieux Sèvres at No. 66, one of the city's finest greengrocers.

◀ *At Marie-Anne Cantin, customers receive expert advice.*

LES FROMAGES FRAIS DE MARIE QUATREHOMME

Marie Quatrehomme's Herb-Flecked Goat Cheese

Marie Quatrehomme is my neighborhood cheese merchant, and I love her fresh goat's-milk cheese rolled in fresh chives. At home, I prepare my own versions, varying the herbs according to the season and desire.

INGREDIENTS:

About 3 tablespoons minced fresh chives, or a mixture of chives, dill, tarragon, and mint

1 disk (about 6 ounces; 180 g) fresh, round goat's-milk cheese

Scatter the herbs in an even layer on a large plate. Roll the cheese in the herbs, completely coating the top and sides. With your fingertips, press any remaining herbs into the cheese. Set the cheese on a plate or platter. Serve.

4 SERVINGS

▶ *A master cheesemonger, Marie Quatrehomme runs one of the finest cheese shops in France.*

9TH ARRONDISSEMENT

PASCAL BEILLEVAIRE (Martyrs)

48, rue des Martyrs
Paris 9
TEL: +33 1 45 26 84 88
fromagerie-beillevaire.com
MÉTRO: Saint-Georges or Pigalle

OPEN: Tuesday through Friday 10AM to 1PM
and 4 to 7:45PM. Saturday 9:30AM to 7:45PM.
Sunday 9:30AM to 1PM.
CLOSED: Monday

A small boutique with a mouthwatering selection of raw-milk cheeses, yogurts, and an irresistible *demi-sel croquant* unpasteurized butter, flecked with crunchy salt. See page 253 for full commentary.

12TH ARRONDISSEMENT

PASCAL BEILLEVAIRE (Nation)

1, rue Marsoulan
Paris 12
TEL: +33 1 43 43 69 21
fromagerie-beillevaire.com

MÉTRO: Picpus
OPEN: Tuesday through Saturday
8:30AM to 8PM. Sunday 9AM to 1PM.
CLOSED: Sunday afternoon and Monday

The prolific Beillevaire cheese empire has over 80 points of sale all over France. See page 253 for full commentary.

14TH ARRONDISSEMENT

ANDROUËT (Montparnasse)

13, rue Daguerre
Paris 14
TEL: +33 1 40 47 53 03
androuet.com
MÉTRO: Denfert-Rochereau

OPEN: Tuesday through Saturday
9:30AM to 1PM and 4 to 7:30PM.
Sunday 9:30AM to 1:30PM.
CLOSED: Sunday afternoon and Monday

Androuët is synonymous with quality aged cheese from all of France. See page 255 for full commentary.

PASCAL BEILLEVAIRE (Montparnasse)

8, rue Delambre
Paris 14
TEL: +33 1 42 79 00 40
fromagerie-beillevaire.com

MÉTRO: Vavin or Edgar Quinet
OPEN: Tuesday through Saturday 8:30AM to
1PM and 4 to 8PM. Sunday 9AM to 1PM.
CLOSED: Sunday afternoon and Monday

Many of Beillevaire's excellent raw-milk cheeses are exclusive to their enterprise. See page 253 for full commentary.

15TH ARRONDISSEMENT

ANDROUËT (Vaugirard)

93, rue Cambronne
Paris 15
TEL: +33 1 47 83 32 05
androuet.com
MÉTRO: Vaugirard or Volontaires

OPEN: Tuesday through Saturday 9:30AM to 1PM and 4 to 7:30PM. Sunday 9:30AM to 1:30PM.
CLOSED: Sunday afternoon and Monday

Before or after visiting this shop, be sure to cross the street for some of baker Frédéric Pichard's golden baguettes and buttery croissants at No. 88. See page 255 for full commentary.

LAURENT DUBOIS (Dupleix)

2, rue de Lourmel
Paris 15
TEL: +33 1 45 78 70 58
fromageslaurentdubois.fr
MÉTRO: Dupleix

OPEN: Tuesday through Friday 9AM to 1PM and 4 to 7:45PM. Saturday 8:30AM to 7:45PM. Sunday 9AM to 1PM.
CLOSED: Sunday afternoon and Monday

Laurent Dubois, who has been awarded the prestigious *Meilleur Ouvrier de France* (Best Artisan in France) status, offers you a universe of picture-perfect cheeses. See page 256 for full commentary.

16TH ARRONDISSEMENT

ANDROUËT (Victor Hugo)

17, rue des Belles Feuilles
Paris 16
TEL: +33 1 45 05 11 77
androuet.com
MÉTRO: Victor Hugo, Rue de la Pompe, or Trocadéro
OPEN: Tuesday through Saturday 9:30AM to 1PM and 4 to 7:30PM. Sunday 9:30AM to 1:30PM. Monday 4 to 7:30PM.
CLOSED: Sunday afternoon and Monday morning

ANDROUËT (Marché de Passy)

1, rue Bois le Vent
Paris 16
TEL: +33 1 42 24 17 52
androuet.com
MÉTRO: La Muette
OPEN: Tuesday through Saturday 8:30AM to 1PM and 3:30 to 7:30PM. Saturday 8:30AM to 7PM. Sunday 8:30AM to 1PM.
CLOSED: Sunday afternoon and Monday

The house of Androuët has been seeking out the best cheeses from all over France to showcase to Parisians for over 100 years. See page 255 for full commentary.

BUTTER

France is the second largest butter producer in the European Union, and the largest consumer of butter in the world (the French consume about 15 pounds of butter per capita per year!).

Although Normandy, with its rolling pastures and black-and-white cows, may be the region first thought of for butter, some of the country's best butter comes from the west of France near Niort, sold under the label *beurre d'Echiré*. This butter is preferred by French pastry chefs because it is less watery than other butters.

There are many other well-known and -loved locally produced butters in France. One of the best, and best known, is *beurre Bordier*, an organic butter produced in small batches in Brittany. *Bordier* butter can be found both salted and unsalted, or seasoned with *algues* (seaweed), *piment d'Espelette* (the mild chile pepper from the Basque region), *yuzu* (Japanese citrus), and *sel fumé* (smoked salt).

Other high-quality brands include one from Île de Ré on the Atlantic Coast, a favorite being that from *La Baratte du Crémier,* which offers an irresistible *demi-sel croquant,* seasoned with coarse sea salt for a fabulous crunch. The Beillevaire brand seasoned with coarse salt is also worth seeking out.

The different labels for butter can be overwhelming, so here is a short lexicon to help you choose your favorite.

BEURRE DOUX: unsalted butter

BEURRE CRU: made with raw cream

BEURRE FIN AND EXTRA FIN: both made with pasteurized cream

BEURRE DEMI-SEL: lightly salted butter, contains .5 to 3 percent salt

BEURRE SALÉ: salted butter, contains 3 percent salt

BEURRE DE BARATTE: made in a traditional butter churn

BEURRE A.O.P.: Two butters in France have this pedigree, those from Isigny (Normandy) and from Charentes-Poitou (in the Southwest). Since 2009, A.O.P., for *Appellation d'Origine Protégée,* has been a European Union designation for agricultural products produced within strict geographical limits, abiding by a strict set of rules. The A.O.P. is a broadening of the A.O.C. (*Appellation d'Origine Controlée,* established in France in 1935) designation to include other European territories and products.

BEURRE ALLEGÉ OR LÉGER: butter having a higher water content and lower fat content than other butters

BEURRE FACILE À TARTINER: butter that's easy to spread. It is made by mixing previously melted and ordinary butter together

In cheese shops and at markets you often see huge, creamy blocks of butter behind the counter. Called *mottes de beurre,* they may be labeled with their origin, and always include a *doux* (unsalted), a *demi-sel* (lightly salted), and a *salé* (fully salted) version. Brittany is the region that traditionally makes and uses salted butter, but it has always had its fans throughout the rest of France as well. (While these mounds of butter are picturesque, beware: They may have been sitting absorbing odors and may not be perfectly fresh.)

The French don't necessarily butter their bread, and often it is absent from the table during mealtimes. The exception is starred restaurants, which often make a fuss over the provenance of the butters, distinguishing salted from unsalted butter. Butter does appear with *charcuterie;* in a sandwich, along with radishes, anchovies, and sardines; and with the rye bread that is served with oysters and other shellfish. Butter is often included with the cheese course, too, and sweet butter may be used to soften the saltiness of Roquefort.

CLAFOUTIS DE BASILIC ET CHÈVRE FRAIS

Fresh Goat Cheese and Basil Clafoutis

We consume plenty of goat's-milk cheese in our house, and the refrigerator is often loaded with bits of odds and ends of the tender young cheese; that's when I bake this quick and easy herb and cheese *clafoutis*.

EQUIPMENT:

A food processor; 9-inch (23-cm) nonstick springform pan

INGREDIENTS:

4 plump, moist garlic cloves, peeled, halved, green germ removed

10 ounces (300 g) fresh goat's-milk cheese

5 large eggs, preferably organic and free-range, lightly beaten

1¾ cups (400 ml) light cream or half-and-half

½ cup (70 g) unbleached all-purpose flour

½ teaspoon fine sea salt

1 cup (250 ml) fresh basil leaves, loosely packed

1. Center a rack in the oven. Preheat the oven to 375°F (190°C).

2. In the food processor, mince the garlic. Add the remaining ingredients and process to blend. Pour the mixture into the springform pan.

3. Place the pan in the oven and bake until firm and golden, about 40 minutes. Remove from the oven to cool. The *clafoutis* will deflate as it cools. Serve at room temperature, cut into thin wedges.

12 SERVINGS

▶ *It's never too early to start your love affair with cheese.*

FROMAGERIE HISADA (Porte de Saint-Cloud)

17, rue le Marois
Paris 16
TEL: +33 1 42 88 34 30
hisada.fr
MÉTRO: Porte de Saint-Cloud

OPEN: Tuesday and Thursday through Saturday
8:30AM to 1PM and 3:30 to 7:30PM. Sunday
8:30AM to 1:30PM.
CLOSED: Sunday afternoon, Monday, and
Wednesday

Unusual French cheeses selected by Japanese owner Sanae Hisada. See page 251 for full commentary.

17TH ARRONDISSEMENT

ALLÉOSSE

13, rue Poncelet
Paris 17
TEL: +33 1 46 22 50 45
fromage-alleosse.com
sa-alleosse@wanadoo.fr

MÉTRO: Ternes
OPEN: Tuesday through Thursday 9AM to 1PM
and 4 to 7PM. Friday and Saturday 9AM to 1PM
and 3:30 to 7PM. Sunday 9AM to 1PM.
CLOSED: Sunday afternoon and Monday

I know few people more devoted to their profession than the Alléosse family: first, father Roger, and now son Philippe and his wife, Rachel. Along with students from my cooking school, I have spent many informative hours visiting the four exquisite aging cellars the family owns near their shop in the 17th *arrondissement*. Every cheese is aged under the most ideal conditions, the proper temperature and humidity levels, to help coax each to perfection. Everyone in this boutique on the rue Poncelet market street shares the Alléosse passion, so be sure to ask for seasonal advice. I have some firm favorites. The well-aged (12 weeks) *Clacbitou fermier*, a clean-tasting, firm white goat's-milk cheese from the Charolais region of Burgundy, always finds its way to my cheese platter. Only one or two people in the world (I am not one of them) know the secret recipe for "washing" their cow's-milk cheese *Reblochon de Savoie au lait cru*—soft, supple, fragrant, and one of the greatest cheeses on earth. The rare *Bleu de Termignon Alpage,* a cow's-milk cheese from the Savoie region of France, shares all the flavors of the rich mountain grasses, wild herbs, and subtle mountain air. Finally, a true Alléosse gift is their rich cow's-milk *Abbaye de Citeaux affiné*, the creamy, assertive offering made by monks in a Burgundian Cistercian abbey. Aged exclusively in the Alléosse cellars, the cheese is brought to its apex by careful washing and nurturing. Be sure to check out the website, which has photos and detailed descriptions of some 125 cheeses on offer through the seasons, many with suggestions for wine pairings.

ANDROUËT (Monceau)

23, rue de la Terrasse
Paris 17
TEL: +33 1 47 54 39 20
androuet.com
MÉTRO: Villiers

OPEN: Tuesday through Friday 9:30AM to 1PM
and 4 to 7:30PM. Saturday 9:30AM to 7:30PM.
Sunday 9:30AM to 1:30PM.
CLOSED: Sunday afternoon and Monday

Not far from the elegant Parc Monceau and linked to the popular rue de Lévis market street, this boutique of quality, aged French cheeses is a great addition to the neighborhood. See page 255 for full commentary.

18ᵀᴴ ARRONDISSEMENT

CHEZ VIRGINIE

54, rue Damrémont
Paris 18
TEL: + 33 1 46 06 76 54
chezvirginie.com
contact@chezvirginie.com

MÉTRO: Lamarck-Caulaincourt
OPEN: Tuesday through Saturday 9:30AM to 1PM and 4 to 8PM. Sunday 10AM to 1PM.
CLOSED: Sunday afternoon, Monday, and August

If you are a cheese lover, run, don't walk to Virginie Boularouah's appealing, spotless little shop in the charming Caulaincourt neighborhood in the 18th. You'll gasp with pleasure as you approach her storefront and, excuse me, perhaps drool at the selection. You just know that this shop is run by a woman (and that's not a sexist remark!) because it is so well tended and well thought out. God is in the details. I thought I knew a lot about cheese until Virginie introduced me to many of her Austrian, Swiss, and Italian specialties. I had never tasted *Calcagno*, an Italian sheep's-milk cheese that could almost rival Parmesan in texture and age. It's the color of candied ginger and has that almost sweet, candied flavor that hard aged cheeses acquire. Equally amazing is her *Testuo* topped with Marc de Barolo, a brilliant, pungent cheese that will, figuratively, put hair on your chest. Another new discovery is her Austrian *tomme aux fleurs*, a cow's-milk cheese in the Gruyère style, aged with an abundant coating of mountain herbs of every color and scent. Mountain perfume! And don't turn your nose up at more common varieties, such as her earthy and fragrant *Comté* from the Jura mountains of eastern France, or a state-of-the-art fresh goat's cheese, *rouelle de chevre*, a tiny, clean, and classic wheel. Virginie offers a cheese-tasting lunch of seven courses with two wines for 90€ per person, for a minimum of two people. Sign me up! Along with cheeses, she has an exquisite selection of olive oils, condiments, and all manner of crackers to pair with your cheese. After your visit, cross the street to No. 57 for Arnaud Delmontel's golden, chewy *baguette Renaissance* and state-of-the-art *Tourte Auvergnate*, a serious, substantive sourdough.

▶ *Owner Virginie Boularouah's pristine store is full of wondrous cheeses from throughout Europe.*

20ᵀᴴ ARRONDISSEMENT

PASCAL BEILLEVAIRE (Belleville)

140, rue de Belleville
Paris 20
TEL: +33 1 46 36 90 81
fromagerie-beillevaire.com

MÉTRO: Jourdain
OPEN: Tuesday through Saturday 9AM to 8PM.
Sunday 9AM to 1PM.
CLOSED: Sunday afternoon and Monday

Choose from the mouthwatering selection of raw-milk cheeses to go with your *baguette tradition* from the next-door bakery *Boulangerie au 140* (see page 245). See page 253 for full commentary.

PARIS ENVIRONS

ANDROUËT (Roissy Charles de Gaulle Airport)

Halls 2E and S3

androuet.com

Found in the main duty-free areas of the Roissy Charles de Gaulle Airport, these two small shops offer a range of prepackaged French cheese selected by Androuët. Packages can be vacuum-packed for travel, and all cheeses sold in the area are authorized on board all the planes. All raw-milk cheeses are aged for more than 60 days and so are authorized for transport into the United States. See page 255 for full commentary.

AT A GLANCE

1ST ARRONDISSEMENT
Fromagerie Hisada (Palais Royal)

3RD ARRONDISSEMENT
Jouannault

4TH ARRONDISSEMENT
Pascal Beillevaire (Marais)

5TH ARRONDISSEMENT
Androuët (Mouffetard)
Laurent Dubois
(Maubert-Mutualité)

7TH ARRONDISSEMENT
Androuët (Musée d'Orsay)
Barthélémy
Griffon

Marie-Anne Cantin
Quatrehomme (Sèvres)

9TH ARRONDISSEMENT
Pascal Beillevaire (Martyrs)

12TH ARRONDISSEMENT
Pascal Beillevaire (Nation)

14TH ARRONDISSEMENT
Androuët (Montparnasse)
Pascal Beillevaire
(Montparnasse)

15TH ARRONDISSEMENT
Androuët (Vaugirard)
Laurent Dubois (Dupleix)

16TH ARRONDISSEMENT
Androuët (Victor Hugo)
Androuët (Marché de Passy)
Fromagerie Hisada (Porte de Saint-Cloud)

17TH ARRONDISSEMENT
Alléosse
Androuët (Monceau)

18TH ARRONDISSEMENT
Chez Virginie

20TH ARRONDISSEMENT
Pascal Beillevaire (Belleville)

PARIS ENVIRONS
Androuët (Roissy Charles de Gaulle Airport)

CHAPTER 378

CHOCOLATE SHOPS

CHOCOLATERIES

The way the French fuss over chocolate, you'd think they invented it. They didn't, but as in so many matters *gastronomique,* the French inspire envy. They have refined the art of fine chocolate making, coaxing and coddling their sweets into existence,

working carefully until they've produced some of the strongest, richest, most intoxicating and flavorful candies to be found anywhere in the world.

The French chocolate-buying public is discriminating, and *chocolatiers,* or chocolate makers, are fortunate to have a clientele willing to pay a premium price for confections prepared with the finest single-plantation cocoa beans from Latin and South America, the best Madagascar vanilla, the freshest Sicilian pistachios.

The world of chocolate is not without its trends. Today the French palate is crazy for *le gout amer,* the bitter, heady flavor of chocolate high in cocoa butter and low in sugar. But beware: A low sugar content is not necessarily a sign of quality. The best bet is to buy in small quantities and judge for yourself.

Before there was chocolate as we know it today—in bars and in flavored squares and rounds, enjoyed as a snack or dessert—chocolate was prepared as a drink. As the brew became popular in Europe during the 17th

century, it also became the subject of discord. Was chocolate healthy? Was it lethal? Was it a dangerous aphrodisiac? The famous 17th-century French letter writer Madame de Sévigné wrote to her daughter: "It flatters you for a while. It warms you for an instant; then it kindles a mortal fever in you." But when her daughter moved from Paris, she worried about how she could get along without a *chocolatière,* or chocolate pot.

Paris's first chocolate shop, located on the rue de l'Arbre Sec in what is now the 1st *arrondissement,* was opened in 1659, when Louis XIV gave one of Queen Anne's officers the exclusive privilege to sell chocolates. Chocolate soon became the rage of the French courts. It was served at least three times a week at Versailles, and it is said that Napoleon preferred chocolate to coffee as a morning pick-me-up. In Voltaire's later years, he consumed 12 cups a day, always between five in the morning and three in the afternoon. (He lived to be 84 years old, true longevity in those days.) Brillat-Savarin, the

18th-century gastronome, put it concisely: "Chocolate is health."

In the early 1800s, two very clever Parisians figured a way around the still-raging dispute over the merits of chocolate. They sold it as medicine. A certain Monsieur Debauve, a *chocolatier*, and Monsieur Gallais, a pharmacist, teamed up and opened an elegant shop at 30, rue des Saints-Pères just off the boulevard Saint-Germain. Soon, the nervous, the sickly, the thin, the obese, were going to Debauve & Gallais for "the chocolate cure." It's no surprise to learn that the chocolate preparations became a bigger business than the other pharmaceuticals, and Debauve & Gallais—where chocolates are still sold in the same shop today—soon became the most important chocolate shop in Paris.

Today in France, chocolate remains synonymous with *gourmandise* and comfort. There is even a *Club des Croqueurs de Chocolat*, a private group of chocolate-loving Parisian connoisseurs who meet regularly to taste and judge the city's latest chocolate creations. Still, the French display a great deal of discipline when it comes to their beloved chocolate. They actually eat less than their neighbors in Switzerland, Germany, Sweden, the United Kingdom, and Norway, downing 16.3 pounds (7.4 kg) annually per capita.

The Parisian world of chocolate continues to grow, with flavors such as salted caramel, *Espelette* pepper from the Basque region of France, as well as both green tea and Japanese *yuzu* teaming up with favorite chocolate confections. And with the addition of two bean-to-bar shops—both Pierre Marcolini and Alain Ducasse take the time to select and roast their own cocoa beans, a process that generally assures fresher flavors, greater intensity—chocolate lovers have even more avenues to explore. ❧

1ST ARRONDISSEMENT

HUGO & VICTOR (Marché Saint-Honoré)

7, rue Gomboust
Paris 1
MÉTRO: Pyramides

OPEN: Monday through Wednesday 10:30AM to 7PM. Thursday through Saturday 10:30AM to 8PM. Sunday 11AM to 5PM.

This dark and sleek shop could easily be mistaken for a jewelry store. The contents are indeed precious treasures, but those of the chocolate and pastry variety. See Pastry Shops, page 287, for full commentary.

LA MAISON DU CHOCOLAT (Louvre)

Carrousel du Louvre
99, rue de Rivoli
Paris 1

TEL: +33 1 42 97 13 50
MÉTRO: Palais Royal Musée du Louvre
OPEN: Daily 10AM to 8PM

A top chocolate destination since 1977, offering a whole universe of chocolate, from simple ganache and pralines and spice-infused creations to chocolate éclairs and a gold-flecked chocolate tart. See box (facing page) for full commentary.

LA MAISON DU CHOCOLAT

lamaisonduchocolat.com
client@lamaisonduchocolat.com

Ahh, La Maison du Chocolat! Each boutique looks and smells like a planet where nothing but chocolate matters. Since 1977, when creator Robert Linxe opened his first Maison du Chocolat in Paris and filled it with never-before-seen bonbons flavored with fresh mint, citrus zest, and other fine and fancy choices, it has tempted chocolate fans. The ganache and pralines are skillful and smooth, the flavors always changing. A recent winner surprises with the tiniest peppery bite from the Basque chile *piment d'Espelette*. The oversize chocolate macaron from la Maison du Chocolat was a sinfully satisfying taste and texture sensation more than 30 years ago (long before the miniature version created a craze) and, delightfully, it is still one of the best offered in the city. Éclairs, a specialty since 1990, are crisp and creamy at once. Fillings are seasonal (though chocolate is a constant) and the wintry, delicate chestnut version is satisfyingly delicious. The chocolate tart, with its tiny gold leaf in the center, recently gained a fine layer of caramel on the bottom, a brilliant link between the very crisp and buttery pastry and the satisfying, deep chocolate filling.

PIERRE HERMÉ (Concorde)

4, rue Cambon
Paris 1

MÉTRO: Concorde

When it comes to chocolates Pierre Hermé is both a visionary and master technician, combining flavors that others can only hope to imitate. See Pastry Shops, page 288, for full commentary.

2ND ARRONDISSEMENT

PIERRE HERMÉ (Opéra)

39, avenue de l'Opéra
Paris 2

MÉTRO: Opéra

Who else but Pierre Hermé could combine chocolate with black olives and olive oil, with such delicious results? See Pastry Shops, page 288, for full commentary.

3RD ARRONDISSEMENT

LA CHOCOLATERIE DE JACQUES GENIN

133, rue de Turenne
Paris 3
TEL: +33 1 45 77 29 01
jacquesgenin.fr
contact@jacquesgenin.fr

MÉTRO: République or Filles du Calvaire
OPEN: Tuesday through Friday 11AM to 7PM.
Saturday 11AM to 8PM. Sunday 11AM to 7PM.
CLOSED: Monday and August

When you enter Jacques Genin's large, sleek shop and tea salon, a moment of reverence is in order as you inhale a glorious blend of chocolate, fruit, butter, and caramel. His caramels are impossibly tender and buttery. Just a bite of one flavored with passion fruit will make you think you're eating the fruit itself. When it comes to chocolates, from the old-fashioned praline to the cinnamon ganache, Genin's selections offer just the right balance of cream with a delicate, crisp coating. You may want to sit and enjoy a cup

of his intense hot chocolate, which is simply chocolate melted into hot milk. Much to the distress of his loyal followers, Genin stopped making individual pastries for sale in the shop in 2013. All is not lost, however, as he has retained the vanilla, chocolate, praline, and—when in season—raspberry *millefeuille* on his tea salon menu, as well as a daily plated pastry, decided on a whim by the pastry chefs. A selection of pastries can be ordered for 4 to 10 people in advance: *Millefeuille* (thick layers of explosive puff pastry layered with soft, delicate cream, minimum 2 people); *Ephemère* (a chocolate mousse cake with a crunchy praline base); *Tarte au Chocolat* (chocolate tart); *Tarte au Citron* (lemon tart); *Tarte Caramel* (caramel tart); *Paris-Brest* (crown-shaped choux pastry filled with praline butter cream; *Saint-Honoré* (mini *choux* puffs, vanilla cream, and chantilly cream atop a base of flaky puff pastry). While in the neighborhood, be sure to hop across the street to *boulanger* Benjamin Turquier's fabulous bread shop at 134, rue de Turenne (see Bakeries, page 224).

5TH ARRONDISSEMENT

PÂTISSERIE SADAHARU AOKI (Port-Royal)

56, boulevard de Port-Royal
Paris 5

MÉTRO: Les Gobelins

Toyko-born pastry chef Sadaharu Aoki is an artist in all he turns his hand to. I love his use of Japanese flavors: *yuzu, matcha,* and sesame, and how his chocolates look like vibrant paint palettes. See Pastry Shops, page 297, for full commentary.

6TH ARRONDISSEMENT

HENRI LE ROUX (Saint-Germain)

1, rue de Bourbon le Château
Paris 6
TEL: +33 1 82 28 49 80
chocolatleroux.com
info@chocolat-leroux.fr

MÉTRO: Saint-Germain-des-Prés, Mabillon, or Odéon
OPEN: Tuesday through Saturday 11AM to 7:30PM. Sunday and Monday 11AM to 2PM and 3PM to 6:30PM.

One might think only world-class chocolate is highlighted in this sober brown-and-orange boutique, tucked away in Saint-Germain des Prés. But no, it's butter and caramel, too, along with the best use of salt by any chocolate maker I know. Henri Le Roux created his *chocolaterie* in Brittany in 1977, the same year he created his patented caramel made with salted butter. The chocolates in this shop are fresh and seasonal—the delicate, warming chocolate with Christmas spices deserves a spot under everyone's tree, and the tomato and basil chocolate is as unusual as it is original. Texture is important at Henri Le Roux, too, and chocolates with a crackly edge, butter-smooth creams, and crisp coatings are signatures. His individual chocolates are all pure, direct, fragrant, and full-flavored: His CBS (*caramel beurre salé*) is a must taste. Good chocolate is like fine wine; the pleasure lingers on the palate long after the treats have been consumed.

PÂTISSERIE SADAHARU AOKI (Saint-Placide)

35, rue de Vaugirard
Paris 6

MÉTRO: Rennes or Saint-Placide

It's no surprise that Sadaharu Aoki counts among his clients such fashion world elites as Kenzo, Chanel, and Christian Dior: His creations are works of art. See Pastry Shops, page 297, for full commentary.

PATRICK ROGER (Rennes)

91, rue de Rennes
Paris 6
TEL: +33 1 45 44 66 13
MÉTRO: Rennes
OPEN: Monday through Saturday 10:30AM to
1:30PM and 2 to 7:30PM
CLOSED: Sunday

PATRICK ROGER (Saint-Germain)

108, boulevard Saint-Germain
Paris 6
TEL: +33 1 43 29 38 42
MÉTRO: Odéon or Cluny–La Sorbonne
OPEN: Daily 10:30AM to 7:30PM

Patrick Roger's ultra-fine yet complex chocolates are among the best in Paris, infused with intense and fragrant flavors: vibrant lime, soothing orange-blossom-flower, earthy pistachio. See box (facing page) for full commentary.

PIERRE HERMÉ (Saint-Germain)

72, rue Bonaparte
Paris 6

MÉTRO: Saint-Sulpice or Mabillon

Here you can sample the full menu of Hermé creations: chocolates, macarons, and pastries. See Pastry Shops, page 288, for full commentary.

PIERRE MARCOLINI (Saint-Germain)

89, rue de Seine
Paris 6
TEL: +33 1 44 07 39 07
marcolini.com
paris@marcolini.fr

MÉTRO: Mabillon or Odéon
OPEN: Monday through Friday 10:30AM to 1PM
and 2 to 7PM. Saturday 10:30AM to 7PM.
CLOSED: Sunday

Pierre Marcolini comes from Belgium—Brussels, to be exact—a fact he advertises loud and clear, not just in words but in his most recent "re-looking" at a Belgian specialty, the *Manon*. He takes a traditional, hefty little nut- and coffee-scented chocolate and gives it his signature touch, reducing its size and transforming it into a delicate little bite of crisp, buttery chocolate pleasure. This finesse, along with the depth of flavor in his chocolates, is what sets him apart from his compatriots. Marcolini regularly travels to cacao-producing countries in search of the best; he speaks of producers with as much passion as he does his chocolates. Focused on quality, he roasts his own cacao beans, then blends and combines them to create depth, a certain intrigue, and indisputable pleasure. His "house" chocolate is an equal blend of cacao from Venezuela and Ghana and it makes a crisp, deeply flavored covering for, among other things, one of his exceptional *palets fins* (thin chocolate disks) of dark chestnut honey or a fluid, tonka-bean-scented caramel. He marries milk chocolate with a tangy passion fruit/vinegar-flavored caramel; his *pavé de Tours* is a crunchy little square of caramelized hazelnut and almond praline and thin lace wafer, all blended into a gorgeous ganache. Design is important to Marcolini and he loves the square, a shape he gives to candies and to his chocolate bars; he uses the round for tiny little bites. His special boxes look as though they might contain a fancy hat.

PATRICK ROGER

patrickroger.com
contact@patrickroger.com

From the moment you enter one of Patrick Roger's turquoise and chocolate–colored boutiques, you are surrounded by great taste, great aroma, and great flavor. His abundant selection of ultra-fine yet complex chocolates, flavored with everything from vivid lime to orange-flower water to pistachio, is displayed in the open, and the temptation to pop one into your mouth is almost irresistible. He has the gift of intensity in color and texture, and of creativity in flavor combinations. Whereas a glistening lime-green chocolate might not tempt from someone else's hand, when offered by this chocolate wizard, it not only tempts but conquers with its tart lime and chocolate flavor. Roger takes lemon and thyme, blends them with ganache, and wow! His praline chocolate almonds are a wonder in toasty, crunchy sweetness; his Sao Tome bar a smoky, sultry pleasure; his "cubes" of *nougatine* and praline a multilevel sensation of nuts, caramelized sugar, and milk or dark chocolate. One has the feeling, on tasting these chocolates, that each bite is a worthwhile occupation, offering satisfaction, delight, interest, and just the right amount of challenge. Roger sculpts chocolate, too, and his windows are a seasonal fantasyland. At Christmas time don't miss his *sapins de Noël*, miniature chocolate trees constructed from his unforgettable *amandes*, perfectly caramelized bits of almonds coated with either dark or milk chocolate.

▲ *Just visiting the Patrick Roger boutique at place de la Madeleine is an experience in itself.*

7TH ARRONDISSEMENT

HUGO & VICTOR (Raspail)

40, boulevard Raspail
Paris 7

MÉTRO: Sèvres-Babylone

This is a world of *haute pâtisserie*, where the fine creations of Hugo & Victor are displayed in jewel cases. Every color, flavor, and design is thought out in immense detail. Even the chocolate boxes are designed to resemble writers' journals, a reference to the literary past of Paris's Rive Gauche (Left Bank). See Pastry Shops, page 287, for full commentary.

LA MAISON DU CHOCOLAT (Sèvres-Babylone)

19, rue de Sèvres
Paris 7
TEL: +33 1 45 44 20 40
MÉTRO: Sèvres-Babylone

OPEN: Monday through Saturday 10AM to 7:30PM
CLOSED: Sunday

Somewhat of an institution in Paris, La Maison du Chocolat offers a whole universe of flavored chocolates, from fennel-infused ganache to Moroccan mint dark chocolates. See page 271 for full commentary.

PIERRE MARCOLINI (Rue du Bac)

78, rue du Bac
Paris 7
TEL: +33 1 45 44 34 02
paris-bac@marcolini.fr

MÉTRO: Rue du Bac
OPEN: Monday through Saturday, 10AM to 7PM
CLOSED: Sunday

A master chocolate maker from Belgium. See page 274 for full commentary.

8TH ARRONDISSEMENT

FOUQUET (Champs-Élysées)

22, rue François 1er
Paris 8
TEL: +33 1 47 23 30 36
MÉTRO: Franklin D. Roosevelt

OPEN: Monday through Saturday 10AM to 7:20PM
CLOSED: Sunday

Intense and lean chocolate of all types: chocolate-covered citrus rinds, chocolate caramels, and nut-and-fruit-studded chocolate bars—all hand-crafted in Paris.

LA MAISON DU CHOCOLAT (Champs-Élysées)

52, rue François 1er
Paris 8
TEL: +33 1 47 23 38 25
MÉTRO: Franklin D. Roosevelt
OPEN: Monday through Saturday 9:30AM to 7PM
CLOSED: Sunday

LA MAISON DU CHOCOLAT (Ternes)

225, rue du Faubourg Saint-Honoré
Paris 8
TEL: +33 1 42 27 39 44
MÉTRO: Ternes
OPEN: Monday through Saturday 10AM to 7:30PM. Sunday 10AM to 1PM.

The "House of Chocolate" offers a whole world of unusual and delicious chocolate inventions. See page 271 for full commentary.

CANDIED CHESTNUTS

Candied chestnuts—*marrons glacés*—are fall and winter specialties that are sold at most of the better chocolate shops in town. They appear around the beginning of November, when the first fresh chestnuts start to arrive from the Ardèche in southeastern France. They generally disappear at the close of the season, around the middle of January. The process of turning fresh raw chestnuts into little candied jewels is painstakingly slow and requires immense patience.

The fresh chestnuts are first boiled several times to free them from their shells and skins. If any bits of skin remain, they are removed by hand. The chestnuts are then wrapped in cheesecloth to prevent their falling apart in the next process—a three- to seven-hour stint in a pressure cooker. Next they are cooked again, this time for 48 hours in a vanilla sugar syrup over very low heat. The chestnuts are often delivered to shops in this form, conserved in syrup. They are then glazed in small quantities by sprinkling with water and baking them, a process that gives the chestnuts their characteristic sugary appearance. Finally they are wrapped in the traditional shiny gold foil paper.

PATRICK ROGER (Ternes)

199, rue du Faubourg Saint-Honoré
Paris 8
TEL: +33 1 45 61 11 46
MÉTRO: Ternes

OPEN: Monday through Saturday 10AM to 1:30PM and 2 to 7:30PM
CLOSED: Sunday and mid-July to beginning of September

Masterful use of color, flavor, and texture makes Patrick Roger one of the finest *chocolatiers* in the capital. See page 275 for full commentary.

PATRICK ROGER (Madeleine)

3, place de la Madeleine
Paris 8
TEL: +33 1 42 65 24 47

MÉTRO: Madeleine
OPEN: Daily 10:30AM to 7:30PM

A veritable chocolate mine, Patrick Roger's boutique on the place de la Madeleine has three floors dedicated to the art of chocolate: the boutique on the ground floor for chocolates, candies, and tastings; the basement and first floor as exhibition spaces for his incredible chocolate sculptures. See page 275 for full commentary.

PIERRE HERMÉ (Champs-Élysées)

Publicis Drugstore
133, avenue des Champs-Élysées

Paris 8
MÉTRO: George V or Charles de Gaulle-Étoile

A small Pierre Hermé counter in Publicis Drugstore selling chocolates and macarons. See Pastry Shops, page 288, for full commentary.

9ᵀᴴ ARRONDISSEMENT

Á L'ÉTOILE D'OR

30, rue Pierre Fontaine
Paris 9
TEL: +33 1 48 74 59 55
MÉTRO: Blanche

OPEN: Tuesday through Saturday
10AM to 7:30PM. Monday 3 to 7PM.
CLOSED: Sunday and August

D enise Acabo, perhaps one of the world's greatest chocolate lovers, is one of a kind, as is her little shop on the rue Pierre Fontaine, a short walk from the Blanche *métro*. Once you've visited Denise's fairyland shop, you won't need to leave Paris, for she brings the best chocolates that France has to offer right to you. Denise is pigtailed and can talk your head off about her favorite subject, even if you don't understand a single word. Show a tiny bit of interest and, no questions asked, she'll take you on a guided tour of her fragrant boutique, covering her travels to Brittany with Henri Le Roux for his irresistible CBS (*caramel beurre salé*, or salted butter caramels), to Lyon with the Bernachons (a family that still makes all chocolates totally from scratch, bean to bar), to La Clayette with Bernard Dufoux, and to Monsieur Bonnat's in Voiron. Her selections are pure, honest, invigorating. If you love chocolate (or think you might one day), don't miss out on this treasure.

▼ *Store owner Denise Acabo offers a tour of France's best chocolates in her unique boutique in the 9th* arrondissement.

FOUQUET (Lafayette)

36, rue Laffitte
Paris 9
TEL: +33 1 47 70 85 00

MÉTRO: Le Peletier or Richelieu Drouot
OPEN: Monday through Friday 11AM to 6:30PM
CLOSED: Saturday and Sunday

Intense and pure hand-crafted chocolates. A favorite has to be their eye-watering chocolate-covered mints, and their flat, small squares of praline dipped in intense dark chocolate.

HENRI LE ROUX (Martyrs)

24, rue des Martyrs
Paris 9
TEL: +33 1 82 28 49 83
MÉTRO: Saint-George or
Notre-Dame-de-Lorette

OPEN: Tuesday through Friday 10:30AM to
3:30PM and 5 to 7:30PM. Saturday 10:30AM to
7:30PM. Sunday 11AM to 1PM.
CLOSED: Monday

Caramel and salt feature prominently in this exquisite chocolate shop by Breton *chocolatier* Henri Le Roux, who patented his caramel made with salted butter in 1977. Be sure to taste the CBS (*caramel beurre salé*). See page 273 for full commentary.

HUGO & VICTOR (Printemps)

Printemps department store
Ground floor, *mode*
64, boulevard Haussmann
Paris 9
MÉTRO: Havre-Caumartin or Saint Lazare

TEL: +33 1 42 82 64 51
OPEN: Monday through Saturday 9:35AM to
8PM, late night Thursday until 10PM
CLOSED: Sunday

A small stand in the Printemps department store, selling chocolates only. See Pastry Shops, page 287, for full commentary.

LA MAISON DU CHOCOLAT (Madeleine)

8, boulevard de la Madeleine
Paris 9
TEL: +33 1 47 42 86 52
MÉTRO: Madeleine
OPEN: Monday through Wednesday
10AM to 7:30PM. Thursday through Saturday
10AM to 8PM. Sunday 10:30AM to 1PM.

LA MAISON DU CHOCOLAT (Printemps)

Printemps Haussmann, 2nd floor
64, boulevard Haussmann
Paris 9
TEL: +33 1 42 82 61 77
MÉTRO: Havre-Caumartin
OPEN: Monday through Wednesday,
Friday, and Saturday 9:35AM to 8PM.
Thursday 9:35AM to 10PM.
CLOSED: Sunday

Whatever your chocolate preferences, you're bound to find something you adore at the House of Chocolate, an institution in Paris since 1977. The stand in the Printemps department store offers a fine selection of La Maison du Chocolat's flavored chocolate creations, including its range of pastries. See page 271 for full commentary.

PIERRE HERMÉ (Galeries Lafayette)

Basement and 1st floor of Lafayette Coupole,
and ground floor Lafayette Maison
Galeries Lafayette department store
35/40, boulevard Haussmann

Paris 9
MÉTRO: Chaussée d'Antin–La Fayette or
Havre-Caumartin

There are no less than three counters in the Galeries Lafayette selling Hermé's chocolates and macarons. See Pastry Shops, page 288, for full commentary.

PIERRE MARCOLINI (Opéra)

3, rue Scribe
Paris 9
TEL: +33 1 44 71 03 74
paris-scribe@marcolini.fr
MÉTRO: Opéra

OPEN: Monday through Wednesday and
Friday through Saturday 10AM to 7PM.
Thursday 10AM to 8PM.
CLOSED: Sunday

Belgian chocolate maker Pierre Marcolini presides over every step in the process of making fine chocolate—from selecting beans to blending flavors—and the results are exquisite. See page 274 for full commentary.

PÂTISSERIE SADAHARU AOKI (Lafayette Gourmet)

Galeries Lafayette department store
48, boulevard Haussmann
Paris 9

MÉTRO: Chaussée d'Antin–La Fayette or
Havre-Caumartin

A large selection of Sadaharu's exquisite chocolates and pastries can be found at this stand in Galeries Lafayette's gourmet supermarket section, Lafayette Gourmet. See Pastry Shops, page 297, for full commentary.

11TH ARRONDISSEMENT

LE CHOCOLAT–ALAIN DUCASSE

40, rue de la Roquette
Paris 11
TEL: +33 1 48 05 82 86
lechocolat-alainducasse.com
lechocolat@alain-ducasse.com

MÉTRO: Bastille
OPEN: Tuesday through Saturday
10:30AM to 7PM
CLOSED: Sunday, Monday, and August

Alain Ducasse's latest food adventure has led him to chocolate, and we are all the better for it. Like a duo of modern-day Willy Wonkas of Paris, Ducasse and his *chef pâtissier,* Nicolas Berger, have created the first bean-to-bar chocolate factory in the capital. This project has been several years in development, and the final results are beyond spectacular. The heady smell of melting chocolate wafting along the rue de la Roquette will draw you off the street, through the courtyard, and into the industrial "showroom" that could be straight out of the set design of Martin Scorsese's film *Hugo*. A pristine glass wall that looks onto the chocolate workshop itself gives a close-up view of the chocolate-making process as Berger and his chocolate makers work away intently. A huge, heavy metal-and-brass cabinet houses a dream of chocolate creations, encased in a giant glass cloche. The flavors are rich and dense, as real chocolate should be—each piece a fine work of art. If you are a lover of chocolate, make this the first stop on your itinerary.

15TH ARRONDISSEMENT

PIERRE HERMÉ (Pasteur)

185, rue de Vaugirard
Paris 15

MÉTRO: Pasteur

This boutique, delicately decorated in hues of pinks and oranges, is like stepping into one of Pierre Hermé's *Ispahan* (a signature flavor combination of rose, lychee, and raspberry) creations. Here you can browse the full range of Hermé wonders: pastries, chocolates, and macarons. See Pastry Shops, page 288, for full commentary.

PÂTISSERIE SADAHARU AOKI (Ségur)

25, rue Pérignon
Paris 15

MÉTRO: Ségur

Sadaharu Aoki is a master at bringing a Japanese twist to traditional French pastries and chocolates. See Pastry Shops, page 297, for full commentary.

16TH ARRONDISSEMENT

LA MAISON DU CHOCOLAT (Victor Hugo)

120, avenue Victor Hugo
Paris 16
TEL: +33 1 40 67 77 83
MÉTRO: Victor Hugo or Rue de la Pompe

OPEN: Monday through Saturday
10AM to 7:30PM. Sunday 10AM to 1PM.
CLOSED: End of July to August 20

You'll undoubtedly find something to please in the world of Maison du Chocolat, from simple ganache and pralines and spice-infused creations to chocolate éclairs and a gold-flecked chocolate tart. See page 271 for full commentary.

PATRICK ROGER (Victor Hugo)

45, avenue Victor Hugo
Paris 16
TEL: +33 1 45 01 66 71
MÉTRO: Kléber or Charles de Gaulle-Étoile

OPEN: Monday through Saturday
10:30AM to 7:30PM
CLOSED: Sunday and end of July to August 20

This eccentrically designed store is like walking into the jungle, an apt setting for the luscious and vibrant flavors of Patrick Roger's chocolates. See page 275 for full commentary.

PIERRE HERMÉ (Passy)

58, avenue Paul Doumer
Paris 16

MÉTRO: Rue de la Pompe or Passy

A master chocolate maker with inspired flavor combinations that others can only hope to imitate. See Pastry Shops, page 288, for full commentary.

PARIS ENVIRONS

LA MAISON DU CHOCOLAT

Roissy Charles de Gaulle Airport: Terminals 2F1, 2E
Orly Ouest Airport: Hall 2

A world of fine chocolates for last-minute airport purchases. See page 271 for full commentary.

AT A GLANCE

1ST ARRONDISSEMENT

Hugo & Victor
  (Marché Saint-Honoré)
La Maison du Chocolat
  (Louvre)
Pierre Hermé (Concorde)

2ND ARRONDISSEMENT

Pierre Hermé (Opéra)

3RD ARRONDISSEMENT

La Chocolaterie de Jacques
  Genin

5TH ARRONDISSEMENT

Pâtisserie Sadaharu Aoki
  (Port-Royal)

6TH ARRONDISSEMENT

Henri Le Roux
  (Saint-Germain)
Pâtisserie Sadaharu Aoki
  (Saint-Placide)
Patrick Roger (Rennes)
Patrick Roger
  (Saint-Germain)

Pierre Hermé
  (Saint-Germain)
Pierre Marcolini
  (Saint-Germain)

7TH ARRONDISSEMENT

Hugo & Victor (Raspail)
La Maison du Chocolat
  (Sèvres-Babylone)
Pierre Marcolini (Rue du Bac)

8TH ARRONDISSEMENT

Fouquet (Champs-Élysées)
La Maison du Chocolat
  (Champs-Élysées)
La Maison du Chocolat
  (Ternes)
Patrick Roger (Ternes)
Patrick Roger (Madeleine)
Pierre Hermé
  (Champs-Élysées)

9TH ARRONDISSEMENT

Á l'Étoile d'Or
Fouquet (Lafayette)
Henri Le Roux (Martyrs)
Hugo & Victor (Printemps)
La Maison du Chocolat
  (Madeleine)

La Maison du Chocolat
  (Printemps)
Pierre Hermé
  (Galeries Lafayette)
Pierre Marcolini (Opéra)
Pâtisserie Sadaharu Aoki
  (Lafayette Gourmet)

11TH ARRONDISSEMENT

Le Chocolat–Alain Ducasse

15TH ARRONDISSEMENT

Pierre Hermé (Pasteur)
Pâtisserie Sadaharu Aoki
  (Ségur)

16TH ARRONDISSEMENT

La Maison du Chocolat
  (Victor Hugo)
Patrick Roger (Victor Hugo)
Pierre Hermé (Passy)

PARIS ENVIRONS

La Maison du Chocolat
  (Roissy Charles de Gaulle
  Airport)
La Maison du Chocolat
  (Orly Ouest Airport)

PASTRY SHOPS AND ICE CREAM

PÂTISSERIES ET GLACES

The Parisian pastry chef is truly a person to be admired. Imagine their responsibility. Day in and day out, season after season, they must attend to the care and feeding of the formidable Parisian sweet tooth.

Everywhere you turn in Paris, someone—man, woman, child—seems to be either munching on a *pain au chocolat*, peering wide-eyed into the window of a pristine, wondrous pastry shop, savoring the last lick of an ice-cream cone, or carrying, with admirable agility, a beribboned cardboard box filled with the day's dessert.

Perhaps the city's per capita consumption of butter, sugar, cream, and eggs is not the highest in the world, but if a population won prizes simply on its level of enthusiasm for all things sweet and satisfying, I think that Parisians would win. I have watched reed-thin women heartily downing three or four desserts in a row—unashamedly, unabashedly, with no remorse. I have eavesdropped as a pair of businessmen huddled at lunchtime, talking in hushed, animated tones; the subject was not politics, or the euro, or racing cars, but chocolates. Chocolates! I have listened as one enthusiastic *pâtissier* explained what went on when several of Paris's pastry chefs gathered together: "I love éclairs, but don't make them in my shop. So when I visit my buddies, I have an éclair feast. Seven is my limit. And I usually meet my limit."

Everywhere, one finds the croissant (along with the chocolate-filled version known as *pain au chocolat*); the brioche (the *mousseline* variety is more buttery and typically Parisian); the madeleine (a lemony tea cake that Proust made famous); and the *financier*—a personal favorite (an almond-flavored rectangle that is part cake, part cookie, and absolutely satisfying when carefully made and fresh).

In recent years, macarons (colorful disks of sweet meringue-based confectionery) have taken the city and world by storm, as have buttery, salted caramels. For many—Parisians as well as those passing through—a day in this city without a pastry is a day not worth living. Why this is so could be the subject of a major treatise, but suffice it to say that Parisians climb the sweet mountain because it is there.

While some pastry shops specialize in just that—sweet delights—there are chocolate shops, tea salons, and bakeries that distinguish themselves in the pastry department, and so they are cross-referenced here. ❧

1ST ARRONDISSEMENT

ANGELINA (Musée du Louvre)

Musée du Louvre
Richelieu Wing
Café Richelieu
Paris 1
MÉTRO: Palais Royal–Musée du Louvre

ANGELINA (Rivoli)

226, rue de Rivoli
PARIS 1
MÉTRO: Tuileries

Essential to visit at least once while in Paris, this classic tea salon will transport you to another, more elegant era as you sip on a thick and luxurious hot chocolate, perhaps Angelina's most famous menu item. The café in the Louvre is not as impressive as the original location on rue de Rivoli, but still inspires a baroque yesteryear, not at all inappropriate for a location in the Louvre museum. See Cafés and Casual Bites, page 129, for full commentary.

ÉRIC KAYSER (Opéra)

33, rue Danielle Casanova
Paris 1

MÉTRO: Opéra

Éric Kayser may be heading for world domination with his 17 stores in Paris, and outposts in 13 countries worldwide, but the quality of his baked goods remains impeccable. His lineup of 50 pastry varieties and 25 *viennoiseries* (sweet breakfast pastries such as croissants) is no less impressive. See Bakeries, page 221, for full commentary.

GOSSELIN (Saint-Honoré)

125, rue Saint-Honoré
Paris 1

MÉTRO: Louvre-Rivoli

In addition to superlative bread, Phillippe Gosselin has an array of delectable-looking pastries and macarons that he also supplies to the Les Deux Magots Café in Saint-Germain. Among my favorites is his *tarte aux figues,* with its cookielike crust and a wisp of pastry cream, topped with delicious fresh figs. See Bakeries, page 220, for full commentary.

HUGO & VICTOR (Marché Saint-Honoré)

7, rue Gomboust
Paris 1
TEL: + 33 1 42 96 10 20
hugovictor.com
MÉTRO: Pyramides

OPEN: Tuesday and Wednesday 10:30AM
to 7PM. Thursday through Saturday
10:30AM to 8PM.
CLOSED: Sunday and Monday

J ust one sample of each pastry is on display at the Hugo & Victor boutiques, either behind or under glass, like a treasured jewel. In fact, if the offerings weren't overflowing with perfect fruit, dusted with cocoa, polka-dotted with white chocolate, it would be easy to mistake these sober boutiques for jewelry stores. And that's what creators Hugues Pouget and Sylvain Blanc, friends since childhood, intend. One a vaunted pastry chef, the other an experienced designer, the two combined their visions to create a dreamily elegant pastry shop where the exotic informs the traditional. They decided to focus on three major flavors—chocolate, vanilla, and caramel—which form the basis for many of their cakes and chocolates. Fruit is another obsession, particularly citrus. Within this flavor realm, Pouget plays with tradition, turning a *Paris-Brest* into a cream-and-fruit-bedecked rectangle, while a milk chocolate and Earl Grey tea tart looks ready to take flight, powered by its decor of elevated chocolate spheres. Tarts aren't round at Hugo & Victor—they're wedges of crisp, filled pastry, allowing patrons to create their own complete tart by mixing and matching slices. This way, if Grandma likes juicy grapefruit slices atop her pastry cream, and Junior prefers lime, and Mom loves clementine, everyone can be happy! Ingredients for some of the more exotic fruit desserts—like *combava* or kaffir lime—come from Blanc's father's garden in southern France. The Hugo & Victor chocolates are delectable, particularly the toasty pralines, and the box they come in appropriately resembles a *grimoire*, or book of magic. Notable, too, are their flaky croissants and *pains au chocolat*.

BOULANGERIE JEAN-NOËL JULIEN (Saint-Honoré)

75, rue Saint-Honoré
Paris 1

MÉTRO: Les Halles or Louvre-Rivoli

An important address to know in a neighborhood lacking good *viennoiseries* (sweet breakfast pastries). Here the croissants are flaky and buttery and the *pain au chocolat* generously filled with rich, dark chocolate. See Bakeries, page 221, for full commentary.

LA MAISON DU CHOCOLAT (Louvre)

99, rue de Rivoli
Paris 1

MÉTRO: Palais Royal-Musée du Louvre

Not only famous for bars of chocolate, La Maison du Chocolat is also known for its crisp and creamy éclairs, a sinful chocolate tart, and a variety of exquisite-looking dessert cakes. See Chocolate Shops, page 271, for full commentary.

PIERRE HERMÉ

pierreherme.com

Pierre Hermé has always been edgy, in a romantic sort of way. He combines rose petals with pastry cream, uses olive oil in surprising places, sprinkles *fleur de sel* with abandon. His pastries are seasonal fashion statements, with all the attendant hype of haute couture. He dusts and sprinkles, swirls and fillips, so that each cake, each tart, each delectable choice is so lovely, you almost want to show it off instead of eat it! He's a master at macarons and his are the perfect overdose of gorgeous flavor, and not too sweet. When it comes to chocolate, he is both a visionary and a master technician, with a grasp of combining sweet and savory as he tries things that others can only hope to imitate. Take his *corso*, a chocolate with shards of black olives and olive oil. It's unconventional, but he made it and it's delicious. His *chocolat au macaron* is brilliant, neither a candy nor a macaron, but somehow better than either, with its almond paste and tender biscuit. And just one little *croquant praliné*, with its perfect balance of crunchy, caramelized nuts and gorgeous ganache, can make you moan with pleasure. For milk chocolate fans, the *Melissa* takes 45 percent milk chocolate to new heights, with its tiny hits of *fleur de sel*.

PIERRE HERMÉ (Concorde)

4, rue Cambon
Paris 1
TEL: +33 1 43 54 47 77
pierreherme.com

MÉTRO: Concorde
OPEN: Monday through Saturday
10AM to 7:30PM
CLOSED: Sunday

A master of macarons, pastries, and chocolates, Pierre Hermé is not just a pastry chef but an artist and an alchemist. Note this particular shop sells only macarons and chocolates. See box (above) for full commentary.

2ND ARRONDISSEMENT

L'ATELIER DE L'ÉCLAIR

16, rue Bachaumont
Paris 2
TEL: + 33 1 42 36 40 54
latelierdeleclair.fr

contact@latelierdeleclair.fr
MÉTRO: Sentier
OPEN: Daily 11AM to 8PM

Step aside, macaron, and move over, cupcake—the latest Parisian pastry obsession is all about *choux*, and there is a flourish of new high-end éclair boutiques across the capital to prove it. The Atelier de l'Éclair is the first boutique entirely dedicated to éclairs, and the shop's haute couture creations are sleek, modern, and absolutely delicious. The salted butter caramel, although sweet, is light and fulfilling; the *citron meringuée* is a dreamy, tart, and lively bite; and the *pistache abricot* is a perfectly balanced creation. You can also try the savory éclair, a large *choux* éclair bun with a variety of sandwich fillings such as chorizo and sun-dried tomatoes, or *chèvre* (goat cheese) and pesto.

FINANCIERS

Almond Cakes

The little rectangular almond cakes known as *financiers* are sold in many of the best pastry shops in Paris. Perfect *financiers* are about as addictive as chocolate. The finest have a firm, crusty exterior and a moist, almondy interior, tasting almost as if they were filled with almond paste. Next to the classic madeleine, the *financier* is probably the most popular little French cake. It was created by *pâtissier* Lasne, who had a pastry shop near the Paris stock exchange in the late 19th century. An entrepreneurial man, he modernized a pastry recipe from the middle ages, inventing a small, tidy pastry resembling a bar of gold. His rich banking clientele could eat the pastry on the run, dirtying neither their hands nor their suits. *Financier*, of course, means "banker" in French. The secret to a good *financier* is in the use of top-quality ingredients, as well as in the baking: For a good crust, it must begin in a hot oven. The temperature is then reduced, keeping the interior nice and moist.

EQUIPMENT:

16 individual 2- by 4-inch (5- by 10-cm) tin *financier* molds

INGREDIENTS:

12 tablespoons (1½ sticks; 180 g) unsalted butter, melted and cooled

1½ cups (140 g) almond meal

1⅔ cups (225 g) confectioners' sugar

½ cups (70 g) unbleached all-purpose flour

⅛ teaspoon fine sea salt

¾ cup (185 g) large egg whites (the whites from 5 to 6 large eggs), preferably organic and free-range

1. Center a rack in the oven. Preheat the oven to 425°F (220°C).

2. With a pastry brush, thoroughly butter the *financier* molds, using some of the melted and cooled butter. Arrange the molds side by side but not touching on a baking sheet. Place the baking sheet with the molds in the freezer for at least 20 minutes to solidify the butter. This will help the *financiers* to unmold easily.

3. In a large bowl, whisk together the almond meal, sugar, flour, and salt. Whisk in the egg whites a little at a time just until thoroughly blended. Gently whisk in the butter until thoroughly blended. The mixture will be fairly thin.

4. Pour or spoon the batter into the molds, filling them almost to the rim. Place the baking sheet in the oven. Bake until the *financiers* are pale gold and begin to firm up, about 7 minutes. Reduce the heat to 400°F (200°C) and bake 7 minutes more. Turn off the oven, keeping the door closed. Leave the *financiers* sitting in the warm oven for 7 minutes.

5. Remove the *financiers* from the oven and let them cool in the molds for 10 minutes, then unmold them onto a wire rack to cool completely.

16 FINANCIERS

NOTE: Almond meal (sometimes called almond flour) is made from whole, unblanched (skin on) almonds. For this recipe, whole, unblanched almonds can be finely ground in a food processor. Do not overprocess.

ÉRIC KAYSER (Bourse)

16, rue des Petits-Carreaux
Paris 2

MÉTRO: Sentier

While in the birthplace of the *financier* (the delicious little pastry was invented in this neighborhood in the late 19th century), you must try Éric Kayser's pistachio version, which is moist and dense with an authentic pistachio flavor. See Bakeries, page 221, for full commentary.

PIERRE HERMÉ (Opéra)

39, avenue de l'Opéra
Paris 2
TEL: +33 1 43 54 47 77
pierreherme.com

MÉTRO: Opéra
OPEN: Monday through Thursday 10AM to 7PM. Friday and Saturday 10AM to 7:30PM. Sunday 10AM to 7PM.

This small boutique sells only macarons and chocolates, but they are among the best you will find in Paris. See box (page 288) for full commentary.

3RD ARRONDISSEMENT

MEERT

16, rue Elzévir
Paris 3
TEL: +33 1 49 96 56 90
meert.fr

MÉTRO: Saint-Paul or Chemin Vert
OPEN: Wednesday through Saturday 11AM to 7PM. Sunday 10AM to 7PM.
CLOSED: Monday and Tuesday

Like an old-fashioned candy shop, this spot demands a certain demeanor—one would not want to misbehave in such a formal setting! Originally from Lille in the north of France, Meert is known for its *speculoos* (the crisp northern French and Belgian spice cookie that has recently taken the whole of France by storm) and its small, flat *gaufres*, or waffle cookies, which hold fillings of either sweet butter and *sucre vergeoise* (a soft, moist brown sugar made from beets) or *speculoos* butter. These alone make a trip to Meert worth it. The spice cakes, both plain and with almonds, are tender and delicious, too, though don't expect gingerbread when you bite into them. When the French say spice cake, they really mean honey cake, and that's the overriding flavor of these dense, delicious slabs. Everything at Meert is gracious, from the bejeweled boxes intended to hold the fruit jellies, chocolate-covered almonds, marshmallows, or candied citrus zests to the well-dressed and professional employees. Meert offers a nostalgic visit to yesteryear. Oh yes, if you like jams, you'll want to try Meert's signature varieties, too.

PAIN DE SUCRE

14, rue Rambuteau
Paris 3
TEL: +33 1 45 74 68 92
patisseriepaindesucre.com

MÉTRO: Rambuteau
OPEN: Thursday through Monday 10AM to 8PM
CLOSED: Tuesday and Wednesday

I s this a pastry shop or is it a gallery offering edible art? Honestly, it's both. The temptingly pretty cakes, the glistening fruit-filled tarts, the children's birthday cakes that look like happy little caterpillars—all are legion and exquisitely conceived and prepared, and so are the displays in this small temple to sweets. Imagination swoops through every offering, from the *chausson aux pommes* (apple turnover) shaped like a small, caramelized baguette to the *désir*, a white orb filled with quince pulp and chestnut mousse on a perfectly crumbly almond pastry. Yet classicism isn't far behind. The textbook-perfect *millefeuille* is a lighter-than-air wonder of layers of buttery puff pastry separated by rosettes of vanilla-scented cream; and the *tarte au citron*, well, it is one of the best in the land. The filling is a blend of lemon and lime, the pastry a delicate shell. It sings, it dances, it disappears way too fast! For beauty, fantasy, imagination—this is the place!

POPELINI (Marais)

29, rue Debelleyme
Paris 3
TEL: +33 1 44 61 31 44
popelini.com

contact@popelini.com
MÉTRO: Filles du Calvaire
OPEN: Daily Monday through Saturday 11AM to 7:30PM. Sunday 10AM to 3PM.

T his adorable boutique, named after the 1540 inventor of *choux* pastry, is dedicated entirely to the making of tiny and perfectly formed *choux à la crème*—mini cream puffs. These bite-size delights are made with all-natural ingredients, no preservatives or artificial flavors, and come in nine year-round flavors plus a *choux du jour,* filled with whipped cream and seasonal fruit that changes daily. These make for a delicious coffee accompaniment, or an original gift for a host when invited to dinner.

▶ *Watch out, macarons! Bite-size cream puffs are stealing the show in Paris right now.*

4TH ARRONDISSEMENT

BERTHILLON

29–31, rue Saint-Louis en l'Île
Paris 4
TEL: +33 1 43 54 31 61
berthillon.fr
MÉTRO: Pont Marie

OPEN: Wednesday through Sunday 10AM
to 8PM
CLOSED: Monday and Tuesday
SPECIALTY: Ice Cream

Although the famous artisanal Berthillon ice creams and sorbets can now be bought at cafés all over Paris, it isn't hard to find the original Berthillon store on the Île Saint-Louis—just look for the immense queue that winds its way from the takeout window as soon as the weather becomes warm.

Still a family-run business, Berthillon creates an extensive array of flavors on-site daily: from the classic *caramel au beurre salé* (salted butter caramel) to the more unusual experimentation of *praliné au citron et coriander* (praline with lemon and coriander). The list of sorbets is no less impressive, including a subtly perfumed *framboise à la rose* (rose-scented raspberry), *cacao extra bitter,* a dark-chocolate-lover's dream, or *fraise de bois* (wild strawberry) that has been on the menu since the company's beginning in 1954. Eat in, in the *salon de thé,* for the full menu of sundae and dessert options. Or join the masses for a takeout cone or cup, savoring your delights as you wander the cobblestone streets; or find a spot among the picnickers along the Seine and watch the *bateaux-mouches* go by.

▲ *Berthillon, a fine* salon de thé, *and an even finer ice-cream maker.*

L'ÉCLAIR DE GENIE (Marais)

14, rue Pavée
Paris 4
TEL: +33 1 42 77 85 11
leclairdegenie.com
contact@leclairdegenie.com

MÉTRO: Saint-Paul
OPEN: Tuesday through Sunday
11AM to 7:30PM
CLOSED: Monday

Christophe Adam has quite the pastry pedigree, having honed his skills in such places as the Crillon and Fauchon. It was at Fauchon where he first began to re-imagine the humble éclair, imbuing the French classic with a contemporary edge. This has since become his full-time occupation, with the opening of two éclair "concept stores" dedicated almost entirely to this cream-filled *choux* dessert. To look at, they are artistic creations in their own right, with modern, colorful icing designs and unusual flavor combinations. The mascarpone *caramel beurre salé* is a winner, with its light and not-too-sweet creamy center. His autumn creation, the *feuille d'automne*, is a veritable construction of *grand cru* chocolate cream, cacao crumble, caramelized almonds and hazelnuts, and chocolate leaves. Sometimes aesthetics trump flavor, and I found his chocolate and *citron yuzu* éclairs lacked punch and balance. That won't keep me from going back, however, to discover what new and wonderful reinventions he will come up with next.

BOULANGERIE JEAN-NOËL JULIEN (Hôtel de Ville)

24, rue Saint-Martin
Paris 4

MÉTRO: Hôtel de Ville or Châtelet

Guaranteed for a buttery, flaky croissant or a winning *pain au chocolat* generously filled with rich, dark chocolate. See Bakeries, page 221, for full commentary.

LA PISTACHERIE (Rambuteau)

67, rue Rambuteau
Paris 4
TEL: +33 1 42 78 84 55
MÉTRO: Rambuteau

OPEN: Daily Monday through
Thursday 11AM to 8PM. Friday
through Sunday 11AM to 8:30PM.

Nut fans will have a field day in La Pistacherie's elegant boutiques, which offer such treasures as top-quality pistachios from Sicily and Turkey, and every other nut imaginable—peanuts, almonds, macadamia nuts, walnuts, pecans—either simply toasted or coated with sweets or with chocolate. The shops are like old-fashioned candy stores, with glass jars filled with varied specialties. They offer a huge line of nut candies, many of them nougatlike and less convincing than the nuts all on their own. The owner, Charles Sakr, is from Lebanon, and according to one friendly salesperson, he just loves to travel and discover new sources for nuts around the world, particularly pistachios.

NOUGAT GLACÉ SORBET
•
Candied Nut and Honey Sorbet

Fresh lemon verbena—or *verveine*—grows like a weed in my Provençal garden, for it's a traditional flavoring for herbal infusions or creamy desserts. I love light and simple ice creams in the hot summer months, and this has become a favorite among family and guests. Here I add a bit of chopped white honey-and-nut nougat candy and a touch of honey. If lemon verbena is not available, try the recipe with a handful of fresh mint, or with less traditional "sweet" herbs, such as thyme or rosemary.

EQUIPMENT:

Ice-cream maker

INGREDIENTS:

2 cups (500 ml) whole milk

1 cup (250 ml) light cream or half-and-half

½ cup (125 ml) honey

3 ounces (90 g) chopped white nougat candy

3 ounces (90 g) toasted pistachio nuts

In a large saucepan, combine the milk, cream, and honey. Stir to dissolve the honey. Heat the mixture over medium heat, stirring from time to time, just until tiny bubbles form around the edges of the pan. Chill thoroughly. Stir in the nougat. Transfer the mixture to an ice-cream maker and freeze according to the manufacturer's instructions. For best results, serve the sorbet as soon as it is made, garnished with toasted pistachio nuts. Do not refreeze.

12 SERVINGS

POZZETTO

39, rue du Roi de Sicile
Paris 4
TEL: +33 1 42 77 08 64
pozzetto.biz
info@pozzetto.biz

MÉTRO: Saint-Paul
OPEN: Monday through Thursday noon to
11:30PM. Friday and Saturday noon to 12:45AM.
Sunday noon to midnight.
SPECIALTY: Ice Cream

A favorite place to indulge in an authentic Italian gelato is Pozzetto, a small *gelateria-caffè* appropriately located on the rue Roi de Sicile (King of Sicily Road) in the Marais. Ice cream is made daily on the premises with fresh whole French milk, and flavors are seasonal, using fresh fruit from the markets, which are pressed daily. Their sorbets hold back on the sugar to let the fresh fruit flavors really come through. Sorrento lemons are used when in season, and in the summer months, you can find Sicilian Granita on the menu—what could be more refreshing on a hot summer's day?

5TH ARRONDISSEMENT

CARL MARLETTI

51, rue Censier
Paris 5
TEL: +33 1 43 31 68 12
carlmarletti.com
boutique@carlmarletti.com

MÉTRO: Censier Daubenton
OPEN: Tuesday through Saturday 10AM to 8PM.
Sunday 10AM to 1:30PM.
CLOSED: Sunday afternoon and Monday

▲ *Pastries from Carl Marletti: the stuff that dreams are made of.*

Each pastry in this shop is decorated, glazed, sprinkled, and dusted to perfection. Like fashion icons, they are set in their pristine case at slight angles, to better accentuate their attributes. Which to buy? Which to taste? What problems! I love them all, but particularly the chocolate tart, a shiny pool of deep chocolate cream in a crisp pastry with the crunch of cacao bean chips that seem to float on the surface of the tart. Every creation in this sparkling shop reveals the deep understanding Marletti has of a valued attribute—what we call the "crunch factor." The *tarte au citron* is lemony and perfectly balanced, the pastry cracks with each bite, and the little piece of candied zest on top is a flavorful bonus. His *millefeuilles*— vanilla, chocolate, praline, berries, and chocolate with passion fruit—are shattery wonders, his caramel éclair sublime. Marletti reveres nuts and salt, too, using them skillfully to offset other flavors. His *tarte Belle-Hélène*, a silken dream of vanilla pastry cream and poached pear, is studded with crunchy toasted hazelnuts; his fat *Paris-Brest* belongs in the pantheon of classics, with its multilayered hazelnut flavoring. The éclairs, a marvel of rich pastry cream and fresh *pâte à choux*, arrive with just the right hint of salt. This shop is worth heading to straight from the airport.

PÂTISSERIE CIEL

3, rue Monge
Paris 5
TEL: +33 1 43 29 40 78
MÉTRO: Maubert-Mutualité

OPEN: Tuesday through Thursday 10:30AM to 11PM. Friday and Saturday 10:30AM to 1AM. Sunday 10AM to 7PM.
CLOSED: Monday

Add to the growing assortment of single-subject pastry shops (éclairs, choux pastry) the aptly named Ciel ("sky" as well as "heaven" in French), which offers just one sweet, welcome product: small, individual angel food cakes. Only they are not really all-egg-white cakes, but rather chiffon cakes, made with the whole egg. The Japanese owner felt the French would be more likely to accept "angel cakes" over "chiffon cakes," so went for the sky. I loved the *yuzu*-flavored version, and though it took me a while to warm up to the black sesame variation, that one left me feeling truly satisfied. One can sample the little cakes right in the airy, open shop, pairing them with a glass of champagne, whiskey, or, better yet, their citrusy, vibrant *yuzu* sake.

ÉRIC KAYSER (Sorbonne)

8, rue Monge
Paris 5
MÉTRO: Maubert-Mutualité

ÉRIC KAYSER (Sorbonne II)

14, rue Monge
Paris 5
MÉTRO: Maubert-Mutualité

This boutique, established in 1996, was the first of Kayser's now vast empire of *boulangeries/ pâtisseries* that includes 17 Paris stores and outposts in 13 countries worldwide. See Bakeries, page 221, for full commentary.

PÂTISSERIE SADAHARU AOKI (Port-Royal)

56, boulevard de Port-Royal
Paris 5
TEL: +33 1 45 35 36 80
sadaharuaoki.com
societe@sadaharuaoki.com

MÉTRO: Les Gobelins
OPEN: Tuesday through Saturday 11AM to 7PM.
Sunday 11AM to 5PM.
CLOSED: Monday and holidays

Sadaharu Aoki's mantra may be simplicity, as borne out in his geometrically narrow éclairs, perfectly round cakes so delicately decorated they resemble Japanese paintings, chocolates like skinny mah-jongg tiles splashed with primary colors instead of characters, but humor and design are ever present, too. One wonders whether providing pastries for many of the top fashion houses in Paris influenced Mr. Aoki, or if his sense of fashion was already firmly in place when he hit the capital in 1991. Whichever came first, it all works seamlessly. He fuses Japanese ingredients and classic French pastry with remarkable finesse and unending flavor. A pinch of black sesame seeds enlivens the white glaze on a toasty black sesame-filled éclair; a dusting of *matcha* on a traditional (though green-tea-flavored) King's cake requires a double take; an intensity of *fleur de sel* in a gorgeous caramel tart inspires an "aha" moment—finally, something made with salted butter that actually tastes salty, and caramelly delicious. Everything offered at Sadaharu Aoki is signature, but favorites include the *matcha* Opéra, a tender layering of *matcha*-scented buttercream and biscuit; his chocolate *duomo*, a chubby chocolate mousse cake that nearly defies description (it's a ginger and chocolate mousse on a crisp hazelnut pastry base), the black sesame éclair, and the unforgettable salted caramel tart. The ethereal *millefeuille*, either dusted with *matcha* or plain, is another heaven-sent delight. Some may just want to visit Aoki's shops to admire the creative packaging: squares of chocolate come in a round, purselike cardboard wrapping, and his original, chocolate-coated macarons are embellished with polka dots and delivered in a see-through round box.

6TH ARRONDISSEMENT

ÉRIC KAYSER (Luxembourg)

87, rue d'Assas
Paris 6
MÉTRO: Vavin or Port-Royal (RER B)

ÉRIC KAYSER (Odéon)

10, rue de l'Ancienne-Comédie
Paris 6
MÉTRO: Odéon or Mabillon

ÉRIC KAYSER (Montparnasse)

1, boulevard du Montparnasse
Paris 6
MÉTRO: Duroc

With three *boulangeries/pâtisseries* in the 6th *arrondissement* alone, Éric Kayser is indeed a formidable force in the baking world. See Bakeries, page 221, for full commentary.

GROM

81, rue de Seine
Paris 6
TEL: +33 1 40 46 92 60
grom.it/eng/
info@grom.it
MÉTRO: Odéon or Mabillon

OPEN: Summer hours Monday through
Wednesday noon to 11PM. Thursday through
Saturday noon to 12AM. Sunday 11AM to 11PM.
Winter hours Monday through Wednesday
1 to 10:30PM. Thursday through Saturday
1PM to 12AM. Sunday noon to 10:30PM.
SPECIALTY: Ice Cream

Winter or summer, rain or shine, customers queue up to sample the delights of true Italian gelato at Grom. Far superior to its rival Amorino around the corner, Grom boasts completely natural ingredients: organic fruit from their own Mura Mura farms in Italy, whole milk, organic eggs—always the best possible ingredients they can source. And the proof is in the creaminess and intensity of flavor. They use minimal cream so the fat content is, well, less guilt inducing. Classics such as chocolate, cream, *stracciatella*, hazelnut, coffee, nougat, and pistachio are year-round fixtures, with various other flavors introduced to their repertoire depending on the season. Their fruit sorbets are nothing more than organic fruit, spring water, and cane sugar, with flavors changing seasonally. A few flavors of granita—coffee, lemon, and the classic Sicilian almond—are also on offer. Try their decadent *cioccolato extra noir* (extra dark chocolate) sorbet alongside the earthy pistachio gelato. And don't miss the *caramello al sale* (salted caramel) with its deep—verging-on-burnt—flavor that is one of the best versions to be found in the city. If, in winter, this is all too cold to think about, try ordering one of their three hot-chocolate offerings: a thick dark *fondente* using Venezuelan Ocumare chocolate, a milkier *al latte* version using Colombian Teyuna chocolate, or *al bacio* with hazelnut chips.

BOULANGERIE JEAN-NOËL JULIEN (Luxembourg)

54, rue Notre-Dame des Champs
Paris 6

MÉTRO: Notre-Dame des Champs or Vavin

A notable address for excellent flaky croissants. See Bakeries, page 221, for full commentary.

LADURÉE (Saint-Germain)

21, rue Bonaparte
Paris 6
TEL: +33 1 44 07 64 87
laduree.com
servicesclients@laduree.com

MÉTRO: Saint-Germain-des-Prés
OPEN: Monday through Friday 8:30AM to
7:30PM. Saturday 8:30AM to 8:30PM.
Sunday and holidays 10AM to 7:30PM.

Settling into a small table at Ladurée is how you begin one of the most romantically nostalgic of Parisian experiences. The dark wood, heavy, embossed menus, and white-aproned servers place Ladurée in a different, more gracious era. Freshly baked and golden croissants, brioches, *pains au chocolat,* and *bretzels* (bready pretzels) stimulate the appetite. And then there's the array of colorful tarts, cakes, and signature macarons displayed in glass cases. The silver pitchers—for coffee, thick dark hot chocolate, and frothed milk—and the little silver trays for pastries add to the elegance. You can spend a morning reading, visiting, lingering until lunchtime, when a delicate finger sandwich or an omelette will satisfy whatever remains of your appetite.

▶ *A last-minute fix at the Ladurée stand at Charles de Gaulle airport.*

LA MAISON DU CHOU

7, place de Furstenberg
Paris 6
TEL: + 33 1 9 54 75 06 05
info@maisonduchou.net

MÉTRO: Saint-Germain-des-Prés or Mabillon
OPEN: Tuesday through Sunday 11AM to 7PM
CLOSED: Monday
SPECIALTY: *Choux à la crème* (cream puffs)

I love simplicity, and that's what you'll find at the tiny Maison du Chou, set within the charming Place de Furstenberg and its towering paulownia trees that take center stage. The shop offers only one product: *choux à la crème*—golden balls of chou pastry filled with a choice of three different fillings: plain (a tangy mix of *fromage blanc* and goat's-milk cheese), coffee, and chocolate. They are ethereally light and delicious. There are a few tables inside, for pairing your cream puff with a cup of espresso.

PIERRE HERMÉ (Saint-Germain)

72, rue Bonaparte
Paris 6
TEL: +33 1 43 54 47 77
pierreherme.com

MÉTRO: Saint-Sulpice or Mabillon
OPEN: Sunday through Wednesday 10AM to 7PM. Thurday and Friday 10AM to 7:30PM. Saturday 10AM to 8PM.

Pierre Hermé's wondrous creations have made him one of France's most famous pastry chefs. Not all his boutiques are created equal, but you can sample pastries, chocolates, and macarons at the Bonaparte boutique. See page 288 for full commentary.

POILÂNE (Cherche-Midi)

8, rue du Cherche-Midi
Paris 6

MÉTRO: Sèvres-Babylone or Saint-Sulpice

Famous for their bread, but loved also for their caramelized apple *tartelettes* and buttery *sablé* (shortbread) cookies. See Bakeries, page 227, for full commentary.

PÂTISSERIE SADAHARU AOKI (Saint-Placide)

35, rue de Vaugirard
Paris 6
TEL: +33 1 45 44 48 90
MÉTRO: Rennes or Saint-Placide

OPEN: Tuesday through Saturday 11AM to 7PM.
Sunday 10AM to 6PM.
CLOSED: Monday and holidays

French pastry with a Japanese twist. See page 297 for full commentary.

7TH ARRONDISSEMENT

ÉRIC KAYSER (Musée d'Orsay)

18, rue du Bac
Paris 7

MÉTRO: Rue du Bac or Solférino

Éric Kayser may be heading for world domination with his 17 stores in Paris and outposts in 13 countries worldwide, but the quality of his baked goods remains impeccable. See Bakeries, page 221, for full commentary.

GOSSELIN (Musée d'Orsay)

258, boulevard Saint-Germain
Paris 7

MÉTRO: Solférino

This bright, spacious boutique at the exit of Solférino *métro,* just steps from the Musée d'Orsay, is full of delectable-looking pastries and macarons (also to be found at Les Deux Magots Café in Saint-Germain). See Bakeries, page 220, for further commentary.

HUGO & VICTOR (Raspail)

40, boulevard Raspail
Paris 7
TEL: +33 1 44 39 97 73

MÉTRO: Sèvres-Babylone
OPEN: Monday through Saturday
9AM to 8PM. Sunday 10AM to 6PM.

You may mistake this elegant boutique for a jewelry store, as each pastry creation is displayed as if a precious jewel. See page 287 for full commentary.

BRIOCHE MOUSSELINE
Denis Ruffel's Feathery Brioche

Paris bakeries offer many variations on the classic brioche, the buttery, egg-rich yeast bread that's enjoyed for luxurious breakfasts or snacks, appearing in various molded forms and sizes. This brioche is known as a *brioche mousseline* because it is richer in butter than classic brioche, and is of course golden and delicious. *Brioche mousseline* is typically Parisian, and the light and sticky dough is often baked in a tin coffee can, making for a nice round loaf. Denis Ruffel, from the Left Bank pastry shop Pâtisserie Jean Millet (see page 302), offers his personal version, baking it in a rectangular loaf pan. Ruffel's special glaze gives this sweet bread a certain glow.

EQUIPMENT:

An electric mixer fitted with a flat paddle; two 6-cup (1.5-l) rectangular loaf pans, preferably nonstick

INGREDIENTS:

BRIOCHE:

1 tablespoon or 1 package active dry yeast

¼ cup (60 ml) whole milk, heated to lukewarm

⅓ cup (65 g) unrefined cane sugar, preferably organic

1 teaspoon salt

8 large eggs, preferably organic and free-range

4 cups (560 g) unbleached, all-purpose flour

1¼ cups (2¼ sticks; 310 g) unsalted butter at room temperature, plus 2 teaspoons unsalted butter for buttering the loaf pans

GLAZE:

1 egg, preferably organic and free-range

1 egg yolk, preferably organic and free-range

⅛ teaspoon fine sea salt

⅛ teaspoon sugar

1 teaspoon milk

2 LOAVES

1. Prepare the bread: In the bowl of the electric mixer, combine the yeast, milk, and sugar. Whisk together by hand, and set aside for 5 minutes until the mixture is bubbly.

2. Whisk in the salt, then the eggs one at a time, mixing until well blended.

3. Add the flour, cup by cup, until the mixture is smooth, then incorporate the butter bit by bit. The dough will be very soft and sticky. Transfer the dough to a bowl, cover securely with plastic wrap, and let rise at room temperature until doubled in bulk, about 1 hour.

4. With a wooden spoon, stir the dough to deflate it. Cover, refrigerate, and let rise until doubled in bulk, 1½ to 3 hours.

5. Center a rack in the oven. Preheat the oven to 350°F (175°C).

6. Butter the 2 loaf pans. Stir down the dough again, and transfer equal portions of the dough into the prepared pans. The dough will remain very soft and sticky. Cover and let rise at room temperature until almost doubled in bulk, about 1 hour. Don't worry if it doesn't double in bulk; it will rise more during the baking.

7. In a small bowl, combine the ingredients for the glaze, and gently brush over the top of each brioche. Place the loaf pans in the oven and bake until golden brown, 35 to 40 minutes. Unmold immediately, and cool on a rack. The brioches can be stored, well wrapped, at room temperature for up to 3 days, or frozen for up to 1 month.

PÂTISSERIE JEAN MILLET

103, rue Saint-Dominique
Paris 7
TEL: +33 1 45 51 49 80
patisserie-jean-millet.com

MÉTRO: École Militaire or La Tour-Maubourg
OPEN: Tuesday through Saturday 8:30AM to
8PM. Sunday 8AM to 5PM.
CLOSED: Monday

Walking into this pastry shop feels like entering a time capsule, for the pastries are ultra-classic and traditional. You won't find polka dots or shards of pastry rising to the heavens here. Instead, you'll weep over the ethereal, vanilla-scented *millefeuille* with layers of the most buttery

puff pastry this side of Vienna, or the sweetly balanced lemon tart in its tender-crisp pastry, or the formal *tarte paysanne* with its tender apples and cloudlike *crème chibouste*. Denis Ruffel is the skill and talent at Pâtisserie Millet, always at the oven unless he's off to Japan, where he has a huge following. His work has remained perfect for decades, and there is nothing quite so comforting as sitting down at one of the small tables in this tiny shop to savor pastry that tastes just as you dreamed it could. As for his croissants and *pains au chocolat,* they define the genres with their buttery flavor and explosive texture. You won't hear much about this shop or the genius behind it, because along with the perfect work, there comes an enviable modesty. Don't hesitate to visit and enjoy everything sweet, and everything savory, too—the sandwiches at Pâtisserie Millet are scrumptious.

LA MAISON DU CHOCOLAT (Sèvres-Babylone)

19, rue de Sèvres
Paris 7

MÉTRO: Sèvres-Babylone or Saint-Sulpice

Not just known for their chocolates, La Maison du Chocolat also excels at éclairs, chocolate tarts, and exquisite sweet desserts. See Chocolate Shops, page 271, for full commentary.

MARTINE LAMBERT

39, rue Cler
Paris 7
TEL: + 33 1 40 62 97 18
martine-lambert.com
MÉTRO: École-Militaire or La Tour-Maubourg

OPEN: Summer hours (April through
September) daily 10AM to midnight. Winter
hours (October through March) Wednesday
through Saturday 10AM to 7:30PM, Sunday
10AM to 1:30PM.
SPECIALTY: Ice Cream

While shopping at the rue Cler market, be sure to stop by the boutique of *glacier* Martine Lambert. Her cream-rich ice creams and fruity sorbets show off the best in French produce: raw milk from Normandy (where the ice cream is made), raspberries from the Dordogne, and Valrhona chocolate for the exquisite chocolate sorbet. Vanilla ice cream is the test of a good ice-cream maker, as the custard has no strong flavors to hide behind. And hers comes out a winner: thick, creamy, and a perfect host for the fresh vanilla seeds. The rue Cler boutique is open year-round, though during the warmer months sales are only by the scoop. During the winter months, you can buy ice cream and sorbet in bulk.

LE MOULIN DE LA VIERGE (Invalides)

64, rue Saint-Dominique
Paris 7

MÉTRO: Invalides or La Tour-Maubourg

I love the pretty exterior and ornate window typography of this charming *boulangerie/pâtisserie*. Basile Kamir is a fine baker but he also has a standout variety of unusual and delicious provincial pastries. A favorite is the addictive *carré au miel*, a biscuit-like pastry square topped with honey, sliced almonds, and dried fruit. And don't miss the vanilla-rich *pain aux raisins* (a spiral-shaped pastry made with sweetened dough and raisins); it's one of the best in Paris. See Bakeries, page 230, for full commentary.

LA PÂTISSERIE DES RÊVES (Rue du Bac)

93, rue du Bac
Paris 7
TEL: +33 1 42 84 00 82
lapatisseriedesreves.com

MÉTRO: Sèvres-Babylone or Rue du Bac
OPEN: Tuesday through Saturday 9AM to 8PM.
Sunday 9AM to 4PM.
CLOSED: Monday

Displayed like clouds in a perfect sky, the pastries in this shop are indeed the stuff of dreams. Chef Philippe Conticini, mastermind of this frothy *pâtisserie*, seems to have as much fun with his wares as his clients have in sampling them. The meringue on his *tarte au citron* finishes with a cheerful fillip, as though it's kicking up its heels. It could be, for it hides some of the most delicate lemon cream in the city. The *Paris-Brest* looks like a sugar-dusted flower, and each puffy, round petal is filled not only with pastry cream but with a drizzle of caramel praline, too. Conticini's *tarte Tatin* is out of the ordinary in every way, with its slowly caramelized apple slices, thin layer of streusel, and apple jelly on a tender crust. Baked in a rectangle, it is served by the tall, golden slice. Another rectangle is the *Saint Honoré*, an entire sweet conversation of puff pastry, whipped cream, pastry cream, and *pâte à choux* (*choux* pastry). No matter the choice here, every one has the last word because each is, amazingly, better than the last. Worth trying, too, is the sweet glazed, perfectly baked brioche and the nuttier-than-nutty hazelnut rolls. Both are sensational.

8ᵀᴴ ARRONDISSEMENT

ÉRIC KAYSER (Monceau)

85, boulevard Malesherbes
Paris 8
MÉTRO: Villiers or Miromesnil

Pick up a picnic lunch of freshly made baguette sandwiches (I swear by his whole-grain baguette) and pastries to take to the nearby Parc Monceau, or dine in for breakfast or lunch in the tea salon seating area. See Bakeries, page 221, for full commentary.

▶ *Parc Monceau is an ideal spot for a fine-weather picnic, for it is one of the few parks in Paris where you can lounge on the grass.*

LADURÉE (Champs-Élysées)

75, avenue des Champs-Élysées
Paris 8
TEL: +33 1 40 75 08 75
MÉTRO: George V
OPEN: Monday through Thursday 7:30AM to 11:30PM. Friday 7:30AM to 12:30AM. Saturday 8:30AM to 12:30AM. Sunday 8:30AM to 11:30PM.

What could be more Parisian than dining on pastries in baroque splendor on one of Paris' most iconic streets? This beautiful tea salon will transport you to another, more gracious era.

See page 298 for full commentary.

LADURÉE (Rue Royal)

18, rue Royale
Paris 8
TEL: +33 1 42 60 21 79
MÉTRO: Madeleine
OPEN: Monday through Thursday 8AM to 7:30PM. Friday and Saturday 8AM to 8PM. Sunday and holidays 10AM to 7PM.

Marvel at the sparkling pastry counter aglow under the light of chandeliers at this pristine boutique next door to the original 1862 café.

LA MAISON DU CHOCOLAT (Champs-Élysées)

52, rue François 1er
Paris 8
MÉTRO: Franklin D. Roosevelt

LA MAISON DU CHOCOLAT (Ternes)

225, rue du Faubourg Saint-Honoré
Paris 8
MÉTRO: Ternes

Not only famous for bars of chocolate, La Maison du Chocolat is also known for its crisp and creamy éclairs, a sinful chocolate tart, and a variety of exquisite-looking dessert cakes. See Chocolate Shops, page 271, for full commentary.

PIERRE HERMÉ (Champs-Élysées)

Publicis Drugstore
133, avenue des Champs-Élysées
Paris 8
TEL: +33 1 43 54 47 77

pierreherme.com
MÉTRO: George V or Charles de Gaulle-Étoile
OPEN: Daily 10AM to 10PM

A counter in the Publicis Drugstore rather than a boutique in its own right, this is good to know about when needing to solve a chocolate and macaron emergency if close to the Champs-Élysées. See page 288 for full commentary.

LA PISTACHERIE (Alma)

5, place de l'Alma
Paris 8
TEL: +33 1 44 43 03 26
lapistacherie.com

MÉTRO: Alma-Marceau
OPEN: Sunday through Thursday 11AM to 8PM.
Friday through Saturday 11AM to 8:30PM.

For nut enthusiasts, toasted and candied nuts of every imaginable variety. See page 293 for full commentary.

9TH ARRONDISSEMENT

ANGELINA (Galeries Lafayette)

Galeries Lafayette, first floor women's fashion
40, boulevard Haussmann

Paris 9
MÉTRO: Havre-Caumartin

Not as spectacular as dining in the main Rivoli tea room, but this small Angelina outpost is a good spot to refuel with a hot chocolate or pastry while shopping up a storm at the Galeries Lafayette. See Cafés and Casual Bites, page 129, for full commentary.

ARNAUD DELMONTEL (Martyrs)

39, rue des Martyrs
Paris 9
TEL: +33 1 48 78 29 33
arnaud-delmontel.com

MÉTRO: Saint-Georges or Pigalle
OPEN: Wednesday through Monday
7AM to 8:30PM
CLOSED: Tuesday

Arnaud Delmontel's shop calls out as surely as if it had blinking lights all over the facade. There is something about its choice of lovely, imaginative pastries and golden, crusty loaves of bread that commands you to walk through the door. Delmontel's cakes look like fairy toys, all frilly and

pink and pistachio green. His wild strawberry *vacherin* (meringue and ice cream cake) looks more like a fancy party dress than a cake; the creamy and light *cerisier,* made with black *griottes* cherries and green tea biscuit, is a marvel, and his strawberry macarons, "sandwiches" with fresh berries and cream inside, are a fragile wonder. He offers, too, a chocolate tart with a delicate minty glaze that is worth trying. Pastries are fragile, so it's recommended that you sample them nearby—they aren't travelers. Don't leave this pastry shop and bakery without a crisp, rustic baguette *à la fleur de sel* or a rich, dark *tourte Auvergnate* tucked under your arm.

LE TEMPS DES CERISES

We say "the good old days," while the French call those lovely days past *"le temps des cerises"* (the time of cherries)—referring to those sweet, sunny, fleeting moments of spring.

ÉRIC KAYSER (Galeries Lafayette)

Lafayette Gourmet
40, boulevard Haussmann
Paris 9

MÉTRO: Havre-Caumartin or Chausée d'Antin-Lafayette

Among the various gourmet food stands at this luxury supermarket, you will find dependable bread and pastries from the Kayser empire. See Bakeries, page 221, for full commentary.

LADURÉE (Printemps)

Printemps de la Maison / Printemps de la Mode
64, boulevard Haussmann
Paris 9
TEL: +33 1 42 82 40 10
MÉTRO: Havre-Caumartin

OPEN: Monday through Wednesday and Friday through Saturday 9:30AM to 8PM. Thursday 9:30AM to 10PM.
CLOSED: Sunday

The small boutique on the second floor of Printemps de la Mode (the women's fashion department) has all the charm of Ladurée's larger cafés, where you will find yourself in a different, more gracious era. Here you can pick up macarons, sweet tarts, and Ladurée merchandise. For carryout treats you can also visit the counters on the ground floor of Printemps de la Mode, or the 2nd floor of Printemps de la Beauté/Maison (the beauty and home goods department). See page 298 for full commentary.

LA MAISON DU CHOCOLAT (Madeleine)

8, boulevard de la Madeleine
Paris 9
MÉTRO: Madeleine

LA MAISON DU CHOCOLAT (Printemps)

Printemps Haussmann, 2nd floor
64, boulevard Haussmann
Paris 9
MÉTRO: Havre-Caumartin

Not only famous for bars of chocolate, La Maison du Chocolat is also known for its crisp and creamy éclairs, a sinful chocolate tart, and a variety of exquisite-looking dessert cakes. See Chocolate Shops, page 270, for full commentary.

PÂTISSERIE DES MARTYRS

22, rue des Martyrs
Paris 9
TEL: +33 1 71 18 24 70
sebastiengaudard.fr
patisserie@sebastiengaudard.com

MÉTRO: Notre-Dame de Lorette
OPEN: Tuesday through Friday 10AM to 8PM.
Saturday 9AM to 8PM. Sunday 9AM to 7PM.
CLOSED: Monday

I s it possible that Sébastien Gaudard has created the perfect Parisian *pâtisserie*? Nostalgia reigns in this beautiful rue des Martyrs boutique with its mottled mirrored walls, marble countertops, a 1960s cash register from his parents' pastry shop in Pont-à-Mousson in Alsace, and the *pâtissier*'s

dedication to classic French pastries. But the bright, airy space and the pristine presentation of Gaudard's creations give just the right touch of modernity. Chocolates to your left with zingy fresh ganache (chocolate and cream) fillings, and to your right a lineup of perfectly formed classics: but which to choose? A *Paris-Brest* perhaps, a pastry with perfect density without which the light and airy praline cream might just fly away. The *tarte au citron* is a creamy perfection in a faultless golden pastry case—although it may have lacked a zesty kick if that's what you're after. The *millefeuille* was delicious in its individual parts, but the ratio was off and

it became dry in the mouth. So perhaps not perfect after all, but close enough for me.

▶ *Making the hard choices in life: a* Paris-Brest *or a* millefeuille?

PIERRE HERMÉ (Galeries Lafayette)

Basement and 1st floor of Lafayette Coupole,
and ground floor Lafayette Maison
35/40, boulevard Haussmann
Paris 9
TEL: +33 1 43 54 47 77
pierreherme.com

MÉTRO: Chaussée d'Antin–La Fayette or
Havre-Caumartin
OPEN: Monday through Saturday 9:30AM
to 8PM.
CLOSED: Sunday

Discover the whole range of Pierre Hermé's exquisite chocolate and macaron creations at three different counters in the Galeries Lafayette department store. See page 288 for full commentary.

PÂTE FEUILLETÉE RAPIDE
Quick Puff Pastry

Even though puff pastry can easily be purchased today, there is nothing more rewarding than the sight of your own homemade, golden, multilayered pastry emerging from the oven. The dough is very pliable and easy to roll out, and can easily be frozen in measured batches for future baking. The malt powder or flakes are there to help with browning and add a deeper, distinctive flavor to the pastry. The lemon juice helps tenderize the dough, adds a light touch of acidity, and prevents the dough from darkening before baking.

EQUIPMENT:

A heavy-duty mixer fitted with a flat paddle

INGREDIENTS:

2½ cups (360 g) unbleached all-purpose flour

16 tablespoons (2 sticks; 250 g) unsalted butter, cubed and chilled

2 teaspoons fine sea salt

2 teaspoons malt powder or malt flakes (see Note)

¾ cup (185 ml) ice water

2 teaspoons lemon juice

1. In the bowl of the mixer, combine the flour, butter, salt, and malt powder. Mix at low speed until the butter is evenly distributed but large chunks are still visible, about 30 seconds.

2. Combine the ice water and lemon juice. Add the lemon water to the flour mixture all at once, mixing at low speed just until the dough forms a ball, about 10 seconds. Do not overmix. The dough will be wet and shaggy.

3. Transfer the dough to a generously floured, clean work surface. Gather the dough into a ball. Flatten it into a 6-inch (15-cm) square. Wrap the dough in foil. Refrigerate it for at least 20 minutes.

4. Lightly flour a clean work surface. Remove the dough from the refrigerator and roll it into a 6- by 18-inch (15- by 45-cm) rectangle. Fold the dough in thirds, resulting in a square. Repeat 1 more time, rolling the dough into a rectangle, folding it in thirds. Wrap the dough in foil and refrigerate it for at least 20 minutes.

5. Remove the dough from the refrigerator and roll and fold the dough a third time. Wrap the dough in foil and refrigerate it for at least 20 minutes.

6. Remove the dough from the refrigerator and roll and fold the dough a fourth time. Wrap the dough in the foil and refrigerate it for at least 20 minutes.

7. Remove the dough from the refrigerator and roll and fold the dough a fifth and final time. Cover and refrigerate for 1 hour. The dough is ready to use. If the dough is not to be used right away, I generally roll it out to desired sizes for tarts or various-sized small pastry rounds and refrigerate or freeze it for future use. Wrapped securely, the dough can be stored in the refrigerator for 1 week or in the freezer for 1 month.

ABOUT 1 ⅔ POUNDS (800 G) PASTRY, ENOUGH FOR 2 TARTS

NOTE: Malt powder, known as diastatic malt powder, can be found in Patricia's Pantry at my Amazon store, accessed via PatriciaWells.com.

POPELINI (Martyrs)

44, rue des Martyrs
Paris 9
TEL: +33 1 42 81 35 79

MÉTRO: Saint-Georges
OPEN: Monday through Saturday 11AM to
7:30PM. Sunday 10AM to 3PM.

A tiny shop dedicated solely to *choux à la crème*, small and perfectly formed cream puffs. See page 291 for full commentary.

CAFÉ POUCHKINE

Printemps Mode department store, ground floor
64, boulevard Haussmann
Paris 9
TEL: +33 1 42 82 43 31
cafe-pouchkine.fr

MÉTRO: Havre-Caumartin
OPEN: Monday through Wednesday and
Friday through Saturday 9:35AM to 8PM.
Thursday 9:35AM to 10PM.
CLOSED: Sunday

This is a pastry shop to make you wake up and pay close attention. At first glance—located as it is on the ground floor of Printemps, girded by Prada, Chanel, and Miu Miu—it looks as though it might be part of the decor. But then the aromas of coffee and chocolate, butter and Russian cheesecake, vanilla, fruit, and poppy seeds draw you into this Franco-Russian pleasure parlor, and they don't easily let you go. The genius behind Café Pouchkine's grandiose pastries is Emmanuel Ryon, a French *Meilleur Ouvrier de France* (Best Artisan in France), who most recently has acquired the accolade of working alongside Michelin-starred chef Anne-Sophie Pic on her pastry creations. He is, clearly, a man with a very well-formed sense of perfection, formality, delight, skill, flair, and a love of vivid color. Each cake is costumed for a fancy dress ball, with caramelized squiggles, concentric circles of color and texture, maddeningly perfect layering, intricately posed fruits and medallions of chocolate, dustings of gold and silver. It is all so decorative it can't possibly be good, but *wait!* Each mouthful is a hymn of balance, delicacy, surprise, subtlety, and simple deliciousness, with palate-defying textures from cream, milk, gelatin, butter, sugar, even buckwheat honey. Café Pouchkine is Russia in Paris, Paris in Russia, and yet, really, it's its own flavorful locus somewhere in between.

PÂTISSERIE SADAHARU AOKI (Lafayette Gourmet)

48, boulevard Haussmann
Paris 9
MÉTRO: Chaussée d'Antin–La Fayette or
Havre-Caumartin

OPEN: Monday through Wednesday and
Friday through Saturday 9:30AM to 8PM.
Thursday 9:30AM to 9PM.
CLOSED: Sunday

The fusion of Japanese ingredients with classic French pastry has exquisite results in Aoki's cakes, pastries, and chocolates. See page 297 for full commentary.

12ᵀᴴ ARRONDISSEMENT

BLÉ SUCRÉ

7, rue Antoine Vollon
Paris 12
TEL: +33 1 43 40 77 73
blesucre.fr

MÉTRO: Ledru Rollin
OPEN: Tuesday through Saturday
7AM to 7:30PM. Sunday 7AM to 7:30PM.
CLOSED: Monday

Blé Sucré is a little neighborhood pastry shop with a huge personality. Tucked away on the small Square Trousseau near the *Marché d'Aligre* (a must-visit), it offers a small selection of shiny individual pastries, all of which share a full, round bombe shape that leads you to believe they are full of explosive flavor, cream, chocolate, fruit, or other delightful ingredients. These shiny, detailed little creations are the first clue that whoever creates them is loaded with imagination, flair, and experience. The other clue is that the owner is Fabrice Lebourdat, a well-known veteran of palaces such as the Hôtel Bristol and the Plaza Athénée. Lebourdat has made a big name for himself in this small, friendly spot with simple things— glazed madeleines, crisp little *financiers,* tiny, thin *sablés.* He keeps people coming back with his buttery croissants and *pains au chocolat,* and his selection of fanciful cakes and overflowing tarts. My favorite? His puckery *tarte au citron* and the house specialty, *le Vollon,* with its dark chocolate glaze and meringue–chocolate mousse filling. He also offers an excellent lunchtime menu of a sandwich, pastry, and drink, which you can enjoy on the sidewalk terrace, with an espresso on the side.

▲ *Don't miss the pristine Blé Sucré* patisserie *when in the 12th* arrondissement.

VANDERMEERSCH

278, avenue Daumesnil
Paris 12

MÉTRO: Porte Dorée

An award-winning pastry chef as well as a great baker, Stéphane Vandermeersh is known for his *galette des rois* (a puff pastry pie filled with sweet almond pastry cream), *millefeuille,* and his orange flower water–scented *kouglof* (a sweet yeast cake with almonds and raisins from Alsace). See Bakeries, page 236, for full commentary.

13TH ARRONDISSEMENT

ÉRIC KAYSER (Bercy)

77, quai Panhard-et-Levassor
Paris 13

MÉTRO: Bibliotheque François Mitterand

As Éric Kayser says, "Good bread doesn't lie," and the quality of his breads and pastries is consistently excellent and dependable. See Bakeries, page 221, for full commentary.

14TH ARRONDISSEMENT

LE MOULIN DE LA VIERGE (Plaisance)

105, rue Vercingétorix
Paris 14

MÉTRO: Plaisance or Pernety

This bright red, old-fashioned, turn-of-the-century bakery is worth the trek to the southern edge of town for Basile Kamir's delicious and dense country loaves and his selection of rustic provincial pastries that are some of the best in Paris. (Here's my route: From the Plaisance *métro* take the rue Décres exit, walk down rue d'Alésia, pass rue de l'Ouest, then right on Vercingétorix.) See Bakeries, page 230, for full commentary.

MADELEINES

Lemon Tea Cakes

Fresh lemon zest permeates these elegant, seashell-shaped little cakes, which not only make for good memories but for lovely moments of conscious pleasure! I like to serve these either with coffee or as a dessert, with a homemade sorbet. Today one finds madeleine molds made from various materials, including the classic tin variety as well as from silicone. I am a classical gal, and prefer the results from tin molds. This also happens to be a classic recipe that's very dear to me, and has been included in each version of this book since 1984.

EQUIPMENT:

3 metal madeleine tins, each with molds for 12 madeleines, each mold measuring 3 inches (8 cm) in height; a flour sifter; a heavy-duty electric mixer fitted with a whisk

INGREDIENTS:

Unsalted butter and flour, for the madeleine tins

1½ cups plus 3 tablespoons (230 g) bleached all-purpose flour (do not use unbleached flour)

⅛ teaspoon fine sea salt

Grated zest of 2 lemons, preferably organic, minced

4 large eggs, preferably organic and free-range

1 cup (200 g) unrefined vanilla cane sugar, preferably organic

12 tablespoons (1½ sticks; 180 g) unsalted butter, melted and cooled

1. Butter and generously flour the madeleine tins and place in the refrigerator.

2. Sift together the flour and salt. Add the lemon zest and, with your fingers, mix it into the flour mixture.

3. Place the eggs and vanilla sugar in the bowl of the electric mixer, and whisk until very thick and lemon colored. Fold in the flour mixture. Add the melted butter and mix until all the ingredients are thoroughly incorporated.

4. Refrigerate the batter in the bowl. Both the batter and the prepared tins should be chilled for at least 1 hour or up to 8 hours.

5. Arrange a rack in the top third of the oven and another rack in the bottom third of the oven. Preheat the oven to 425°F (220°C).

6. Spoon a generous tablespoon of batter into each mold, nearly filling each one.

7. Place the tins in the oven and bake until the madeleines are golden brown and puffed, and your fingers leave a slight indentation in the top of each when lightly touched, about 10 to 12 minutes, rotating the tins from one rack to the other and turning them front to back halfway through.

8. Remove the madeleines from their tins as soon as they are baked, and cool them on a wire rack. (Note: Wash the tins immediately with a stiff brush but no detergent so that they retain their seasoning.) The madeleines are best eaten slightly warm or at room temperature the same day they are baked.

MAKES THIRTY-SIX 3-INCH (8-CM) MADELEINES

15ᵀᴴ ARRONDISSEMENT

ÉRIC KAYSER (Émile Zola)

79, rue du Commerce
Paris 15

MÉTRO: Commerce

Éric Kayser may be heading for world domination with stores all over Paris (17 in total), as well as locations in 13 countries around the world, but the quality of his baked goods is excellent and dependable. See Bakeries, page 221, for full commentary.

LE MOULIN DE LA VIERGE (Breteuil)

166, avenue de Suffren
Paris 15

MÉTRO: Sèvres-Lecourbe

Basile Kamir's sweet provincial pastries and unbeatable vanilla-rich *pain aux raisin* (a spiral pastry made from sweetened dough with raisins) are worth seeking out while in the neighborhood. See Bakeries, page 230, for full details.

PIERRE HERMÉ (Pasteur)

185, rue de Vaugirard
Paris 15
TEL: +33 1 47 83 89 97
pierreherme.com

MÉTRO: Pasteur
OPEN: Daily Monday through Thursday 10AM to 7PM. Friday and Saturday 10AM to 8PM. Sunday 9AM to 5PM.

Entering this boutique, decorated in delicate hues of pinks and oranges, is like stepping into one of Pierre Herme's *Ispahan* (a signature flavor combination of rose, lychee, and raspberry) creations. It has the full range of Hermé wonders: pastries, chocolates, and macarons. See page 288 for full commentary.

POILÂNE (Grenelle)

49, boulevard de Grenelle
Paris 15

MÉTRO: Dupleix or Bir-Hakeim

Not only is their bread some of the best you will find in Paris, their caramelized apple *tartelettes* and buttery *sablé* (shortbread) cookies also rank among the finest in the capital. See Bakeries, page 227, for full commentary.

PÂTISSERIE SADAHARU AOKI (Ségur)

25, rue Pérignon
Paris 15
TEL: +33 1 43 06 02 71

MÉTRO: Ségur
OPEN: Monday through Saturday 11AM to 7PM
CLOSED: Sunday and holidays

A Japanese take on French *pâtisserie*. See page 297 for full commentary.

16TH ARRONDISSEMENT

ANGELINA (Jardin d'Acclimatation)

Bois de Boulogne
Paris 16

MÉTRO: Les Sablons

Sip hot chocolate with the angels in this small Angelina café situated in the *Jardin d'Acclimatation*, the children's fun park and petting zoo in the Bois de Boulogne forest. See Cafés and Casual Bites, page 129, for full commentary.

L'ÉCLAIR DE GENIE (Passy)

Galerie Commerciale du Passy Plaza
53, rue de Passy
Paris 16
TEL: +33 9 72 30 59 72

leclairdegenie.com
MÉTRO: Passy or La Muette
OPEN: Tuesday through Sunday 11AM to 7:30PM
CLOSED: Monday

Christophe Adam elevates the humble éclair to contemporary sophistication in his concept store dedicated almost entirely to éclairs. See page 293 for full commentary.

ÉRIC KAYSER (Auteuil)

79, avenue Mozart
Paris 16

MÉTRO: Jasmin

Éric Kayser may be heading for world domination with stores all over Paris (17 in total), as well as locations in 13 countries around the world, but you can always rely on the quality of his breads and pastries. See Bakeries, page 221, for full commentary.

LA MAISON DU CHOCOLAT (Victor Hugo)

120, avenue Victor Hugo
Paris 16

MÉTRO: Victor Hugo

Seek out this Parisian institution for its take on chocolate éclairs and tarts. See Chocolate Shops, page 271, for full commentary.

BOUTIQUE NOURA

33, avenue Pierre 1er de Serbie
Paris 16
noura.com
TEL: +33 1 47 23 02 20

MÉTRO: Iéna or Alma-Marceau
OPEN: Daily 8:30AM to 11:30PM

Lebanese pastries are remarkable for their finesse, and those at Noura are perhaps the most elegant and sophisticated of the North African or Middle Eastern-style pastries that you will find in Paris. The baklava stuffed with either cashews or pine nuts is light and delicately sweetened. The honey cake with almonds is satisfyingly nutty, the date-stuffed butter cookies a sheer delight.

Everything at Noura is fresh, the staff pleasant, the offerings abundantly generous. You can eat your pastries *sur place*, or take them away.

LA PÂTISSERIE DES RÊVES (Victor Hugo)

111, rue de Longchamp
Paris 16
TEL: +33 1 47 04 00 24
MÉTRO: Rue de la Pompe or Victor Hugo

OPEN: Tuesday through Friday 10AM to 8PM.
Saturday and Sunday 9AM to 8PM.
CLOSED: Monday

A pastry shop not to be missed, as the rear of this store is a tearoom that leads to an outdoor garden terrace, a rare commodity in Paris. See page 303 for full commentary.

PIERRE HERMÉ (Passy)

58, avenue Paul Doumer
Paris 16
TEL: +33 1 43 54 47 77
pierreherme.com

MÉTRO: Rue de la Pompe or Passy
OPEN: Tuesday through Sunday 10AM to 7:30PM. Monday 1 to 7:30PM.
CLOSED: Monday morning

This little boutique sells only Hermé's macarons and chocolates, but his remarkable pastries can be ordered in the shop or by phone with 24 hours notice. See page 288 for full commentary.

17TH ARRONDISSEMENT

ANGELINA (Palais du Congrès)

2, place de la Porte Maillot
Paris 17

MÉTRO: Porte Maillot

A delicious rest stop before or after shopping at the Galeries Gourmands luxury supermarket. See Cafés and Causal Bites, page 129, for full commentary.

ARNAUD DELMONTEL (Villiers)

25, rue de Lévis
Paris 17
TEL: +33 1 42 27 15 45
MÉTRO: Villiers

OPEN: Wednesday through Monday 7AM to 8:30PM
CLOSED: Tuesday

It's almost impossible to pass a Delmontel shop without stopping to gaze in at his beautiful pastry creations. See page 305 for full commentary.

▲ *A popular bakery terrace in the Marais neighborhood.*

ÉRIC KAYSER (Ternes)

19, avenue des Ternes   **MÉTRO**: Ternes
Paris 17

Éric Kayser may be heading for world domination with his 17 stores in Paris and outposts in 13 countries worldwide, but the quality of his baked goods remains impeccable. See Bakeries, page 221, for full commentary.

GONTRAN CHERRIER (Wagram)

8, rue Juliette-Lamber   **MÉTRO**: Wagram
Paris 17

This is the place to head to for a flaky croissant or a zesty *tarte au citron* while in the Wagram neighborhood. See Bakeries, page 242, for full commentary.

LE MOULIN DE LA VIERGE (Batignolles)

6, rue de Lévis   **MÉTRO**: Villiers
Paris 17

Visit this traditional *boulangerie/pâtisserie*, not far from the beautiful and historic Parc Monceau. La Moulin de la Vierge also has a small stand at the Saturday morning organic Batignolles market (see Markets, page 000). See Bakeries, page 230, for full commentary.

TARTE AU CHOCOLAT, MIEL, ET NOIX DE GONTRAN CHERRIER

Gontran Cherrier's Chocolate, Honey, and Nut Tart

Gontran Cherrier is one of Paris's best bakers and pastry chefs and I never leave his boutique without picking up at least half a dozen samples from the buffetlike counter of his charming, bustling *boulangerie/pâtisserie*. This chocolate tart is totally decadent and thoroughly delicious. A very slim wedge is truly satisfying.

EQUIPMENT:

A 10-inch (25-cm) tart pan with a removable bottom

INGREDIENTS:

A 14-ounce (400-g) sheet of Quick Puff Pastry (page 308), well chilled, or purchased all-butter puff pastry, thawed if frozen (see Note)

3 tablespoons (45 g) unsalted butter

½ cup (90 g) light brown sugar, lightly packed

½ teaspoon fine sea salt

1 tablespoon (15 g) honey

3 tablespoons (45 g) maple syrup

2 tablespoons coarsely ground walnuts

2 tablespoons coarsely ground almonds

2 tablespoons coarsely ground hazelnuts

2 tablespoons minced dried apricots, preferably organic

2 tablespoons minced dried figs, preferably organic

2 tablespoons minced candied lemon or orange peel, preferably organic

1 cup (250 ml) heavy (whipping) cream

8 ounces (250 g) bittersweet chocolate, such as Valrhona Guanaja 70%, broken into pieces

1. Center a rack in the oven. Preheat the oven to 375°F (190°C).

2. On a well-floured surface, roll the pastry into a 13-inch (33-cm) round.

3. Arrange the pastry in the tart pan, trimming the edges so that the pastry neatly fits the pan.

4. In a saucepan, combine the butter and brown sugar over low heat just until melted and blended. Stir to blend. Over low heat, stir in the salt, honey, and maple syrup. Remove the pan from the heat. Spread the mixture over the bottom of the prepared pastry. Sprinkle with all the nuts, and the dried and candied fruit.

5. Place in the center of the oven and bake until the crust is dark golden and the topping is bubbly, 15 to 20 minutes. Let cool for 25 minutes.

6. Meanwhile, prepare the ganache topping. In a saucepan, heat the cream over medium heat. Add the chocolate pieces and stir until they melt. Spread the ganache over the top of the tart. Refrigerate for at least 3 hours before serving, then cut into very thin wedges.

16 SERVINGS

NOTE: In France my choice for purchased all-butter puff pastry is Marie's brand. In the United States, I favor Dufour brand frozen puff pastry, available at most specialty supermarkets. Be sure to leave ample time—at least 6 hours—for thawing frozen dough.

18TH ARRONDISSEMENT

ARNAUD DEMONTEL (Montmartre)

57, rue Damrémont
Paris 18
TEL: +33 1 42 64 59 63
MÉTRO: Lamarck-Caulaincourt

OPEN: Tuesday through Saturday 7AM to
8:30PM
CLOSED: Sunday and Monday

While the *viennoiseries* (sweet breakfast pastries) here might leave you indifferent, the beautifully created sweet dessert pastries will have you pressing your nose against the window. See page 305 for full commentary.

GONTRAN CHERRIER (Montmartre)

22, rue Caulaincourt
Paris 18

MÉTRO: Lamarck-Caulaincourt or Blanche

Flaky croissants and irresistible pastries are among the lineup at this bright and airy Montmartre *pâtisserie/boulangerie*. See Bakeries, page 242, for full commentary.

AT A GLANCE

1ST ARRONDISSEMENT

Angelina (Musée du Louvre)
Angelina (Rivoli)
Éric Kayser (Opéra)
Gosselin (Saint-Honoré)
Hugo & Victor (Marché
    Saint-Honoré)
Boulangerie Jean-Noël Julien
    (Saint-Honoré)
La Maison du Chocolat
    (Louvre)
Pierre Hermé (Concorde)

2ND ARRONDISSEMENT

L'Atelier de L'Éclair
Éric Kayser (Bourse)
Pierre Hermé (Opéra)

3RD ARRONDISSEMENT

Meert
Pain de Sucre
Popelini (Marais)

4TH ARRONDISSEMENT

Berthillon
L'Éclair de Génie (Marais)
Boulangerie Jean-Noël Julien
    (Hôtel de Ville)
La Pistacherie (Rambuteau)
Pozzetto

5TH ARRONDISSEMENT

Carl Marletti
Pâtisserie Ciel
Éric Kayser (Sorbonne)
Éric Kayser (Sorbonne II)
Pâtisserie Sadaharu Aoki
    (Port-Royal)

6TH ARRONDISSEMENT

Éric Kayser (Luxembourg)
Éric Kayser (Montparnasse)
Éric Kayser (Odéon)
Grom
Boulangerie Jean-Noël Julien
    (Luxembourg)
Ladurée (Saint-Germain)
La Maison du Chou
Pierre Hermé (Saint-Germain)

Poilâne (Cherche-Midi)
Pâtisserie Sadaharu Aoki
    (Saint-Placide)

7TH ARRONDISSEMENT

Éric Kayser (Musée d'Orsay)
Gosselin (Musée d'Orsay)
Hugo & Victor (Raspail)
Pâtisserie Jean Millet
La Maison du Chocolat
    (Sèvres-Babylone)
Martine Lambert
Le Moulin de la Vierge
    (Invalides)
La Pâtisserie des Rêves
    (Rue du Bac)

8TH ARRONDISSEMENT

Éric Kayser (Monceau)
Ladurée (Champs-Élysées)
Ladurée (Rue Royal)
La Maison du Chocolat
    (Champs-Élysées)
La Maison du Chocolat
    (Ternes)
Pierre Hermé (Champs-
    Élysées)
La Pistacherie (Alma)

9TH ARRONDISSEMENT

Angelina (Galeries Lafayette)
Arnaud Delmontel (Martyrs)
Éric Kayser (Galeries
    Lafayette)
Ladurée (Printemps)
La Maison du Chocolat
    (Madeleine)
La Maison du Chocolat
    (Printemps)
Pâtisserie des Martyrs
Pierre Hermé
    (Galeries Lafayette)
Popelini (Martyrs)
Café Pouchkine
Pâtisserie Sadaharu Aoki
    (Lafayette Gourmet)

12TH ARRONDISSEMENT

Blé Sucré
Vandermeersch

13TH ARRONDISSEMENT

Éric Kayser (Bercy)

14TH ARRONDISSEMENT

Le Moulin de la Vierge
    (Plaisance)

15TH ARRONDISSEMENT

Éric Kayser (Émile Zola)
Le Moulin de la Vierge
    (Breteuil)
Pierre Hermé (Pasteur)
Poilâne (Grenelle)
Pâtisserie Sadaharu Aoki
    (Ségur)

16TH ARRONDISSEMENT

Angelina (Jardin
    d'Acclimatation)
L'Éclair de Génie (Passy)
Éric Kayser (Auteuil)
La Maison du Chocolat
    (Victor Hugo)
Boutique Noura
La Pâtisserie des Rêves
    (Victor Hugo)
Pierre Hermé (Passy)

17TH ARRONDISSEMENT

Angelina (Palais du Congrès)
Arnaud Delmontel (Villiers)
Éric Kayser (Ternes)
Gontran Cherrier (Wagram)
Le Moulin de la Vierge
    (Batignolles)

18TH ARRONDISSEMENT

Arnaud Delmontel
    (Montmartre)
Gontran Cherrier
    (Montmartre)

WINE SHOPS

CAVES À VIN

Parisian wine lovers are lucky to have such an array of devoted and intelligent wine-shop owners, people with a passion for finding just the right bottle at the right price for any occasion. Most of the shops listed here are small and specialized, reflecting the personal tastes of their owners. They are not wine supermarkets, so don't expect to find an infinite selection. Rather, think of each visit as a step toward a greater understanding and appreciation of wine. Parisian wine shops each have their own personality and clientele. From the romantic, old-Paris Legrande Fille & Fils in one of the city's historic *passages,* to the funky Les Caves du Marais, and the always-on-top-of-it La Dernière Goutte (hosting regular weekend wine tastings with independent French winemakers), there is no reason to ever go thirsty in Paris. ❧

WHAT'S NATURAL ABOUT NATURAL WINES?

Throughout France and in Parisian wine bars and wine shops, the trend has been to favor "natural" wines. While there is no legal definition of what a natural wine must be, generally it is a wine made in small quantities by an independent producer, with low-yielding vineyards, and grapes that are organically or biodynamically grown and hand-harvested. As a rule, the wines are neither filtered nor fined (a process of adding a product to improve clarity, color, bouquet, and/or flavor). There should be no added sugars, no adjustments for acidity. Natural winemakers intervene as little as possible in the winemaking process, using only natural, indigenous yeasts and adding a minimal amount of sulfur dioxide—or none at all—traditionally used in winemaking to stabilize the wine and as an insurance policy that the wine will not re-ferment in the bottle.

But the "natural" label poses many problems. First, it forces consumers to assume that any wine lacking the "natural" label is unnatural. All too often defenders of the trend jump on the bandwagon simply because of the label, not taking into account the fact that the quality of many of these wines is often under par, a good number of them resembling fizzy fruit juice.

As with all products, a label is simply an indicator. I know winemakers who make organic wines but do not label them as such, saying, "I want people to buy my wine because it's mine, not because it is organic."

So what is the consumer to do? Wine lovers need to do a great deal of experimentation, sampling a good number of wines until settling on a vineyard and a winemaker whose product fits the definition of a pleasing beverage. "Natural" is not a trend that is going to go away, so rather than fighting the trend, embrace it with careful research.

1ST ARRONDISSEMENT

JUVENILES

47, rue de Richelieu
Paris 1
TEL: +33 1 42 97 46 49
MÉTRO: Palais-Royal–Musée du Louvre,

Bourse, or Pyramides
OPEN: Monday 6 to 11PM. Tuesday through Saturday noon to 11PM.
CLOSED: Sunday, and Monday lunch

Scotsman Tim Johnston has made Juveniles a Parisian institution, not just for having a great time at the table, with his sturdy bistro fare (see Wine Bars, page 170), but also for sharing in his well-selected wines. The wine shop/bistro is always stacked to the ceiling with his latest finds, which might include new discoveries from the Rhône, Italy, Australia, or Lebanon. He has a good stock of sherry and whiskey, as well as a variety of sparkling wines.

2ND ARRONDISSEMENT

LEGRANDE FILLE & FILS

1, rue de la Banque
Paris 2
TEL: +33 1 42 60 07 12
caves-legrand.com
info@caves-legrand.com

MÉTRO: Bourse or Pyramides
OPEN: Monday 11AM to 7PM, Tuesday through Friday 10AM to 7:30PM, Saturday 10AM to 7PM
CLOSED: Sunday

There are several reasons to go out of your way to visit this lovely, well-stocked wine shop. One reason, of course, is the carefully chosen selection of wines (more than 700 from around the world), but you can also order from their website and have wine delivered anywhere in Paris! Regular tastings might include wines from the famed Domaine Dagueneau in the Loire, Le Cos des Lambrays in Burgundy, or Domaine Sottimano in the Piedmont.

4TH ARRONDISSEMENT

LES CAVES DU MARAIS

64, rue Francois Miron
Paris 4
TEL: +33 1 42 78 54 64
MÉTRO: Saint-Paul or Pont Marie

OPEN: Tuesday through Saturday 10:30AM to 1PM and 4 to 8PM
CLOSED: Sunday and Monday

For more than two decades the chatty, outgoing owner Jean-Jacques Bailly has held court in this crammed-to-the-rafters little wine shop, a place that certainly expresses his tastes. His wife is Australian and he lived there for many years, so his command of English is excellent. All the best Northern and Southern Rhônes are there, including names like Cuilleron, Clape, Janasse, Chaupin, Beaucastel, and Pierre Usseglio. Bailly introduced me to some fine unsulfured wines from Alsace, all from the Binner family. I loved the clean lines of the Pinot Noir, the wine made biodynamically, unfiltered, with no sulfites added. And I love the winemaker's dedication to replace the traditional cork seal: His stoppers are made of clean, elegant, modern glass.

▶ *A view of the Seine and Notre Dame from the Left Bank.*

5TH ARRONDISSEMENT

DE VINIS ILLUSTRIBUS

48, rue de la Montagne-Sainte-Geneviève
Paris 5
TEL: +33 1 43 36 12 12
devinis.fr
lionel.michelin@devinis.fr

MÉTRO: Cardinal Lemoine or Maubert-Mutualité
OPEN: Monday through Saturday 2 to 7PM
CLOSED: Sunday
WINE TASTINGS: By reservation 7 days a week

For those who have been around long enough to remember, this address in the 5th *arrondissement* was once the domain of Jean-Baptiste Besse, who in 1932 opened what I once described as "a tumble-down corner grocery." I remember ordering a bottle of wine and Monsieur Besse climbing his

wooden ladder to reach the prize, stocked almost at the ceiling. Today this gem of a shop is the domain of Lionel Michelin, a man passionate about wine and wine knowledge. He has impeccably restored the beautifully appointed shop, with its carefully lit walls of stone, complete with a cellar for wine tastings in both English and French. The outgoing Michelin will happily search out the wine of your dreams and even sit down and share it with you!

▶ *Owner Lionel Michelin will happily share his recommendations with you.*

6TH ARRONDISSEMENT

LA DERNIÈRE GOUTTE

6, rue Bourbon le Château
Paris 6
TEL: +33 1 43 29 11 62
ladernieregoutte.net
goutte@club-internet.fr
MÉTRO: Saint-Germain-des-Prés, Mabillon, or Odéon

OPEN: Sunday 11AM to 7PM, Monday 3 to 8PM, Tuesday through Friday 10:30AM to 1:30PM and 3 to 8PM, Saturday 10:30AM to 8PM
WINE TASTINGS: Friday and Saturday afternoons

My good friend Juan Sanchez moved his wine shop into the Saint-Germain neighborhood about the same time that I installed my cooking school studio there in the mid-1990s, and we have spent many an hour together since, either talking wine, sipping it, or sharing our passions for wine and food. Juan has a rare palate and is a great teacher, and I have probably learned more about wine from him than I have from anyone else. You can count on quality here, with a carefully sourced selection of largely organic or biodynamic wines from small independent winemakers. My list of favorites is long, but they include the everyday white Picpoul de Pinet from Domaine Félines Jourdan in the Languedoc; the always-dependable red Cairanne Côtes-du-Rhône-Villages from Domaine Oratoire St. Martin; the 100 percent Chardonnay Mâcon-Fuissé from Domaine la Soufrandise; and Cédric Bouchard's irresistible line of Champagnes. The shop offers a small but unique selection of wineglasses, wine accoutrements, artisanal steak knives, olive oil, vinegars, and chocolate. Check the website for details of Friday afternoon wine and cheese tastings and Saturday tastings with the winemakers. Juan will also arrange special group wine tastings in the shop.

▼ *La Dernière Goutte, my go-to wine shop in the 6th* arrondissement.

PARISIAN VINEYARDS

Vineyards in Paris: Their history dates back to the 12th century, when a Benedictine abbey built on the hills of Montmartre included a wine-press operated by the nuns. Other vineyards dotted the city and the wines they produced found their way to the noblest tables. (It was, in fact, the white claret from the suburb of Suresnes that François I said was "as light as a tear in the eye.") A white wine from Montmartre gave its name—la Goutte d'Or, golden drop—to what is now a neighborhood in the 18th arrondissement.

Today the tradition continues: Tucked away in the hills of Montmartre in north central Paris there is a minuscule vineyard of 1,900 vines with an amazing number of varieties of grapes (27), though mainly red Gamay and Pinot Noir. The vineyard is owned by the city of Paris, and annually, this plot produces about 500 bottles of a red wine simply labeled Clos Montmartre—clos translating as a vineyard enclosed by fences, gates, or other types of barriers. The current vines were planted in 1933 by the city of Paris.

The harvest party, or Fête des Vendanges, is a traditional celebration full of pageantry (parades, fireworks, street performances, concerts, and giant picnics) that takes place the first Saturday of October, following the grape harvest. For the vinification itself, the basement of the local town hall, or mairie, of the 18th arrondissement is turned into a winemaking cellar, and later bottles from the previous vintage are sold at auction.

A second vineyard lies in the suburban community of Suresnes, on the western boundary of the city of Paris. Once considered the best vineyard in the Île-de-France region that includes Paris, the Suresnes vines were replanted in 1965 with mostly Chardonnay grapes, and it is the only commercial vineyard in the Paris suburbs.

Legend has it that in 918 AD, the head of the Benedictine abbey in Paris's Saint-Germain-des-Prés was presented the vineyard as a gift from Charles III the Simple.

After the 14th-century Hundred Years War, the wines of Suresnes were considered the best drink to treat all illnesses. Soon the wines of Suresnes became the favorite vin de soif, or daily drinking wines, of the kings of France, including Henri IV.

Today the vineyard is classified as a site protected by the government, to be preserved indefinitely. It produces about 6,000 bottles of white Clos du Pas-Saint-Maurice, and bottles from the previous vintage are sold on the first Saturday morning of October at the village's central market (place du 8 Mai 1945), and the first Sunday of October beginning at noon near the Théatre de Suresnes Jean Vilar (place Stalingrad).

In 1983, in an apparent effort to revitalize its illustrious wine heritage, the city of Paris planted another 720 vines of Pinot Noir grapes on the south side of the Georges-Brassens Square in the 15th arrondissement park built on the site of the former stockyards. The vineyard produces a total of 300 bottles of red wine, carefully aged in oak casks. The wine is sold at the mairie, the 15th arrondissement city hall.

MONTMARTRE: MAIRIE OF THE 18TH ARRONDISSEMENT
1, rue Jules-Joffrin
Paris 18
TEL: + 33 1 42 52 42 00
MÉTRO: Jules Joffrin

SURESNES: MAIRIE DE SURESNES
2, rue Carnot
92150 Suresnes
TEL: +33 1 41 18 19 20
suresnes.fr

Accessible via RER A from Châtelet–Les Halles to La Defense (Grande Arche), changing to Local SNCF L, line 48. The stop is Suresnes–Mont Valérien.

CLOS DE MORILLONS: MAIRIE OF THE 15TH ARRONDISSEMENT
31, rue Péclet
Paris 15
TEL: +33 1 48 28 40 12
MÉTRO: Vaugirard

7TH ARRONDISSEMENT

LA CAVE DE JOËL ROBUCHON

3, rue Paul-Louis Courier
Paris 7
TEL: +33 1 42 22 11 02
joel-robuchon.net/fr/boutique/

laboutique@lacavedejoelrobuchon.com
MÉTRO: Rue du Bac
OPEN: Monday through Saturday 11AM to 9PM
CLOSED: Sunday

Just a few steps from the famed L'Atelier de Joël Robuchon Saint-Germain (see Restaurants, page 157), you'll find this tidy shop loaded with wines selected by Robuchon's longtime *sommelier* Antoine Hernandez.

Some wines I love here include anything from Remy Pedreno's Roc d'Anglade in the Languedoc, the Gevrey-Chambertin Village from the Domaine de la Vougeraie, and the Riesling from Weingut Sander in Germany. It's nice to know that they are open until 9PM, for those later shoppers.

LES GRANDES CAVES (Invalides)

70, rue Saint-Dominque
Paris 7
TEL: +33 1 47 05 69 28
lesgrandescaves.fr

MÉTRO: Solférino or Invalides
OPEN: Monday through Saturday
10AM to 1PM and 3:30 to 7:15PM,
Sunday 9:30AM to 1PM

With four shops in Paris, this family-owned business, which started on the outskirts of Paris in Clichy in 1946, offers a stunning selection of wines from around the world, and free delivery within Paris. With more than 1,500 selections, their choices from France include Billecart-Salmon and Egly-Ouriet Champagne, Dagueneu from the Loire, Domaine Leflaive and Anne Gros in Burgundy, Domaine de Marcoux in the Southern Rhône, Roc d'Anglade in the Languedoc, as well as wines from Italy, Argentina, Australia, and New Zealand.

LE LIVRE DE CAVE

3, rue Casimir-Périer
Paris 7
TEL: +33 9 51 20 00 62
lelivredecave.com
frederic.beal@lelivredecave.com

MÉTRO: Solférino
OPEN: Monday 7 to 9PM, Tuesday through
Friday 10AM to 2PM and 4 to 9PM,
Saturday 10AM to 9PM, Sunday 11AM to 1:30PM

Wine lovers in search of bottles old and rare would do well to make a visit to Frédéric Beal's shop or website. Nestled in the lovely corner of the 7th near the Basilique Sainte-Clotilde, this boutique specializes in old Bordeaux and Champagnes. Services include wine tastings in the cellar of the shop, organization of personal wine cellars, and estimates on personal wine collections.

8ᵀᴴ ARRONDISSEMENT

CAVES AUGÉ

16, boulevard Haussmann
Paris 8
TEL: +33 1 45 22 16 97
cavesauge.com
cavesauge@wanadoo.fr

MÉTRO: Miromesnil or Saint-Augustin
OPEN: Monday through Saturday 10AM to 7:30PM
CLOSED: Sunday
WINE TASTINGS: Regularly; check website

This elegant, classic wine shop, with its black marble front and antique gold lettering, offers not just a carefully chosen selection of wines but also a fine assortment of port, Cognac, Armagnac, Champagne, vodka, Calvados, and even absinthe. The list of offerings is encyclopedic, and includes Egly-Ouriet Champagne and some of my personal favorites, Michèle Aubéry Laurent's Domaine Gramenon and Vieille Julienne from the Southern Rhône. Wines from outside France include selections from Italy, Spain, Chile, Greece, New Zealand, Switzerland, Australia, Morocco, Israel, Lebanon, and Hungary. Check the website for the entire listing as well as regular tastings.

▶ *Dust, age, and anticipation.*

LES CAVES DE TAILLEVENT

199, rue du Faubourg Saint-Honoré
Paris 8
TEL: +33 1 45 61 14 09
taillevent.com/les-caves-de-taillevent-boutique
lescavesparis@taillevent.com
MÉTRO: Ternes or Courcelles

OPEN: Monday through Saturday 10AM to 7:30PM
CLOSED: Sunday
WINE TASTINGS: Regularly; check website. Private tastings by arrangement.

You can walk into this trustworthy shop with your eyes closed, and among the more than 1,500 wine offerings, find happiness. The shop has been described as a "window into the winemaking of France." All the greats are here, from Coche-Dury to Zind-Humbrecht, along with ancient Armagnacs and Cognacs. Wine tastings with food are held regularly, while private tastings can be arranged.

CURNONSKY

Curnonsky, the French food critic named "prince of gastronomes" by his peers, designated the five best white wines in France, perhaps the world:

CHÂTEAU D'YQUEM: "The matchless sweet wine: true liquid gold."

CHÂTEAU-CHALON: "The prince of the Jura yellow wines, full-bodied, with the penetrating bouquet of walnuts."

CHÂTEAU-GRILLET: "The legendary wine of the Côtes-du-Rhône, with a stunning aroma of violets and wildflowers; as changing as a pretty woman."

MONTRACHET: "The splendid lord of Burgundy, which Alexander Dumas counseled to drink, bareheaded, while kneeling."

SAVENNIÈRES COULÉES DE SERRANT: "The dazzling dry wine from the vineyards of the Loire."

AU VERGER DE LA MADELEINE

4, boulevard Malesherbes
Paris 8
TEL: +33 1 42 65 51 99
verger-madeleine.com

MÉTRO: Madeleine
OPEN: Monday through Saturday 10AM to 8PM
CLOSED: Sunday

This classic wine shop has been near the Madeleine since 1932, and it won't disappoint. You'll find Comte Lafon Montrachet, as well as a large selection of Leflaive Burgundies, and Rayas and Clos des Papes from Châteauneuf-du-Pape.

11TH ARRONDISSEMENT

LA CAVE LE VERRE VOLÉ

38, rue Oberkampf
Paris 11
TEL: +33 1 43 14 99 46
leverrevole.fr
leverrevole@wooz.com

MÉTRO: Oberkampf or Parmentier
OPEN: Daily 11AM to 3PM and 4:40 to 8PM
SPECIALTY: Natural wines

Part of a culinary triumvirate that includes a wine shop, a bistro, and an *épicerie,* this spot should help any wine lover discover something new. There's a huge selection of varied wines, many from young winemakers heralding "natural" wines with no added sulfur. Some wines I've loved include Thierry Puzelat's gamay from Clos du Tue-Boeuf, the Beaumes-de-Venise from the Ferme Saint Martin, various offerings from Domaine Gramenon, and a selection of well-priced wines from the progressive cooperative Cave des d'Estezargues in the Gard.

14ᵀᴴ ARRONDISSEMENT

CAVE DES GRANDS VINS

144, boulevard du Montparnasse
Paris 14
TEL: +33 1 43 20 89 38
cave-des-grands-vins.com
contact@cavedesgrandsvins.fr

MÉTRO: Vavin
OPEN: Monday 4 to 7:45PM, Tuesday through Saturday 10AM to 7:45PM
CLOSED: Sunday

If you are searching for a rare Romanée Conti, a Richbourg, a La Tâche, this is the place for you. But you'll also find Château de Beaucastel Châteauneuf-du-Pape, De Vogüe Chambolle-Musigny, Clos de Tart from Morey-Saint-Denis, and Domaine Dagueneau from Pouilly-Fumé. The shop offers a service that buys wines from personal cellars.

16ᵀᴴ ARRONDISSEMENT

LES GRANDES CAVES (La Muette)

38, rue de l'Annonciation
Paris 16
TEL: +33 1 45 25 80 97
MÉTRO: La Muette

OPEN: Monday through Saturday 10AM to 1PM and 3:30 to 7:15PM, Sunday 9:30AM to 1PM

A stunning selection of wines from around the world. See page 327 for full commentary.

VINS RARES PETER THUSTRUP

11–13, rue Pergolèse
Paris 16
TEL: +33 1 45 01 46 00
vins-rares.fr

infos@vins-rares.fr
MÉTRO: Argentine
OPEN: By appointment only

Peter Thustrup has been a fixture in the Paris wine world since 1983. And since 1977 he has kept notes on every single wine he has sampled, logging in more than 25,000 commentaries. While he has no shop, he searches out and purchases rare wines for connoisseurs—bottles that he calls "les introuvables," or wines that are virtually impossible to find in the open market. By appointment, Thustrup regularly organizes custom-designed wine tastings.

17TH ARRONDISSEMENT

CAVES PETRISSANS

30, bis avenue Niel
Paris 17
TEL: +33 1 42 27 52 03
cavespetrissans.fr
MÉTRO: Ternes or Pereire

OPEN: Monday through Friday 12:15 to 2:15PM
and 7:30 to 10:15PM
CLOSED: Saturday, Sunday, public holidays,
and August

This old-fashioned, family-run neighborhood wine shop/wine bar offers some fine selections, including Vacheron's Sancerre, Coudoulet de Beaucastel from the Southern Rhône, J. M. Gerin's Condrieu from the Northern Rhône, and Roblet Monnot's Volnay from Burgundy.

LES GRANDES CAVES (Poncelet)

9, rue Poncelet
Paris 17
TEL: +33 1 43 80 40 37
MÉTRO: Ternes

OPEN: Monday 4 to 7:30PM, Tuesday through
Saturday 9:30AM to 2PM and 3 to 7:30PM,
Sunday 9:30AM to 1:30PM

This family-run business has four shops in Paris, and a stunning selection of over 1,500 wines from around the world. See page 327 for full commentary.

18ᵀᴴ ARRONDISSEMENT

18 SUR VIN

154, rue Ordener
Paris 18
TEL: +33 9 81 44 10 16
18survin.com
alban.lecam@18survin.com
MÉTRO: Jules Joffrin

OPEN: Monday 5 to 9PM. Tuesday through Thursday 10:30AM to 1:30PM and 4:30 to 9PM. Friday 4 to 9PM. Saturday 10AM to 9PM.
CLOSED: Sunday
SPECIALTY: Nautral wines

Owner Albon Le Cam is committed to offering a carefully selected assortment of independently produced wines—he can tell you the story of almost every winemaker behind each bottle—made as naturally as possible, largely following organic and biodynamic rules, adding the least possible amount of sulfites when bottling. Some of his choices include those from the passionate Languedoc winemaker Leon Barral, the Chenin Blanc from Jean-Pierre Robinot's Domaine L'Angevin, the mineral-rich selections from Gérard Eyraud's Domaine de Rapatel near Nimes, and Isabelle Jolly and Jean-Luc Cossart's wines from the Roussillon.

LES GRANDES CAVES (Damrémont)

63, rue Damrémont
Paris 18
TEL: +33 1 53 41 06 77
MÉTRO: Lamarck-Caulaincourt

OPEN: Monday through Saturday 10AM to 1PM and 3:30 to 7:15PM, Sunday 9:30AM to 1PM

A stunning array of wines from around the world. See page 327 for full commentary.

AT A GLANCE

1ST ARRONDISSEMENT

Juveniles

2ND ARRONDISSEMENT

Legrande Fille & Fils

4TH ARRONDISSEMENT

Les Caves du Marais

5TH ARRONDISSEMENT

De Vinis Illustribus

6TH ARRONDISSEMENT

La Dernière Goutte

7TH ARRONDISSEMENT

La Cave de Joël Robuchon
Les Grandes Caves (Invalides)
Le Livre de Cave

8TH ARRONDISSEMENT

Caves Augé
Les Caves de Taillevent
Au Verger de la Madeleine

11TH ARRONDISSEMENT

La Cave Le Verre Volé

14TH ARRONDISSEMENT

Cave des Grands Vins

16TH ARRONDISSEMENT

Les Grandes Caves
  (La Muette)
Vins Rares Peter Thustrup

17TH ARRONDISSEMENT

Caves Petrissans
Les Grandes Caves (Poncelet)

18TH ARRONDISSEMENT

18 Sur Vin
Les Grandes Caves
  (Damrémont)

SPECIALTY FOOD SHOPS

SPECIALITÉS GASTRONOMIQUES

The specialty food shops of Paris, now more than ever, offer a veritable selection of rare, unusual, and wonderful food items from all corners of the world. These shops are places to find your favorite traditional ingredients, and to discover rarely found and delicious new foods. Along with the classic *foie gras* and French mustard, sample buckwheat honey the color of ink, hand-rolled couscous from an organic farm in Tunisia, fragrant wild pepper from Madagascar, or the Sicilian olive oils used by some of Paris's most famous chefs. From fresh black truffles to salted butter caramels, from the exotic to the commonplace, here is a list of favorite Paris food shops to tantalize your taste buds. ❧

1ˢᵀ ARRONDISSEMENT

LE COMPTOIR DE TUNISIE

TUNISIAN GOURMET FOODS
30, rue de Richelieu
Paris 1
TEL: +33 1 42 97 14 04
lecomptoirdetunisie.com

contact@lecomptoirdetunisie.com
MÉTRO: Pyramides or Palais Royal–Musée du Louvre
OPEN: Monday through Saturday 11AM to 7PM
CLOSED: Sunday

All the products sold at this Tunisian gourmet food shop are sourced from the family-run Moulins Mahjoub in northern Tunisia. Everything is organic and prepared using traditional methods. Try a jar of traditional *harissa* or cured wild mountain capers. Once you've had their hand-rolled couscous, you'll never settle for the supermarket variety again.

MARIAGE FRÈRES (Louvre)

TEA SHOP / TEA SALON
Carrousel du Louvre
99, rue de Rivoli
Paris 1
TEL: +33 1 40 20 18 54

mariagefreres.com
info@mariagefreres.com
MÉTRO: Palais Royal–Musée du Louvre
OPEN: Daily 10AM to 8PM (*salon de thé* noon to 7PM)

Mariage Frères is one of France's oldest and most respected tea importers, boasting possibly the world's largest tea collection. The tea emporium evokes the world of old colonial France with its dark wooden counters and wall-to-wall shelves of classical Mariage Frères tea canisters. The company meticulously researches and imports the highest quality teas, offering a selection of over 600 types of tea from all corners of the globe: China, India, Nepal, Sri Lanka, Japan, Thailand, Kenya,

MARIAGE FRÈRES'S 5 GOLDEN RULES OF MAKING TEA

Preheat your teapot and tea strainer or filter with boiling water.

Place one teaspoon of tea per cup into the warm tea strainer or filter, letting the leaves steamed by the boiling water begin to release their aroma.

Fill the teapot by pouring hot water (the temperature of the water varying with the type of tea) over the tea leaves until they are covered.

Leave the tea to infuse for several minutes, ranging from 1 to 15 minutes depending on the type of tea.

Remove the tea strainer or filter and stir the tea before serving—this is a very important step.

Mauritius, Rwanda, South Africa, Australia, and New Zealand. They also have an impressive selection of tea blends and perfumed teas. Serious and knowledgeable staff will talk you through the menu of teas, which is dense and can be overwhelming.

For the uninitiated a small 3½-ounce (100-g) bag may do. For those more interested in immersing themselves in the world of tea, there are no limits. Peruse the numerous styles of teapots and other tea paraphernalia; sample teas in the tea salon; or for the really serious, sit down for a Tea Club *Atelier de Découverte et de Dégustation* tea tasting with an in-house tea connoisseur. Prices range from 65€ per person

for an hour and a half to 300€ for three hours. A sky's-the-limit option with on-request prices is available for private groups.

▶ *Seriously dressed, Mariage Frères's staff is also serious about their tea.*

CAFÉ VERLET

COFFEE MERCHANT / CAFÉ
256, rue Saint-Honoré
Paris 1
TEL: +33 1 42 60 67 39
verlet.fr

MÉTRO: Palais Royal–Musée du Louvre or Pyramides
OPEN: Monday through Saturday 9:30AM to 7PM. Tearoom open 9:30AM to 6:30PM.
CLOSED: Sunday, August 31, December 31 to January 6

A s soon as you walk in the door of Café Verlet, your senses are seduced by the smooth, rich smell of coffee. Dark wood paneling recalls the company's colonial beginnings. The shop itself dates back to the early 1900s, when an intrepid traveler and navigator first opened it on the rue Saint-Honoré to sell exotic ingredients from around the world. But for decades, Café Verlet has largely specialized in coffee. You can enjoy one of the many varieties from South America, Africa, and Asia in the tea salon section of the shop, or you can buy roasted beans by the gram to take away. Favorites include the Papua New Guinean Sigri, a *grand cru* bean that is balanced and full-bodied, with soft notes of chocolate, and the gentle yet "do take note" Colombie, with more undertones of

▶ *Enjoying an espresso at the Café Verlet.*

chocolate. Or you can pick up a house blend mixed for the season—tart in the spring, warmer in the winter months. They have a serious range of teas, also spanning the continents, and a selection of spices, vanilla, and artisanal jams.

2ND ARRONDISSEMENT

ÉPICES ROELLINGER

SPICE SHOP
51, bis rue Sainte-Anne
Paris 2
TEL: +33 1 42 60 46 88

epices-roellinger.com
MÉTRO: Pyramides or Quatre-Septembre
OPEN: Tuesday through Saturday 10AM to 7PM
CLOSED: Sunday and Monday

Entering Épices Roellinger is like stepping into a market on an ancient spice route. Inspired by 30 years of travel, Michelin-starred chef Olivier Roellinger and his wife, Jane, have created an exotic world of spices and flavors stretching from Africa and Asia to the South Pacific. Shelves offer all the ground spices you could imagine: sumac, cinnamon, turmeric, as well as Roellinger's own concoctions such as *Poudre Grande Caravan,* a delicate mixture of cardamom, fenugreek, cinnamon, nora pepper, and sesame, to season vegetables or lamb. Or pick up a jar of his Equinox powder, a beguiling mix of cinnamon, vanilla, and black pepper, to add to hot chocolate or to sprinkle over chocolate ice cream. The boutique also offers an excellent selection of salts, aromatic oils, and a vanilla "cellar," with a selection of plump *grand cru* pods. Madagascar pods are the true Rolls-Royce of vanilla, but you can choose a Congolese variety for a heady carnal flavor, or a pod from the island of Réunion for a more delicate aroma. The Indian variety is deep and spicy and best with poached fruits, while the Tahitian vanilla is best with whipped cream. For seafood and shellfish, go for the more sensual Papua New Guinean vanilla, with its spicy honey notes.

G. DETOU

ÉPICERIE
58, rue Tiquetonne
Paris 2
TEL: +33 1 42 36 54 67
gdetou.com

MÉTRO: Étienne Marcel or Sentier
OPEN: Monday through Saturday 8:30AM to 6:30PM
CLOSED: Sunday

This tiny shop is truly a pastry chef's dream. A very French play on words, G. Detou sounds like *j'ai de tout,* meaning "I have everything." And as its name suggests, it is stacked floor to ceiling with every imaginable baking ingredient, for both professionals and home cooks. They really do have everything, from dextrose and invert sugar for the serious ice-cream maker to vanilla beans, spices, unusual crystallized confectionary and cake decorations, a huge selection of chocolate

(Valrhona, Michel Cluizel, Bonnat, Voisin, Weiss, Cacao Barry), and raw, untreated nuts. No wonder the shop has been dubbed Ali Baba's Cave. Savory items can be found here, too: stacks of tinned sardines with gorgeous retro packaging designs and Edmond Fallot whole-grain mustard, one of the last authentic Dijon mustard brands.

À LA MÈRE DE FAMILLE (Montorgueil)

CONFECTIONARY AND CHOCOLATE SHOP
82, rue Montorgueil
Paris 2
TEL: +33 1 53 40 82 78

lameredefamille.com
contact@lameredefamille.com
MÉTRO: Les Halles
OPEN: Monday through Saturday 9:30AM to 8PM, Sunday 10AM to 1PM

I love this Old World candy store, full of jams and conserves, jars of caramels and flavored marshmallows, decorated tins of old-fashioned hard candies, and gift boxes of assorted treats. The chocolates are excellent, as is the friendly service. Be sure to seek out the original 1761 store if you're in the 9th *arrondissement* (see page 363).

TÉLESCOPE

COFFEE
5, rue Villedo
Paris 2

MÉTRO: Pyramides or Palais Royal-Musée du Louvre

Coutume-roasted coffee beans and other coffee paraphernalia are available at this beautiful little café near the Palais Royal gardens. See Cafés and Casual Bites, page 134, for full commentary.

TERROIR D'AVENIR

FISHMONGER, BUTCHER, AND GROCER
6, 7, and 8, rue de Nil
Paris 2
TEL: +33 1 45 08 48 80
MÉTRO: Sentier

OPEN: Tuesday through Friday 9:30AM to 2PM and 4 to 8PM. Saturday 9:30AM to 2PM and 3:30 to 8PM. Sunday 9AM to 1:30PM.
CLOSED: Monday

The young entrepreneurial duo Alexandre Drouard and Samuel Nahon first began supplying superlative produce to top restaurants in 2008. Word of their enterprise spread quickly and the name Terroir d'Avenir (which translates as "land of the future") has become synonymous with great produce in Parisian restaurants because Drouard and Nahon seek out the best fruit and vegetables, meat, poultry, and fish from small French producers. Since 2013, the two have brought their findings to the streets: rue du Nil, to be exact (the fastest-growing gastronomic destination in Paris, thanks to this pair, along with neighbor Gregory Marchand of Frenchie, Frenchie Bar à Vins, and Frenchie To-Go). Terroir d'Avenir has taken over three premises along this small cobblestone street, to house a *poissonnerie* (fish market) selling line-caught fish arriving directly from the Île d'Yeu and Saint Jean de Luz, a *boucherie* (butcher) selling the likes of salt-marsh lamb from Brittany and milk-fed lamb from the Pyrénées, and a *primeur* (fresh food grocer) selling unusual fruit and vegetables (although at times I have found the freshness questionable), as well as an excellent selection of cheese, milk, and cream products. Whether you're planning on home cooking or not, this is an excellent place to discover new produce and the *crème de la crème* of small French producers.

TETREL

CONFECTIONERY SHOP
44, rue des Petits-Champs
Paris 2
TEL: +33 1 42 96 59 58

MÉTRO: Pyramides
OPEN: Monday through Saturday 11AM to 7PM
CLOSED: Sunday

Stepping into the Tetrel *confiserie*—with its shelves filled with old-fashioned jars of colorful sweets and beautifully packaged fine foods from around France—among them sardines, *confits,* and *foie gras*—is like

stepping back in time to 19th-century Paris. And this is exactly how the fourth-generation owners prefer it: No photos allowed here; you'll have to savor the moment as you browse the glass jars filled with candied violet and bergamot bonbons, or linger over which brand of salted butter caramels to buy.

WORKSHOP ISSÉ

JAPANESE GOURMET FOODS
11, rue Saint Augustin
Paris 2
TEL: +33 1 1 42 96 26 74
workshop@ksm.fr

MÉTRO: Quatre-Septembre
OPEN: Monday through Friday 9AM to 8PM.
Saturday 9AM to 6PM.
CLOSED: Sunday

Workshop Issé has one of the finest selections of Japanese imported ingredients that you will find anywhere in Paris: soy sauces, vinegars and dressings, unusual condiments and seasonings, excellent-quality fresh

and dried noodles, *dashi* broth in liquid form or dried sachets, and all kinds of *yuzu*-flavored products from that Japanese citrus, including sweet dried *yuzu* zest and *yuzu* miso—all in predictably lovely packaging. There is a small but beautifully selected range of tea and sake ceramics, and traditional Hirota glassware.

SARDINES

Pierre-Joseph Colin, from Brittany, invented the tinned sardine in 1810. The first tins—well soldered and opened with a hammer—departed with Napoleon on his Russian campaign of 1812. Today many French gourmands tuck tins of fine, delicate Brittany sardines away in their basement *caves* (wine cellars), sometimes aging the tender little fish for a decade or more. Vintage, or *millesimé*, sardines can be found in most Parisian specialty shops, tinned and carefully dated. The tins should be stored in a cool spot and turned every six months. As the delicate fish age—most experts recommend aging from four to ten years—they become softer, more refined, and tender, ready to be enjoyed with a slice of crusty rye bread and a glass of white Muscadet wine.

Sardines destined for *millesimé* stardom bear no resemblance to the cheap garden-variety canned fish. Vintage sardines are always preserved fresh, whereas most ordinary sardines are frozen, then fried and processed. To prepare vintage sardines for processing, the fish are delivered fresh from the Atlantic Ocean, from April to September, though early spring sardines are said to be more firm and offer better flavor. The sardines are weighed and brined immediately, then cleaned by hand, air-dried, and deep-fried in sunflower oil (traditionally, for the time it takes to say a Hail Mary!) before being packed, by hand and head-to-tail, into small, flat tins. The fish are then covered with extra-virgin olive oil and perhaps a touch of salt, then sealed and stored for at least six months before being distributed. Brands to look for include those from La Confrérie de la Sardine de Saint Gilles Croix de Vie, La Quiberonnaise, Albert Menès, Gonidec (their sardines are sold under the label les Mouettes d'Arvor), Les Perles des Dieux, La Belle Illoise, Connetable, Rodel, and Capitaine Cook.

Check for the processing date stamped on the tin so that you know how long to keep them. Experts recommend the sardines be kept no more than four years, but some sardine lovers hold them up to ten years, being sure to turn the tins regularly.

The following are just a few of the shops offering vintage sardines.

LA GRANDE ÉPICERIE
38, rue de Sèvres
Paris 7
TEL: + 33 1 44 39 81 00
MÉTRO: Sèvres-Babylone

ALBERT MENÈS
41, boulevard Malesherbes
Paris 8
TEL: +33 1 42 66 95 63
MÉTRO: Saint-Augustin

HÉDIARD
21, place de la Madeleine
Paris 8
TEL: +33 1 42 66 44 36
MÉTRO: Madeleine

SHOP ORGANIC

Buying and eating organic is easier than ever in Paris. It may cost more than nonorganic, but there is an immense number of options to choose from all over the capital. Organic items are known as *produits biologique* or simply *bio*. Paris Biotiful has good listings of organic shops in France. Search by shop type: parisobiotiful.com.

REGULAR SUPERMARKETS

Most leading supermarkets now have an organic section and several home-brand organic options. Organic items will be clearly labeled *bio*, or look for the green label *Agriculture Biologique*.

ORGANIC SUPERMARKETS

For a wider selection of organic goods, there are a number of organic supermarket chains where you can pick up dried and packaged foods, fresh fruit and vegetables (the quality varies from shop to shop, so best to check out your local store to see if that is your best option), bread, dairy products, vitamins and supplements, baby food, cleaning products, and beauty products.

BIOCOOP: An excellent chain that has been operating since the 1970s, it offers the full range of organic supermarket items. See full listings of all their Paris stores on biocoop.fr.

BIO C' BON: The bright, modern shops of Paris's newest organic supermarket chain offer a good range of items, including fresh fruit and vegetables from France and abroad, as well as a *fromagerie*. For full listings of all their Paris stores see bio-c-bon.eu.

NATURALIA: Run by the Monoprix group, the Naturalia stores vary widely in quality. Some stores can feel a little musty and the freshness of the fruit and vegetables can be dubious, but this differs from neighborhood to neighborhood. The new Naturalia concept store in the 3rd *arrondissement* (84, rue Beaubourg) is a light, airy space, full of fresh, inspiring produce. For full listings of all their Paris stores, see naturalia.fr.

LES NOUVEAUX ROBINSONS: Stores are found outside of Paris, with one exception: 78, boulevard Saint-Michel, Paris 5.

LA VIE CLAIRE: A large chain with over 200 stores around Paris, offering organic foods at a reasonable price. For full listings of all their Paris stores see lavieclaire.com.

ORGANIC MARKETS

There are three roving organic markets in Paris: Raspail in the 6th *arrondissement* (see page 190), Batignolles in the 8th (see page 195), and Brancusi in the 14th. Prices at these markets can be astronomical and can vary from stall to stall, so it is always wise to browse the markets first to decide where it is you really want to spend your money.

INDEPENDENT ORGANIC SHOPS

For specialty organic items, small, independent shops are your best bet.

AQUOLINA IN BOCCA

7, rue du Général Blaise
Paris 11
TEL: +33 1 43 55 43 84
acquolinainbocca.fr
MÉTRO: Saint-Ambroise
OPEN: Tuesday through Saturday 10:30AM to 9:30PM. Sunday 11:30AM to 3PM.
CLOSED: Monday

This excellent organic Italian *épicerie* stocks fresh and dried pasta, polenta, cheese, *charcuterie*, and a selection of delicious deli items and homemade dishes for eat-in or carryout.

CLAUS

14, rue Jean-Jacques Rousseau
Paris 1
MÉTRO: Palais Royal-Musée du Louvre or Louvre-Rivoli

A breakfast café and *épicerie*. See page 130 for full commentary.

LE COMPTOIR DE TUNISIE

30, rue de Richelieu
Paris 1
lecomptoirdetunisie.com
MÉTRO: Pyramides or Palais-Royal

▲ *Shopping organic has long been popular in Paris, as well as the rest of France.*

Sells specialties including hand-rolled couscous and traditional harissa from an organic farm in Tunisia. See page 336 for full commentary.

LA DERNIÈRE GOUTTE
6, rue Bourbon le Château
Paris 6
MÉTRO: Mabilllon or Saint-Germain-des-Pres

Offers a range of organic and biodynamic wines from small independent winemakers. See page 324 for full commentary.

HEDONIE
6, rue de Mézières
Paris 6
TEL: +33 1 45 44 19 16
hedonie.com
MÉTRO: Rennes
OPEN: Monday noon to 8PM. Tuesday through Saturday 11AM to 8PM.
CLOSED: Sunday

An *épicerie fine*, with a diverse range of organic products: jams, coffee, oils, mustards, wines and Champagnes, gluten-free products, and organic baby food.

DOMINIQUE SAIBRON
77, avenue du Général Leclerc
Paris 14

Visit Dominique Saibron for great organic bread. See page 237 for full commentary.

L'AUTRE BOULANGE
43, rue de Montreuil
Paris 11
TEL: +33 1 43 72 86 04
MÉTRO: Rue des Boulets or Faidherbe-Chaligny
OPEN: Monday to Friday 7:30AM to 1:30PM and 3:30 to 7:30PM. Saturday 7:30AM to 1PM.
CLOSED: Saturday afternoon, Sunday, and August

Great organic bread.

L'ÉPICERIE BREIZH
111, rue Vieille du Temple
Paris 3
MÉTRO: Saint-Sébastien-Froissart

Stocks artisanal Breton products. Not all the products are organic, but many come from small producers in Brittany. See page 135 for full commentary.

LE PAIN QUOTIDIEN
Many locations.

A great organic spot for pastries, bread, and light meals. See page 222 for full commentary.

ROSE BAKERY
Many locations.

Along with its organic menu for eat-in or carryout, Rose Bakery stocks a number of British organic items, from fruit and vegetables to cereal, teas, and chocolate. See page 138 for full commentary.

18 SUR VIN
154, rue Ordener
Paris 18
MÉTRO: Jules Joffrin

Stocks organic, biodynamic, and natural wines. See page 332 for full commentary.

3ᴿᴰ ARRONDISSEMENT

LA CHAMBRE AUX CONFITURES (Marais)

JAMS AND MARMALADES
60, rue Vieille du Temple
Paris 3
lachambreauxconfitures.com

MÉTRO: Saint-Paul or Rambuteau
OPEN: Monday through Friday 11:30AM to 8PM.
Saturday and Sunday 10AM to 8PM.

Lise Bienaimé inherited her love of jams from her great-grandfather, a master jam maker who once owned a fine foods store on rue Saint-Honoré. Now with two pristine stores in the Marais and rue des Martyrs entirely dedicated to jams, jellies, and marmalades, she shares her passion for jams with all of Paris. She works closely with four trusted jam makers to produce a nothing-less-than-wondrous collection of jam flavors, all natural and free of preservatives and colorings. The fruits span the seasons of the year and are paired with clever ingredients that enhance the natural flavors of the fruit and really make them pop: Orange and orange blossom marmalade in winter, rhubarb and elderflower in the spring. Raspberry combined with samba flower is an unusual and intense flavor pairing that is particularly good, as is the apricot and lavender from the summer fruits collection. If you love jam, don't miss this *bienaimé* (well-loved) boutique.

L'ÉPICERIE BREIZH CAFÉ

BRETON *ÉPICERIE*
111, rue Vieille du Temple
Paris 3
TEL: +33 1 42 71 39 44

MÉTRO: Saint-Sébastien–Froissart
OPEN: Wednesday through Sunday 11:30AM to 9PM
CLOSED: Monday and Tuesday

If, like many Parisians, you just can't get enough of Breton cuisine, the expansion of the much-loved Breizh Café (see Cafés, page 135) into a next-door *épicerie Breton* will be good news. You'll find a well-curated selection of Brittany's finest produce: Bordier butter, organic buckwheat (*sarrasin*) flour for *galettes* and *crêpes,* and for caramel lovers, a whole wall of salted caramels and caramel spreads (try the *Keramel Caramel Breton au Sarrasin,* with a hint of chocolate and buckwheat for an earthy twist on caramel sauce). And of course, there is a fantastic selection of local *cidres,* or apple ciders, as well as a good-value carryout sandwich lunch menu.

GOUMANYAT & SON ROYAUME

GOURMET FOODS AND SPICES
3, rue Charles-François Dupuis
Paris 3
TEL: +33 1 44 78 96 74
goumanyat.com

contact@goumanyat.com
MÉTRO: Temple or République
OPEN: Tuesday through Saturday 11AM to 7PM
CLOSED: Sunday and August

Run by the seventh generation of the Thiercelin family (since 1809), and frequented by the *grands chefs de Paris* for its exotic array of spices and aromatics, Goumanyat & Son Royaume has a vast selection of unusual ingredients for the adventurous chef or baker: sugars flavored with coconut, lavender, and violet; syrups, honeys, and crystallized flowers; pink Himalaya saffron salt; ayurvedic spices; smoked oil; shellfish oil; coffee, teas. In the basement, you will find a selection of wines from Burgundy, Alsace, and the Loire Valley, as well as Thiercelin Champagne, which the family has been producing since 1893. The shop also sells a range of German-made Rösle cooking utensils.

OLIVIERS & CO. (Marais)

OLIVE OIL SPECIALIST
60, rue Vieille du Temple
Paris 3
TEL: +33 1 42 74 38 40

oliviers-co.com/en
MÉTRO: Saint-Paul
OPEN: Monday through Saturday 1:30 to 8PM.
Sunday 10:30AM to 1:30PM.

You feel like you are walking right into the olive grove when you enter one of the fresh and welcoming Oliviers & Co. stores, dotted with olive trees and replete with a huge variety of exceptional olive oils from some of Provence's finest growers, *grand cru* organic oils from Tuscany, and select oils from Portugal. For many years Oliviers & Co. has teamed up with some of France's top chefs to create a fantastic range of olive oil pastes, including a black olive and tomato paste from a favored Parisian chef, Eric Frechon of Epicure au Bristol. All their products are available on their website. One of my favorite things here is their *poudre de*

▲ *It's like stepping into an olive grove at the Oliviers & Co. Marais boutique.*

tomate, a brilliant red powder consisting of 100 percent dried tomatoes—perfect as a flavor as well as a color booster for sprinkling on everything from soft cheese to pasta to a tomato bruschetta. I also always have on hand their exquisite *huile de citron,* the real deal here. Pressed in Sicily, olives and lemons from the property are crushed together for this exquisite oil, ideal for any lemon and olive oil dressing.

4ᵀᴴ ARRONDISSEMENT

IZRAËL ÉPICERIE DU MONDE

GOURMET FOODS AND SPICES
30, rue François-Miron
Paris 4
TEL: +33 1 42 72 66 23

MÉTRO: Saint-Paul
OPEN: Tuesday to Friday 11AM to 1PM and 2 to 7PM; Saturday 11AM to 7PM
CLOSED: Sunday

This Ali Baba–type shop opened more than seventy-five years ago, specializing in North African products. Today, the cluttered and delicious-smelling boutique continues to supply many of the city's chefs with its wondrous assortment of products from all over the world: huge sacks of grains, pulses, rice, and nuts; spices, condiments, curry powders, and a delicious spread of deli items—Lucques olives, marinated artichokes, stuffed peppers, and a tempting variety of tapenades and spreads. Try a bag of the Madagascan wild pepper; you won't be disappointed.

LA MAISON DE LA PRASLINE MAZET

37, rue des Archives
Paris 4
TEL: +33 1 44 05 18 08
mazetconfiseur.com
mazetparis@mazetconfiseur.com

MÉTRO: Rambuteau
OPEN: Monday through Saturday 10AM to 7PM, Sunday 11AM to 7PM
SPECIALTY: Confectionary shop

The decor of this shop is a replica of the original store in Montargis and reflects the company's 17th-century origins, with its wooden and stain-glassed cabinetry. Sticking with tradition, the grilled almond pralines are true to the original 1636 recipe. Try some of their other nutty combinations, too: hazelnuts enrobed in nougat and dipped in bittersweet chocolate, or almond nougat rolled in cocoa—all are generously available for sampling in the store. Or perhaps try a box of their classic ganache or praline chocolates.

MARIAGE FRÈRES (Marais)

TEA SHOP / TEA SALON
30, rue du Bourg-Tibourg
Paris 4
TEL: +33 1 42 72 28 11

MÉTRO: Hôtel de Ville
OPEN: Daily 10:30AM to 7:30PM
(restaurant open daily noon to 3PM; *salon de thé* open daily 3 to 7PM)

On entering the store on rue du Bourg-Tibourg (inhabited by the family since 1845) you are transported to another slower, more pleasurable world. The delicate perfumes of hundreds of teas from around the world mix in the air, classical music envelopes you gently, and suddenly the modern world of the bustling Marais simply falls away. With antique adornments like Chinese tea chests, scales, tea strainers, and the old colonial counter, it could be more like a museum than a tea shop. See page 336 for full commentary.

À L'OLIVIER

OLIVE OIL SPECIALIST
23, rue de Rivoli
Paris 4
TEL: +33 1 48 04 86 59
alolivier.com

alorivoli@gmail.com
MÉTRO: Saint-Paul
OPEN: Monday 2 to 7PM, Tuesday through Saturday 9:30AM to 7PM
CLOSED: Sunday

You can find over 50 excellent-quality olive, nut, and seed oils in this warm and welcoming boutique on the southern edge of the Marais. Olive oils are selected for their aromatic, fruity, and floral tones from groves all over the Mediterranean: A.O.P. (*Appellation d'Origine Protégée,* a European Union designation for agricultural products produced within strict geographical limits, abiding by a strict set of rules) products from the South of France; and single-variety olive oils from Spain, Italy, and Greece. Whatever your preference for oils, you will be able to find it here: a complex and peppery olive oil from Provence, an earthy truffle and porcini

infusion (all natural extracts and aromas), or perhaps a smoky sesame seed oil from Burkina Faso. They also stock a variety of vinegars and the excellent *Terre Exotique* brand of spices. Their oil and vinegar handbook is useful for those overwhelmed by the choices, and breaks down their oils by origin, predominant flavors, and suggested uses.

OLIVIERS & CO. (Île Saint-Louis)

OLIVE OIL SPECIALIST
81, rue Saint-Louis en l'Île
Paris 4
oliviers-co.com/en

TEL: +33 1 40 46 89 37
MÉTRO: Sully-Morland
OPEN: Daily 11AM to 1:30PM and 2:30 to 7:30PM

A selection of some of the finest olive oils from across the Mediterranean. See page 345 for full commentary.

LA PISTACHERIE (Rambuteau)

NUT AND CONFECTIONERY SHOP
67, rue Rambuteau
Paris 4
TEL: +33 1 42 78 84 55

lapistacherie.boolkit.com
MÉTRO: Rambuteau
OPEN: Monday through Thursday 11AM to 8PM. Friday through Sunday 11AM to 8:30PM.

Nut fans will have a field day in La Pistacherie's elegant boutiques, which offer such jewels as top-quality pistachios from Sicily and Turkey, and every other nut imaginable—peanuts, almonds, macadamia nuts, walnuts, pecans—either simply toasted or coated with sugar or with chocolate. The shops are like old-fashioned candy stores, with glass jars filled with varied specialties. They offer a huge line of nut candies, many of them nougat-like and less convincing than the nuts all on their own. The owner, Charles Sakr, is from Lebanon, and according to one friendly salesperson, he just loves to travel and discover new sources for nuts around the world, particularly pistachios.

5TH ARRONDISSEMENT

MAISON DES TROIS THÉS

TEA SHOP AND TEA TASTING
1, rue Saint Médard
Paris 5
TEL: +33 1 43 36 93 84
maisondestroisthes.com

info@maisondestroisthes.com
MÉTRO: Place Monge
OPEN: Tuesday through Sunday 11AM to 7:30PM. Tea tastings 1 to 6:30PM.
CLOSED: Monday

Immerse yourself in the ancient tradition of *gong fu cha*, the Chinese tea ceremony that dates back to the Ming Dynasty, at the exquisite teahouse of tea master Yu Hui Tseng (*Maître* Tseng). The unique preparation method brings out the best in the teas, allowing the tea drinker to appreciate the complex perfumes of the tea as well as its evolving flavors. Time will slow down as you are seated at one of the heavy wooden antique tables for an intimate *dégustation* of some of the world's most refined natural teas. *Maître* Tseng is among 10 of the most renowned tea masters in the world, and the first and only female tea master. She spends 7 to 8 months of the year traveling to China in search of the finest teas, of which she has collected over a thousand varieties. These include many varieties of *grand cru* oolong (*bleu-vert*) teas, and 500 *pu-erh* vintages of aged tea, comprising some extremely rare and precious teas dating back to the 19th century, and teas from trees that are over a thousand years old. For those willing to pay a premium, teas in her *cave* are worth up to 800,000€ per kilo. However, a simple tasting of one *grand cru* tea, selected by the very gracious and knowledgeable staff, is more likely to come to around 20 to 30€. You can also find a selection of *Maître* Tseng's teas at the *salon de thé* of *chocolatier* Jacques Genin (see Chocolate Shops, page 272), as well as sample tea-infused chocolates that are the result of their collaboration.

OLIVIERS & CO. (Mouffetard)

OLIVE OIL SPECIALIST
128, rue Mouffetard
Paris 5
TEL: +33 1 43 37 04 38
oliviers-co.com/en
oco-mouffetard@oliviers-co.com

MÉTRO: Censier-Daubenton
OPEN: Tuesday through Friday 10AM to 2PM and 3:30 to 7:30PM. Saturday 10AM to 7PM. Sunday 9:30AM to 2PM.
CLOSED: Monday

Fine olive oils and unusual gourmet items for your pantry. Of note are the olive oil pastes developed by some of France's leading chefs, and the *poudre de tomate*, a punchy red powder made from dried tomatoes. See page 345 for full commentary.

6ᵀᴴ ARRONDISSEMENT

DA ROSA

ÉPICERIE
62, rue de Seine

Paris 6
MÉTRO: Mabillon or Saint-Germain-des-Prés

A casual eatery with a wonderful selection of carryout deli items from Spain, Italy, and France. See Cafés and Casual Bites, page 149, for full commentary.

MARIAGE FRÈRES (Saint-Germain)

TEA SHOP / TEA SALON
13, rue des Grands-Augustins
Paris 6
TEL: +33 1 40 51 82 50

MÉTRO: Odéon or Saint-Michel
OPEN: Daily 10:30AM to 7:30PM
(restaurant open daily noon to 3PM;
salon de thé open daily 3 to 7PM)

Mariage Frères is one of France's oldest and most respected tea importers, boasting possibly the world's largest tea collection. See page 336 for full commentary.

À LA MÈRE DE FAMILLE (Cherche-Midi)

**CONFECTIONERY AND
CHOCOLATE SHOP**
39, rue du Cherche-Midi
Paris 6

TEL: +33 1 42 22 29 99
MÉTRO: Rennes
OPEN: Monday through Saturday 9:30AM to
8PM, Sunday 10AM to 1PM

This shop does not quite have the charm of the original 1761 shop in the 9th *arrondissement*, but the contents of this old-world candy store are just as good, and it's handy to know about when shopping for confectionary gifts in the 6th *arrondissement*. See page 339 for full commentary.

OLIVIERS & CO. (Saint-Germain)

OLIVE OIL SPECIALIST
28, rue de Buci
Paris 6
TEL: +33 1 44 07 15 43
oliviers-co.com/en

oco-buci@oliviers-co.com
MÉTRO: Rennes or Sèvres-Babylone
OPEN: Monday through Saturday 10:30AM to
8PM, Sunday 10:30AM to 1PM.

A selection of fine olive oils and unusual gourmet pantry items. See page 345 for full commentary.

TOMAT'S ÉPICERIE FINE

ÉPICERIE
12, rue Jacob
Paris 6
TEL: +33 1 44 07 36 58
tomats.fr

MÉTRO: Saint-Germain-des-Prés
OPEN: Tuesday through Saturday
11AM to 7:30PM
CLOSED: Sunday and Monday

This little shop, in a charming courtyard off the artistic rue Jacob, offers a bundle of culinary treasures, including the incomparable Leblanc oils (pistachio and pumpkin-seed oil are my favorites), Bonnat chocolates, top-quality olives, smoked salmon, tinned sardines and tuna, vodka, and a small selection of wines.

7TH ARRONDISSEMENT

COUTUME

COFFEE
47, rue de Babylone
Paris 7

MÉTRO: Saint-Françoise-Xavier or
Sevres-Babylone

Here you will find some of the best Arabica coffee in Paris, roasted and brewed onsite. Beans can be bought by the gram, whole or ground to your specifications, or enjoyed at the café prepared by one of their highly skilled baristas. See also Cafés and Casual Bites, page 151.

LE GIGOT D'AGNEAU DES VIANDES DU CHAMPS DE MARS

Les Viandes du Champ de Mars's Leg of Lamb

In France, you hardly need a cookbook to know how to cook meat and poultry. Butchers always offer a quick, surefire recipe for whatever it is you're buying that day. On my first visit to Jean-Marie Boedec's fabulous shop (see page 354) one rainy day in October, I purchased a tiny, 2-pound (1-kg) leg of lamb and followed his instructions to the letter. The same recipe will work for a larger leg of lamb, generally roasting for 12 to 15 minutes per pound (500 g). I like to roast this "weeping style," with the lamb set on a rack just above the potatoes in a roasting pan, allowing the meat juices to drip onto the potatoes.

EQUIPMENT:

A roasting pan fitted with a roasting rack; an instant-read thermometer

INGREDIENTS:

1 whole bone-in leg of lamb (about 6 pounds; 3 kg), fat trimmed

1½ pounds (750 g) tiny spring potatoes, scrubbed but not peeled

2 tablespoons unsalted butter

Fine sea salt

Coarse, freshly ground black pepper

1. Remove the meat from the refrigerator at least 20 minutes before roasting.

2. Center a rack in the oven. Preheat the oven to 475°F (245°C).

3. Arrange the potatoes in a single layer in the roasting pan. Arrange a roasting rack over the potatoes. Place the lamb, fat side up, on the roasting rack. Rub the lamb with butter and season generously with salt and pepper. Place in the oven and immediately reduce heat to 400°F (200°C). Roast the lamb, turning once during the roasting time, for 12 minutes per pound (500 g) for medium-rare meat and 15 minutes per pound (500 g) for medium, or until the internal temperature of the lamb registers 120°F (49°C) to 125°F (52°C) on an instant-read thermometer for medium rare. When cooked to the desired doneness, remove from the oven and season once again with salt and pepper. Check to be sure the potatoes are cooked through. If necessary, leave them in the oven to complete cooking while the lamb rests. Tent the lamb loosely with aluminum foil and let it rest for 20 minutes before carving into thick slices cut on the diagonal. Serve with potatoes on the side.

8 SERVINGS

FOIE GRAS

*F*oie gras—one of the crown jewels of French gastronomy—is the smooth and buttery liver from a fattened duck or goose. Seasoned lightly with salt and pepper, then cooked gently in a porcelain terrine, this highly perishable delicacy demands no further embellishment than a slice of freshly toasted country bread and a glass of chilled sweet Sauternes. At its best, *foie gras* is one of the world's most satisfying foods. Earthy and elegant, a single morsel of it melts slowly on the palate, invading one's senses with an aroma and flavor that's gracefully soothing, supple, and rich, with a lingering and delicate toasted-nut aftertaste. Depending on its origin and length of cooking time, the color of the fattened livers ranges from a slightly golden brown to a peach-blushed rose. Rich in calories, *foie gras* is best enjoyed slowly and parsimoniously. *Foie gras* has traditionally been an expensive delicacy, but in recent years the French government has assisted farmers with their *foie gras* production, dropping the price considerably.

Which is better, goose or duck *foie gras*? It is purely a matter of preference. Fattened goose liver (*foie gras d'oie*), which was the traditional sort, is much less common and more expensive than fattened duck liver (*foie gras de canard*) because geese are more fragile than ducks, and require more intensive care. Their livers are more fragile, too, and the cooking necessitates much more care than the liver from a duck. The French government has championed the production of *foie gras de canard* because it is easier to produce, and the French public has supported this by developing a palate for the more intensely flavored *foie gras de canard*.

What does one look for in cooked *foie gras*? Ideally, it should be the same color throughout, a sign that it is from the same liver and has been carefully and uniformly cooked. It should always have a fresh, appealing, mild, liverlike aroma.

When serving cooked *foie gras*, remove it from the refrigerator 15 to 20 minutes before serving, so the flavors will emerge. If it's too cold, flavors are masked. But do not serve *foie gras* too warm, as it can become soft, losing its seductive charm.

The following are the legal French definitions and preparations for *foie gras*. When purchasing it preserved, look for *foie gras* packed in terrines or glass jars rather than tins, so you can see what you are buying. The best *foie gras* has a fresh color, slices neatly, is generally free of blood vessels, and is not too heavily surrounded by fat. Many shops also sell *foie gras* by the slice, cut from a larger terrine. This should be refrigerated and is best eaten within a few hours. *Foie gras* that can legally enter the United States must have been sterilized—cooked at a temperature of 230°F (110°C)—and is generally marked as *foie gras de conserve*.

FOIE GRAS CRU: Raw liver, the ultimate if it is of good quality. Usually found in select Paris *charcuteries* and specialty shops around the end of the year, it is delicious sliced raw and spread on warm, toasted bread; it can also be preserved in a terrine at home. Often sold vacuum-packed. The best are the smallest, a little over 1 pound (500 to 600 g) for goose, a little less for duck (400 g). Lobes should be supple, round, smooth rather than granular, and without spots. A good buy when purchased from a reputable merchant.

FOIE GRAS MI-CUIT OR NATURE: The lightly cooked and pasteurized *foie gras* of connoisseurs, and the best way to sample *foie gras* for the first time. Ideally, only the highest quality livers are preserved in this manner. The terms *mi-cuit* and *nature* are used interchangeably with *foie gras frais*, denoting that the livers have been pasteurized at 175° to 200°F (80° to 90°C). Next to raw this is the best way to enjoy *foie gras*, for it is barely cooked, retaining its pure, agreeably rich flavor. Sold in terrines, vacuum-packed, in aluminum foil–wrapped rolls, or in a can or jar, it requires refrigeration. Depending on packaging, it will last several days to several weeks.

FOIE GRAS ENTIER: An entire lobe of the fattened liver, lightly seasoned and generally cooked in a terrine or a glass jar. If the container is large, additional pieces of another liver may be added to fill it. Sold fresh (*frais*), it requires refrigeration and must be consumed within a few weeks or months, depending on the cooking time.

FOIE GRAS EN CONSERVE: Fattened livers, whole or in pieces, that have been seasoned, then sterilized in a jar or can at 230° to 240°F (108° to 115°C). This requires no refrigeration. Carefully conserved, high-quality *foie gras* will actually ripen and improve with age. It should be stored in a cool, dry place and turned from time to time.

BLOC DE FOIE GRAS: By law, composed of 100 percent fattened duck or goose liver that has been blended. If it has chunks, it must be mentioned on the label (*contient morceaux*). Not the best buy.

FOIE GRAS TRUFFE: *Foie gras* with at least 3 percent black truffles. A bad buy, for the flavor of the expensive truffle is totally lost, and the price greatly inflated.

FOIE GRAS PARFAIT: A mechanically mixed blend of usually mediocre-quality *foie gras*, *foie gras parfait* must contain 75 percent *foie gras*, which is mixed with chicken livers. A bad buy.

FOIE GRAS PÂTÉ, GALANTINE, MOUSSE, OR PURÉE: Various products with a base of *foie gras*. Usually composed of lowest-quality livers mixed with pork, chicken, or veal, surrounded by barding fat. The word *gras* may be missing, but the mixtures must contain a minimum of 50 percent *foie gras*. A bad buy.

À LA MÈRE DE FAMILLE (Rue Cler)

**CONFECTIONERY AND
CHOCOLATE SHOP**
47, rue Cler
Paris 7

TEL: +33 1 45 55 29 74
MÉTRO: École Militaire
OPEN: Monday through Saturday 9:30AM to
8PM, Sunday 10AM to 1PM

This small outpost of the Faubourg-Montmartre confectionery store does not have the unique charm of the original shop, but the chocolate, jellies, and other sweet treats are of the same high quality and are worth a stop if strolling on the rue Cler market street. See page 339 for full commentary.

PETROSSIAN

CAVIAR MERCHANT
18, boulevard de Latour-Maubourg
Paris 7
TEL: +33 1 44 11 32 22
petrossian.fr
info.petrossian@petrossian.fr

MÉTRO: La Tour-Maubourg or Invalides
OPEN: Monday through Saturday 9:30AM to
8PM. August hours Tuesday through Saturday
10AM to 7PM.
CLOSED: Sunday

As the Petrossians like to say, "We sell dreams." And dreams are made of Russian caviar, smoked salmon, *foie gras,* truffles, and Sauternes. Everything here is of high quality, but the prices are competitive. I rarely buy caviar anywhere else in Paris—the Petrossians make regular trips to the Caspian Sea to monitor its processing. Other specialties in this well-appointed shop include Russian pastries, fresh blinis, assorted herring, vodka, and delicious black Georgian tea, which can be sampled at their café with its sidewalk terrace.

LES VIANDES DU CHAMP DE MARS / JEAN-MARIE BOEDEC

BUTCHER
122, rue Saint-Dominque
Paris 7
TEL: +33 1 47 05 53 52

MÉTRO: École Militaire
OPEN: Monday 2PM to 7PM, Tuesday through
Saturday 9:30AM to 7PM
CLOSED: Sunday

Walk into this tiny, tidy storefront shop on any day and you'll see at least five adept butchers hard at work, slicing, paring, butchering with finesse and passion, all the while waiting on the line of very patient customers who come here knowing they will get top quality and friendly service. The lean, athletic owner Jean-Marie Boedec is there carefully creating a masterpiece as he takes apart an entire baby lamb from the salty *pré salé* (salt marsh) fields of Normandy (generally available from Easter to November). A single leg of lamb, or *gigot,* weighs just under 2 pounds (1 kg) and roasts to perfection in about 40 minutes (see recipe, page 351). Any cut of meat or poultry you desire is here: well-marbled *cote de boeuf* (rib steak) aged up to two months, chicken from Bresse and duck from Challans, guinea hen (*pintade*) from the Dombes, and my favorite Levoni sausage from the Abruzzo in Italy.

Ask a butcher for a few kilos of beef cheeks for long, slow cooking, and he'll spend a good 10 minutes carefully trimming off every bit of fat and sinew, then offer you a veal or beef bone to make for a smooth, shiny, gelatinous sauce. Laurance, Madame Beodec, is there at the cash register, cheerful and well-mannered, as is this entire *boucherie*. The array of terrines, homemade sausages, and hams are pure pleasure to the eye. The shop has been there since 2005, and in 2008 the owner became an honored *maître artisan*.

8ᵀᴴ ARRONDISSEMENT

BETJEMAN & BARTON

TEA SHOP
23, boulevard Malesherbes
Paris 8
TEL: +33 1 42 65 86 17
betjemanandbarton.com

contact@betjemanandbarton.com
MÉTRO: Madeleine
OPEN: Monday through Saturday 10AM to 7PM
CLOSED: Sunday

An English tea shop with *thé à la francaise* credentials, offering a selection of more than 200 teas from India, China, Japan, Brazil, Laos, and Kenya, among others. The perfumed teas, seldom-seen flower and herbal mixtures, are particularly interesting. Why not try some of their old-English fruitcakes or shortbread to complete your British tea experience?

CAVIAR KASPIA

CAVIAR MERCHANT
17, place de la Madeleine
Paris 8
TEL: +33 1 42 65 66 21
caviarkaspia.com

gourmandisedeluxe.com/fr
MÉTRO: Madeleine
OPEN: Monday through Saturday
10AM to midnight
CLOSED: Sunday

This small, pristine shop has some of the best caviar and finest seafood in Paris. They offer a large selection of caviar; delicious *taramas,* a variety of salmon smoked using ancestral methods; and Kamchatka king crab, its huge claws displayed in the window. Kaspia also specializes in the finest in Iberico cured meat products from Spain, including *pata negra* and chorizo. You can order a tray of cocktail canapés for a reasonable 29€, or buy their fresh blinis to make up your own. There is a small restaurant upstairs overlooking the *Eglise Madeleine,* where you can sample the house specialties.

FAUCHON

GOURMET ÉPICERIE
24–26, place de la Madeleine
Paris 8
TEL: +33 1 70 39 38 00
fauchon.com

MÉTRO: Madeleine
OPEN: Monday through Saturday
9AM to 8:30PM
CLOSED: Sunday

If you are in search of unusual upscale products, head for the legendary Fauchon on the place de la Madeleine. Fauchon may have modernized its look with a makeover in shocking pink against sleek black, but the attention to quality and sourcing unusual products is as old as the shop itself, originally founded in 1886. The shop is pristine and light, cakes reminiscent of modern architectural structures adorn the window displays, while inside glass cases are filled with pastries, macarons, éclairs, bread, and no fewer than seven flavors of madeleines. At the far end of the shop, past the delicatessen counter and stacks of *foie gras,* you will find the seafood and caviar bar. Here you can sip Champagne and sample caviar, oysters, and crab, or, if you come in July or at Christmas, pick up some wild smoked salmon from the Adour River in Southwest France. For excellent cheeses, seek out the Fauchon *fromager,* François Robin, who has been awarded the title *Meilleur Ouvrier de France,* the highest achievement that can be earned by a French artisan. Every section of Fauchon has a specialist with considerable knowledge of the products in their area, and all speak English.

Across the street in their second shop at 30, place de la Madeleine, you will find the Fauchon wine cellar, chocolate section, and gourmet *épicerie;* specialty pastas; dried *girolles* (chanterelles); black salt colored by lava rocks, or *fleur de sel de l'Île de Ré,* which has a subtle scent of violets and is perfect paired with fish. And of course, all the classic prepared French foods can be found, including duck *confit, cassoulet, choucroute garnie d'Alsace.* Need to catch your breath after all this? Then how about some Oxygen tea that promises to evoke a walk in the wild? Or perhaps a stroll in Provence? That's an infusion of lavender, licorice, and lemon. There is a café on the first floor of the 30, place de la Madeleine store, open 8AM to midnight for breakfast, lunch, tea, cocktails, and dinner.

HÉDIARD (George V)

GOURMET ÉPICERIE
31, avenue George V
Paris 8
TEL: +33 1 47 20 44 44
hediard.com

georgeV@hediard.fr
MÉTRO: George V
OPEN: Monday through Saturday
9AM to 8:30PM
CLOSED: Sunday

One of the chicest gourmet shops in France, Hédiard earned the title Living Heritage Company from the French government in 2007 for its dedication to *haute gastronomie.* They stock everything you could imagine for a gourmet *épicerie,* from their famous spice blends and unusual seasonings (such as Cypriot golden salt or wasabi powder) to exotic vinegars, mustards, and oils (the Chateau d'Establon spray olive oil bottled in a cologne-like decanter makes for a fun gift), carryout deli items, and exotic fruits and vegetables. Or for the sweet-toothed, chocolates, fruit jellies, jams, honeys, cakes, and biscuits. The wine cellar includes Hédiard wines and Champagnes as well as the Hédiard *caviste's* own wine choices. An excellent one-stop shop for gourmet gifts.

VIVE LES SUPERMARCHÉS GOURMANDES!

For out-of-the-ordinary supermarket items or when preparing an elaborate meal just isn't in the cards, Paris's gourmet supermarkets are an excellent place to pick up high-quality produce and ready-made deli items on your way home (many even deliver). You'll have a ready-made dinner for family or friends in no time.

LA GRANDE ÉPICERIE
38, rue de Sèvres (magasin 2)
Paris 7
TEL: +33 1 44 39 81 00
lagrandeepicerie.fr
MÉTRO: Sèvres-Babylone
OPEN: Monday through Saturday 8:30AM to 9PM
CLOSED: Sunday

I call this immense supermarket my 7-Eleven. Fauchon on the place de la Madeleine may have more history and tradition, but this is the place to go to find the latest and best in nearly every food product you can imagine: a fabulous selection of Italian products; *foie gras* in a dozen different preparations; a wine shop downstairs; a bread shop; a pastry shop; and one of the best butchers in the city. The cheese selection is extensive, but offerings are generally not well aged. (Shoppers are better off walking a few blocks to Quatrehomme at 62, rue de Sèvres.) Produce can vary from best-ever to tasteless and wilted, depending on the season and time of day.

LAFAYETTE GOURMET
48, boulevard Haussmann
Paris 8
TEL: +33 1 48 74 46 06
haussmann.galerieslafayette.com/fr/category/gourmet-4/
MÉTRO: Chausée-d'Antin or Havre-Caumartin
OPEN: Monday through Wednesday, Friday, and Saturday 9:30AM to 8PM. Thursday 9:30AM to 9PM.
CLOSED: Sunday

Here's a Right Bank alternative to La Grande Épicerie with butcher shops; specialty wine, fish, and cheese departments; fresh produce and packaged items from around the world; and even a Petrossian tasting bar and counter. You will also find special departments run by such names as Pierre Hermé, Éric Kayser, Mavrommatis, and Sadaharu Aoki.

GALERIES GOURMANDES
Palais des Congrès (Level -1)
2, place de la Porte Maillot
Paris 17
TEL: +33 1 56 68 85 50
PARKING VINCI AT LEVEL 5BIS

This luxury supermarket offers an excellent variety of high-quality French and international products, including fresh produce (even fresh truffles by order); and organic, gluten free, and kosher foods. Other services like refrigerated Champagnes and wines, parking in the Palais de Congrès, free delivery services, and open seven days a week, make this a handy supermarket destination for those based in the west of Paris.

MARKS AND SPENCER
marksandspencer.fr
100, avenue des Champs-Élysées
Paris 8
TEL: +33 1 56 69 19 20
OPEN: Monday through Saturday 10am to 10pm, Sunday 11am to 10pm

LEVALLOIS-PERRET: SO OUEST SHOPPING CENTER
21-39, rue d'Alsace
Paris 8
TEL: +33 1 47 30 10 35
MÉTRO: Porte de Champerret or Louise Michel
OPEN: Monday through Saturday 10AM to 9PM
CLOSED: Sunday

The tiny food section of this British supermarket chain is always packed full of Parisians and foreigners alike, seeking their favorite treats from across the channel: pork and leek sausages, clotted and thick whipping cream, tea bags, British jams and chutneys, and spiced hot cross buns. For die-hard M&S fans, the Levallois-Perret store just outside of Paris has an extensive food hall, and a large kitchen and tableware department.

HÉDIARD (Madeleine)

GOURMET ÉPICERIE
Place de la Madeleine
Paris 8
TEL: +33 1 42 66 44 36
madeleine@hediard.fr

MÉTRO: Madeleine
OPEN: Monday through Saturday
9AM to 8:30PM
CLOSED: Sunday

Their excellent selection of coffee beans is roasted right in the middle of the place de la Madeleine store. See page 357 for full commentary.

BOUTIQUE MAILLE

MUSTARD, OIL, AND VINEGAR
6, place de la Madeleine
Paris 8
TEL: +33 1 40 15 06 00

maille.com
MÉTRO: Madeleine
OPEN: Monday through Saturday 10AM to 7PM
CLOSED: Sunday

Walking into this beautifully lit, warm golden-oak boutique delivers you instantly to a Paris of the past. It is little known that at one time housewives bought mustard fresh the way we now buy bread—for that meal. As the mustard wasn't pasteurized, it quickly lost its zest, flavor, and heady hotness once exposed to the heat and air. The Maille company boutique has revived this tradition by offering mustard "on tap," pumped from giant containers at the wooden counter into beautiful little gray crockery jars, which are then sealed with a cork. The sales assistants advise against keeping the mustard for more than six months and will happily package the crocks for long-distance travel. Here, you can also pick from Maille's extensive range of flavored mustards, vinegars, and condiments such as cornichons (small cucumber pickles) and capers. A collector's range of hand-painted mustard jars features designs that date back to the company's founding in 1747. Very tempting, they add to the romance of the shop.

LA MAISON DE LA TRUFFE (Madeleine)

TRUFFLE MERCHANT
19, place de la Madeleine
Paris 8
TEL: +33 1 42 65 53 22
maison-de-la-truffe.com

MÉTRO: Madeleine
OPEN: Monday through Saturday 10AM to
10PM. Tasting room open noon to 10PM.
CLOSED: Sunday

As soon as you enter La Maison de la Truffe, you are hit by the unmistakable earthy aroma of the "black diamond of gastronomy." The luxury food shop on the left sells fresh black truffles in season (November to March) as well as the white truffle from Alba (October to December). From May to August shoppers will find the less fragrant but still delicious "summer" truffles known as Burgundy truffles. Exquisitely prepared truffle products are available year-round: preserved truffles, truffle juice, truffle-infused cheeses, truffle potato puree, and a variety of *charcuterie*, goose and duck *foie gras*, duck rillettes, and pâté, all flavored by the Maison de la Truffe with black or white truffles. The adjacent tasting room offers many different dishes with which to experience the truffle, from a simple omelet to a decadent truffled *millefeuille* of goose *foie gras*.

LA MAISON DE LA TRUFFE (Champs-Élysées)

TRUFFLE MERCHANT
14, rue Marbeuf
Paris 8
TEL: +33 1 53 57 41 00

MÉTRO: Alma-Marceau
OPEN: Monday through Saturday 10AM to
10PM. Tasting room open noon to 10PM.
CLOSED: Sunday

A specialist in the highly prized black and white truffle. See above for full commentary.

LA MAISON DU MIEL

HONEY
24, rue Vignon
Paris 8
TEL: +33 1 47 42 26 70
maisondumiel.com

MÉTRO: Madeleine, Havre-Caumartin,
or Opéra
OPEN: Monday through Saturday
9:30AM to 7PM
CLOSED: Sunday and holidays

From the second you lay eyes on the colorful blue and honey–toned storefront of La Maison du Miel—The House of Honey—you know that you are in for a treat. Jars of honey line the store windows as well as the shelves inside. Family run since 1905, this specialty shop founded in 1898 speaks of pride and experience. You can't go wrong here, whether it's a jar of fragrant eucalyptus honey from Italy, the rare New Zealand manuka honey, or heather honey from Spain, not to mention all the varieties of French honey from throughout the land. There are fragrant honey candles, an entire assortment of beauty products, and health-related remedies for breathing, improving one's energy, or curing a sore throat. You may from time to time find bees flying around the shop: They come visiting from the *ruches* (hives) on the roof of the nearby Opéra! And don't forget to look down at the elegantly tiled floor, decorated, of course, with images of bees.

MARIAGE FRÈRES (Étoile)

TEA SHOP / TEA SALON
260, rue du Faubourg Saint-Honoré
Paris 8
TEL: +33 1 46 22 18 54
MÉTRO: Ternes or Charles de Gaulle–Etoile
OPEN: Daily 10:30AM to 7:30PM
(restaurant open daily noon to 3PM;
salon de thé open daily 3 to 7PM)

MARIAGE FRÈRES (Madeleine)

TEA SHOP / TEA SALON
17, place de la Madeleine
Paris 8
TEL: +33 1 42 68 18 54
MÉTRO: Madeleine
OPEN: Monday through Saturday
10:30AM to 7:30PM
CLOSED: Sunday

Mariage Frères is one of France's oldest and most respected tea importers, boasting the world's largest tea collection. See page 336 for full commentary.

BOUCHERIES NIVERNAISES SAINT-HONORÉ

BUTCHER
99, rue du Faubourg Saint-Honoré
Paris 8
TEL: +33 1 43 59 11 02
boucheries-nivernaises.com

boucheries@nivernaisessthonore.fr
MÉTRO: Saint-Philippe-du-Roule
OPEN: Tuesday through Saturday 7:30AM to 1PM and 3:30 to 7PM. Sunday 7AM to 12:30PM.
CLOSED: Monday

Guy Bissonnet is butcher to the stars—Michelin stars, that is. When you dine in the city's finest establishments, that *agneau de Pauillac, boeuf de Normandie, poulet de Bresse,* or *canard de Challans* probably passed through the Bissonnet family's hands. What better reference can there be?

LA PISTACHERIE (Alma)

NUT AND CONFECTIONERY SHOP
5, place de l'Alma
Paris 8
TEL: +33 1 44 43 03 26

MÉTRO: Alma-Marceau
OPEN: Sunday through Thursday 11AM to 8PM.
Friday and Saturday 11AM to 8:30PM.

Top-quality pistachios from Sicily and Turkey. See page 348 for full commentary.

9ᵀᴴ ARRONDISSEMENT

CAUSSES

ÉPICERIE

55, rue Notre-Dame de Lorette
Paris 9
TEL: +33 1 53 16 10 10
causses.org

contact@causses.org
MÉTRO: Saint-Georges or Pigalle
OPEN: Monday through Saturday
10ᴀᴍ to 9:30ᴘᴍ
CLOSED: Sunday

A grocery store for those who like to shop in season and in style. It won't be hard to fill the woven shopping basket you pick up at the door as you wander around this bright, modern *épicerie*. The seasonal fruit and vegetables are fresh and inviting—so don't expect to find tomatoes and strawberries in the winter. In season, local when possible, chemical- and additive-free is their motto. Here you'll find *charcuterie* that is free of gluten and preservatives, and an excellent selection of mostly raw-milk cheeses with the protective European A.O.P. label (*Appellation d'Origine Protégée*, a designation of origin guaranteeing the provenance and savoir faire of a food item's origin and production). Huge ceramic pots hold smoked salt, pepper, herbs, and excellent-quality olives. The pantry section of pastas, flours, spices, and condiments will give you a mini world tour.

> Someone who's tall and lanky is known as a "bean pole" in English—*une asperge,* or "asparagus," in French.

LA CHAMBRE AUX CONFITURES (Martyrs)

JAMS AND MARMALADES

9, rue des Martyrs
Paris 9
MÉTRO: Notre-Dame de Lorette

OPEN: Tuesday through Friday 11ᴀᴍ to 2:30ᴘᴍ and 3:30 to 7:30ᴘᴍ. Saturday 10ᴀᴍ to 7:30ᴘᴍ. Sunday 10ᴀᴍ to 2:30ᴘᴍ.
CLOSED: Monday

A warm and inviting shop lined wall-to-wall with lovingly created gourmet jams. See page 344 for full commentary.

HÉDIARD (Printemps Haussmann)

GOURMET ÉPICERIE

115, rue de Provence
2nd floor of Printemps department store
Paris 9
TEL: +33 1 42 82 62 98

yasmina.aboudrar@hediard.fr
MÉTRO: Havre-Caumartin
OPEN: Monday through Saturday 9:35ᴀᴍ to 8ᴘᴍ
CLOSED: Sunday

A small selection of Hédiard's gourmet food items can be found on the 2nd floor of the Printemps department store. See page 357 for full commentary.

▲ *The original À la Mère de Famille in the 9th is worth visiting just for its incredible storefront and elaborate window displays.*

À LA MÈRE DE FAMILLE (Faubourg-Montmartre)

CONFECTIONERY AND CHOCOLATE SHOP
35, rue du Faubourg-Montmartre
Paris 9

TEL: +33 1 47 70 83 69
MÉTRO: Le Peletier or Richelieu-Drouot
OPEN: Monday through Saturday 9:30AM to 8PM. Sunday 10AM to 1PM.

It's worth coming just for the window displays and vintage exterior of this Old World shop that has been open on rue du Faubourg-Montmartre since 1761. See page 339 for full commentary.

10TH ARRONDISSEMENT

LA TÊTE DANS LES OLIVES

SICILIAN GOURMET FOODS
2, rue Sainte-Marthe
Paris 10
TEL: +33 9 51 31 33 34
latetedanslesolives.com
info@latetedanslesolives.com

MÉTRO: Colonel Fabien, Belleville, or Goncourt
OPEN: Tuesday through Friday 2 to 7PM.
Saturday 11AM to 6PM.
CLOSED: Sunday, Monday, July 30 to August 31, December 25 to January 3

Good things come in small packages and this is certainly true of La Tête Dans les Olives, a cubbyhole of a shop hidden among the brightly colored shutters, artist workshops, and neighborhood restaurants of the adorable rue Sainte-Marthe in the 10th *arrondissement.* Open since 2008, this Italian *épicerie* has become the olive oil supplier for such heavyweights as Alain Ducasse and Inaki Aizpitarte of Le Chateaubriand fame. All the extra-virgin olive oils come from small olive groves in the northwestern region of Sicily (as do all the products in the store) and are affectionately named after their growers: Paolo, Francesco, Marco. Oils are sold by the bottle, or at cheaper prices if you bring in your own vessel.

Owner Cedric Casanova imports a number of other Sicilian products: capers, semi-dried tomatoes, wild oregano, strong, rich Pecorino cheese, all of which can be sampled at lunchtime and evenings when the Paris shop transforms itself into the city's smallest restaurant of one table, seating five people. By reservation only (generally about a six-month wait). Restaurant hours: Monday to Friday noon to 1:30PM for lunch and from 8PM in the evenings. See their website for more details.

12TH ARRONDISSEMENT

OLIVIERS & CO. (Bercy Village)

OLIVE OIL SPECIALIST
20, Cour Saint-Émilion
Bercy Village
Paris 12
TEL : +33 1 43 42 07 83

oliviers-co.com/en
oco-bercy@oliviers-co.com
MÉTRO: Cour Saint-Émilion
OPEN: Monday through Saturday 11AM to 9PM.
Sunday 10:30AM to 1PM.

Fine olive oils, olive oil pastes, and other unusual gourmet pantry items. See page 345 for full commentary.

13TH ARRONDISSEMENT

LES ABEILLES

HONEY
21, rue de la Butte aux Cailles
Paris 13
TEL: +33 1 45 81 43 48
lesabeilles.biz

les.abeilles@wanadoo.fr
MÉTRO: Corvisart
OPEN: Tuesday through Saturday 11AM to 7PM
CLOSED: Sunday and Monday

This tiny shop supplies everything to fulfill the dreams of a beekeeper, a bee lover, and a honey nut, including huge slabs of *pain d'épices,* the French answer to gingerbread. It doesn't have any ginger in it—it's generally a moist, rich-flavored honey and rye-flour bread/cake, supposedly made from a recipe first created by . . . Charlemagne! It's delicious, and the origins of this particular bread are kept a secret by store owner, Jean-Jacques Schakmundès. It's the only honey secret he keeps, however. Besides strong opinions about honey, he offers dozens of varieties ranging from the typical to the obscure (cork oak honey from southern France; buckwheat honey as black as ink; limpid Paris honey from Schakmundès's own hives in the 13th *arrondissement*); even a full beekeeper's outfit; and certainly slabs, rolls, and chunks of beeswax. If you're sincerely interested, you'll walk out of his store filled with honey from his generous samples, laden with jars of honey, and holding a doctorate in apiary science.

14ᵀᴴ ARRONDISSEMENT

BOUCHERIE HUGO DESNOYER

BUTCHER
45, rue Boulard
Paris 14
TEL: +33 1 45 40 76 67
regalez-vous.com

MÉTRO: Mouton-Duvernet
OPEN: Tuesday through Friday 7AM to 1PM and 4 to 8PM. Saturday 7AM to 5PM.
CLOSED: Sunday and Monday

B utcher to the stars Hugo Desnoyer has a long list of celebrity chefs and conscientious bistro owners who he supplies from his modest shop in the 14th *arrondissement*. He counts the Élysée Palace, Joël Robuchon, and Pascal Barbot of the Michelin three-star Astrance among his most loyal clientele. Scores of Parisian home cooks cross the city to sample some of France's best meats: three-month-old lamb from the Lozère, milk-fed by their mothers, who graze on wild cumin,

▼ *Hugo Desnoyer's expert butcher team hard at work.*

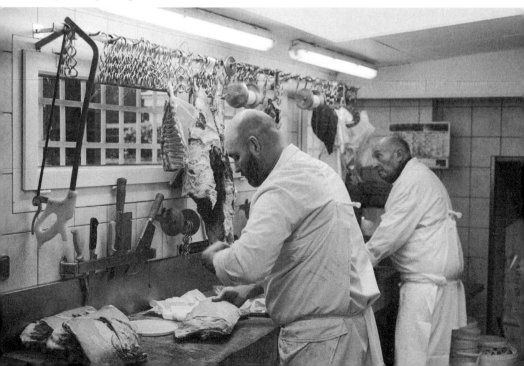

salade burnet, and sweet clover; well-marbled beef from an ancient breed of cow that has strong, forward flavors and (some say) a mild perfume of hazelnuts; as well as free-range, milk-fed veal from the Limousin. You can also find ready-to-cook preparations such as veal roast with olives and Gruyère; pork roast stuffed with apricots, prunes, figs, or peaches; a shoulder of lamb with escargot (snail) butter; or duck with green pepper. See his website (*regalez-vous* translates as "treat yourself") for a more detailed list of the restaurants he supplies.

15TH ARRONDISSEMENT

OLIVIERS & CO. (Grenelle)

OLIVE OIL SPECIALIST
85, rue du Commerce
Paris 15
TEL: +33 1 55 76 42 26
oliviers-co.com/en
oco-commerce@oliviers-co.com

MÉTRO: Commerce
OPEN: Monday 2:30 to 7:30PM. Tuesday through Saturday 10:30AM to 1:30PM and 2:30 to 7:30PM.
CLOSED: Sunday

A top address for *grand cru* and flavored olive oils, olive oil pastes, and other gourmet pantry items. See page 345 for full commentary.

16TH ARRONDISSEMENT

HÉDIARD (La Muette)

GOURMET ÉPICERIE
70, avenue Paul-Doumer
Paris 16
TEL: +33 1 45 04 51 92

doumer@hediard.fr
MÉTRO: Trocadéro or Muette
OPEN: Monday through Saturday 9AM to 9PM
CLOSED: Sunday

A chic and elegant *épicerie*, stocking everything you need for a gourmet pantry: house spice blends, exotic vinegars and mustards, chocolates and cakes. See page 357 for full commentary.

À LA MÈRE DE FAMILLE (rue de la Pompe)

CONFECTIONERY AND CHOCOLATE SHOP
59, rue de la Pompe
Paris 16

TEL: +33 1 45 04 73 19
MÉTRO: Rue de la Pompe
OPEN: Monday through Saturday 9:30AM to 8PM, Sunday 10AM to 1PM

A small version of the larger, more romantic Old World shop in the 9th *arrondissement*. See page 339 for full commentary.

PÂTÉ AUX FOIE DE VOLAILLE
Chicken Liver Spread

I roast chickens with great regularity. I chop up the gizzards and heart and stuff them back into the cavity to enrich the flavors of the poultry. But I always set aside the tasty chicken livers. I freeze them until I have gathered up half a dozen, then prepare this spread, always a winner at our table.

EQUIPMENT:

A fine-mesh sieve; a mini food processor or a standard food processor fitted with a small bowl

INGREDIENTS:

6 chicken livers, trimmed

3 tablespoons best-quality red wine vinegar

1 small onion, peeled and minced

1 tablespoon extra-virgin olive oil

Fine sea salt

3 tablespoons white wine

3 oil-cured anchovy filets, drained

2 fresh or dried bay leaves

Coarse, freshly ground black pepper

2 tablespoons capers in vinegar, drained

4 to 6 slices toasted sourdough bread, for serving

1. In a bowl, combine the chicken livers and the vinegar and set aside for 5 minutes. Place the livers in the mesh sieve, draining and discarding the vinegar.

2. In a small saucepan with a lid, combine the onion, oil, and a pinch of salt and sweat—cook, covered, over low heat until soft, 2 to 3 minutes. Add the chicken livers, wine, anchovies, bay leaves, another pinch of salt, and the pepper. Cook over low heat for 10 minutes, stirring regularly. Remove and discard the bay leaves.

3. Transfer the liver mixture to the food processor and puree. Return the mixture to the saucepan, add the capers, and cook over low heat for 2 minutes more, stirring regularly, to allow flavors to blend. The mixture should be smooth, dotted with capers. Taste for seasoning. Serve warm, on toast, seasoned with plenty of black pepper.

4 TO 6 SERVINGS

▶ *Hugo Desnoyer, sharpening his butcher's knife.*

17ᵀᴴ ARRONDISSEMENT

HÉDIARD (Monceau)

GOURMET ÉPICERIE
106, boulevard de Courcelles
Paris 17
TEL: +33 1 47 63 32 14
hediard.com
courcelles@hediard.fr
MÉTRO: Courcelles
OPEN: Monday through Saturday
9AM to 8:30PM
CLOSED: Sunday

HÉDIARD (Palais des Congrès)

GOURMET ÉPICERIE
Palais des Congrès
Porte Maillot
Paris 17
TEL: +33 1 56 68 85 50
hediard.com
MÉTRO: Porte Maillot
OPEN: Tuesday through Saturday
10AM to 12:30PM and 3 to 7:30PM
CLOSED: Sunday

The perfect boutique for gourmet gift items. See page 357 for full commentary.

À LA MÈRE DE FAMILLE (Wagram)

**CONFECTIONERY AND
CHOCOLATE SHOP**
107, rue Jouffroy d'Abbans
Paris 17

TEL: +33 1 47 63 52 95
MÉTRO: Wagram
OPEN: Monday through Sunday
9:30AM to 8PM, Sunday 10AM to 1PM

This small sister boutique of the original 1761 store in the 9th *arrondissement* sells beautiful Old World candies, chocolates, and jellies, and charming tins of assorted treats. See page 339 for full commentary.

OLIVIERS & CO. (Batignolles)

OLIVE OIL SPECIALIST
8, rue de Levis
Paris 17
TEL: +33 1 53 42 18 04
oliviers-co.com/en

oliviers.co.levis@free.fr
MÉTRO: Villiers
OPEN: Monday 1 to 7:30PM. Tuesday through Saturday 10AM to 7:30PM. Sundays 9:30AM to 1:30PM.

For top-quality *grand cru* and flavored olive oils and gourmet pantry items. See page 345 for full commentary.

AT A GLANCE

1ST ARRONDISSEMENT

Le Comptoir de Tunisie
Mariage Frères (Louvre)
Café Verlet

2ND ARRONDISSEMENT

Épices Roellinger
G. Detou
À la Mère de Famille
    (Montorgueil)
Télescope
Terroir d'Avenir
Tetrel
Workshop Issé

3RD ARRONDISSEMENT

La Chambre aux Confitures
    (Marais)
L'Épicerie Breizh Café
Goumanyat & Son Royaume
Oliviers & Co. (Marais)

4TH ARRONDISSEMENT

Izraël Épicerie du Monde
La Maison de la Prasline
    Mazet
Mariage Frères (Marais)
À L'Olivier
Oliviers & Co.
    (Île Saint-Louis)
La Pistacherie (Rambuteau)

5TH ARRONDISSEMENT

Maison des Trois Thés
Oliviers & Co. (Mouffetard)

6TH ARRONDISSEMENT

Da Rosa
Mariage Frères
    (Saint-Germain)
À la Mère de Famille
    (Cherche-Midi)
Oliviers & Co.
    (Saint-Germain)
Tomat's Épicerie Fine

7TH ARRONDISSEMENT

Coutume
À la Mere de Famille
    (Rue Cler)
Petrossian
Les Viandes du Champ de
    Mars / Jean-Marie Boedec

8TH ARRONDISSEMENT

Betjeman & Barton
Caviar Kaspia
Fauchon
Hédiard (George V)
Hédiard (Madeleine)
Boutique Maille
La Maison de la Truffe
    (Madeleine)
La Maison de la Truffe
    (Champs-Élysées)
La Maison du Miel
Mariage Frères (Étoile)
Mariage Frères (Madeleine)
Boucheries Nivernaises
    Saint-Honoré
La Pistacherie (Alma)

9TH ARRONDISSEMENT

Causses
La Chambre aux Confitures
    (Martyrs)
Hédiard (Printemps
    Haussmann)
À La Mère de Famille
    (Faubourg-Montmartre)

10TH ARRONDISSEMENT

La Tête dans les Olives

12TH ARRONDISSEMENT

Oliviers & Co. (Bercy Village)

13TH ARRONDISSEMENT

Les Abeilles

14TH ARRONDISSEMENT

Boucherie Hugo Desnoyer

15TH ARRONDISSEMENT

Oliviers & Co. (Grenelle)

16TH ARRONDISSEMENT

Hédiard (La Muette)
À la Mère de Famille
    (Rue de la Pompe)

17TH ARRONDISSEMENT

Hédiard (Monceau)
Hédiard (Palais des Congrès)
À la Mère de Famille
    (Wagram)
Oliviers & Co. (Batignolles)

KITCHEN AND TABLEWARE SHOPS

POUR LA MAISON

I f you have been searching for just the right antique champagne flute, antique knife rests *(porte couteaux),* colorful asparagus or oyster plates, modern silicone baking molds, or need to round out a knife collection, you will find your *bonheur,* or happiness, in these shops. I have always had a weakness for each and every antique object used in the kitchen or dining room, so many of these shops are ones I frequent regularly, in search of a 1930s cookie jar, a lovely linen tablecloth with someone else's embroidered initials (or sometimes I may find one with my own!), a special spoon for serving cured olives. On the modern side, I am a gadget girl, so I love to be set loose inside the city's many emporiums devoted to the kitchen and the table. Note that some of the shops are small and may be casually run, so opening and closing hours might not always be followed to the letter. ❧

1ST ARRONDISSEMENT

ASTIER DE VILLATTE

TABLEWARE AND HOME DECOR
173, rue Saint-Honoré
Paris 1
TEL: +33 1 42 60 74 13
astierdevillatte.com

MÉTRO: Palais-Royal–Musée du Louvre,
Pyramides, or Tuileries
OPEN: Monday through Saturday 11AM to
7:30PM
CLOSED: Sunday

What used to be the workshop of a silversmith to Napoleon 200 years ago is now home to the beautifully handmade wares of Astier de Villatte. There is a large collection of charming white ceramics, each piece a small artwork of its own. Most are designed and made in Paris by founders Ivan Pericoli and Benoît Astier de Villatte, but you will also find exquisite handcrafted pieces by Parisian artist Nathalie Lété. The shop covers three floors, so be sure to visit the first floor and basement for the Astier de Villatte furniture collection.

▶ *Astier de Villatte's ceramics.*

E. DEHILLERIN

COOKING SUPPLY STORE
18–20, rue Coquillière
Paris 1
TEL: +33 1 42 36 53 13
e-dehillerin.fr

info@e-dehillerin.fr
MÉTRO: Les Halles
OPEN: Monday 9AM to 12:30PM and 2 to 6PM.
Tuesday through Saturday 9AM to 6PM.
CLOSED: Sunday

A fabulous but somewhat overwhelming professional cookware store, E. Dehillerin is not for the faint of heart. In a setting more like a warehouse than a shop, the stock covers every available wall, floor, and

▲ *E. Dehillerin is copper heaven!*

ceiling space, as well as a basement level. They have a remarkable selection of cooking tools, copper pots, carbon and stainless alloy knives, silicon and fiberglass baking molds, and unusual kitchen tools that include copper tabletop potato warmers for raclette and *cremaillères,* or hooks to hang from the hearth. English is spoken by the staff, who can be friendly, if not a little gruff and impatient. A comprehensive merchandise catalog is available on their website in English. The shop will ship purchases.

FRAGONARD (Louvre)

TABLEWARE AND TABLE LINENS
Carrousel du Louvre
99, rue de Rivoli
Paris 1

TEL: +33 1 42 96 96 96
fragonard.com
MÉTRO: Louvre-Rivoli
OPEN: Daily 10AM to 8PM

With a handful of appealing boutiques sprinkled around Paris, the landmark perfume-maker Fragonard expands to the table, with all matter of fanciful (and practical) embroidered napkins, as well as unusual cutlery and table ornaments. Their selection never remains static, so if you find what you like, jump on it, for it may not be there on the next visit! I have an extensive collection of their "themed" napkins, including those sporting colorful vegetables, fish, shellfish, poultry, herbs, and fruits. They make perfects gifts for the host or hostess, or, when you feel worthy, for yourself!

MORA

COOKING SUPPLY STORE
13, rue Montmartre
Paris 1
TEL: 33 1 45 08 19 24
mora.fr

moracontact@mora.fr
MÉTRO: Les Halles
OPEN: Monday through Friday 9AM to 6:15PM.
Saturday 10AM to 1PM and 1:45 to 6:30PM.
CLOSED: Sunday

Walking into Mora makes you want to fill your basket with kitchen equipment and head straight back to your kitchen to start cooking.

This cooking-supply store in the old Les Halles neighborhood is for both professionals and the ambitious amateur. There is a huge range of cooking utensils, molds, and baking tins in every imaginable shape and size, chocolate molds, and pots and pans in stainless steel and copper—although be sure to come with the dimensions of your oven: Many objects are oversize, made to fit large professional ovens. You can also find an extensive selection of food dyes, cake decorations, paperware, and all sizes of disposable pastry boxes.

2ND ARRONDISSEMENT

A. SIMON

COOKING SUPPLY STORE
48, rue Montmartre
Paris 2
TEL: +33 1 42 33 71 65

MÉTRO: Sentier or Les Halles
OPEN: Monday through Friday 9AM to 7PM,
Saturday 10:30AM to 7PM
CLOSED: Sunday

This store is a serious cook's dream, whether professional or amateur. A. Simon has stocked French restaurants since the late 1800s and can

supply you with almost any kind of kitchen implement or machine your heart can dream of. Next door, at No. 52, their sister store stocks a huge variety of tableware.

LIBRAIRIE GOURMANDE

COOKBOOK STORE
92–96, rue Montmartre
Paris 2
TEL: +33 1 43 54 37 27

librairiegourmande.fr
OPEN: Monday through Saturday 11AM to 7PM
CLOSED: Sunday

If you're in need of inspiration for your own culinary creations, or just like to explore the world through cookbooks, seek out the Librairie Gourmande, a favorite cookbook store of Parisian chefs. I could get lost in this store for days, browsing the two floors of their hugely diverse collection, which includes over 200 titles from French chefs and an extensive baking and pastry section, including 85 books just on chocolate! For the serious researcher, there is a whole section dedicated to the literature, history, and the sociology of cooking and food. The impressive foreign-language section has over 300 titles in English, including English translations of publications by some of Paris's star chefs, such as Pierre Gagnaire, Eric Briffard of Le Cinq, Alain Ducasse, and famed pastry chef Pierre Hermé. All their titles are online and can be ordered from their website.

3RD ARRONDISSEMENT

KITCHEN BAZAAR (Marais)

COOKING SUPPLY STORE
4, rue de Bretagne
Paris 3
TEL: +33 1 44 78 97 04
kitchenbazaar.fr

info@kitchenbazaar.net
MÉTRO: Filles du Calvaire
OPEN: Monday 1:30 to 7:30PM. Tuesday through Saturday 10:30AM to 7:30PM.
CLOSED: Sunday

Name a kitchen gadget and they most likely will have it here—especially if it's stainless steel or silicone. For decades, Kitchen Bazaar has been at the forefront of modern kitchenware design, offering items that are not only beautiful but functional—Japanese mandolines, Rösle truffle slicers, anti-adhesive silicone whisks, and all kinds of mixers and blenders. They also stock much larger items such as elegant shopping carts, garbage cans, and espresso makers. I never leave here without finding something I *have* to have.

MERCI

CONCEPT STORE
111, boulevard Beaumarchais
Paris 3
TEL: +33 42 77 00 33

merci-merci.com
MÉTRO: Saint-Sébastien–Froissard
OPEN: Monday through Saturday 10AM to 7PM
CLOSED: Sunday

The basement of this super-hip concept store is dedicated to your designer kitchenware needs, from clever Japanese cooking gadgets to chic plastic and tin picnicware. Two flights up in the top-floor housewares section, you can find beautiful porcelain and ceramic dinner sets, elegant glassware, linen tableware, and cute and quirky table decorations. Take a break after shopping in one of the store's three cafés. The basement café looks out onto an inner courtyard garden and serves up fresh, tasty salads, tarts, and risotto. Or you can settle into a vintage leather armchair in the Used Book Café to order coffee, cake, or light snacks. The Cinema Café next door offers soups, salads, and small-snack plates, such as organic meaty country *terrine de campagne* or the prized Spanish *pata negra* ham, served with toast scrubbed with juicy, fresh tomatoes, or *pan con tomate*. All are delicious, healthy, and well priced. And for guilt-free shopping, it's nice to know that all company profits go to charity.

LE PETIT ATELIER DE PARIS

CERAMICS
31, rue de Montmorency
Paris 3
TEL: +33 1 44 54 91 40
lepetitatelierdeparis.com

contact@lepetitatelierdeparis.com
MÉTRO: Rambuteau
OPEN: Thursday through Saturday 1 to 7PM
CLOSED: Sunday through Wednesday

Le Petit Atelier de Paris is the showroom of ceramic designer husband-and-wife duo Stéphane and Jae Froger. Using simple industrial molds in their on-site atelier they create a variety of fine porcelain housewares, then finish each piece by hand. You can pick up stylish espresso cup sets, individual tart molds imprinted with simple sentiments (*bonheur, santé, prosperité*, which translate as "happiness, health, prosperity"), as well as elegant star-embossed plates. They also print their own quirky vintage-style tea towels. Note the odd opening hour to avoid disappointment.

▶ *You will find beauty in simplicity at the Petit Atelier de Paris.*

4TH ARRONDISSEMENT

ARGENTERIE D'ANTAN

SILVERWARE
6, rue de Birague
Paris 4
TEL: +33 1 42 71 31 91
argenterie-dantan.com

argenterie-dantan@argenterie-dantan.com
MÉTRO: Saint-Paul
OPEN: Tuesday through Saturday 10:30AM to 1PM and 2 to 7PM. Sunday 2 to 7PM.
CLOSED: Monday

Just south of the Place des Vosges, this small but tightly packed silverware shop has a beautiful range of antique and secondhand pieces, from extraordinarily crafted silver flatware and tableware (including Christofle, Ercuis, Puiforcat, and Odiot) to original 1950s oyster spoons. A perfect spot to augment your collection.

FLEUX

TABLEWARE AND HOME DECOR
52, rue Sainte-Croix de la Bretonnerie
Paris 4
TEL: +33 1 42 78 27 20
fleux.com

MÉTRO: Hôtel de Ville
OPEN: Monday through Friday 10:45AM to 7:30PM. Saturday 10:30AM to 8PM. Sunday 2 to 7PM.

A modern houseware store with a nod to the vintage, Fleux has a fun range of designer table and kitchenware that makes for original gifts or a memorable addition to your kitchen collection. They have a range of European, Asian, and French tableware designs, including beautiful Eno plates and trays and a vast choice of quirky designer mugs and tea sets. Fleux has a second location across the road at No. 39, but most of the kitchenware can be found at No. 52.

FRAGONARD (Marais)

TABLEWARE AND TABLE LINENS
51, rue des Francs-Bourgeois
Paris 4
TEL: +33 1 44 78 01 32

fragonard.com
MÉTRO: Saint-Paul
OPEN: Monday through Saturday 10:30AM to 7:30PM. Sunday noon to 7PM.

This is my go-to store for colorful, themed napkins for the table. See page 373 for full commentary.

LAGUIOLE

KNIVES
35, rue des Deux Ponts
Paris 4
TEL: +33 1 43 29 10 57
laguiole-en-aubrac.fr
magasins-paris.com/magasins/laguiole-ile-
saint-louis

laguiole-ile-saint-louis@orange.fr
MÉTRO: Pont Marie
OPEN: Monday through Saturday
10:30AM to 7PM. Sunday 2 to 7PM.

This small boutique on the Île Saint-Louis offers the largest range of authentic, high-quality Laguiole knives (see box on facing page for some background) in Paris—indeed, anywhere in France outside of Laguiole.

Their vast selection includes the whole Laguiole en Aubrac collection, including their classic folding pocketknife, contemporary knife designs from the artisan manufacturer Forge de Lagioule, and a range of pocket- knives from the well-known Opinel brand. The boutique also offers a repair service for all Laguiole en Aubrac knives, which come with a lifetime guarantee. The pronunciation, by the way, is "lay-ole," with the g silent.

MUJI (Marais)

TABLEWARE AND HOME DECOR
47, rue des Francs Bourgeois
Paris 4
TEL: +33 1 49 96 41 41
muji.eu

MÉTRO: Rambuteau or Saint-Paul
OPEN: Monday through Friday 10AM to
7:30PM. Saturday 10AM to 8PM.
CLOSED: Sunday

Paris and Tokyo may be worlds apart but one thing they do have in common is small-apartment living. This minimalist Japanese store has simply designed cookware and tableware, and clever storage solutions for the *petit cuisine*. See box (below) for full commentary.

MUJI

France's love affair with Japan is evident in the number of Muji stores found all over Paris. They are always bustling, full of customers browsing in search of clever Japanese home-storage solutions. I could happily stock my kitchen cupboards with their clean, simply designed glass, porcelain, wood, and plastic kitchenware. Whether it be a plastic cling-film dispenser, binders for recipes, or a set of wooden miso bowls, I always come away with something. Their range of plastic travel bottles is also very useful to avoid problems with hand luggage at airport security.

LAGUIOLE KNIVES

"A knife in the pocket: Let's say, an Opinel n°6, or a Laguiole. A knife that could belong to a hypothetical and perfect grandfather … a knife that could be pulled from his pocket at lunchtime, to stab slices of *saucisson* with its tip, to peel his apple slowly … a knife that we would have thought wonderful if we were children: a knife for the bow and the arrow, to shape the wooden sword, the hilt sculpted from bark. … For a few seconds we feel both the pastoral white-moustached grandfather and the child, close to the water with the scent of elderflower. Between the moment of opening and closing the blade, we are no longer between two ages, but both ages at the same time. That is the secret of the knife."
—Philippe Delerm, *La Première Gorgée de Bière (The First Sip of Beer)*

The Laguiole (pronounced "lay-ole") folding knife has become a cult symbol in the French consciousness, one that conjures sentimental images—as French author Philippe Delerm so wistfully puts it—of childhood and a hypothetical and perfect grandfather. Invented in 1829, the original Laguiole pocketknife was modeled on a Spanish knife and was traditionally a gift from father to son, to be treasured over a lifetime. The blades are made from extra-hard surgical steel that never rusts and needs only infrequent sharpening. (The official Laguiole website tells how to do it.) The handles of both table and pocketknives were historically made of wood, bone, or ivory, though some contemporary designs are now all steel. The bee or fly symbol (there is controversy over which it actually is) on the back of the knife handle is a trademark of this traditional Occitan pocketknife. Due to the fact that the design has never been trademarked, cheap knockoffs

abound. But with knives such as these, for which just the sculpting of the handle can take anywhere from a few hours to a couple of days, don't expect to pay anything less than around 100€. And look for the label Laguiole Origine Guarantie for a guarantee of authenticity.

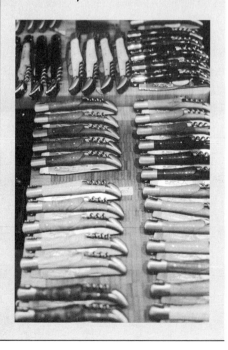

▶ *Authentic Laguiole corkscrew pocketknives.*

▲ *If vintage kitchenware is your thing, then you will surely find happiness at Au Petit Bonheur La Chance.*

AU PETIT BONHEUR LA CHANCE

VINTAGE KITCHENWARE
13, rue Saint-Paul
Paris 4
TEL: +33 1 42 74 36 38
aupetitbonheurlachance.fr

MÉTRO: Saint-Paul
OPEN: Wednesday through Sunday 11AM to 1PM
and 2:30 to 6:30PM
CLOSED: Monday and Tuesday

This minuscule shop on the rue Saint-Paul antique alley is a trove of vintage kitchenware collected from flea markets all over France. Straight from the 1950s country kitchen of *la grandmère,* the shop is stacked floor to ceiling with all manner of wonderful old objects: jam jars and tins, blue-and-white sugar and flour pots, *café au lait* bowls, canning labels, and cheese markers. Note the odd hours, but if you catch them open, you'll be sure to find a treasure.

LA VAISSELLERIE (Marais)

TABLEWARE
92, rue Saint-Antoine
Paris 4
TEL: +33 1 42 72 76 66
lavaissellerie.fr

lavaissellerie@orange.fr
MÉTRO: Saint-Paul
OPEN: Monday through Saturday 10AM to 7PM
CLOSED: Sunday

With several shops dotted around Paris, cheap and cheerful La Vaissellerie is the perfect place to pick up small porcelain ramekins, *café au lait* bowls, or a Limoges porcelain dining set for next to nothing.

6TH ARRONDISSEMENT

COUTELLERIE CECCALDI

KNIVES
15, rue Racine
Paris 6
TEL: +33 1 46 33 87 20
couteaux-ceccaldi.com

couteaux.ceccaldi@live.fr
MÉTRO: Odéon or Luxembourg (RER)
OPEN: Monday through Saturday 9AM to noon
and 2 to 6PM
CLOSED: Sunday

This charming boutique with its adjacent workshop turns out precious, unique, artisanal cutlery for the table, the kitchen, and yes, the pasture.

The Corsican family of artisans began in 1978, creating special knives for shepherds. Their line has now grown to include knives for hunting, for cutting paper, for the table and the kitchen. Most items can be purchased online. Each item is special, hand-forged with handles made of wood, horn, silver, and ebony.

MAISON DE FAMILLE (Saint-Sulpice)

TABLEWARE AND HOME DECOR
29, rue Saint-Sulpice
Paris 6
TEL: +33 1 40 46 97 47
maisondefamille.fr

MÉTRO: Mabillon
OPEN: Monday through Saturday
10:30AM to 7PM
CLOSED: Sunday

Maison de Famille's collection of tableware and home decor is understated but with a flair for fun, with a large collection of classic, modern, and ethnic pieces. Pick up charming additions to your dining room decor, such as feathered place mats and etched-glass Champagne flutes, or invest in a larger piece from their beautiful range of extendable dining tables. Quality is good and prices are within reason.

MUJI (Saint-Sulpice)

TABLEWARE AND HOME DECOR
27 and 30, rue Saint-Sulpice
Paris 6
TEL: +33 1 44 07 37 30
muji.eu

MÉTRO: Mabillon or Odéon
OPEN: Monday through Friday 10AM to
7:30PM. Saturday 10AM to 8PM.
CLOSED: Sunday

This is my local Muji store, which I find indispensible. See box (page 378) for full commentary.

LA VAISSELLERIE (Saint-Germain)

TABLEWARE AND COOKWARE
85, rue de Rennes
Paris 6
TEL: +33 42 22 61 49

lavaissellerie@orange.fr
MÉTRO: Saint-Sulpice or Rennes
OPEN: Monday through Saturday 10AM to 7PM
CLOSED: Sunday

See facing page for full commentary.

POUR LA CUISINE MODERNE

Parisian kitchens are notoriously small. Making the most of these tiny spaces is made much easier by the many modern kitchenware stores—both foreign and French-owned—that are now all over the capital. These stores have endless creative ideas for fun kitchen design at very affordable prices.

THE CONRAN SHOP has an excellent kitchen section where you will be sure to find something you love. While some items have a high price tag, there's usually something for every budget and fantastic bargains are to be had during sale season. Pick up a shiny new espresso machine, or just cheer up your kitchen with a chic new tea towel.

At **CULINARION** you'll find almost every kind of kitchen implement you can think of, including the more unusual—blini pans, bamboo cookbook stands, and sturdy metal oyster gloves.

HABITAT has everything you could want for setting up a modern, fun kitchen, from furniture to state-of-the-art kitchenware. Whether you are searching for pottery and affordable dining sets with bold graphic prints, or a hot pink cake stand, you'll no doubt find something to brighten up your kitchen.

GENEVIÈVE LETHU has more of a country style, with a huge selection of handmade baskets, brightly striped cotton and cotton-linen fabric for making tea towels, Alsatian cookie stamps, white porcelain *chocolatiers*, painted pottery dishes, and pretty wicker shopping carts to take to the market.

ZARA HOME is surprisingly inexpensive for its elegantly designed diningware. They have a very appealing collection of wineglasses and carafes, and all manner of table decorations that will transform any dining room.

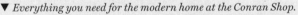

▼ *Everything you need for the modern home at the Conran Shop.*

THE CONRAN SHOP

117, rue du Bac
Paris 7
TEL: +33 1 42 84 10 01
conranshop.fr
bac@conranshop.fr
MÉTRO: Sèvres-Babylone
OPEN: Monday through
Friday 10AM to 7PM. Saturday
10AM to 7:30PM.
CLOSED: Sunday

CULINARION

99, rue de Rennes
Paris 6
TEL: +33 1 45 48 94 76
culinarion.com
contact@culinarionparis.com
MÉTRO: Rennes
OPEN: Monday and Tuesday
10:30AM to 7PM. Wednesday
through Saturday 10:15AM
to 7PM.
CLOSED: Sunday

HABITAT

habitat.fr
8, rue du Pont-Neuf
Paris 1
TEL: +33 1 63 00 99 88
MÉTRO: Pont-Neuf
OPEN: Monday through
Saturday 10AM to 7:30PM
CLOSED: Sunday

30, boulevard des Capucines
Paris 9
TEL: +33 1 42 68 12 76
MÉTRO: Madeleine
OPEN: Monday through
Friday 10:30AM to 7PM,
Saturday 11am to 7:30PM
CLOSED: Sunday

10, place de la République
Paris 11
TEL: +33 1 48 07 13 14
MÉTRO: République
OPEN: Monday through
Saturday 11AM to 8PM
CLOSED: Sunday

91, rue du Faubourg
Saint-Antoine
Paris 12
TEL: +33 1 53 02 02 54
MÉTRO: Bastille or
Ledru-Rollin
OPEN: Monday through
Saturday 10AM to 7:30PM
CLOSED: Sunday

Centre Commercial
Maine-Montparnasse
11, rue de l'Arrivée
Paris 15
TEL: +33 1 45 38 69 90
MÉTRO: Montparnasse-
Bienvenüe
OPEN: Daily 10AM to 7:30PM

35, avenue de Wagram
Paris 17
TEL: +33 1 55 37 75 00
MÉTRO: Ternes
OPEN: Monday through
Friday 10:30AM to 7:30PM,
Saturday 10AM to 8PM
CLOSED: Sunday

GENEVIÈVE LETHU

genevievelethu.com

95, rue de Rennes
Paris 6
TEL: +33 1 45 44 40 35
MÉTRO: Rennes
OPEN: Monday through
Saturday 10:15AM to 7PM
CLOSED: Sunday

317, rue de Vaugirard
Paris 15
TEL: +33 1 45 31 77 84
MÉTRO: Convention
OPEN: Monday 1:30 to 7PM.
Tuesday through Saturday
10:30AM to 7PM.
CLOSED: Sunday and some
days between 1 and 2PM for
lunch.

ZARA HOME

zarahome.com

38–40, avenue des Champs-
Élysées
Paris 8
TEL: +33 1 56 59 97 10
MÉTRO: Franklin D. Roosevelt
OPEN: Daily 10AM to 9PM

2, boulevard de la Madeleine
Paris 9
TEL: +33 1 58 18 38 20
MÉTRO: Madeleine
OPEN: Monday through
Friday 10AM to 7:30PM
CLOSED: Sunday

54, avenue Victor Hugo
Paris 16
TEL: +33 1 58 44 99 50
MÉTRO: Victor Hugo
OPEN: Monday through
Friday 10AM to 7:30PM
CLOSED: Sunday

Passy Plaza
53, rue de Passy
Paris 16
TEL: +33 1 55 74 01 61
MÉTRO: Passy or La Muette
OPEN: Monday through
Friday 10AM to 7:30PM
CLOSED: Sunday

7TH ARRONDISSEMENT

AU BAIN MARIE

KITCHEN AND TABLEWARE
56, rue de l'Université
Paris 7
TEL: +33 1 42 71 08 69

aubainmarie.fr
MÉTRO: Rue du Bac
OPEN: Tuesday through Saturday 11AM to 7PM
CLOSED: Sunday and Monday

Think of Aude Clément's fantasy-like Au Bain Marie as a candy store for those with a passion for unique kitchen and tableware items. She offers a spectacular selection of antique and modern silver and a large collection of antique *barbotines*, such as decorative asparagus, artichoke, and oyster plates. Items can also be purchased directly from her website.

▶ *Au Bain Marie: a kitchen and tableware lover's dream.*

LA CORNUE

STOVES AND TABLEWARE
54, rue de Bourgogne
Paris 7
TEL: +33 1 46 33 84 74
lacornue.com

MÉTRO: Varenne
OPEN: Monday through Saturday
10:30AM to 6:30PM
CLOSED: Sunday

La Cornue is what dream kitchens are made of! Their sturdy, giant stoves are legendary (I am lucky enough to have Julia Childs's 1960s white model in my kitchen in Provence). But La Cornue president Xavier Dupuy is not content to rest on history and laurels, and in this shiny, modern 7th *arrondissement* boutique, he now offers a huge line of ultramodern cookware (wall ovens as well as high-tech induction counters). But he does not let down the old-timers who are just looking for sturdy kitchen gadgets, hefty copper cookware, and well-designed materials for cooking and grilling.

FRAGONARD (Saint-Germain)

TABLEWARE AND TABLE LINENS
196, boulevard Saint-Germain
Paris 7
TEL: +33 1 42 84 12 12
fragonard.com

MÉTRO: Rue du Bac or Saint-Germain-des-Prés
OPEN: Monday through Saturday 10AM to 6PM
CLOSED: Sunday

This is my neighborhood Fragonard boutique, which I pass every day on my way to the office/cooking school. I love to window shop in the early hours, then return to "browse" when they are open later in the day. Their themed napkins often end up as gifts for myself or my host or hostess. See page 373 for full commentary.

MURIEL GRATEAU BOUTIQUE

CERAMIC TABLEWARE AND LINENS
37, rue de Beaune
Paris 7
TEL: +33 1 40 20 42 82
murielgrateau.com

info@murielgrateau.com
MÉTRO: Rue du Bac
OPEN: Monday through Saturday 11AM to 7PM
CLOSED: Sunday

Muriel Grateau has moved her stunning boutique, formerly in the Galerie de Valois in the Palais Royal Gardens, to the rue de Beaune on the Left Bank. As always you can find her rich array of brightly colored table linens. Her new collection of tableware includes an exquisite range of extremely fine porcelain dinnerware in subtle hues of pinks and blues as well as striking black ceramic. Prices are high but the workmanship is perfect.

SIÈCLE

TABLEWARE
24, rue du Bac
Paris 7
TEL: +33 1 47 03 48 03

siecle-paris.com
boutique@siecle-paris.com
MÉTRO: Rue du Bac
OPEN: Daily 11AM to 7PM

It's hard to walk past this fanciful boutique devoted to aesthetic, often playful items for the table and not go in and browse. Once inside, it's even harder to walk out empty-handed. Fortunately, most items here are reasonably priced, ranging from simple white porcelain tableware (which I use at my Paris table each day) to decorative drawer pulls in the shape of butterflies (which adorn my Paris kitchen as well). You'll also find table linens, a strong line of unique cutlery for the table, glassware, and caviar spoons, as well as well-priced, one-of-a-kind jewelry items. Browsing is encouraged and the service is always friendly. Items from the boutique can also be purchased online.

▶ *Siècle founder and owner Philippe Chupin.*

8ᵀᴴ ARRONDISSEMENT

LA CARPE

COOKING SUPPLY STORE
14, rue Tronchet
Paris 8
TEL: +33 1 47 42 73 25
lacarpe75.com
MÉTRO: Madeleine or Havre-Caumartin

OPEN: Monday 2 to 6:45PM. Tuesday through Saturday 10AM to 6:45PM. Sundays in December only, 10AM to 6:45PM.
CLOSED: Sunday (exept in December) and August

Since 1921, this full-service kitchenware shop has served Parisian households. Just about every piece of contemporary cookware and gadgetry can be found here, including a generous selection of knives, modern shopping carts, cheese-serving equipment, and many brands of cutlery. The shop also repairs equipment and will ship abroad.

FORGE DE LAGUIOLE

KNIVES
29, rue Boissy d'Anglas
Paris 8
TEL: +33 1 40 06 09 75
forge-de-laguiole.com

MÉTRO: Madeleine
OPEN: Monday through Saturday 10AM to noon and 2 to 7PM
CLOSED: Sunday

The Laguiole folding knife has become a cult symbol in the French consciousness, one that conjures sentimental images of the perfect

MARCHÉS AUX PUCES (FLEA MARKETS)

There are two main flea markets in Paris, Marché aux Puces Saint-Ouen, just on the other side of the *Peripherique* border in the north of Paris in Saint-Ouen, and Marché aux Puces de la Porte de Vanves, in the 15th *arrondissement* in the south of Paris. However, there are many roving flea markets called *brocantes et vides greniers* (literally, "to empty the attic," and similar to yard sales), which pop up in every neighborhood in Paris. Some are better than others, but if you strike a good one, there are some fantastic bargains to be found. You can find listings of all the upcoming markets, by *arrondissement*, at vide-greniers.org. Just type *Paris* into the search field.

MARCHÉS AUX PUCES

SAINT-OUEN
Clignancourt Flea Market
marcheauxpuces-
saintouen.com
MÉTRO: Porte de
Clignancourt or Garibaldi
OPEN: Saturday and Sunday
9AM to 6PM. Monday 10AM
to 6PM.
CLOSED: Tuesday through
Friday

DE LA PORTE DE VANVES
Avenue Marc Sangnier and
avenue Georges Lafenestre
MÉTRO: Porte de Vanves
OPEN: Every weekend
without exception, 7AM
to 2PM

AT MARCHÉ AUX PUCES SAINT-OUEN

Some favorite spots in the Saint-Ouen market:

BACHELIER ANTIQUITÉS
Marché Paul Bert
17, Allée 1
93400 Saint-Ouen
Expensive, but great for
finding old copper pots,
etc.

LA PUCE D'ARGENT
Marché Vernaison
Allée 1 Stand 24
93400 Saint-Ouen
A treasure trove for finding
unusual oyster forks, ice-
cream spoons, and more.

Where to eat in the Saint-Ouen market:

MA COCOTTE
106, rue des Rosiers
93400 Saint-Ouen
TEL: +33 1 49 51 70 00
macocotte-lespuces.com
MÉTRO: Porte de
Clignancourt

See page 124 for full
commentary.

---

grandfather and a simple country life where such a knife might be used at a picnic to peel an apple or spear a slice of *saucisson*. Forge de Laguiole, an artisan manufacturer of the Laguiole knife, was established in 1987 in the town of Laguiole itself in central France, to preserve the town's knife-forging traditions, which date back to 1828. Each knife is handcrafted by a single master cutler, from the forging of the steel blade to the shaping, polishing, and finishing of the handle, traditionally made from bone, wood, or ivory. Their stunning collection of knives ranges from simple traditional folding blades with wooden handles to sleek modern tableset collections, created by select designers such as Philippe Starck.

The small boutique near the Madeleine *métro* is the only Forge de Laguiole shop in Paris, but they stock almost their entire collection, including some impressively ornate display knives, costing upward of 2,000€.

MAISON DE FAMILLE (Madeleine)

TABLEWARE AND HOME DECOR
10, place de la Madeleine
Paris 8
TEL: +33 1 53 45 82 00
maisondefamille.fr

vpt@maisondefamille.fr
MÉTRO: Madeleine
OPEN: Monday through Saturday
10:30AM to 7PM
CLOSED: Sunday

Understated tableware and home decor with a flair for fun. See page 381 for full commentary.

LA VAISSELLERIE (Haussmann)

TABLEWARE AND COOKWARE
80, boulevard Haussmann
Paris 8
TEL: +33 1 45 22 32 47

MÉTRO: Saint-Augustin or Saint-Lazare
OPEN: Monday through Saturday 10AM to 7PM
CLOSED: Sunday

See page 380 for full commentary.

VIS-À-VIS PARIS

LINENS
14, rue du Faubourg Saint-Honoré, in the
courtyard
Paris 8
TEL: +33 1 46 28 56 56
visavisparis.com

visavisparis@visavisparis.com
MÉTRO: Concorde
OPEN: Monday through Saturday 10:30AM to
6:30PM
CLOSED: Sunday

When I walk into Vis-à-Vis—one of the more elegant linen shops in the world—I want to lock the door behind me and simply be alone with all this refinement. Table linens and bed linens—all painstakingly hand-embroidered—are displayed in this courtyard shop, a large, airy room that once served as a meeting room for the 8th *arrondissement*'s *mairie*, or city hall. Each item is made to order, with themes varying from floral to vegetal to ephemeral.

9TH ARRONDISSEMENT

LA VAISSELLERIE (Saint-Lazare)

TABLEWARE AND COOKWARE
79, rue Saint Lazare
Paris 9
TEL: +33 1 42 85 07 27

MÉTRO: Trinité–d'Estienne d'Orves
OPEN: Monday through Saturday 10AM to 7PM
CLOSED: Sunday

See page 380 for full commentary.

BOUTIQUE ZWILLING

COOKING SUPPLY STORE
12, boulevard de la Madeleine
Paris 9
TEL: +33 1 42 68 88 00
zwilling.com

shop.paris@zwilling
MÉTRO: Madeleine
OPEN: Monday 2 to 7PM. Tuesday through
Saturday 10AM to 7PM.
CLOSED: Sunday

For professional-quality knives and cookware you will find plenty of choice at the spacious Zwilling Boutique just off the place de la Madeleine.

The boutique stocks steel chef's knives, pots, pans, and grill plates, as well as knife and cookware ranges, by German design company Zwilling J.A. Henckels. You'll also find products by Zwilling's subsidiary brands Staub (known for its cast-iron casseroles, or *cocottes*) and Miyabi (ultra-sharp Japanese knives). They also have a small but well-selected range of Laguiole knives.

11TH ARRONDISSEMENT

MUJI (Ledru-Rollin)

TABLEWARE AND HOME DECOR
91–93, rue du Faubourg Saint-Antoine
Paris 11
TEL: +33 1 53 33 48 48

MÉTRO: Ledru-Rollin
OPEN: Monday through Friday 10AM to 7:30PM. Saturday 10AM to 8PM.
CLOSED: Sunday

My kitchen is organized with military precision, and Muji is my go-to store for storage solutions to make sure my supplies are always in order. See box (page 378) for full commentary.

12TH ARRONDISSEMENT

KITCHEN BAZAAR (Nation)

COOKING SUPPLY STORE
32, bis boulevard de Picpus
Paris 12
TEL: +33 1 43 47 14 98

MÉTRO: Nation
OPEN: Tuesday through Saturday 10:30AM to 2PM and 3 to 7PM
CLOSED: Monday and Sunday

Dream up any modern cooking implement and Kitchen Bazaar will most likely have it. See page 375 for full commentary.

14TH ARRONDISSEMENT

MUJI (Alésia)

TABLEWARE AND HOME DECOR
32, avenue General LeClerc
Paris 14
TEL: +33 1 43 95 60 72

MÉTRO: Mouton-Duvernet
OPEN: Monday through Friday 10AM to 7:30PM, Saturday 10AM to 8PM
CLOSED: Sunday

For clean, simple design and kitchen organization Japanese-style, Muji is a favorite. See box (page 378) for full commentary.

15TH ARRONDISSEMENT

KITCHEN BAZAAR (Montparnasse)

COOKING SUPPLY STORE
11, avenue du Maine
Paris 15
TEL: +33 1 42 22 91 17

MÉTRO: Montparnasse-Bienvenüe
OPEN: Monday through Saturday 10:30AM to 7PM
CLOSED: Sunday

See page 375 for full commentary.

16TH ARRONDISSEMENT

MAISON DE FAMILLE (La Muette)

TABLEWARE AND HOME DECOR
90, avenue Paul Doumier
Paris 16
TEL: +33 1 42 88 12 46

MÉTRO: La Muette
OPEN: Monday through Saturday 10:30AM to 7PM
CLOSED: Sunday

See page 381 for full commentary.

KITCHEN BAZAAR (Trocadéro)

COOKING SUPPLY STORE
31, avenue Raymond Poincaré
Paris 16
TEL: +33 1 56 26 04 23

MÉTRO: Trocadéro
OPEN: Monday through Friday 10:30AM to 7PM. Saturday 10:30AM to 7:30PM.
CLOSED: Sunday

See page 375 for full commentary.

17TH ARRONDISSEMENT

MUJI (Ternes)

TABLEWARE AND HOME DECOR
51, avenue des Ternes
Paris 17
TEL: +33 1 40 55 55 90

MÉTRO: Argentine or Ternes
OPEN: Monday through Saturday 10AM to 7:30PM
CLOSED: Sunday

There's a lot to love about this Japanese homeware design store, with its wooden miso bowls, heatproof glass mugs, and clever solutions for kitchen organization. See box (page 378) for full commentary.

18TH ARRONDISSEMENT

FRAGONARD (Montmartre)

TABLEWARE AND TABLE LINENS
1, bis rue Tardieu
Paris 18

TEL: +33 1 42 23 03 03
MÉTRO: Anvers or Abesses
OPEN: Daily 10:30AM to 7PM

The newest Fragonard is two shops in one: One half is devoted to the famed Fragonard fragrances, the other to collections that include souvenirs from travels, including special trunks for touring. Always, there are my favorite collections of themed napkins—colorful and useful. See page 373 for full commentary.

AT A GLANCE

1ST ARRONDISSEMENT
Astier de Villatte
E. Dehillerin
Fragonard (Louvre)
Mora

2ND ARRONDISSEMENT
A. Simon
Librairie Gourmande

3RD ARRONDISSEMENT
Kitchen Bazaar (Marais)
Merci
Le Petit Atelier de Paris

4TH ARRONDISSEMENT
Argenterie d'Antan
Fleux
Fragonard (Marais)
Laguiole
Muji (Marais)
Au Petit Bonheur La Chance
La Vaissellerie (Marais)

6TH ARRONDISSEMENT
Coutellerie Ceccaldi
Maison de Famille
   (Saint-Sulpice)
Muji (Saint-Sulpice)
La Vaissellerie (Saint-
   Germain)

7TH ARRONDISSEMENT
Au Bain Marie
La Cornue
Fragonard (Saint-Germain)
Muriel Grateau Boutique
Siècle

8TH ARRONDISSEMENT
La Carpe
Forge de Laguiole
Maison de Famille
   (Madeleine)
La Vaissellerie (Haussmann)
Vis-à-Vis Paris

9TH ARRONDISSEMENT
La Vaissellerie (Saint-Lazare)
Boutique Zwilling

11TH ARRONDISSEMENT
Muji (Ledru-Rollin)

12TH ARRONDISSEMENT
Kitchen Bazaar (Nation)

14TH ARRONDISSEMENT
Muji (Alésia)

15TH ARRONDISSEMENT
Kitchen Bazaar
   (Montparnasse)

16TH ARRONDISSEMENT
Maison de Famille
   (La Muette)
Kitchen Bazaar (Trocadéro)

17TH ARRONDISSEMENT
Muji (Ternes)

18TH ARRONDISSEMENT
Fragonard (Montmartre)

FRENCH/ENGLISH FOOD GLOSSARY

For many diners, the restaurant menu can present a confusing and intimidating barrier to the pleasures of dining out. The French language, of course, is no help with so many soundalike words. It is so easy to confuse *tourteau* (crab) with *tortue* (turtle), *ail* (garlic) with *aile* (a poultry wing), *chevreau* (young goat) with *chevreuil* (venison).

The variety of fish and shellfish found in France's waters can be equally confusing, particularly when one is faced with a multitude of regional or local names given to each species. The large, meaty monkfish, for example, might be called *baudroie, lotte,* or *gigot de mer,* depending upon the region or the whim of the chef.

In preparing this glossary, I have tried to limit the list to contemporary terms, making this a practical guide for today's traveler in France. Translations are generally offered for those dishes, foods, and phrases one is most likely to encounter on menus, in markets, and in shops. I have also added regional terms one might not find explained elsewhere, as well as non-French words (such as *harissa, bento, yuzu,* and *boquerones*) that will show up on contemporary Parisian menus.

A

A POINT: cooked medium rare
ABAT(S): organ meat(s)
ABATI(S): giblet(s) of poultry or game fowl
ABBACCHIO: young lamb; specialty of Corsica
ABONDANCE: firm thick wheel of cow's-milk cheese from the Savoie, a *département* in the Alps
ABRICOT: apricot
ACACIA: the acacia tree, the blossoms of which are used for making fritters; also, honey made from the blossom
ACHATINE: land snail, or escargot, imported from China and Indonesia; less prized than other varieties
ADDITION: bill
AFFAMÉ: starving
AFFINAGE: process of aging cheese
AFFINÉ: aged, as with cheese
AGNEAU (DE LAIT): lamb (young, milk-fed)

AGNEAU CHILINDRON: sauté of lamb with potatoes and garlic; specialty of the Basque country
AGNEAU DE PAUILLAC: breed of lamb from the Southwest
AGNELET: baby milk-fed lamb
AGRUME(S): citrus fruit(s)
AÏADO: roast lamb shoulder stuffed with parsley, chervil, and garlic
AIGLEFIN, AIGREFIN, ÉGLEFIN: small fresh haddock, a type of cod
AÏGO BOUIDO: garlic soup, served with oil, over slices of bread; specialty of Provence
AÏGO SAOU: "water-salt" in Provençal; a fish soup that includes, of course, water and salt, plus a mixture of small whitefish, onions, potatoes, tomatoes, garlic, herbs, and olive oil; specialty of Provence
AIGRE: bitter; sour
AIGRE-DOUX: sweet and sour
AIGRELETTE, SAUCE: a type of tart sauce

AIGUILLETTE: a long, thin slice of poultry, meat, or fish. Also, top part of beef rump
AIL: garlic
AIL DES OURS: Wild garlic—also known as ramsons, buckrams, broad-leaved garlic, wood garlic, bear leek, or bear's garlic
AILE: wing of poultry or game bird
AILE ET CUISSE: used to describe white breast meat (*aile*) and dark thigh meat (*cuisse*), usually of chicken
AILLADE: garlic sauce; also, dishes based on garlic
AILLÉ: with garlic
AILLET: shoot of mild winter baby garlic; specialty of the Poitou-Charentes region along the Atlantic coast
AÏOLI, AILLOLI: garlic mayonnaise. Also, combination of salt cod, hard-cooked eggs, boiled snails, and vegetables served with garlic mayonnaise; specialty of Provence
AIRELLE: wild cranberry

AISY CENDRÉ: thick disk of cow's-milk cheese, washed with *eau-de-vie* and patted with wood ashes; also called *cendre d'aisy*; specialty of Burgundy

ALBUFÉRA: *béchamel* (sauce of butter, flour, and milk) with sweet peppers, prepared with chicken stock instead of milk; classic sauce for poultry

AL DENTE: a stage of doneness at which pasta and rice are firm to the bite

ALGUE(S): seaweed

ALIGOT: mashed potatoes with *tomme* (the fresh curds used in making Cantal cow's-milk cheese) and garlic; specialty of the Auvergne

ALISIER, ALIZIER: *eau-de-vie* with the taste of bitter almonds, made with the wild red serviceberries (also known as Juneberries) that grow on shrubs in the forests of Alsace

ALLUMETTE: "match"; puff pastry strips; also fried matchstick potatoes

ALOSE: shad, a spring river fish plentiful in the Loire and Gironde rivers

ALOUETTE: lark

ALOYAU: loin area of beef; beef sirloin, butcher's cut that includes the rump and *contrefilet*

ALSACIENNE, À L': in the style of Alsace, often including sauerkraut, sausage, or *foie gras*

AMANDE: almond

AMANDE DE MER: smooth-shelled shellfish, like a small clam, with a sweet, almost almond flavor

AMANDINE: a dish with almonds

AMBROISIE: ambrosia

AMER: bitter, as in unsweetened chocolate

AMÉRICAINE, AMORICAINE: sauce of white wine, Cognac, tomatoes, and butter

AMI DU CHAMBERTIN: "friend of Chambertin wine"; moist and buttery short cylinder of cow's-milk cheese with a rust-colored rind, made near the village of Gevrey-Chambertin in Burgundy. Similar to Époisses cheese

AMOURETTE(S): spinal bone marrow of calf or ox

AMUSE-BOUCHE OR AMUSE GUEULE: "amuse the mouth"; appetizer

ANANAS: pineapple

ANCHOÏADE: a sauce of olive oil, anchovies, and garlic, usually served with raw vegetables; specialty of Provence; also, a paste of anchovies and garlic, spread on toast

ANCHOIS (DE COLLIOURE): anchovy (prized salt or olive oil–cured anchovy from Collioure, a port town near the Spanish border of the Languedoc), fished in the Atlantic and the Mediterranean

ANCIENNE, À L': in the old style

ANDOUILLE: large smoked chitterling (tripe) sausage, usually served cold

ANDOUILLETTE: small chitterling (tripe) sausage, usually served grilled

ANETH: dill

ANGE À CHEVAL: "angel on horseback"; grilled bacon-wrapped oyster

ANGLAISE, À L': English style, plainly cooked

ANGUILLE (AU VERT): eel (poached in herb sauce)

ANIS: anise or aniseed

ANIS ÉTOILÉ: star anise; also called *badiane*

ANON: haddock, also called *aiglefin, églefin*. Usually sold in filets, excellent for *ceviche*

APPELLATION D'ORIGINE CONTRÔLÉE (A.O.C.): When the A.O.C. was officially created by the French government in the 1935, it was to specify a badge of authenticity and quality of an agricultural product. The A.O.C. certifies excellence for wines, cheeses, butters, honey, poultry, and other products. In modern times, as the number of A.O.C. products grows, it is clear that its importance is also a marketing tool to promote the brand. Never awarded lightly, all A.O.C.-certified products retain a specific quality: Each bears a

special label; each plays a role in French agricultural history based on its authenticity, regional lineage, and method of production. All are required to adhere to strict standards established by the French government, and production is rigorously controlled. The A.O.C. label remains a serious badge of confidence for consumers.

APPELLATION D'ORIGINE PROTÉGÉE (A.O.P.): A European Union designation, equivalent to the French A.O.C. for agricultural products produced within strict geographical limits, abiding by certain sets of rules of production and preparation, using established industry know-how. French producers whose products meet these guidelines can choose whether to promote their product under the A.O.C. or A.O.P. label.

APÉRITIF: a before-dinner drink that stimulates the appetite, usually somewhat sweet or mildly bitter

ARACHIDE (HUILE D'; PÂTÉ D'): peanut (oil; butter)

ARAIGNÉE DE MER: spider crab

ARBOUSIER (MIEL D'): trailing arbutus, a small evergreen shrub of the heather family, with strawberry-like fruit dotted with tiny bumps (honey of). Used for making liqueurs, jellies, and jams

ARC EN CIEL (TRUITE): rainbow (trout)

ARDENNAISE, À L': in the style of the Ardennes, a *département* in northern France; generally a dish with juniper berries

ARDI GASNA: Basque name for sheep's-milk cheese

ARDOISE: blackboard; bistros often use a blackboard to list specialties in place of a printed menu

ARÊTE: fish bone

ARLÉSIENNE, À L': in the style of Arles, a town in Provence; with tomatoes, onions, eggplant, potatoes, rice, and sometimes olives

ARMAGNAC: brandy from the Armagnac area of southwestern France

AROMATE: aromatic herb, vegetable, or flavoring

ARÔMES À LA GÊNE: generic name for a variety of tangy, lactic cheeses of the Lyon area that have been steeped in *gêne,* or dry marc, the dried grapeskins left after grapes are pressed for wine. Can be of cow's milk, goat's milk, or a mixture

AROSÉ(E): sprinkled, basted, moistened with liquid

ARPAJON: a town in the Île-de-France; dried-bean capital of France; a dish containing dried beans

ARTICHAUT (CAMUS): variety of large green artichoke from Brittany

ARTICHAUT POIVRADE (VIOLET): variety of small purple artichoke from Provence

ARTICHAUT À LA BARIGOULE: in original form, artichokes cooked with mushrooms and oil; also, artichokes stuffed with ham, onion, and garlic, browned in oil with onions and bacon, then cooked in water or white wine; specialty of Provence

ASPERGE (VIOLETTE): asparagus (purple-tipped asparagus, a specialty of the Côte d'Azur)

ASSAISONNÉ: seasoned; seasoned with

ASSIETTE ANGLAISE: assorted cold meats, usually served as a first course

ASSIETTE DE PÊCHEUR: assorted fish platter

ASSOIFFÉ: parched, thirsty

ASSORTI(E): assorted

AUBERGINE: eggplant

AULX: plural of *ail* (garlic)

AUMÔNIÈRE: "beggar's purse"; thin *crêpe,* filled and tied like a bundle

AURORE: tomato and cream sauce

AUVERGNAT(E): in the style of the Auvergne; often with cabbage, sausage, and bacon

AVELINE: hazelnut or filbert, better known as *noisette*

AVOCAT: avocado

AVOINE: oat

AXOA: a dish of ground veal, onions, and the local fresh chilies, *piment d'Espelette*; specialty of the Basque region

AZYME, PAIN: unleavened bread; matzo

B

BABA AU RHUM: sponge cake soaked in rum syrup

BABA GHANOUSH: smoky eggplant dip

BADIANE: star anise

BAECKEOFFE, BAEKAOFFA, BACKAOFA, BACKENOFF: "baker's oven"; stew of wine, beef, lamb, pork, potatoes, and onions; specialty of Alsace

BAGNA CAUDÀ: sauce of anchovies, olive oil, and garlic, for dipping raw vegetables; specialty of Nice

BAGUETTE: "wand"; classic long, thin loaf of bread

BAGUETTE AU LEVAIN OR À L'ANCIENNE: sourdough baguette

BAIE: berry

BAIE ROSE: pink peppercorn

BAIGNÉ: bathed

BALLOTINE: usually poultry, boned, stuffed, and rolled

BANANE: banana

BANON: village in Provence, source of dried chestnut leaves traditionally used to wrap fresh, young goat's-milk cheese, which was then washed with *eau-de-vie* and aged for several months; today, refers to various goat's-milk cheese or mixed goat's- and cow's-milk cheese from the region, sometimes wrapped in fresh green or dried brown chestnut leaves and tied with raffia. Raw-milk version A.O.C./A.O.P.

BAR: sea bass, an ocean fish, known as *loup* on the Mediterranean coast, *louvine* or *loubine* in the Southwest, and *barreau* in Brittany

BARBOUILLADE: stuffed eggplant, or an eggplant stew; also, a combination of beans and artichokes

BARBUE: brill, a flatfish related to turbot, found in the Atlantic and the Mediterranean

BARDER: to cover poultry or meat with strips of uncured bacon in order to add moisture while cooking

BARON D'AGNEAU: hindquarters of lamb, including both legs

BARQUETTE: "small boat"; pastry shaped like a small boat

BASILIC: basil

BASQUAISE, À LA: Basque style; usually with ham or tomatoes or red peppers

BÂTARD, PAIN: "bastard bread"; traditional long, thin loaf, wider than a baguette

BATAVIA: salad green, a broad, flat-leafed lettuce

BÂTON: small white wand of bread, smaller than a baguette

BÂTONNET: literally, "little stick;" food cut at a size that's ¼ inch (½ cm) wide and 2¼ inches (5.75 cm) to 3 inches (7.5 cm) long

BAUDROIE: in Provence, the name for monkfish or anglerfish, the large, firm-fleshed ocean fish also known as *lotte* and *gigot de mer*; also a specialty of Provence, a fish soup that includes potatoes, onions, fresh mushrooms, garlic, fresh or dried orange zest, artichokes, tomatoes, and herbs

BAVAROISE: cold dessert; a rich custard made with cream and gelatin

BAVETTE: skirt steak

BAVEUSE: "drooling"; method of cooking an omelet so that it remains moist and juicy

BÉARNAISE: tarragon-flavored sauce of egg yolks, butter, shallots, white wine, vinegar, and herbs

BÉATILLE: "tidbit"; dish combining various organ meats

BÉCASSE: small bird, a woodcock

BÉCASSINE: small bird, a snipe

BÉCHAMEL: white sauce made with butter, flour, and milk, usually flavored with onion, bay leaf, pepper, and nutmeg

BEIGNET: fritter or doughnut

BEIGNET DE FLEUR DE COURGETTE: batter-fried zucchini blossom, native to Provence and the Mediterranean, now popular all over France

BELLE HÉLÈNE (POIRE): classic dessert of chilled poached fruit (pear), served on ice cream and topped with hot chocolate sauce

BELLEVUE, EN: classic presentation of whole fish, usually in aspic on a platter

BELON: river in Brittany identified with a prized flat-shelled (*plate*) oysters

BELONDINES: Brittany *creuses,* crinkle-shelled oysters that are *affinées,* or finished off in the Belon river

BENTO: traditional Japanese meal in a box-shaped container, usually rice, fish, or meat with cooked vegetables

BERAWECKA, BIEREWECKE, BIREWECK, BIREWECKA: dense, moist Christmas fruit bread stuffed with dried pears, figs, and nuts; specialty of Kaysersberg, a village in Alsace

BERCY: fish stock–based sauce thickened with flour and butter and flavored with white wine and shallots

BERGAMOT (THÉ À LA BERGAMOTE): name for a variety of both an orange and a pear often used as a flavor infusion for Earl Grey tea

BERRICHONNE: garnish of bruised cabbage, glazed baby onions, chestnuts, and lean bacon; named for the old province of Berry

BETTERAVE: beet

BEURRE: butter

Blanc: classic reduced sauce of vinegar, white wine, shallots, and butter

Charentes-Poitou, des: finely textured unctuous French butter with the flavor of hazelnuts, from the region of Poitou-Charentes along the Atlantic coast. A.O.C./A.O.P.

Cru: butter from raw, unpasteurized cream

De Montpellier: classic butter sauce seasoned with olive oil, herbs, garlic, and anchovies

Demi-sel: butter (lightly salted)

Echiré, d': brand of fine French butter with an A.O.C. and A.O.P. pedigree; from the region of Poitou-Charentes along the Atlantic coast

Isigny: Noted as superior since the 16th century, this full-flavored butter profits from the temperate climate of the Normandy region and the iodine-rich air. A.O.C./A.O.P.

Noir: sauce of browned butter, lemon juice or vinegar, parsley, and sometimes capers; traditionally served with *raie,* or skate

Noisette: lightly browned butter

Vierge: whipped butter sauce with salt, pepper, and lemon juice

BIBELSKÄS, BIBBELSKÄSE: fresh cheese seasoned with horseradish, herbs, and spices; specialty of Alsace

BICHE: female deer

BIEN CUIT(E): cooked well done

BIÈRE (EN BOUTEILLE, À LA PRESSION): beer (bottled, on tap)

BIFTECK: steak

BIGARADE: a variety of bitter Seville orange; also a sauce made from the orange

BIGGAREAU: red, firm-fleshed variety of cherry

BIGORNEAU: periwinkle, tiny sea snail

BIGOUDÈNE, À LA: (*pommes*) (*ragôut*): in the style of Bigouden, a province in Brittany (baked slices of unpeeled potato) (sausage stewed with bacon and potato)

BILLY BI, BILLY BY: cream of mussel soup, specialty of the Atlantic coast

BIOLOGIQUE: organic

BISCUIT À LA CUILLÈRE: ladyfinger

BISTROTIER: bistro owner

BLANC (DE POIREAU): white portion (of leek)

BLANC (DE VOLAILLE): usually breast (of chicken)

BLANC-MANGER: chilled pudding of almond milk with gelatin

BLANQUETTE: classic stew of poached veal, lamb, chicken, or seafood, enriched with an egg and cream sauce

BLÉ (NOIR): wheat (buckwheat)

BLETTE, BETTE: Swiss chard

BLEU: "blue"; cooked rare, usually for steak. See also *truite au bleu*

BLEU D'AUVERGNE: a strong, firm, and moist flattened cylinder of blue-veined cheese made from raw cow's milk in the Auvergne, sold wrapped in foil; some still made on small farms. A.O.C./A.O.P.

BLEU DE BRESSE: a cylinder of mild blue-veined cow's-milk cheese from the Bresse area in the Rhône-Alps region; industrially made

BLEU DE GEX: thick, savory blue-veined disk of raw cow's-milk cheese from the Jura; made in a handful of small dairies in the *département* of the Ain. A.O.C./A.O.P.

BLEU DES CAUSSES: a firm, pungent, flat cylinder of blue-veined raw cow's-milk cheese, cured in cellars similar to those used in making Roquefort. A.O.C./A.O.P.

BLINI: small, thick pancake, usually eaten with caviar

BOEUF À LA FICELLE: beef tied with string and poached in broth

BOEUF À LA MODE: beef marinated and braised in red wine, served with carrots, mushrooms, onions, and turnips

BOEUF GROS SEL: boiled beef, served with vegetables and coarse salt

BOHÉMIENNE, À LA: gypsy style; with rice, tomatoes, onions, sweet peppers, and paprika, in various combinations

BOISSON (NON) COMPRISE: drink (not) included

BOLET: type of wild boletus mushroom. See *cèpe*

BOMBE: molded, layered ice-cream dessert

BONBON: candy or sweet

BON-CHRÉTIEN: "good Christian"; a variety of pear, also known as *poire Williams,* often used to make an *eau-de-vie* or clear liqueur

BONDON: small cylinder of delicately flavored, mushroomy cow's-milk cheese made in the Neufchâtel area in Normandy

BONITE: tuna, or oceanic bonito

BONNE FEMME (CUISINE): meat garnish of bacon, potatoes, mushrooms, and onions; fish garnish of shallots, parsley, mushrooms, and potatoes; or white wine sauce with shallots, mushrooms, and lemon juice; (homestyle cooking)

BORDELAISE: Bordeaux style; also refers to a brown sauce of shallots, red wine, and bone marrow

BOUCHÉE: "tiny mouthful"; may refer to a bite-size pastry or to a *vol-au-vent,* a small shell of puff pastry with varied fillings

BOUCHOTEUR: mussel fisherman; a dish containing mussels

BOUDIN: technically, a meat sausage, but generically, any sausage-shaped mixture

BOUDIN BLANC: white sausage of veal, chicken, or pork

BOUDIN NOIR: pork blood sausage

BOUDOUSES: literally, "to pout"; tiny oysters from Brittany that refuse to grow to normal size; iodine rich and prized

BOUILLABAISSE: popular Mediterranean fish soup, most closely identified with Marseille, ideally prepared with the freshest local fish, preferably rockfish. Traditionally might include dozens of different fish, but today generally includes the specifically local *rascasse* (scorpion fish), Saint-Pierre (John Dory), *fiéla* (conger eel), *galinette* (gurnard or grondin), *vive* (weever), and *baudroie* (monkfish) cooked in a broth of water, olive oil, onions, garlic, tomatoes, parsley, and saffron. The fish is served separately from the broth, which is poured over garlic-rubbed toast and seasoned with *rouille* (a colorful rust-colored sauce of olive oil, garlic, chile peppers, bread, and fish broth), which is stirred into the broth. Varied additions include boiled potatoes, orange peel, fennel, and shellfish. Expensive shellfish are often added in restaurant versions, but this practice is considered inauthentic.

BOUILLITURE: eel stew with red wine and prunes; specialty of the Poitou-Charentes on the Atlantic coast

BOUILLON: stock or broth

BOULANGÈRE, À LA: in the style of the "baker's wife"; meat or poultry baked or braised with onions and potatoes

BOULE: "ball"; a large round loaf of white bread, also known as a *miche*

BOULE DE PICOULAT: meatball from Languedoc, combining beef, pork, garlic, and eggs, traditionally served with cooked white beans

BOULETTE D'AVESNES: a soft, conical-shaped cow's-milk cheese flavored with parsley, pepper, tarragon, and cloves. The exterior is dusted with paprika or annatto, a natural food coloring; named for Avesnes, a village on the French-Belgian border.

BOUQUERONES: fresh anchovies marinated in white vinegar

BOUQUET: large reddish shrimp. See also *crevette rose*

BOUQUET GARNI: typically, fresh whole parsley, bay leaf, and thyme tied together with string and tucked into stews; the package is removed prior to serving

BOUQUETIÈRE: garnished with bouquets of vegetables

BOURDALOUE: hot poached fruit, sometimes wrapped in pastry, often served with vanilla custard; often, pear

BOURGEOISE, À LA: with carrots, onions, braised lettuce, celery, and bacon

BOURGUIGNONNE, À LA: Burgundy-style; often with red wine, onions, mushrooms, and bacon

BOURIBOT: spicy red-wine duck stew

BOURRIDE: a Mediterranean fish soup that generally includes a mixture of small white fish, onions, tomatoes, garlic, herbs, and olive oil, thickened with egg yolks and *aïoli* (garlic mayonnaise); there are many variations

BOURRIOLE: rye flour pancake, both sweet and savory; specialty of the Auvergne

BOUTARGUE, POUTARGUE: salty paste prepared from dried mullet or tuna roe, mashed with oil; specialty of Provence

BOUTON DE CULOTTE: "trouser button"; tiny buttons of goat cheese from the Lyon area; traditionally made on farms, aged until rock hard and pungent; today found in many forms, from soft and young to hard and brittle

BRAISER: to braise; to cook meat by browning in fat, then simmering in a covered dish with a small amount of liquid

BRANCHE, EN: refers to whole vegetables or herbs

BRANDADE (DE MORUE): a warm garlicky puree (of salt cod) with milk or cream or oil, and sometimes mashed potatoes; specialty of Provence; currently used to denote a variety of flavored mashed potato dishes

BRASSADO: a doughnut that is boiled, then baked, much like a bagel; specialty of Provence

BRAYAUDE, GIGOT: leg of lamb studded with garlic, cooked in white wine, and served with red beans, braised cabbage, or chestnuts

BREBIS (FROMAGE DE): sheep (sheep's-milk cheese)

BRÉSI (BREUZI): smoked, salted, and dried beef from the Jura

BRETONNE, À LA: in the style of Brittany; a dish served with white beans; or may refer to a white wine sauce with carrots, leeks, and celery

BRETZEL: a pretzel; specialty of Alsace

BRIE DE MEAUX: "king of cheese"; the flat wheel of cheese made only with raw cow's milk and aged at least four weeks; from Meaux, just east of Paris; Brie made with pasteurized milk does not have the right to be called brie de Meaux. A.O.C./A.O.P.

BRIE DE MELUN: smaller than Brie de Meaux, another raw cow's-milk cheese, aged at least one month, with a crackly rust-colored rind. A.O.C./A.O.P.

BRILLAT-SAVARIN: (1755–1826) famed gastronome, coiner of food aphorisms, and author of *The Physiology of Taste*; the high-fat, supple cow's-milk cheese from Normandy is named for him

BRIOCHE: buttery egg-enriched yeast bread

BROCCIU: soft, young, ricotta-like sheep's-milk or goat's-milk cheese, or mix of the two, from Corsica, made from the whey of cheese, with added sheep or goat's milk. A.O.C./A.O.P.

BROCHE, À LA: spit-roasted

BROCHET(ON): freshwater pike (small pike)

BROCHETTE: cubes of meat or fish and vegetables on a skewer

BROCOLI: broccoli

BROUET: old term for soup

BROUILLADE: a mixture of ingredients as in a stew or soup; also, scrambled eggs

BROUILLÉ(S): scrambled, usually eggs

BROUSSE: a very fresh and unsalted sheep's- or goat's-milk cheese, not unlike Italian ricotta; specialty of Provence

BROUTARD: young goat

BRUGNON: nectarine

BRÛLÉ(E): "burnt"; usually refers to caramelization

BRUNOISE: tiny diced vegetables

BRUT: very dry, particularly in reference to Champagne

BUCCIN: large sea snail or whelk, also called *bulot*

BÛCHE DE NOËL: Christmas cake shaped like a log (*bûche*), a sponge cake often flavored with chestnuts and chocolate

BUFFET FROID: variety of dishes served cold, sometimes from a buffet

BUGNE: deep-fried yeast-dough fritter or doughnut dusted with confectioner's sugar; popular in and around Lyon before Easter

BUISSON: "bush"; generally, a dish including vegetables arranged like a bush; classically, a crayfish presentation

BULOT: large sea snail or whelk, also called *buccin*

BURON: traditional stone barn in which cow's-milk cheese—Cantal, Laguiole, and Saint-Nectaire—is made from May to October in the Auvergne mountains in the center of France

C

CABÉCOU(S): small, round goat's-milk cheese from the Southwest, sometimes made with a mix of goat's and cow's milk

CABILLAUD: fresh codfish, also called *morue*; known as *doguette* in the north, *bakalua* in the Basque region

CABRI: young goat

CACAHOUÈTE, CACAHOUETTE, CACACHUÈTE: prepared peanut—roasted, dry roasted, or salted. A raw peanut is *arachide*

CACAO: cocoa; powdered cocoa

CACHAT: a very strong goat cheese; generally, a blend of various ends of leftover cheese, mixed with seasonings that might include salt, pepper, brandy, and garlic, and aged in a crock; specialty of Provence

CAEN, À LA MODE DE: in the style of Caen, a town in Normandy; a dish cooked in Calvados and white wine and/or cider

CAFÉ: coffee, as well as a place where coffee is served

 Allongé: weakened espresso, often served with a small pitcher of hot water so clients may thin the coffee themselves

 Au lait or crème: espresso with warmed or steamed milk

 Déca or décaféiné: decaffeinated coffee

 Express: plain black espresso

 Faux: decaffeinated coffee

 Filtre: filtered American-style coffee

 Glacé: iced coffee

 Liégeois: iced coffee served with ice cream (optional) and whipped cream; also, coffee ice cream with whipped cream

 Noir: plain black espresso

 Noisette: espresso with tiny amount of milk

 Serré: extra-strong espresso, made with half the normal amount of water

CAFÉINE: caffeine

CAGOUILLE: on the Atlantic coast, name for small *escargot*, or land snail; also called *petit gris*

CAILLE: quail

CAILLÉ: clotted or curdled; curds of milk

CAILLETTE: round pork sausage including chopped spinach or Swiss chard, garlic, onions, parsley, bread, and egg and wrapped in *crépine* (caul fat);

served hot or cold; specialty of northern Provence

CAISSE: cash register; cash desk

CAISSETTE: literally, "small box"; bread, brioche, or chocolate shaped like a small box

CAJASSE: a sort of *clafoutis* from the Dordogne, made with black cherries

CAJOU: cashew nut

CALAMAR: small squid, similar to *encornet*, with interior transparent cartilage instead of a bone. Also called *chipiron* in the Southwest.

CALISSON D'AIX: delicate, diamond-shaped Provençal sweet prepared with almonds; candied oranges, melon, or apricots; egg white; sugar; and jam of oranges or apricots

CALVADOS: a *département* in Normandy known for the famed apple brandy

CAMEMBERT (DE NORMANDIE): village in Normandy that gives its name to a supple, fragrant cow's-milk cheese. Only Camembert labeled Camembert de Normandie is made from raw milk, with the right to the A.O.C./A.O.P. designation.

CAMOMILLE: camomile herb tea

CAMPAGNARD(E) (ASSIETTE): country-style, rustic; (an informal buffet of cold meats, terrines, etc.)

CAMPAGNE, À LA: country-style

CANADA GRIS: cooking apple

CANAPÉ: originally, a slice of crustless bread; now also used to refer to a variety of hors d'oeuvres consisting of toasted or fried bread spread with forcemeat, cheese, and other flavorings

CANARD: duck

CANARD À LA PRESSE: roast duck served with a sauce of juices obtained from pressing the carcass, combined with red wine and Cognac

CANARD SAUVAGE: wild duck, usually mallard

CANCOILLOTTE: spreadable cheese from the Jura; usually

blended with milk, spices, or white wine when served

CANETON: young male duck

CANETTE: young female duck

CANNELLE: cinnamon

CANNOISE, À LA: in the style of Cannes

CANON: marrow bone

CANTAL: large, cylindrical cow's-milk cheese (raw or pasteurized) made in the Cantal mountains of the Auvergne. *Cantal Fermier* is made from raw milk on farms, while *Cantal Laitier* is made from pasteurized milk in dairies. *Cantal jeune* is aged for 1 to 2 months; *Cantal entre-deux* or *Cantal doré* is aged 2 to 6 months; *Cantal vieux* is aged for 6 months to 1 year. A.O.C./A.O.P.

CANTALOUP: cantaloupe melon

CAPILOTADE: basically, any leftover meat or poultry cooked to tenderness in a well-reduced sauce

CAPRE: caper

CAPUCINE: nasturtium; the leaves and flowers are used in salads

CARAFE (D'EAU): pitcher (of tap water). House wine is often offered in a carafe. A full carafe contains one liter; a *demi-carafe* contains half a liter; a *quart* contains one-fourth liter

CARAÏBES: Caribbean, usually denotes chocolate from the Caribbean

CARAMELISÉ: cooked with high heat to brown sugar and heighten flavor

CARBONNADE: braised beef stew prepared with beer and onions; specialty of the north

CARDAMOME: cardamom

CARDE: white rib, or stalk, portion of Swiss chard

CARDON: cardoon; large celery-like vegetable in the artichoke family, popular in Lyon, Provence, and the Mediterranean area

CARGOLADE: a copious mixed grill of snails, lamb, pork sausage, and sometimes blood sausage, cooked over vine clippings; specialty of Catalan, an area of southern Languedoc

CAROTTE: carrot

CARPACCIO: traditionally, thinly sliced raw meat, but can refer to thinly sliced fish and vegetables as well

CARPE: carp fish

CARPE À LA JUIVE: braised marinated carp in aspic

CARRÉ D'AGNEAU: rack (ribs) or loin of lamb; also crown roast

CARRÉ DE PORC: rack (ribs) or loin of pork; also crown roast

CARRÉ DE VEAU: rack (ribs) or loin of veal; also crown roast

CARRELET: see *plaice*

CARTE, À LA: menu dishes that are priced individually, selected from a restaurant's full list of offerings

CARTE PROMOTIONELLE OR CONSEILLÉE: a simple and less expensive fixed-price meal

CARVI (GRAIN DE): caraway (seed)

CARY: curry

CASHER: kosher

CASSE-CROÛTE: "break bread"; slang for snack

CASSERON: cuttlefish

CASSIS (CRÈME DE): black currant (black currant liqueur)

CASSOLETTE: usually, a dish presented in a small casserole

CASSONADE: soft brown sugar; demerara sugar

CASSOULET: popular Southwestern casserole of white beans, including various combinations of sausages, duck, pork, lamb, mutton, and goose

CAVAILLON: a town in Provence, known for its small, flavorful orange-fleshed melons

CAVIAR D'AUBERGINE: cold seasoned eggplant puree

CAVIAR DU PUY: green lentils from Le Puy, in the Auvergne

CÉBETTE: a mild, leeklike vegetable, sliced and eaten raw in salads; native to Provence, but seen occasionally outside the region

CÉDRAT: a variety of Mediterranean lemon

CÉLERI (EN BRANCHE): celery (stalk)

CÉLERI-RAVE: celeriac, celery root

CÉLERI REMOULADE: popular first-course bistro dish consisting of julienne of celery root with tangy mayonnaise

CENDRE (SOUS LA): ash (cooked by being buried in embers); some cheeses made in wine-producing regions are aged in the ash of burnt rootstocks

CÈPE: large, meaty wild boletus mushroom

CERDON: sparkling (*pétillant*) pink wine from the Bugey in the *département* of the Ain, south of Lyon

CÉRÉALE: cereal

CERF: stag, or male deer

CERFEUIL: chervil

CERFEUIL TUBEREUX: chervil root

CERISE: cherry

CERISE NOIRE: black cherry

CERNEAU: walnut meat

CERVELAS: garlicky cured pork sausage; now also refers to fish and seafood sausage

CERVELLE(S): brain(s), of calf or lamb

CERVELLE DE CANUT: a soft, fresh herbed cheese known as silkworker's brains; specialty of Lyon

CÉTEAU(X): small ocean fish, *solette* or baby sole, found in the gulf of Gascony and along the Atlantic coast

CÉVENOLE, À LA: Cevennes style; garnished with chestnuts or mushrooms

CEVICHE, CEBICHE, SEVICHE: generally, raw fish or shellfish marinated in citrus juice and other flavorings, often onions, avocado, and hot peppers

CHALUTIER: trawler; any flat fish caught with a trawl

CHAMPÊTRE: rustic; describes a simple presentation of a variety of ingredients

CHAMPIGNON: mushroom
À la bague: parasol mushroom with a delicate flavor; also called *coulemelle, cocherelle,* and *grisotte*
De bois: wild mushroom, from the woods

De Paris: most common cultivated mushroom
Sauvage: wild mushroom

CHAMPVALLON, CÔTELETTE D'AGNEAU: traditional dish of lamb chops baked in alternating layers of potatoes and onions; named for a village in northern Burgundy

CHANTERELLE: prized pale-orange wild mushroom; also called *girolle*

CHANTILLY: sweetened whipped cream

CHAOURCE: soft and fruity cylindrical cow's-milk cheese, with a 50 percent fat content; takes its name from a village in Champagne

CHAPEAU: "hat"; small round loaf, topped with a little dough hat

CHAPELURE: bread crumbs

CHAPON: capon, or castrated chicken

CHAPON DE MER: Mediterranean fish, in the *rascasse* or scorpion-fish family

CHARBON DE BOIS, AU: charcoal-grilled

CHARENTAIS: variety of sweet cantaloupe, or melon, originally from the Charentes on the Atlantic coast

CHARLOTTE: classic dessert in which a dish is lined with ladyfingers, filled with custard or other filling, and served cold; in the hot version, the dish is lined with crustless white bread sautéed in butter, filled with fruit compote, and baked. Also, a potato variety.

CHAROLAIS: area of Burgundy; light-colored cattle producing high-quality beef; also, firm white cylinder of raw goat's-milk cheese made in Burgundy. A.O.C./A.O.P.

CHARTREUSE: dish of braised partridge and cabbage; also herb- and spice-based liqueur made by the Chartreuse monks in the Savoie

CHASSEUR: "hunter"; sauce with white wine, mushrooms, shallots, tomatoes, and herbs

CHÂTAIGNE: chestnut, smaller than *marron*, with multiple nut meats

CHATEAUBRIAND: thick filet steak, traditionally served with sautéed potatoes and a sauce of white wine, dark beef stock, butter, shallots, and herbs, or with a *béarnaise* sauce

CHÂTELAINE, À LA: elaborate garnish of artichoke hearts and chestnut puree, braised lettuce, and sautéed potatoes

CHAUD(E): hot or warm

CHAUD-FROID: "hot-cold"; cooked poultry dish served cold, usually covered with a cooked sauce, then with aspic

CHAUDRÉE: Atlantic fish stew, often including sole, skate, small eels, potatoes, butter, white wine, and seasoning

CHAUSSON: a filled pastry turnover, sweet or savory

CHEMISE, EN: wrapped with pastry

CHEVAL: horse, horse meat

CHEVEUX D'ANGE: "angel's hair"; thin vermicelli pasta

CHÈVRE (FROMAGE DE): goat (goat's-milk cheese)

CHEVREAU: young goat

CHÈVRE CHAUD (SALADE DE): grilled goat's-milk cheese on toasted bread, served on a bed of salad leaves

CHEVREUIL: young roe buck or roe deer; venison

CHEVRIER: small pale green, dried kidney-shaped bean, a type of *flageolet*

CHICHI: doughnut-like, deep-fried bread spirals sprinkled with sugar; often sold from trucks at open-air markets; specialty of Provence and the Mediterranean

CHICONS DU NORD: Belgian endive

CHICORÉE (FRISÉE): a bitter salad green (curly endive); also chicory, a coffee substitute

CHICORÉE DE BRUXELLES: Belgian endive

CHIFFONNADE: fresh herbs cut into tiny ribbons

CHINCHARD: also called *saurel, scad,* or horse mackerel; Atlantic and Mediterranean fish similar to mackerel

CHIPIRON (À L'ENCRE): Southwestern name for small

squid, or *encornet* (in its own ink)

CHIPOLATA: small sausage

CHIPS, POMMES: potato chips

CHOCOLAT: chocolate
- **Amer:** bittersweet chocolate, with very little sugar
- **Au lait:** milk chocolate
- **Chaud:** hot chocolate
- **Mi-amer:** bittersweet chocolate, with more sugar than *chocolat amer*
- **Noir:** used interchangeably with *chocolat amer*

CHOIX, AU: a choice; usually meaning one may choose from several offerings

CHORIZO: spiced Spanish sausage

CHORON, SAUCE: *béarnaise* sauce with tomatoes

CHOU: cabbage

CHOU DE BRUXELLES: Brussels sprout

CHOU DE MER: sea kale

CHOU DE MILAN: Savoy cabbage

CHOU-FLEUR: cauliflower

CHOU FRISÉ: kale

CHOU-NAVET: rutabaga

CHOU-RAVE: kohlrabi

CHOU ROUGE: red cabbage

CHOU VERT: curly green Savoy cabbage

CHOUCAS: jackdaw; European blackbird, like a crow, but smaller

CHOUCROUTE (NOUVELLE): sauerkraut (the season's first batch of sauerkraut, still crunchy and slightly acidic); also, main dish of sauerkraut, various sausages, bacon, and pork, served with potatoes; specialty of Alsace and brasseries all over France

CHOUX, PÂTE À: cream pastry dough

CIBOULE: spring onion, or scallion

CIBOULETTE: chives

CIDRE: bottled, mildly alcoholic cider, either apple or pear

CIGALE DE MER: "sea cricket"; tender, crayfish-like, blunt-nosed rock lobster

CÎTEAUX: creamy, ample disk of cow's-milk cheese with a rust-colored rind made by the Cistercian monks at the Abbaye de Cîteaux in Burgundy

CITRON: lemon

CITRON, ORANGE, OR PAMPLEMOUSSE PRESSÉ(E): lemon, orange, or grapefruit juice served with a carafe of tap water and sugar; for sweetening to taste

CITRON VERT: lime

CITRONNELLE: lemon grass, an oriental herb; also lemon balm (*mélisse*)

CITROUILLE: pumpkin, gourd. Also called *courge, potiron, potimarron*

CIVE: spring onion

CIVELLE: spaghetti-like baby eel, also called *pibale*

CIVET: stew, usually of game traditionally thickened with blood

CIVET DE LIÈVRE: jugged hare, or wild rabbit stew

CIVET DE TRIPES D'OIES: a stew of goose innards, sautéed in fat with onions, shallots, and garlic, then cooked in wine vinegar, diluted with water, and thickened with goose blood; from Gascony

CLAFOUTIS: traditional custard tart, usually made with black cherries; specialty of the Southwest

CLAIRE: oyster; also a designation given to certain oysters to indicate they have been put in *claires*, or oyster beds in salt marshes, where they are fattened up for several months before going to market

CLAMART: Paris suburb once famous for its green peas; today, a garnish of peas

CLÉMENTINE: small tangerine, from Morocco or Spain

CLOUTÉ: studded with (as in studding an onion with cloves for stock)

CLOVISSE: variety of very tiny clams, generally from the Mediterranean

COCHERELLE: parasol mushroom with a delicate flavor; also called *champignon à la bague, coulemelle*, and *grisotte*

COCHON (DE LAIT): pig (suckling)

COCHONNAILLE(S): pork product(s); usually an assortment of sausages and/or pâtés served as a first course

COCO BLANC (ROUGE): type of small white (red) shell bean, both fresh and dried, popular in Provence, where it is a traditional ingredient of the vegetable *soupe au pistou*; also, coconut

COCOS DE MOLLANS: prized white shell bean with a rich, buttery flavor, from the village of Mollans in the Drôme department of Provence. An essential ingredient in the vegetable *soupe au pistou*. Each year the village holds a festival and elects a "Miss Coco."

COCOS DE PAIMPOL: Cream-colored shell bean striated with purple, from Brittany, in season from July to November; the first bean in France to receive A.O.C./A.O.P.

COCOTTE: a high-sided cooking pot (casserole) with a lid; a small ramekin dish for baking and serving eggs and other preparations

COEUR: heart

COEUR DE FILET: thickest (and best) part of beef filet, usually cut into chateaubriand steaks

COEUR DE PALMIER: delicate shoots of the palm tree, generally served with a vinaigrette as an hors d'oeuvre

COFFRE: "chest"; refers to the body of a lobster or other crustacean, or of a butchered animal

COIFFE: traditional lacy hat; sausage patty wrapped in caul fat

COING: quince

COLVERT: wild ("green-collared") mallard duck

COLBERT: method of preparing fish, coating with egg and bread crumbs and then frying

COLÈRE, EN: "anger"; method of presenting fish in which the tail is inserted into the mouth, so it appears agitated

COLIN: hake, ocean fish related to cod; known as *merluche*

in the north, *merluchon* in Brittany, *bardot* or *merlan* along the Mediterranean

COLOMBE: dove

COLOMBO: a mixture of spices, like a curry powder, used to season shellfish, meat, or poultry. Like curry, the mix may vary, but usually contains turmeric, rice powder, coriander, pepper, cumin, and fenugreek.

COLZA: rape, a plant of the mustard family, colorful yellow field crop grown throughout France, usually pressed into vegetable (rapeseed) oil

COMMANDER AVANT LE REPAS, À: a selection of desserts that should be ordered when selecting first and main courses, as they require longer cooking

COMPLET: filled up, with no more room for customers

COMPOTE: stewed fresh or dried fruit

COMPOTIER: fruit bowl; also stewed fruit

COMPRIS: see *service (non) compris*

COMTÉ: large wheel of cheese of cooked and pressed cow's milk; the best is made of raw milk and aged for up to several years, still made by independent cheesemakers in the Jura mountains

CONCASSÉ: coarsely chopped

CONCOMBRE: cucumber

CONFÉRENCE: a variety of pear

CONFISERIE: candy, sweet, or confection; a candy shop

CONFIT: a preserve, generally pieces of duck, goose, or pork cooked and preserved in their own fat; also, fruit or vegetables preserved in sugar, alcohol, or vinegar

CONFITURE: jam

CONFITURE DE VIEUX GARÇON: varied fresh fruits macerated in alcohol

CONGELER: to freeze

CONGRE: conger eel; a large ocean fish resembling a freshwater eel (*anguille*); often used in fish stews

CONSEILLÉ: advised, recommended

CONSOMMATION(S): "consumption"; drinks, meals, and snacks available in a café or bar

CONSOMMÉ: clear soup

CONTRE-FILET: cut of sirloin taken above the loin on either side of the backbone, tied for roasting or braising (can also be cut for grilling)

CONVERSATION: puff pastry tart with sugar glazing and an almond or cream filling

COPEAU(X): shaving(s), such as from chocolate, cheese, or vegetables

COQ (AU VIN): mature male chicken (stewed in wine sauce)

COQ AU VIN JAUNE: chicken cooked in the sherry-like *vin jaune*, the golden wine of the Jura region, with cream, butter, and tarragon, often garnished with morels; specialty of the Jura

COQ DE BRUYÈRE: wood grouse

COQUE: cockle, a tiny, mild-flavored, clamlike shellfish

COQUE, À LA: served in a shell. See *oeuf à la coque*

COQUELET: young male chicken

COQUILLAGE(S): shellfish

COQUILLE: shell

COQUILLE SAINT-JACQUES: sea scallop

CORAIL: coral-colored egg sac found in scallops, spiny lobster, and crayfish

CORB: Mediterranean bluefish

CORIANDRE: coriander; either the fresh herb or dried seeds

CORNE D'ABONDANCE: "horn of plenty"; dark brown wild mushroom, also called *trompette de la mort*

CORNET: cornet-shaped; usually refers to foods rolled conically; also, an ice-cream cone, and a conical pastry filled with cream

CORNICHON: gherkin; tiny, tart cucumber pickle

CÔTE D'AGNEAU: lamb chop

CÔTE DE BOEUF: beef blade or rib steak

CÔTE DE VEAU: veal chop

CÔTELETTE: thin chop or cutlet

COTRIADE: a fish stew, usually including mackerel, whiting, conger eel, sorrel, butter, potatoes, and vinegar; specialty of Brittany

COU D'OIE (DE CANARD) FARCI: neck skin of goose (or duck), stuffed with meat and spices, much like sausage

COULANT: refers to runny cheese

COULEMELLE: parasol mushroom with a delicate flavor; also called *champignon à la bague, cocherelle*, and *grisotte*

COULIBIAC: classic, elaborate, hot Russian pâté, usually layers of salmon, rice, hard-cooked eggs, mushrooms, and onions, wrapped in brioche

COULIS: puree of raw or cooked vegetables or fruit

COULOMMIERS: town in the Île-de-France that gives its name to a supple, fragrant disk of cow's-milk cheese, slightly larger than Camembert

COURGE (MUSCADE): generic term for squash or gourd (bright orange pumpkin)

COURGETTE: zucchini

COURONNE: "crown"; ring or circle, usually of bread

COURT-BOUILLON: broth, or aromatic poaching liquid

COUSCOUS: granules of semolina, or hard wheat flour; also, refers to a hearty North African dish that includes the steamed, grainlike pasta, broth, vegetables, meats, hot sauce, and sometimes chickpeas and raisins

COUTEAU: razor clam

COUVERT: a place setting, including dishes, silver, glassware, and linen

COUVERTURE: bittersweet chocolate high in cocoa butter; used for making the shiniest chocolates

CRABE: crab

CRAMBE: sea kale, or *chou de mer*

CRAMIQUE: brioche with raisins or currants; specialty of the north

CRAPAUDINE: preparation of grilled poultry or game bird with backbone removed

CRAQUANT: crunchy

CRAQUELOT: smoked herring

CRÉCY: a dish garnished with carrots

CRÉMANT: sparkling wine

CRÈME: cream

Aigre: sour cream

Anglaise: light egg-custard cream

Brûlée: rich custard dessert with a top of caramelized sugar

Caramel: vanilla custard with caramel sauce

Catalane: creamy anise-flavored custard from the southern Languedoc

Chantilly: sweetened whipped cream

Épaisse: thick cream

Fleurette: liquid light or heavy cream

Fouettée: whipped cream

Fraîche: thick, sour, heavy cream

D'Isigny: sweet and acidulated butter from Normandy, matured for 16 to 18 hours to help develop its aromas and gustatory textures. A.O.C./A.O.P.

Pâtissière: custard filling for pastries and cakes

Plombières: custard filled with fresh fruits and egg whites

CRÊPE: thin pancake

CRÊPE SUZETTE: hot *crêpe* dessert flambéed with orange liqueur

CRÉPINE: caul fat

CRÉPINETTE: traditionally, a small sausage patty wrapped in caul fat; today, boned poultry wrapped in caul fat

CRESSON(ADE): watercress (watercress sauce)

CRÊTE (DE COQ): (cock's) comb

CREUSE: elongated, crinkle-shelled oyster

CREVETTE: shrimp

CREVETTE GRISE: tiny soft-fleshed shrimp that turns gray when cooked

CREVETTE ROSE: small firm-fleshed shrimp that turns pink when cooked; when large, called *bouquet*

CRIQUE: potato pancake from the Auvergne

CRISTE MARINE: a plant that grows between rocks at the water's edge in the Mediterranean. Often pickled like cucumbers and used as a condiment.

CROQUE AU SEL, À LA: served raw, with a small bowl of coarse salt for seasoning; tiny purple artichokes and cherry tomatoes are served this way

CROQUE-MADAME: toasted ham and cheese sandwich with an egg grilled on top

CROQUE-MONSIEUR: toasted ham and cheese sandwich

CROQUEMBOUCHE: *choux* pastry rounds filled with cream and coated with a sugar glaze, often served in a conical tower at special events

CROQUETTE: ground meat, fish, fowl, or vegetables bound with eggs or sauce, shaped into various forms, usually coated in bread crumbs, and deep fried

CROSNE: small, unusual tuber with a subtle artichoke-like flavor, known as Chinese or Japanese artichoke

CROTTIN DE CHAVIGNOL: small flattened disk of goat's-milk cheese from the Loire valley

CROUSTADE: usually small pastry-wrapped dish; also regional southwestern pastry filled with prunes and/or apples

CROÛTE (EN): crust; (in) pastry

CROÛTE DE SEL (EN): (in) a salt crust

CROÛTONS: small cubes of toasted or fried bread

CRU: raw

CRUDITÉ: raw vegetable

CRUSTACÉ(S): crustacean(s)

CUILLIÈRE (À LA): (to be eaten with a) spoon; meat that is so tender one could eat it with a spoon

CUISSE (DE POULET): leg or thigh (chicken drumstick)

CUISSOT, CUISSEAU: haunch of veal, venison, or wild boar

CUIT(E): cooked

CUL: haunch or rear; usually of red meat

CULOTTE: rump, usually of beef

CULTIVATEUR: "truck farmer"; fresh vegetable soup

CURCUMA: turmeric

CURE-DENT: toothpick

D

DAMIER: "checkerboard"; arrangement of vegetables or other ingredients in alternating colors like a checkerboard; also, a cake with such a pattern of light and dark pieces

DARNE: a rectangular portion of fish filet; also a fish steak, usually of salmon

DARIOLE: truncated cone or oval-shaped baking mold

DARTOIS: puff pastry rectangles layered with an almond cream filling as a dessert, or stuffed with meat or fish as an hors d'oeuvre

DATTE (DE MER): date (prized date-shaped wild Mediterranean mussel)

DAUBE: a stew, usually of beef, lamb, or mutton, with red wine, onions, and/or tomatoes; specialty of many regions, particularly Provence and the Atlantic coast

DAUPHIN: cow's-milk cheese shaped like a *dauphin*, or dolphin; from the north

DAURADE: sea bream, similar to porgy; the most prized of a group of ocean fish also known as *dorade*

DÉCAFÉINÉ OR DÉCA: decaffeinated coffee

DÉCORTIQUÉ(E): shelled or peeled

DÉGUSTATION: tasting or sampling

DÉJEUNER: lunch

DEMI: half; also, an 8-ounce (250-ml) glass of beer; also, a half-bottle of wine

DEMI-DEUIL: "in half mourning"; poached fowl (usually chicken) with sliced truffles inserted under the skin; also, sweetbreads with a truffled white sauce

DEMI-GLACE: concentrated beef-based sauce lightened

with consommé, or a lighter brown sauce

DEMI-SEC: usually refers to goat cheese that is in the intermediate aging stage between one extreme of soft and fresh and the other extreme of hard and aged

DEMI-SEL (BEURRE): lightly salted (butter)

DEMI-TASSE: small cup; after-dinner coffee cup

DEMOISELLE DE CANARD: marinated raw duck tenderloin; also called *mignon de canard*

DEMOISELLES DE CHERBOURG: small lobsters from the town of Cherbourg in Normandy, cooked in a court-bouillon and served in cooking juices. Also, restaurant name for Breton lobsters weighing 10 to 13 ounces (300 to 400 grams).

DENTELLE: "lace"; a portion of meat or fish so thinly sliced as to suggest a resemblance to lace. Also, large lace-thin sweet crêpe.

DENT, DENTÉ: one of a generic group of Mediterranean fish known as *dorade*, similar to porgy

DENTS-DE-LION: dandelion salad green; also called *pissenlit*

DÉS: diced pieces

DÉSOSSÉ: boned

DIABLE: "devil"; method of preparing poultry with a peppery sauce, often mustard-based. Also, a round pottery casserole.

DIEPPOISE: Dieppe-style; usually white wine, mussels, shrimp, mushrooms, and cream

DIGESTIF: general term for spirits served after dinner, such as Armagnac, Cognac, *marc, eau-de-vie*

DIJONNAISE: Dijon style; usually with mustard

DIM SUM: small, bite-size Chinese steamed dumplings and other delicacies

DINDE: turkey hen

DINDON(NEAU): male turkey (young turkey)

DÎNER: dinner; to dine

DIOT: pork sausage cooked in wine, often served with a potato gratin; specialty of the Savoy

DISCRÉTION, À: on menus, usually refers to wine, which may be consumed without limit at the customer's discretion

DODINE: cold stuffed, boned poultry

DORADE: generic name for group of ocean fish, the most prized of which is *daurade royale*, similar to porgy

DORÉ: browned until golden

DOS: back; also the meatiest portion of fish

DOUCETTE: lamb's lettuce; see *mâche*

DOUCEUR: sweet or dessert

DOUILLON, DUILLON: a whole pear wrapped and cooked in pastry; specialty of Normandy

DOUX, DOUCE: sweet

DOYENNÉ DE COMICE: a variety of pear

DUGLÉRÉ: white flour–based sauce with shallots, white wine, tomatoes, and parsley

DUR (OEUF): hard (hard-cooked egg)

DUXELLES: minced mushrooms and shallots sautéed in butter, then mixed with cream

E

EAU DU ROBINET: tap water

EAU DE SOURCE: spring water

EAU-DE-VIE: literally, "water of life"; brandy, usually fruit-based

EAU GAZEUSE: carbonated water

EAU MINÉRALE: mineral water

EAU PLAT: flat (not carbonated) water

ÉCAILLER: to scale fish or to open oysters; also used as a noun to refer to someone who sells and opens oysters and other shellfish

ECHALOTE (GRIS): shallot (prized gray shallot)

ECHALOTE BANANE: banana-shaped onion

ECHINE: pork shoulder, encompassing the blade bone and spare ribs

ECHOURGNAC: delicately flavored, ocher-skinned cheese made of cow's milk by the monks at the Echourgnac abbey in the Dordogne in Southwestern France

ECLADE DE MOULES: mussels grilled under a fire of pine needles until the shells open; specialty of the Atlantic coast

ECRASÉ: crushed; with fruit, pressed to release juice

ECREVISSE: freshwater crayfish

EFFILOCHÉ: frayed, shredded

EGLANTINE: wild rose jam; specialty of Alsace

EGLEFIN, ÉGREFIN, AIGLEFIN: small fresh haddock, a type of cod

ELZEKARIA: soup made with green beans, cabbage, and garlic; specialty of the Basque region

EMBEURRÉ DE CHOU: buttery cooked cabbage

EMINCÉ: thin slice, usually of meat

EMMENTAL: large wheel of cooked and pressed cow's-milk cheese, very mild in flavor, with large interior holes; made in large commercial dairies in the Jura

EMONDÉ: skinned by blanching, a method often used with almonds

EN SUS: see *service en sus*

ENCHAUD: pork filet with garlic; specialty of the Dordogne

ENCORNET: small illex squid, also called *calmar*; in Basque region called *chipiron*

ENCRE: squid ink

ENDIVE: Belgian endive; also chicory salad green

ENTIER, ENTIÈRE: whole, entire

ENTRECÔTE: beef rib steak

ENTRECÔTE MAÎTRE D'HÔTEL: beef rib steak with sauce of red wine and shallots

ENTRÉE: first course

ENTREMETS: dessert

EPAIS(SE): thick

EPAULE: shoulder (of veal, lamb, mutton, or pork)

ÉPEAUTRE: a grain (*triticum*

monococcum) grown in Provence since the Middle Ages, often called "poor man's wheat" because it will grow in dry climates and poor soil. Similar to spelt, *farro*, wheatberry. Cooked and used like rice.

ÉPERLAN: smelt or whitebait, usually fried, often imported but still found in the estuaries of the Loire

EPI DE MAÏS: ear of sweet corn

EPICE: spice

EPIGRAMME: classic dish of grilled breaded lamb chop and a piece of braised lamb breast shaped like a chop, breaded and grilled; crops up on modern menus as an elegant dish of breaded and fried baby lamb chops paired with lamb sweetbreads and tongue

EPINARD: spinach

EPINE VINETTE: highbush cranberry

ÉPOISSES: Village in Burgundy that gives its name to a buttery disk of cow's-milk cheese with a pungent flavor and rust-colored rind. Only cheese labeled Époisses de Bourgogne has A.O.C./A.O.P. status.

ÉPOISSES BLANC: fresh white Époisses cheese

EQUILLE: sand eel, a long silvery fish that buries itself in the sand; eaten fried on the Atlantic coast

ESCABÈCHE: a Provençal and Southwestern preparation of small fish, usually sardines or *rouget*, in which the fish are browned in oil, then marinated in vinegar and herbs and served very cold. Also, raw fish marinated in lemon or lime juice and herbs

ESCALIVADA: Catalan roasted vegetables, usually sweet peppers, eggplant, and onions

ESCALOPE: thin slice of meat, poultry, or fish

ESCARGOT: land snail

ESCARGOT DE BOURGOGNE: land snail prepared with butter, garlic, and parsley

ESCARGOT PETIT-GRIS: small land snail

ESCAROLE: bitter salad green of the chicory family with thick broad-lobed leaves, found in both flat and round heads

ESPADON: swordfish found in the Gulf of Gascony, the Atlantic, and the Mediterranean

ESPAGNOLE, À L': Spanish style; with tomatoes, peppers, onions, and garlic

ESQUEIXADA: in Catalan, literally "shredded"; a shredded salt cod salad

ESTIVAL: summer, used to denote seasonality of ingredients

ESTOFICADO: a puree-like blend of dried codfish, olive oil, tomatoes, sweet peppers, black olives, potatoes, garlic, onions, and herbs; also called stockfish *niçoise*; specialty of Nice

ESTOFINADO: a puree-like blend of dried codfish, potatoes, garlic, parsley, eggs, walnut oil, and milk, served with triangles of toast; specialty of the Auvergne

ESTOUFFADE À LA PROVENÇALE: beef stew with onions, garlic, carrots, and orange zest

ESTRAGON: tarragon

ETOFFÉ: stuffed

ETOILE: star; star-shaped

ETOUFFÉ; ÉTUVÉ: literally "smothered"; method of cooking very slowly in a tightly covered pan with almost no liquid

ÉTRILLE: small swimming crab

EXPRESS: espresso coffee

F

FAÇON (À MA): (my) way of preparing a dish

FAGOT: "bundle"; meat shaped into a small ball

FAISAN(E): pheasant

FAISANDÉ: game that has been hung to age

FAIT: usually refers to a cheese that has been well aged and has character—runny if it's a Camembert, hard and dry if

it's a goat cheese; also means ready to eat

FAIT, PAS TROP: refers to a cheese that has been aged for a shorter time and is blander

FALAFEL: deep-fried patties made from spiced, ground chickpeas, often served with pita bread

FALETTE: veal breast stuffed with bacon and vegetables, browned, and poached in broth; specialty of the Auvergne

FANES: green tops of root vegetables such as carrots, radishes, turnips

FAR: Breton sweet or savory pudding-cakes; the most common, similar to *clafoutis* from the Dordogne, is made with prunes

FARCI(E): stuffed

FARIGOULE(TTE): Provençal name for wild thyme

FARINE: flour
  Complète: whole-wheat flour
  D'avoine: oat flour
  De blé: wheat flour; white flour
  De maïs: corn flour
  De sarrasin: buckwheat flour
  De seigle: rye flour
  De son: bran flour

FAUX-FILET: sirloin steak

FAVORITE D'ARTICHAUT: classic vegetable dish of artichoke stuffed with asparagus, covered with a cheese sauce, and browned

FAVOUILLE: in Provence, tiny male (female) crab often used in soups

FENOUIL: fennel

FER À CHEVAL: "horseshoe"; a horseshoe-shaped baguette

FÉRA, FERET: salmon-like lake fish, found in Lac Léman, in the Morvan, in Burgundy, and in the Auvergne

FERME (FERMIER, FERMIÈRE): farm (farmer); in cheese, refers to farm-made cheese, often used to mean raw-milk cheese; in poultry, refers to free-range chickens

FERMÉ: closed

FERNKASE: young cheese shaped like a flying saucer and sprinkled with coarsely ground pepper; specialty of Alsace

FEU DE BOIS, AU: cooked over a wood fire

FEUILLE DE CHÊNE: oak-leaf lettuce

FEUILLE DE VIGNE: vine leaf

FEUILLETAGE (EN): (in) puff pastry

FEUILLETÉE (PÂTÉ): puff pastry

FÉVES (FÉVETTES): broad, fava, coffee, or cocoa beans (miniature beans); also, the porcelain figure baked into the Twelfth Night cake, or *galette des rois*

FIADONE: Corsican flan made from fresh, ricotta-like cheese and citrus

FICELLE, À LA: a way to order wine in some cafés and bistros, where one orders a bottle of wine but only pays for what is consumed

FICELLE (BOEUF À LA): "string"; (beef suspended on a string and poached in broth); also, a small thin baguette; also, a small bottle of wine, as in carafe of Beaujolais

FICELLE PICARDE: thin crêpe wrapped around a slice of ham and topped with a cheesy cream sauce; specialty of Picardy, in the north

FIGUE: fig

FINANCIER: small rectangular almond cake

FINANCIÈR(E): Madeira sauce with truffle juice

FINE DE CLAIRE: elongated crinkle-shelled oyster that stays in fattening beds (*claires*) a minimum of two months

FINES HERBES: mixture of herbs, usually chervil, parsley, chives, tarragon

FLAGEOLET: small white or pale green kidney-shaped dried bean

FLAGNARDE, FLAUGNARDE, FLOGNARDE: hot, fruit-filled batter cake made with eggs, flour, milk, and butter, and sprinkled with sugar before serving; specialty of the Southwest

FLAMANDE, À LA: Flemish style; usually with stuffed cabbage leaves, carrots, turnips, potatoes, and bacon

FLAMBER: to burn off the alcohol by igniting. Usually the brandies or other liqueurs to be flambéed are warmed first, then lit as they are poured into the dish

FLAMICHE (AU MAROILLES): a vegetable tart with rich bread dough crust, commonly filled with leeks, cream, and cheese; specialty of Picardy, in the north; (filled with cream, egg, butter, and Maroilles cheese)

FLAMMEKUECHE: thin-crusted savory tart, much like a pizza, covered with cream, onions, and bacon; also called *tarte flambée*; specialty of Alsace

FLAN: sweet or savory tart; also, a crustless custard pie

FLANCHET: flank of beef or veal, used generally in stews

FLÉTAN: halibut, found in the English Channel and North Sea

FLEUR (DE SEL): flower (fine, delicate sea salt, from Brittany or the Camargue)

FLEUR DE COURGETTE: zucchini blossom

FLEURON: puff pastry crescent

FLORENTINE: with spinach; also, a cookie of *nougatine* and candied fruit brushed with a layer of chocolate

FLÛTE: "flute"; usually a very thin baguette; also, form of Champagne glass

FOIE: liver

FOIE BLOND DE VOLAILLE: chicken liver; sometimes, a chicken-liver mousse

FOIE DE VEAU: calf's liver

FOIE GRAS D'OIE (DE CANARD): liver of fattened goose (duck)

FOIN (DANS LE): (cooked in) hay

FOND: cooking juices from meat, used to make sauces; also the bottom of a vessel

FOND D'ARTICHAUT: heart and base of an artichoke

FONDANT: "melting"; refers to worked sugar (sugar that has been beaten until it reaches a creamy consistency) that is cooked and flavored, then used for icing cakes; also, the bittersweet chocolate

high in cocoa butter used for making the shiniest chocolates; also, pureed meat, fish, or vegetables shaped into croquettes

FONDU(E): melted

FONTAINEBLEAU: creamy, white fresh dessert cow's-milk cheese from the Île-de-France

FORESTIÈRE: garnish of wild mushrooms, bacon, and potatoes

FORMULE: set menu

FOUACE: a kind of brioche; specialty of the Auvergne

FOUCHTRA: a young goat's or cow's-milk cheese from the Saint-Nectaire area of the Auvergne

FOUDJOU: a pungent goat-cheese spread, a blend of fresh and aged grated cheese mixed with salt, pepper, brandy, and garlic and cured in a crock; specialty of northern Provence

FOUGASSE: a crusty lattice-like bread made of baguette dough or puff pastry often flavored with anchovies, black olives, herbs, spices, or onions; specialty of Provence and the Mediterranean; also a sweet bread of Provence flavored with orange-flower water, oil, and sometimes almonds

FOUR (AU): (baked in an) oven

FOURME D'AMBERT: cylindrical blue-veined cow's-milk cheese, made in dairies and small farms around the town of Ambert in the Auvergne; A.O.C./A.O.P.

FOURRÉ: stuffed or filled

FOYOT: classic sauce made of *béarnaise* with meat glaze

FRAIS, FRAÎCHE: fresh or chilled

FRAISE: strawberry

FRAISE DES BOIS: wild strawberry

FRAMBOISE: raspberry

FRANÇAISE, À LA: classic garnish of peas with lettuce, small white onions, and parsley

FRANGIPANE: almond custard filling

FRAPPÉ: usually refers to a drink served very cold or with ice, often shaken

FRÉMI: "quivering"; often refers to barely cooked oysters

FRIANDISE: sweetmeat, petit four

FRICADELLE: fried minced meat patty

FRICANDEAU: thinly sliced veal or a rump roast, braised with vegetables and white wine

FRICASSÉE: classically, ingredients braised in wine sauce or butter with cream added; currently denotes any mixture of ingredients—fish or meat—stewed or sautéed

FRICOT (DE VEAU): veal shoulder simmered in white wine with vegetables

FRISÉ(E): "curly"; usually curly endive, the bitter salad green of the chicory family sold in enormous round heads

FRIT(E): fried

FRITES: French fries

FRITONS: coarse pork *rillettes,* or a minced spread that includes organ meats

FRITOT: small organ meat fritter, where meat is partially cooked, then marinated in oil, lemon juice, and herbs, dipped in batter and fried just before serving; also, can refer to any small fried piece of meat or fish

FRITURE: fried food; also a preparation of small fried fish, usually whitebait or smelt

FROID(E): cold

FROMAGE: cheese

Blanc: a smooth low-fat cheese similar to cottage cheese

D'alpage: cheese made in mountain pastures during the prime summer milking period

Fort: pungent cheese

Frais: smooth, runny fresh cheese, like cottage cheese

Frais, bien égouté: well-drained fresh cheese

Maigre: low-fat cheese

FROMAGE DE TÊTE: headcheese, usually pork

FRUIT CONFIT: whole fruit preserved in sugar

FRUITS DE MER: seafood

FUMÉ: smoked

FUMET: fish stock

G

GALANGA: a ginger-like plant stem used in Asian cuisine

GALANTINE: classical preparation of boned meat or whole poultry that is stuffed or rolled, cooked, then glazed with gelatin and served cold

GALETTE: round flat pastry, pancake, or cake; can also refer to pancake-like savory preparations; in Brittany, usually a savory buckwheat *crêpe* known as *blé noir*

GALETTE BRESSANE, GALETTE DE PÉROUGES: cream and sugar tart from the Bresse area of the Rhône-Alpes

GALETTE DES ROIS: puff pastry filled with almond pastry cream, traditional Twelfth Night celebration cake

GALINETTE: Mediterranean fish of the mullet family

GAMBAS: large prawn

GANACHE: classically, a rich mixture of chocolate and *crème fraîche* used as a filling for cakes and chocolate truffles

GARBURE: a hearty stew that includes cabbage, beans, and salted or preserved duck, goose, turkey, or pork; specialty of the Southwest

GARDIANE: stew of beef or bull (*toro*) meat, with bacon, onions, garlic, and black olives, served with rice; specialty of the Camargue, in Provence

GARGOUILLAU: pear cake or tart; specialty of the northern Auvergne

GARNI(E): garnished

GARNITURE: garnish

GASCONNADE: roast leg of lamb with garlic and anchovies; specialty of the Southwest

GASPACHO: a cold soup, usually containing tomatoes, cucumber, onions, and sweet peppers; originally of Spanish origin

GÂTEAU: cake

Basque: a chewy sweet cake filled with pastry cream or, historically, with black cherry jam; also called *pastiza*; specialty of the Basque region

Breton: a rich round pound cake; specialty of Brittany

Opéra: classic almond sponge cake layered with coffee and chocolate butter cream, and covered with a sheet of chocolate; seen in every pastry shop window

Saint-Honoré: classic cake of *choux* puffs dipped in caramel and set atop a cream-filled *choux* crown on a pastry base

GAUDE: thick corn-flour porridge served hot, or cold and sliced, with cream

GAUFRE: waffle

GAVE: Southwestern term for mountain stream; indicates fish from the streams of the area

GAYETTE: small sausage patty made with pork liver and bacon, wrapped in caul fat and bacon

GELÉE: aspic

GENDARME: salted and smoked herring

GENIÈVERE: juniper berry

GÉNOISE: sponge cake

GENTIANE: gentian; a liqueur made from this mountain flower

GERMINY: garnish of sorrel; also, sorrel and cream soup

GERMON: albacore or long-fin tuna

GÉSIER: gizzard

GIBASSIER: round sweet bread from Provence, often flavored with lemon or orange zest, orange-flower water, and/ or almonds; also sometimes called *fougasse* or *pompe à l'huile*

GIBELOTTE: fricassée of rabbit in red or white wine

GIBIER: game, sometimes designated as *gibier à plume* (feathered) or *gibier à poil* (furry)

GIGOT (DE PRÉ SALÉ): usually a leg of lamb (lamb grazed on the salt meadows along the Atlantic and Normandy coasts)

GIGOT DE MER: a preparation, usually of large pieces of monkfish (*lotte*), oven-roasted like a leg of lamb

GIGUE (DE): haunch of certain game meats

GILLARDEAU: prized oyster raised in Normandy and finished in *claires*, or fattening beds on the Atlantic coast

GINGEMBRE: ginger

GIROFLE: clove

GIROLLE: prized pale orange wild mushroom; also called *chanterelle*

GIVRÉ; ORANGE GIVRÉ: frosted; orange sherbet served in its skin

GLACE: ice cream

GLACÉ: iced, crystallized, or glazed

GNOCCHI: dumplings made of *choux* paste, potatoes, or semolina

GORET: young pig

GOUGÈRE: cheese-flavored *choux* pastry

GOUJON: small catfish; generic name for a number of small fish. Also, preparation in which the central part of a larger fish is coated with bread crumbs, then deep fried.

GOUJONNETTE: generally used to describe a small strip of fish, such as sole, usually breaded and fried

GOURMANDISE(S): a taste and relish for good food

GOUSSE D'AIL: clove of garlic

GOUSSE DE VANILLE: vanilla bean

GOÛT: taste

GOÛTER (LE): to taste, to try (children's afternoon snack)

GRAINE DE LIN: flaxseed or linseed

GRAINE DE MOUTARDE: mustard seed

GRAISSE: fat

GRAISSERONS: crisply fried pieces of duck or goose skin; cracklings

GRAND CRÈME: large or double espresso with milk

GRAND CRU: top-ranking wine

GRAND VENEUR: "chief huntsman"; usually, a brown sauce for game, with red currant jelly

GRANITÉ: a type of sherbet or sorbet; a sweetened, flavored ice

GRAPPE (DE RAISINS): cluster; bunch (of grapes)

GRAS (MARCHÉ AU): fatty (market of fattened poultry and their livers)

GRAS-DOUBLE: tripe baked with onions and white wine

GRATIN: crust formed on top of a dish when browned in broiler or oven; also the dish in which such food is cooked

GRATIN DAUPHINOIS: baked casserole of sliced potatoes, usually with cream, milk, and sometimes cheese and/or eggs

GRATIN SAVOYARD: baked casserole of sliced potatoes, usually with bouillon, cheese, and butter

GRATINÉ(E): having a crusty, browned top

GRATINÉE LYONNAISE: bouillon flavored with port, garnished with beaten egg, topped with cheese, and browned under a broiler

GRATTONS, GRATTELONS: crisply fried pieces of pork, goose, or duck skin; cracklings

GRATUIT: free

GRECQUE, À LA: cooked in a seasoned mixture of oil, lemon juice, and water; refers to cold vegetables, usually mushrooms

GRELETTE, SAUCE: cold sauce with a base of whipped cream

GRELOT: small, white bulb onion

GRENADE: pomegranate

GRENAILLE: refers to a small, bite-size new potato of any variety

GRENADIN: small veal scallop

GRENOUILLE (CUISSE DE): frog (leg)

GRESSINI: breadsticks

GRIBICHE, SAUCE: mayonnaise with capers, cornichons, hard-cooked eggs, and herbs

GRILLADE: grilled meat

GRILLÉ(E): grilled

GRIOTTE: shiny, slightly acidic, reddish black cherry

GRISOTTE: parasol mushroom with a delicate flavor; also called *champignon à la bague*, *cocherelle*, and *coulemelle*

GRIVE: small wild bird, thrush

GROIN D'ÂNE: "donkey's snout"; Lyonnais name for a bitter winter salad green similar to dandelion greens

GRONDIN: red gurnard, a bony ocean fish, a member of the mullet family, used in fish stews such as bouillabaisse

GROS SEL: coarse salt

GROSEILLE: red currant

GRUYÈRE: strictly speaking, cheese from the Gruyère area of Switzerland; in France, generic name for a number of hard, mild cooked cheeses from the Jura, including Comté, Beaufort, and Emmental

GYROMITE: group of wild mushrooms, or *gyromitra*, known as false morels

H

HACHIS: minced or chopped meat or fish preparation

HADDOCK: small fresh cod that has been salted and smoked

HALLOUMI: a salty, brined, unripened cheese originally from Cyprus, served fried or grilled

HARENG: herring, found in the Atlantic, the English Channel (the best between Dunkerque and Fécamp), and the mouth of the Gironde River

HARENG À L'HUILE: herring cured in oil, usually served with a salad of warm sliced potatoes

HARENG BALTIQUE, BISMARK: marinated herring

HARENG BOUFFI: herring that is salted, then smoked

HARENG PEC: freshly salted young herring

HARENG ROLL-MOP: marinated herring rolled around a small pickle

HARENG SAUR: smoked herring

HARICOT: bean
  Beurre: yellow bean

Blancs (à la Bretonne): white beans, fresh or dried (white beans in a sauce of onions, tomatoes, garlic, and herbs)

De Mouton: stew of mutton and white beans (also called haricots)

Gris: green string bean mottled with purplish black; also called *pélandron;* a specialty of the Côte d'Azur

Mais: white bean (usually dried) with a thin skin, similar to *haricot blanc*

Rouge: red kidney bean; also mottled red *borlotti* bean; also, preparation of red beans in red wine

Sec: dried bean

Vert: green bean, usually fresh

HARICOT DE MOUTON: see *navarin*

HÂTELET, ATTELET: decorative skewer; currently used to mean meat or fish cooked on a skewer

HELIANTHUS TUBEROSUS: Jerusalem artichoke, sunchoke, *topinambour*

HERBES DE PROVENCE: A mix of dried herbs that bears an official French badge, *Label Rouge* (see *Label Rouge*), a guarantee of quality and authenticity. By law a mixture of rosemary (26%), summer savory (26%), oregano (26%), thyme (19%), and basil (3%). Herb mixtures not bearing the label may also include lavender and may come from outside Provence, including Central and Eastern Europe, North Africa, and China. Generally used to flavor stocks and sauces, or to sprinkle on vegetables, fish, poultry, or meat to be grilled.

HIRONDELLE: swallow

HOCHEPOT: a thick stew, usually of oxtail; specialty of Flanders, in the north

HOLLANDAISE: sauce of butter, egg yolks, and lemon juice

HOMARD (À L'AMORICAINE, À L'AMÉRICAINE): lobster (a classic dish of many variations, in which lobster is cut into sections and browned, then simmered with shallots, minced onions, tomatoes, Cognac, and white wine; served with a sauce of the reduced cooking liquid, enriched with butter)

HONGROISE, À LA: Hungarian style; usually with paprika and cream

HORS D'OEUVRE: appetizer; can also refer to a first course

HORTILLON: picturesque market garden plot built between crisscrossed canals on the outskirts of Amiens, a city in the north

HUILE: oil

D'arachide: peanut oil

De colza: rapeseed oil

De maïs: corn oil

De noisette: hazelnut oil

De noix: walnut oil

De pépins de raisins: grapeseed oil

De pistache: pistachio oil

De sésame: sesame oil

De tournesol: sunflower oil

De truffe: Artificially flavored with the "essence" of black truffles. To be avoided: more of a perfume than a worthy food product.

D'olive (extra vierge): olive oil (extra virgin)

HUÎTRE: oyster

HUMMUS: a dip made from cooked, pureed chickpeas and sesame paste

HURE DE PORC OR DE MARCASSIN: head of pig or baby wild boar; usually refers to headcheese preparation

HURE DE SAUMON: a salmon "headcheese," or pâté, prepared with salmon meat—not actually the head

HYSOPE: hyssop; fragrant, mintlike thistle found in Provence, used in salads and in cooking

I

ÎLE FLOTTANTE: "floating island"; most commonly used interchangeably with *oeufs à la neige,* poached meringue floating in *crème anglaise;* classically, a layered cake covered with whipped cream and served with custard sauce

IMPÉRATRICE, À L': usually, a rice pudding dessert with candied fruit

IMPÉRIALE: variety of plum; also, a large bottle for wine, holding about 4 quarts (4 liters)

IMPÉRIALE, À L': classic haute cuisine garnish of mussels, cockscombs, crayfish, and other extravagant ingredients

INDIENNE, À L': East Indian style, usually with curry powder

INFUSION: herb tea

ISMAN BAYALDI, IMAM BAYALDI: "the priest fainted," in Turkish; a dish of eggplant stuffed with sautéed onions, tomatoes, and spices; served cold

J

JALOUSIE: louvered window; a classic small, latticed, flaky pastry filled with almond paste and spread with jam

JAMBON: ham; also refers to the leg, usually of pork, but also of poultry

À l'os: ham with the bone in

Blanc: lightly salted, unsmoked or very lightly smoked ham, served cooked; sold cold, in *charcuteries* as *jambon de Paris, glacé,* or *demi-sel*

Cru: salted or smoked ham that has been cured but not cooked

Cuit: cooked ham

D'Auvergne: raw, dry, salt-cured smoked ham

De Bayonne: raw, dry, salt-cured ham, very pale in color

De Bourgogne: see *jambon persillé*

De montagne: any mountain ham, cured according to local custom

De Paris: pale, lightly salted cooked ham

De Parme: Italian prosciutto from Parma; air-dried and salt-cured ham, sliced thin and served raw

De pays: any country ham, cured according to local custom

De poulet: boned stuffed chicken leg

De Westphalie: German Westphalian ham, raw, cured, and smoked

De York: smoked English-style ham, usually poached

D'oie (or de canard): breast of fattened goose (or duck), smoked, salted, or sugar cured, somewhat resembling ham in flavor

Fumé: smoked ham

Persillé: cold cooked ham, cubed, and preserved in parsleyed gelatin, usually sliced from a terrine; a specialty of Burgundy

Salé: salt-cured ham

Sec: dried ham

JAMBONNEAU: cured ham shank or pork knuckle

JAMBONNETTE: boned and stuffed knuckle of ham or poultry

JARDINIÈRE: a garnish of fresh cooked vegetables

JARRET DE VEAU, DE PORC, DE BOEUF: knuckle (of veal or pork), shin (of beef)

JAUNE: yellow

JEREZ: sherry

JÉSUS DE MORTEAU: plump smoked pork sausage that takes its name from the town of Morteau in the Jura; distinctive because a wooden peg is tied in the sausage casing on one end; traditionally, the sausage is made at Christmas, hence its name; also called *saucisson de Morteau*

JEUNE: young

JONCHÉE: rush basket in which certain fresh sheep's- or goat's-milk cheeses of Poitou (along the Atlantic coast) are contained; thus, by extension, the cheese itself

JOUE: cheek

JOUE DE LOTTE: monkfish cheeks, generally breaded and pan-fried

JULIENNE: cut into matchstick-like slivers, usually vegetables

JURANÇON: district in the Béarn, the area around Pau in southwestern France, known for its dry as well as sweet white wine

JUS: juice

K

KATAIFI, KATAIF: thin strands of vermicelli-like shredded phyllo dough, used in Greek and Middle Eastern pastries and in some modern French preparations

KAKI: persimmon, grown in Provence

KARI: variant spelling of *cary*

KEBBE (KIBBE, KIBBEH)

BATATA: a Lebanese layered and baked pie of mashed potatoes, onions, spices, and grains; may contain chickpeas

KIEV: deep-fried breast of chicken stuffed with herb and garlic butter

KIR: an apéritif made with *crème de cassis* (black currant liqueur) and most commonly dry white wine, but sometimes red wine

KIR ROYAL: a Kir made with Champagne

KIRSCH: *eau-de-vie* of black cherries

KNEPFLA: Alsatian dumpling, sometimes fried

KOMBU, KONBU: an edible kelp or seaweed, mostly harvested off the northern coast of Hokkaido, Japan

KOUGELHOPH, HOUGELHOF, KOUGLOF, KUGELHOPH: sweet crown-shaped yeast bread, with almonds and raisins; specialty of Alsace

KOUIGH-AMANN: sweet, buttery pastry from Brittany

KUMMEL: caraway seed liqueur

L

LABEL ROUGE: A French label of quality awarded to various agricultural products, including flour, bread, fruits, vegetables, poultry, fish and shellfish, meat and *charcuterie*,

plants, seeds, herbs, dairy, and other products; all bear a distinctive red and white label.

LABNÉ: a thick, fresh, creamy Lebanese cheese, seasoned with garlic and mint; the result of draining and discarding the residual liquid from yogurt

LACTAIRE: the edible *Lactaire pallidus* mushroom, also called *sanguine* and *lactaire délicieux*; apricot colored, with bloodred juices when raw

LAGUIOLE: Large wheel (55 to 110 pounds; 25 to 50 kg) of raw cow's-milk cheese from the area around the village of Laguiole in the southern Auvergne. Can be aged up to two years. A.O.C./A.O.P.

LAIT: milk

Demi-écremé: semi-skimmed milk

Écremé: skimmed milk

Entier: whole milk

Microfiltré: a filtering process that removes undesirable bacteria from raw milk while retaining the flavor

Ribot: buttermilk from Brittany, served with *crêpes*

Stérilizé: milk heated to a higher temperature than pasteurized milk, so that it stays fresh for several weeks

LAITANCE: soft roe (often of herring), or eggs

LAITIER: made of or with milk; also denotes a commercially made product as opposed to *fermier*, meaning farm made

LAIT RIBOT: fermented milk from Brittany, similar to cultured buttermilk

LAITUE: lettuce

LAMELLE: very thin strip

LAMPROIE (À LA BORDELAISE): lamprey eel, ocean fish that swim into rivers along the Atlantic in springtime (hearty stew of lamprey eel and leeks in red wine)

LANÇON: tiny fish, served fried

LANDAISE, À LA: from the Landes region in southwestern France; classically, a garnish of garlic, pine nuts, and goose fat

LANGOUSTE: clawless spiny lobster or rock lobster; sometimes called crawfish, and mistakenly, crayfish

LANGOUSTINE: clawed crustacean, smaller than either *homard* or *langouste*, with very delicate meat; known in British waters as Dublin Bay prawn

LANGRES: supple, tangy cylindrical cow's-milk cheese with a rust-colored rind; named for a village in Champagne

LANGUE (DE CHAT): tongue ("cat's tongue"; thin, narrow, delicate cookie often served with sorbet or ice cream)

LANGUEDOCIENNE: garnish, usually of tomatoes, eggplant, and wild *cèpe* mushrooms

LAPEREAU: young rabbit

LAPIN: rabbit

LAPIN DE GARENNE: wild rabbit

LARD: bacon

LARDER: to thread meat, fish, or liver with strips of fat for added moisture

LARDON: cube or small strip of bacon

LARME: "teardrop"; a very small portion of liquid

LAURIER: bay laurel or bay leaf

LAVARET: lake fish of the Savoie, similar to salmon

LÉGER (LÉGÈRE): light

LÉGUME: vegetable

LENTILLES (DE PUY): lentils (prized green lentils from the village of Puy in the Auvergne)

LIEU JAUNE: green pollack, in the cod family, a pleasant, inexpensive, small yellow fish; often sold under the name *colin*; found in the Atlantic

LIEU NOIR: pollack, also called black cod; in the cod family, a pleasant, inexpensive fish found in the English Channel and the Atlantic

LIÈVRE (À LA ROYALE): hare (cooked with red wine, shallots, onions, and cinnamon, then rolled and stuffed with *foie gras* and truffles)

LIMACES À LA SUÇARELLE: snails cooked with onions,

garlic, tomatoes, and sausage; specialty of Provence

LIMAÇON: land snail

LIMANDE: lemon sole, not as firm or prized as sole; found in the English Channel, the Atlantic, and rarely, in the Mediterranean; also called dab or sand dab

LINGOT: type of kidney-shaped dry white bean, generally used in the preparation of *cassoulet*

LISETTE: small *maquereau*, or mackerel

LIVAROT: village in Normandy that gives its name to an elastic, pungent thick disk of cow's-milk cheese with reddish golden stripes around the edge; A.O.C./A.O.P.

LOTTE: monkfish or angler fish; a large firm-fleshed ocean fish

LOTTE DE RIVIÈRE (OR DE LAC): fine-fleshed river (or lake) fish, prized for its large and flavorful liver; not related to the ocean fish *lotte*, or monkfish

LOU MAGRET: breast of fattened duck

LOUP DE MER: wolf fish or ocean catfish; a sea bass in the Mediterranean

LOUVINE: Basque name for striped bass, fished in the Bay of Gascony

LUCULLUS: a classic, elaborate garnish of truffles cooked in Madeira and stuffed with chicken forcemeat

LUMAS: a land snail in the Poitou-Charentes region along the Atlantic coast

LUZIENNE, À LA: prepared in the manner popular in Saint-Jean-de-Luz, a Basque fishing port

LYONNAISE, À LA: in the style of Lyon; often garnished with onions

M

MACARON: Delicate meringue cookies made from almonds, egg whites, and sugar. Traditionally two cookies are sandwiched together while warm, but macarons are most

commonly found held together by a cream or ganache filling. Found in many colors and flavors.

MACARONADE: A rich blend of wild and domestic mushrooms and chunks of *foie gras*, tossed with fresh pasta; specialty of France's Southwest. Also, macaroni with mushrooms, bacon, white wine, and Parmesan cheese; an accompaniment to a beef stew, or *daube*; specialty of Provence.

MACCHERONI: a variety of dry durum wheat pasta with a short, curved, hollow shape

MACÉDOINE: diced mixed fruit or vegetables

MÂCHE: dark small-leafed salad green known as lamb's lettuce or corn salad; also called *doucette*

MÂCHON: early morning snack of sausage, wine, cheese, and bread; also, the café that offers the snack; particular to Lyon

MACIS: mace, the spice

MADELEINE (DE COMMERCY): small scallop-shaped teacake made famous by Marcel Proust; the town in the Lorraine where the teacakes are commercialized

MADÈRE: Madeira

MADRILÈNE, À LA: with tomatoes, literally, in the style of Madrid; classically, a garnish of peeled chopped tomatoes for consommé

MAGRET DE CANARD (OR D'OIE): breast of fattened duck (or goose)

MAIGRE: meager fish (also known as giant sea bass, drum, croaker, shadefish, and salmon bass); a thin, non-fatty, white-fleshed fish similar to a European sea bass found in the Atlantic Ocean and the Mediterranean Sea

MAÏS: corn

MAISON, DE LA: of the house, or restaurant

MAÎTRE D'HÔTEL: headwaiter; also sauce of butter, parsley, and lemon

MALTAISE: orange-flavored hollandaise sauce

MALVOISIE, VINAIGRE DE: vinegar made from the malvasia grape, used for the sweet, heavy Malmsey wine

MANDARINE: tangerine

MANGE-TOUT: "eat it all"; a podless green runner bean; a sweet pea; a snow pea; also, a variety of apple

MANGUE: mango

MANIÈRE, DE: in the style of

MAQUEREAU: mackerel; *lisette* is a small mackerel

MARA DE BOIS: tiny, fragrant strawberry that's a cross of four hybrid strawberries, created in France

MARAÎCHÈR(E) (À LA): market gardener or truck farmer (market-garden style; usually refers to a dish or salad that includes various greens)

MARBRÉ: striped sea bream, a Mediterranean fish that is excellent grilled

MARC: *eau-de-vie* distilled from pressed grape skins and seeds or other fruits

MARCASSIN: young, wild, or domesticated boar; at one year of age, a wild boar will weigh 20 pounds (40 kg) while a domesticated boar of the same age will weigh 60 pounds (120 kg)

MARCECHAL, LE: A raw cow's-milk cheese made by 14 farmers in Granges Marnand in Switzerland. In addition to their normal diet, the cattle are fed flaxseed, which aids blood flow and creates a cheese rich in omega-3 fatty acids. The cheese is wrapped in cloth and a mix of aromatic, organic herbs are pressed into the cloth, and the cheese is ripened for 120 days minimum.

MARCHAND DE VIN: wine merchant; also, sauce made with red wine, meat stock, and chopped shallots

MARÉE, LA: "the tide"; usually used to indicate seafood that is fresh

MARENNES: flat-shelled green-tinged *plate* oyster; also, the French coastal area where flat-shelled oysters are raised

MARINADE: Seasoned liquid in which food, usually meat, is soaked for several hours. The liquid seasons and tenderizes at the same time.

MARINÉ: marinated

MARJOLAINE: marjoram; also, a multilayered chocolate and nut cake

MARMELADE: traditionally, a thick puree of fruit, or sweet stewed fruit; today, a puree of vegetables or stewed vegetables

MARMITE: small covered pot; also, a dish cooked in a small casserole

MAROILLES: village in the north that gives its name to a strong-tasting, thick, square cow's-milk cheese with a pale brick-red rind; A.O.C./A.O.P.

MARQUISE (AU CHOCOLAT): mousselike (chocolate) cake

MARRON (GLACÉ): large (candied) chestnut

MATCHA: powdered green tea leaves

MATELOTE (D'ANGUILLES): freshwater fish (or eel) stew

MATIGNON: a garnish of mixed stewed vegetables

MAUVIETTE: wild meadowlark or skylark

MÉDAILLON: round piece or slice, usually of fish or meat

MÉLANGE: mixture or blend

MÉLI-MÉLO: an assortment of fish and/or seafood

MELON DE CAVAILLON: small canteloupe melon from Cavaillon, a town in Provence known for its wholesale produce market

MÉNAGÈRE, À LA: "in the style of the housewife"; usually, a simple preparation including onions, potatoes, and carrots

MENDIANT, FRUITS DU: Traditional mixture of figs, almonds, hazelnuts, and raisins, whose colors suggest the robes of the mendicants it is named after; also a traditional French confection composed of a chocolate disk studded with nuts and dried fruits representing the four mendicant orders: Dominicans, Augustinians,

Franciscans, and Carmelites. Modern versions also include a greater variety of fruits, dried citrus peels, and seeds.

MENTHE: mint

MERGUEZ: small, spicy North African sausage, made from lamb, mutton, or beef, or a mix of the meats

MERLAN: whiting

MERLE: blackbird

MERLU: hake, a member of the codfish family, often incorrectly identified in Paris markets as *colin*; found in the English Channel, Atlantic, and Mediterranean

MÉROU: a large grouper, an excellent tropical or near-tropical fish, generally imported from North Africa but sometimes found in the Atlantic and Mediterranean

MERVEILLE: hot sugared doughnut

MESCLUM, MESCLUN: a mixture of at least seven multishaded salad greens from Provence

METS: dish or preparation

METS SELON LA SAISON: seasonal preparation; according to the season

MÉTURE: corn bread from the Basque region

MEULE: a large (70 to 99 lbs; 32 to 45 kg) cylindral wheel of cheese

MEUNIÈRE, À LA: "in the style of the miller's wife"; refers to a fish that is seasoned, rolled in flour, fried in butter, and served with lemon and parsley

MEURETTE: in, or with, a red wine sauce; also, a Burgundian fish stew

MI-CRU: half raw

MI-CUIT: half cooked

MICHE: a large, round country-style loaf of bread; also, Basque name for aniseed cakelike bread

MIE: interior or crumb of the bread (see *pain de mie*)

MIEL: honey

MIGNARDISE: see *petit four*

MIGNON DE CANARD: see *demoiselle de canard*

MIGNONETTE: small cubes, usually of beef; also refers to coarsely ground black or white pepper

MIJOTÉ(E) (PLAT): simmered (dish or preparation)

MILLEFEUILLE: refers to puff pastry with many thin layers; usually a cream-filled rectangle of puff pastry, or a Napoleon

MIMOSA: garnish of chopped, hard-cooked egg yolks

MINUTE (À LA): "minute"; something quickly grilled or fried in butter with lemon juice and parsley (prepared at the last minute)

MIQUE: generally, a large breaded dumpling, poached and served with stews and meats; specialty of France's Southwest

MIRABEAU: garnish of anchovies, pitted olives, tarragon, and anchovy butter

MIRABELLE: small, sweet yellow plum; also, colorless fruit brandy or *eau-de-vie* made from yellow plums

MIREPOIX: cubes of carrots and onions or mixed vegetables, usually used in braising to boost the flavor of a meat dish

MIROIR: "mirror"; a dish that has a smooth glaze; currently, a fruit mousse cake with a layer of fruit glaze on top

MIROTON (DE): slice (of); also, a stew of meats flavored with onions

MISO: fermented bean paste; an important staple in Japanese cooking, used in dressings, as a spread on grilled foods, or as the base of the ubiquitous *miso shiru* (miso soup)

MITONNÉE: a simmered, souplike dish

MODE DE, À LA: in the style of

MOËLLE: beef bone marrow

MOGETTE, MOJETTE, MOUGETTE: a variety of dried white bean from the Atlantic coast, often used in *cassoulet*

MOKA: refers to coffee; coffee-flavored dish

MOLLUSQUE: mollusk

MONT BLANC: rich classic pastry of baked meringue, chestnut puree, and whipped cream

MONTAGNE, DE LA: from the mountains

MONTMORENCY: garnished with cherries; historically, a village known for its cherries, now a suburb of Paris

MORBIER: supple cow's-milk cheese from the Jura; a thin sprinkling of ashes in the center gives it its distinctive black stripe and light smoky flavor; A.O.C./A.O.P.

MORCEAU: piece or small portion

MORILLE: wild morel mushroom, dark brown and conical

MORNAY: classic cream sauce enriched with egg yolks and cheese

MORUE: salt cod; also currently used to mean fresh cod, which is *cabillaud*

MORVANDELLE, JAMBON À LA: in the style of the Morvan in Burgundy (ham in a piquant creamy sauce made with white wine, vinegar, juniper berries, shallots, and cream)

MORVANDELLE, RÂPÉE: grated potato mixed with eggs, cream, and cheese, baked until golden

MOSAÏQUE: "mosaic"; a presentation of mixed ingredients

MOSTÈLE: forkbeard mostelle; small Mediterranean fish of the cod family

MOUCLADE: creamy mussel stew from the Poitou-Charentes on the Atlantic Coast, generally flavored with curry or saffron

MOUFFLON: wild sheep

MOULE: mussel; also, a mold

MOULE DE BOUCHOT: small, highly prized cultivated mussel, raised on stakes driven into the sediment of shallow coastal beds

MOULE DE BOUZIGUES: iodine-strong mussel from the village of Bouzigues, on the Mediterranean coast

MOULE D'ESPAGNE: large, sharp-shelled mussel, often served raw as part of a seafood platter

MOULES DE LA BAIE DU MONT SAINT-MICHEL: the first A.O.C./A.O.P. of the sea, these prized mussels from Brittany appear in French markets from July to February

MOULE DE PARQUES: Dutch cultivated mussel, usually raised in fattening beds or diverted ponds

MOULES MARINIÈRE: mussels cooked in white wine with onions, shallots, butter, and herbs

MOULIN (À POIVRE): mill (peppermill); also, oil and flour mills

MOURONE: Basque name for red bell pepper

MOURTAYROL, MOURTAÏROL: a *pot-au-feu* of boiled beef, chicken, ham, and vegetables, flavored with saffron, and served over slices of bread; specialty of the Auvergne

MOUSSE: light, airy mixture usually containing eggs and cream, either sweet or savory

MOUSSELINE: refers to ingredients that are usually lightened with whipped cream or egg whites, as in sauces, or with butter, as in *brioche mousseline*

MOUSSERON: tiny, delicate, sandy-colored wild fairy ring mushroom

MOUTARDE (À L'ANCIENNE, EN GRAINES): mustard (old-style, coarse-grained)

MOUTON: mutton

MUGE: gray mullet

MULARD: breed of duck common to France's Southwest, fattened for its delicate liver for *foie gras*

MULET: the generic group of mullet found in the English Channel, Atlantic, and Mediterranean

MUNSTER: village in Alsace that gives its name to a disk of soft, tangy cow's-milk cheese with a brick-red rind and a penetrating aroma; the cheese is also sometimes aged with cumin seeds

MÛRE (DE RONCES): blackberry (bush)

MUSCADE: nutmeg

MUSCAT DE HAMBOURG:
variety of popular purple table
grape grown in Provence, with
its own A.O.C./A.O.P.

**MUSEAU DE PORC (OR DE
BOEUF):** vinegared pork (or
beef) muzzle

MYRTILLE: bilberry (bluish
black European blueberry)

MYSTÈRE: truncated cone-
shaped ice-cream dessert;
also, dessert of cooked
meringue with ice cream and
chocolate cake

N

NAGE (À LA): "swimming";
aromatic poaching liquid
(served in)

NANTUA: sauce of crayfish,
butter, cream, and traditionally,
truffles; also garnish of crayfish

NAPOLÉON, LE: firm,
thick-crusted, modern raw
sheep's-milk cheese from
the Basque region, made on
farms and carefully aged for
at least 10 months and up to
several years; firm, fragrant,
memorable

NAPPÉ: covered, as with a sauce

NATTE: woven, often braided
loaf of bread

NATURE: refers to simple,
unadorned natural
preparations

NAVARIN: lamb or mutton stew

NAVARRAISE, À LA: Navarre-
style, with sweet peppers,
onions, and garlic

NAVET: turnip

NAVETTE: "little boat"; small
pastry boats

NÈFLE: medlar; also
called Japanese loquat; tart
fruit that resembles an apricot
and tastes like a mango

NEUFCHÂTEL: white, creamy,
delicate (and often heart-
shaped) cow's-milk cheese,
named for the village in
Normandy where it is made

NEWBURG: lobster preparation
with Madeira, egg yolks, and
cream

NIVERNAISE, À LA: in the style
of Nevers; with carrots and
onions

NOILLY: a vermouth or a
vermouth-based sauce

NOISETTE: hazelnut; also refers
to any of the following: a small
round piece (such as from a
potato), generally the size of
a hazelnut, lightly browned
in butter; center cut of lamb
chop; dessert flavored with
hazelnuts; espresso coffee
with just a touch of cream

NOIX: general term for nut;
also, walnut; also, nut-size,
typically *une noix de beurre*,
or lump of butter

NOIX DE VEAU: bottom round
filet of veal, the tender, fine-
grained muscle from the top
of the back leg

NON COMPRIS: see *service
(non) compris*

NONAT: small river fish in
Provence, usually fried; also
known as *poutine*

NORMANDE: in the style of
Normandy; sauce of seafood,
cream, and mushrooms; also
refers to fish or meat cooked
with apple cider or Calvados
(apple brandy); or dessert with
apples, usually served with
cream

NOTE: another word for
addition, bill, or tab

NOUGAT: candy of roasted
almonds, egg whites,
and honey; specialty of
Montélimar in Northern
Provence

NOUGAT GLACÉ: frozen
dessert of whipped cream and
candied fruit

NOUILLES: noodles

NOUVEAU, NOUVELLE: new
or young

NOUVEAUTÉ: a new offering

O

OEUF: egg
À la coque: soft-cooked egg
Brouillé: scrambled egg
Dur: hard-cooked egg
En meurette: poached egg in
red wine sauce
Miroir: a fried egg cooked with
the lid on the pan so that the
yolk's membrane turns an
opaque white

Mollet: egg simmered in water
for 6 minutes
Oeufs à la neige: "eggs in the
snow"; sweetened whipped
egg whites poached in milk
and served with vanilla
custard sauce
Poché: poached egg
**Sauté à la poêle or oeuf sur le
plat:** fried egg

OFFERT: offered; free or given

OIE: goose

OIGNON: onion

OISELLE: sorrel

OLIVE NOIRE (VERTE): black
olive (green olive)

OLIVE DE NYONS: wrinkled
black olive, first olive in
France to receive A.O.C.; also
used for oil

OLIVES CASSÉES: fresh green
olives cured in a rich fennel-
infused brine; specialty of
Provence

OMBLE (OMBRE) CHEVALIER:
lake fish, similar to salmon
trout, with firm, flaky flesh
varying from white to deep
red; found in lakes in the
Savoie

OMELETTE NORVEGIENNE:
French version of baked
Alaska; a concoction of sponge
cake covered with ice cream
and a layer of sweetened,
stiffly beaten egg whites, then
browned quickly in the oven

ONGLET: cut similar to beef
flank steak; also cut of beef
sold as *biftek* and *entrecôte*,
usually a tough cut, but better
than flank steak

OREILLE DE PORC: cooked
pig's ear; served grilled, with
a coating of egg and bread
crumb

OREILLETTE: thin, crisp
rectangular dessert fritters,
flavored with orange-flower
water; specialty of Provence

ORGE (PERLE): barley (pearl
barley)

ORIENTALE, À L': general
name for vaguely Eastern
dishes cooked with saffron,
tomatoes, and sweet red
peppers

ORIGAN: oregano

ORTIE: nettle

OSEILLE: sorrel

OSSO BUCCO À LA NIÇOISE: sautéed veal braised with tomatoes, garlic, onions, and orange zest; specialty of the Mediterranean

OSTRÉICULTEUR: oyster grower

OURSIN: sea urchin

OURSINADE: creamy sea urchin soup

OUVERT: open

P

PAGEOT: A type of sea bream or porgy. The finest is *pageot rouge*, wonderful grilled. *Pageot blanc* is drier and needs to be marinated in oil before cooking.

PAILLARDE (DE VEAU): thick slice (of veal); also, a piece of meat pounded flat and sauteéed

PAILLES (POMMES): fried potato sticks

PAILLETTE: cheese straw, usually made with puff pastry and Parmesan cheese

PAIN: bread; also, loaf of any kind

  Aux cinq céréales: five-grain bread

  Aux noix (aux noisettes): bread, most often rye or wheat, filled with walnuts (hazelnuts)

  Aux raisins: bread, most often rye or wheat, filled with raisins

  Azyme: unleavened bread, matzoh

  Bis: made with whole wheat flour

  Brié: very dense, elongated loaf of unsalted white bread; specialty of Normandy

  Complet: bread made partially or entirely from whole-wheat flour, with bakers varying proportions according to their personal tastes

  Cordon: seldom-found regional country loaf decorated with a strip of dough

  D'Aix: variously shaped sourdough loaves, sometimes like a sunflower, other times a chainlike loaf of four linked rounds

  De campagne: country loaf; can vary from a white bread simply dusted with flour to give it a rustic look to a truly hearty loaf that may be a blend of white, whole wheat, and perhaps rye flour with bran added; comes in every shape

  Décoré: decorated

  De fantaisie: generally, any odd or imaginatively shaped bread; even *baguette de campagne* falls into this category

  De gênes: classic almond sponge cake

  De mie: rectangular white sandwich loaf that is nearly all *mie* (interior crumb) and very little crust. It is made for durability, its flavor and texture developed for use in sandwiches. Unlike most French breads, it contains milk, sugar, and butter.

  D'épices: spice bread, a specialty of Dijon

  De seigle: bread made from 60 to 70 percent rye flour and 40 to 30 percent wheat flour

  De son: legally, a dietetic bread that is quality controlled, containing 20 percent bran mixed with white flour

  Grillé: toast

  Paillé: country loaf from the Basque region

  Sans sel: salt-free bread

  Viennois: bread shaped like a baguette, with regular horizontal slashes, usually containing white flour, sugar, powdered milk, water, and yeast

PALERON: shoulder of beef

PALESTINE: classically, a soup or garnish of Jerusalem artichokes

PALETTE: upper shoulder of pork

PALMIER: palm leaf–shaped cookie made of sugared puff pastry

PALMIER, COEUR DE: heart of palm

PALOMBE: wild pigeon, wood pigeon, or ring dove

PALOURDE: prized medium-size clam

PAMPLEMOUSSE: grapefruit

PAN BAGNA: traditionally a large round bun (now more often a baguette), split, brushed with olive oil, and filled with a variable mixture including fresh tomatoes, cured anchovies, scallions, canned tuna, hard-cooked eggs, green bell peppers, fava beans, and basil; café specialty of Nice

PAN CON TOMATE: a Spanish Catalan specialty of toasted bread rubbed with fresh garlic, fresh tomatoes, and drizzled with olive oil

PANACHÉ: mixed; now liberally used menu term to denote any mixture

PANADE: panada, a thick mixture used to bind forcemeats and *quenelles*, usually flour and butter based, but can also contain fresh or toasted bread crumbs, rice, or potatoes; also refers to soup of bread, milk, and sometimes cheese

PANAIS: parsnip

PANÉ(E): breaded

PANISSE: a thick fried pancake of chickpea flour, served as accompaniment to meat; specialty of Provence

PANNEQUET: rolled *crêpe*, filled and/or covered with sweet or savory mixture

PANOUFLE: generally, discarded belly flap from saddle of lamb, veal, and beef; sometimes grilled

PANTIN: small pork pastry

PAPETON: eggplant fried, pureed, and often cooked in a ring mold or a bread pan; specialty of Provence

PAPILLON: "butterfly"; small crinkle-shelled *creuse* oyster from the Atlantic coast

PAPILLOTE, EN: baked in sealed parchment paper or aluminum foil

PAQUET (EN): (in) a package or parcel

PARFAIT: a dessert mousse; also, mousse-like mixture of chicken, duck, or goose liver

PARFUM: flavor

PARIS-BREST, GÂTEAU: classic, large, crown-shaped *choux* pastry filled with praline butter cream and topped with chopped almonds

PARISIENNE, À LA: varied vegetable garnish that generally includes potato balls that have been fried and tossed in a meat glaze

PARMENTIER: a dish containing or garnished with potatoes

HACHIS PARMENTIER: a dish of minced meat, usually beef, topped with mashed potatoes and browned in the oven

PASSE CRASSANE: flavorful variety of winter pear

PASSE-PIERRE: edible seaweed

PASTEL DE NATA (PL. PASTEIS DE NATA): a Portuguese tart filled with baked egg custard, traditionally served warm with a sprinkling of cinnamon and icing sugar

PASTÈQUE: watermelon

PASTIS: anise-flavored alcohol that becomes cloudy when water is added (the most famous brands are Pernod and Ricard); also, name for *tourtière*, the flaky prune pastry from France's Southwest

PASTIZA: see *gâteau basque*

PATA NÉGRA (JAMBON): prized ham from Spain, literally "black feet"

PATAGOS: clam

PÂTE: pastry dough
  Brisée: butter-rich, tart pastry dough
  D'amande: almond paste
  Sablée: pastry dough that is sweeter, richer, and more crumbly than *pâte sucrée*, sometimes leavened
  Sucrée: sweet, tart pastry dough

PÂTÉ: minced meat that is molded, spiced, baked, and served hot or cold

PÂTES (FRAÎCHES): pasta (fresh)

PATTE BLANCHE: small crayfish weighing less than 2½ ounces (75 g)

PATTE ROUGE: large crayfish

PAUCHOUSE, POCHOUSE: stew of river fish that generally includes *tanche* (tench), *perche* (perch), *brochet* (pike), and *anguille* (eel); specialty of Burgundy

PAUPIETTE: slice of meat or fish filled, rolled, then wrapped and served warm

PAVÉ: "paving stone"; usually, a thick slice of boned beef or calf's liver

PAVÉ D'AUGE: thick, ocher-colored square of cow's-milk cheese that comes from the Auge area of Normandy

PAVOT (GRAINE DE): poppy (seed)

PAYSAN(NE) (À LA): country style (garnish of carrots, turnips, onions, celery, and bacon)

PEAU: skin

PÈBRE D'AIL: see *poivre d'âne*

PÊCHE: peach; also, fishing

PÊCHE ALEXANDRA: cold dessert of poached peaches with ice cream and pureed strawberries

PÊCHE MELBA: poached peach with vanilla ice cream and raspberry sauce

PÊCHEUR: "fisherman"; usually refers to fish preparations

PÉLANDRON: see *haricot gris*

PÉLARDON: small, flat, dried, pungent disk of goat's-milk cheese; specialty of the Languedoc

PÈLERINE: another name for scallop or *coquille Saint-Jacques*

PENNE: a variety of dry durum wheat pasta with a cylindrical shape, either ribbed or smooth

PÉPITE (AU CHOCOLAT): nugget (chocolate chip)

PEQUILLO: small red Spanish pepper, often stuffed with salt cod puree

PERCE-PIERRE: samphire, edible seaweed

PERCHE: perch

PERDREAU: young partridge

PERDRIX: partridge

PÉRIGOURDINE, À LA, OR PÉRIGUEUX: sauce, usually with truffles and *foie gras,* named for the Périgord in southwestern France

PERSIL (PLAT): parsley (flatleaf)

PERSILLADE: blend of chopped parsley and garlic

PERSILLÉ: "parsleyed"; describes certain blue-veined cheeses; see also *jambon persillé*

PERSIL TUBEREUX: parsley root

PET DE NONNE: "nun's fart"; small, dainty beignets, or fried doughnut-like pastry

PÉTALE: "petal"; very thin slice

PETIT-BEURRE: popular tea cookie made with butter

PETIT DÉJEUNER: breakfast

PETIT-FOUR (SUCRÉ OR SALÉE): tiny cake or pastry (sweet or savory); in elegant restaurants, served with cocktails before dinner or with coffee afterward; also called *mignardise*

PETIT-GRIS: small land snail

PETIT-POIS: small green pea

PETIT SALÉ: salt-cured portions of lean pork belly, often served with lentils

PETITE MARMITE: earthenware casserole; the broth served from it

PÉTONCLE: tiny scallop, similar to the American bay scallop

PHO: Vietnamese soup of broth, rice noodles, herbs, and beef

PIBALE: tiny eel, also called *civelle*

PICHOLINE, PITCHOULINE: a variety of green olive, generally used to prepare *olives casseés* (crushed olives); specialty of Provence

PICODON: small disk of raw goat's-milk cheese, aged a minimum of 14 days; also Picodon de Dieulefit, aged a minimum of 1 month and washed and dried 7 times during the aging process; A.O.C./A.O.P.; specialty of northern Provence

PIÈCE: portion, piece

PIECH: poached veal brisket stuffed with vegetables, herbs, and sometimes rice, ham, eggs, or cheese; specialty of the Mediterranean

PIED DE CHEVAL: "horse's foot"; giant Atlantic coast oyster

PIED DE MOUTON: meaty cream-colored wild mushroom; also, sheep's foot

PIEDS ET PAQUETS: "feet and packages"; mutton tripe rolled and cooked with the meat from sheep's feet, white wine, and tomatoes; specialty of Provence and the Mediterranean

PIERRE-QUI-VIRE: "stone that moves"; a supple, tangy, flat disk of cow's-milk cheese with a reddish rind, made by the Benedictine monks at the Abbaye de la Pierre-Qui Vire in Burgundy

PIGEON (NEAU): pigeon or squab (young pigeon or squab)

PIGNONS: pine nuts, found in the cones of pine trees growing in Provence and along the southwestern Atlantic coast

PILAU, PILAF: rice sautéed with onion and simmered in broth

PILCHARD: name for sardines on the Atlantic coast

PIMENT: red pepper or pimento

PIMENT (OR POIVRE) DE JAMAÏQUE: allspice

PIMENT D'ESPELETTE: slender, mildly hot red chile pepper from Espelette, a village in the Basque region; sold fresh in markets or oven-dried and ground like a spice

PIMENT DOUX: sweet pepper

PIMENTÉ: hot, peppery, spicy

PIMPERNELLE: salad burnet, a salad green with a cucumber-like flavor

PINCE: claw; also, tongs used when eating snails or seafood

PINEAU DES CHARENTES: sweet fortified wine from the Cognac region on the Atlantic coast, served as an *apéritif*

PINTADE(AU): (young) guinea fowl

PIPÉRADE: a dish of pepper, onions, tomatoes, and often ham and scrambled eggs; specialty of the Basque region

PIQUANT(E): sharp or spicy tasting

PIQUÉ: larded; studded

PIQUENCHAGNE, PICANCHAGNE: a pear tart with a walnut or brioche crust;

specialty of the Bourbonnais, a historic province of central France

PISSALADIÈRE: a flat, open-faced tart like a pizza, garnished with onions, olives, and anchovies; specialty of Nice; usually made with a puff-pastry base

PISSENLIT: dandelion green

PISTACHE: pistachio nut

PISTIL DE SAFRAN: thread of saffron

PISTOU: sauce of basil, garlic, and olive oil; specialty of Provence; also a colorful soup of summer vegetables, fresh white beans, and pasta, flavored with *pistou* sauce

PITHIVIERS: a town in the Loire valley that gives its name to a classic large puff pastry filled with almond cream; also, lark *pâté*

PLAICE: a small, orange-spotted flounder or fluke, a flat ocean fish; also known as *plie franch* or *carrelet*; found in the English Channel

PLANCHA: flat griddle

À la plancha: a Spanish term applied to cooking meat, fish, and vegetables on a flat griddle

PLAT CUISINÉ: dish containing ingredients that have cooked together, usually in a sauce

PLAT DU JOUR: daily special

PLAT PRINCIPAL: main dish

PLATE: flat-shelled oyster

PLATEAU: platter

PLATEAU DE FRUITS DE MER: seafood platter combining raw and cooked shellfish; usually includes oysters, clams, mussels, *langoustines*, periwinkles, whelks, crabs, and tiny shrimp

PLATES CÔTES: part of beef ribs usually used in *pot-au feu*

PLEUROTE: very soft-fleshed, feather-edged wild oyster mushrooms; now being cultivated commercially in several regions of France

PLIE: see *plaice*

PLOMBIÈRE: classic dessert of vanilla ice cream, candied fruit, kirsch, and apricot jam

PLUCHE: small sprig of herbs or plants, generally used for garnish

POCHÉ: poached

POCHOUSE: see *pauchouse*

POÊLÉ: pan-fried

POGNE: brioche flavored with orange-flower water and filled with fruits; specialty of Romans-sur-Isère in the Rhône-Alpes

POINT(E) (D'ASPERGE): tip (of asparagus)

POINT (À): ripe or ready to eat, the perfect moment for eating a cheese or fruit; also, cooked medium rare

POIRE: pear

POIRE WILLIAMS: variety of pear; colorless fruit brandy, or *eau-de-vie*, often made from this variety of pear

POIREAU: leek

POIS (CHICHE): pea (chickpea)

POISSON: fish

D'eau douce: freshwater fish

De lac: lake fish

De mer: ocean fish

De rivière: river fish

De roche: rockfish

Fumé: smoked fish

Noble: prized, thus expensive, variety of fish

POITRINE: breast (of meat or poultry)

POITRINE DEMI-SEL: unsmoked slab bacon

POITRINE D'OIE FUMÉE: smoked goose breast

POITRINE FUMÉE: smoked slab bacon

POIVRADE: a peppery brown sauce made with wine, vinegar, and cooked vegetables and strained before serving

POIVRE: pepper

D'ain: Provençal name for the herb wild savory; also, small disk of goat's-milk cheese garnished with sprigs of savory; the cheese is also known as *pèbre d'ail* and *pèbre d'ase*

En grain: peppercorn

Frais de Madagascar: green peppercorn

Gris: a mix of white and black peppercorns, either whole or ground

Moulu: ground pepper
Noir: black peppercorn
Rose: pink peppercorn
Vert: green peppercorn
POIVRON (DOUX): (sweet bell) pepper
POJARSKI: finely chopped meat or fish shaped like a cutlet and fried
POLENTA: cooked dish of cornmeal and water, usually with added butter and cheese; also, cornmeal
POMMADE (BEURRE EN): usually refers to a thick, smooth paste (creamed butter)
POMME: apple
POMMES DE TERRE: potatoes
À l'anglaise: boiled
Allumettes: "matchsticks"; cut into very thin julienne strips and fried
Boulangère: potatoes cooked with the meat they accompany; also, a gratin of sliced potatoes, baked with milk or poultry stock and sometimes flavored with onions, bacon, and tomatoes
Darphin: grated potatoes shaped into a cake
Dauphine: mashed potatoes mixed with *choux* pastry, shaped into small balls and fried
Dauphinoise: a gratin of sliced potatoes, baked with milk and/or cream, garlic, cheese, and eggs
Duchesse: mashed potatoes with butter, egg yolks, and nutmeg, used for garnish
En robe des champs, en robe de chambre: potatoes boiled or baked in their skin; potatoes in their jackets
Frites: French fries
Gratinées: browned potatoes, often with cheese
Lyonnaise: potatoes sautéed with onions
Macaire: classic side dish of pureed potatoes shaped into small balls and fried or baked in a flat cake
Mousseline: potato puree enriched with butter, egg yolks, and whipped cream
Paillasson: fried pancake of grated potatoes

Pailles: potatoes cut into julienne strips, then fried
Pont-Neuf: classic fries
Sarladaise: sliced potatoes cooked with goose fat and (optionally) truffles
Soufflées: small, thin slices of potatoes fried twice, causing them to inflate so they resemble little pillows
Sous la cèndre: baked under cinders in a fireplace
Vapeur: steamed or boiled potatoes
POMMES EN L'AIR: caramelized apple slices, usually served with *boudin noir* (blood sausage)
POMPE À L'HUILE, POMPE DE NOËL: see *gibassier*
POMPE AUX GRATTONS: bread containing cracklings
PONT L'EVÊQUE: village in Normandy that gives its name to a very tender, fragrant square of cow's-milk cheese; A.O.C./A.O.P.
PONZU: a light and tangy Japanese sauce made with citrus juice, *mirin* (rice wine similar to sake), rice vinegar, dark soy sauce, kelp, and dried bonito (tuna) flakes, recommended as a dipping sauce for paper-thin slices of sashimi (raw fish)
PORC (CARRÉ DE): pork (loin)
PORC (CÔTE DE): pork (chop)
PORCELET: young suckling pig
PORCHETTA: young pig stuffed with offal, herbs, and garlic, and roasted; seen in *charcuteries* in Nice
PORTO (AU): (with) port
PORTUGAISE: elongated, crinkle-shell oyster
POT-AU-FEU: traditional dish of beef simmered with vegetables, often served in two or more courses; today, chefs often use it to mean fish poached in fish stock with vegetables
POT BOUILLI: another name for *pot-au-feu*
POT-DE-CRÈME: individual classic custard dessert, often chocolate

POTAGE: soup
POTÉE: traditional hearty meat soup, usually containing pork, cabbage, and potatoes
POTIMARRON: see *citrouille*
POTIRON: see *citrouille*
POTJEVLEISCH: a mixed meat terrine, usually of veal, pork, and rabbit; specialty of the north
POULARDE: fatted hen
POULE AU POT: boiled stuffed chicken with vegetables; specialty of the city of Béarn in the Southwest
POULE D'INDE: turkey hen
POULE FAISANE: female pheasant
POULET (RÔTI): chicken (roast)
Basquaise: Basque-style chicken, with tomatoes and sweet peppers
De Bresse: breed of high-quality free-range chicken raised on farms to exacting specifications, from the Rhône-Alpes; A.O.C./A.O.P.
De grain: corn-fed chicken
Fermier: free-range chicken
POULETTE: tiny chicken
POULIGNY-SAINT-PIERRE: village in the Loire valley that gives its name to a raw goat's-milk cheese shaped like a truncated pyramid with a mottled, grayish rind and a smooth-grained, ivory-white interior; A.O.C./A.O.P.
POULPE: octopus
POUNTI, POUNTY: a pork meat loaf that generally includes Swiss chard or spinach, eggs, milk, herbs, onions, and prunes; specialty of the Auvergne
POUSSE-EN-CLAIRE: oysters that have been aged and fattened in *claires*, or oyster beds, for 4 to 8 months
POUSSE-PIERRE: edible seaweed; also called sea beans
POUSSIN: baby chicken
POUTARGUE, BOUTARGUE: salted, pressed, and flattened mullet roe, generally spread on toast as an appetizer; specialty of Provence and the Mediterranean
POUTINE: see *nonat*
PRAIRE: small clam

PRALIN: ground caramelized almonds

PRALINE: caramelized almonds

PRÉ-SALÉ (AGNEAU DE): Delicately flavored lamb raised on the salt marshes of Normandy in the meadows of Mont Saint-Michel. The animals graze in coastal pastures with a high salinity and iodine content, imparting a delicate, distinct flavor to their meat.

PRESSKOPH: pork headcheese, often served with vinaigrette; specialty of Alsace

PRIMEUR(S): refers to early fresh fruits and vegetables; also, to new wine

PRINTANIÈRE: garnish of a variety of spring vegetables cut into dice or balls

PRIX FIXE: fixed-price menu

PRIX NET: service included

PROFITEROLE(S): classic *chou* (cream puff) pastry dessert, usually puffs of pastry filled with vanilla ice cream and topped with hot chocolate sauce

PROVENÇALE: in the style of Provence; usually includes garlic, tomatoes, and/or olive oil

PRUNE (D'ENTE): fresh plum (variety of plum grown in the famed Agen region of Southwestern France)

PRUNEAU: prune or dried plum; also an *eau-de-vie* made with fresh plums

PUITS D'AMOUR: "wells of love"; classic small pastry crowns filled with pastry cream

Q

QUASI (DE VEAU): standing rump (of veal)

QUATRE ÉPICES: spice blend of ground ginger, nutmeg, white pepper, and cloves

QUATRE-QUARTS: "four quarters"; pound cake made with equal weights of eggs, flour, butter, and sugar

QUENELLE: dumpling, usually of veal, fish, or poultry

QUETSCHE: small purple Damson plum

QUEUE (DE BOEUF): tail (of beef; oxtail)

QUICHE LORRAINE: savory custard tart made with bacon, eggs, and cream

R

RÂBLE DE LIÈVRE (LAPIN): saddle of hare (rabbit)

RACLETTE: rustic dish, from Switzerland and the Savoie, of melted cheese served with boiled potatoes, tiny pickled cucumbers, and onions; also, the cheese used in the dish

RADIS: small red, white, or yellow radish

RADIS NOIR: large black radish, often served with cream, as a salad

RAFRAÎCHI: cool, chilled, or fresh

RAGOÛT: stew, usually of meat

RAIE (BOUCLÉE): skate or ray, found in the English Channel, Atlantic, and Mediterranean

RAIFORT: horseradish

RAISIN: grape; raisin
  De corinthe: currant
  De smyrne: sultana
  Sec: raisin

RAÏTO: red wine sauce that generally includes onions, tomatoes, garlic, herbs, olives, and capers, usually served warm over grilled fish; specialty of Provence

RAMEQUIN: small individual casserole; also, a small tart; also, a small raw or pasteurized goat's-milk cheese from the Bugey, an area in the northern Rhône valley

RAMIER: wood or wild pigeon

RÂPÉ: grated or shredded

RASCASSE: *gurnard,* or scorpion fish in the rockfish family; an essential ingredient of bouillabaisse, the fish stew of the Mediterranean

RATAFIA: liqueur made by infusing nut or fruit in brandy

RATATOUILLE: a cooked dish of eggplant, zucchini, onions, tomatoes, peppers, garlic, and olive oil, served hot or cold; specialty of Provence

RATTE: variety of small potato, often used for purees

RAVIGOTE: classic thick vinaigrette sauce with vinegar, white wine, shallots, and herbs; also, cold mayonnaise with capers, onions, and herbs

RAVIOLE DU DAUPHINÉ: tiny squares of ravioli pasta filled with cow's-milk cheese and herbs, from the village of Saint-Jean-en-Royans in the Rhône-Alpes

RAVIOLI À LA NIÇOISE: square or round pasta filled with meat and/or Swiss chard and baked with grated cheese

REBLOCHON: smooth, supple, creamy cow's-milk cheese with a burnished light orange, almost saffron-colored rind, from the Savoie in the Alps; A.O.C./A.O.P.

RÉGLISSE: licorice

REINE-CLAUDE: greengage plum

REINETTE, REINE DE: fall and winter variety of apple, deep yellow with a red blush

RELIGIEUSE, PETITE: "nun"; a small version of a classic pastry consisting of two *choux* puffs filled with chocolate, coffee, or vanilla pastry cream, placed one on top of another, and frosted with chocolate or coffee icing to resemble a nun in her habit

RÉMOULADE (CÉLERI): sauce of mayonnaise, capers, mustard, herbs, anchovies, and gherkins (dish of shredded celery root with mayonnaise)

REPAS: meal

RHUHARBE: rhubarb

RHUM: rum

RIGOTTE: small cow's-milk cheese from the Lyon region

RILLETTES (D'OIE): spreadable pâté of pork (goose); can also be made with duck, fish, or rabbit

RILLONS: usually pork belly, cut up and cooked until crisp, then drained of fat; also made of duck, goose, or rabbit

RIS D'AGNEAU (DE VEAU):
lamb (veal) sweetbreads
RISSOLÉ: browned by frying,
usually potatoes
RIZ: rice
À l'impératrice: cold rice
pudding with candied fruit
Complet: brown rice
De camargue: nutty, fragrant
rice grown in the Camargue,
the swampy area just south
of Arles in Provence; can be
white, brown, red
Sauvage: wild rice
RIZOTTO, RISOTTO: creamy
rice made by stirring rice
constantly in stock as it
cooks, then mixing in other
ingredients such as cheese or
mushrooms
**ROBE DES CHAMPS, ROBE DE
CHAMBRE (POMMES EN):**
potatoes boiled or baked in
their skin; potatoes in their
jackets
ROCAMADOUR: village in
southwestern France that
gives its name to a tiny disk
of raw goat's- or sheep's-milk
cheese; also called Cabécou de
Rocamadour; A.O.C./A.O.P.
ROGNONNADE: veal loin with
kidneys attached
ROGNONS: kidneys
ROLLOT: spicy cow's-milk
cheese with a washed ocher-
colored rind, in a small
cylinder or heart shape; from
the North
ROMANOFF: fruit, often
strawberries, macerated
in liqueur and topped with
whipped cream
ROMARIN: rosemary
RONDELLE: thin round slice—
of lemon, for example
ROQUEFORT: blue-veined
cheese of raw sheep's milk
from the Auvergne region of
south central France, aged in
the village of Roquefort-sur-
Soulzon; A.O.C./A.O.P.
ROQUETTE: rocket or arugula,
a spicy salad green
ROSÉ: rare; used for beef, lamb,
veal, duck, or liver; also rose-
colored wine
ROSETTE (DE BOEUF): large
dried pork (beef) sausage,
from area around Lyon

RÔTI: roast; meat roast
ROUELLE: slice of meat
or vegetable cut at an angle
ROUENNAISE (CANARD À LA):
in the style of Rouen; (classic
dish of duck stuffed with its
liver in a blood-thickened
sauce)
**ROUGET BARBET, ROUGET DE
ROCHE:** red mullet, a prized
rockfish with sweet flesh and
red skin; its flavorful liver is
reserved for sauces
ROUGET GRONDIN: red
gurnard, a large, common
rockfish, less prized than
rouget barbet; a variety of
galinette; an ingredient in
bouillabaisse
ROUGETTE: a small red-leafed
butterhead lettuce, specialty
of Provence
ROUILLE: a mayonnaise of
olive oil, garlic, chile peppers,
bread, and fish broth; usually
served with fish soups, such as
bouillabaisse
ROULADE: meat or fish roll, or
rolled-up vegetable soufflé;
larger than a *paupiette*, and
often stuffed
ROULÉ(E): rolled
ROUSSETTE: dogfish, also
called *salmonette* because of
its pinkish skin, found on the
Atlantic coast
ROUX: sauce base or thickening
of flour and butter
ROVE: Breed of goat; also small
golf ball–shaped round of soft,
fresh Provençal goat's-milk
cheese. The goats feed on
wild herbs, giving an intense,
herbal flavor and fragrance to
the cheese.
ROYALE, À LA: "royal-style";
rich classic preparation,
usually with truffles and a
cream sauce
RUMSTECK: rump steak

S

SABAYON, ZABAGLIONE:
frothy sweet sauce of egg
yolks, sugar, wine, and
flavoring that is whipped
while being cooked in a water
bath

SABODET: strong, earthy pork
sausage of pig's head and skin,
served hot; specialty of Lyon
SAFRAN: saffron
SAIGNANT(E): cooked rare, for
meat, usually beef
SAINDOUX: lard or pork fat
SAINT-FÉLICIEN: A "cousin" of
Saint-Marcellin cow's-milk
cheese; has a slightly higher
fat content (28 percent versus
24 percent), a small (3 ounces;
100 g) disk—cured for just
1 week—that is delicate,
almost nutty-flavored, firm
and supple when young, and
more pungent once aged for
2 to 3 weeks
SAINT-GERMAIN: with peas
SAINT-HUBERT: *poivrade* sauce
with chestnuts and bacon
added
SAINT-JACQUES, COQUILLE:
sea scallop
SAINT-MARCELLIN: Small
flat disk of cow's-milk cheese
(once prepared from goat's
milk) made in dairies in the
Isère, outside Lyon. The best
is well aged and runny. Found
in Paris, the Lyon area, and
Northern Provence.
**SAINTE-MAURE DE
TOURAINE:** Village in the
Loire valley that gives its
name to a soft, elongated
cylinder of goat's-milk cheese
with a distinctive straw in the
middle and a mottled, natural
blue rind. Due to fraudulent
imitation of the cheese, the
straw is engraved with a laser,
which notes the name and
identification number of the
cheesemaker. A.O.C./A.O.P.
SAINT-NECTAIRE: Village
in the Auvergne that gives
its name to a supple, thick
disk of cow's-milk cheese
with a mottled gray rind.
Saint-Nectaire Fermier is
made twice daily after each
milking, from raw milk, and
is indentified with an oval
stamp. *Saint-Nectaire Laitier*
can be made from either raw
or pasteurized milk and is
identified with a square green
stamp. Aged for 3 to 6 weeks.
A.O.C./A.O.P.

SAINT-NICOLAS: a small, rectangular cheese made of raw goat's milk, produced at a Greek Orthodox monastery near Montpéllier in the south of France; with a huge reputation, this cheese is perfumed with the flavors and aromas of thyme and rosemary

SAINT-PIERRE: John Dory, a prized mild, flat, white ocean fish; known as *soleil* and *Jean Doré* in the north, and *poule de mer* along the Atlantic coast

SAINT-VINCENT: moist, buttery, thick cylinder of cow's-milk cheese from Burgundy with a rust-colored rind; similar to Époisses, but aged a bit longer, therefore stronger

SALADE: salad; also, a head of lettuce

Folle: mixed salad, usually including green beans and *foie gras*

Lyonnaise: green salad with cubed bacon and soft-cooked eggs, often served with herring and anchovies, and/or sheep's feet and chicken livers; specialty of Lyon; also called *saladier lyonnais*

Niçoise: salad with many variations, but usually with tomatoes, green beans, anchovies, tuna, potatoes, black olives, capers, and artichokes

Panachée: mixed salad

Russe: cold mixed salad of peas and diced carrots and turnips in mayonnaise

Verte: green salad

SALADIER (LYONNAIS): see *salade lyonnaise*

SALÉ: salted

SALERS: A whole, raw-milk cow's-milk cheese produced only when the cows are nurtured on the abundant herbs and grass in the Auvergne's mountain pastures, from April 15 to November 15. Only made on farms, the firm, fragrant, prized cheese is made from the breed of Salers cows. It must be aged a minimum of 3 months. A.O.C./A.O.P.

SALICORNE: encompasses some 30 varieties of green, stringy edible seaweed; often pickled and served as a condiment

SALMIS: classic preparation of roasted game birds or poultry, with sauce made from the pressed carcass

SALPICON: diced vegetables, meat, and/or fish in a sauce, used as a stuffing, garnish, or spread

SALSIFIS: salsify, oyster plant

SANDRE: pickerel, a perchlike river fish, found in the Saône and Rhine rivers

SANG: blood

SANGLIER: adult wild boar

SANGUE: Corsican black pudding, usually with grapes or herbs

SANGUINE: "blood" orange, so named for its red juice

SANSONNET: starling or thrush

SAR, SARGUE: blacktail, a tiny flat fish of the sea bream family, best grilled or baked

SARCELLE: teal, a species of wild duck

SARDINE: small sardine (large sardines are called *pilchards*); found year-round in the Mediterranean, from May to October in the Atlantic

SARLADAISE: as prepared in Sarlat in the Dordogne; with truffles

SARRASIN: buckwheat

SARRIETTE: summer savory; see *poivre d'ain*

SAUCISSE: small fresh sausage

SAUCISSE CHAUDE: warm sausage

SAUCISSE DE FRANCFORT: hot dog

SAUCISSE DE STRASBOURG: red-skinned hot dog

SAUCISSE DE TOULOUSE: mild country-style pork sausage

SAUCISSON: most often, a large air-dried sausage, such as salami, eaten sliced as a cold cut; when fresh and cooked, usually called *saucisson chaud,* or hot sausage

SAUCISSON À L'AIL: garlic sausage, usually to be cooked and served warm

SAUCISSON D'ARLES: dried salami-style sausage that blends pork, beef, and gentle seasoning; a specialty of Arles, in Provence

SAUCISSON DE CAMPAGNE: any country-style sausage

SAUCISSON DE LYON: air-dried pork sausage, flavored with garlic and pepper and studded with chunks of pork fat

SAUCISSON DE MORTEAU: see *Jésus de Morteau*

SAUCISSON EN CROÛTE: sausage cooked in a pastry crust

SAUCISSON SEC: any dried sausage, or salami

SAUGE: sage

SAUMON (SAUVAGE): salmon ("wild," to differentiate from commercially raised salmon)

SAUMON D'ECOSSE: Scottish salmon

SAUMON DE FONTAINE: small, commercially raised salmon

SAUMON FUMÉ: smoked salmon

SAUMON NORVÉGIEN: Norwegian salmon

SAUMONETTE: see *roussette*

SAUPIQUET: classic aromatic wine sauce thickened with bread

SAUTÉ: browned in fat

SAUVAGE: wild

SAVARIN: yeast-leavened cake shaped like a ring, soaked in sweet syrup

SAVOIE (BISCUIT DE): sponge cake

SAVOYARDE: in the style of Savoy, usually flavored with Gruyère cheese

SBRISOLONA: a crunchy northern Italian almond and butter dessert with a cookie-like texture, traditionally set on the table as one whole piece; guests break off an end and enjoy it with a sip of sweet wine

SCAROLE: escarole

SCHIEFFELE, SCHIEFFALA, SCHIFELA: smoked pork shoulder, served hot and garnished with pickled turnips or a potato and onion salad

SÉBASTE: ocean perch
SEC (SÈCHE): dry or dried
SEICHE: cuttlefish
SEIGLE (PAIN DE): rye (bread)
SEL (GROS): coarse salt
SELLE: saddle (of meat)
SEL GRIS: gray sea salt
SEL MARIN: sea salt
SELLES-SUR-CHER: village in the Loire Valley identified with a small, flat, truncated cylinder of raw goat's-milk cheese with a mottled bluish-gray rind (sometimes patted with powdered ash) and a pure white interior; A.O.C./A.O.P.
SELON GROSSEUR (S.G.): according to size; usually said of lobster or other seafood
SELON LE MARCHÉ: according to what is in season or available
SELON POID (S.P.): according to weight; usually said of seafood
SEMOULE: semolina or finely ground wheat; also used in France as a savory garnish, particularly in North African dishes such as couscous
SERPOLET: wild thyme
SERVICE: Meal, mealtime, the serving of the meal. A restaurant has two services if it serves lunch and dinner; a dish *en deux services*, like *canard pressé*, is served in two courses.
SERVICE (NON) COMPRIS: service charge (not) included in the listed menu prices (but invariably included on the bill)
SERVICE EN SUS: service charge to be made in addition to menu prices; same as *service non compris*
SIMPLE: simple, plain, unmixed; also, a single scoop of ice cream
SMITANE: sauce of cream, onions, white wine, and lemon juice
SOCCA: a very thin, round *crêpe* made with chickpea flour, sold on the streets of Nice and eaten as a snack
SOISSONS: fresh or dried white beans, from the area around Soissons, northeast of Paris

SOJA (POUSSE DE): soy bean (soy bean sprout)
SOJA, SAUCE DE: soy sauce
SOLETTE: small sole
SOMMELIER (SOMMELIÈRE): male wine steward (female wine steward)
SORBET: sherbet
SOT L'Y LAISSE: Poultry "oysters"—two small oyster-size pieces of prized, tender dark meat found on the back of the poultry in a hollow near the thigh. Because carvers often ignore the meat, the literal French translation is a "fool leaves it there." Traditionally, the cook is given first preference to the oyster meat.
SOUBISE: a *béchamel*-based sauce (of butter, flour, and milk) with strained or pureed cooked onions
SOUFFLÉ: light mixture of pureed ingredients, egg yolks, and whipped egg whites, which puffs up when baked; sweet or savory, hot or cold
SOUMAINTRAIN: a spicy, supple flat disk of cow's-milk cheese with a reddish-brown rind; from Burgundy
SOUPIR DE NONNE: "nun's sighs"; fried *choux* (cream puff) pastry dusted with confectioner's sugar; created by a nun in an Alsatian abbey; also called *pet de nonne*
SOURIS: "mouse"; muscle that holds the leg of lamb to the bone; lamb shanks
SPÄTZEL, SPAETZLE, SPETZLI: noodlelike Alsatian egg-and-flour dumpling, served poached or fried
SPOOM: wine or fruit juice mixed with egg whites, whipped, and frozen to create a frothy iced dessert
STEAK FRITES: classic French dish of grilled steak served with French-fried potatoes
STOCKFISH, STOCAFICADA, ESTOFICADA, ESTOFICADO, MORUE PLATE: flattened, dried cod found in southern France; also, a puree-like

blend of dried codfish, olive oil, tomatoes, sweet peppers, black olives, potatoes, garlic, onions, and herbs; specialty of Nice; sometimes served with a basil and olive oil sauce (*pistou*)
STRASBOURGEOISE, À LA: ingredients typical of Strasbourg, including sauerkraut, *foie gras*, and salt pork
SUCCÈS À LA PRALINE: cake made with praline meringue layers, frosted with meringue and butter cream
SUCETTE DE VOLAILLE: small, meatball-like morsels of minced, seasoned chicken breast, pan-fried
SUCRE: sugar
   Cassonade: raw (unrefined) cane or beet sugar
   Sucre en poudre: superfine or castor sugar
   Vergeoise: moist soft brown sugar
SUPION, SUPIOUN, SUPPION: cuttlefish
SUPRÊME: a veal- or chicken-based white sauce thickened with flour and cream; also, a boneless breast of poultry or a fillet of fish

T

TABLE D'HÔTE: open table or board; often found in the countryside, these are private homes that serve fixed meals and often have one or two guest rooms as well; also, in restaurants, refers to a large table that is shared by several guests
TABLETTE (DE CHOCOLAT): bar (of chocolate)
TABLIER DE SAPEUR: "fireman's apron"; tripe that is marinated, breaded, and grilled; specialty of Lyon
TACAUD: small fish from the cod family, found in the Atlantic and Mediterranean, usually fried
TAGINE: spicy North African stew of veal, lamb, chicken, or pigeon, and vegetables

TALMOUSE: savory pastry triangle of cheese-flavored *choux* (cream puff) dough baked in puff pastry

TAMIÉ: flat disk of cheese, made of cow's milk at the Trappist monastery in the Savoie village of Tamié; similar to Reblochon

TANCHE: tench, a river fish with a mild, delicate flavor; often an ingredient in *matelote* and *pauchouse*, freshwater fish stews

TAPENADE: a blend of black or green olives, anchovies, capers, olive oil, and lemon juice, sometimes with rum or canned tuna added; specialty of Provence

TARAMA: carp roe, often made into a spread of the same name

TARBAS: variety of large fresh or dried white bean

TARTARE (DE POISSON): traditionally, chopped raw beef, seasoned and garnished with raw egg, capers, chopped onion, and parsley (today, a popular, highly seasoned raw fish dish)

TARTE: tart; open-faced pie or flan, usually sweet

TARTE ENCALAT: name for cheesecake in the Auvergne

TARTE FLAMBÉE: thin-crusted savory tart, much like a round or rectangular pizza, covered with cream, onions, and bacon; specialty of Alsace; also called *Flammekueche*

TARTE TATIN: caramelized upside-down apple pie, made famous by the Tatin sisters in their hotel in Lamotte-Beuvron, in the Sologne; a popular dessert, seen on menus all over France

TARTINE: open-faced sandwich; buttered bread

TASSE: cup; a coffee or tea cup

TELLINE: a tiny violet-streaked clam, the size of a fingernail, seen in Provence and the Camargue; generally seared with a bit of oil in a hot pan to open the shells, then seasoned with minced parsley and garlic

TENDRE: tender

TENDRON: cartilaginous meat cut from beef or veal ribs

TEPPANYAKI: a style of Japanese cooking in which meat, fish, or vegetables are cooked on a large griddle, often built into, or in front of, the diner's table

TEURGOULE: a sweet rice pudding with cinnamon; specialty of Normandy

TERRINE: Earthenware container used for cooking meat, game, fish, or vegetable mixtures; also the pâté cooked and served in such a container. It differs from a pâté proper in that the terrine is actually sliced out of the container, while a pâté has been removed from its mold.

TÊTE DE VEAU (PORC): head of veal (pork), usually used in headcheese

TÉTRAGONE: spinach-like green, found in Provence

THÉ: tea

THERMIDOR (HOMARD): classic lobster dish; lobster split lengthwise, grilled, and served in the shell with a cream sauce

THON (BLANC) (GERMON): tuna (white) (albacore)

THON ROUGE: bluefin tuna

THYM: thyme

TIAN: an earthenware gratin dish; also vegetable gratins baked in such a dish; from Provence

TIÈDE: lukewarm

TILLEUL: linden tree; linden-blossom herb tea

TIMBALE: small round mold with straight or sloping slides; also, a mixture prepared in such a mold

TOMATES À LA PROVENÇALE: baked tomato halves sprinkled with garlic, parsley, and bread crumbs

TOMME: generic name for cheese, usually refers to a variety of cheeses in the Savoie; also, the fresh cheese used to make Cantal in the Auvergne

TOMME ARLÉSIENNE:

rectangular cheese made with a blend of goat's and cow's milk and sprinkled with summer savory; also called *tomme de Camargue*; a specialty of the Languedoc and Arles, in Provence

TOMME FRAÎCHE: pressed cake of fresh milk curds, used in the regional dishes of the Auvergne

TOPINAMBOUR: Jerusalem artichoke

TORO (TAUREAU): bull; meat found in butcher shops in Provence, the Languedoc and Pays Basque, and sometimes on restaurant menus

TORRÉFIÉE: roasted, as in coffee beans and chocolate

TORTEAU AU FROMAGE: goat-cheese cheesecake from the Poitou-Charentes along the Atlantic coast; a blackened, spherical loaf found at cheese shops throughout France; once a homemade delicacy, today prepared industrially

TORTUE: turtle

TOUCY: village in Burgundy that gives its name to a local fresh goat's-milk cheese

TOURAIN, TOURIN, TOURRIN: generally, a peasant soup of garlic, onions (and sometimes tomatoes), and broth or water, thickened with egg yolks and seasoned with vinegar; specialty of the Southwest

TOURNEDOS: center portion of beef filet, usually grilled or sautéed

TOURNEDOS ROSSINI: sauteed *tournedos* garnished with *foie gras* and truffles

TOURON: marzipan loaf, or a cake of almond paste, often layered and flavored with nuts or candied fruits and sold by the slice; specialty of the Basque region

TOURTE (AUX BLETTES): pie (common Niçoise dessert pie filled with Swiss chard, eggs, cheese, raisins, and pine nuts); also, name for giant rounds of country bread found in the Auvergne and the Southwest

TOURTEAU: large crab

TOURTIÈRE: shallow three-legged cooking vessel, set over hot coals for baking; also, Southwestern pastry dish filled with apples and/or prunes and sprinkled with Armagnac

TRAIN DE CÔTES: rib of beef

TRAITEUR: caterer; delicatessen

TRANCHE: slice

TRAPPISTE: name given to the mild, lactic cow's-milk cheese made in a Trappist monastery in Echourgnac, in the Southwest

TRAVERS DE PORC: spareribs

TRÉVISE: radicchio, a bitter red salad green of the chicory family

TRIPES À LA MODE DE CAEN: beef tripe, carrots, onions, leeks, and spices, cooked in water, cider, and Calvados (apple brandy); specialty of Normandy

TRIPLE CRÈME: legal name for cheese containing more than 75 percent butterfat, such as Brillat-Savarin

TRIPOUX: mutton tripe

TRIPOXA: Basque name for sheep's- or calf's-blood sausage served with spicy red Espelette peppers

TROMPETTES DE LA MORT: dark brown wild mushroom, also known as "horn of plenty"

TRONÇON: cut of meat or fish resulting in a piece that is longer than it is wide; generally refers to slices from the largest part of a fish

TROUCHIA: flat omelet filled with spinach or Swiss chard; specialty of Provence

TRUFFADE: a large layered and fried potato pancake made with bacon and fresh Cantal cheese; specialty of the Auvergne

TRUFFE (TRUFFÉ): truffle (with truffles)

TRUFFES SOUS LA CENDRE: truffles wrapped in pastry or foil and gently warmed by burying in hot ashes

TRUITE (AU BLEU): trout (a preferred method of cooking trout, not live—as often assumed—but rather in a "live condition." The trout is gutted just moments prior to cooking, but neither washed nor scaled. It is then plunged into a hot mixture of vinegar and water, and the slimy lubricant that protects the skin of the fish appears to turn the trout a bluish color. The fish is then removed to a broth to finish its cooking).

De lac: lake trout

De mer: sea trout or brown trout

De rivière: river trout

Saumoneé: salmon trout

TTORO: Fish soup from the Basque region. Historically, the liquid that remained after poaching cod was seasoned with herbs and used to cook vegetables and potatoes. Today, a more elaborate version includes the addition of *lotte*, mullet, mussels, conger eel, *langoustines*, and wine.

TUILE: literally, "curved roofing tile"; delicate almond-flavored cookie

TULIPE: tulip-shaped cookie for serving ice cream or sorbet

TURBAN: usually, a mixture or combination of ingredients cooked in a ring mold

TURBOT(IN): prized flatfish found in the Atlantic and Mediterranean (small turbot)

V

VACHE: cow

VACHERIN: dessert of baked meringue, with ice cream and whipped cream; also, a strong, supple winter cheese encircled by a fragrant band of dried spruce bark, from the Jura

VADOUVAN: Indian spice mix of dried onions, garlic, Indian lentils, fenugreek, cumin, fennel, turmeric, curry leaves, and vegetable oils

VALLÉE D'AUGE: area of Normandy; also, garnish of cooked apples and cream or Calvados and cream

VANILLE: vanilla

VAPEUR, À LA: steamed

VEAU: veal

VELOUTÉ: classic sauce based on veal, chicken, or fish stock, thickened with a roux of butter and flour; also, variously seasoned classic soups thickened with cream and egg yolks

VENTRE: belly or stomach

VENTRÈCHE: pork belly

VERDURE (EN): garnish of green vegetables

VERDURETTE: herb vinaigrette

VERJUS: the juice of unripe grapes, used to make condiments; also used much like vinegar in sauces

VERNIS: large, fleshy clam with small red tongue and shiny varnish-like shell

VÉRONIQUE, À LA: garnish of peeled white grapes

VERT-PRÉ: a watercress garnish, sometimes including potatoes

VERVEINE: the herb lemon verbena, often used in herb tea infusions

VESSIE, EN: cooked in a pig's bladder (usually chicken)

VIANDE: meat

VICHY: with glazed carrots; also, a brand of mineral water

VICHYSSOISE: cold, creamy leek and potato soup

VIENNOISE: coated in egg, breaded, and fried

VIERGE: "virgin"; term for virgin olive oil, with less than 1.5 percent acidity and generally good flavor

VIERGE, EXTRA: "extra virgin"; term for the best quality olive oil, with the lowest level of acidity, 0.8 percent

VIERGE, SAUCE: sauce of olive oil, lemon juice, garlic, tomatoes, and fresh herbs

VIEUX (VIELLE): old

VIEUX LILLE: thick, square cheese named for the old part of Lille, the North's largest city, made in the same way as Maroilles—with cow's milk—only salted more, then aged 6 months until extremely fragrant and ripe; also called *vieux puant,* or "old stinker"

VIN JAUNE: an amber yellow wine made in the Jura with late harvested grapes; stored in oak casks, it can last up to a century

VINAIGRE (VIEUX): vinegar (aged)

VINAIGRE DE XÉRÈS: sherry vinegar

VINAIGRETTE: oil and vinegar dressing

VIOGNIER: increasingly popular white grape of the Rhône, used for the famed Condrieu

VIOLET OR FIGUE DE MER: unusual iodine-strong, soft-shelled edible sea creature, with a yellowish interior; a delicacy along the Mediterranean, particularly in Marseille

VIOLET DE PROVENCE: plump garlic with mottled white and purple skin or casing, a specialty of Provence and the Côte d'Azur

VIOLETTE: violet; its crystallized petals are a specialty of Toulouse

VIROFLAY: classic garnish of spinach for poached or soft-cooked eggs

VITELLO TONNATO: an Italian dish of cold, sliced veal, served coated with a tuna mayonnaise, or *tonnato* sauce

VIVE OR VIPÈRE DE MER: weever; a small firm-fleshed ocean fish used in soups, such as bouillabaisse, or grilled; the venomous spine is removed before cooking

VOL-AU-VENT: puff pastry shell

VOLONTÉ (À): at the customer's discretion

VONNAISSIENNE, À LA: in the style of Vonnas, a village in the Rhône-Alpes; also, *crêpes* made with potatoes

WATERZOOI: Flemish chicken stew cooked with aromatic herbs and vegetables in a sauce of cream and chicken broth

---

XÉRÈS (VINAIGRE DE): sherry (vinegar)

YAOURT: yogurt

YUZU: A pungent, fragrant citrus fruit used in East Asian cooking, particularly Japanese

---

ZA'TAR: Middle Eastern seasoning mix of ground sesame seeds, sumac berrries, thyme, and salt

ZESTE: zest, or citrus peel with white pith removed

ZEWELMAI, ZEWELWAI: Alsatian onion tart

ZINGARA, À LA: gypsy style; with tomato sauce; also, classically, a garnish of ham, tongue, mushrooms, and truffles

READY REFERENCE

WHERE TO EAT: BY ARRONDISSEMENT

(Includes restaurants, bistros, brasseries, cafés, casual eateries, and wine bars)

1st ARRONDISSEMENT:

Angelina (Musée du Louvre)
Angelina (Rivoli)
Carré des Feuillants, Le
Claus
Dame de Pic, La
Chez Denise / La Tour de
  Montlhéry
Fines Gueules, Les
Izakaya Issé
Juveniles
Kotteri Ramen Naritake
Café Marly, Le
Pain Quotidien, Le
  (Palais Royal)
Pain Quotidien, Le
  (Saint-Honoré)
Racines 2
Rubis, Le
Spring
Verjus Bar à Vins
Verjus Restaurant
Willi's Wine Bar
Yam'Tcha

2nd ARRONDISSEMENT:

Frenchie
Frenchie Bar à Vins
Frenchie To Go
Chez Georges
Goust
Grillé
Gyoza Bar
Liza
Pain Quotidien, Le
  (Montorgueil)
Passage 53
Saturne
Télescope

3rd ARRONDISSEMENT:

Al Taglio (Marais)
Ambassade d'Auvergne, L'
Ami Louis, L'
Breizh Café
Cuisine de Bar (Marais)
Grazie
Chez Jenny
Loustic
Merci: Cinéma Café, Used
  Book Café & Merci Cantine
Café des Musées
Nanashi (Charlot)
Rose Bakery (Marais)

4th ARRONDISSEMENT:

Ambroisie, L'
As du Fallafel, L'
Benoit
Claude Colliot
Comme à Lisbonne
Isami
Mon Vieil Ami
Pain Quotidien, Le (Marais)

5th ARRONDISSEMENT:

A.O.C., L'
Atelier Maître Albert
Brasserie Balzar
Dans les Landes
Mosquée Salon de Thé, La
Chez René
Terroir Parisien
Zyriab by Noura, Le
  (Institut du Monde Arabe)

6th ARRONDISSEMENT:

21, Le
Ambassade de Bourgogne
Avant Comptoir, L'
Azabu
Bonaparte, Le
Bouquinistes, Les
Closerie de Lilas, La
Comptoir du Relais, Le

Cosi
Bar de la Croix Rouge
Cuisine de Bar
  (Saint-Germain)
Deux Magots, Les
Fish la Boissonnerie
Café de Flore
Fogón
Huîtrerie Régis
Ladurée (Saint-Germain)
Brasserie Lipp
Little Breizh
Nanashi (Bonpoint)
Oenosteria
Pavillon de la Fontaine, Le
Petit Lutetia, Le
Pied de Fouet, Au
  (Saint-Germain)
Pizza Chic
Rosa, Da
Semilla
Société, La
Timbre, Le
Toyo
Tsukizi
Yen
Yoom (Saint-Germain)
Ze Kitchen Galerie

7th ARRONDISSEMENT:

35° Ouest
Aida
Affable, L'
Ami Jean, L'
Arpège
Atelier de Joël Robuchon
  Saint-Germain, L'
Attendant Rosa, En
Botanistes, Les
Cinq Mars, Le
Cocottes de Christian
  Constant, Les
Coutume
Restaurant ES
Fables de la Fontaine, Les

Fontaine de Mars, La
Restaurant Jean-François Piège
Jules Verne, Le
Mozza & Co. (food truck)
Omnivore Rives (food truck)
Pain Quotidien, Le
  (Rue du Bac)
Pied de Fouet, Au (Babylone)
Pottoka
Brasserie aux PTT
Rose Bakery (Bon Marché)
Table d'Aki, La
Tourette by Ibérique Gourmet,
  Le
Café Varenne
Yuzu

8TH ARRONDISSEMENT:

Restaurant Alain Ducasse au
  Plaza Athénée
Chez André
Atelier de Joël Robuchon
  Étoile, L'
Cinq, Le (Four Seasons)
Restaurant du Dominique
  Bouchet
Epicure au Bristol
Ladurée (Champs-Élysées)
Ladurée (Rue Royale)
Laurent
Lazare
Mini Palais
Pavillon Ledoyen
Neva Cuisine
Okuda
Pierre Gagnaire
Taillevent, Le

9TH ARRONDISSEMENT:

Angelina (Lafayette)
Kiku
Ladurée (Printemps
  de la Mode)
Orient d'Or, L'
Pantruche, Le
Pâtes Vivantes, Les
Rose Bakery (Martyrs)
Yoom (Martyrs)

10TH ARRONDISSEMENT:

Abri
Albion
Galopin, Le
Krishna Bhavan

Chez Michel
Nanashi (Paradis)
Philou
Sunken Chip, The
Ten Belles
Vivant Table

11TH ARRONDISSEMENT:

6 Paul Bert, Le
Chez Aline
Al Taglio
  (Oberkampf)
Astier
Bones
Chateaubriand, Le
Caffé dei Cioppi
Come a Casa
Dauphin, Le
Deux Fois Plus de Piment
Écailler du Bistrot, L'
Jeanne A
Mansouria, Le
Passage, Au
Bistrot Paul Bert
Pied du Fouet, Au
  (Oberkampf)
Sassotondo
Septime
Septime Cave
Sot-l'y-Laisse, Le
Unico
Villaret, Le
West Country Girl

12TH ARRONDISSEMENT:

Biche au Bois, À la
Rose Bakery
  (La Maison Rouge)
Trou Gascon, Au

13TH ARRONDISSEMENT:

Pho 14

14TH ARRONDISSEMENT:

Dome, Le
Duc, Le
Jeu de Quilles
Severo, Le
Spice and Wine

15TH ARRONDISSEMENT:

Afaria
Epicuriste, L'
Grand Pan, Le

16TH ARRONDISSEMENT:

Akrame
Angelina (Jardin d'Acclimatation
  children's park)
Astrance
Pré Catelan, Le
Shang Palace (Shangri-La
  Hotel)

17TH ARRONDISSEMENT:

Angelina (Porte Maillot)
Éntredgeu Restaurant, L'
Frédéric Simonin
Guy Savoy

18TH ARRONDISSEMENT:

Coq Rico, Le
Gontran Cherrier
Guilo Guilo
Jeanne B
Marcel
Rallonge, La
Soul Kitchen
Table d'Eugène, La

19TH ARRONDISSEMENT:

Quedubon

20TH ARRONDISSEMENT:

Baratin, Le
Chatomat
Roseval

PARIS ENVIRONS:

Cocotte, Ma (Saint-Ouen)

BRASSERIES

Brasserie Balzar (5th)
Dome, Le (14th)
Chez Jenny (3rd)
Brasserie Lipp (6th)
Petit Lutetia, Le (7th)

BISTROS (CLASSIC)

Ambassade d'Auvergne, L'
  (6th)
Ami Jean, L' (7th)
Ami Louis, L' (3rd)
Chez André (8th)
Astier (11th)
Benoit (4th)
Biche au Bois, À la (12th)
Botanistes, Les (7th)

Chez Denise / La Tour de
Montlhéry (1st)
Éntredgeu Restaurant, L' (17th)
Epicuriste, L' (15th)
Fables de la Fontaine, Les (7th)
Fontaine de Mars, La (7th)
Chez Georges (2nd)
Chez Michel (10th)
Café des Musées (3rd)
Bistrot Paul Bert (11th)
Petit Lutetia, Le (7th)
Pied de Fouet, Au (Babylone)
(7th)
Pied de Fouet, Au (Saint-
Germain) (6th)
Pied du Fouet, Au
(Oberkampf) (11th)
Quedubon (19th)
Chez René (5th)
Severo, Le (14th)
Villaret, Le (11th)

BISTROS (MODERN)

Affable, L' (15th)
Atelier Maître Albert (5th)
Bouqinistes, Les (6th)
Chateaubriand, Le (11th)
Cinq Mars, Le (7th)
Cocottes de Christian
Constant, Les (7th)
Comptoir du Relais, Le (6th)
(bistro menu weeknights
only)
Coq Rico, Le (18th)
Frenchie (2nd)
Galopin, Le (10th)
Pantruche, Le (9th)
Philou (10th)
Pottoka (7th)
Racines 2 (1st)
Septime (11th)
Sot-l'y-Laisse, Le (11th)
Terroir Parisien (5th)
Timbre, Le (6th)
Mon Vieil Ami (4th)

MODERN FRENCH
RESTAURANTS

35° Ouest (7th)
Abri (10th)
Afaria (15th)
Akrame (16th)
Restaurant Alain Ducasse au

Plaza Athénée (8th)
Ambroisie, L' (4th)
Arpège (7th)
Astrance (16th)
Atelier de Joël Robuchon
Étoile, L' (8th)
Atelier de Joël Robuchon
Saint-Germain, L' (7th)
Carré des Feuillants, Le (1st)
Cinq, Le (Four Seasons) (8th)
Claude Colliot (4th)
Cocotte, Ma (Saint-Ouen)
Dame de Pic, La (1st)
Restaurant du Dominique
Bouchet (8th)
Epicure au Bristol (8th)
Restaurant ES (7th)
Frédéric Simonin (17th)
Goust (2nd)
Guy Savoy (17th)
Restaurant Jean-François Piège
(7th)
Jules Verne, Le (7th)
Laurent (8th)
Mini Palais (8th)
Neva Cuisine (8th)
Passage 53 (2nd)
Pavillon Ledoyen (8th)
Pierre Gagnaire (8th)
Pré Catelan, Le (16th)
Roseval (20th)
Semilla (6th)
Société, La (6th)
Spring (1st)
Table d'Aki, La (7th)
Table d'Eugène, La (18th)
Terroir Parisien (5th)
Vivant Table (10th)
Yam'Tcha (1st)
Ze Kitchen Galerie (6th)

RESTAURANTS WITH
MICHELIN STAR RATINGS

35° Ouest (1 star) (7th)
Aida (1 star) (7th)
Akrame (1 star) (16th)
Restaurant Alain Ducasse au
Plaza Athénée (3 star) (8th)
Ambroisie, L' (3 star) (4th)
Arpège (3 star) (7th)
Astrance (3 star) (16th)
Atelier de Joël Robuchon
Étoile, L' (2 star) (8th)
Atelier de Joël Robuchon

Saint-Germain, L' (2 star)
(7th)
Benoit (1 star) (4th)
Carré des Feuillants, Le (2 star)
(1st)
Cinq, Le (Four Seasons)
(2 star) (8th)
Dame de Pic, La (1 star) (1st)
Epicure au Bristol (3 star) (8th)
Fables de la Fontaine, Le
(1 star) (7th)
Frédéric Simonin (1 star) (17th)
Guy Savoy (3 star) (17th)
Restaurant Jean-François Piège
(2 star) (7th)
Jules Verne, Le (1 star) (7th)
Laurent (1 star) (8th)
Passage 53 (2 star) (2nd)
Pavillon Ledoyen (3 star) (8th)
Pierre Gagnaire (3 star) (8th)
Pré Catelan, Le (3 star) (16th)
Shang Palace (Shangri-La
Hotel) (1 star) (16th)
Taillevent (2 star) (8th)
Trou Gascon, Au (1 star) (12th)
Yam'Tcha (1 star) (1st)
Ze Kitchen Galerie (1 star)
(6th)

CARRYOUT

Chez Aline (11th)
Al Taglio (Marais) (3rd)
Al Taglio (Oberkampf) (11th)
As du Fallafel, L' (4th)
Camion Qui Fume, Le
(food truck) (7th)
Claus (1st)
Cusi (6th)
Cuisine de Bar (Marais) (3rd)
Cuisine de Bar (Saint-Germain)
(6th)
Frenchie To Go (2nd)
Gontran Cherrier (18th)
Grillé (2nd)
Huîtrerie Régis (6th)
Jeanne A (11th)
Jeanne B (18th)
Krishna Bhavan (10th)
Mansouria, Le (11th)
Mozza & Co. (food truck) (7th)
Omnivore Rives (food truck)
(7th)
Pain Quotidien, Le (Lepic)
(18th)

Pain Quotidien, Le (Marais)
(4th)
Pain Quotidien, Le
(Montorgueil) (2nd)
Pain Quotidien, Le
(Palais Royal) (1st)
Pain Quotidien, Le
(Rue du Bac) (7th)
Pain Quotidien, Le
(Saint-Honoré) (1st)
Pain Quotidien, Le
(Victor Hugo) (16th)
Rose Bakery (Bon Marché)
(7th)
Rose Bakery (Marais) (3rd)
Rose Bakery (Martyrs) (9th)
Soul Kitchen (18th)
Sunken Chip, The (10th)
Télescope (2nd)
Ten Belles (10th)
Verjus Bar à Vins (lunchtime;
sandwiches only) (1st)

CONTINUOUS SERVICE

Al Taglio (Marais) (3rd)
Al Taglio (Oberkampf) (11th)
Chez Aline (11th)
Ambassade de Bourgogne (6th)
Chez Andre (8th)
Angelina (Musée du Louvre)
(1st)
Angelina (Rivoli) (1st)
As du Fallafel, L' (4th)
Avant Comptoir, L' (6th)
Brasserie Balzar (5th)
Bonaparte, La (6th)
Breizh Café (3rd)
Claus (1st)
Cocotte, Ma (Saint-Ouen)
Comptoir du Relais, Le (6th)
Cosi (6th)
Coutume (7th)
Bar de la Croix Rouge (6th)
Cuisine de Bar (Marais) (3rd)
Cuisine de Bar (Saint-Germain)
(6th)
Dans les Landes (5th)
Café de Flore (6th)
Frenchie To Go (2nd)
Gontran Cherrier (18th)
Grazie (3rd)
Jeanne A (11th)
Jeanne B (18th)
Chez Jenny (3rd)

Krishna Bhavan (10th)
Brasserie Lipp (6th)
Loustic (3rd)
Marcel (18th)
Café Marly, Le (1st)
Mini Palais (8th)
Nanashi (Bonpoint) (6th)
Nanashi (Charlot) (3rd)
Nanashi (Paradis) (10th)
Oenosteria (6th)
Pain Quotidien, Le (Lepic)
(18th)
Pain Quotidien, Le (Marais)
(4th)
Pain Quotidien, Le
(Montorgueil) (2nd)
Pain Quotidien, Le
(Palais Royal) (1st)
Pain Quotidien, Le
(Rue du Bac) (7th)
Pain Quotidien, Le
(Saint-Honoré) (1st)
Pain Quotidien, Le
(Victor Hugo) (16th)
Pavillon de la Fontaine
(6th)
Pho 14 (13th)
Brasserie aux PTT (7th)
Rosa, Da (6th)
Rose Bakery (Bon Marché)
(7th)
Rose Bakery (La Maison
Rouge) (12th)
Rose Bakery (Marais) (3rd)
Rose Bakery (Martyrs) (9th)
Rubis, Le (1st)
Société, La (6th)
Soul Kitchen (18th)
Télescope (2nd)
Ten Belles (10th)
Café Varenne (7th)

WORTHY WINE LIST

Restaurant Alain Ducasse au
Plaza Athénée (8th)
Albion (10th)
Ambassade de Bourgogne (6th)
Ambroisie, L' (4th)
Ami Louis, L' (3rd)
Avant Comptoir, L' (6th)
Carré des Feuillants (1st)
Cinq, Le (Four Seasons) (8th)
Comptoir du Relais, Le (6th)
Dame de Pic, La (1st)

Epicure au Bristol (8th)
Epicuriste, L' (15th)
Goust (2nd)
Guy Savoy (17th)
Restaurant Jean-François Piège
(7th)
Jeu de Quilles (14th)
Jules Verne, Le (7th)
Juveniles (1st)
Laurent (8th)
Oenosteria (6th)
Bistrot Paul Bert (11th)
Rallonge, La (18th)
Rubis, Le (1st)
Verjus Bar à Vins (1st)
Villaret, Le (11th)
Vivant Table (10th)
Willi's Wine Bar (1st)

GARDEN OR SIDEWALK TERRACE

Afaria (15th)
Chez Aline (11th)
Ambassade de Bourgogne (6th)
Chez André (8th)
A.O.C., L' (5th)
Azabu (6th)
Bonaparte, Le (6th)
Botanistes, Les (7th)
Brasserie Balzar (5th)
Caffé dei Cioppi (11th)
Closerie de Lilas, La (6th)
Cocotte, Ma (Saint-Ouen)
Comptoir du Relais, Le (6th)
Bar de la Croix Rouge (6th)
Dans les Landes (5th)
Deux Magots, Les (6th)
Écailler du Bistrot, L' (11th)
Epicure au Bristol (8th)
Fables de la Fontaine, Les (7th)
Café de Flore (6th)
Fontaine de Mars, La (7th)
Frenchie Bar à Vins (2nd)
Grazie (3rd)
Grillé (2nd)
Huîtrerie Régis (6th)
Izakaya Issé (1st)
Jeanne A (11th)
Jeanne B (18th)
Chez Jenny (3rd)
Jeu de Quilles (14th)
Laurent (8th)
Brasserie Lipp (6th)
Marcel (18th)

Café Marly, Le (1st)
Chez Michel (10th)
Mini Palais (8th)
Mosquée Salon de Thé, La (5th)
Pain Quotidien, Le (Lepic) (18th)
Pain Quotidien, Le (Marais) (4th)
Pain Quotidien, Le (Montorgueil) (2nd)
Pain Quotidien, Le (Saint-Honoré) (1st)
Pain Quotidien, Le (Victor Hugo) (16th)
Pantruche, Le (9th)
Bistrot Paul Bert (11th)
Pavillon de la Fontaine (6th)
Petit Lutetia, Le (6th)
Philou (10th)
Pho 14 (13th)
Pizza Chic (6th)
Pré Catelan, Le (16th)
Brasserie aux PTT (7th)
Racines 2 (1st)
Rallonge, La (18th)
Chez René (5th)
Rosa, Da (6th)
Roseval, Le (20th)
Sassotondo (11th)
Société, La (6th)
Soul Kitchen (18th)
Ten Belles (10th)
Café Varenne (7th)
Zyriab by Noura, Le (5th)

GOOD FOR CHILDREN

Al Taglio (Marais) (3rd)
Al Taglio (Oberkampf) (11th)
Angelina (Musée du Louvre) (1st)
Angelina (Rivoli) (1st)
As du Fallafel, L' (4th)
Brasserie Balzar (5th)
Bonaparte, La (6th)
Breizh Café (3rd)
Cinq, Le (Four Seasons) (8th)
Caffé dei Cioppi (11th)
Cocottes de Christian Constant, Les (7th)
Come a Casa (11th)
Cosi (6th)
Bar de la Croix Rouge (6th)
Cuisine de Bar (Marais) (3rd)

Cuisine de Bar (Saint-Germain) (6th)
Deux Magots, Les (6th)
Café de Flore (6th)
Frenchie To Go (2nd)
Gontran Cherrier (18th)
Grillé (2nd)
Jeanne A (11th)
Jeanne B (18th)
Chez Jenny (3rd)
Krishna Bhavan (10th)
Little Breizh (6th)
Mansouria, Le (11th)
Marcel (18th)
Café Marly, Le (1st)
Nanashi (Bonpoint) (6th)
Nanashi (Charlot) (3rd)
Nanashi (Paradis) (10th)
Oenosteria (6th)
Pain Quotidien, Le (Lepic) (18th)
Pain Quotidien, Le (Marais) (4th)
Pain Quotidien, Le (Montorgueil) (2nd)
Pain Quotidien, Le (Palais Royal) (1st)
Pain Quotidien, Le (Rue du Bac) (7th)
Pain Quotidien, Le (Saint-Honoré) (1st)
Pain Quotidien, Le (Victor Hugo) (16th)
Pâtes Vivantes, Les (9th)
Pavillon de la Fontaine (6th)
Pho 14 (13th)
Rose Bakery (Bon Marché) (7th)
Rose Bakery (Marais) (3rd)
Rose Bakery (Martyrs) (9th)
Semilla (6th)
Soul Kitchen (18th)
Sunken Chip, The (10th)
Télescope (2nd)
Ten Belles (10th)
Unico (11th)
Café Varenne (7th)
Mon Vieil Ami (4th)
West Country Girl (11th)

GOOD VALUE

Abri (19th)
Al Taglio (Marais) (3rd)
Al Taglio (Oberkampf) (11th)

Albion (19th)
As du Fallafel, L' (4th)
Avant Comptoir, L' (6th)
Biche au Bois, À la (12th)
Bones (11th)
Breizh Café (3rd)
Chatomat (20th)
Come a Casa (11th)
Cosi (6th)
Dans les Landes (5th)
Epicuriste, L' (15th)
Frenchie To Go (2nd)
Gyoza Bar (2nd)
Krishna Bhavan (10th)
Little Breizh (6th)
Neva Cuisine (8th)
Oenosteria (6th)
Pantruche, Le (9th)
Passage, Au (11th)
Pâtes Vivantes, Les (9th)
Philou (10th)
Pho 14 (13th)
Pied de Fouet, Au (Babylone) (7th)
Pied de Fouet, Au (Saint-Germain) (6th)
Pied du Fouet, Au (Oberkampf) (11th)
Quedubon (19th)
Rallonge, La (18th)
Roseval, Le (20th)
Rubis, Le (1st)
Table d'Eugène, La (18th)
Terroir Parisien (5th)
Tourette by Ibérique Gourmet, La (7th)
Villaret, Le (11th)
West Country Girl (11th)
Willi's Wine Bar (1st)

WELL-PRICED LUNCH MENU

35° Ouest (7th)
6 Paul Bert, Le (11th)
Abri (10th)
Afaria (15th)
Akrame (16th)
Astier (11th)
Astrance (16th)
Atelier Maître Albert (5th)
Avant Comptoir, L' (6th)
Baratin, Le (20th)
Botanistes, Les (7th)

Carré des Feuillants (1st)
Cinq, Le (Four Seasons)
  (8th)
Cinq Mars, Le (7th)
Caffè dei Cioppi (11th)
Claude Colliot (4th)
Coq Rico, Le (18th)
Cosi (6th)
Dame de Pic, La (1st)
Écailler du Bistrot, L' (11th)
Epicuriste, L' (15th)
Fables de la Fontaine, Les
  (7th)
Fish la Boissonnerie (6th)
Frédéric Simonin (17th)
Guy Savoy (17th)
Izakaya Issé (1st)
Jeanne A (11th)
Jeanne B (18th)
Jeu de Quilles (14th)
Juveniles (1st)
Laurent (8th)
Little Breizh (6th)
Liza (2nd)
Mansouria, Le (11th)
Mini Palais (8th)
Café des Musées (3rd)
Pantruche, Le (9th)
Passage 53 (2nd)
Passage, Au (11th)
Bistrot Paul Bert (11th)
Pierre Gagnaire (8th)
Pré Catelan, Le (16th)
Quedubon (19th)
Sassotondo (11th)
Semilla (6th)
Septime (11th)
Sot-l'y-Laisse, Le (11th)
Table d'Eugène, La (18th)
Taillevent (8th)
Trou Gascon, Au (12th)
Tsukizi (6th)
Unico (11th)
Mon Vieil Ami (4th)
Villaret, Le (11th)
Willi's Wine Bar (1st)
Yuzu (7th)
Ze Kitchen Galerie (6th)

LATE DINING (KITCHEN OPEN AFTER 10PM)

(Note that some are open only
  until 10:30PM, so check
  times in main listings or call
  ahead to confirm.)
Afaria (15th)
Al Taglio (Marais) (3rd)
Al Taglio (Oberkampf) (11th)
Ambassade de Bourgogne
  (6th)
Ami Louis, L' (3rd)
Chez André (8th)
As du Fallafel, L' (4th)
Atelier de Joël Robuchon
  Saint-Germain, L' (7th)
Atelier Maître Albert (5th)
Avant Comptoir, L' (6th)
Bouqinistes, Les (6th)
  (except Sundays)
Brasserie Balzar (5th)
Cocotte, Ma (Saint-Ouen)
Come a Casa (11th)
Cosi (6th)
Dans les Landes (5th)
Chez Denise / La Tour de
  Montlhéry (1st)
Dome, Le (14th)
Fish la Boissonnerie (6th)
Café de Flore (6th)
Fogón (6th)
Gyoza Bar (2nd)
Chez Jenny (3rd)
Krishna Bhavan (10th)
Brasserie Lipp 6th)
Café Marly, Le (1st)
Chez Michel (10th)
Mini Palais (8th)
Café des Musées (3rd)
Oenosteria (6th)
Passage, Au (11th)
Rosa, Da (6th)
Semilla (6th)
Septime La Cave (11th)
Société, La (6th)
Sunken Chip, The (10th)
Terroir Parisien (5th)
Unico (11th)
Vivant Table (10th)
Willi's Wine Bar (1st)
Zyriab by Noura, Le (5th)

OPEN IN AUGUST

(Note that closing dates vary
  yearly, and some restaurants
  are open only part of
  August, so always call first
  to confirm.)
Ambassade d'Auvergne,
  L' (3rd)
Chez André (8th)
Angelina (Musée du Louvre)
  (1st)
Angelina (Rivoli) (1st)
Arpège (7th)
Atelier de Joël Robuchon
  Étoile, L' (7th)
Atelier de Joël Robuchon
  Saint-Germain, L' (8th)
Avant Comptoir, L' (6th)
Benoit (4th)
Bonaparte, La (6th)
Chatomat (20th)
  (2 weeks only)
Cinq, Le (Four Seasons) (8th)
Cinq Mars, Le (7th)
Cocottes de Christian
  Constant, Les (7th)
Comptoir du Relais, Le (6th)
Coq Rico, Le (18th)
Cosi (6th)
Epicure au Bristol (8th)
Fines Gueules, Les (1st)
Fish la Boissonnerie (6th)
  (3 weeks only)
Café de Flore (6th)
Galopin, Le (10th)
Grazie (3rd)
Chez Jenny (3rd)
Jules Verne, Le (7th)
Kotteri Ramen Naritake (1st)
  (2 weeks only)
Laurent (8th)
Brasserie Lipp (6th)
Liza (2nd)
Mansouria, Le (11th)
Marcel (18th)
Café Marly, Le (1st)
Mini Palais (8th)
Café des Musées (3rd)
Oenosteria (6th)
Pain Quotidien, Le (Lepic)
  (18th)
Pain Quotidien, Le (Marais)
  (4th)
Pain Quotidien, Le

(Montorgueil) (2nd)
Pain Quotidien, Le
(Palais Royal) (1st)
Pain Quotidien, Le
(Rue du Bac) (7th)
Pain Quotidien, Le
(Saint-Honoré) (1st)
Pain Quotidien, Le
(Victor Hugo) (16th)
Pavillon de la Fontaine (6th)
Petit Lutetia, Le (6th)
Pho 14 (13th)
Pizza Chic (6th)
Quedubon (19th)
Racines 2 (1st) (one week only)
Rosa, Da (6th)
Rose Bakery (Marais) (3rd)
Semilla (6th) (2 weeks only)
Société, La (6th)
Sot-l'y-Laisse, Le (11th)
(2 weeks only)
Café Varenne (7th)
(2 weeks only)
Mon Vieil Ami (4th)
Willi's Wine Bar (1st)
Yen (6th) (2 weeks only)
Ze Kitchen Galerie (6th)
Zyriab by Noura, Le (5th)

OPEN MONDAY

6 Paul Bert, Le (11th)
Abri (sandwiches only) (10th)
Affable, L' (7th)
Akrame (16th)
Al Taglio (Marais) (3rd)
Al Taglio (Oberkampf) (11th)
Restaurant Alain Ducasse au
Plaza Athénée (8th)
Albion (10th)
Ambassade d'Auvergne,
L' (3rd)
Ambassade de Bourgogne (6th)
Chez André (8th)
Angelina (Musée du Louvre)
(1st)
Angelina (Rivoli) (1st)
As du Fallafel, L' (4th)
Atelier de Joël Robuchon
Étoile, L' (8th)
Atelier de Joël Robuchon
Saint-Germain, L' (7th)
Atelier Maître Albert (5th)
Avant Comptoir, L' (6th)
Brasserie Balzar (5th)

Baratin, Le (20th)
Benoit (4th)
Biche au Bois, À la (12th)
(dinner only)
Bonaparte, La (6th)
Botanistes, Les (7th)
Bouqinistes, Les (6th)
Carré des Feuillants, Le (1st)
Cinq, Le (Four Seasons) (8th)
Cinq Mars, Le (7th)
Claus (1st)
Closerie de Lilas, La (6th)
Cocotte, Ma (Saint-Ouen)
Cocottes de Christian
Constant, Les (7th)
Come a Casa (11th)
Coq Rico, Le (18th)
Cosi (6th)
Bar de la Croix Rouge (6th)
Coutume (7th)
Dans les Landes (5th)
Chez Denise / La Tour de
Montlhéry (1st)
Deux Fois Plus de Piment (11th)
Dome, Le (14th)
Restaurant du Dominique
Bouchet (8th)
Epicure au Bristol (8th)
Fables de la Fontaine, Les (7th)
Fines Gueules, Les (1st)
Fish la Boissonnerie (6th)
Café de Flore (6th)
Fontaine de Mars, La (7th)
Frenchie Bar à Vins (2nd)
(dinner only)
Chez Georges (2nd)
Gontran Cherrier (18th)
Grand Pan, Le (15th)
Grazie (3rd)
Grillé (2nd)
Gyoza Bar (2nd)
Izakaya Issé (1st)
Restaurant Jean-François Piège
(7th)
Jeanne A (11th)
Jeanne B (18th)
Chez Jenny (3rd)
Jules Verne, Le (7th)
Juveniles (dinner only) (1st)
Kiku (9th) (evening only)
Kotteri Ramen Naritake (1st)
Krishna Bhavan (10th)
Laurent (8th)
Pavillon Ledoyen (8th)

Brasserie Lipp (6th)
Loustic (3rd)
Mansouria, Le (11th)
(dinner only)
Marcel (18th)
Café Marly, Le (1st)
Chez Michel (10th)
(dinner only)
Mini Palais (8th)
Mosquée Salon de Thé, La (5th)
Café des Musées (3rd)
Nanashi (Charlot) (3rd)
Nanashi (Paradis) (10th)
Neva Cuisine (8th)
Oenosteria (6th)
Pain Quotidien, Le (Lepic)
(18th)
Pain Quotidien, Le (Marais)
(4th)
Pain Quotidien, Le
(Montorgueil) (2nd)
Pain Quotidien, Le (Palais
Royal) (1st)
Pain Quotidien, Le (Rue du
Bac) (7th)
Pain Quotidien, Le (Saint-
Honoré) (1st)
Pain Quotidien, Le (Victor
Hugo) (16th)
Pantruche, Le (9th)
Passage, Au (11th)
Pavillon de la Fontaine (6th)
Petit Lutetia, Le (6th)
Pho 14 (13th)
Pied de Fouet, Au (Babylone)
(7th)
Pied de Fouet, Au
(Saint-Germain) (6th)
Pied du Fouet, Au
(Oberkampf) (11th)
Pierre Gagnaire (8th)
Pizza Chic (6th)
Pottoka (7th)
Brasserie aux PTT (7th)
Racines 2 (1st)
Rosa, Da (6th)
Rose Bakery (Bon Marché)
(7th)
Roseval (20th)
Rubis, Le (1st)
Sassotondo (11th)
Saturne (2nd)
Semilla (6th)
Septime (11th)

Severo, Le (14th)
Shang Palace (Shangri-La
  Hotel) (16th)
Société, La (6th)
Sot-l'y-Laisse, Le (dinner only)
  (11th)
Spice and Wine (14th)
Taillevent (8th)
Télescope (1st)
Ten Belles (10th)
Terroir Parisien (5th)
Tourette by Ibérique Gourmet,
  La (7th) (lunch only)
Toyo (6th) (dinner only)
Trou Gascon, Au (12th)
Unico (11th)
Café Varenne (7th)
Mon Vieil Ami (4th)
Verjus Bar à Vins (1st)
Verjus Restaurant (1st)
Villaret, Le (11th)
Vivant Table (10th)
Willi's Wine Bar (1st)
Yen (6th)
Yoom (Martyrs) (9th)
Ze Kitchen Galerie (6th)

OPEN SUNDAY

Al Taglio (Marais) (3rd)
Al Taglio (Oberkampf) (11th)
Restaurant Alain Ducasse au
  Plaza Athénée (8th)
Ambassade d'Auvergne,
  L' (3rd)
Ambassade de Bourgogne (6th)
Ami Louis, L' (3rd)
Chez André (8th)
Angelina (Musée du Louvre)
  (1st)
Angelina (Rivoli) (1st)
As du Fallafel, L' (4th)
Atelier de Joël Robuchon
  Étoile, L' (8th)
Atelier de Joël Robuchon
  Saint-Germain, L' (7th)
Atelier Maître Albert (5th)
Avant Comptoir, L' (6th)
Azabu (6th)
Brasserie Balzar (5th)
Benoit (4th)
Bonaparte, La (6th)
Bouquinistes, Les (6th)
  (except Sundays)
Breizh Café (3rd)

Chatomat (20th) (first Sunday
  of the month only)
Cinq, Le (Four Seasons) (8th)
Claus (1st)
Closerie de Lilas, La (6th)
Cocotte, Ma (Saint-Ouen)
Cocottes de Christian
  Constant, Les (7th)
Coq Rico, Le (18th)
Cosi (6th)
Bar de la Croix Rouge (6th)
Cuisine de Bar (Marais) (3rd)
Cuisine de Bar (Saint-Germain)
  (6th)
Dans les Landes (5th)
Deux Fois Plus de Piment (11th)
Dome, Le (14th)
Epicure au Bristol (8th)
Fables de la Fontaine, Les (7th)
Fines Gueules, Les (1st)
Fish la Boissonnerie (6th)
Café de Flore (6th)
Fogón (6th)
Fontaine de Mars, La (7th)
Gontran Cherrier (18th)
Grazie (3rd)
Guilo Guilo (18th)
  (only during odd months)
Huîtrerie Régis (6th)
Jeanne A (11th)
Jeanne B (18th)
Chez Jenny (3rd)
Jules Verne, Le (7th)
Krishna Bhavan (10th)
Brasserie Lipp (6th)
Loustic (3rd)
Marcel (18th)
Café Marly, Le (1st)
Mini Palais (8th)
Mosquée Salon de Thé, La (5th)
Café des Musées (3rd)
Nanashi (Charlot) (3rd)
Nanashi (Paradis) (10th)
Oenosteria (6th)
Okuda (8th)
Orient d'Or, L' (9th)
Pain Quotidien, Le (Lepic)
  (18th)
Pain Quotidien, Le (Marais)
  (4th)
Pain Quotidien, Le
  (Montorgueil) (2nd)
Pain Quotidien, Le
  (Palais Royal) (1st)

Pain Quotidien, Le
  (Rue du Bac) (7th)
Pain Quotidien, Le
  (Saint-Honoré) (1st)
Pain Quotidien, Le
  (Victor Hugo) (16th)
Pavillon de la Fontaine (6th)
Petit Lutetia, Le (6th)
Pizza Chic (6th)
Pottoka (7th)
Rosa, Da (6th)
Rose Bakery (La Maison
  Rouge) (12th)
Rose Bakery (Marais) (3rd)
Rose Bakery (Martyrs) (9th)
Sassotondo (11th)
Semilla (6th)
Shang Palace (Shangri-La
  Hotel) (16th)
Société, La (6th)
Soul Kitchen (18th)
Sunken Chip, The (10th)
Ten Belles (10th)
Terroir Parisien (5th)
Tsukizi (6th) (dinner only)
Mon Vieil Ami (4th)
Yoom (Martyrs) (6th)
Yuzu (lunch only) (7th)
Zyriab by Noura, Le
  (lunch only) (5th)

PRIVATE DINING

Aida (7th)
Ambassade d'Auvergne,
  L' (3rd)
Ambroisie, L' (4th)
Arpège (7th)
Atelier de Joël Robuchon
  Étoile, L' (8th)
Atelier Maître Albert (5th)
Benoit (4th)
Carré des Feuillants, Le (1st)
Cinq, Le (Four Seasons) (8th)
Dame de Pic, La (1st)
Guy Savoy (17th)
Chez Jenny (3rd)
Laurent (8th)
Pavillon Ledoyen (8th)
Liza (2nd)
Mansouria, Le (11th)
Okuda (8th)
Pierre Gagnaire (8th)
Shang Palace
  (Shangri-La Hotel) (16th)

Taillevent (8th)
Toyo (6th)
Verjus Bar à Vins (1st)
Verjus Restaurant (1st)

SPECIAL OCCASION

Aida (7th)
Restaurant Alain Ducasse au
    Plaza Athénée (8th)
Ambroisie, L' (4th)
Arpège (7th)
Astrance (16th)
Atelier de Joël Robuchon
    Étoile, L' (8th)
Atelier de Joël Robuchon
    Saint-Germain, L' (7th)
Carré des Feuillants, Le (1st)
Cinq, Le (Four Seasons) (8th)
Dame de Pic, La (1st)
Epicure au Bristol (8th)
Frédéric Simonin (17th)
Guy Savoy (17th)
Restaurant Jean-François Piège
    (7th)
Jules Verne, Le (7th)
Laurent (8th)
Okuda (8th)
Passage 53 (2nd)
Pierre Gagnaire (8th)
Pré Catelan, Le (16th)
Saturne (2nd)
Septime (11th)
Shang Palace (Shangri-La
    Hotel) (16th)
Table d'Eugène, La (18th)
Taillevent (8th)
Yam'Tcha (1st)

TASTING MENU
(MENU DÉGUSTATION)

Afaria (15th)
Aida (6th)
Restaurant Alain Ducasse au
    Plaza Athénée (8th)
Arpège (7th)
Astrance (16th)
Atelier de Joël Robuchon
    Étoile, L' (8th)
Atelier de Joël Robuchon
    Saint-Germain, L' (7th)
Carré des Feuillants, Le (1st)
Dame de Pic, La (1st)
Epicure au Bristol (8th)

Fables de la Fontaine (7th)
Frédéric Simonin (evening
    only) (17th)
Guy Savoy (17th)
Restaurant Jean-François Piège
    (7th)
Jules Verne, Le (7th)
Kiku (9th) (evening only)
Laurent (8th)
Okuda (8th)
Passage 53 (2nd)
Pavillon Ledoyen (8th)
Pierre Gagnaire (8th)
Pottoka (7th)
Pré Catelan, Le (16th)
Shang Palace (Shangri-La
    Hotel) (16th)
Taillevent (8th)
Toyo (6th)
Verjus Restaurant (1st)
Villaret, Le (11th)
Vivant Table (10th)
Yam'Tcha (1st)
Yuzu (7th)
Ze Kitchen Galerie (6th)

INVENTIVE CUISINE

Akrame (16th)
Restaurant Alain Ducasse au
    Plaza Athénée (8th)
Ambroisie, L' (16th)
Arpège (7th)
Astrance (16th)
Atelier de Joël Robuchon
    Étoile, L' (8th)
Atelier de Joël Robuchon
    Saint-Germain, L' (7th)
Bones (11th)
Carré des Feuillants, Le (1st)
Chateaubriand, Le (11th)
Chatomat (20th)
Cinq, Le (Four Seasons) (8th)
Claude Colliot (4th)
Dame de Pic, La (1st)
Epicure au Bristol (8th)
Restaurant ES (7th)
Frédéric Simonin (17th)
Frenchie (2nd)
Guilo Guilo (18th)
Guy Savoy (17th)
Restaurant Jean-François Piège
    (7th)
Jules Verne, Le (7th)
Laurent (8th)

Passage 53 (2nd)
Pierre Gagnaire (8th)
Pré Catelan, Le (16th)
Roseval (20th)
Saturne (2nd)
Septime (11th)
Spring (1st)
Table d'Eugène, La
    (18th)
Taillevent (8th)
Verjus Bar à Vins (1st)
Verjus Restaurant (1st)
Yam'Tcha (1st)
Ze Kitchen Galerie (6th)

VEGETARIAN FRIENDLY

Al Taglio (Marais) (3rd)
Al Taglio (Oberkampf) (11th)
As du Fallafel, L' (4th)
Brasserie Balzar (5th)
Breizh Café (3rd)
Come a Casa (11th)
Cosi (6th)
Cuisine de Bar (Marais)
    (3rd)
Cuisine de Bar
    (Saint-Germain)
    (6th)
Deux Magots, Les (6th)
Café de Flore (6th)
Grazie (3rd)
Jeanne A (11th)
Jeanne B (18th)
Krishna Bhavan (10th)
Little Breizh (6th)
Mansouria, Le (11th)
Marcel (18th)
Nanashi (Bonpoint) (6th)
Nanashi (Charlot) (3rd)
Nanashi (Paradis) (10th)
Pain Quotidien, Le (Lepic)
    (18th)
Pain Quotidien, Le (Marais)
    (4th)
Pain Quotidien, Le
    (Montorgueil) (2nd)
Pain Quotidien, Le
    (Palais Royal) (1st)
Pain Quotidien, Le
    (Rue du Bac) (7th)
Pain Quotidien, Le
    (Saint-Honoré) (1st)
Pain Quotidien, Le (Victor
    Hugo) (16th)

Pâtes Vivantes, Les (9th)
Pho 14 (13th)
Pizza Chic (6th)
Rose Bakery (Bon Marché)
  (7th)
Rose Bakery (La Maison
  Rouge) (12th)
Rose Bakery (Marais) (3rd)
Rose Bakery (Martyrs) (9th)
Sassotondo (11th)
Semilla (6th)
Shang Palace (Shangri-La
  Hotel) (16th)
Société, La (6th)
Mon Vieil Ami (4th)
West Country Girl (11th)
Yoom (Martyrs) (6th)
Yoom (Saint-Germain) (6th)

NON-FRENCH CUISINE

ARGENTINIAN
Unico (11th)

AMERICAN
Le Camion Qui Fume
  (food truck)

BRITISH
Rose Bakery (Bon Marché)
  (7th)
Rose Bakery (La Maison
  Rouge) (12th)
Rose Bakery (Marais) (3rd)
Rose Bakery (Martyrs) (9th)
Sunken Chip, The (10th)

CHINESE
Deux Fois Plus de Piment (11th)
Orient d'Or, L' (9th)
Pâtes Vivantes, Les (9th)
Shang Palace (Shangri-La
  Hotel) (16th)
Yoom (Martyrs) (9th)
Yoom (Saint-Germain) (6th)

JAPANESE
Aida (7th)
Azabu (6th)
Guilo Guilo (18th)
Gyoza Bar (2nd)
Isami (4th)
Izakaya Issé (1st)
Kiku (9th)
Kotteri Ramen Naritake (1st)
Nanashi (Bonpoint) (6th)
Nanashi (Charlot) (3rd)
Nanashi (Paradis) (10th)
Okuda (8th)
Toyo (6th)
Tsukizi (6th)
Yen (6th)
Yuzu (7th)

GERMAN
Claus (1st)

INTERNATIONAL
Akrame (16th)
Bones (11th)
Cosi (6th)
Coutume (7th)
Frenchie To Go (2nd)
Holybelly (10th)
Loustic (3rd)
Marcel (18th)
Café Marly, Le (1st)
Omnivores Rives (Les Berges)
  (7th)
Saturne (2nd)
Semilla (6th)
Société, La (6th)
Soul Kitchen (18th)
Télescope (2nd)
Ten Belles (10th)
Verjus Bar à Vins (1st)
Verjus Restaurant (1st)
Ze Kitchen Galerie (6th)

INDIAN
Krishna Bhavan (10th)

ITALIAN
Al Taglio (Marais) (3rd)
Al Taglio (Oberkampf) (11th)
Caffè dei Cioppi (11th)
Come a Casa (11th)
Grazie (3rd)
Mozza & Co. (Les Berges) (7th)
Oenosteria (6th)
Pizza Chic (6th)
Rosa, Da (6th)
Sassotondo (11th)
Vivant (10th)

MIDDLE EASTERN
As du Fallafel, L' (4th)
Grillé (2nd)

MOROCCAN
Mansouria, Le (11th)
Mosquée Salon de Thé,
  Le (5th)

LEBANESE
Liza (2nd)
Zyriab by Noura, Le (5th)

PORTUGUESE
Comme à Lisbonne (4th)

THAI
Spice and Wine (14th)

SPANISH
En Attendant Rosa
  (Les Berges, 7th)
Fogón (6th)
Rosa, Da (6th)
Tourette Bistrot Cantine,
  La (7th)

VIETNAMESE
Pho 14 (13th)

INDEX

Following French style, any articles such as *au, la,* or *le* and the words *bistro, brasserie, café,* or *chez* appearing before the proper name of the establishment are ignored in the alphabetizing. For example, Bistrot Paul Bert and Le Petit Lutetia are listed under the letter *P*.

RECIPE INDEX